DEADLINE ARTISTS

He speaks in your voice, American,
and there's a shine in his eye that's halfway hopeful.
—DON DELILLO

DEADLINE ARTISTS

America's Greatest Newspaper Columns

Edited by John Avlon, Jesse Angelo & Errol Louis

THE OVERLOOK PRESS
New York, NY

This edition published in paperback in the United States in 2012 by
The Overlook Press, Peter Mayer Publishers, Inc.

141 Wooster Street
New York, NY 10012
www.overlookpress.com

For bulk and special sales, please contact sales@overlookny.com

PHOTOGRAPH PERMISSIONS:
Theodore Roosevelt and Richard Harding Davis: Strohmeyer & Wyman, Library of Congress, Prints & Photographs Division, LC-USZ62-23023; H.L. Mencken: Photo by Leonard McCombe/Time Life Pictures/Getty Images; Will Rogers: The Will Rogers Memorial Museum, Claremore, Oklahoma; Heywood Broun: Library of Congress, Prints & Photographs Division, LC-USZ62-73280; Langston Hughes: Photo by Carl Van Vechten courtesy of the Van Vechten Trust; Dorothy Thompson: Harris & Ewing, Library of Congress, Prints & Photographs Division, LC-DIG-hec-26561; Ernie Pyle: Bettmann/CORBIS; Walter Lippmann: Photo by Carl Mydans/Time Life Pictures/Getty Images; Westbrook Pegler: Photo by John Phillips/Time Life Pictures/Getty Images; William F. Buckley Jr.: Photo courtesy of the Estate of William F. Buckley Jr.; Damon Runyon: Bettmann/CORBIS; Murray Kempton: *World Telegram & Sun* photo by Al Ravenna, Library of Congress, Prints & Photographs Division, LC-USZ62-126477; Mike Royko: *Chicago Tribune*/MCT via Getty Images; Jimmy Breslin: Ron Galella/WireImage; Jack Newfield: Photo by Joey Newfield courtesy of Janie Eisenberg; Red Smith: Photo by Don Rice, Library of Congress, Prints & Photographs Division, NYWT&S Collection, LC-USZ62-118851; Molly Ivins: Photo by Melanie West; Pete Hamill: Deirdre Hamill/Quest Imagery; Mary McGrory: Photo by Gjon Mili/Time & Life Pictures/Getty Images; Mike Barnicle: Courtesy of the author; Peggy Noonan: Courtesy of the author; Carl Hiaasen: Photo by Fenia Hiaasen. Leonard Pitts: Courtesy of the author; Thomas L. Friedman: Photo by Josh Haner/*The New York Times*; Kathleen Parker: Courtesy of CNN; Steve Lopez: Photo by Gilles Mingasson.

Cataloging-in-Publication Data is available from the Library of Congress

Book design and typeformatting by Bernard Schleifer
Manufactured in the United States of America

10 9 8 7 6 5 4 3 2 1

ISBN 978-1-4683-0054-3

TO "THE LIFE OF KINGS"

Contents

INTRODUCTION

It is a great American art form, read by millions every day.

Taped on refrigerators and tacked up over desks, its wisdom is folded in wallets and e-mailed among friends. The best of it rises to the level of literature: balancing the urgency of news with the precision of poetry.

Deadline Artists is a celebration of the American newspaper column—a reminder that compelling stories told by engaging personalities can resonate beyond their era. Newspaper columnists are their readers' advisers, advocates, and confidants, helping them make sense of current events while subtly defining the spirit of the age. They hold a special place in people's hearts. When the iconic Chicago columnist Mike Royko died, his memorial service was held at Wrigley Field. *San Francisco Chronicle* mainstay Herb Caen—credited with coining the terms "Beatnik" and "Hippie"—was memorialized in one of the largest public gatherings in the city's history.

That's because columnists speak in a voice readers understand—their own, but just a bit better. It is the voice of the bar room, the locker room and the smoke-filled back room. It is a voice that comforts and confronts. A great column is both a witness and a work of art—helping people understand the world around them while making them feel a little less alone.

This book began with a simple proposition: it was the book we wanted to read. As young journalists, we wanted to mine it for inspiration, education, and entertainment. To our surprise, we found that a comprehensive anthology of America's greatest newspaper columns had never been compiled.

Two of us—John Avlon and Errol Louis—were working as columnists for the *New York Sun* at the time and asked our colleague Jack Newfield about his favorite columns. He and his friend Jimmy Breslin named the same column as among the very best—"The Death of Frankie Jerome" by Westbrook Pegler, published in 1924. It had not been anthologized since, and hunting it down took months. Reading the opening line made it clear that this was not just a newspaper column—this was a short story:

> A yellow-haired kid with a mashed nose and scalloped lips dipped his fingers
> in the holy water fount of St. Jerome's Church, crossed himself with the fist that
> killed Frankie Jerome and went to his knees on the cold marble to pray when
> all that was left of the little fellow was wheeled up the aisle to the altar yesterday
> for the funeral mass that preceded the journey to the grave.

And so the process of putting this book together began. The inclusion of some columns were matters of clear consensus, such as Breslin's classic profile of JFK's grave-digger, "It's an Honor," and Ernie Pyle's "The Death of Captain Waskow." Conversations with journalism professors and research through books and microfilm were helpful, but the best suggestions came from columnists themselves. In all cases, great writing was our guide.

The emergence of the popular newspaper column we now take for granted has been centuries in the making. Historians of journalism date the first American multi-page newspaper to Boston's *Publick Occurrences Both Forreign and Domestick* in 1690. It lasted one issue before being shut down by the government. Next came the *Boston News-Letter*, in 1704. It lasted for two decades, during which period other newspapers began to pop up among the coastal colonies.

The influential publishers and pamphleteers of the Revolutionary era, like Benjamin Franklin and Thomas Paine, offered insights and incitements that became enduring American wisdom. The Federalist Papers—penned by James Madison, Alexander Hamilton, and John Jay—first appeared in the pages of New York's *Daily Advertiser* and other newspapers as anonymous columns arguing for the ratification of the Constitution.

In the evolutionary slog from pamphlets and unsigned editorials to the signed column, the mid-1800s began to see the regular publication of local voices like "Fanny Fern"—the pen-name of Sara Willis Parton, the best known and best compensated chronicler of her time, earning an un-heard of $100 a week for her column in the *New York Ledger*. Humor and light verse printed alongside editorials were also popular early versions of the column. The newspaper column as we know it today emerged gradually, taking more defined shape by the late nineteenth century with pioneers of first-person literary journalism like Richard Harding Davis, who became not just a chronicler but a character in contemporary dramas, a national figure in his own right.

The common denominator shared by all columns is personal perspective, combining observation with opinion. As newspapers proliferated across the United States at the turn of the last century, each sought the competitive advantage that a marquee columnist could provide. As Professor Hallam Walker Davis's 1926 book, *The Column,* confidently asserted, "With the public, the successful columnist bears the same relation to the rest of the newspaper force that a predatory home-run hitter bears to the rest of a winning baseball team."

For well-known public figures, writing a newspaper column became a prestigious and profitable sideline: Theodore Roosevelt, O. Henry, Will Rogers, Woody Guthrie, Orson Welles, Eleanor Roosevelt, Langston Hughes, and Hunter S. Thompson all wrote regular newspaper columns, at least for a time. In general, however, these celebrity voices don't compare to the workaday professionals whose columns still set the standard for excellence: H. L. Mencken,

Damon Runyon, Dorothy Thompson, Murray Kempton, Jimmy Breslin, and Mike Royko. In our time, voices like Peggy Noonan, Tom Friedman, Carl Hiaasen, Mike Barnicle, and Steve Lopez carry on this tradition.

The opportunity and obligation of the newspaper columnist, Finley Peter Dunne once famously said, is to "comfort the afflicted and afflict the comfortable." Columnists are supposed to be truth tellers—literary private eyes working for the public good.

We have sought to create a broad anthology, taking into account different eras, perspectives, and places. In cutting down the columns to a manageable number, we have undoubtedly excluded some worthy voices from a list that could never be anything but subjective. We don't consider it definitive—we consider it a start.

In the process of reading many hundreds of columns, it has been striking to see which pieces endure. Those centered around storytelling and historic events best retain their power—the more original reporting, the better. But what might be called the "Mount Olympus" column, in which the author-analyst surveys the nation and passes policy pronouncements down from on high, tends not to age as well. Likewise, early columns that rely too heavily on dialect or homespun tales often grow stale.

A once-popular form of column seemed to borrow its style from the telegram—staccato riffs, bits of gossip and innuendo alongside breaking news, all strung together. This style was frequently used by influential figures like Walter Winchell and Drew Pearson, but without much narrative structure, they don't read as well today or merit reprinting. (The iconic Winchell's work is included here, however, with "Waiting for Lepke," a first-person account of a wanted criminal turning himself in, to the columnist.)

The columns in this book give readers the chance to see history first hand—to storm the beach at Normandy on D-Day, to cheer Bobby Thompson's pennant-winning "Shot Heard 'Round the World" at the Polo Grounds, and to wrestle the gun from Sirhan Sirhan in the chaos of the kitchen at the Ambassador Hotel in Los Angeles. It is a chance to be there at the moments when America changes, for better or worse.

But our goal is not to give a history lesson. Some of the best columns include appreciations of everyday life: stories of love, loss, laughter, and faith—struggles against the odds and long shots that come in. In these pages are the sound of celebrations and the echoes of a wake. Most of all, we want to share great writing. With an average length of eight hundred words, these morsels are tailor-made for today's short attention spans and never-ending travel schedules. And the vast majority are not available online.

We are living in a time of transition in the news media, when obituaries for newspapers are being written every day. In our Internet age, there is a danger that the classic reported column is becoming a lost art. Search engine research is no substitute for getting out from behind the desk and knocking on doors. Before the rise of television, reporters and columnists had to make a scene come alive in the mind of a reader. The result was vivid descriptive writing, aided by more actual reporting—making much of the current opinion crop seem like mere typing in comparison.

This is not to say that the future is bleak for opinion journalism—it's potentially brighter than ever, with a broader array of perspectives and wider access to publication, both digital and print. The classic craftsmanship of these columns can inspire some healthy competition between the generations and serve as a source of durable inspiration for today's columnists and bloggers—opinion writers, all—looking to learn from the best of their predecessors.

A final word about our selection process. Because *Deadline Artists* is an anthology of *newspaper* columns, legendary magazine columnists, feature writers, and accomplished authors of the occasional Op-Ed piece are not included. It can be argued that magazine columns are not inherently different from newspaper columns except in their day-to-day deadlines—but that, as our title suggests, is the key consideration.

The improvisational nature of the newspaper column is what sets it apart, the near-miracle that stories composed on punishing daily deadlines can resonate with beauty and power decades later. Jimmy Breslin's "Are You John Lennon?" was completed less than three hours after the murder it described was committed, while Pete Hamill's first-person account of the attacks of 9/11 from lower Manhattan was filed the same day. These Deadline Artists beat the odds and created something transcendent in a disposable medium.

Whether it's a game-day riff off "Casey at the Bat," the way-to-wealth aphorisms of Benjamin Franklin's Poor Richard, or the wise kindness behind "Yes, Virginia—There is a Santa Claus," the greatest newspaper columns continue to resonate. They have worked their way into the language of everyday American life.

By reading beloved but half-remembered columns that were gathering dust in libraries or moldering on microfilm, you are joining a conversation across the generations. Flip to the subjects that interest you, or seek out the writers you already know and love. We know you will find powerful writing—clear voices offering wit, wisdom, and some unforgettable characters. Enjoy.

I: WAR

In wartime, columnists serve as witnesses on the front lines, trying to cut through the fog of war to bring a bit of truth to those back home.

Richard Harding Davis was one of the first great war columnists in our history, covering the Spanish-American War and the First World War with first person journalism, as when he captured the terrible beauty of an oncoming assault as German troops crossed into Belgium: "Like a river of steel it flowed, gray and ghostlike." The archetypal American war columnist is Ernie Pyle, the "GI journalist." He covered the Second World War from the perspective of his beloved "God-Damned Infantry" and ultimately lost his life in the process.

First Lady Eleanor Roosevelt penned her syndicated "My Day" column from within the walls of the White House the day Pearl Harbor was attacked. Sometimes columnists seek to warn us of a conflict to come. Dorothy Thompson dedicated herself to speaking out against the rise of Nazi power in the *Herald Tribune*, deriding Neville Chamberlain's naïve hopes for "peace in our time."

The Vietnam War lacked the self-evident moral clarity of earlier conflicts but resulted in some enduring journalism. Pete Hamill's dispatches from the front honored the soldiers as they struggled to do the right thing in firefights fraught with ambiguity. Art Hoppe expressed his horror at finding himself rooting against our side in the war while Peter Kann penned an obituary for the South Asian nation fifty-seven thousand Americans died trying to save.

The end of the cold war brought celebrations—such as William F. Buckley's "Hallelujah!"—along with the hope for a new era of peaceful and prosperous globalization. Those hopes were crushed on a blue Tuesday morning in the fall of 2001. Pete Hamill was again a witness on the front lines, now to a new war unfolding in the streets of his hometown. The *Miami Herald*'s Leonard Pitts captured the fury and defiance of the nation in his column that day, which inspired twenty-six thousand e-mailed responses and was read aloud by congressional leaders as a way of expressing our grief and outrage.

The *New York Times*' Thomas L. Friedman is a globe-trotting chronicler of globalization and its discontents, while Nicholas Kristof has kept the tradition of the front-line columnist alive, reporting from war zones in Africa and around the world. His columns amplify the voices of remote villagers while stirring our collective conscience to help stop a slaughter before it begins.

The best columns filed from a combat zone bring out the humanity obscured by the savagery of war.

Like a River of Steel It Flowed, Gray and Ghostlike
RICHARD HARDING DAVIS—*The New York Tribune*—8/23/1914

BRUSSELS, FRIDAY, AUGUST 21, 2 P.M.—The entrance of the German army into Brussels has lost the human quality. It was lost as soon as the three soldiers who led the army bicycled into the Boulevard du Régent and asked the way to the Gare du Nord. When they passed the human note passed with them.

What came after them, and twenty-four hours later is still coming, is not men marching, but a force of nature like a tidal wave, an avalanche or a river flooding its banks. At this minute it is rolling through Brussels as the swollen waters of the Conemaugh Valley swept through Johnstown.

At the sight of the first few regiments of the enemy we were thrilled with interest. After three hours they had passed in one unbroken steel-gray column we were bored. But when hour after hour passed and there was no halt, no breathing time, no open spaces in the ranks, the thing became uncanny, inhuman. You returned to watch it, fascinated. It held the mystery and menace of fog rolling toward you across the sea.

The gray of the uniforms worn by both officers and men helped this air of mystery. Only the sharpest eye could detect among the thousands that passed the slightest difference. All moved under a cloak of invisibility. Only after the most numerous and severe tests at all distances, with all materials and combinations of colors that give forth no color, could this gray have been discovered. That it was selected to clothe and disguise the German when he fights is typical of the German staff in striving for efficiency to leave nothing to chance, to neglect no detail.

After you have seen this service uniform under conditions entirely opposite you are convinced that for the German soldier it is his strongest weapon. Even the most expert marksman cannot hit a target he cannot see. It is a gray green, not the blue gray of our Confederates. It is the gray of the hour just before daybreak, the gray of unpolished steel, of mist among green trees.

I saw it first in the Grand Palace in front of the Hôtel de Ville. It was impossible to tell if in that noble square there was a regiment or a brigade. You saw only a fog that melted into the stones, blended with the ancient house fronts, that shifted and drifted, but left you nothing at which you could point.

Later, as the army passed below my window, under the trees of the Botanical Park, it merged and was lost against the green leaves. It is no exaggeration to say that at a hundred yards you can see the horses on which the uhlans ride, but you cannot see the men who ride them.

If I appear to overemphasize this disguising uniform it is because of all the details of the German outfit it appealed to me as one of the most remarkable. The other day when I was with the rear guard of the French Dragoons and the Cuirassiers and they threw out pickets, we could distinguish them against the yellow wheat or green gorse at half a mile, while these men passing in the street, when they have reached the next crossing, become merged into the gray of the paving stones and the earth swallows them. In comparison the yellow khaki of our own American army is about as invisible as the flag of Spain.

Yesterday Major General von Jarotsky, the German Military Governor of Brussels, assured Burgomaster Max that the German army would not occupy the city, but would pass through it. It is still passing. I have followed in campaigns six armies, but excepting not even our own, the Japanese, or the British, I have not seen one so thoroughly equipped. I am not speaking of the fighting qualities of any army, only of the equipment and organization. The German army moved into this city as smoothly and as compactly as an Empire State Express. There were no halts, no open places, no stragglers.

This army has been on active service three weeks, and so far there is not apparently a chin strap or a horseshoe missing. It came in with the smoke pouring from cookstoves on wheels, and in an hour had set up post-office wagons, from which mounted messengers galloped along the line of columns, distributing letters, and at which soldiers posted picture postcards.

The infantry came in in files of five, two hundred men to each company; the Lancers in columns of four, with not a pennant missing. The quick-firing guns and fieldpieces were one hour at a time in passing, each gun with its caisson and ammunition wagon taking twenty seconds in which to pass.

The men of the infantry sang *Fatherland, My Fatherland.* Between each line of song they took three steps. At times two thousand men were singing together in absolute rhythm and beat. When the melody gave way the silence was broken only by the stamp of iron-shod boots, and then again the song rose. When the singing ceased, the bands played marches. They were followed by the rumble of siege guns, the creaking of wheels, and of chains clanking against the cobblestones and the sharp bell-like voices of the bugles.

For seven hours the army passed in such solid columns that not once might a taxicab or trolley car pass through the city. Like a river of steel it flowed, gray and ghostlike. Then, as dusk came and as thousands of horses' hoofs and thousands of iron boots continued to tramp forward, they struck tiny sparks from the stones, but the horses and the men who beat out the sparks were invisible.

At midnight pack wagons and siege guns were still passing. At seven this morning I was awakened by the tramp of men and bands playing jauntily. Whether they marched all night or not I do not know; but now for twenty-six hours the gray army has rumbled by with the mystery of fog and the pertinacity of a steam roller.

The Chauffeurs of Madrid

ERNEST HEMINGWAY—*New York Times*—5/23/1937

We had a lot of different chauffeurs in Madrid. The first one was named Tomas, was 4 feet 11 inches high and looked like a particularly unattractive, very mature dwarf out of Velasquez put into a suit of blue dungarees. He had several front teeth missing and seethed with patriotic sentiments. He also loved Scotch whisky.

We drove up from Valencia with Tomas and, as he sighted Madrid rising like a great white fortress across the plain from Alcala de Henares, Tomas said, through missing teeth:

"Long live Madrid, the capital of my soul!"

"And of my heart," I said, having had a couple myself. It had been a long, cold ride.

"Hurray!" shouted Tomas and abandoned the wheel temporarily in order to clap me on the back. We just missed a lorry full of troops and a staff car.

"I am a man of sentiment," said Tomas.

"Me, too," I said, "but hang onto that wheel."

"Of the noblest sentiment," said Tomas.

"No doubt of it, comrade," I said, "but just try to watch where you are driving."

"You can place all confidence in me," said Tomas.

But the next day we were stalled on a muddy road up near Brihuega by a tank which had lurched around a little too far on a hairpin bend and held up six other tanks behind it. Three Rebel planes sighted the tanks and decided to bomb them. The bombs hit the wet hillside above us, lifting mud geysers in sudden, clustered, bumping shocks.

Next morning Tomas couldn't get the car to start. And every day when anything of that sort happened from then on, no matter how well the car had run coming home at night, Tomas never could start her in the morning.

The way he felt about the front became sort of pitiful, finally, along with his size, his patriotism and his general inefficiency, and we sent him back to Valencia with a note to the Press Department thanking them for Tomas, a man of the noblest sentiments and the finest intentions; but could they send us something just a little braver?

So they sent one with a note certifying him as the bravest chauffeur in the whole department. I don't know what his name was, because I never saw him. Sid Franklin (the Brooklyn bullfighter), who bought us our food, cooked breakfasts, typed articles, wangled petrol, wangled cars, wangled chauffeurs and covered Madrid and all its gossip like a human Dictaphone, evidently instructed this chauffeur very strongly.

Sid put forty liters of petrol in the car, and petrol was the correspondents' main problem, being harder to obtain than Chanel's and Molyneux's perfumes or Bols gin. He took the chauffeur's name and address and told him to hold himself ready to roll whenever he was called. We were expecting an attack.

The chauffeur was to check in at the hotel the next night at 7:30 to see if there were any new orders. He didn't come and we called up his rooming house. He had left that same morning for Valencia with the car and the forty liters of petrol. He is in jail in Valencia now. I hope he likes it.

Then we got David. David was an Anarchist boy from a little town near Toledo. Being with David has changed my whole conception of profanity. He was absolutely brave, and he had only one real defect as a chauffeur: he couldn't drive a car. He was like a horse which has only two gaits—walking and running away.

David could sneak along in second speed and hit practically no one in the streets, due to his clearing a swathe ahead of him with his vocabulary. He could also drive with the car wide open, hanging to the wheel, in a sort of fatalism that was, however, never tinged with despair. We solved the problem by driving David ourselves.

The only thing that developed in David was his vocabulary. He went off to the village where the motion-picture outfit was making a film.

After having one more particularly useless chauffeur that there is no point in going into, we got Hipolito. Hipolito is the point of this story.

Hipolito was not much taller than Tomas, but he looked carved out of a granite block. He walked with a roll, putting his feet down flat at each stride; and he had an automatic pistol so big it came halfway down his leg. He always said, "Salud" with a rising inflection, as though it were something you said to hounds—good hounds that knew their business. He knew motors, he could drive; and if you told him to show up at 6 a.m. he was there ten minutes before the hour. He had fought at the taking of Montana Barracks in the first days of the war, and he had never been a member of any political party. He was a trade union man for the last twenty years in the Socialist union, the U.G.T. He said, when I asked him what he believed in, that he believed in the republic.

He was our chauffeur in Madrid and at the front during a nineteen-day bombardment of the capital that was almost too bad to write anything about. All the time he was as solid as the rock he looked to be cut from, as sound as a good bell and as regular and accurate as a railway man's watch.

He made you realize why Franco [Insurgent General Francisco Franco] never took Madrid when he had the chance. Hipolito and the others like him would have fought from street to street and house to house as long as any one of them was left alive, and the last ones left would have burned the town. They are tough and they are efficient.

On the day we had over three hundred shells come into Madrid, so the main streets were a glass-strewn, brick-dust-powdered, smoking shambles, Hipolito had the car parked in the lee of a building in a narrow street beside the hotel. It looked like a good safe place, and after he had sat around the room while I was working until he was thoroughly bored, he said he'd go down and sit in the car. He hadn't been gone ten minutes when a six-inch shell hit the hotel just at the junction of the main floor and the sidewalk. It went deep in out of sight and didn't explode. If it had burst, there would not have been enough left of Hipolito and the car to take a picture of. They were about fifteen feet away from where the shell hit. I looked out of the window, saw he was all right, and then went downstairs.

"How are you?" I was fairly average breathless.

"Fine," he said.

"Put the car farther down the street."

"Don't be foolish," he said. "Another one wouldn't drop there in a thousand years. Besides, it didn't explode."

"Put it farther along the street."

"What's the matter with you?" he asked. "You getting windy?"

I tried to give him some money when I left Madrid.

"I don't want anything from you," he said.

"No," I said. "Take it. Go on. Buy something for the family."

"No," he said. "Listen, we had a good time, didn't we?"

You can bet on Franco, or Mussolini, or Hitler, if you want; but my money goes on Hipolito.

"Peace"—And the Crisis Begins
DOROTHY THOMPSON—*New York Herald Tribune*—10/4/1938

"Perhaps the pacifist-humane idea is quite a good one in cases where the man at the top has first thoroughly conquered and subdued the world to the extent of making himself the sole master of it."   —Adolf Hitler, in Mein Kampf

What happened on Friday is called "Peace." Actually it is an international Fascist *coup d'état*.

The "Four-Power Accord" is not even a diplomatic document. It is certainly not a normal treaty. It is such a fantastic piece of paper that it is difficult to describe except as a hurriedly concocted armistice made in advance of a war to permit the occupation by German troops of a territory which by sheer threat and demonstration of force they have conquered by "agreement."

All of the territory where there are more than fifty per cent of German-speaking peoples will be evacuated by the Czechoslovaks and occupied by the German Army within ten days, although there are hundreds of thousands of people in this territory who are either not German or are anti-Nazi and therefore constitute a racial and political minority.

This document provides no protection whatsoever for their lives, their properties or their existences.

Not a clause indicates that they are to be protected in any manner from this occupation.

Those of us who know and have seen what the Nazi authorities do to political minorities realize that this can only result in a panicky flight into the interior of Czechoslovakia. It means the open establishment of terror.

No consideration is paid anywhere in this fantastic document to the reapportionment of financial and industrial interests—banks or industries the ownership of which is not necessarily on the spot—and this in spite of the fact that the British and French governments know that in the occupation of Austria the property of political minorities, and in particular of Jews, was simply confiscated.

There is not the most elementary consideration of justice.

An international commission will determine further territories in which a plebiscite is to be held, and will fix the conditions.

This will give plebiscites in areas containing more than fifty per cent Czechs, although no plebiscites will be held in areas containing more than fifty per cent Germans.

The pressure of the Nazis in contiguous territories occupied by German troops, their immense and cunningly organized propaganda, their house-by-house and name-by-name political organization; the ever-present threat that if the territories go German the political minorities will be exterminated, will assure the outcome of these plebiscites. *One might just as well cede them to Germany in the first place.*

Czechs and political minorities are given the right of option in and out of the ceded territories, but they must move within six months, and the conditions for exercising the option are left to a German-Czechoslovak commission. Which simply means that they are left to the Germans, considering the relative power position.

Compared with this the Treaty of Versailles is a great humane document and a normal and reasonable treaty.

The Treaty of Versailles allowed German nationals incorporated in the then new Czechoslovak state to opt for German nationality. They were given two years in which to make a decision and then twelve months in which to exercise it—three years in all—and the treaty guaranteed their right to retain ownership of their landed property in the territory of the state that they left, guaranteed their right to carry with them movable property of every description and prohibited the imposition of any export or import duties to be made upon them in connection with the removal of such property.

We know that the political minorities in Austria since the Nazi occupation have not been allowed to move anything, and that the property left behind by those who fled was confiscated in the form of an "emigration tax," a treatment of property usually described as Bolshevism.

The Treaty of Versailles was made after five months of deliberations, into which scores of experts were called—as experts and not as partisans.

But on Friday Czechoslovakia was disposed of by four men who in four hours made a judgment of the case in which the defendant was not even allowed to present a brief or be heard.

The very basis and spirit of Anglo-Saxon law was violated. What ruled that conference was Nazi law. Not one of the four men who thus arbitrarily disposed of a nation had ever set foot in Czechoslovakia, nor did any of them understand the other's language—except Mussolini. They had a German interpreter. They decided on the primary basis of a report issued by a man who also until two months ago had never spent any time at all in Czechoslovakia.

Furthermore, Lord Runciman's Report, though it recommends the ceding of the territories to Germany, categorically denies that the Germans had ever been "terrorized," fixes the blame for the failure of negotiations on Germans, states that at the time of his arrival many Sudetens still desired to remain in Czechoslovakia and accuses the Sudeten extremists, egged on by Germany, of provoking the demonstrations which, on the German side, were made an excuse for demanding armed occupation.

Even on the basis of what by internal evidence would seem to be a rigged report, Germany is guilty of provoking what was nearly an all-European war. And the punishment for this guilt is that she received everything that she was going to fight the war over.

This "everything" is more than the Sudeten territories. It is more than a free hand in the east. It is the domination of Europe.

In this whole affair, described as an attempt to keep peace, the democratic process has been completely suspended. In both Britain and France the facts have been suppressed by the exercise of government pressure on the controlled radio and on the newspapers. The people of England and France are confronted with a *fait accompli* without even being able to gain in advance possession of the facts on which it is based.

The Runciman Report was published the day before the *fait accompli*!

Not only is Czechoslovakia dismembered—what is left is destroyed as a democratic republic. *It will be utterly impossible for the new state to exist, under the conditions created, as anything except a military and semi-Fascist dictatorship. There will be no civil liberties. There will be enforced labor. There must be—in order to save the nation at all!*

Let us not call this peace. Peace is not the absence of war. Peace is a positive condition—the rule of law.

This peace has been estblished on lawlessness, and can only maintain itself by further lawlessness.

This peace has been established by dictatorship, and can only maintain itself by further dictatorship.

This peace has been established on betrayal, and can only maintain itself by further betrayal.

"Peace," said Spinoza, "is virtue caused by strength of spirit." This is not peace without victory, for the victory goes to Mr. Hitler.

This is peace without virtue. Therefore, it is not peace—but the initiation of a terrific world crisis.

Jock Evans Was on Duty That Night
ROBERT J. CASEY—*Chicago Daily News*—9/17/1940

HOTSPOT, SOUTHEAST ENGLAND—In the larger matters of threatened invasion by aerial bombs and artillery fire people have given little thought to Jock Evans, upon whose thin breast nobody will ever pin any medals, even posthumously.

He will never have a public funeral with muffled drums, muted trumpets, and suchlike tokens of civic gratitude. It is most unlikely he will ever have any funeral at all.

In the years before the war he had done nothing to distinguish himself. He had some sort of dock job where the dust hadn't been too good for his lungs. Because of bad eyes and other deficiencies, he had been rejected for military service even at the end of the last war, when medical examiners hadn't been too particular.

In other words, though nobody noticed it at the time, he was made of the stuff heroes are made of.

So far as concerns the elements that have made England to date, he was an architect's model for the spirit of the British Empire.

Jock Evans, to get on with it, was in his most recent career an air-raid-precautions warden. In a year's drill on how to put on the gas mask, how to revive fainting women, how to direct people to the nearest shelter, he had never shown more than ordinary aptitude.

Jock Evans was on duty that night. He had been on duty most nights in the past month, as he would be now with warnings on all the time and never an all-clear. He had phoned to central control at eleven p.m. that he had seen a bright light somewhere—his superiors, remembering Jock, suspected it might be somebody with a too-bright cigar.

He had stationed himself near the telephone kiosk near the edge of an out-lying suburb where the artillery shells still land each day when the town is shelled. He had had no occasion to move from his post at midnight when the big crump fell.

The big crump was a dud. For a moment Jock felt glad of that. The shriek of it had been pretty nerve-racking. But after a while, when he remembered he had better go run over and look at it, he wasn't reassured. It wasn't a dud. He had looked at enough diagrams and sketches to know. It was a time bomb—and a big one.

He told all this to his chief in his report a minute later.

"Where is it?" inquired his chief.

"In the garden," said Jock.

Then the same order:

"Get people out, empty near-by houses, and keep people away!"

"Yes, sir," said Jock Evans.

Maybe it might be as well to mention here something of the nature of a time bomb, especially for Americas, who so far haven't had much experience with such things.

In the first place it is not like the old-type torpedo with nose fuse which could be unscrewed by a handy man with a monkey wrench. This is more complicated. The timing device is a simple interior arrangement of acid working on metal.

By varying the thickness of the metal density, the acid rate of corrosion may be set for anything between one minute and one month. Eventually the acid reaches the fulminating charge and the neighborhood goes to pieces.

There have been some hints that in what followed after his report Jock didn't show any great judgment, but the same might have been said of Dewey if he had run into a mine at Manila Bay. He followed out his orders. In less than an hour he had evacuated the few homes in the immediate vicinity. Then he stationed himself to warn off traffic.

There wasn't much to do until about seven o'clock in the morning, when workers and sight-seers began to pass afoot, on bicycles, and in automobiles.

The odd feature of a community which is being continuously bombed is the inquisitive interest in lethal hazards. Jock Evans suddenly found himself alone in a two-man job. The bomb lay almost at the junction of two lanes, giving access to it from four directions.

Mr. Evans solved this problem as best he could. He roped off the street a hundred yards behind the bomb, then took up his post at the middle of the crossing.

Dozens of persons heard and heeded his call during the next two hours. "Time bomb here. Keep away, keep away."

One of those who passed was the priest of the neighborhood Anglican church, to whom is owing the best description of Jock Evans' last stand.

"He hardly needed to point out the bomb," said the padre. "It was lying there in a grass plot right behind him, and it was evident he knew all about it. His face was white and drawn, but there wasn't any tremor in his voice. I couldn't get it out of my head, as he sang out the warning and blew his whistle, that he was the psychological equivalent of the medieval leper, ringing his bell and shouting, 'Unclean! Unclean!'"

"I had told him to get away from the corner, block off the streets with ropes. But he said, 'My duty is to stay here. Please go on, sir; don't set a bad example.' I went to telephone for help."

The bomb went off at 9:10, blew a crater forty feet wide. No trace has been found of Evans.

Pearl Harbor
ELEANOR ROOSEVELT—"My Day"—United Features Syndicate—12/8/1941

I was going out in the hall to say goodbye to our cousins, Mr. and Mrs. Frederick Adams and their children, after luncheon, and, as I stepped out of my room, I knew something had happened. All the secretaries were there, two telephones were in use, the senior military aides were on their way with messages. I said nothing because the words I heard over the telephone were quite sufficient to tell me that, finally, the blow had fallen, and we had been attacked.

Attacked in the Philippines, in Hawaii, and on the ocean between San Francisco and Hawaii. Our people had been killed not suspecting there was an enemy, who attacked in the usual ruthless way which Hitler has prepared us to suspect.

Because our nation has lived up to the rules of civilization, it will probably take us a few days to catch up with our enemy, but no one in this country will doubt the ultimate outcome. None of us can help but regret the choice which Japan has made, but having made it, she has taken on a coalition of enemies she must underestimate; unless she believes we have sadly deteriorated since our first ships sailed into her harbor.

The clouds of uncertainty and anxiety have been hanging over us for a long time. Now we know where we are. The work for those who are at home seems to be obvious. First, to do our own job, whatever it is, as well as we can possibly do it. Second, to add to it everything we can do in the way of civilian defense. Now, at last, every community must go to work to build up protections from attack.

We must build up the best possible community services, so that all of our people may feel secure because they know we are standing together and that whatever problems have to be met, will be met by the community and not one lone individual. There is no weakness and insecurity when once this is understood.

The God-Damned Infantry
ERNIE PYLE—Scripps Howard—5/2/1943

In the front lines before Mateur, Northern Tunisia—We're now with an infantry outfit that has battled ceaselessly for four days and nights.

This northern warfare has been in the mountains. You don't ride much anymore. It is walking and climbing and crawling country. The mountains aren't big, but they are constant. They are largely treeless. They are easy to defend and bitter to take. But we are taking them.

The Germans lie on the back slope of every ridge, deeply dug into foxholes. In front of them the fields and pastures are hideous with thousands of hidden mines. The forward slopes are left open, untenanted, and if the Americans tried to scale these slopes they would be murdered wholesale in an inferno of machine-gun crossfire plus mortars and grenades.

Consequently we don't do it that way. We have fallen back to the old warfare of first pulverizing the enemy with artillery, then sweeping around the ends of the hill with infantry and taking them from the sides and behind.

I've written before how the big guns crack and roar almost constantly throughout the day and night. They lay a screen ahead of our troops. By magnificent shooting they drop shells on the back slopes. By means of shells timed to burst in the air a few feet from the ground, they get the Germans even in their foxholes. Our troops have found that the Germans dig foxholes down and then under, trying to get cover from the shell bursts that shower death from above.

Our artillery has really been sensational. For once we have enough of something and at the right time. Officers tell me they actually have more guns than they know what to do with.

All the guns in any one sector can be centered to shoot at one spot. And when we lay the whole business on a German hill the whole slope seems to erupt. It becomes an unbelievable cauldron of fire and smoke and dirt. Veteran German soldiers say they have never been through anything like it.

Now to the infantry—the God-damned infantry, as they like to call themselves.

I love the infantry because they are the underdogs. They are the mud-rain-frost-and-wind boys. They have no comforts, and they even learn to live without the necessities. And in the end they are the guys that wars can't be won without.

I wish you could see just one of the ineradicable pictures I have in my mind today. In this particular picture I am sitting among clumps of sword-grass on a steep and rocky hillside that we have just taken. We are looking out over a vast rolling country to the rear.

A narrow path comes like a ribbon over a hill miles away, down a long slope, across a creek, up a slope and over another hill.

All along the length of this ribbon there is now a thin line of men. For four days and nights they have fought hard, eaten little, washed none, and slept hardly at all. Their nights have been violent with attack, fright, butchery, and their days sleepless and miserable with the crash of artillery.

The men are walking. They are fifty feet apart, for dispersal. Their walk is slow, for they are dead weary, as you can tell even when looking at them from behind. Every line and sag of their bodies speaks their inhuman exhaustion.

On their shoulders and backs they carry heavy steel tripods, machine-gun barrels, leaden boxes of ammunition. Their feet seem to sink into the ground from the overload they are bearing.

They don't slouch. It is the terrible deliberation of each step that spells out their appalling tiredness. Their faces are black and unshaven. They are young men, but the grime and whiskers and exhaustion make them look middle-aged.

In their eyes as they pass is not hatred, not excitement, not despair, not the tonic of their victory—there is just the simple expression of being here as though they had been here doing this forever, and nothing else.

The line moves on, but it never ends. All afternoon men keep coming round the hill and vanishing eventually over the horizon. It is one long tired line of antlike men.

There is an agony in your heart and you almost feel ashamed to look at them. They are just guys from Broadway and Main Street, but you wouldn't remember them. They are too far away now. They are too tired. Their world can never be known to you, but if you could see them just once, just for an instant, you would know that no matter how hard people work back home they are not keeping pace with these infantrymen in Tunisia.

The Death of Captain Waskow
ERNIE PYLE—Scripps Howard—1/10/1944

AT THE FRONT LINES IN ITALY—In this war I have known a lot of officers who were loved and respected by the soldiers under them. But never have I crossed the trail of any man as beloved as Capt. Henry T. Waskow of Belton, Texas.

Capt. Waskow was a company commander in the 36th Division. He had led his company since long before it left the States. He was very young, only in his middle twenties, but he carried in him a sincerity and gentleness that made people want to be guided by him.

"After my own father, he came next," a sergeant told me.

"He always looked after us," a soldier said. "He'd go to bat for us every time."

"I've never knowed him to do anything unfair," another one said.

I was at the foot of the mule trail the night they brought Capt. Waskow's body down. The moon was nearly full at the time, and you could see far up the trail, and even part way across the valley below. Soldiers made shadows in the moonlight as they walked.

Dead men had been coming down the mountain all evening, lashed onto the backs of mules. They came lying belly-down across the wooden pack-saddles, their heads hanging down on the left side of the mule, their stiffened legs sticking out awkwardly from the other side, bobbing up and down as the mule walked.

The Italian mule-skinners were afraid to walk beside dead men, so Americans had to lead the mules down that night. Even the Americans were reluctant to unlash and lift off the bodies at the bottom, so an officer had to do it himself, and ask others to help.

The first one came early in the morning. They slid him down from the mule and stood him on his feet for a moment, while they got a new grip. In the half light he might have been merely a sick man standing there, leaning on the others. Then they laid him on the ground in the shadow of the low stone wall alongside the road.

I don't know who that first one was. You feel small in the presence of dead men, and ashamed at being alive, and you don't ask silly questions.

We left him there beside the road, that first one, and we all went back into the cowshed and sat on water cans or lay on the straw, waiting for the next batch of mules.

Somebody said the dead soldier had been dead for four days, and then nobody said anything more about it. We talked soldier talk for an hour or more. The dead man lay all alone outside in the shadow of the low stone wall.

Then a soldier came into the cowshed and said there were some more bodies outside. We went out into the road. Four mules stood there, in the moonlight, in the road where the trail came down off the mountain. The soldiers who led them stood there waiting. "This one is Captain Waskow," one of them said quietly.

Two men unlashed his body from the mule and lifted it off and laid it in the shadow beside the low stone wall. Other men took the other bodies off. Finally there were five lying end to end in a long row, alongside the road. You don't cover up dead men in the combat zone. They just lie there in the shadows until somebody else comes after them.

The unburdened mules moved off to their olive orchard. The men in the road seemed reluctant to leave. They stood around, and gradually one by one I could sense them moving close to Capt. Waskow's body. Not so much to look, I think, as to say something in finality to him, and to themselves. I stood close by and I could hear.

One soldier came and looked down, and he said out loud, "God damn it." That's all he said, and then he walked away. Another one came. He said, "God damn it to hell anyway." He looked down for a few last moments, and then he turned and left.

Another man came; I think he was an officer. It was hard to tell officers from men in the half light, for all were bearded and grimy dirty. The man looked down into the dead captain's face, and then he spoke directly to him, as though he were alive. He said: "I'm sorry, old man."

Then a soldier came and stood beside the officer, and bent over, and he too spoke to his dead captain, not in a whisper but awfully tenderly, and he said:

"I sure am sorry, sir."

Then the first man squatted down, and he reached down and took the dead hand, and he sat there for a full five minutes, holding the dead hand in his own and looking intently into the dead face, and he never uttered a sound all the time he sat there.

And finally he put the hand down, and then reached up and gently straightened the points of the captain's shirt collar, and then he sort of rearranged the tattered edges of his uniform around the wound. And then he got up and walked away down the road in the moonlight, all alone.

After that the rest of us went back into the cowshed, leaving the five dead men lying in a line, end to end, in the shadow of the low stone wall. We lay down on the straw in the cowshed, and pretty soon we were all asleep.

D-Day: A Pure Miracle
ERNIE PYLE—Scripps Howard—6/12/1944

NORMANDY BEACHHEAD—Due to a last-minute alteration in the arrangements, I didn't arrive on the beachhead until the morning after D-day, after our first wave of assault troops had hit the shore.

By the time we got here the beaches had been taken and the fighting had moved a couple of miles inland. All that remained on the beach was some sniping and artillery fire, and the occasional startling blast of a mine geysering brown sand into the air. That plus a gigantic and pitiful litter of wreckage along miles of shoreline.

Submerged tanks and overturned boats and burned trucks and shell-shattered jeeps and sad little personal belongings were strewn all over these bitter sands. That plus the bodies of soldiers lying in rows covered with blankets, the toes of their shoes sticking up in a line as though on drill. And other bodies, uncollected, still sprawling grotesquely in the sand or half hidden by the high grass beyond the beach.

That plus an intense, grim determination of work-weary men to get this chaotic beach organized and get all the vital supplies and the reinforcements moving more rapidly over it from the stacked-up ships standing in droves out to sea.

Now that it is over it seems to me a pure miracle that we ever took the beach at all. For some of our units it was easy, but in this special sector where I am now our troops faced such odds that our getting ashore was like my whipping Joe Louis down to a pulp.

In this column I want to tell you what the opening of the second front in this one sector entailed, so that you can know and appreciate and forever be humbly grateful to those both dead and alive who did it for you.

Ashore, facing us, were more enemy troops than we had in our assault waves. The advantages were all theirs, the disadvantages all ours. The Germans were dug into positions that they had been working on for months, although these were not yet all complete. A one-hundred-foot bluff a couple of hundred yards back from the beach had great concrete gun emplacements built right into the hilltop. These opened to the sides instead of to the front, thus making it very hard for naval fire from the sea to reach them. They could shoot parallel with the beach and cover every foot of it for miles with artillery fire.

Then they had hidden machine-gun nests on the forward slopes, with cross-fire taking in every inch of the beach. These nests were connected by networks of trenches, so that the German gunners could move about without exposing themselves.

Throughout the length of the beach, running zigzag a couple of hundred yards back from the shoreline, was an immense V-shaped ditch fifteen feet deep. Nothing could cross it, not even men on foot, until fills had been made. And in other places at the far end of the beach, where the ground is flatter, they had great concrete walls. These were blasted by our naval gunfire or by explosives set by hand after we got ashore.

Our only exits from the beach were several swales or valleys, each about one hundred yards wide. The Germans made the most of these funnel-like traps, sowing them with buried mines. They contained, also, barbed-wire entanglements with mines attached, hidden ditches, and machine guns firing from the slopes.

This is what was on the shore. But our men had to go through a maze nearly as deadly as this before they even got ashore. Underwater obstacles were terrific. The Germans had whole fields of evil devices under the water to catch our boats. Even now, several days after the landing, we have cleared only channels through them and cannot yet approach the whole length of the beach with our ships. Even now some ship or boat hits one of these mines every day and is knocked out of commission.

The Germans had masses of those great six-pronged spiders, made of railroad iron and standing shoulder-high, just beneath the surface of the water for our landing craft to run into. They also had huge logs buried in the sand, pointing upward and outward, their tops just below the water. Attached to these logs were mines.

In addition to these obstacles they had floating mines offshore, land mines buried in the sand of the beach, and more mines in checkerboard rows in the tall grass beyond the sand. And the enemy had four men on shore for every three men we had approaching the shore.

And yet we got on.

Beach landings are planned to a schedule that is set far ahead of time. They all have to be timed, in order for everything to mesh and for the following waves of troops to be standing off the beach and ready to land at the right moment.

As the landings are planned, some elements of the assault force are to break through quickly, push on inland, and attack the most obvious enemy strong points. It is usually the plan for units to be inland, attacking gun positions from behind, within a matter of minutes after the first men hit the beach.

I have always been amazed at the speed called for in these plans. You'll have schedules calling for engineers to land at H-hour plus two minutes, and service troops at H-hour plus thirty minutes, and even for press censors to land at H-hour plus seventy-five minutes. But in the attack on this special portion of the beach where I am—the worst we had, incidentally—the schedule didn't hold.

Our men simply could not get past the beach. They were pinned down right on the water's edge by an inhuman wall of fire from the bluff. Our first waves were on that beach for hours, instead of a few minutes, before they could begin working inland.

You can still see the foxholes they dug at the very edge of the water, in the sand and the small, jumbled rocks that form parts of the beach.

Medical corpsmen attended the wounded as best they could. Men were killed as they stepped out of landing craft. An officer whom I knew got a bullet through the head just as the door of his landing craft was let down. Some men were drowned.

The first crack in the beach defenses was finally accomplished by terrific and wonderful naval gunfire, which knocked out the big emplacements. They tell epic stories of destroyers that ran right up into shallow water and had it out point-blank with the big guns in those concrete emplacements ashore.

When the heavy fire stopped, our men were organized by their officers and pushed on inland, circling machine-gun nests and taking them from the rear.

As one officer said, the only way to take a beach is to face it and keep going. It is costly at first, but it's the only way. If the men are pinned down on the beach, dug in and out of action, they might as well not be there at all. They hold up the waves behind them, and nothing is being gained.

Our men were pinned down for a while, but finally they stood up and went through, and so we took that beach and accomplished our landing. We did it with every advantage on the enemy's side and every disadvantage on ours. In the light of a couple of days of retrospection, we sit and talk and call it a miracle that our men ever got on at all or were able to stay on.

Before long it will be permitted to name the units that did it. Then you will know to whom this glory should go. They suffered casualties. And yet if you take the entire beachhead assault, including other units that had a much easier time, our total casualties in driving this wedge into the continent of Europe were remarkably low—only a fraction, in fact, of what our commanders had been prepared to accept.

And these units that were so battered and went through such hell are still, right at this moment, pushing on inland without rest, their spirits high, their egotism in victory almost reaching the smart-alecky stage.

Their tails are up. "We've done it again," they say. They figure that the rest of the army isn't needed at all. Which proves that, while their judgment in this regard is bad, they certainly have the spirit that wins battles and eventually wars.

Dispatches from the End of the War

Orson Welles—*New York Post*—May 1945

Editors' Note: These paragraphs from "Orson Welles' Today" are culled from columns after the Nazi surrender, as newsreel footage of the concentration camps was shown in movie theaters across the United States.

I think you'll be glad with me that it has been made so difficult to avoid those hideous sights. They are the proof of the nightmare. The heaped-up dead in evidence. The burdened ovens. The ingenious machinery for the pit of pain. The eyeball blinking in the open grave. The tawdry skeleton that turns out to be still alive. The survivor squatting among the cadavers, opening his toothless mouth and naming the guilty without speech. Patton and Bradley, their eyes choked full of this. Eisenhower moving slowly with immense dignity through the long tableau.

* * *

Then there are the Germans—-the householders, the solid citizens. They are dressed like people. You recognize the costumes. A doctor, a school teacher, a shopkeeper, a factory foreman, a mother. Stock types, but in all a very unpersuasive masquerade. These creatures are less alive than the dead they have been called to view and bury.

The MP's are gentle with the Herrenvolk. You realize that they have need to be gentle or they would strike them down each with a single blow.

* * *

One place of torture you will learn was camouflaged as a madhouse. Here the most grisly of all grand guignol conceits was realized. Here the wardens were the lunatics. You can watch the chief of these being interviewed in the newsreels. The subject is poison. He is very businesslike. Between phrases he touches his upper lip with a fat lizard's tongue. The frown is professional. He is the man of science, called for expert consultation. The poison gives him away. And his chin—it is wet with drool.

* * *

If your stomach is weak you are the one they were after when they decided to show these films in the movie house. No, you must not miss the newsreels. They make a point this week no man can miss: The war has strewn the world with corpses, none of them very nice to look at. The thought of death is never pretty, but the newsreels testify to the fact of quite another sort of death—quite another level of decay. This is a putrefaction of the soul, a perfect spiritual garbage.

* * *

Said Mussolini at the point of a partisan's pistol. "Let me have my life and I will give you an empire."

These people really talk that way. They're actually the jibbering lunatics we said they were, I think that's why their downfall hasn't yet been dignified with a mighty sentence for the history books. The great and terrible names of Fascism are checked off, one by one, and there isn't anything to say.

The line equaling the event is often very casually spoken. A sequence in history is many times lassoed by the most accidental sort of prose and often goes unrecognized as the conclusive word. I nominate this last item from a news dispatch. Please read it slowly and carefully out loud.

"Lieut. Jerome Shapiro, New York City, guarded Goering's door last night."

There Are No Young Guys Here
PETE HAMILL—*New York Post*—1/10/1966

Perhaps we, who come from the fortunate places of the earth, shall never understand about places like Cam Ne. Where I come from, a place with shattered windows and no steam heat in winter is thought of as a slum. We think it criminal if rats scurry between the walls, or if children are forced to work at sixteen, or if a man loses one shot at decency and comfort because his education was incomplete or the color of his skin was unacceptable to others.

But in the Cam Nes of the world, to live past three is a success, and to make it to thirty is a triumph. I wish I could bring you here somehow; I wish you could see the faces of the old women, the light in their eyes extinguished, their small, shrinking heads looking dumbly from under conical hats, their skin eroded, clay-dry, pitted with the half-healed gashes of the swamp leech.

When they smile, which is seldom, their teeth show tar black from chewing betel nuts. If I could make that clear, make clear that these women have ceased being women at all, that their bodies have gone fallow and bone-hard like some strange new vertical beast of burden, make clear how disease has sapped them, and the filth of the rice paddies has flaked their skins, and ruined their blood, and shortened their very lives—if I could make that clear to you, you would begin to understand something about Cam Ne and perhaps about Vietnam.

You would begin to understand about Vietnam and the wretchedness of the land, if you could see the roads in the morning, clogged by people on the move, all of them old men and old women and young children. They carry on their backs all that they own: bamboo struts that make up their houses, small sacks of clothing, chickens, and an occasional pig. It is all they have. No books, no paintings, no radios, none of the soft ornaments of the twentieth century. Last year alone, 750,000 people in this country moved their place of residence, trying to keep a few hundred feet ahead of the violence. The whole country has been doing this for a quarter of a century.

But perhaps you should see Cam Ne on a trip with a couple of Marines. On this morning, I took a walk with two sergeants, Chuck Burzamato and Harold R. Hoerning. Burzamato is a short, red-faced guy, who came from Mott Street, lived in Brooklyn, and has been in the Marines for seventeen years. His wife and children live in San Clemente, California, and his parents live at 1402 East Third Street in Brooklyn. Hoerning has been a Marine for twenty-one years. His wife and four kids live in Oceanside, California, and his father, a retired New York cop, lives in Bayside, Long Island. They are professional Marines. They are also men.

We walked together down the dirt road which leads from the Marine camp to Cam Ne. The thick, gluey mud of Asia stuck to our boots and made a sucking sound as we walked. Hoerning was carrying a carbine, and Burzamato held a shotgun.

"The funny thing in Cam Ne," Burzamato said, "is that we got through to the children, and we even are getting through to the old people. But there's no young guys here. None."

"That's right," Hoerning said. "The young guys are all off with the VC."

The town is a collection of scattered huts and houses, laced with thick, crawling jungle. The Marines have been urging the people who live there to cut down the undergrowth, to clear the area of jungle. We saw an old man, with a Ho Chi Minh beard, slashing at the tangle with a machete.

"Hey, Pop!" Burzamato shouted. The old man stopped and smiled. "He's got swell-lookin' gums, don't he?" Burzamato said. We walked into the bush to talk to him. "Numbah One!" Burzamato said, using the local phrase which means something is very good. "You do number one job, Pop. You come today one o'clock, see boxie [doctor], get food! Numbah one."

The old man bowed, and shook his head yes, and said, "Numbah one, Numbah one." Burzamato gave him a cigarette and we moved into the jungle.

Everywhere in the jungle we saw trenches and long, narrow slots dug under the roots of trees. When the battle was fought here, the Vietcong were dug into the holes, covered with foliage, firing machine guns at the Marines, as they moved in. "If Charlie's dug into one of those holes," Hoerning said, "you'd need a direct hit with artillery to get him out."

The jungle itself had a sinister quality. I suppose if you come from cities, there is always something treacherous about uncontrolled nature. If it is in Vietnam, the possibility of violence around each turn makes it even more so. It must have been terrible to fight here; we literally could not see 20 feet on any side of us. "You could have twenty VC in there," Burzamato said, gesturing toward a dripping dark area to the right, "and never see them."

Suddenly we came to a small clearing. On a knoll, up above a small untended private rice paddy, stood a brick house. There had once been a walk leading to the door, but it was cracked and smashed now, with scrub growing in the broken places. Bougainvillaea ran up the sides of the house, and on its porch stood a small young girl, maybe six or seven, a boy about four, and no one else. All of it—the children, the house, the small 10-foot-by-20-foot rice paddy—all seemed about to be swallowed or suffocated by the jungle.

"Hal-looo," Burzamato shouted. We walked up to the porch. The house was bare and empty. Not a single piece of furniture, no food, nothing. In one corner stood a neat Buddhist altar. The girl looked terrified. "Don't be afraid, beautiful. Me numbah one." He reached in his pocket and pulled out some candy. The little girl was afraid to take it. The boy reached out, and Burzamato gave it to him, explaining with gestures that he should share it with his sister. We started to leave when I saw something move in the corner. It was an infant, huddled in a kind of thatch nest, coverd with flies. The child's skin was gray, its eyes clamped shut, its stomach swollen. It was obviously dying.

"Jesus," Burzamato said. "Jesus, Jesus, Jesus."

I thought he was going to cry.

We walked through the village for two hours. Everywhere the old people were clearing away the tangle of undergrowth, chopping away the 35-foot bamboo, taking cigarettes from the two Marines. One old man had cut away about 10 square yards, and Burzamato gave him a whole pack of smokes.

We came across one little girl whose eye had been split by a piece of flying bamboo, and Burzamato called a Marine corpsman, David Luck, from St. Paul, Minnesota, and had the eye cleaned and treated. He gave out eighteen packs of candy, and when we started back later, the children followed him all the way to the base camp. He looked like a squat, gun-toting pied piper.

At one o'clock, the people of Cam Ne had lined up, and the Marines had spread the donated clothing across sheets of cardboard. The children came into the compound two at a time, and the Marines sorted out the clothing, trying to find things of the correct size. "Lookit this," Burzamato said, holding up a sheep-skin-lined jacket. "That's for when it goes under a hundred."

He took out a nightgown, made of a diaphanous material. "Just what the mama-san needs for a big Saturday night in Cam Ne." There was a lot of joking and laughter, but the children walked away from the place, past the ruined shell of the house which served as headquarters, and they were smiling.

Perhaps we do not have either a legal or moral right to be in this country, and certainly the war itself is a disgusting and an abstract thing. But believe me, the Americans who are here are as decent as anyone I've ever met. It should be unnecessary to say so, but the Marine Corps is not the Wehrmacht, and if I had my choice of dinner companions between Staughton Lynd and Chuck Burzamato, I would not be long in the choosing.

To Root Against Your Country
ART HOPPE—*San Francisco Chronicle*—3/5/1971

The radio this morning said the Allied invasion of Laos had bogged down. Without thinking, I nodded and said, "Good."

And having said it, I realized the bitter truth: Now I root against my own country.

This is how far we have come in this hated and endless war. This is the nadir I have reached in this winter of my discontent. This is how close I border on treason:

Now I root against my own country.

How frighteningly sad this is. My generation was raised to love our country and we loved it unthinkingly. We licked Hitler and Tojo and Mussolini. Those were our shining hours. Those were our days of faith.

They were evil; we were good. They told lies; we spoke the truth. Our cause was just, our purposes noble, and in victory we were magnanimous. What a wonderful country we are! I loved it so.

But now, having descended down the torturous, brutalizing years of this bloody war, I have come to the dank and lightless bottom of the well: I have come to root against the country that once I blindly loved.

I can rationalize it. I can say that if the invasion of Laos succeeds, the chimera of victory will dance once again before our eyes—leading us once again into more years of mindless slaughter. Thus, I can say, I hope the invasion fails.

But it is more than that. It is that I have come to hate my country's role in Vietnam.

I hate the massacres, the body counts, the free fire zones, the napalming of civilians, the poisoning of rice crops. I hate being part of My Lai. I hate the fact that we have now dropped more explosives on these scrawny Asian peasants than we did on all our enemies in World War II.

And I hate my leaders, who, over the years, have conscripted our young men and sent them there to kill or be killed in a senseless cause simply because they can find no honorable way out—no honorable way out for them.

I don't root for the enemy. I doubt they are any better than we. I don't give a damn anymore who wins the day. But because I hate what my country is doing in Vietnam, I emotionally and often irrationally hope that it fails.

It is a terrible thing to root against your own country. If I were alone, it wouldn't matter. But I don't think I am alone. I think many Americans must feel these same sickening emotions I feel. I think they share my guilt. I think they share my rage.

If this is true, we must end this war now—in defeat, if necessary. We must end it because all of Southeast Asia is not worth the hatred, shame, guilt and rage that is tearing Americans apart. We must end it not for those among our young who have come to hate America, but for those who somehow manage to love it still.

I doubt that I can ever again love my country in that unthinking way that I did when I was young. Perhaps this is a good thing.

But I would hope the day will come when I can once again believe what my country says and once again approve of what it does. I want to have faith once more in the justness of my country's causes and the nobleness of its ideals.

What I want so very much is to be able once again to root for my own, my native land.

Obituary for South Vietnam
PETER R. KANN—*Wall Street Journal*—5/2/1975

South Vietnam, or rather the South Vietnam that I have known for several years, has passed away.

There probably are a great many Americans who breathed a sigh of relief when they heard the end had come. There undoubtedly are some Americans who wished, for whatever reason, that South Vietnam had expired much sooner. But surely there also are some Americans who mourn the passing. I am one of them.

For me the collapse of South Vietnam was like the death of an old acquaintance. Much as I often criticized South Vietnam I don't think it deserved to die.

South Vietnam's faults and failings always were much more visible than its strengths and I, like most reporters, tended to focus at least my professional attention on what South Vietnam was doing wrong. Few societies, and certainly few small and frail ones, ever have been subjected to the degree of sustained critical attention that Vietnam was. I and a thousand other reporters dissected its every aspect, analyzed its every mistake, exposed its every flaw. This is not to say South Vietnam would have fared better or survived longer had the spotlights been turned off, but conceivably there might be a few more sympathizers at the funeral.

In the end, of course, the severest critics and profoundest pessimists proved to be right. South Vietnam may have survived longer than some pessimists expected, but it did collapse—suddenly, chaotically, completely. And I think, tragically.

South Vietnam was, to my mind, no better but no worse than a great many other societies around the world. In at least some ways it was not so very different from our own. Obviously South Vietnam's social structure, government and army ultimately were too weak to resist the Vietnamese Communists. Less obvious is the thought that South Vietnam did manage to resist for a great many years and not always with a great deal of American help. Few nations or societies that I can think of would have struggled so long.

THE COMMUNIST CRUSADE

It is true that South Vietnam lacked a unifying and motivating cause that could compete with the Communist crusade. Anti-communism never was compelling or even comprehensible to most South Vietnamese Capitalism, as represented by Honda motorbikes and other imported goodies, was not a cause that captured hearts and minds. Nationalism was a contested cause and if only because the American presence had been so great in South Vietnam the Communists seemed to be the *true* nationalists. So South Vietnam was a country without a cause. But now stop to consider: What cause would motivate you or me to fight for 25 years?

It is true that South Vietnam lacked the kind of creative, dynamic leadership that conceivably might have coaxed more spirit and sacrifice from a war-weary nation. President Nguyen van Thieu was no charismatic statesman. He was an introverted and suspicious military man who proved surprisingly adept at playing palace politics but who never truly learned to lead. But was Mr. Thieu really any less of a leader than scores of other retired generals who rule semi-developed nations around the world? I think not. He was, by his own lights, a Vietnamese patriot. And, before being too hard on failed South Vietnamese leaders, perhaps one ought to stop to list the names of truly popular and successful statesmen anywhere in the non-Communist world today. My own list could be written on a Bandaid.

It is true that South Vietnam's politicians and people never seemed able to unite, that the society seemed divisive and sounded discordant. Saigon's chaotic traffic frequently was cited as symbolizing the society's lack of order and discipline. But what non-Communist society these days can claim any great degree of political unity or social cohesion? Do we, by our values, venerate order and discipline as social goals or moral virtues? Are the best societies really those in which the trains all run on time and the people all march in step?

It is true that South Vietnam never was really democratic. Its democratic institutions, imported from America along with bombs and bulgur wheat, were more show than substance. And yet, if only because the South Vietnamese government never was very efficient, South Vietnam, unlike North Vietnam, never qualified as a totalitarian state. There were political prisoners and torture chambers and other elements of sometimes harsh authoritarianism. But there also were some limitations on the power of the president, there was fairly widespread—and not always whispered—criticism of government policies, there was a surprising diversity of individual opinion and behavior. Might South Vietnam have fared better had it been more authoritarian, more rigid and ruthless? I doubt it. But I also doubt that it would have fared better had the legislature exercised more power or had press controls been relaxed.

THE CORRUPTION ISSUE

It is true that South Vietnam was corrupt. The corruption was more widespread and more serious than simply a few fat generals salting away millions in Swiss bank accounts. The whole system was in some sense corrupt. At the lowest level it was a simple matter of government clerks supplementing meager incomes with petty bribes. At a higher level it all too often was a case of jobs being sold to men who could pay rather than given to men who could perform. At the highest levels there were some cases of outright venality. But not all, perhaps not even most, South Vietnamese officers or administrators were corrupt. It is not excusing Vietnamese corruption to point out that it exists to roughly the same degree in almost every Southeast Asian country. Nor is it excusing Asian corruption to note that few Western societies are so pure that they can cast many stones.

It is true that South Vietnamese society was inegalitarian and elitist. Its rich were too rich and its poor too poor and the disparities were all too visible. Money and position bought privileges like draft deferments and, at the end, escape. Yet the disparities in Vietnam actually were less glaring than those in a score of other American-allied states from the Philippines to Brazil. The South Vietnamese peasant, when the war was not being fought in his particular paddy, was a prosperous small farmer by Asian standards. I am not minimizing the misery of the millions who passed through refugee camps when I note that there also were some millions of small farmers who owned their own land and made a fair living from their crops. The South Vietnamese peasant, in short, was not a downtrodden serf waiting for liberation from some slave master.

It also should be said, or confessed if you will, that there were many likeable people among the elite who ruled Vietnam. Almost every reporter who spent any time in the country befriended some government official, army officer, businessman, politician—some member of that elite. These people frequently were all too remote from their own countrymen and countryside. Many were too wealthy or too Western-oriented to have much rapport with peasants or soldiers. They were not the best sort of people according to some biblical, or Buddhist, value scale. But some of them were my friends and I will miss them.

It is true that the South Vietnamese army (ARVN) in the end proved to be no match for the North Vietnamese army. The end was an inglorious six weeks of retreats, routs, chaos, and collapse. Still, the ARVN was not an army of bumblers and cowards. It was an army that stood and fought with great courage and competence on a few occasions you may remember, like the siege of An Loc. It stood and fought well at a score of places whose names we have forgotten. And it stood and fought well in a thousand little engagements and in a thousand little mudwalled outposts whose names no American ever knew.

It was an army of soldiers who deserved better leadership than they got. It was an army that for years watched the Americans try to combat the Communists with every wonder of modern weaponry and which then, all too suddenly, was left to face the Communists with American-style tactics but without American-style resources. It was a Vietnamese army that perhaps never should have been Americanized and thus never would have required Vietnamization. It was an army that for years was ordered to defend every inch of Vietnamese territory and which tried, with greater or lesser success, to do just that. When suddenly it was told to abandon cities and provinces it effectively abandoned the war.

It was not an army of officers and men who tended to charge impregnable enemy positions, or who would have been willing to live for years in holes in the ground with B-52 bombers pounding the earth around them, or who would have made the long and terrible trek down the Ho Chi Minh Trail, or who went into battle motivated by the thought that their almost certain deaths would serve some noble goal. The North Vietnamese army is that kind of army, but how many others, including our own, are fashioned in that mold? The South Vietnamese army was an army of simple soldiers who, without a cause, fought on for more than two decades. Several hundred thousand of these soldiers died. More than half a million were wounded. And, in the final weeks of the war, when every American in Saigon knew the war was lost, some of these soldiers continued to fight at places like Xuan Loc and thereby bought a bit of time for the Americans and their chosen Vietnamese to escape with their lives. It was a much better army than it appeared to be at the end.

It is true that South Vietnam got a great deal of help from America and became too reliant upon us. Soviet and Chinese troops never fought in Vietnam as American troops did. For much of a decade South Vietnam was, for most practical purposes, an American colony. The U.S. army took over the war and for a time promised to win it. The U.S. taxpayer financed Vietnam. Washington set Saigon's policies and the U.S. Embassy in Saigon largely fashioned Vietnam's politics. South Vietnam was not always a docile puppet and at times it failed to dance to American tunes. But over the years South Vietnam came to assume, indeed was led to assume, that America was its patron and protector. It was not an unreasonable assumption. Nor then was it entirely unreasonable for Vietnamese to sometimes shrug off responsibility for their own failings, to blame the U.S. for their problems, and, toward the end, when America lost heart for the war and lost interest in Vietnam, to be bitter at America and Americans.

THE VICTORS

In the end the stronger side won. The Vietnamese Communists had more strength and more stamina. They had a cause, a combination of communism and nationalism, and they pursued that cause with almost messianic motivation. They persisted against all obstacles and at times against all odds and they finally succeeded.

But the stronger side is not necessarily the better side. "Better" becomes a question of values and much as I may respect Communist strength and stamina I cannot accept that the Spartan Communist society of North Vietnam is *better* than the very imperfect South Vietnamese society that I knew.

This is an obituary for that South Vietnam. It cannot be an obituary for the country of Vietnam or even the people of Vietnam. Countries don't die. South Vietnam will continue to exist for some months or perhaps a few years with a new government, new policies, a new social system. Then it presumably will merge with North Vietnam and this enlarged Vietnam will dominate Indochina and will become a major force in Asia as a whole. It will be a nation of 40 million hardy and hardened people. It will be rich in natural resources. It will have one of the finest, maybe the finest, army in the world.

Perhaps the energies of 40 million Vietnamese will be devoted to reconstruction and economic progress. Perhaps they will be devoted to further political and military expansion. In either case Vietnam will merit, and probably command, world attention in years ahead. Some South Vietnamese enthusiastically will embrace a new system and new society. Some will have trouble adjusting but eventually will find a place in the new order. Some will be unable to accept the new order, or will be unacceptable to it. They will be discarded in one manner or another, but their children will be brought up to be part of the new society.

The new Vietnam will be powerful and successful and those are the qualities that seem to count among nations, as among men. History books tend to deal with the same themes and history thus is unlikely to look kindly on the South Vietnam that failed to survive. But this is not history. It's just an obituary for the South Vietnam that I knew.

Hallelujah
WILLIAM F. BUCKLEY JR.—United Press Syndicate—11/10/1989

When the news came in, President Bush sat quietly in his large chair in the Oval Office and said in grave tones that we must not overreact. He is absolutely right about this. *Jingle Bells! Jingle Bells! Jingle at the Waaaay!* It is proper to deem it a historical development, but its significance must not affect our judgment. *Oh what a beau-ti-ful morn-ing! Oh what a beau-ti-ful day!!!* After all, there is tomorrow to think about in Germany. *Germany?!?! What do you mean, "Germany"? You mean West Germany or you mean East Germany?*—and the score allows for many variations. Calmness is in order.

I remember the day in 1973 when, as a delegate to the General Assembly of the United Nations, occupying the chair, I had to sit there and listen to the ambassador from the German Democratic Republic lecturing to the Third Committee (Human Rights Committee) on the differences between life in his own country, where the pastures of the people were evergreen and life was pleasant, just and equable, in contrast to "elsewhere" in Europe, dominated by strife, competition and all the vexations of bourgeois life. I interrupted the speaker to make some reference or another to the Wall that obscured the view of the Communists' green pastures, but all the professional diplomats of course knew all about the wall and about communist rhetoric—I learned early during my brief service at the United Nations that the thing to remember is that nobody pays any attention whatever to anything anybody says at the United Nations, which is one up for sanity. But as a freshman diplomat, who never graduated, the insolence of the East German diplomat stayed with me.

And so I wrote a book about the United Nations, and made reference to the special hypocrisies of totalitarian states, which, instead of isolating in such secrecy as is possible what goes on there, actually go about the world boasting about their civil depravity. But the wall and what it represented stuck in the mind, as it did with so many people—the antipodes of the Statue of Liberty; the great symbol of Gulag life. A few years later I wrote a novel based on a young idealist's determination in 1952 to attempt to reunite Germany, a political effort finally frustrated by the assassination of the young, upward-bound idealist. By the KGB? No, by my hero, Blackford Oakes, under orders from Washington, because Stalin had said the alternative was a Third World War. I dramatized that novel (*Stained Glass*) and in March of this year, on Good Friday, it was splendidly produced by the Actors Theatre in Louisville, Kentucky.

Still, the ugliness of divided Germany hadn't left me, and in 1978 I went to Berlin actually to look. It is hard to describe the impacted loathsomeness of it. Every season, the communists added one more obstacle to stand in the way of the occasional Houdini who managed to get through. That was the winter they added the dogs. It had begun with a concrete wall. Then barbed wire. Then watchtowers with machine-gunners. Then huge spotlights. Then land mines. Then mountains of shards of glass. It is a comment on the limited resources of the communist imagination that they forgot to plant poison ivy alongside the wall.

And so I wrote a novel based on another young German idealist, determined to prevent the construction of the wall when on Aug. 13, 1961, all of a sudden it began to materialize. My young German, who as a Jewish child had been secreted to England for safety, his parents being left to die in a Nazi camp, had his contact in East Berlin, a secretary to the monster Ulbricht. And the word from the secretary was that if three NATO tanks charged through the wall that first day during its flimsy stage, the East Germans, backed by the Russians, would make a great show of opposition, but actually they would yield, as Khrushchev did not want a showdown with the West—not in August 1961, a full year before the missile crisis in Cuba. But the U.S. military, under orders, seized the little column of tanks that had been secretly pulled out from the U.S. armory by young, trained resistance Germans—and so we never knew what would have happened if we had asserted our rights to co-governing East Berlin. My young German hero, Henri Tod, did not live to see the sun set on the growing wall.

It was a great day, Nov. 9, 1989, and one day must be nominated for international celebration. *Joshua fit the Battle of Jericho, Jericho, Jericho! Joshua fit the Battle of Jericho! and the walls came tumblin' Down!*

Word of the Year: Freedom
WILLIAM SAFIRE—*New York Times*—12/31/1989

In his recent meeting with President Bush, Mikhail S. Gorbachev was reported to have suggested that the American stop using the phrase Western values, as in "the triumph of Western values." This hint that the West had won the cold war smacked too much of gloating.

Mr. Bush, an ardent anti-triumphalist, agreed to change his rhetoric; he and his Secretary of State immediately switched to democratic values, a concept that his Communist counterpart professes to share.

That adjective was inoffensive to Mr. Gorbachev because democracy is a word long adopted by Communism, along with people. Many Marxist-Leninist regimes styled themselves democratic peoples' republics, though this is redundant: demos is the Greek root for "people." (Kratos means "strength" or "power.") A democracy is a system of government in which the power comes directly from the people; past mislabeling is tacitly recognized in the Soviet Union today, which is undergoing what Mr. Gorbachev calls the process of democratization.

One word, however, is generally recognized to be a Western value, to use the provocative term, which orators often use with the phrase Judeo-Christian heritage. The key word is freedom, certainly 1989's Word of the Year.

In a curious but longstanding agreement, speech writers of the left and right have come to respect each other's primary rhetorical turf: Communists call their countries and allies peaceloving (not hyphenated); conservative ideologues call their countries freedom-loving (hyphenated).

Many Westerners hasten to add peace, as in "to live in freedom and peace," often adding Abraham Lincoln's adjectives "just and lasting," but their emphasis differs from the Communists'. Few would accept Picasso's symbol of a dove of peace as their own. The West's appropriation of the word freedom is apparent in a Communist spokesman's reference to "the so-called free world"; that phrase, now used mainly by unreconstructed cold warriors, has effectively cast aspersions on the state of liberty in Communist-dominated nations.

Freedom has even triumphed over liberty. The two words are synonyms, but resonate differently.

Liberty, from the Latin liber, "free," taken from the Greek eleutheros, is a product of the Romance languages—in French, liberte; Spanish libertad; Rumanian liberdade. In American English, the revered word has the happy connotation of a Liberty Bell with its invocations to "proclaim Liberty throughout the land" and calls up images of the pre-Civil War liberty poles ("What's liberty without a pole?" asked William Seward, defending the idea of a proclamation of emancipation).

Perhaps because of recent bicentennial celebrations, the word liberty, unmodified by the controversializing civil, has gained a historical connotation; we tend to associate it with a symbolic spread eagle, and think reverently of liberty as the remembered goal of the philosophy of self-government.

Freedom is a hammer of a word, without a Greek or Latin pedigree, from the proto-Germanic frijaz that came into Old English as freodom. These Germanic words are punchier than their Romance-language counterparts: rich and hard are more telling than affluent and arduous.

The root freo, in Dutch vrij, was among our earliest English words, making its appearance in the eighth century. The first meaning was "dear, beloved, close," to identify family members in contrast to servants or slaves; the Indo-European prei-, "to be fond of," is the root of "friend," and is related to the Sanskrit priyas, "beloved."

Loved ones had privileges: one held in freedom by the authority of the house had fewer restrictions on speech or movement. The free had the capacity to act without the many constraints imposed on those in bondage, and that ability came to be valued highly. "I remember a proverb said of old," wrote John Lydgate in 1430. "'Who loseth his freedom, in faith he loseth all.'"

In time, freedom—the state of the loved ones—came to mean more than a guiding principle of householding or government; in its passionate political sense, the thundering word now means a way of life unbounded by arbitrary power.

Freiheit was the word shouted at the opening of the Berlin wall. (Metaphorical problem: a wall does not "open" like a gate; a wall falls, crumbles, or is climbed over, breached or torn down. That did not happen as movement within Berlin was permitted, leaving commentators straining for a suitable verb. Orators pray for a tearing-down, with remnants left standing as reminders and platforms.) In Prague, Czechs call for svoboda, which is also the word in Russian and Bulgarian. In Warsaw, you hear wolnosc, pronounced VOL-nosch. In Budapest, Hungarians say szabadsag, pronounced SAH-bahd-shag, and in Riga, Latvians demand briviba, pronounced BREE-VEE-ba. In Albania, there's not much liri, but it will come one day. Same with azadi in Afghanistan, laisve in Lithuania and zi uyou in China.

Diplomats still talk carefully about peaceful change, measured reform and progress toward self-determination, but the blunt and thrilling words for freedom can be heard in the streets, bouncing off satellites to television screens and inspiring others to hit the streets around the world. (And if a T-shirt manufacturer would print all these words for freedom on single shirts, machine washable, demonstrators everywhere would buy them.) "Sir," said Robert Young Hayne of South Carolina in the Senate more than a century and a half ago, "there have existed, in every age and every country, two distinct orders of men—the lovers of freedom and the devoted advocates of power." The year 1990 may see order or stability, the euphemisms for the imposition of power, come roaring malevolently back; but in 1989, at least in most places, freedom was the rallying cry.

What's the name of this era, anyway?

"We're going through some very fundamental changes," intoned Robert Stalla, a forecaster for McDonald & Company Securities, at a December 1985 luncheon in Cleveland, "that would indicate we're entering the post, postwar period."

Nearly three years later, Joseph C. Harsch used the phrase (properly punctuated) in his column, which The Christian Science Monitor headlined "Welcome to the 'post-postwar' era."

The global strategist Hal Sonnenfeldt, in March of 1989, gave the phrase a push at a Brookings Institution seminar, and Britain's Daily Telegraph a couple of months later characterized the 40th anniversary of the North Atlantic Treaty Organization as "Europe's entry to the post-postwar era."

Neo-post-modernist phrase-watchers gave the double posting up for dead until Secretary of State James A. Baker 3d announced earlier this month: "I think it's fair to say we are moving into the post post-war era." (He went on to Berlin to float out the new Europe, the new Atlanticism, the new Architecture and the old-fashioned new era, in a tie salesman's approach to phrasemaking.) Is this the best the pre-millennial decade can do? (Sometimes you have to play the hyphens by ear.) Post post-which war—World War II or cold? (I must have missed the entire pre pre-war period, which presumably overlapped the post post-World War I era.) Seers, sages, historico-futurists, era-ushers and even quasi neo-post-modernists are invited to send their characterizations of these days of our years to Safire's Names for Nowadays, The New York Times, 1627 Eye Street, Washington, D.C. 20006. Prize is immortality.

Death Takes Hold Among the Living
PETE HAMILL—*New York Daily News*—9/12/2001

We were gathered at a large table in the Tweed Courthouse, discussing over bagels and coffee its future as a symbol of civilization, a museum of the history of New York. About 8:45, we heard a boom. It was not a ferocious boom, but the sort too common in a city where construction jobs are a constant. A few made nervous jokes and the meeting went on. We heard sirens now. Then, just before 9, a man came in and told us that an American Airlines jetliner had slammed into one of the twin towers.

I grabbed my coat and ran down the marble stairs, passing construction workers, and hurried onto Chambers St. Sirens were now splitting the air and there were police lines being set up on Broadway. Several hundred New Yorkers were on the north side of the street gazing up at the World Trade Center. A great gray cloud billowed in slow motion, growing larger and larger, like some evil genie released into the cloudless sky. Twisted hunks of metal were falling off the ruined facade. Sheets of paper fluttered against the grayness like ghostly snowflakes.

Then, at 9:03, there was another boom, and now an immense ball of orange flame exploded out of a high floor of the second tower.

"Oh, —, man, oh, —, oh, wow," a man said, backing away, eyes wide with fear and awe, while a few others began running toward the Municipal Building. "No way!" shouted another man. "You believe this?" While a fourth said: "They gotta be dyin' up there."

None of us on that street had seen the second plane coming from the west. Through the clouds of smoke, we couldn't see it smash into the immense tower, loaded with fuel. But there was this expanding, fearful, insidious orange ball: about seven stories high, full of dumb, blind power. For one heart-stopping moment it seemed capable of rolling all the way to where we were standing, charring everything in its path. And then it seemed to sigh and contract, retreating into the building, to burn whatever human beings might still be alive.

Calm & Orderly

The odd thing on the street was that so few New Yorkers panicked. The photographs of weeping women and distraught men were exceptions, not the rule. Some stoic New York cool took over. People walked north on Broadway, but few ran. All looked back to see the smoke flowing darkly to the east, toward Brooklyn.

"Go, go, go, go," a police sergeant was shouting, pointing east. And people followed his orders, but didn't grow runny with fear. Now the sky was dark with blacker clouds. Near the corner of Duane St., two women called to a policewoman: "Officer, officer, where can we go to give blood?" The policewoman said, "I don't know, ma'am, but please keep moving north."

The great stream moved steadily north. My wife and I walked south, gazing up at the beautiful facade of the Woolworth Building, all white and ornate against the clouds of smoke. By now we all knew that this was terrorism; one plane hitting a tower could be an accident, but two were part of a plan. On Vesey St., outside the Jean Louis David hair salon on the corner of Church St., we could see a wheel rim from an airplane, guarded by a man in an FBI jacket. Another anonymous hunk of scorched metal was lying on the ground across Vesey St. from St. Paul's, where George Washington once kneeled in prayer.

Near the curb beside the police lines, I could see a puddle of blood already darkening, a woman's black shoe now sticky with blood, an unopened bottle of V-8 Splash, a cheese danish still wrapped in cellophane. Someone had been hurt here, on her way to breakfast at an office desk.

Tumbling Bodies

But when we looked up, the fires and smoke shifted from ghastly spectacle to specific human horror. It was 9:40. From the north facade of the uptown tower, just below the floor that was spewing orange flame, a human being came flying into the air.

A man.

Shirtless.

Tumbling head over heels at first, until the weight of his torso carried him face-first, story after story, hundreds of feet, in the last terrifying seconds of his life.

We did not see him smash into the ground. He just vanished.

"That's 14 by my count," a cop said. "These poor bastards. . . . "

He didn't finish the sentence. He turned away, talked on a cell phone, hung up, turned to another cop. "Believe this? My mother says they crashed a plane into the—Pentagon!"

The Pentagon? Could that be?

But there was no time to call for details, to see how wide this day would be.

For above us, at 9:55, the first of the towers began to collapse. We heard snapping sounds, pops, little explosions, and then the walls bulged out, and we heard a sound like an avalanche, and here it came.

Everything then happened in fragments, scribble. I yell to my wife, "Run!" And we start together, and this immense cloud, perhaps 25 stories high, is rolling at us.

But bodies come smashing together in the doorway of 25 Vesey St. and I can't see my wife, and when I push to get out, I'm driven into the lobby. I keep calling her name, and saying, "I've got to get out of here, please, my wife. . . ."

No Way Out

We're in the building, deep in the lobby, behind walls, and the clear glass doors are gray-brown, locked tight, but the dust whooshes into the lobby. "Don't open that door!" someone says. "Get away from that—door!" As I write, it remains present tense. We look for a back door. There is none. Joey Newfield, a photographer for the *New York Post*, the son of a close friend, is covered with powder and dust and still making photographs. He is told by a building employee there might be an exit in the basement. A half-dozen of us go down narrow stairs. There is no exit. But there is a water cooler, and we rinse the dust from our mouths.

I'm desperate now to get out, to find my wife, to be sure she's alive, to hug her in the horror. But I'm sealed with these others inside in the tomblike basement of an office building. "Come on, come up here!" a voice calls, and we start climbing narrow stairs. Back in the lobby, police emergency workers are caked with white powder, coughing, hacking, spitting, like figures from a horror movie. Then there's a sound of splintering glass. One of the emergency workers has smashed open the glass doors. I feel as if I've been there for an hour; only 14 minutes have passed.

"Get going!" a cop yells. "But don't run!"

Ashen Faces, Streets

The street before us is now a pale gray wilderness. There is powdery white dust on gutter and sidewalk, and dust on the roofs of cars, and dust on the tombstones of St. Paul's. Dust coats all the walking human beings, the police and the civilians, white people and black, men and women. It's like an assembly of ghosts. Dust has covered the drying puddle of blood and the lone woman's shoe and the uneaten cheese danish. To the right, the dust cloud is still rising and falling, undulating in a sinister way, billowing out and then falling in upon itself. The tower is gone.

I start running toward Broadway, through dust 2 inches deep. Park Row is white. City Hall Park is white. Sheets of paper are scattered everywhere, orders for stocks, waybills, purchase orders, the pulverized confetti of capitalism. Sirens blare, klaxons wail. I see a black woman with dazed eyes, her hair coated with dust, and an Asian woman masked with powder. I don't see my wife anywhere. I look into store windows. I peer into an ambulance. I ask a cop if there's an emergency center.

"Yeah," he says. "Everywhere."

Searching amid Exodus

Then we're all walking north, streams of New Yorkers, thousands of us, holding handkerchiefs to noses, coughing, a few in tears. Many are searching for friends or lovers, husbands or wives. I try a pay phone. Not working. Another. Dead. At Chambers St., when I look back, City Hall is covered with white powder. So is the dome of the Potter Building on Park Row.

A few more blocks and I'm home, my own face and clothes a ghastly white, and my wife is coming out the door, after checking telephone messages, about to race back into the death-stained city to search for me.

We hug each other for a long time.

All around us, the fine powder of death is falling, put into the New York air by lunatics. Religious war, filled with the melodrama of martyrdom, had come to New York. Almost certainly, it was welded to visions of paradise. And in some ways, on the day of the worst single disaster in New York history, there was a feeling that the dying had only begun.

We'll Go Forward From This Moment
Leonard Pitts Jr.—*Miami Herald*—9/12/2001

It's my job to have something to say.

They pay me to provide words that help make sense of that which troubles the American soul. But in this moment of airless shock when hot tears sting disbelieving eyes, the only thing I can find to say, the only words that seem to fit, must be addressed to the unknown author of this suffering.

You monster. You beast. You unspeakable bastard.

What lesson did you hope to teach us by your coward's attack on our World Trade Center, our Pentagon, us? What was it you hoped we would learn? Whatever it was, please know that you failed.

Did you want us to respect your cause? You just damned your cause.

Did you want to make us fear? You just steeled our resolve.

Did you want to tear us apart? You just brought us together.

Let me tell you about my people. We are a vast and quarrelsome family, a family rent by racial, social, political and class division, but a family nonetheless. We're frivolous, yes, capable of expending tremendous emotional energy on pop cultural minutiae—a singer's revealing dress, a ball team's misfortune, a cartoon mouse.

We're wealthy, too, spoiled by the ready availability of trinkets and material goods, and maybe because of that, we walk through life with a certain sense of blithe entitlement. We are fundamentally decent, though—peace-loving and compassionate. We struggle to know the right thing and to do it. And we are, the overwhelming majority of us, people of faith, believers in a just and loving God.

Some people—you, perhaps—think that any or all of this makes us weak. You're mistaken. We are not weak. Indeed, we are strong in ways that cannot be measured by arsenals.

Yes, we're in pain now. We are in mourning, and we are in shock. We're still grappling with the unreality of the awful thing you did, still working to make ourselves understand that this isn't a special effect from some Hollywood blockbuster, isn't the plot development from a Tom Clancy novel.

Both in terms of the awful scope of their ambition and the probable final death toll, your attacks are likely to go down as the worst acts of terrorism in the history of the United States and, probably, the history of the world. You've bloodied us as we have never been bloodied before.

But there's a gulf of difference between making us bloody and making us fall. This is the lesson Japan was taught to its bitter sorrow the last time anyone hit us this hard, the last time anyone brought us such abrupt and monumental pain. When roused, we are righteous in our outrage, terrible in our force. When provoked by this level of barbarism, we will bear any suffering, pay any cost, go to any length, in the pursuit of justice.

I tell you this without fear of contradiction. I know my people, as you, I think, do not. What I know reassures me. It also causes me to tremble with dread of the future.

In the days to come, there will be recrimination and accusation, fingers pointing to determine whose failure allowed this to happen and what can be done to prevent it from happening again. There will be heightened security, misguided talk of revoking basic freedoms. We'll go forward from this moment sobered, chastened, sad. But determined, too. Unimaginably determined.

You see, the steel in us is not always readily apparent. That aspect of our character is seldom understood by people who don't know us well. On this day, the family's bickering is put on hold.

As Americans, we will weep; as Americans, we will mourn; and as Americans, we will rise in defense of all that we cherish.

So I ask again: What was it you hoped to teach us? It occurs to me that maybe you just wanted us to know the depths of your hatred. If that's the case, consider the message received. And take this message in exchange: You don't know my people. You don't know what we're capable of.

You don't know what you just started.

But you're about to learn.

Boots on the Ground, Hearts on Their Sleeves
David Brooks—*New York Times*—12/2/2003

Soldiers in all wars are called upon to be heroes, but our men and women in Iraq are called upon to define a new sort of heroism. First, they must endure the insanity of war, fighting off fedayeen ambushes, withstanding the suicide bombings and mortars, kicking down doors and searching homes.

But a day or an hour or a few minutes later, they are called upon to enter an opposite moral universe. They are asked to pass out textbooks, improvise sewer systems and help with budgets. Some sit in on town council meetings to help keep the discussions on track. Some act like foundation program officers, giving seed money to promising local initiatives.

Trained as trigger-pullers, many are also asked in theater to be consultants and aldermen. They are John Wayne, but also Jane Addams.

Can anybody think of another time in history when a comparable group of young people was asked to be at once so brave, fierce and relentless, while also being so sympathetic, creative and forbearing?

When you read the dispatches from Iraq, or the online diaries many soldiers keep, or the e-mail they send home, you quickly sense how hard it is to commute between these two universes. Yet the most important achievements seem to occur on the border between chaos and normalcy.

At spontaneous moments, when order threatens to break down, the soldiers, aviators and marines jump in and coach the Iraqis on the customs and habits of democracy. They try to weave that fabric of civic trust that can't be written into law, but without which freedom becomes anarchy.

For example, in a *New Yorker* article, George Packer describes an incident in the life of Capt. John Prior. He was inside a gas station when a commotion erupted outside. A mob of people was furiously accusing a man of butting in line and stealing gasoline. Prior established that the man was merely a government inspector checking the quality of the fuel. Frazzled and exhausted, Prior took the chance to teach the mob a broader lesson: "The problem is that you people accuse each other without proof! That's the problem!"

Another soldier, who keeps a Weblog, collects toys and passes them out to Iraqi children. He brought a pile of toys to an orphanage, but the paid staff at the place rushed the pile to grab the toys for themselves—"like sharks in a feeding frenzy," he writes. He has learned that if he stations himself with an M-16 over the toys, things go smoothly.

Another soldier writes of his dismay at seeing Iraqi parents give their kids toy guns as presents after Ramadan. He wonders, Haven't they had enough death? Don't they realize how dangerous it is for a kid to wander the street with a piece of plastic that looks like an AK-47?

When you read the diaries and the postings of the soldiers in Iraq, you see how exhausted they are. You see that their feelings about the Iraqis are as contradictory as the Iraqis' feelings about them. You see their frustration and yearning to go home.

But despite all this, their epic bouts of complaining are interrupted by bursts of idealism. Most of them seem to feel, deep down, some elemental respect for the Iraqis and sympathy for what they have endured. Far more than the population at home, the soldiers in the middle of the conflict believe in their mission and are confident they will succeed.

When you read their writings you see what thorough democrats they are. They are appalled at the thought of dominating Iraq. They want to see the Iraqis independent and governing themselves. If some president did want to create an empire, he couldn't do it with these people. Their faith in freedom governs their actions.

Most of all, you see what a challenging set of tasks they have been given, and how short-staffed they are. And yet you sense that in this war, as in so many others, the improvising skill of the soldiers on the ground will make up for the cosmic screw-ups of the people up the chain of command.

If anybody is wondering: Where are the young idealists? Where are the people willing to devote themselves to causes larger than themselves? They are in uniform in Iraq, straddling the divide between insanity and order.

A Village Waiting for Rape and Murder
NICHOLAS D. KRISTOF—*New York Times*—3/12/2006

Politely but insistently, the people in this town explained that they were about to be massacred.

"The janjaweed militias have already destroyed all the villages east of Koloy," Adam Omar, a local sheik, explained somberly. "Any moment, they will attack us here."

This remote market town of thatch-roof mud huts near the Chad-Sudan border is on the front line of the genocidal fury that Sudan has unleashed on several black African tribes. After killing several hundred thousand people in its own Darfur region, Sudan's government is now sending its brutal janjaweed militias to kill the same tribes here in Chad.

President Bush is showing signs that he may be ready to stand up to the thugs in Sudan, but China is protecting Sudan, Europe is inert, and the African Union can't even muster the courage to call for immediate U.N. peacekeepers. So the people here are probably right to resign themselves to be slaughtered— if not sooner, then later.

Koloy has no electricity and no phones, so the people could not call for help. But even if they could, no one could help them. Chad's small army had sent a few trucks of troops the previous day, but after learning that they faced more than 500 janjaweed armed with heavy machine guns, the Chadian soldiers had dashed away again. As I drove into town, the town's police force was fleeing on horseback.

I visited the "hospital"—an open-sided tent that lacked any medical personnel but was filled with gunshot victims. Local leaders told me that the janjaweed were only three miles away and had sent word that they would attack Koloy that day.

"When they see you, they shoot you," said Adam Zakaria, the sheik of a nearby village, Gindeiza, that had been attacked the day before. Mr. Adam had one bullet wound in his foot and another in his thigh.

"I know the man who shot me," Mr. Adam said. "He used to be my friend." That man, Hussein al-Beheri, is an Arab neighbor. But last year, according to Mr. Adam's account, Mr. Hussein joined the janjaweed and now regularly attacks non-Arabs.

"I told him, 'Don't shoot me!'" Mr. Adam recalled. "Three or four times, I pleaded, 'Don't shoot me.' And then he shot me."

Ten people are known dead in his village, Mr. Adam said, but many others are missing—and no one has been able to look for dead bodies because the janjaweed still occupy the village. Among those missing, he said, are his two wives and four children.

"I have not seen them since yesterday, when they were in the village," he said. "In my heart, I think they are dead."

This entire area gets no visits from diplomats and no help from the U.N. or aid groups, because it is too risky. Only one organization, Doctors Without Borders, sticks it out, sending in a convoy of intrepid doctors three days a week to pull bullets out of victims.

It was nerve-racking to be in Koloy, and my local interpreter kept insisting that we rush away. But I've never felt more helpless than the moment I pulled away in my Toyota Land Cruiser, waving goodbye to people convinced that they would soon be murdered.

In the end, there was no janjaweed attack that day. Perhaps that's because the janjaweed have found that it is inconvenient to drive away absolutely all

Africans; now the janjaweed sometimes leave market towns alone so that their own families can still have places to shop.

The people of Koloy are still waiting to be massacred. Think for a moment what it would be like to huddle with your family every day, paralyzed by fear, waiting for the end.

And then remember that all this can be stopped. You can go to http://www .millionvoicesfordarfur.org and send a postcard to President Bush, encouraging him to do more. At http://www.genocideintervention.net you can find a list of "10 things you can do right now."

Maybe it seems that you have no real power to change anything in Koloy, but, frankly, right now you're the only hope that the people in Koloy have.

Farewell to Geronimo
THOMAS L. FRIEDMAN—*New York Times*—5/3/2011

There is only one good thing about the fact that Osama bin Laden survived for nearly 10 years after the mass murder at the World Trade Center and the Pentagon that he organized. And that is that he lived long enough to see so many young Arabs repudiate his ideology. He lived long enough to see Arabs from Tunisia to Egypt to Yemen to Syria rise up peacefully to gain the dignity, justice and self-rule that Bin Laden claimed could be obtained only by murderous violence and a return to puritanical Islam.

We did our part. We killed Bin Laden with a bullet. Now the Arab and Muslim people have a chance to do their part—kill Bin Ladenism with a ballot—that is, with real elections, with real constitutions, real political parties and real progressive politics.

Yes, the bad guys have been dealt a blow across the Arab world in the last few months—not only Al Qaeda, but the whole rogues' gallery of dictators, whose soft bigotry of low expectations for their people had kept the Arab world behind. The question now, though, is: Can the forces of decency get organized, elected and start building a different Arab future? That is the most important question. Everything else is noise.

To understand that challenge, we need to recall, again, where Bin Ladenism came from. It emerged from a devil's bargain between oil-consuming countries and Arab dictators. We all—Europe, America, India, China—treated the Arab world as a collection of big gas stations, and all of us sent the same basic message to the petro-dictators: Keep the oil flowing, the prices low and don't bother Israel too much and you can treat your people however you like, out back, where we won't look. Bin Laden and his followers were a product of all the pathologies that were allowed to grow in the dark out back—crippling deficits of freedom, women's empowerment and education across the Arab world.

These deficits nurtured a profound sense of humiliation among Arabs at how far behind they had fallen, a profound hunger to control their own futures and a pervasive sense of injustice in their daily lives. That is what is most striking about the Arab uprisings in Egypt and Tunisia in particular. They were almost apolitical. They were not about any ideology. They were propelled by the most basic human longings for dignity, justice and to control one's own life. Remember, one of the first things Egyptians did was attack their own police stations—the instruments of regime injustice. And since millions of Arabs share these longings for dignity, justice and freedom, these revolutions are not going to go away.

For decades, though, the Arab leaders were very adept at taking all that anger brewing out back and redirecting it onto the United States and Israel. Yes, Israel's own behavior at times fed the Arab sense of humiliation and powerlessness, but it was not the primary cause. No matter. While the Chinese autocrats said to their people, "We'll take away your freedom and, in return, we'll give you a steadily rising education and standard of living," the Arab autocrats said, "We'll take away your freedom and give you the Arab-Israel conflict."

This was the toxic "out back" from which Bin Laden emerged. A twisted psychopath and false messiah, he preached that only through violence—only by destroying these Arab regimes and their American backers—could the Arab people end their humiliation, restore justice and build some mythical uncorrupted caliphate.

Very few Arabs actively supported Bin Laden, but he initially drew significant passive support for his fist in the face of America, the Arab regimes and Israel. But as Al Qaeda was put on the run, and spent most of its energies killing other Muslims who didn't toe its line, even its passive support melted away (except for the demented leadership of Hamas).

In that void, with no hope of anyone else riding to their rescue, it seems—in the totally unpredictable way these things happen—that the Arab publics in Tunisia, Egypt, Yemen and elsewhere shucked off their fears and decided that they themselves would change what was going on out back by taking over what was going on out front.

And, most impressively, they decided to do it under the banner of one word that you hear most often today among Syrian rebels: "Silmiyyah." It means peaceful. "We will do this peacefully." It is just the opposite of Bin Ladenism. It is Arabs saying in their own way: We don't want to be martyrs for Bin Laden or pawns for Mubarak, Assad, Gaddafi, Ben Ali and all the rest. We want to be "citizens." Not all do, of course. Some prefer more religious identities and sectarian ones. This is where the struggle will be.

We cannot predict the outcome. All we can hope for is that this time there really will be a struggle of ideas—that in a region where extremists go all the way and moderates tend to just go away, this time will be different. The moderates will be as passionate and committed as the extremists. If that happens, both Bin Laden and Bin Ladenism will be resting at the bottom of the ocean.

II: Politics

Life in a democracy is a never-ending debate. In print, vibrant voices from the left, right, and center argue across the decades, helping our nation evolve into a more perfect union in the process.

The columnist is supposed to be the honest broker in politics—independent-minded, writing without fear or favor. His or her eternal enemies are hypocrisy, ignorance, injustice, and unbridled self-interest. The columnist can bring a broader perspective to the civic conversation.

H. L. Mencken set the standard for the modern political columnists with his transcendent skepticism. He loved the newspaper life—"the life of kings," he called it. His dispatches from the Scopes Monkey trial are American classics that inspired both the play and film *Inherit the Wind*. His dissection of President Warren G. Harding's soapbox bloviating—"It is so bad that a sort of grandeur creeps into it"—is still cited every campaign season.

The Alsop brothers' column "Mad-Hatter Loyalty Purge" was an early indictment of McCarthyism that resonates whenever purity tests intrude on our political discourse. Mary McGrory's work for the *Washington Star* captured the question put to McCarthy himself: "Have you no sense of decency, sir?"

William F. Buckley Jr. skewers the self-righteous assumptions of the left by asking the trenchant question: "Are You Against the Handicapped?" James Reston defines the electoral strength of centrism in "The Decisive Political Center" written as the pendulum swung to the left after LBJ's 1964 landslide. Likewise, Heywood Broun and Molly Ivins put an engaging face on liberalism's call to expand the circle of self-interest.

From Watergate to Monica-gate, Washington columnists like David Broder and Maureen Dowd have helped us see through the Beltway spin. Charley McDowell's look at the reaction to Nixon's resignation from a small town in the Shenandoah Valley finds an unexpected and haunting angle. Likewise, Thomas L. Friedman's meditation on his daughter's middle school as a microcosm of America's strength after the attacks of 9/11 comes through as a modern classic.

Long-ball columns still emerge, like Kathleen Parker's campaign '08 bombshell calling for Sarah Palin to drop off McCain's ticket ("My cringe reflex is exhausted"), provoking over seven thousand hate-fueled responses in a matter of days. Some of the best contemporary political columnists—like David Brooks—dedicate themselves to trying to heal the hyper-partisanship that can poison our civic debates. Enduring political columns offer not just heat, but light—they help us see the present with a sense of perspective.

What's the Matter with Kansas?
WILLIAM ALLEN WHITE—*Emporia Gazette*—8/15/1896

Today the Kansas Department of Agriculture sent out a statement which indicates that Kansas has gained less than two thousand people in the past year. There are about two hundred and twenty-five thousand families in the state, and there were about ten thousand babies born in Kansas, and yet so many people have left the state that the natural increase is cut down to less than two thousand net.

This has been going on for eight years.

If there had been a high brick wall around the state eight years ago, and not a soul had been admitted or permitted to leave, Kansas would be a half million souls better off than she is today. And yet the nation has increased in population. In five years ten million people have been added to the national population, yet instead of gaining a share of this—say, half a million—Kansas has apparently been a plague spot and, in the very garden of the world, has lost population by ten-thousands every year.

No one brings any money into Kansas any more. What community knows over one or two men who have moved in with more than $5,000 in the past three years? And what community cannot count half a score of men in that time who have left, taking all the money they could scrape together?

Yet the nation has grown rich; other states have increased in population and wealth—other neighboring states. Missouri has gained over two million, while Kansas has been losing half a million. Nebraska has gained in wealth and population while Kansas has gone downhill. Colorado has gained every way, while Kansas has lost every way since 1888.

What's the matter with Kansas?

There is no substantial city in the state. Every big town save one has lost in population. Yet Kansas City, Omaha, Lincoln, St. Louis, Denver, Colorado Springs, Sedalia, the cities of the Dakotas, St. Paul and Minneapolis, Des Moines—all cities and towns in the West—have steadily grown.

Take up the Government Blue Book and you will see Kansas is virtually off the map. Two or three little scrubby consular places in yellow-fever-stricken communities that do not aggregate ten thousand dollars a year is all the recognition that Kansas has. Nebraska draws about one hundred thousand dollars; little old North Dakota draws about fifty thousand dollars; Oklahoma doubles Kansas; Missouri leaves her a thousand miles behind; Colorado is almost seven times greater than Kansas—the whole west is ahead of Kansas.

Take it by any standard you please, Kansas is not in it.

Go east and you hear them laugh at Kansas; go west and they sneer at her; go south and they "cuss" her; go north and they have forgotten her. Go into any crowd of intelligent people gathered anywhere on the globe, and you will find the Kansas man on the defensive. The newspaper columns and magazines once devoted to praise of her, to facts and startling figures concerning her resources, are now filled with cartoons, jibes and Pefferian speeches. Kansas just naturally isn't in it. She has traded with Arkansas and Timbuctoo.

What's the matter with Kansas?

We all know; yet here we are at it again. We have an old mossback Jacksonian who snorts and howls because there is a bathtub in the state house; we are running that old jay for Governor. We have another shabby, wild-eyed, rattle-brained fanatic who has said openly in a dozen speeches that "the rights of the user are paramount to the rights of the owner"; we are running him for Chief Justice, so that capital will come tumbling over itself to get into the state. We have raked the old ash heap of failure in the state and found an old human hoop-skirt who has failed as a businessman, who has failed as an editor, who has failed as a preacher, and we are going to run him for Congressman-at-Large. He will help the looks of the Kansas delegation at Washington. Then we have discovered a kid without a law practice and have decided to run him for Attorney General. Then, for fear some hint that the state had become respectable might percolate through the civilized portions of the nation, we have decided to send three or four harpies out lecturing, telling the people that Kansas is raising hell and letting the corn go to weeds.

Oh, this is a state to be proud of! We are a people who can hold up our heads! What we need is not more money, but less capital, fewer white shirts and brains, fewer men with business judgment, and more of those fellows who boast that they are "just ordinary clodhoppers but they know more in a minute about finance than John Sherman"; we need more men who are "posted," who can bellow about the crime of '73, who hate prosperity and who think, because a man believes in national honor, he is a tool of Wall Street. We have had a few of them, some hundred fifty thousand—but we need more.

We need several thousand gibbering idiots to scream about the "Great Red Dragon" of Lombard Street. We don't need population, we don't need wealth, we don't need well-dressed men on the streets, we don't need standing in the nation, we don't need cities on the fertile prairies; you bet we don't! What we are after is the money power. Because we have become poorer and ornerier all and meaner than a spavined, distempered mule, we, the people of Kansas, propose to kick; we don't care to build up, we wish to tear down.

"There are two ideas of government," said our noble Bryan at Chicago. "There are those who believe that if you just legislate to make the well-to-do prosperous, this prosperity will leak through on those below. The Democratic idea has been that if you legislate to make the masses prosperous their prosperity will find its way up through every class which rests upon them."

That's the stuff! Give the prosperous man the dickens! Legislate the thriftless man into ease, whack the stuffings out of the creditors and tell debtors who borrowed the money five years ago when money "per capita" was greater than it is now, that the contraction of currency gives him a right to repudiate.

Whoop it up for the ragged trousers; put the lazy, greasy fizzle, who can't pay his debts, on an altar, and bow down and worship him. Let the state ideal be high. What we need is not the respect of our fellow men, but the chance to get something for nothing.

Oh, yes, Kansas is a great state. Here are people fleeing from it by the score every day, capital going out of the state by the hundreds of dollars; and every industry but farming paralyzed, and that crippled, because its products have to go across the ocean before they can find a laboring man at work who can afford to buy them. Let's don't stop this year. Let's drive all the decent, self-respecting men out of the state. Let's keep the old clodhoppers who know it all. Let's encourage the man who is "posted." He can talk, and what we need is not mill hands to eat our meat, nor factory hands to eat our wheat, nor cities to oppress the farmer by consuming his butter and eggs and chickens and produce. What Kansas needs is men who can talk, who have large leisure to argue the currency question while their wives wait at home for that nickel's worth of bluing.

What's the matter with Kansas?

Nothing under the shining sun. She is losing wealth, population and standing. She has got her statesmen, and the money power is afraid of her. Kansas is all right. She has started in to raise hell, as Mrs. Lease advised, and she seems to have an over-production. But that doesn't matter. Kansas never did believe in diversified crops. Kansas is all right. There is absolutely nothing wrong with Kansas. "Every prospect pleases and only man is vile."

Good Luck to the Anti-Bolshevists
THEODORE ROOSEVELT—*Kansas City Star*—9/12/1918

The absolute prerequisite for successful self-government in any people is the power of self-restraint which refuses to follow either the wild-eyed extremists of radicalism or the dull-eyed extremists of reaction. Either set of extremists will wreck the Nation just as certainly as the other. The Nation capable of self-government must show the Abraham Lincoln quality of refusing to go with either. The dreadful fall which has befallen Russia is due to the fact that when her people cast off the tyranny of the autocracy, they did not have sufficient self-control and common sense to avoid rushing into the gulf of Bolshevist anarchy.

In this country there are plenty of highbrow Bolsheviki who like to think of themselves as intellectuals, and who in parlors and at pink teas preach Bolshevism as a fad. They are fatuously ignorant that it may be a dangerous fad. Some of them are mere make-believe, sissy Bolsheviki, almost or quite harmless. Others are sincere and foolish fanatics, who mean well and who do not realize that their doctrines tend toward moral disintegration. But there are practical Bolsheviki in this country who are in no sense highbrows. The I.W.W. [International Workers of the World] and the Non-Partisan League, just as long and so far as its members submit to the dominion of leaders like Mr. Townley, represent the forces that under Lenine and Trotzky have brought ruin to Russia. If these organizations obtained power here, they would cast this country into the same abyss with Russia.

The I.W.W. activities may have been officially set forth by the Chicago jury which found the I.W.W. leaders guilty of treasonable practices. These leaders protested that they were only trying to help "the wage slave of to-day," and had not taken German money. But the jury found them guilty as charged. The American people, when fully awake and aroused, will tolerate neither treason nor anarchy. No Americans are more patriotic than the honest American labor men, and these above all had cause to rejoice in the verdict. Undoubtedly there are plenty of poor ignorant men who join the I.W.W. because they feel they do not receive justice. We should all of us actively unite in the effort to right any wrongs from which these men suffer. But we should set our faces like flint against such criminal leadership as that of the I.W.W.

The Non-Partisan League endeavored to ally itself with the I.W.W. since we entered the war. When the League was started, I felt much sympathy with its avowed purposes. I hope for and shall welcome wisely radical action on behalf of the farmer. But only destruction to all of us can come from the venous class hatred preached by the present leadership of the League. Some of its leaders have been convicted and imprisoned for treasonable activities. Some of the League's representatives have been actively pro-Germans. Some are Socialists or Socialist-Anarchists. For the first six months of the war and until it became too dangerous, they were openly against the war, against our allies, and for Germany. The only half-secret alliance between these leaders and certain high Democratic politicians is deeply discreditable to the latter. The victory of the League in its recent efforts to gain control of the Republican Party in Minnesota and Montana would have given immense strength to the pro-German and Bolshevist element throughout the country and its defeat was a matter of rejoicing to all right-minded and patriotic men.

Mr. Townley's leadership in its moral purpose and national effect entitles him to rank with Messrs. Lenine and Trotzky, and the utterances of the League's official organ, especially in its appeals to class hatred, puts the official representatives of the League squarely in the clan with the Bolshevist leaders who have done such evil in Russia.

I have before me an official letter from the League written in January last refusing to coöperate in non-political work for the benefit of the farmers, saying, "This organization is a political one, the farmers being organized for the purpose of controlling legislation in their own interests." In other words, the title, Non-Partisan, is a piece of pure hypocrisy, and its league is really partisan in the narrowest and worst sense. Americans should organize politically as Americans and not as bankers, or lawyers, or farmers, or wage-workers. To organize politically on the basis adopted by the League is thoroughly anti-American and unpatriotic, and if copied generally by our citizens, would mean the creation in this country of rival political parties based on cynically brutal class selfishness.

I have no doubt that the rank and file of the members of the League are good, honest people who have been misled. I am certain that there has been much neglect of the rights of the farmers and that it is a high duty for this country to begin a constructive, practical agricultural policy. But no good American can support the League while it is dominated by its present leadership. The Kansans who have joined to fight the League because it represents Bolshevism are rendering a patriotic service to America.

Gamalielese
H. L. MENCKEN—*Baltimore Sun*—3/7/1921

On the question of the logical content of Dr. Harding's harangue of last Friday I do not presume to have views. The matter has been debated at great length by the editorial writers of the Republic, all of them experts in logic; moreover, I confess to being prejudiced. When a man arises publicly to argue that the United States entered the late war because of a "concern for preserved civilization," I can only snicker in a superior way and wonder why he isn't holding down the chair of history in some American university. When he says that the United States has "never sought territorial aggrandizement through force," the snicker arises to the virulence of a chuckle, and I turn to the first volume of General Grant's memoirs. And when, gaining momentum, he gravely informs the boobery that "ours is a constitutional freedom where the popular will is supreme, and minorities are sacredly protected," then I abandon myself to a mirth that transcends, perhaps, the seemly, and send picture postcards of A. Mitchell Palmer and the Atlanta Penitentiary to all of my enemies who happen to be Socialists.

But when it comes to the style of a great man's discourse, I can speak with a great deal less prejudice, and maybe with somewhat more competence, for I have earned most of my livelihood for twenty years past by translating the bad English of a multitude of authors into measurably better English. Thus qualified professionally, I rise to pay my small tribute to Dr. Harding. Setting aside a college professor or two and half a dozen dipsomaniacal newspaper reporters, he takes the first place in my Valhalla of literati. That is to say, he writes the worst English I have even encountered. It reminds me of a string of wet sponges; it reminds me of tattered washing on the line; it reminds me of stale bean-soup, of college yells, of dogs barking idiotically through endless nights. It is so bad that a sort of grandeur creeps into it. It drags itself out of the dark abysm (I was about to write abscess!) of pish, and crawls insanely up the topmost pinnacle of posh. It is rumble and bumble. It is flap and doodle. It is balder and dash.

But I grow lyrical. More scientifically, what is the matter with it? Why does it seem so flabby, so banal, so confused and childish, so stupidly at war with sense? If you first read the inaugural address and then heard it intoned, as I did (at least in part), then you will perhaps arrive at an answer. That answer is very simple. When Dr. Harding prepares a speech he does not think of it in terms of an educated reader locked up in jail, but in terms of a great horde of stoneheads gathered around a stand. That is to say, the thing is always a stump speech; it is conceived as a stump speech and written as a stump speech. More, it is a stump speech addressed primarily to the sort of audience that the speaker has been used to all of his life, to wit, an audience of small town yokels, of low political serfs, or morons scarcely able to understand a word of more than two syllables, and wholly unable to pursue a logical idea for more than two centimeters.

Such imbeciles do not want ideas—that is, new ideas, ideas that are unfamiliar, ideas that challenge their attention. What they want is simply a gaudy series of platitudes, of threadbare phrases terrifically repeated, of sonorous nonsense driven home with gestures. As I say, they can't understand many words of more than two syllables, but that is not saying that they do not esteem such words. On the contrary, they like them and demand them. The roll of incomprehensible polysyllables enchants them. They like phrases which thunder like salvos of artillery. Let that thunder sound, and they take all the rest on trust. If a sentence begins furiously and then peters out into fatuity, they are still satisfied. If a phrase has a punch in it, they do not ask that it also have a meaning. If a word slips off the tongue like a ship going down the ways, they are content and applaud it and wait for the next.

Brought up amid such hinds, trained by long practice to engage and delight them, Dr. Harding carries his stump manner into everything he writes. He is, perhaps, too old to learn a better way. He is, more likely, too discreet to experiment. The stump speech, put into cold type, maketh the judicious to grieve. But roared from an actual stump, with arms flying and eyes flashing and the old flag overhead, it is certainly and brilliantly effective. Read the inaugural address, and it will gag you. But hear it recited through a sound-magnifier, with grand gestures to ram home its periods, and you will begin to understand it.

Let us turn to a specific example. I exhume a sentence from the latter half of the eminent orator's discourse:

> I would like government todo all it an to mitigate, then, in understanding, in mutuality of interest, in concern for the common goodk our tasks will be solved

I assume that you have read it. I also assume that you set it down as idiotic— a series of words without sense. You are quite right; it is. But now imagine it intoned as it were designed to be intoned. Imagine the slow tempo of a public speech. Imagine the stately unrolling of the first clause, the delicate pause upon the word "then"—and then the loud discharge of the phrase "in understanding," "in mutuality of interest," "in concern for the common good," each with its attendant glare and roll of the eyes, each with a sublime heave, each with its gesture of a blacksmith bringing down his sledge upon an egg—imagine all this, and then ask yourself where you have got. You have got, in brief, to a point where you don't know what it is all about. You hear and applaud the phrases, but their connection has already escaped you. And so, when in violation of all sequence and logic, the final phrase, "our tasks will be solved," assaults you, you do not notice its disharmony—all you notice is that, if this or that, already forgotten, is done, "our tasks will be solved." Whereupon, glad of the assurance and thrilled by the vast gestures that drive it home, you give a cheer.

That is, if you are the sort of man who goes to political meetings, which is to say, if you are the sort of man that Dr. Harding is used to talking to, which is to say, if you are a jackass.

The whole inaugural address reeked with just such nonsense. The thing started off with an error in English in its very first sentence—the confusion of pronouns is the *one-he* combination, so beloved of bad newspaper reporters. It bristled with words misused: *Civic* for *civil*, *luring* for *alluring*, *womanhood* for *women*, *referendum* for *reference*, even *task* for *problem*. "The *task* is to be *solved*"—what could be worse? Yet I find it twice. "The expressed views of world opinion"—what irritating tautology! "The expressed conscience of progress"—what on earth does it mean? "This is not selfishness, it is sanctity"—what intelligible idea do you get out of that? "I know that Congress and the administration will favor every wise government policy to aid the resumption and encourage continued progress"—the resumption of what? "Service is the supreme *commitment* of life"—*ach, du heiliger!*

But is such bosh out of place in a stump speech? Obviously not. It is precisely and thoroughly in place in a stump speech. A tight fabric of ideas would weary and exasperate the audience; what it wants is simply loud burble of words, a procession of phrases that roar, a series of whoops. This is what it got in the inaugural address of the Hon. Warren Gamaliel Harding. And this is what it will get for four long years—unless God sends a miracle and the corruptible puts on incorruption. . . . Almost I long for the sweeter song, the rubber-stamps of more familiar design, the gentler and more seemly bosh of the late Woodrow.

Scopes Monkey Trial
H. L. MENCKEN—*Baltimore Sun*—7/13/1925

DAYTON, TENNESSEE—There is a Unitarian clergyman here from New York, trying desperately to horn into the trial and execution of the infidel Scopes. He will fail. If Darrow ventured to put him on the stand the whole audience, led by the jury, would leap out of the courthouse windows and take to the hills. Darrow himself, indeed, is as much as they can bear. The whisper that he is an atheist has been stilled by the bucolic make-up and by the public report that he has the gift of prophecy and can reconcile Genesis and evolution. Even so, there is ample space about him when he navigates the streets. The other day a newspaperwoman was warned by her landlady to keep out of the courtroom when he was on his legs. All the local sorcerers predict that a bolt from heaven will fetch him in the end. The night he arrived there was a violent storm, the town water turned brown, and horned cattle in the lowlands were afloat for hours. A woman back in the mountains gave birth to a child with hair four inches long, curiously bobbed in scallops.

The Book of Revelation has all the authority, in these theological uplands, of military orders in time of war. The people turn to it for light upon all their problems, spiritual and secular. If a text were found in it denouncing the antievolution law, then the antievolution law would become infamous overnight. But so far the exegetes who roar and snuffle in the town have found no such text. Instead they have found only blazing ratifications and reinforcements of Genesis. Darwin is the devil with seven tails and nine horns. Scopes, though he is disguised by flannel pantaloons and a Beta Theta Pi haircut, is the harlot of Babylon. Darrow is Beelzebub in person and Malone is the Crown Prince Friedrich Wilhelm.

I have hitherto hinted an Episcopalian down here in the Coca-Cola belt is regarded as an atheist. It sounds like one of the lies that journalists tell, but it is really an understatement of the facts. Even a Methodist, by Rhea county standards, is one a bit debauched by pride of intellect. It is the four Methodists on the jury who are expected to hold out for giving Scopes Christian burial after he is hanged. They all made it plain, when they were examined, that they were freethinking and independent men, and not to be run amuck by the superstitions of the lowly. One actually confessed that he seldom read the Bible, though he hastened to add that he was familiar with its principles. The fellow had on a boiled shirt and a polka-dot necktie. He sits somewhat apart. When Darrow withers to a cinder under the celestial blowpipe, this dubious Wesleyan, too, will lose a few hairs.

Even the Baptists no longer brew a medicine that is strong enough for the mountaineers. The sacrament of baptism by total immersion is over too quickly for them, and what follows offers nothing that they can get their teeth into. What they crave is a continuous experience of the divine power, an endless series of evidence that the true believer is a marked man, ever under the eye of God. It is not enough to go to a revival once a year or twice a year; there must be a revival every night. And it is not enough to accept the truth as a mere statement of indisputable and awful fact: it must be embraced ecstatically and orgiastically, to the accompaniment of loud shouts, dreadful heavings and gurglings, and dancing with arms and legs.

This craving is satisfied brilliantly by the gaudy practices of the Holy Rollers, and so the mountaineers are gradually gravitating toward the Holy Roller communion, or, as they prefer to call it, the Church of God. Gradually, perhaps, is not the word. They are actually going in by whole villages and townships. At the last count of noses there were 20,000 Holy Rollers in these hills. The next census, I have no doubt, will show many more. The cities of the lowlands, of course, still resist, and so do most of the county towns, including even Dayton, but once one steps off the state roads the howl of holiness is heard in the woods, and the yokels carry on an almost continuous orgy.

A foreigner in store clothes going out from Dayton must approach the sacred grove somewhat discreetly. It is not that the Holy Rollers, discovering him, would harm him; it is simply that they would shut down their boiling of the devil and flee into the forests. We left Dayton an hour after nightfall and parked our car in a wood a mile or so beyond the little hill village of Morgantown. Far off in a glade a flickering light was visible and out of the silence came a faint rumble of exhortation. We could scarcely distinguish the figure of the preacher; it was like looking down the tube of a dark field microscope. We got out of the car and sneaked along the edge of a mountain cornfield.

Presently we were near enough to see what was going on. From the great limb of a mighty oak hung a couple of crude torches of the sort that car inspectors thrust under Pullman cars when a train pulls in at night. In their light was a preacher, and for a while we could see no one else. He was an immensely tall and thin mountaineer in blue jeans, his collarless shirt open at the neck and his hair a tousled mop. As he preached he paced up and down under the smoking flambeaux and at each turn he thrust his arms into the air and yelled, "Glory to God!" We crept nearer in the shadow of the cornfield and began to hear more of his discourse. He was preaching on the day of judgment. The high kings of the earth, he roared, would all fall down and die; only the sanctified would stand up to receive the Lord God of Hosts. One of these kings he mentioned by name—the king of what he called Greece-y. The King of Greece-y, he said, was doomed to hell.

We went forward a few more yards and began to see the audience. It was seated on benches ranged round the preacher in a circle. Behind him sat a row of elders, men and women. In front were the younger folk. We kept on cautiously, and individuals rose out of the ghostly gloom. A young mother sat suckling her baby, rocking as the preacher paced up and down. Two scared little girls hugged each other, their pigtails down their backs. An immensely huge mountain woman, in a gingham dress cut in one piece, rolled on her heels at every "Glory to God." To one side, but half visible, was what appeared to be a bed. We found out afterward that two babies were asleep upon it.

The preacher stopped at last and there arose out of the darkness a woman with her hair pulled back into a little tight knot. She began so quietly that we couldn't hear what she said, but soon her voice rose resonantly and we could follow her. She was denouncing the reading of books. Some wandering book agent, it appeared, had come to her cabin and tried to sell her a specimen of his wares. She refused to touch it. Why, indeed, read a book? If what was in it was true, then everything in it was already in the Bible. If it was false, then reading it would imperil the soul. Her syllogism complete, she sat down.

There followed a hymn, led by a somewhat fat brother wearing silver-rimmed country spectacles. It droned on for half a dozen stanzas, and then the first speaker resumed the floor. He argued that the gift of tongues was real and that education was a snare. Once his children could read the Bible, he said, they had enough. Beyond lay only infidelity and damnation. Sin stalked the cities. Dayton itself was a Sodom. Even Morgantown had begun to forget God. He sat down, and the female aurochs in gingham got up.

She began quietly, but was soon leaping and roaring, and it was hard to follow her. Under cover of the turmoil we sneaked a bit closer. A couple of other discourses followed, and there were two or three hymns. Suddenly a change of mood began to make itself felt. The last hymn ran longer than the others and dropped gradually into a monotonous, unintelligible chant. The leader beat time with his book. The faithful broke out with exultations. When the singing ended there was a brief palaver that we could not hear and two of the men moved a bench into the circle of light directly under the flambeaux. Then a half-grown girl emerged from the darkness and threw herself upon it. We noticed with astonishment that she had bobbed hair. "This sister," said the leader, "has asked for prayers." We moved a bit closer. We could now see faces plainly and hear every word.

What followed quickly reached such heights of barbaric grotesquerie that it was hard to believe it real. At a signal all the faithful crowded up to the bench and began to pray—not in unison, but each for himself. At another they all fell on their knees, their arms over the penitent. The leader kneeled, facing us, his head alternately thrown back dramatically or buried in his hands. Words spouted from his lips like bullets from a machine gun—appeals to God to pull the penitent back out of hell, defiances of the powers and principalities of the air, a vast impassioned jargon of apocalyptic texts. Suddenly he rose to his feet, threw back his head, and began to speak in tongues—blub-blub-blub, gurgle-gurgle-gurgle. His voice rose to a higher register. The climax was a shrill, inarticulate squawk, like that of a man throttled. He fell headlong across the pyramid of supplicants.

A comic scene? Somehow, no. The poor half-wits were too horribly in earnest. It was like peeping through a knothole at the writhings of a people in pain. From the squirming and jabbering mass a young woman gradually detached herself—a woman not uncomely, with a pathetic homemade cap on her head. Her head jerked back, the veins of her neck swelled, and her fists went to her throat as if she were fighting for breath. She bent backward until she was like half of a hoop. Then she suddenly snapped forward. We caught a flash of the whites of her eyes. Presently her whole body began to be convulsed—great convulsions that began at the shoulders and ended at the hips. She would leap to her feet, thrust her arms in air, and then hurl herself upon the heap.

Her praying flattened out into a mere delirious caterwauling, like that of a tom-cat on a petting party.

I describe the thing as a strict behaviorist. The lady's subjective sensations I leave to infidel pathologists. Whatever they were they were obviously contagious, for soon another damsel joined her, and then another and then a fourth. The last one had an extraordinary bad attack. She began with mild enough jerks of the head, but in a moment she was bounding all over the place, exactly like a chicken with its head cut off. Every time her head came up a stream of yells and barkings would issue out of it. Once she collided with a dark, undersized brother, hitherto silent and stolid. Contact with her set him off as if he had been kicked by a mule. He leaped into the air, threw back his head, and began to gargle as if with a mouthful of BB shot. Then he loosened one tremendous stentorian sentence in the tongues and collapsed.

By this time the performers were quite oblivious to the profane universe. We left our hiding and came up to the little circle of light. We slipped into the vacant seats on one of the rickety benches. The heap of mourners was directly before us. They bounced into us as they cavorted. The smell that they radiated, sweating there in that obscene heap, half suffocated us. Not all of them, of course, did the thing in the grand manner. Some merely moaned and rolled their eyes. The female ox in gingham flung her great bulk on the ground and jabbered an unintelligible prayer. One of the men, in the intervals between fits, put on spectacles and read his Bible.

Beside me on the bench sat the young mother and her baby. She suckled it through the whole orgy, obviously fascinated by what was going on, but never venturing to take any hand in it. On the bed just outside the light two other babies slept peacefully. In the shadows, suddenly appearing and as suddenly going away, were vague figures, whether of believers or of scoffers I do not know. They seemed to come and go in couples. Now and then a couple at the ringside would step back and then vanish into the black night. After a while some came back. There was whispering outside the circle of vision. A couple of Fords lurched up in the wood road, cutting holes in the darkness with their lights. Once someone out of sight loosed a bray of laughter.

All this went on for an hour or so. The original penitent, by this time, was buried three deep beneath the heap. One caught a glimpse, now and then, of her yellow bobbed hair, but then she would vanish again. How she breathed down there I don't know; it was hard enough ten feet away, with a strong five-cent cigar to help. When the praying brothers would rise up for a bout with the tongues their faces were streaming with perspiration. The fat harridan in gingham sweated like a longshoreman. Her hair got loose and fell down over her face. She fanned herself with her skirt. A powerful old gal she was, equal in her day to obstetrics and a week's washing on the same morning, but this was worse than a week's washing. Finally, she fell into a heap, breathing in great, convulsive gasps.

We tired of it after a while and groped our way back to our automobile. When we got to Dayton, after eleven o'clock—an immensely late hour in these parts—the whole town was still gathered on the courthouse lawn, hanging upon the disputes of theologians. The Bible champion of the world had a crowd. The Seventh Day Adventist missionaries had a crowd. A volunteer from faraway Portland, Oregon, made up exactly like Andy Gump, had another and larger crowd. Dayton was enjoying itself. All the usual rules were suspended and the curfew bell was locked up. The prophet Bryan, exhausted by his day's work for Revelations, was snoring in his bed up the road, but enough volunteers were still on watch to keep the battlements manned.

Such is human existence among the fundamentalists, where children are brought up on Genesis and sin is unknown. If I have made the tale too long, then blame the spirit of garrulity that is in the local air. Even newspaper reporters, down here, get some echo of the call. Divine inspiration is as common as the hookworm. I have done my best to show you what the great heritage of mankind comes to in regions where the Bible is the beginning and end of wisdom, and the mountebank Bryan, parading the streets in his seersucker coat, is pointed out to sucklings as the greatest man since Abraham.

There Is a Ship
HEYWOOD BROUN—*New York World-Telegram*—6/9/1939

EDITORS' NOTE: The *St. Louis* was a ship carrying Jewish refugees from Nazi-era Germany to the supposed safety of the New World in 1939. The 937 passengers were denied permission to land in Cuba and amid the subsequent outcry were denied asylum via executive order by President Franklin Delano Roosevelt despite advocacy by Treasury Secretary Henry Morgenthau and others. The *St. Louis* ultimately returned to Europe, where the passengers were admitted by Belgium, the Netherlands, and France shortly before the Nazi invasion of the continent.

There is a ship. It is called the *St. Louis*. If suddenly the vessel flashed an SOS to indicate that the crew and the 900 passengers were in danger every other steamer within call would be hurrying to the rescue. That is the rule of the sea.

And no vessel which got the flash would pause to inquire the economic, political, religious or national position of those in distress. It would want no more than the position of the ship.

And the captain on the bridge, according to the prevailing tradition, would ask the engineer to put on all speed so that the work of rescue could be completed as expeditiously as possible. And this would be true of the skipper of a totalitarian merchantman, one from a democratic nation or a ship flying under the flag of a monarchy, liberal or otherwise.

But there is a ship. It carries 900 passengers—men, women and small children. This is a group of God-fearing people guilty of no crime whatsoever. And they are in peril.

They are in peril which threatens not only their lives but their very souls and spiritual freedom. It would be better for them by far if the *St. Louis* has ripped its plates in a collision with some other craft, or if an impersonal iceberg had slashed the hull below the water line.

Then there would be not the slightest hesitation in a movement of all the allied fleets to save these members of the human race in deep and immediate distress.

But this is not an iceberg or a plate which has been ripped away. The passengers—men, women and children—are Jewish. It is not an accident of nature but an inhuman equation which has put them in deadly peril. It is quite true that when the *St. Louis* gets back to Hamburg these 900, with possibly a few exceptions, will not die immediately. They will starve slowly, since they have already spent their all. Or they will linger in concentration camps—I refer to the men and women. God knows what will happen to the children.

And so the whole world stuffs its ears and pays no attention to any wireless.

There is a ship. And almost two thousand years have elapsed since the message of universal brotherhood was brought to earth.

What have we done with that message? After so many years we have not yet put into practice those principles to which we pay lip service. Nine hundred are to suffer a crucifixion while the world passes by on the other side.

At any luncheon, banquet or public meeting the orator of the occasion can draw cheers if he raises his right hand in the air and pledges himself, his heart and soul to the declaration that he is for peace and amity and that all men are brothers. He means it, generally, and so do the diners who pound the table until the coffee cups and the cream dishes rattle into a symphony of good feeling and international sympathy.

But there is a ship. If one were to look upon it with cold logic it would be better for every one of the 900 if the vessel suddenly buckled and went down in forty fathoms. That would be more merciful.

Against the palpable threat of death we can muster brotherhood. But against the even more plain sentence of life in death we pretend to be helpless.

Our answer is, "We must look after ourselves. What can we do about it? Life is greater than death." We agree. Here is our test. What price civilization? There is a ship. Who will take up an oar to save 900 men, women and children?

The Mad-Hatter Loyalty Purge
JOSEPH AND STEWART ALSOP—*New York Herald Tribune*—8/21/1948

There is not the slightest doubt in these times the American government must have the right to protect itself from attack from within. The immensely delicate and difficult problem of national security exists and it must somehow be solved. No sensible man believes that J. Parnell Thomas's headline hunts can solve it. And any one who believes that the solution is to be found in the present loyalty program should consider certain questions which the conduct of the loyalty program has posed.

First, there is the whole troubling question of guilt by association. Obviously, a man who has constantly associated with Communists and promoted Communist fronts should not have access to state secrets. But how far should this principal be carried?

Take the recent case of a State Department employee. He was charged with having associated with ten persons, all presumably suspect. He had never heard of five of them and has had only the most casual contacts with four. But he had known one of the ten intimately for several years.

This man was a banker, and stood high in the banking community, a community not conspicuous for its radical tendencies. The State Department man could only defend himself by defending the banker, and neither he nor the banker had any notion why the banker was suspect. It finally developed that the banker had lived briefly in Albuquerque, N.M., several years before, and that an anonymous landlady had reported to the F.B.I. that he kept Communist literature in the basement. On further inquiry, it was established that the Communist literature consisted of accumulated copies of *The New Republic* which the banker had discarded.

This sort of thing is making the loyalty program a pretty sour joke. Moreover, the case of the State Department man is typical in that in a great majority of cases of guilt by association, at least half of the supposed associates are wholly unknown to the accused.

Second, it seems obvious enough that an intellectual pro-Communist, who accepts unhesitatingly the Communist dogma, should hold no sensitive position —this was the sort of individual who figured conspicuously in the Canadian spy case. But, again, how far should this principle be carried?

Here are a few verbatim quotes from recent loyalty hearings: "What type of books did your associates have—any on political or social economy?" "What kind of books, by title, did you purchase, what kind of literature?" "How many copies of Howard Fast's novels have you read?" "Do you read 'The Newspaper PM'?" "Have you a book by John Reed?"

All government employees know that such questions are asked in loyalty cases, and the assumption that any kind of intellectual or political curiosity provides grounds for suspicion is inevitable. If this country wants a government service in which ignorance is at a premium, it will doubtless get what it deserves.

Third, does it really matter in America whether a man's maternal grandparents came over from Poland, or whether all his ancestors landed decorously on Plymouth Rock? There have been countless instances when, during loyalty hearings, individuals have been asked where their parents and grandparents were born. An entirely American response would be that it was none of the loyalty board's damn business where a man's forebears came from.

Finally, there is a question of confrontation. Take the case of a man who has one item of "derogatory information" in his dossier. His file notes that F.B.I. source X-32 has said that the accused is known to have attended a meeting of high Communist leaders in Seattle. The accused man hotly denies it. The loyalty board has no way whatsoever of knowing whether X-32 or the accused man is lying, and the board knows nothing at all about X-32.

It is the F.B.I. position to allow those charged to confront their accusers might compromise F.B.I. sources. This seems logical enough. It is also the F.B.I. position that F.B.I. agents should not be allowed to make estimates of the trustworthiness of their sources, and this too seems logical. Yet surely loyalty boards which must decide cases certain to affect the whole future of government employees should know the identity of sources of their information. They should also, in case of necessity, be able to confront and cross-question such sources in secret.

Obviously there is no easy solution to the problem of national security. But a government of drones and boneheads and toadies hardly contributes to national security. And if the sort of thing outlined about is allowed to continue indefinitely, that is the kind of government we shall get.

Welch Defends One Friend and Finds He's Made Many
MARY MCGRORY—*Washington Star*—6/10/1954

Mr. Welch came to Washington to defend the army. But he had his finest hour defending a friend.

In lighter moments, Mr. Welch has often said that he was here "just to ask a few questions."

And yesterday, he asked one that went to the heart of the matter, even if it no more bore on the issues in the case than the charges which provoked it.

He asked it of Senator McCarthy, in tones of shock and outrage, twice. The question was: "Have you no sense of decency, Senator?"

Senator McCarthy did not answer Mr. Welch. He went rumbling along in his allegations against a member of Mr. Welch's Boston law firm.

The young man's former membership in an organization which the attorney general has sought to brand subversive was known to Mr. Welch. He explained this was the factor that decided him against allowing the young man's participation in the case.

It was a precaution, however, that was taken in vain. Senator McCarthy, sitting one seat away from Mr. Welch, and gaining momentum with every word, accused Mr. Welch of trying to "foist" the young man on the committee.

During six stormy weeks of the hearings, Mr. Welch has borne Senator McCarthy's personal attacks on him with equanimity and grace, sometimes merely acknowledging them with an interested nod.

But the senator's attack on Mr. Welch's friend brought an end to silent toleration of McCarthyism. It also brought forth a display of eloquence and indignation that rocked the caucus room.

"Until this moment, Senator," said Mr. Welch, "I think I never really gauged your cruelty or your recklessness."

Acting Chairman Mundt intervened twice during the hearing's most dramatic moments, to say that Mr. Welch had not recommended the young man in question to the committee.

He might as well have saved his breath.

Senator McCarthy roared on. He tried to equate his allegations about Mr. Welch's friend with what he called Mr. Welch's "baiting" of the young chief counsel of the McCarthy Committee, Roy Cohn, who was then on the witness stand.

Mr. Welch and Mr. Cohn had had some barbed exchanges about Mr. Cohn's nightclub activities, but Mr. Welch turned to him with hand outstretched.

"I did you no personal injury, I think, Mr. Cohn?" he asked.

And Mr. Cohn shook his head and said, "No, sir."

Mr. Welch returned to the defense of his absent friend. "Let us not assassinate this lad, further, Senator. You have done enough. Have you no sense of decency, sir, at long last? Have you left no sense of decency?"

Mr. Welch ended by saying he had no further questions of Mr. Cohn. After a moment's silence, the caucus room broke out into its applause—an "audible manifestation" forbidden by the rules. But Mr. Mundt banged his gavel only for a recess.

Mr. Welch, his face working, made his way quickly to the door. A woman there patted his arm and then burst into tears.

Mr. Welch walked down the hall.

The caucus room's greatest wit, he is also its greatest walker. The first day of the hearing—before he and Senator McCarthy had taken each other's measure—he had been observed strolling down the hall, in typical toes-out fashion, with his hands in his pockets, bemusedly observing the would-be spectators crowded behind the velvet ropes in the rotunda.

On another happier day, to the ill-contained wrath of Senator McCarthy, he took another walk. That time, with a troop of reporters and photographers at his heels, he went down the broad staircase to make a telephone call to find out Mr. Stevens's sentiments about cutting off the hearings.

But yesterday, Mr. Welch walked alone. The corporal who carries his briefcase and guides him through the labyrinthine ways of the Capitol and the Pentagon, followed him a little apart. A little group of photographers and reporters stood at a distance.

Finally, with an obvious effort, Mr. Welch, looking for once, every minute of his sixty-three years, went back into the caucus room.

He took his seat, two places away from Senator McCarthy at the end of the committee table. He appeared a sickened and shaken man as he leaned his head on his hand. He listened to Special Counsel Jenkins's jovial direct examination of the senator, who whacked large maps and charts with two pointers. He heard, with no change in his stricken expression, the junior senator from Wisconsin say in his self-styled "Hog-caller's voice," that communism had made more converts than Christianity.

The Ninth Life
MURRAY KEMPTON—*New York Post*—5/14/1958

Harold E. Stassen, fighting through what the professionals think has to be his ninth political life, stood in the morning sun in front of the Wynnewood shopping center yesterday and gazed upon the unpeopled vista of marked-down John Wanamaker outdoor furniture and said that he was glad to be among his neighbors and fellow-citizens.

A couple in their autumn years walking with their backs to him along the sidewalk in front of his sound truck stopped at that, and turned and looked at him briefly and turned away. A few women stopped in the driveway; a salesman sat down on the merchandise. Far, far away, a haze in the distance, a woman stood waiting for her bus, the sound of his amplifier beating at her back. He spoke of the big issues—the need to back President Eisenhower and Vice President Nixon in their fight for peace; then the amplifier died in a silence altered only by the passing of cars.

Harold Stassen came down. A station wagon drove up with its chauffeur in front and the lady of the house in the back. The chauffeur got out and said, "Gosh, that's Staysen." His mistress cast a cold eye upon the enemy of the Pennsylvania Manufacturers Association and, true to her class and her kind, waddled into John Wanamaker's. Harold Stassen leaned over the shake hands with the chauffeur and with a mother and her moppet and raised his head and looked about and there was nobody there. The first public meeting of his Main Line tour was over.

Here is almost the last serious political figure who was a factor in the 1940 Republican convention. Harold Stassen has fought and lost to all the giants whose names are a catalogue of our afflictions since—Dewey and Eisenhower and Nixon. Now he is running for the Republican nomination for governor of Pennsylvania next Tuesday, and the chances are that he will lose to someone named McGonigle.

Yesterday morning he had scheduled public meetings at Bala Cynwyd shopping center and at Narberth. They were abandoned, because nobody came. At Narberth, he walked from his car, along an empty sidewalk to his sound truck by the railroad station and talked to its driver for a while—gravely courteous, undefeated—and walked back, alone with no sign of grievance. This is a primary; in a primary, after so many years, without the organization you expect these things.

He is that much alone. It is even said that, when some brave soul from the organization sends an overture, Harold Stassen himself must conduct the negotiations; there is no one else. He is only fifty-two, but a time that began too soon for him has worn him badly around the eyes; there is something oddly old-fashioned about the sweep of the hair back over his neck, the pockets bulging with papers; the Homburg with the patch at the back of its fold. He has missed too many boats. Yet there is nothing pathetic about him; Harold Stassen is a gallant man. If he must go, he will not sneak off to some law firm; he will go down in an uneven fight with his head up.

Life went on around him in these towns no sun could warm yesterday, indifferent, unremarking—the thinnest lines of the curious on the streets, and far larger clumps of the incurious in the Ardmore drugstore sealed off from the sound of his voice.

Yesterday Harold Stassen, who has won Presidential primaries, was visiting the editors of weekly newspapers. He explained very gravely that this could mean stories in four papers before the primary. He knows that the organization will vote; he has no chance unless somebody comes out in a state which hasn't had a Republican gubernatorial primary in twenty years. His enemies in the Pennsylvania Republican Party would rather beat him than the Democrats, although the bitterness with which they began has ebbed a little in the terrible indifference which is all the surface of this campaign.

He is not, of course, an insurgent by choice; his is a gallantry enforced by circumstances. Yesterday, Bernard Kramer, editor of the *Main Line Chronicle,* observed that he had the organization scared and Harold Stassen said very quickly: "We'd like to get 'em to join us." He is, after all, no longer a young man.

He made his speeches in Pottstown, and Ardmore, and Phoenixville as the cars went by and then he went back to the television station for the last of the Tuesday night talks on which he has staked most of the hopes he may be casting into empty air.

He sat there and made a very few notes; he no longer needs to write a speech. The paragraphs come now to his mind in blocks; he can finish on the second, conceiving and framing a respectable sentence which sounds like a peroration with just eight or nine seconds left.

He had brought a few props, and he sat there and explained, to the cameramen how they should treat a still picture of self and running mates and wives; "Can you close in and pan down the line from left to right?"

There were about three minutes left and Frank Chirkinian, his director—does Lynn Fontanne need a director?—went to the control room. The tube showed Harold Stassen running through his pockets. He looked strangely like President Eisenhower, which is the tonic which his trade even in this dull market works upon him. When he is just working at a job these days, Harold Stassen looks a little like Herbert Hoover; when he is running for an office, even against these odds, he looks like Dwight D. Eisenhower. "Look at the pockets," said Frank Chirkinian with real affection. "I never saw a man with such bulgy pockets." When you've been this long on the road, you travel alone without baggage.

A Day of Endless Fitness
MARY McGRORY—*Washington Star*—11/26/1963

Of John Fitzgerald Kennedy's funeral it can be said he would have liked it.

It had that decorum and dash that were in his special style. It was both splendid and spontaneous. It was full of children and princes, of gardeners and governors.

Everyone measured up to New Frontier standards.

A million people lined every inch of his last journey. Enough heads of state filed into St. Matthew's Cathedral to change the shape of the world.

The weather was superb, as crisp and clear as one of his own instructions.

His wife's gallantry became a legend. His two children behaved like Kennedys. His 3-year-old son saluted his coffin. His 6-year-old daughter comforted her mother. Looking up and seeing tears, she reached over and gave her mother's hand a consoling squeeze.

The procession from the White House would have delighted him. It was a marvelous eye-filling jumble of the mighty and the obscure, all walking behind his wife and his two brothers.

There was no cadence of order, but the presence of Gen. de Gaulle alone in the ragged line of march was enough to give it grandeur. He stalked splendidly up Connecticut Avenue, more or less beside Queen Frederika of Greece and King Baudouin of Belgium.

The sounds of the day were smashingly appropriate. The tolling of the bells gave way to the skirling of the Black Watch Pipers whose lament blended with the organ music inside the Cathedral.

At the graveside there was the thunder of jets overhead, a 21-gun salute, taps, and finally the strains of the Navy hymn, "Eternal Father Strong to Save."

He would have seen every politician he ever knew, two ex-Presidents, Truman and Eisenhower, and a foe or two. Gov. Wallace of Alabama had trouble finding a place to sit in the Cathedral.

His old friend, Cardinal Cushing of Boston, who married him, baptized his children and prayed over him in the icy air of his Inaugural, said a low mass. At the final prayers, after the last blessing, he suddenly added, "Dear Jack."

There was no eulogy. Instead, Bishop Philip M. Hannan mounted the pulpit and read passages from the President's speeches and evoked him so vividly that tears splashed on the red carpets and the benches of the Cathedral. Nobody cried out, nobody broke down.

And the Bishop read a passage the President had often noted in the Scriptures: "There is a time to be born and a time to die." He made no reference to the fact that no one had thought last Friday was a time for John Fitzgerald Kennedy to die—a martyr's death—in Dallas. The President himself had spent no time in trying to express the inexpressible. Excess was alien to his nature.

The funeral cortege stretched for miles. An old campaigner would have loved the crowd. Children sat on the curbstones. Old ladies wrapped their furs around them.

The site of the grave, at the top of one slope, commands all of Washington. Prince Philip used his sword as a walking stick to negotiate the incline.

His brother, Robert, his face a study in desolation, stood beside the President's widow. The children of the fabulous family were all around.

Jacqueline Kennedy received the flag from his coffin, bent over and with a torch lit a flame that is to burn forever on his grave—against the day that anyone might forget that her husband had been a President and a martyr.

It was a day of such endless fitness, with so much pathos and panoply, so much grief nobly borne that it may extinguish that unseemly hour in Dallas, where all that was alien to him—savagery, violence, irrationality—struck down the 35th President of the United States.

Touring Dixie with LBJ
JAMES RESTON—*New York Times*—5/10/1964

Touring the South with President Johnson is a little bit like going back to the old evangelical Chautauqua Circuit. He is Andy Jackson in a jetliner vaulting in the Appalachian Range in half an hour, and loving and exhorting the South at every stop. The exhausted Washington press corps chases after him in amazement, noting all the flattery and exaggeration, but this combination of his Southern origins, his present power, and his political skill may very well prove the most significant part of his Administration.

He turned out more than half a million people in the streets of Atlanta this week. In Rocky Mount, N.C., and Gainesville, Ga., his audiences were larger than the total population of the two towns, and his message was perfectly clear. His speech, his manner and address, his stories, his reminiscences of the past, his emphasis on family and friendship, his fantastic personal recollections of local and state politicians, were all so genuinely Southern that nobody could possibly challenge him.

But his point was unmistakable. "Justice," he said, referring to the motto of the State of Georgia—Wisdom, Justice and Moderation—"means justice among the races. . . . I will never feel that I have done justice to my high office until every section of this country is linked to a single purpose, a joint devotion to bring an end to injustice, to bring an end to poverty and to bring an end to the threat of conflict among nations."

The South would probably hesitate to take this from anybody else, but even the most segregationist Southerner cannot wholly disown President Johnson.

When his daughter Lynda was born twenty years ago, the first man he called up to announce the news was Representative Carl Vinson of Georgia, who was on the platform with the President here this week. When Lynda was introduced to the Georgia legislators at Friday's breakfast, she said simply that she felt at home in Georgia and referred to Georgia's Senator Russell, who is leading the fight against her father's civil-rights bill and was conspicuously absent at the breakfast, as "my beloved friend, who helped raise me."

Even the members of the Georgia Legislature, who hate Johnson's civil-rights bill and who applaud Senator Russell's decision not to attend the Johnson breakfast, knew that this just happened to be true.

They may disagree with the President, but he is one of them. When he talks about civil rights he quotes not Northerners but Southerners like Atticus Haygood, the president of Emory College, who said in 1880: "We in the South have no Divine call to stand eternal guard by the grave of dead issues."

When the President talks about poverty, he says: "Over my bed in the While House in Washington I keep a little picture of the tiny, three-room home where I was born, the son of a tenant farmer who worked on the 'halves,' and his cotton crop was about eight bales a year. It reminds me every day where I came from. But, more important, it reminds me of the people I serve."

He knows the history of the South and he tells them exactly what role Georgians played in the writing of the Constitution and how many went to the last three wars and how many died. He knows they still respect Franklin D. Roosevelt, and he has Franklin D. Roosevelt, Jr., on the platform with him. He knows most of them oppose his program of equal rights, yet he says, using the Biblical idiom of the South:

"In God's praise and under God's guidance, let all of us resolve this morning to help heal the last fading scars of old battles. . . . Heed not those who would come waving the tattered and discredited banners of the past, who seek to stir old hostilities and kindle old hatreds, who preach battle between neighbors and bitterness between states. That is the way back toward the anguish from which we all came."

The South has never lacked for spokesmen who have urged it to look to the future. It has produced probably more good newspaper editors in the last generation than any other section of the country. It has listened attentively but skeptically over the generations to Walter Prescott Webb telling it what oil, modern insecticides, the new fertilizers, water power, milo maize, and air-conditioning were going to do for the South in the last half of the twentiethth century. It has heard the faith and the wondrously disarming stories of Henry Grady about the glorious future of the South, but all this was less important.

Now it is the President of the United States who speaks not only for the South, and the difference is important. It is a long time since the South has had a voice in the White House that it really listened to, and this may prove a most important fact of our time.

The Decisive Political Center
JAMES RESTON—*New York Times*—11/7/1965

The history of American politics since the war of 1939–45 seems to support three propositions: (1)—The political spirit of the majority of American people varies from moderate to progressive; (2)—either major party that takes its stand on this middle ground with an attractive world-minded candidate can win the Presidency; and (3)—there is plenty of room for vigorous and constructive party welfare on this center battlefield between the Tweedledum Republicans a little right of center and the Tweedledee Democrats a little left of center.

These propositions may not be true in some areas of the country—for example, in some predominantly Democratic states of the South and some predominatly Republican states of the Middle West, where the spirit of the people is more conservative. But in national terms, it is difficult to argue from the record that either party can win the Presidency or even an effective national opposition if it defies these propositions.

Dwight D. Eisenhower accepted all three propositions and won for the Republicans in 1952 and 1956. Lyndon Johnson accepted them in 1964 and won by the largest margin in the history of the Presidency. Barry Goldwater defied them and not only lost but weakened his party's capacity—in the Congress and in the state capitals—to serve as an effective opposition party. Even in so Democratic a city as New York, John Lindsay saved the Republican party by repudiating it, and won the mayoral election by appealing beyond his party to all moderates and progressives, while the Democrats lost by appealing on narrow partisan grounds.

Individuals may ignore and even resent the success of these moderate-to-progressive candidates of both parties, but political parties cannot. For the function of a political party in this country is not to preside over a philosophical debate, but to control and direct the struggle for power, and no party can do this successfully unless it appeals to many diverse economic, regional, religious, and racial groups all over the continental United States.

Ideological conservatives like Goldwater and Buckley in New York are quite right in asserting that acceptance of the policies of the American "center" means acceptance of a strong trend toward "the welfare state" and "the planned economy." They are right too—though their opponents usually will not admit to it—in charging that American politics are moving to the left.

Where they are wrong, or so it seems to me, is in basing the political action of a large national party on narrow ideological grounds and on what people say or pretend instead of on what people really do. Almost everybody says he is against "the welfare state" and "the planned economy," but most of them vote for both without thinking much about either.

Almost everybody in this country is for "the common welfare," and the most successful "planners" in the United States are the Republican big businessmen who plan every automobile or other commercial product to attract popular support. People are not as rigid as political doctrines. They often denounce in theory the things they support in practice, and the successful politicians of the last generation have been those who have appealed to the people's interests and not to the people's pretenses.

The record simply does not support the notion that moving the Republican party from the center to the conservative right strengthens the Republican opposition and helps restore a balance in American political life. It does the opposite. It gives the people a clear "choice" all right, but a choice they are not prepared to accept. It does not balance or weaken the left but strengthens the left. It increases the noise and it envenoms the political argument, but it actually reduces the power of the Republican opposition.

Eisenhower and the British Conservatives have demonstrated that the best way to gain national power in a Western democracy is not by moving to the right and exaggerating the differences with the party of the left, but by commanding the center, accepting the best of liberal policies, and arguing that the moderates can administer them more efficiently. Eisenhower accepted all the domestic and foreign policy forms which the Democrats introduced and his own party opposed in the Thirties and Forties, and thus managed to be the only Republican President in the last thirty-three years. Goldwater gave the impression that he was against these reforms and was overwhelmingly defeated.

This is still the main political lesson of the postwar era. The decisive battleground of American politics lies in the center and cannot be captured from either of the extremes, and any party that defies this principle does not improve its chances of national power or even effective opposition, but precisely the opposite.

Are You Against the Handicapped?

WILLIAM F. BUCKLEY Jr.—Universal Press Syndicate—4/7/1973

The reaction to Richard Nixon's veto of the aid-to-the-handicapped bill brilliantly illustrates a difference between the Democratic and the Republican modes of operation; indeed, a difference between the always-elusive "liberal" and "conservative" ways of looking at things.

Never mind for a moment any structural defect in the proposed law. Consider it simply as a means of helping the handicapped by voting federal dollars for their use.

Senator Hubert Humphrey emerged as the best, i.e. quintessential, spokesman for the Democratic approach to such questions. For Senator Humphrey it was very simply this: Do you or do you not believe in helping handicapped children? Pure and simple. The senator went so far as to personalize the argument going even beyond his abstract identification with the cause of the handicapped. He spoke his rage over Nixon's veto on the floor of the Senate, saying, "I am the grandfather of a mentally retarded child. Our family can afford to take care of that child, but many families can't. I ask every senator here to search his own conscience. I don't believe the president of the United States knew what he was doing. If he did, he ought to be ashamed of himself." Such language is highly volatile. It spreads like wildfire through the college campuses.

From such an onslaught the conservative reels. If the critic will listen, the conservatives can patiently ask a few questions.

1. Do the Democrats believe that there is as much public money available as there are worthy causes in the world on which it might be spent?

No one, on reflection—not even Teddy Kennedy—would answer that question with a categorical yes.

2. Do the Democrats acknowledge that we have at this moment in American history strained the safe level of government spending?

No one, on reflection, can safely say that we have not. To do so would mean to interrupt his own criticism of the high price of meat, for one thing. All Democrats deplore the effects of inflation, and all Democrats recognize that the dollar's humiliation in the money markets abroad is the direct result of inflation at home.

3. Did the Democrats suggest that the billion-dollar aid-to-the-handicapped bill take the place of a billion dollars already appropriated for another social service? Did Senator Humphrey propose that Congress reduce by a billion dollars appropriations for medical aid to the elderly? For education for the young? For purification of our water and our air?

We nudge up against the argument that we should commensurately reduce the military budget.

4. As a matter of fact, the military budget has been reduced. In constant dollars we would need to spend $105 billion to maintain the same level of spending the Democratic Congress judged necessary when Mr. Nixon assumed office, subtracting the cost of the Vietnamese operation. Now, spending on defense is what a society, resolved to maintain its sovereignty, begins with, even as you begin a house by building a foundation. To economize by pouring more sand and less cement into the concrete is to be compared with economizing by offering the sick man a half million units of penicillin when the doctor has prescribed one million.

5. Since approximately one half of the states of the Union send more money for social expenditures to Washington than they receive for social expenditures from Washington, what is to keep these states from appropriating their own funds for the help of the handicapped? Senator Javits, for instance, who voted to override President Nixon's veto, comes from a state that sends Washington $1.60 for every dollar it gets back. Why doesn't Senator Javits satisfy himself to recommend to New York State that it look after its own handicapped?

In his classic book, *Economics in One Lesson*, Mr. Henry Hazlitt remarks that it is distinctively the conservative who looks beyond the immediate effect of any particular expenditure; that the liberal foreshortens his perspective, so that he is able to talk only in terms of, Are you or aren't you in favor of helping invalids? It is an onerous responsibility that the conservative needs to bear under the pressure of such demagogy, and we can only be grateful that Mr. Nixon and a few senators have had the courage to think in strategic terms.

Nixon's Resignation
CHARLES McDOWELL—*Richmond Times-Dispatch*—8/9/1974

The Shenandoah Valley was rainy, peaceful and eternal. The voice on the radio, from Washington, sounded unduly excited, no matter how big the news.

The voice was saying that Richard M. Nixon was expected to announce his resignation as president before the end of the day, Thursday, Aug. 8, 1974.

George Macheras, proprietor of the Southern Inn in Lexington, rang up a lunch bill and said very softly, Six months ago a lot of people like me were still for this fellow, still hoping he could pull it out. Now hes got no alternative. None.

A few doors down Main Street, in front of McCrums drugstore, two other men were discussing the president. They had discussed the weather and a couple of other things before they got to him.

Well, I hope he doesnt do it, the first man said. When I think back to how it was when he took over, I have to say he did great things for this country.

I believe I can tell you what his problem was, said the second man, smiling slightly and exaggerating his mountain accent. He got in bad trouble with the law.

At 12:45 p.m. the radio in the car was playing "Wildwood Flower" and some other numbers like that. There was a drizzle. The fields looked shiny green and fog hid the tops of mountains.

The radio in the Texaco station was on a shelf above the little cans of gas and oil additives. A large man in blue coveralls and a wiry man in farmer's clothes and a straw hat were sitting in the station talking. When the 1 o'clock news came on, they stopped talking and listened.

Ronald L. Ziegler said in a choked voice that the President would speak to the nation at 9 p.m. An announcer said the President had told Vice President Gerald R. Ford he would resign.

When that was over, the wiry man said, Cecil, what ever happened to that little truck Albert Straub had?

The big man replied, He traded it in on another.

Back in the car, the strongest radio station was one in Waynesboro, the big No. 1, Radio97 from the power tower. The big No. 1 broke into its music and commercials for an editorial. It was about a parking controversy in Waynesboro. The big No. 1 sided with the retail merchants against more or higher parking fees.

There was news at 1:30. A bank robber had been sentenced to jail. The second item was that Virginia Congressman Robert W. Daniel Jr., a Republican, had said the President's resignation would be wise and proper. Virginia Congressman Stanford E. Parris, another Republican, had said he would vote for impeachment if the President did not resign.

The first copies of the afternoon Waynesboro News-Virginian came off the press at 1:47, just two minutes late. A traveler bought a stickily fresh one at the front counter of the newspaper office.

The streamer headline said: Nixon to Quit. It was printed in red ink.

Pat Velenovsky, the managing editor, was sitting at a desk in the newsroom looking at the red headline. It was the first red one he had ever used. The type was the largest he could get, 72 point, and it had been doubled in size by a photographic process.

Velenovsky had written the headline early in the morning, and decided about noon to use it when a wire service reported that the Republican leader in the House, John J. Rhodes, had said the President definitely was resigning.

Edward P. Berlin Jr., the editor of *The News-Virginian*, walked in looking at the red headline and said he hoped Velenovsky would like it as much after the President's speech as he did right now.

Velenovsky said he was not coming to work Friday if the red headline was wrong.

Berlin went back to his office and resumed drafting an editorial for today. Gazing at the paper in the typewriter, he said, I have never known a man who wanted to be remembered by history as much as Richard Nixon. I have a sympathetic feeling for the man. Maybe Ford will have a chance to pull things back together.

There was sunshine on Afton mountain, puddles beside Interstate 64. The big No. 1 had an announcement at 2:15: at the Greater Shenandoah Valley Agricultural Fair there would be a greased-pole-climbing at contest at 10 p.m.

There was fog at the very top of the mountain, and nobody could see anything from the great glass dining room of the Holiday Inn perched over Rockfish Valley. A few people were eating quietly, looking at their food.

A sign on the dining room cash register said: If you think our beef is high, cigarettes are $11.60 a pound.

In the lobby, a middle-aged couple was talking with the clerk about a reservation for the night at another Holiday Inn, perhaps in Kingsport, Tenn., or Abingdon, or in the Roanoke area. The man was getting as far down the road as possible. His wife wanted to be sure to be settled for the evening by 9 p.m.

The man could not seem to understand her concern about 9 p.m., and the wife said, You know, the program on television.

What program? he said. He was a little irritated.

You know, the speech, she said.

Yes, the speech, he said, and they told the clerk to try for a reservation in Roanoke, but for some reason they were shy of mentioning what speech they were talking about.

The sunshine was bright again on the eastern side of the mountain, and the Rockfish Valley looked like a picture in a book. The big No. 1 gave one more resignation bulletin at 3 o'clock and began to fade. A Washington station came in huskily. Two voices were discussing problems of tact in removing the Nixons' possessions from the White House.

Just beyond Charlottesville, at the Shadwell Gulf station and u-Day Jr. Store, a radio was playing behind the counter and a trim, dark-haired woman was listening to it. The voice on the radio was not quite sure of the resignation.

I doubt if he'll quit, the woman said. I sure don't expect him to, anyway. They're all alike, really. They never quit.

Along the back road to Gordonsville, the white fences of the horse farms were freshly washed and the sun was pale and soft, and the Washington radio station was talking of thundershowers and the transfer of power in the White House.

The drive-in movie at Gordonsville was advertising *Teenage Milkmaid* for adults only.

At the traffic circle where Rt. 15 and 231, among others, converge in Gordonsville, there is a sandwich shop operated by Mrs. J.S. Hall. She grew up in Madison County, has lived in Waynesboro, and has run the sandwich shop for three years.

When a traveler asked for coffee, she said: I sometimes don't get a call for a cup of coffee in a whole day, so I don't make that big pot. Now, if we were in West Virginia, say, I'd get lots of calls for coffee.

The traveler settled for instant without trying to understand the whole thing, and asked Mrs. Hall if she thought the President would resign.

Today or tomorrow is what they say, she said. It's the awfulest thing I ever heard of. We'll just have to get along the best we can without a president.

The one other customer in the place, a jolly-looking woman, coughed. There was a silence, and then Mrs. Hall said: I guess the vice president will take over, won't he? What's his name?

Gerald Ford.

Ford, yes. Well, what I wonder is, is why this president, if he didn't do all those things, couldn't show us the papers or the proof that he did'nt do them, Mrs. Hall said.

The jolly-looking woman said, Because he knew he did 'em, I guess.

A 4:10 p.m., in the neighborhood of Orange, the Washington station began a retrospective on The Nixon Years. The past tense was pervasive and created a strange kind of unreality in the automobile.

Somewhere between the Wilderness and Chancellorsville, a sports announcer came on the Washington station and said he almost had a great interview with Billy Kilmer, the Redskins quarterback, but the announcer had forgotten to push the record button on his tape recorder.

During the drive on Interstate 95, at Fredericksburg, the radio said the President's resignation was now taken for granted, Nelson Rockefeller had been approached about the vice presidency, and there was a massive tie-up in Washington in all directions.

It was not much worse than normal. Everything in Washington looked oddly normal. There was some fog. The Washington Monument was partly hidden, but it was there and it seemed peaceful and eternal.

Being Spied On Has Benefits of Sorts
JACK ANDERSON—*Washington Post*—1/31/1975

I don't know how other middle-aged men, beset by menopausal quirks and temptation, manage to keep on the straight and narrow. But I have found a method.

More precisely, the method has found me.

For illustration, just the other day I was browsing through the morning paper and came unexpectedly upon the admission by Central Intelligence Agency chief William E. Colby that the agency has been spying on me.

Well there was a time when such tidings might have left me somewhat greenish. But I can now accept the CIA in my life with an inner serenity. I have developed this simple philosophy:

If men would but live their lives as though gumshoes from seven government agencies were always half a block behind, the appeal of the virtuous life would soon be made manifest to them.

I also get some comfort from the security which all this government attention provides. To waylay me, a bad man would have to get past a whole posse of federal flatfeet. Here is the latest count:

- In late 1970, the White House assigned Jack Caulfield, the precursor of the plumbers, to investigate me. His aim, according to a confidential Feb. 11, 1971, memo, was to make "the ability of the Andersons of the world to gain White House information both difficult and hazardous." He spent three months on the assignment, without notable results.
- The Pentagon's sleuths got on my trail in early 1971. They produced a bespectacled clerk, Eugene Smith, as our master spy and, after third-degree grillings that left him with ulcers dragged him before a grand jury in Norfolk, Va. The U.S. attorney there, Brian Gettings, quickly concluded that Smith was the wrong man.
- Shortly thereafter, *The Washington Post* reported that the White House "is directing a major effort to discredit columnist Jack Anderson"—an effort *The Post* said involved the Justice Department, Republican National Committee and the Committee for the Re-election of the President. These groups were to feed "negative material about Anderson" to the press and to simpatico senators.
- By this time, the CIA and the FBI had joined the posse. A separate investigation was directed by Robert C. Mardian, then an assistant attorney general, whose plainclothesmen collaborated behind the scenes with Intertel, the private eye firm, which had been hired by the International Telephone and Telegraph Corp. to spy on me. Mardian has now been convicted in the Watergate case.
- In 1972, the maladroit White House "plumbers" turned their attention from Pentagon Papers' leaker Daniel Ellsberg and scrawled my name on their blackboard as their new Public Enemy No. 1. Their relentlessness search for my sources led them at last to a gentle Navy yeoman, and they browbeat a confession out of him that he was, indeed, a spy—not for me but for the Joint Chiefs of Staff.

All this surveillance, meanwhile has toned me up marvellously for the future.

I have a sensitive eye and memory for the location of pay phones, and in conversation, my evasive code has become so effective that half the time my own staff doesn't understand my instructions.

Other pitfalls are avoided. For other men, the Washington whirl is full of lures— massage parlors, Fannie Foxe–type bistros, get-rich-quick schemes, lobbyists who can offer all that comfort and cupidity hold dear. Temptation is everywhere.

But not for me. The thought of all those cops back there, tripping over their night-sticks but gaining on me, turns me right off.

Reagan Shot: End of an Era?
DAVID S. BRODER—*Washington Post*—4/1/1981

The honeymoon has ended and a new legend has been born.

The gunfire that shattered the stillness of a rainy Washington Monday afternoon broke not just four bodies, but the mood of euphoria that has buoyed this capital since the inauguration of a new president and the return of the hostages from Iran.

But it also created a new hero in Ronald Reagan, the chipper gipper who took a .22 caliber slug in his chest but walked into the emergency room on his own power and joked with the anxious doctors on his way into surgery.

This being Washington, the politicians no sooner learned that the president was out of danger than they started sorting out the political implications of the day's drama.

That is a process that will take some time, but one fact is so obvious it cannot be missed even in a capital that sometimes understands everything but the most important thing. What happened to Reagan on Monday is the stuff of which legends are made.

From primitive days, heroic tales have been fashioned from incidents in which brave men escape danger. That tradition has been carried intact into the presidency—from Andy Jackson, the hero of New Orleans, to Teddy Roosevelt, the hero of San Juan Hill, and Jack Kennedy on PT109.

In these and other cases, the survival of the hero in conditions of imminent danger is taken as a sign of divine favor—a token that he has been saved for a reason. So much more so when the threat strikes at the president in office, from a seemingly deranged assassin, and he survives what the entire television-watching world sees could easily have been a calamity.

Ten weeks earlier, Reagan struck an unusual theme in his inaugural address, when he turned from a recital of the nation's problems to say, "We have every right to dream heroic dreams. Those who say we're in a time when there are no heroes, they just don't know where to look."

In his first weeks in office, Reagan demonstrated repeatedly a kind of personal ease and charm that not only delighted his audience but disarmed his critics. He was the first to kid his own supposed shortcomings—his age, his hearing, his eyesight, even his grasp of issues—in a way untinged by any sympathy-seeking self-pity.

When he displayed that same wit and grace in the hours after his own life was threatened, he elevated those appealing human qualities to the level of legend. As long as people remember the hospitalized president joshing his doctors and nurses—and they will remember—no critic will be able to portray Reagan as a cruel or callous or heartless man.

Criticism of his policies will be—probably forever—separated from criticism of the man. Reagan now enjoys an aura of good will and a presumption of good motive that no president since war hero Dwight D. Eisenhower has had as a shield in a political arena.

Tragically, that arena is now a far bloodier place than it was in the innocent Eisenhower era. The fragility of our governmental structure to the assassin's bullet has been demonstrated again.

Last Saturday night, at the Gridiron dinner, where Washington correspondents entertain the politicians with satirical songs and skits, Reagan and his press secretary Jim Brady laughed uproariously when a Tip O'Neill character, dressed incongruously as a bulky bride, sang, "Honeymoon, it could last until June."

It lasted less than 48 hours more. Then Reagan was on his way to the hospital and Brady was lying on the sidewalk in his own blood, a bullet in his brain. The sense that was so strong in January, when the hostages came home and the new administration took office, that perhaps the frustrations and agonies of the '60s and '70s had been put behind us—that dream was over.

"Then one noon," the Tip O'Neill character sang, "I will pop the balloon. And I'll reveal that Tip O'Neill calls the Capitol tune." But in reality, the balloon was popped by the all-too-well-remembered sound of gunfire, and a demented individual came within inches of erasing the voters' mandate.

This society, which stubbornly resists even the most modest effort to discipline its own appetite for handguns, had once again paid the price for its folly. It appears that a sick man, arrested once before in threat-to-the-president circumstances, had procured a new weapon with ridiculous ease—and this time had struck.

I have a chilling thought that mocks the merry mood of the Gridiron dinner. A year ago, we lost Sen. Ted Kennedy as our scheduled speaker because his friend—and mine—Allard Lowenstein had just been shot to death. This year's Gridiron is indelibly linked with the last glimpse of the lovely, loving man we knew as Jim Brady in his customary rollicking good humor.

Next year—God knows what awaits us.

Slats Mistakes GOP for GOD
MIKE ROYKO—*Chicago Tribune*—3/9/1984

I could tell something was wrong. President Reagan had been on the TV at the end of the bar for ten minutes. But Slats Grobnik hadn't said even one unkind word.

Normally, Slats hoots, jeers, snorts, hisses, or puts his thumb to his nose and wiggles his bony fingers at any Republican—especially a Republican president.

As he once said: "That's why I love TV. My father was a lifelong Democrat, just like me. But he didn't have the same advantages. There was nothing but newspapers and radio in his day, and it wasn't nearly as much fun thumbing your nose at the front page or a radio dial."

But this time Slats sat silently staring at his beer and occasionally glancing at the TV screen. I finally walked over and asked him if something was wrong.

He nervously cracked his knuckles, then said: "I got a problem. It has to do with my soul."

Your what?

"My soul. You know, that thing inside ya."

Oh, your soul. What's the problem with it?

"I'm worried about losing it or having it burn in hell or something. Look, you know how I am about politics. I was born a Democrat. I never voted for a Republican even once. I always figured that with all my other vices, I don't need one more."

Yes, we all know that.

"But now I'm thinking about voting for . . . Gee, I hate to even say it. Let me whisper. I'm thinking of voting for Reagan."

And you think you'll lose your soul if you do?

"No, I'm thinking that I might lose it if I don't."

Why should that happen?

"Well, what if God is a Republican?"

That's ridiculous.

"You think so. Then tell me. Who's Reagan's running mate?"

It will surely be Vice President George Bush.

"No it won't. Take it from me, it's God."

What are you talking about?

"Just listen to Reagan. Every speech lately, who does he talk about? God. Do you remember any president who talked about God as much as he does?"

Now that you mention it, no.

"And what gets me is that he talks like he knows God and knows exactly what He likes or doesn't like. I mean, sometimes Reagan sounds like God is his campaign adviser."

It does sound that way.

"And look how he's got Congress spending its time. All they do these days is argue if God wants the kids to pray out loud or pray quiet or to pray at all, and who writes the prayer. You'd think it was some kind of Bible meeting instead of a bunch of politicians cutting deals."

But that's just politics. Reagan and the Republicans are trying to hustle the fundamentalist vote. Don't worry. God is not a Republican.

"You don't think so? Well, tell me this. I'm not religious, but I always heard that God is all-powerful, right?"

True.

"And you break His rules and—bam—you're in big trouble, right?"

Some people believe that, yet.

"And if you goof up, He's liable to smite you with His mighty and swift sword, right?"

So it has been said.

"Well, if that don't sound like a Republican to me, I don't know what does."

But what about God's son? Do you think Jesus was a Republican? Or a Concervative?

"Well, Republicans usually pass it on. I think in Lake Forest, they put it in their wills with the stocks and bonds."

Would a Republican have said, blessed are the poor in spirit, the meek, the merciful, and the peacemakers?

"If he wanted to get elected in the suburbs, he wouldn't."

And what about all this silly business of organized, vocal, school prayer? Would a Republican have said he was against it?

"You're not saying Jesus was against it?"

Some people think he might have been. He said: "But thou, when thou prayest, enter into thy closet, and when thou hast shut thy door, pray to thy Father which is in secret; and thy Father which seeth in secret shall reward thee openly." Does that sound like something Reagan's supporters are screaming at congressmen to pass?

"No. And I'm all for putting a lot of those noisy kids in closets, too."

And if Jesus was a Republican, would he have spent most of his life hanging around with the poor, the afflicted, the social riff-raff of his day, and raising hell with the government, the rich, and the powerful?

"No, that doesn't sound like something Ed Meese or Jim Watt would go in for. Unless they just wanted to see the poor and the afflicted so they could tell them that they brought it on themselves."

And one more thing. Would any Republican have said this: "And again I say to you, it is easier for a camel to go through the eye of the needle, than for a rich man to enter into the kingdom of God"?

"A Republican? That sounds to me like somebody whose phone they would have tapped."

All right, then stop worrying.

"I think you're probably right. Except for one thing. About the camel going through the eye of the needle."

What about it?

"With all their money, I figure they'd just build a bigger needle."

The Sound of a Lapdog
GEORGE F. WILL—*Washington Post*—1/30/1986

The optimistic statement "George Bush is not as silly as he frequently seems" now seems comparable to Mark Twain's statement that Wagner's music is better than it sounds. Bush's recent New York performance suggests that although the

1988 nomination is his to lose, he has a gift for doing things like that.

Before his New York debacle, his most recent splash was in the waning days of the 1984 campaign when he had debates with the Geraldine Ferraro and himself, winning only the former, and only sort of winning it. His performance earned—yes, earned—him *The Washington Post*'s designation as "the Cliff Barnes of American politics," a reference to the *Dallas* character whom *The Post* characterized as "blustering, opportunistic, craven and hopelessly ineffective all at once." Kinder critics referred to Bush's "hyperkinesis."

After the debate, he bragged about how he had "kicked a little ass." Actually, he had applied his foot firmly to the inside of his mouth as when he claimed Walter Mondale and Ferraro had said the Marines killed by the Beirut truck bomb had "died in shame." His charge was flatly false, and if it was not initially a lie it quickly became one as he refused to retract it.

That rancid episode is relevant to Bush's New York shambles because, yet again, the question of his intention arises: Did he intend to talk rot? It is hard to believe that premeditation was involved in what he said about Mario Cuomo but, alas, he was not improvising: he was reading from a prepared text. Does he read such texts before rising to speak?

A few days before Bush addressed the New York State Conservative Party, Cuomo, no slouch in the silliness sweepstakes, said he might run for president to disprove ethnic "slurs," by which he means speculation that an Italian American cannot win. That is among the silliest reasons ever offered for trying to become leader of the Free World. Besides, speculation about the consequences of a particular ethnicity hardly constitutes a "slur."

Cuomo is right to raise the matter of the sort of thinking that I have heard phrased this way: "If Cuomo looked like Bush, he would be the odds-on favorite for the Democratic nomination." Ah, but what if Cuomo had the handicap of sounding like Bush? This is how Bush sounded when characterizing Cuomo's thought in New York:

"He's telling us to ignore the millions of blacks, Jews, Irish, Italians, Latins and Poles who shattered the bonds of discrimination and built this great land. . . ."

You blew it, Bush—you blew the Samoan American vote by neglecting to pander to them too. But, unwilling to leave wretched enough alone, Bush slogged on:

"Worst of all, he's telling us to be ashamed to stand up and be proud of this great land. . . ."

There he goes again, dishonestly tossing around the idea of shame. What Bush said is gibberish, but not just gibberish. It is a lie. And it suggests how bare Bush's mental cupboard is of themes. He began by accusing Cuomo of "divisiveness," another echo of the Ferraro debate, in which Bush accused Mondale of "telling the American people to divide [by] class—rich and poor." Bush's syntax was as muddled as his thought.

But Bush's low point came with this smarmy sentence: "I can tell you one thing about the difference between a liberal politician and a conservative one: Gov. Ronald Reagan kept cop-killers in jail." That was a ten-thumbed attempt to squeeze political advantage from a complicated case in which Cuomo recommended clemency for a man who has spent 18 years in jail and who may—but who never was found to—have directly killed a policeman. Among those who have campaigned for clemency is William F. Buckley Jr., not hitherto famous as a coddler of "cop-killers." Anyway, anyone can tell Bush one difference between a real conservative and a charlatan: a real conservative does not consider an office such as the vice presidency a license to meddle in a state's system of criminal justice.

The unpleasant sound Bush is emitting as he traipses from one conservative gathering to another is this, tinny "arf"—the sound of a lapdog. He is panting along Mondale's path to the presidency.

When Normal Mailer published a particularly dreadful novel, a critic—an optimist—titled his review "Mailer Hits Bottom." Realists replied: Not unless he (Mailer) never again gets near a typewriter. Concerning Bush, optimists say: Well, er, perhaps in New York he got the demagoguery out of his system. Realists say: That was not a momentary dereliction of taste; that was part of a pattern.

A Supreme Court Buzzword Guide
MICHAEL KINSLEY—*Washington Post*—7/26/1990

President Bush is either a liar or a fool when he says he has no idea where David Souter stands on abortion, affirmative action and so on. Seeking a formula that will reassure liberals without alarming conservatives, and vice versa, he said there was no "litmus test" but that his Supreme Court nominee would "interpret the Constitution and not legislate." And thus the Summer Supreme Court hypocrisy festival is underway once more. Herewith a handy buzzword guide.

Advice and Consent: A "strict construction" (see below) of these words would seem to entitle the Senate to a major say in choosing Supreme Court justices. Yet conservatives generally interpret this phrase to mean that the Senate must approve anyone the president nominates unless he actually can't tie his shoes on the third attempt.

Balance: What liberals now claim they want among the nine justices. History does not record any liberal calls for "balance" when the court was tilted to the left and liberal presidents were doing the appointing.

Conservative: This can mean two things. It can mean a principled belief that unelected judges shouldn't thwart democracy by sticking their own political values into the Constitution. Or it can mean, "Here is a golden opportunity to stick conservative political values into the Constitution. Liberals did it for years—why shouldn't we?"

Election Returns: Commentators can't resist Mr. Dooley's line, "th' supreme coort follows th'iliction returns"—even though the entire controversy over the court centers on the fact that it does not follow the election returns. Conservatives resent this. However, when liberals campaign against a nominee, conservatives complain about the "politicization" of the judiciary. They've got it backward. The sitting Supreme Court is supposed to be above politics. Choosing justices is where politics is supposed to come into it.

Ideology: Very bad for a judge to have, everyone agrees. (But see "philosophy" below.) In announcing Souter, Bush reaffirmed the traditional pretense that he sought "excellence" and that he would never dream of finding out whether a potential justice agreed with him on issues he has long claimed to be vitally important.

Judicial Activism and Judicial Restraint: Conservatives believe that activism is bad, and restraint is good. Except that the 1988 Republican platform calls for judges who hold that "the 14th Amendment's protections apply to unborn children," which means judges who ban abortion no matter what the legislature votes. Oh, yes, and conservatives think the special prosecutor law is unconstitutional, and so is affirmative action, and maybe New York City rent control, and so on and so forth.

Litmus Tests: Sometimes called "single-issue litmus tests." Bad, very bad. Especially the other side's. While pro-choice senators were warning President Bush not to apply a pro-life "litmus test" to his nominee, pro-choice groups were sending out mass mailings promising to oppose anyone who would vote to reverse *Roe v. Wade*.

Philosophy: Good to have, as long as it doesn't make you an "ideologue" (see above) or suggest that you have "pre-judged" (see below). There is a germ of a legitimate distinction here, between having a theory of the role of the judiciary (philosophy) and merely being determined to impose your political will (ideology). But usually a "philosophy" is what I have, and an "ideology" is what you have.

Original Intent: What conservatives say they want judges to follow. Makes it sound simple, which it isn't.

Pre-Judge: A very, very bad thing to do, it seems. Preferable: an "open mind." In the Bork episode, Republicans savaged Democrats for having "pre-judged" his suitability before the hearings. Then Democrats savaged Bork for having "pre-judged" constitutional issues that might come before him on the court.

The whole point of having a judicial "philosophy"—good, remember?—is that it leads you to understandings on specific issues. Abortion, for example, has been the predominant constitutional issue for almost two decades. Anyone who hasn't thought it through and reached a conclusion by now shouldn't be eligible to graduate law school, let alone sit on the Supreme Court.

Questions on Specific Issues: Should a Supreme Court nominee have to answer them? Of course. Except for Bush's understandable desire to have it both ways, why should this be a guessing game? That would indeed—as Robert Bork has charged—put a premium on candidates with no record of having thought about the matters they will have to deal with. Nominees shouldn't have to answer an endless string of hypotheticals. But on the great constitutional questions— does the Bill of Rights apply to the states?—and the big 5-to-4 issues of recent years—abortion, reverse discrimination, flag-burning—there's no reason the Senate shouldn't expect an answer and an explanation of how it was derived.

Pro-Choice: Should mean: believes in a woman's right to choose abortion. Usually does mean: believes the right to abortion is in the Constitution. Not the same thing at all.

Strict Constructionism: The third component of the great conservative judicial trinity, along with "judicial restraint" and "original intent." These values are not always compatible. For example, the First Amendment says, "Congress shall make no law . . . abridging the freedom of speech." A strict construction of those words would lead to a broad, "activist" approach. Yet few self-proclaimed strict constructionists are First Amendment absolutists. Where does Souter stand? The only way to find out is to ask.

When Clinton Talks, People Listen—and Vice Versa
MOLLY IVINS—*Fort Worth Star-Telegram*—8/30/1992

ON THE CLINTON BUS—It is a show, and a good one at that. I'd recommend it for everyone, regardless of political persuasion, who enjoys vintage American politics.

Our political life is now so dominated by television that it's wonderfully pleasant to be able to wander down to the courthouse—or the mall—in your own hometown to hear and see the guy who wants to be president while he's out there sweating in the sun with everyone else.

That the entire show is carefully orchestrated for television is just one of the facts of contemporary life. Clinton is an exceptionally good campaigner. I make this observation in the same spirit in which one would note that Joe Montana is an artist on the football field, even if one were a Cowboys fan. What is, is. The "liberal media" is not inventing Clinton.

As a campaigner, Clinton has great stamina. He tends to get stronger as the day goes on. He blends gentle ridicule of the whole Bush era with a "We-can-do-it" pitch that is actually classic Reagan. We're the optimists; they're the pessimists.

He has a standard litany of what he plans to do if elected. To my surprise, the one that crowds like most is the national-service idea. Clinton wants to set up a national college trust fund, so any American can get a loan to go to college. Then, he emphasizes that the student will have to pay back the loan, either with a small percentage of his or her earnings after graduation, or by giving two years to public service—as a teacher, as a cop, working with inner-city kids, helping old folks.

As the list goes on, the applause swells. "We can rebuild this country. We can save our cities. We can do it. We can!"

Clinton and Al Gore have a lot of material to work with, given Bush's record, his dingbat mode and latest goofy proposals. Both men needle the president constantly and are rapidly turning the "family-values" convention to their own advantage. Meanwhile, the Bush team, now under Jim Baker, is already quicker at responding and has now dropped family values.

Bush probably made a mistake when he told the evangelical crowd in Dallas last weekend that the Democrats left G-O-D out of their platform (that was before Baker nixed "family values").

An Episcopalian really should know better than to try to out-Bible a couple of Baptist boys. Both Clinton and Gore can quote Scripture to a fare-thee-well, but the ever-magisterial Barbara Jordan, daughter of a Baptist preacher, used it most witheringly at the enormous rally in Austin (best guess, twenty thousand). "Everyone who calleth to me, 'Lord, Lord,' will not get in. Who will get in? Those who do the Lord's work."

Much of the Texas tour, viewed as a whole, is an exercise in inoculation.

The Clinton campaign fully expects Bush to go on television with massive negative buys. In Texas, two obvious targets are guns and gays. If past Republican performance is a reliable indicator, the gay-bashing will be down below radar, on radio.

Clinton tried to defuse the gun issue (he supports the Brady bill, the seven-day hold on gun purchases) by citing Ronald Reagan's support for the Brady bill and touting it as a common-sense measure to help law enforcement.

The Republicans' Texas attack plan, titled "September Storm," contains a memorable wincer. The R's refer to the political operatives with whom they plan to flood East Texas as "Stormtroopers." You don't have to be Jewish to flinch at that lack of historical sensitivity.

Energy, stamina, and joy are key factors that make Clinton such an effective campaigner. Of pols I have watched, he is most like Hubert Humphrey and Ralph Yarborough. He loves doing this. He gets energy from people.

A lot of politicians, Lloyd Bentsen for example, move through crowds smiling and shaking hands. But the smile never reaches their eyes. You can tell they'd much rather be back in Washington cutting deals with other powerful people. In his book *What It Takes: The Way to the White House*, writer Richard Ben Cramer suggests that Bush despises politics, considers it a dirty business, and consequently believes anything is permitted.

The different thing about Clinton is that he listens to people as he moves among them. Humphrey and Yarborough were always talking. Clinton listens and remembers and repeats the stories he hears.

I have read several of the poetic effusions produced by my journalistic colleagues about Clinton's bus tours and laughed. On Thursday evening, in the late dusk, moving among the thousands gathered on the old suspension bridge over the Brazos in Waco, I realized why so many of us wax poetic about these scenes.

It's not Clinton who's so wonderful. It's America.

No Guardrails
DANIEL HENNINGER—*Wall Street Journal*—3/18/1993

The gunning down of abortion doctor David Gunn in Florida last week shows us how small the barrier has become that separates civilized from uncivilized behavior in American life. In our time, the United States suffers every day of the week because there are now so many marginalized people among us who don't understand the rules, who don't think that rules of personal or civil conduct apply to them, who have no notion of self-control. We are the country that has a TV commercial on all the time that says: "Just do it." Michael Frederick Griffin just did it.

An anti-abortion protester of intense emotions, he walked around behind the Pensacola Women's Medical Services Clinic and pumped three bullets into the back of Dr. Gunn. Emptied himself, Michael Griffin then waited for the police to take him away. A remark by his father-in-law caught our eye: "Now we've got to take care of two grandchildren."

As the saying goes, there was a time. And indeed there really was a time in the United States when life seemed more settled, when emotions, both private and public, didn't seem to run so continuously at breakneck speed, splattering one ungodly tragedy after another across the evening news. How did this happen to the United States? How, in T. S. Eliot's phrase, did so many become undone?

We think it is possible to identify the date when the U.S., or more precisely when many people within it, began to tip off the emotional tracks. A lot of people won't like this date, because it makes their political culture culpable for what has happened. The date is August 1968, when the Democratic National Convention found itself sharing Chicago with the street fighters of the anti–Vietnam War movement.

The real blame here does not lie with the mobs who fought bloody battles with the hysterical Chicago police. The larger responsibility falls on the intellectuals—university professors, politicians and journalistic commentators—who said then that the acts committed by the protesters were justified or explainable. That was the beginning. After Chicago, the justifications never really stopped. America had a new culture, for political action and personal living.

With great rhetorical firepower, books, magazines, opinion columns and editorials defended each succeeding act of defiance—against the war, against university presidents, against corporate practices, against behavior codes, against dress codes, against virtually all agents of established authority.

What in the past had been simply illegal became "civil disobedience." If you could claim, and it was never too hard to claim, that your group was engaged in an act of civil disobedience—taking over a building, preventing a government official from speaking, bursting onto the grounds of a nuclear cooling station, destroying animal research, desecrating Communion hosts—the shapers of opinion would blow right past the broken rules to seek an understanding of the "dissidents" (in the '60s and '70s) and "activists" (in the '80s and now).

Concurrently, the personal virtue known as self-restraint was devalued. In the process, certain rules that for a long time had governed behavior also became devalued. Whatever else was going on here, we were repeatedly lowering the barriers of acceptable political and personal conduct.

You can argue, as many did and still do, that all this was necessary because the established order wouldn't respond or change. But then you still need to account for the nation's simultaneous dive into extensive social and personal dysfunction. You need to account for what is happening to those people within U.S. society who seem least able to navigate the political and personal torrents that they become part of, like Michael Griffin.

Those torrents began with the antiwar movement in the 1960s. Those endless demonstrations, though, were merely one part of a much deeper shift in American culture—away from community and family rules of conduct and toward more autonomy, more personal independence. As to limits, you set your own.

The people who provided the theoretical underpinnings for this shift—the intellectuals and political leaders who led the movement—did very well, or at least survived. They are born with large reservoirs of intelligence and psychological strength. The fame and celebrity help, too.

But for a lot of other people it hasn't been such an easy life to sustain. Not exceedingly sophisticated, neither thinkers nor leaders, never interviewed for their views, they're held together by faith, friends, fun and, at the margins, by fanaticism. The big political crackups make the news—a Michael Griffin or the woman on trial in Connecticut for the attempted bombing of the CEO of a surgical-device company or the '70s radicals who accidentally blew themselves up in a New York brownstone. But the personal crackups just float like flotsam through the country's hospitals and streets. You can also see some of them on daytime TV, America's medical museum of personal autonomy.

It may be true that most of the people in Hollywood who did cocaine survived it, but many of the weaker members of the community hit the wall. And most of the teenage girls in the Midwest who learn about the nuances of sex from magazines published by thirtysomething women in New York will more or less survive, but some continue to end up as prostitutes on Eighth Avenue.

Everyone today seems to know someone who couldn't handle the turns and went over the side of the mountain.

These weaker or more vulnerable people, who in different ways must try to live along life's margins, are among the reasons that a society erects rules. They're guardrails. It's also true that we need to distinguish good rules from bad rules and periodically re-examine old rules. But the broad movement that gained force during the anti-war years consciously and systematically took down the guardrails. Incredibly, even judges pitched in. All of them did so to transform the country's institutions and its codes of personal behavior (abortion, for instance).

In a sense, it has been a remarkable political and social achievement for them. But let's get something straight about the consequences. If as a society we want to live under conditions of constant challenge to institutions and limits on personal life, if we are going to march and fight and litigate over every conceivable grievance, then we should stop crying over all the individual casualties, because there are going to be a lot of them.

Michael Griffin and Dr. David Gunn are merely two names on a long list of confrontations and personal catastrophe going back 25 years. That today is the status quo. The alternative is to start rethinking it.

Pulp Nonfiction
MAUREEN DOWD—*New York Times*—9/13/1998

The President must not lose his job.

Not over this.

Certainly, Bill Clinton should be deeply ashamed of himself. He has given a bad name to adultery and lying. He has made wickedness seem pathetic, and that's truly a sin.

Kenneth Starr, all these years and all these millions later, has not delivered impeachable offenses. He has delivered a 445-page Harold Robbins novel.

If we are going to dump our President, it should be for something big and bold and black and original. Not for the most tired story ever told.

Middle-aged married man has affair with frisky and adoring young office girl. Man hints to girl he might be single again in three or four years. Man gets bored with girl and dumps her. Girl cries and rants and threatens, and tells 11 people what a creep he is.

The dialogue in this potboiler, compiled with sanctimonious, even voyeuristic relish by Reverend Starr, is so trite and bodice-ripping that it makes *Titanic* look profound.

In fact, Monica identified with Rose, the feisty, zaftig young heroine of *Titanic*. Last January, the former intern wrote the President what she called an embarrassing mushy note inspired by the movie, asking her former boyfriend if they could have sex (the lying-down kind).

Despite the fact that it takes place in the most powerful spot on the planet, the romance does not sizzle.

Bill Clinton fancies himself another Jack Kennedy and invoked his idol's name last week to defend himself. But Kennedy was cool. His women were glamorous. The Rat Pack was good copy. He may have been just as immoral, but his carousing at least had style.

Mr. Clinton's escapades are just cheesy and depressing. The sex scenes are flat, repetitive, juvenile and cloying, taking place in the windowless hallway outside the Oval Office study or in the President's bathroom.

The props are uninspiring. Monica always pretends she's carrying papers to get into the Oval Office, and she gives the President a frog figurine, a letter opener decorated with a frog and *Oy Vey! The Things They Say: A Guide to Jewish Wit.*

Their meetings, often when the First Lady is traveling, are more needy than erotic.

Monica recalled, "I asked him why he doesn't ask me any questions about myself, and . . . is this just about sex . . . or do you have some interest in trying to get to know me as a person?"

By way of riposte, she said, the President laughed, said he cherished their time together and then "unzipped his pants and sort of exposed himself."

When she complained to the President that she had not had any hugs for months, he quipped, "Every day can't be sunshine."

Thankfully, Mr. Clinton grew tired of his little pizza girl. She sensed he was "putting up walls."

"This was another one of those occasions when I was babbling on about something," she said of their last rendezvous, "and he just kissed me, kind of to shut me up, I think."

He didn't call. He didn't write. She began to suspect she was being "strung along." Trapped in a stereotype, Monica became the raging, vengeful Glenn Close character in *Fatal Attraction.*

"PLEASE DO NOT DO THIS TO ME," she wrote in a draft of a note to the President. "I feel disposable, used and insignificant."

She demanded a big job at the United Nations or in the business world in New York, as compensation for his ruining her life.

"I don't want to have to work for this position," she said. "I just want it to be given to me." She sent the President a "wish list" of jobs ("I am NOT someone's administrative/executive assistant") and enclosed an erotic postcard and her thoughts on education reform.

Now if the President was taking Monica's advice on education reform, that might be an impeachable offense.

She sent him a note that read: "I am not a moron. I know that what is going on in the world takes precedence . . . I need you right now not as president, but as a man. PLEASE be my friend."

Getting nervous over her fits, Mr. Clinton reminded her, "It's illegal to threaten the President."

This is the document on which the fate of the Republic has been hanging? These are not grounds for impeachment. These are grounds for divorce.

Eastern Middle School

THOMAS L. FRIEDMAN—*New York Times*—10/2/2001

I recently attended meet-the-teacher night at Eastern Middle School, my daughter Natalie's school in Silver Spring, Md. The evening began with the principal noting that Eastern, a public school in suburban Washington, had 40 different nationalities among its students. Before the teachers were introduced, the school's choir and orchestra, a Noah's ark of black, Hispanic, Asian and white kids, led everyone in "God Bless America." There was something about the way those kids sang together, and the earnest, if not always melodious, way the school orchestra pounded out the National Anthem, that was both moving and soothing. As I took in the scene, it occurred to me how much the Islamic terrorists who just hit America do not understand about America.

Their constant refrain is that America is a country with wealth and power but "no values." The Islamic terrorists think our wealth and power is unrelated to anything in the soul of this country—that we are basically a godless nation, indeed the enemies of God. And if you are an enemy of God you deserve to die. These terrorists believe that wealth and power can be achieved only by giving up your values, because they look at places such as Saudi Arabia and see that many of the wealthy and powerful there lead lives disconnected from their faith.

Of course, what this view of America completely misses is that American power and wealth flow directly from a deep spiritual source—a spirit of respect for the individual, a spirit of tolerance for differences of faith or politics, a respect for freedom of thought as the necessary foundation for all creativity and a spirit of unity that encompasses all kinds of differences. Only a society with a deep spiritual energy, that welcomes immigrants and worships freedom, could constantly renew itself and its sources of power and wealth.

Which is why the terrorists can hijack Boeing planes, but in the spiritless, monolithic societies they want to build, they could never produce them. The terrorists can exploit the U.S.-made Internet, but in their suffocated world of one God, one truth, one way, one leader, they could never invent it.

Lord knows, ours is hardly a perfect country. Many times we have deviated from the American spirit or applied it selfishly. But it is because we come back to this spirit more times than not, in more communities than not, that our country remains both strong and renewable.

Why can't we convey that? In part, we're to blame. President Bush denigrated Washington during his campaign and repeated the selfish mantra about the surplus that "it's your money—not the government's money." How thankful we are today that we have a Washington, D.C., with its strong institutions—FEMA, the F.A.A., the F.B.I. and armed forces—not to mention a surplus to help manage our way out of this crisis.

In part we don't talk about these issues so we don't embarrass our autocratic allies in the Middle East. But this negative view of America as a nation that achieved wealth and power without any spiritual values is also deliberately nurtured by governments and groups in the Middle East. It is a way of explaining away their own failures to deliver a better life for their own people: The Americans are powerful only because they stole from us or from others—not because of anything intrinsically spiritual or humane in their society.

A society that will dig until it has found every body in the World Trade Center rubble—because at some level it believes every individual is created in the image of God—a society that raises $600 million for the victims in two weeks, is a godless, spiritless place? Guess again.

These terrorists so misread America. They think our strength lies only in the World Trade Center and the Pentagon—the twin pillars of our wealth and power—and if they can just knock them down we'll start to fold: as if we, like them, have only one truth, one power center.

Actually, our strength lies in the slightly dilapidated gym of Eastern Middle School on parent-teacher night, and in thousands of such schools across the land. That is where you'll find the spirit that built the twin towers and can build them over again anytime we please.

So in these troubled times, if you want to feel reassured about how strong this country is, or what we're fighting to preserve, just attend a P.T.A. meeting. It's all there, hiding in plain sight.

In Defense of the F-Word
CHARLES KRAUTHAMMER—*Washington Post*—7/2/2004

I am sure there is a special place in heaven reserved for those who have never used the F-word. I will never get near that place. Nor, apparently, will Dick Cheney.

Washington is abuzz with the latest political contretemps. Cheney, taking offense at Sen. Pat Leahy's imputation of improper vice presidential conduct regarding Halliburton contracts in Iraq, let the senator know as much during a picture-taking ceremony on the floor of the Senate. The F-word was used. Washington is scandalized.

The newspapers were full of it. Lamentations were heard about the decline of civility. *The Post* gave special gravitas to the occasion, spelling out the full four letters (something that it had done only three times previously). Democrats, feeling darned outraged, demanded apologies. The vice president remained defiant, offering but the coyest concession—that he "probably" cursed—coupled with satisfaction: "I expressed myself rather forcefully, felt better after I had done it."

The Federal Communications Commission just last year decreed that the F-word could be used as an adjective, but not as a verb. Alas, this Solomonic verdict, fodder for a dozen PhD dissertations, was recently overturned. It would not get Cheney off the hook anyway. By all accounts, he deployed the pungent verb form, in effect a suggestion as to how the good senator from Vermont might amuse himself.

Flood-the-zone coverage by investigative reporters has not, however, quite resolved the issue of which of the two preferred forms passed Cheney's lips: the priceless two-worder—"[verb] you"—or the more expansive three-worder, a directive that begins with "go."

Though I myself am partial to the longer version, I admit that each formulation has its virtues. The deuce is the preferred usage when time is short and concision is of the essence. Enjoying the benefits of economy, it is especially useful in emergencies. This is why it is a favorite of major league managers going nose to nose with umpires. They know that they have only a few seconds before getting tossed out of the game, and as a result television viewers have for years delighted in the moment the two-worder is hurled, right on camera. No need for sound. The deuce was made for lip reading.

Which makes it excellent for drive-by information conveyance. When some jerk tailgater rides my bumper in heavy traffic, honking his horn before passing and cutting me off, I do a turn-to-the-left, eyeball-to-eyeball, through-the-driver's-window two-worder—mouthed slowly and with exaggerated lip movements. No interlocutor has yet missed my meaning.

Nonetheless, while the two-worder has the directness of the dagger, the three-worder has the elegance of the wide-arced saber slice. It is more musical and, being more clearly spelled out, more comprehensible to the non-English speaker (a boon in major urban areas). It consists of a straightforward directive containing both a subject and an object—charmingly, the same person.

According to *The Post*, the local authority on such matters, Cheney went for a variant of the short form, employing the more formal "yourself." And given the location, the floor of the Senate, it seems a reasonable choice: Time was short, and he undoubtedly reserves the right to revise and extend his remarks.

Ah, but the earnest chin-pullers are not amused. Cheney's demonstration of earthy authenticity in a chamber in which authenticity of any kind is to be valued has occasioned anguished meditations on the loss of civility in American politics. Liberals in particular have expressed deep concern about this breach of decorum.

Odd. The day before first reports of Cheney's alleged indiscretion, his Democratic predecessor, Al Gore, delivered a public speech in which he spoke of the administration's establishing a "Bush gulag" around the world and using "digital brown shirts" to intimidate the media. The former vice president of the United

States compared the current president to both Hitler and Stalin in the same speech—a first not just in hyperbole but in calumny—and nary a complaint is heard about a breach of civility.

If you suspect that this selective indignation may be partisan, you guessed right. But here's an even more important question. In the face of Gore's real breach of civil political discourse, which of the following is the right corrective: (a) offer a reasoned refutation of the charge that George Bush is both Stalinist and Hitlerian; (b) suggest an increase in Gore's medication; or (c) do a Cheney.

The correct answer is "C." And given the circumstances, go for the deuce.

The End of Placeness
PEGGY NOONAN—*Wall Street Journal*—8/15/2008

The end of placeness is one of the features of the campaign. I do not like it.

Pretend you are not a political sophisticate and regular watcher of the presidential race as it unfolds on all media platforms. Pretend, that is, that you are normal.

OK, quick, close your eyes. Where is Barack Obama from?

He's from Young. He's from the town of Smooth in the state of Well Educated. He's from TV.

John McCain? He's from Military. He's from Vietnam Township in the Sunbelt state.

Chicago? That's where Mr. Obama wound up. Modern but Midwestern: a perfect place to begin what might become a national career. Arizona? That's where Mr. McCain settled, a perfect place from which to launch a more or less conservative career in the 1980s.

Neither man has or gives a strong sense of place in the sense that American politicians almost always have, since Mr. Jefferson of Virginia, and Abe Lincoln of Illinois, and FDR of New York, and JFK of Massachusetts. Even Bill Clinton was from a town called Hope, in Arkansas, even if Hope was really Hot Springs. And in spite of his New England pedigree, George W. Bush was a Texan, as was, vividly, LBJ.

Messrs. Obama and McCain are not from a place, but from an experience. Mr. McCain of course was a Navy brat. He bounced around, as members of the families of our military must, and wound up for a time in the suburbs of Washington. Mr. Obama's mother was somewhat itinerant, in search of different climes. He was born in Hawaii, which Americans on the continent don't experience so much as a state as a destination, a place of physical beauty and singular culture. You go there to escape and enjoy. Then his great circling commenced: Indonesia, back to Hawaii, on to the western coast of America, then to the eastern coast, New York and Cambridge. He circled the continent, entering it, if you will, in Chicago, where he settled in his 30s.

The lack of placeness with both candidates contributes to a sense of their disjointedness, their floatingness. I was talking recently with a journalist who's a podcaster. I often watch him in conversation on the Internet. I told him I'm always struck that he seems to be speaking from No Place, with some background of beige wall that could exist anywhere. He leans in and out of focus. It gives a sense of weightlessness. He's like an astronaut floating without a helmet.

That's a little what both candidates are like to me.

Mr. Obama hails from Chicago, but no one would confuse him with Chicagoans like Richard Daley or Dan Rostenkowski, or Harold Washington. "There is something colorless and odorless about him," says a friend, "like an inert gas." And Mr. McCain, in his experience, history and genes, is definitely military, and could easily come from Indiana or South Carolina or California, and could easily speak of upholding the values of those places.

What are the political implications of candidates seeming unconnected to regional roots, or being shorn of them? I suppose the question first surfaced in 2000, when Al Gore won the national popular vote and lost Tennessee, his home state. But he hadn't ever really seemed of Tennessee. He was born and grew up in Washington, D.C., the son of a senator. That was his formative experience. They liked him better in New York and California than down South.

They like Mr. Obama in Illinois, but he hasn't locked up neighboring Michigan, just as Mr. McCain has strong support in Arizona but still lags in Colorado and New Mexico.

On a policy level, the end of placeness may have implications. It may, for instance, lead a president to more easily oppose pork-barrel spending. If you're not quite from anywhere, you'll be slower to build a bridge to nowhere. If you don't feel the constant tug of Back Home—if it is your natural habit to think of the nation not first in specific and concrete terms but in abstract ones—then you might wind up less preoccupied by the needs and demands of the people Back Home. Mr. McCain is already a scourge of pork. Mr. Obama? Not clear. One doesn't sense any regional tug on his policy.

All this is part of a national story that wasn't new even a quarter century ago. Americans move. They like moving. Got a lot of problems? The answer may be geographical relocation. New problem in the new place? GTT. Gone to Texas.

It's in us. And yet.

I was at a gathering a few weeks ago for an aged Southern sage, a politico with an accent so thick you have to lean close and concentrate to understand every word, so thick, as they used to say, you could pour it on pancakes. Most of the people there were from the South, different ages and generations but Southerners—the men grounded and courteous in a certain way, the women sleeveless and sexy in a certain way. There was a lot of singing and toasting and drinking, and this was the thing: Even as an outsider, you knew them. They were Mississippi Delta people—Mizz-izz-DEHLT people—and the sense of placeness they brought into the room with them was sweet to me. It allowed you to know them, in the same way that at a gathering of, say, Irish Catholics from the suburbs of Boston, you would be able to know them, pick up who they are, with your American antennae. You grow up, move on, and bring the Delta with you, but as each generation passes, the Delta disappears, as in time the ward and the parish disappear.

I miss the old geographical vividness. But we are national now, and in a world so global that at the Olympics, when someone wins, wherever he is from, whatever nation or culture, he makes the same movements with his arms and face to mark his victory. South Korea's Park Tae-hwan moves just like Michael Phelps, with the "Yes!" and the arms shooting upward and the fists. This must be good. Why does it feel like a leveling? Like a squashing and squeezing down of the particular, local and authentic.

I end with a thought on the upcoming announcements of vice presidential picks. Major props to both campaigns for keeping it tight, who it's going to be, for by now they should know and have, please God, fully vetted him or her. On the Democrats, who are up first, I firmly announce I like every name floated so far, for different reasons (Joe Biden offers experience and growth; Evan Bayh seems by nature moderate; Sam Nunn is that rare thing, a serious man whom all see as a serious man.) But part of me tugs for Tim Kaine of Virginia, because he has a wonderful American Man haircut, not the cut of the man in first but the guy in coach who may be the air marshal. He looks like he goes once every 10 days to Jimmy Hoffa's barber and says, "Gimme a full Detroit."

Detroit: that's a place.

Palin Problem
KATHLEEN PARKER—*Washington Post*—9/26/2008

If at one time women were considered heretical for swimming upstream against feminist orthodoxy, they now face condemnation for swimming downstream—away from Sarah Palin.

To express reservations about her qualifications to be vice president—and possibly president—is to risk being labeled anti-woman.

Or, as I am guilty of charging her early critics, supporting only a certain kind of woman.

Some of the passionately feminist critics of Palin who attacked her personally deserved some of the backlash they received. But circumstances have changed since Palin was introduced as just a hockey mom with lipstick—what a difference a financial crisis makes—and a more complicated picture has emerged.

As we've seen and heard more from John McCain's running mate, it is increasingly clear that Palin is a problem. Quick study or not, she doesn't know enough about economics and foreign policy to make Americans comfortable with a President Palin should conditions warrant her promotion.

Yes, she recently met and turned several heads of state as the United Nations General Assembly convened in New York. She was gracious, charming and disarming. Men swooned. Pakistan's president wanted to hug her. (Perhaps Osama bin Laden is dying to meet her?)

And, yes, she has common sense, something we value. And she's had executive experience as a mayor and a governor, though of relatively small constituencies (about 6,000 and 680,000, respectively).

Finally, Palin's narrative is fun, inspiring and all-American in that frontier way we seem to admire. When Palin first emerged as John McCain's running mate, I confess I was delighted. She was the antithesis and nemesis of the hirsute, Birkenstock-wearing sisterhood—a refreshing feminist of a different order who personified the modern successful working mother.

Palin didn't make a mess cracking the glass ceiling. She simply glided through it. It was fun while it lasted.

Palin's recent interviews with Charles Gibson, Sean Hannity, and now Katie Couric have all revealed an attractive, earnest, confident candidate. Who Is Clearly Out Of Her League.

No one hates saying that more than I do. Like so many women, I've been pulling for Palin, wishing her the best, hoping she will perform brilliantly. I've also noticed that I watch her interviews with the held breath of an anxious parent, my finger poised over the mute button in case it gets too painful. Unfortunately, it often does. My cringe reflex is exhausted.

Palin filibusters. She repeats words, filling space with deadwood. Cut the verbiage and there's not much content there. Here's but one example of many from her interview with Hannity: "Well, there is a danger in allowing some obsessive partisanship to get into the issue that we're talking about today. And that's something that John McCain, too, his track record, proving that he can work both sides of the aisle, he can surpass the partisanship that must be surpassed to deal with an issue like this."

When Couric pointed to polls showing that the financial crisis had boosted Obama's numbers, Palin blustered wordily: "I'm not looking at poll numbers. What I think Americans at the end of the day are going to be able to go back and look at track records and see who's more apt to be talking about solutions and wishing for and hoping for solutions for some opportunity to change, and who's actually done it?"

If BS were currency, Palin could bail out Wall Street herself.

If Palin were a man, we'd all be guffawing, just as we do every time Joe Biden tickles the back of his throat with his toes. But because she's a woman—and the first ever on a Republican presidential ticket—we are reluctant to say what is painfully true.

What to do?

McCain can't repudiate his choice for running mate. He not only risks the wrath of the GOP's unforgiving base, but he invites others to second-guess his executive decision-making ability. Barack Obama faces the same problem with Biden.

Only Palin can save McCain, her party, and the country she loves. She can bow out for personal reasons, perhaps because she wants to spend more time with her newborn. No one would criticize a mother who puts her family first.

Do it for your country.

Morning in America
EUGENE ROBINSON—*Washington Post*—12/6/2008

I almost lost it Tuesday night when television cameras found the Rev. Jesse Jackson in the crowd at Chicago's Grant Park and I saw the tears streaming down his face. His brio and bluster were gone, replaced by what looked like awestruck humility and unrestrained joy. I remembered how young he was in 1968 when he stood on the balcony of the Lorraine Motel with the Rev. Martin Luther King Jr., moments before King was assassinated and hours before America's cities were set on fire.

I almost lost it again when I spoke with Rep. John Lewis (D-Ga.), one of the bravest leaders of the civil rights crusade, and asked whether he had ever dreamed he would live to see this day. As Lewis looked for words beyond "unimaginable," I thought of the beating he received on the Edmund Pettus Bridge and the scars his body still bears.

I did lose it, minutes before the television networks projected that Barack Obama would be the 44th president of the United States, when I called my parents in Orangeburg, S.C. I thought of the sacrifices they made and the struggles they endured so that my generation could climb higher. I felt so happy that they were here to savor this incredible moment.

I scraped myself back together, but then almost lost it again when I saw Obama standing there on the stage with his family—wife Michelle, daughters Malia and Sasha, their outfits all color-coordinated in red and black. I thought of the mind-blowing imagery we will see when this young, beautiful black family becomes the nation's First Family.

Then, when Michelle's mother, brother and extended family came out, I thought about "the black family" as an institution—how troubled it is, but also how resilient and how vital. And I found myself getting misty-eyed again when Barack and Michelle walked off the stage together, clinging to one another, partners about to embark on an adventure, full of possibility and peril, that will change this nation forever.

It's safe to say that I've never had such a deeply emotional reaction to a presidential election. I've found it hard to describe, though, just what it is that I'm feeling so strongly.

It's obvious that the power of this moment isn't something that only African Americans feel. When President Bush spoke about the election yesterday, he mentioned the important message that Americans will send to the world, and to themselves, when the Obama family moves into the White House.

For African Americans, though, this is personal.

I can't help but experience Obama's election as a gesture of recognition and acceptance—which is patently absurd, if you think about it. The labor of black people made this great nation possible. Black people planted and tended the tobacco, indigo and cotton on which America's first great fortunes were built. Black people fought and died in every one of the nation's wars. Black people fought and died to secure our fundamental rights under the Constitution. We don't have to ask for anything from anybody.

Yet something changed on Tuesday when Americans—white, black, Latino, Asian—entrusted a black man with the power and responsibility of the presidency. I always meant it when I said the Pledge of Allegiance in school. I always meant it when I sang the national anthem at ball games and shot off fireworks on the Fourth of July. But now there's more meaning in my expressions of patriotism, because there's more meaning in the stirring ideals that the pledge and the anthem and the fireworks represent.

It's not that I would have felt less love of country if voters had chosen John McCain. And this reaction I'm trying to describe isn't really about Obama's policies. I'll disagree with some of his decisions, I'll consider some of his public statements mere double talk and I'll criticize his questionable appointments. My job will be to hold him accountable, just like any president, and I intend to do my job.

For me, the emotion of this moment has less to do with Obama than with the nation. Now I know how some people must have felt when they heard Ronald Reagan say "it's morning again in America." The new sunshine feels warm on my face.

III: Sports

"In the era before television, sportswriters served as the nation's tribe of story-tellers, popular artists invested with enormous powers to reinforce cultural mores and shape the public imagination." So wrote David Maraniss in his biography of football great Vincent Lombardi.

When it comes to classic sports columns, though, all sports are not created equal. Baseball and boxing are overrepresented in shortlists of the best columns ever written.

Maybe it's because baseball lends itself to literature with its contemplative pace. It has been called a haunted game, where current players are always compared to the best of those who came before them, stat by stat. Boxing offers all the drama a writer could ask for—physical conflict where the best man wins. It is a sport custom-made for the columnist, who can detail the action in the ring while casting the human contest in a larger arena.

We've taken care to make sure that the other American sports are well represented—and columns like W. C. Heinz's "Death of a Racehorse" or Grantland Rice's "The Four Horsemen" are classics in any competitive field. What's most heartening to the person who turns to the sports pages first is how, pound for pound, the best sportswriters match up against the best political columnists or war correspondents.

Sportswriters have mastered the art of the opening lede. Here's Shirley Povich on Lou Gehrig's farewell: "I saw strong men weep this afternoon, expressionless umpires swallow hard, and emotion pump the hearts and glaze the eyes of 61,000 baseball fans in Yankee Stadium." Red Smith opens the ode to joy that is "Miracle of Coogan's Bluff": "Now it is done. Now the story ends. And there is no way to tell it. The art of fiction is dead. Reality has strangled invention. Only the utterly impossible, the inexpressibly fantastic, can ever be plausible again."

Jimmy Cannon's work dots the landscape with distinction, no matter which sport he was called on to chronicle. Grantland Rice's classic piece on the thoroughbred Seabiscuit ("a little horse with the heart of a lion and the flying feet of a gazelle") helped inspire the book and the movie of the same name a half-century later.

Thomas Bowsell of the *Washington Post* carries the torch of the best sportswriters of the past. Detroit's Mitch Albom has transcended his beginnings as a sportswriter to become a beloved multifaceted phenomenon with nonfiction books, charities, and radio shows to his name. The column selected to close the section deserves special mention—Bill Plaschke's "Her Blue Haven" delivers a gut-punching twist, a stunning testament to a true fan's love for her team.

Casey at the Bat

ERNEST LAWRENCE THAYER—*San Francisco Examiner*—6/3/1888

The Outlook wasn't brilliant for the Mudville nine that day:
The score stood four to two, with but one inning more to play.
And then when Cooney died at first, and Barrows did the same,
A sickly silence fell upon the patrons of the game.

A straggling few got up to go in deep despair. The rest
Clung to that hope which springs eternal in the human breast;
They thought, if only Casey could get but a whack at that—
We'd put up even money, now, with Casey at the bat.

But Flynn preceded Casey, as did also Jimmy Blake,
And the former was a lulu and the latter was a cake;
So upon that stricken multitude grim melancholy sat,
For there seemed but little chance of Casey's getting to the bat.

But Flynn let drive a single, to the wonderment of all,
And Blake, the much despis-ed, tore the cover off the ball;
And when the dust had lifted, and the men saw what had occurred,
There was Jimmy safe at second and Flynn a-hugging third.

Then from 5,000 throats and more there rose a lusty yell;
It rumbled through the valley, it rattled in the dell;
It knocked upon the mountain and recoiled upon the flat,
For Casey, mighty Casey, was advancing to the bat.

There was ease in Casey's manner as he stepped into his place;
There was pride in Casey's bearing and a smile on Casey's face.
And when, responding to the cheers, he lightly doffed his hat,
No stranger in the crowd could doubt 'twas Casey at the bat.

Ten thousand eyes were on him as he rubbed his hands with dirt;
Five thousand tongues applauded when he wiped them on his shirt.
Then while the writhing pitcher ground the ball into his hip,
Defiance gleamed in Casey's eye, a sneer curled Casey's lip.

And now the leather-covered sphere came hurtling through the air,
And Casey stood a-watching it in haughty grandeur there.
Close by the sturdy batsman the ball unheeded sped—
"That ain't my style," said Casey. "Strike one," the umpire said.

From the benches, black with people, there went up a muffled roar,
Like the beating of the storm-waves on a stern and distant shore.
"Kill him! Kill the umpire!" shouted someone on the stand;
And it's likely they'd a-killed him had not Casey raised his hand.

With a smile of Christian charity great Casey's visage shone;
He stilled the rising tumult; he bade the game go on;
He signaled to the pitcher, and once more the spheroid flew;
But Casey still ignored it, and the umpire said, "Strike two."

"Fraud!" cried the maddened thousands, and echo answered fraud;
But one scornful look from Casey and the audience was awed.
They saw his face grow stern and cold, they saw his muscles strain,
And they knew that Casey wouldn't let that ball go by again.

The sneer is gone from Casey's lip, his teeth are clenched in hate;
He pounds with cruel violence his bat upon the plate.
And now the pitcher holds the ball, and now he lets it go,
And now the air is shattered by the force of Casey's blow.

Oh, somewhere in this favored land the sun is shining bright;
The band is playing somewhere, and somewhere hearts are light,
And somewhere men are laughing, and somewhere children shout;
But there is no joy in Mudville—mighty Casey has struck out.

The Four Horsemen
GRANTLAND RICE—*New York Herald Tribune*—10/18/1924

Outlined against a blue-gray October sky, the Four Horsemen rode again. In dramatic lore they are known as Famine, Pestilence, Destruction and Death. These are only aliases. Their real names are Stuhldreher, Miller, Crowley and Layden. They formed the crest of the South Bend cyclone before which another fighting Army football team was swept over the precipice at the Polo Grounds yesterday afternoon as 55,000 spectators peered down on the bewildering panorama spread on the green plain below.

A cyclone can't be snared. It may be surrounded, but somewhere it breaks through to keep on going. When the cyclone starts from South Bend, where the candle lights still gleam through the Indiana sycamores, those in the way must take to storm cellars at top speed.

Yesterday the cyclone struck again as Notre Dame beat the Army, 13 to 7, with a set of backfield stars that ripped and crashed through a strong Army defense with more speed and power than the warring cadets could meet.

Notre Dame won its ninth game in twelve Army starts through the driving power of one of the greatest backfields that ever churned up the turf of any gridiron in any football age. Brilliant backfields may come and go, but in Stuhldreher, Miller, Crowley and Layden, covered by a fast and charging line, Notre Dame can take its place in front of the field.

Coach McEwan sent one of his finest teams into action, an aggressive organization that fought to the last play around the first rim of darkness, but when Rockne rushed his Four Horsemen to the track they rode down everything in sight. It was in vain that 1,400 gray-clad cadets pleaded for the Army line to hold. The Army line was giving all it had, but when a tank tears in with the speed of a motorcycle, what chance had flesh and blood to hold? The Army had its share of stars as Garbisch, Farwick, Wilson, Wood, Ellinger, and many others, but they were up against four whirlwind backs who picked up at top speed from the first step as they swept through scant openings to slip on by the secondary defense. The Army had great backs in Wilson and Wood, but the Army had no such quartet, who seemed to carry the mixed blood of the tiger and the antelope.

Rockne's light and tottering line was just about as tottering as the Rock of Gibraltar. It was something more than a match for the Army's great set of forwards, who had earned their fame before. Yet it was not until the second period that the first big thrill of the afternoon set the great crowd into a cheering whirl and brought about the wild flutter of flags that are thrown to the wind in exciting moments. At the game's start Rockne sent in almost entirely a second-string cast. The Army got the jump and began to play most of the football. It was the Army attack that made three first downs before Notre Dame had caught its stride. The South Bend cyclone opened like a zephyr.

And then, in the wake of a sudden cheer, our rushed Stuhldreher, Miller, Crowley and Layden, the four star backs who helped to beat Army a year ago. Things were to be a trifle different now. After a short opening flurry in the second period, Wood, of the Army, kicked out of bounds on Notre Dame's 20 yard line. There was no sign of a tornado starting. But it happened to be at just this spot that Stuhldreher decided to put on his attack and began the long and dusty hike.

On the first play the fleet Crowley peeled off fifteen yards and the cloud from the west was now beginning to show signs of lightning and thunder. The fleet, powerful Layden got six yards more and then Don Miller added ten. A forward pass from Stuhldreher to Crowley added twelve yards, and a moment later Don Miller ran twenty yards around Army's right wing. He was on his way to glory when Wilson, hurtling across the right of way, nailed him on the 10 yard line and threw him out of bounds. Crowley, Miller and Layden—Miller, Layden and Crowley—one or another, ripping and crashing through, as the Army defense threw everything it had in the way to stop this wild charge that had now come seventy yards. Crowley and Layden added five yards more and then, on a split play, Layden went ten yards across the line as if he had just been fired from the black mouth of a howitzer.

In that second period Notre Dame made eight first downs to the Army's none, which shows the unwavering power of the Western attack that hammered relentlessly and remorselessly without easing up for a second's breath. The Western line was going its full share, led by the crippled Walsh with a broken hand.

But there always was Miller or Crowley or Layden, directed through the right spot by the cool and crafty judgment of Stuhldreher, who picked his plays with the finest possible generalship. The South Bend cyclone had now roared eighty-five yards to a touchdown through one of the strongest defensive teams in the game. The cyclone had struck with too much speed and power to be stopped. It was the preponderance of Western speed that swept the Army back.

The next period was much like the second. The trouble began when the alert Layden intercepted an Army pass on the 48 yard line. Stuhldreher was ready for another march.

Once again the cheering cadets began to call for a rallying stand. They are never overwhelmed by any shadow of defeat as long as there is a minute of fighting left. But silence fell over the cadet sector for just a second as Crowley ran around the Army's right wing for 15 yards, where Wilson hauled him down on the 33 yard line. Walsh, the Western captain, was hurt in the play but soon resumed. Miller got 7 and Layden got 8 and then, with the ball on the Army's 20 yard line, the cadet defense rallied and threw Miller in his tracks. But the halt was only for the moment. On the next play Crowley swung out and around the Army's left wing, cut in and then crashed over the line for Notre Dame's second touchdown.

On two other occasions the Notre Dame attack almost scored. Yeomans saved one touchdown by intercepting a pass on his 5 yard line as he ran back 35 yards before he was nailed by two tacklers. It was a great play in the nick of time. On the next drive Miller and Layden in two hurricane dashes took the ball 42 yards to the Army's 14 yard line, where the still game Army defense stopped four plunges on the 9 yard line and took the ball.

Up to this point the Army had been outplayed by a crushing margin. Notre Dame had put underway four long marches and two of these had yielded touchdowns. Even the stout and experienced Army line was meeting more than it could hold. Notre Dame's brilliant backs had been provided with the finest possible interference, usually led by Stuhldreher, who cut down tackler after tackler by diving at some rival's flying knees. Against this, each Army attack had been smothered almost before it got underway. Even the great Wilson, the star from Penn State, one of the great backfield runners of his day and time, rarely had a chance to make any headway through a massed wall of tacklers who were blocking every open route.

The sudden change came late in the third quarter, when Wilson, raging like a wild man, suddenly shot through a tackle opening to run 34 yards before he was finally collared and thrown with a jolt. A few minutes later Wood, one of the best of all punters, kicked out of bounds on Notre Dame's 5 yard line. Here was the chance. Layden was forced to kick from behind his own goal. The punt soared up the field as Yeomans called for a free catch on the 35 yard line. As he caught the ball he was nailed and spilled by a Western tackler, and the penalty gave the Army 15 yards, with the ball on Notre Dame's 20 yard line.

At this point Harding was rushed to quarter in place of Yeomans, who had been one of the leading Army stars. On the first three plays the Army reached the 12 yard line, but it was now fourth down, with two yards to go. Harding's next play was the feature of the game.

As the ball was passed, he faked a play to Wood, diving through the line, held the oval for just a half breath, then, tucking the same under his arm, swung out around Notre Dame's right end. The brilliant fake worked to perfection. The entire Notre Dame defense had charged forward in a surging mass to check the line attack and Harding, with open territory, sailed on for a touchdown. He traveled those last 12 yards after the manner of food shot from guns. He was over the line before the Westerners knew what had taken place. It was a fine bit of strategy, brilliantly carried over by every member of the cast.

The cadet sector had a chance to rip open the chilly atmosphere at last, and most of the 55,000 present joined in the tribute to football art. But that was Army's last chance to score. From that point on, it was seesaw, up and down, back and forth, with the rivals fighting bitterly for every inch of ground. It was harder now to make a foot than it had been to make ten yards. Even the all-star South Bend cast could no longer continue to romp for any set distances, as Army tacklers, inspired by the touchdown, charged harder and faster than they had charged before.

The Army brought a fine football team into action, but it was beaten by a faster and smoother team. Rockne's supposedly light, green line was about as heavy as Army's, and every whit as aggressive. What is even more important, it was faster on its feet, faster in getting around.

It was Western speed and perfect interference that once more brought the Army doom. The Army line couldn't get through fast enough to break up the attacking plays; and once started, the bewildering speed and power of the Western backs slashed along for 8, 10, and 15 yards on play after play. And always in front of these offensive drivers could be found the whirling form of Stuhldreher, taking the first man out of the play as cleanly as though he had used a hand grenade at close range. This Notre Dame interference was a marvelous thing to look upon.

It formed quickly and came along in unbroken order, always at terrific speed, carried by backs who were as hard to drag down as African buffaloes. On receiving the kick-off, Notre Dame's interference formed something after the manner of the ancient flying wedge, and they drove back up the field with the runner covered from 25 and 30 yards at almost every chance. And when a back such as Harry Wilson finds few chances to get started, you can figure upon the defensive strength that is barricading the road. Wilson is one of the hardest backs in the game to suppress, but he found few chances yesterday to show his broken-field ability. You can't run through a broken field unless you get there.

One strong feature of the Army play was its headlong battle against heavy odds. Even when Notre Dame had scored two touchdowns and was well on its way to a third, the Army fought on with fine spirit until the touchdown chance came at last. And when the chance came, Coach McEwan had the play ready for the final march across the line. The Army has a better team than it had last year. So has Notre Dame. We doubt that any team in the country could have beaten Rockne's array yesterday afternoon, East or West. It was a great football team brilliantly directed, a team of speed, power and team play. The Army has no cause to gloom over its showing. It played first-class football against more speed than it could match.

Those who have tackled a cyclone can understand.

Louis Knocks Out Schmeling

BOB CONSIDINE—International News Service—6/22/1938

Listen to this, buddy, for it comes from a guy whose palms are still wet, whose throat is still dry, and whose jaw is still agape from the utter shock of watching Joe Louis knock out Max Schmeling.

It was a shocking thing, that knockout—short, sharp, merciless, complete. Louis was like this:

He was a big lean copper spring, tightened and retightened through weeks of training until he was one pregnant package of coiled venom.

Schmeling hit that spring. He hit it with a whistling right-hand punch in the first minute of the fight—and the spring, tormented with tension, suddenly burst with one brazen spang of activity. Hard brown arms, propelling two unerring fists, blurred beneath the hot white candelabra of the ring lights. And Schmeling was in the path of them, a man caught and mangled in the whirring claws of a mad and feverish machine.

The mob, biggest and most prosperous ever to see a fight in a ball yard, knew that there was the end before the thing had really started. It knew, so it stood up and howled one long shriek. People who had paid as much as $100 for their chairs didn't use them—except perhaps to stand on, the better to let the sight burn forever in their memories.

There were four steps to Schmeling's knockout. A few seconds after he landed his only punch of the fight, Louis caught him with a lethal little left hook that drove him into the ropes so that his right arm was hooked over the top strand, like a drunk hanging to a fence. Louis swarmed over him and hit him with everything he had—until Referee Donovan pushed him away and counted one.

Schmeling staggered away from the ropes, dazed and sick. He looked drunkenly toward his corner, and before he had turned his head back Louis was on him again, first with a left and then that awe-provoking right that made a crunching sound when it hit the German's jaw. Max fell down, hurt and giddy, for a count of three.

He clawed his way up as if the night air were as thick as black water, and Louis—his nostrils like the mouth of a double-barreled shotgun—took a quiet lead and let him have it with both barrels.

Max fell almost lightly, bereft of his senses, his fingers touching the canvas like a comical stew-bum doing his morning exercises, knees bent and the tongue lolling in his head.

He got up long enough to be knocked down again, this time with his dark unshaven face pushed in the sharp gravel of the resin.

Louis jumped away lightly, a bright and pleased look in his eyes, and as he did the white towel of surrender which Louis' handlers had refused to use two years ago tonight came sailing into the ring in a soggy mess. It was thrown by Max Machon, oblivious to the fact that fights cannot end this way in New York. The referee snatched it off the floor and flung it backwards. It hit the ropes and hung there, limp as Schmeling. Donovan counted up to five over Max, sensed the futility of it all, and stopped the fight.

The big crowd began to rustle restlessly toward the exits, many only now accepting Louis as champion of the world. There were no eyes for Schmeling, sprawled on his stool in the corner.

He got up eventually, his dirty gray-and-black robe over his shoulders, and wormed through the happy little crowd that hovered around Louis. And he put his arm around the Negro and smiled. They both smiled and could afford to—for Louis had made around $200,000 a minute and Schmeling $100,000 a minute.

But once he crawled down in the belly of the big stadium, Schmeling realized the implications of his defeat. He, who won the title on a partly phony foul, and beat Louis two years ago with the aid of a crushing punch after the bell had sounded, now said Louis had fouled him. That would read better in Germany, whence earlier in the day had come a cable from Hitler, calling on him to win.

It was a low, sneaking trick, but a rather typical last word from Schmeling.

Seabiscuit: The Gamest Thoroughbred
GRANTLAND RICE—*New York Tribune*—11/3/1938

PIMLICO RACETRACK, MD.—A little horse with the heart of a lion and the flying feet of a gazelle, today proved his place as the gamest thoroughbred that ever raced over an American track. In one of the greatest match races ever run in the ancient history of the turf at 1³⁄₁₆ miles, the valiant Seabiscuit not only conquered the great War Admiral, but, beyond this, he ran the beaten son of Man o' War into the dirt and dust of Pimlico.

Head and head around the last far turn, Seabiscuit, ably ridden by George Woolf, beat War Admiral by a full four lengths down the last furlong, with a dazzling burst of speed than not only cracked the heart of the Admiral, but, in addition, broke the track record, which he now holds at 1.56⅖.

The drama and the melodrama of the match race, held before a record crowd keyed to the highest tension I have ever seen in the sport, set an all-time mark.

You must get the picture from the start to absorb the thrill of this perfect autumn day over a perfect track. As the two thoroughbreds paraded to the post, there was no emotional outburst. The big crowd was too full of tension, the type that locks the human throat.

You looked at the odds flashed upon the mutuel board—War Admiral 1 to 4—Seabiscuit 2 to 1. Even those backing War Admiral, the great majority of the crowd, felt their pity for the son of Hark Tack and Swing On, who had come along the hard way and had churned up the dust of almost every track from the Great Lakes to the Gulf, from the Atlantic to Pacific.

After two false walking starts, they were set off. But it wasn't the fast flying War Admiral who took the lead. It was Seabiscuit, taking the whip from Woolf, who got the jump. It was Seabiscuit who had a full length lead as they passed the first furlong. The Admiral's supporters were dazed as the Biscuit not only held his lead, but increased the gap to two lengths before they passed the first quarter.

The Biscuit was moving along as smoothly as a Southern breeze. Then the first roar of the big crowd swept over Maryland. The Admiral was moving up. Stride by stride, Man o' War's favorite offspring was closing up the open gap.

The Admiral was under full steam. He cut away a length. He cut away a length, as they came to the half-mile post—and now they were running head and head. The Admiral looked Seabiscuit in the eye at the three-quarters—but Seabiscuit never got the look. He was too busy running, with his shorter, faster stride.

For almost a half mile they ran as one horse, painted against the green, red and orange foliage of a Maryland countryside. They were neck and neck—head and head—nose and nose.

The great Admiral had thrown his challenge. You could see that he expected Seabisquit to quit and fold up. But Seabiscuit has never been that brand of horse. I had seen him before in two $100,000 races at Santa Anita, boxed out, knocked to his knees, taking the worst of all racing luck—almost everything except facing a firing squad or a machine gun nest—and yet, through all this barrage of trouble, Seabiscuit was always there, challenging at the wire.

So, when War Admiral moved up on even terms, and 40,000 throats poured out their tribute to the Admiral, I still knew that the Biscuit would be alongside at the finish. The Biscuit had come up the hard way. That happens to be the only way worth while. The Admiral had only known the softer years—the softer type of competition.

He had never met a combination of grizzly bear and a running fool.

Head and head they came to the mile. There wasn't a short conceded putt between them. It was a question now of the horse that had the heart. Seabiscuit had lost his two length margin. His velvet had been shot away. He was on his own where all races are won—down the stretch.

He had come to the greatest kingdom of all sport—the kingdom of heart.

The Admiral had shown his reserve speed. From two lengths away he was now on even terms. But as they passed the mile post with three-sixteenths left— the vital test—the stretch that always tells the story—where 40,000 looked for the fleet War Admiral to move away—there was another story. Seabiscuit was still hanging on. Seabiscuit hadn't quit. With barely more than a final furlough left, the hard-way son of Hard Tack must have said to the Admiral—"Now let's start running. Let's see who is the better horse."

Foot by foot and yard by yard, Woolf and Seabiscuit started moving away. Charley Kurtsinger gave the Admiral the whip. But you could see from the stands that the Admiral suddenly knew that he had nothing left in heart or feet to match this wild, crazy five-year-old which all his life had known only the uphill, knock-down devil-take-the-loser route, any track—any distance—any weight—any time.

War Admiral had no answer. Down the final furlong the great-hearted Biscuit put on extra speed. He moved on by. Then he opened a small gap. Forty thousand expected the Admiral to move up. Close the gap again. But the Admiral was through. He had run against too many plow horses and platers in his soft and easy life. He had never tackled a Seabiscuit before.

"Iron Horse" Breaks
SHIRLEY POVICH—*Washington Post*—7/4/1939

I saw strong men weep this afternoon, expressionless umpires swallow hard, and emotion pump the hearts and glaze the eyes of 61,000 baseball fans in Yankee Stadium. Yes, and hard-boiled news photographers clicked their shutters with fingers that trembled a bit.

It was Lou Gehrig Day at the stadium, and the first 100 years of baseball saw nothing quite like it. It was Lou Gehrig, tributes, honors, gifts heaped upon him, getting an overabundance of the thing he wanted least—sympathy. But it wasn't maudlin. His friends were just letting their hair down in their earnestness to pay him honor. And they stopped just short of a good, mass cry.

They had Lou out there at home plate between games of the double-header, with the 60,000 massed in the triple tiers that rimmed the field, microphones and cameras trained on him, and he couldn't take it that way. Tears streamed down his face, circuiting the most famous pair of dimples in baseball, and he looked chiefly at the ground.

Seventy-year-old Ed Barrow, president of the Yankees, who had said to newspapermen, "Boys, I have bad news for you," when Gehrig's ailment was diagnosed as infantile paralysis two weeks ago, stepped out of the background halfway through the presentation ceremonies, draped his arm across Gehrig's shoulder. But he was doing more than that. He was holding Gehrig up, for big Lou needed support.

RUTH, MEUSEL, HOYT, PENNOCK

As he leaned on Barrow, Gehrig said: "Thanks, Ed." He bit his lip hard, was grateful for the supporting arm, as the Yankees of 1927 stepped to the microphone after being introduced. Babe Ruth, Bob Meusel, Waite Hoyt, Herb Pennock, Benny Bengough, Bob Shawkey, Mark Koenig, Tony Lazzeri, all of the class of '27 were there. And Gehrig had been one of them, too. He had been the only one among them to bestride both eras.

Still leaning on Barrow, Gehrig acknowledged gifts from his Yankee mates, from the Yankee Stadium ground crew, and the hot dog butchers, from fans as far as Denver, and from his New York rivals, the Giants. There was a smile through his tears, but he wasn't up to words. He could only shake the hands of the small army of officials who made the presentations.

He stood there twisting his doffed baseball cap into a braid in his fingers as Manager Joe McCarthy followed Mayor La Guardia and Postmaster General Farley in tribute to "the finest example of ball player, sportsman and citizen that baseball has ever known," but Joe McCarthy couldn't take it that way, either. The man who has driven the highest-salaried prima donnas of baseball into action, who has baited a thousand umpires, broke down.

"YOU WERE NEVER A HINDRANCE"

McCarthy openly sobbed as he stood in front of the microphone and said, "Lou, what else can I say except that it was a sad day in the life of everybody who knew you when you came to my hotel room that day in Detroit and told me you were quitting as a ball player because you felt yourself a hindrance to the team. My God, man, you were never that."

And as if to emphasize the esteem in which he held Gehrig though his usefulness to the Yankees as a player was ended, McCarthy, too, stepped out of the fringe full into the circle where Gehrig and Barrow stood and half embraced the big fellow.

Now it was Gehrig's turn to talk into the microphone, to acknowledge his gifts. The 60,000 at intervals had set up the shout, "We want Lou!" even as they used to shout, "We want Ruth"—yells that they reserved for the only two men at Yankee Stadium for which the crowd ever organized a cheering section.

But Master of Ceremonies Sid Mercer was anticipating Gehrig. He saw the big fellow choked up. Infinitesimally Gehrig shook his head, and Mercer announced: "I shall not ask Lou Gehrig to make a speech. I do not believe that I should."

THEN LOU MADE A SPEECH
They started to haul away the microphones. Gehrig half turned toward the dugout, with the ceremonies apparently at an end. And then he wheeled suddenly, strode back to the loud-speaking apparatus, held up his hand for attention, gulped, managed a smile and then spoke.

"For weeks," said Gehrig, "I have been reading in the newspapers that I am a fellow who got a tough break. I don't believe it. I have been a lucky guy. For 16 years, into every ball park in which I have ever walked, I received nothing but kindness and encouragement. Mine has been a full life."

He went on, fidgeting with his cap, pawing the ground with his spikes as he spoke, choking back emotions that threatened to silence him, summoning courage from somewhere. He thanked everybody. He didn't forget the ball park help; he told of his gratitude to newspapermen who had publicized him. He didn't forget the late Miller Huggins, or his six years with him; or Manager Joe McCarthy, or the late Col. Ruppert, or Babe Ruth, or "my roommate, Bill Dickey."

And he thanked the Giants—"The fellows from across the river, who we would give our right arm to beat"—he was more at ease in front of the mike now, and he had a word for Mrs. Gehrig and for the immigrant father and mother who had made his education, his career, possible. And he denied again that he had been the victim of a bad break in life. He said, "I've lots to live for, honest."

And thousands cheered.

The Graziano-Zale Fight
JIMMY CANNON—*New York Post*—7/17/1947

They played the organ between the rounds of the preliminaries at the Chicago Stadium last night and instead of the music of funerals and solemn happenings, the pompous instrument jingled with the small music of the dance hall.

It tinkled excitedly, the way a child's toy might if tipped over, as Rocky Graziano came down the aisle, lunging toward the ring with a twitching impatience.

It trembled hoarsely with the happiness of "The Sidewalks of New York" but changed suddenly to "Back Home in Indiana" because Tony Zale of Gary, Ind., first came into the ring. The little rickety sonnet of New York ended with a strangling grumble of embarrassment as though the pipes of the organ were choking with asthma.

The song of Indiana came full and big into the body smell heat of the arena where the lights hang from the ceiling on long silver painted stems like metallic and mysterious flowers in an inverted garden. The metropolitan song dying, unfinished, in a grumbling discord reminded me of the last Zale-Graziano fight when Rocky fell with an unexpected suddenness after punching Tony into the aching blackness where the mind ceases to function and the body operates under the instructions of the subconscious.

But that was a year ago and last night Graziano, half blind and splashed with blood, became the middleweight champion of the world when the referee, Johnny Behr, stopped the second fight between those two in the sixth round.

There are some who explain Zale's collapse by explaining the oven heat of the red-chaired arena baked the stamina out of his pale body. Others will say the years beat him and such was my opinion before the fight. But Graziano has been a man who has dedicated himself to a selfish crusade in this year of his life. There were those who accused him of deliberately loafing on the canvas until the referee counted ten in their last fight. Rocky, who has the pride of a professional prize fighter, considered this a disgrace he must bear forever if he did not lick Zale last night.

The first round was Zale's, and the crowd muttered with sadistic excitement as the champion moved with a brutal smugness, the calmness of him menacing and contemptuous. In that round Zale crossed a right swiftly to the body. It made Rocky move sidewise with the grotesque clumsiness of a man suddenly crippled. It was Zale's big punch and Graziano's mouth slowly as though he were about to vomit.

It was such a punch which knocked him out the last time but on this night he sagged and then retreated, holding himself erect as the pain struggled to bend him over. In that round a left hook and a right made him wobble and at the end of it his left eye was cut and trickling a lazy thread of blood.

The second round belonged to Rocky, although he was hit good punches which made him shake his head as though this motion was a mysterious anecdote to end all suffering of the mind and body. Zale left-jabbed Rocky's bleeding eye with a taunting impatience as he searched for the big punch.

But two rights and a left made Zale do a small wandering dance and he strolled to the wrong corner, pulling his shoulders back in a deceitful pose of superiority, as the round closed.

Zale had evaded the dream which Rocky's punches had beckoned him into and in the third on he jabbed at Rocky's eyes, one blurred by the running blood, the other pinched by the bruised and swelling flesh. Rocky, changing his posture as the range of his vision faded, let go aimlessly, heavy punches out of his controlled agony.

Zale waited and then hit Graziano with a right which knocked him.

It was the slowest round of the fight but the energy was gone from Zale's fat-muscled white body and Rock was like a man who had climbed many flights of stairs and now gets his breath back on a landing. He churned right hands, shifting all the time to get the range, dodging the approaching blindness, ignoring Zale, as though the darkness was the most important foe.

Rocky was fumbling towards him in the fifth, grabbing at his eyes with his gloves. After Tony slammed him into the ropes with a powerful left hook to the body, Rocky banged him with the rights which seemed more the punches of an angry man in a street fight than one who was to be middle weight champion of the world less than three minutes later.

Zale was jabbing in the sixth but he was an exhausted man. The right Rocky let go on the chin. The punch had allies in the heat and the years. Zale was suddenly worthless as a pugilist. All those in the stadium, even those up in the top tier with the discs of their opera glasses shining like cats' eyes in the gloom, realized it.

Rocky went at him and I counted the punches. Thirty-six times Rocky hit Zale, and they were every punch any fighter ever threw. Zale walked backwards in slow retreat, a man backing into insensibility and you could see him going as the punches changed his angular face into a flat-faced bloody mess. He leaned back through the ropes and Rocky was still hitting him, Rocky on top of the middleweight champion, hitting him short punches the way a man hits nails with a hammer.

They were both leaning out across the ropes in a writhing embrace, when the referee pulled Rocky back. The round had gone two minutes and 10 seconds and Rocky Graziano was again the middleweight champion of the world.

Death of a Racehorse
W. C. HEINZ—*New York Sun*—7/29/1949

They were going to the post for the sixth race at Jamaica, two year olds, some making their first starts, to go five and a half furlongs for a purse of four thousand dollars. They were moving slowly down the backstretch toward the gate, some of them cantering, others walking, and in the press box they had stopped their working or their kidding to watch, most of them interested in one horse.

"Air Lift," Jim Roach said. "Full brother of Assault."

Assault, who won the triple crown . . . making this one too, by Bold Venture, himself a Derby winner, out of Igual, herself by the great Equipoise . . . Great names in the breeding line . . . and now the little guy making his first start, perhaps the start of another great career.

They were off well, although Air Lift was fifth. They were moving toward the first turn, and now Air Lift was fourth. They were going into the turn, and now Air Lift was starting to go, third perhaps, when suddenly he slowed, a horse stopping, and below in the stands you could hear a sudden cry, as the rest left him, still trying to run but limping, his jockey—Dave Gorman—half falling, half sliding off.

"He broke a leg!" somebody, holding binoculars to his eyes, shouted in the press box. "He broke a leg!"

Down below they were roaring for the rest, coming down the stretch now, but in the infield men were running toward the turn, running toward the colt and the boy standing beside him, alone. There was a station wagon moving around the track toward them, and then, in a moment, the big green van they call the horse ambulance.

"Gorman was crying like a baby," one of them, coming out of the jockey room, said. "He said he must have stepped in a hole, but you should have seen him crying."

"It's his left front ankle," Dr. J. G. Catlett, the veterinarian, was saying. "It's a compound fracture, and I'm waiting for confirmation from Mr. Hirsch to destroy him."

He was standing outside one of the stables beyond the backstretch, and he had just put in a call to Kentucky where Max Hirsch, the trainer, and Robert Kleberg, the owner, were attending the yearling sales.

"When will you do it?" one of them said.

"Right as soon as I can," the doctor said. "As soon as I get confirmation. If it was an ordinary horse, I'd done it right there."

He walked across the road and around another barn to where they had the horse. The horse was still in the van, about twenty stable hands in dungarees and sweat-stained shirts, bare-headed or wearing old caps, standing around quietly and watching with Dr. M. A. Gilman, the assistant veterinarian.

"We might as well get him out of the van," Catlett said, "before we give him the novocaine. It'll be better out in the air."

The boy in the van with the colt led him out then, the colt limping, tossing his head a little, the blood running down and covering his left foreleg. When the say him, standing there outside the van now, the boy holding him, they started talking softly.

"Full brother of Assault." . . . "It don't make no difference now. He's done." . . . "But damn, what a grand little horse." . . . "Ain't he a horse?"

"It's a funny thing," Catlett said. "All the cripples that go out, they never break a leg. It always happens to a good-legged horse."

A man, gray-haired and rather stout, wearing brown slacks and a blue shirt, walked up.

"Then I better not send for the wagon yet?" the man said.

"No," Catlett said. "Of course, you might just as well. Max Hirsch may say no, but I doubt it."

"I don't know," the man said.

"There'd be time in the morning," Catlett said.

"But in this hot weather—" the man said.

They had sponged off the colt, after they had given him the shot to deaden the pain, and now he stood, feeding quietly from some hay they had placed at his feet. In the distance, you could hear the roar of the crowd in the grandstand, but beyond it and above it you could hear thunder and see the occasional flash of lightning.

When Catlett came back the next time he was hurrying, nodding his head and waving his hands. Now the thunder was louder, the flashes of lightning brighter, and now rain was starting to fall.

"All right," he said, shouting to Gilman. "Max Hirsch talked to Mr. Kleberg. We've got confirmation."

They moved the curious back, the rain falling faster now, and they moved the colt over close to a pile of loose bricks. Gilman had the halter and Catlett had the gun, shaped like a bell with a handle at the top. This bell he placed, the crowd silent, on the colt's forehead, just between the eyes. The colt stood still and then Catlett, with the hammer in his other hand, struck the handle of the bell. There was a short, sharp sound and the colt toppled onto his left side, his eyes staring, his legs straight out, the free legs quivering.

"Aw,——" someone said.

That was all they said. They worked quickly, the two vets removing the broken bones as evidence for the insurance company, the crowd silently watching. Then the heavens opened, the rain pouring down, the lightning flashing, and they rushed for cover of the stables, leaving alone on his side near a pile of bricks, the rain running off his hide, dead an hour and a quarter after his first start, Air Lift, son of Bold Venture, full brother of Assault.

Miracle of Coogan's Bluff

RED SMITH—*New York Herald Tribune*—10/4/1951

Now it is done. Now the story ends. And there is no way to tell it. The art of fiction is dead. Reality has strangled invention. Only the utterly impossible, the inexpressibly fantastic, can ever be plausible again.

Down on the green and white and earth-brown geometry of the playing field, a drunk tries to break through the ranks of ushers marshaled along the foul lines to keep profane feet off the diamond. The ushers thrust him back and he lunges at them, struggling in the clutch of two or three men. He breaks free, and four or five tackle him. He shakes them off, bursts through the line, runs head-on into a special park cop, who brings him down with a flying tackle.

Here comes a whole platoon of ushers. They lift the man and haul him, twisting and kicking, back across the first-base line. Again he shakes loose and crashes the line. He is through. He is away, weaving out toward center field where cheering thousands are jammed beneath the windows of the Giants' clubhouse.

At heart, our man is a Giant, too. He never gave up.

From center field comes burst upon burst of cheering, pennants are waving, uplifted fists are brandished, hats are flying. Again and again, the dark clubhouse windows blaze with the light of photographers' flash bulbs. Here comes that same drunk out of the mob, back across the green turf to the infield. Coattails flying, he runs the bases, slides into third. Nobody bothers him now.

And the story remains to be told, the story of how the Giants won the 1951 pennant in the National League. The tale of their barreling run through August and September and into October. . . . Of the final day of the season, when they won the championship and started home with it from Boston, to hear on the train how the dead, defeated Dodgers had risen from the ashes in the Philadelphia twilight. . . . Of the three-game playoff in which they won, and lost, and were losing again with one out in the ninth inning yesterday when—Oh, why bother?

Maybe this is the way to tell it: Bobby Thomson, a young Scot from Staten Island, delivered a timely hit yesterday in the ninth inning of an enjoyable game of baseball before 34,320 witnesses in the Polo Grounds. . . . Or perhaps this is better:

"Well," said Whitey Lockman, standing on second base in the second inning of yesterday's playoff game between the Giants and Dodgers.

"Ah, there," said Bobby Thomson, pulling into the same station after hitting a ball to left field. "How've you been?"

"Fancy," Lockman said, "meeting you here!"

"Ooops!" Thomson said. "Sorry."

And the Giants' first chance for a big inning against Don Newcombe disappeared as they tagged Thomson out. Up in the press section, the voice of Willie Goodrich came over the amplifiers announcing a macabre statistic: "Thomson has now hit safely in fifteen consecutive games." Just then the floodlights were turned on, enabling the Giants to see and count their runners on each base.

It wasn't funny, though, because it seemed for so long that the Giants weren't going to get another chance like the one Thomson squandered by trying to take second base with a playmate already there. They couldn't hit Newcombe, and the Dodgers couldn't do anything wrong. Sal Maglie's most splendorous pitching would avail nothing unless New York could match the run Brooklyn had scored in the first inning.

The story was winding up, and it wasn't the happy ending which such a tale demands. Poetic justice was a phrase without meaning.

Now it was the seventh inning and Thomson was up, with runners on first and third base, none out. Pitching a shutout in Philadelphia last Saturday night, pitching again in Philadelphia on Sunday, holding the Giants scoreless this far, Newcombe had now gone twenty-one innings without allowing a run.

He threw four strikes to Thomson. Two were fouled off out of play. Then he threw a fifth. Thomson's fly scored Monte Irvin. The score was tied. It was a new ball game.

Wait a moment, though. Here's Pee Wee Reese hitting safely in the eighth. Here's Duke Snider singling Reese to third. Here's Maglie, wild —pitching a run home. Here's Andy Pafko slashing a hit through Thomson for another score. Here's Billy Cox batting still another home. Where does his hit go? Where else? Through Thomson at third.

So it was the Dodgers ball game, 4 to 1, and the Dodgers' pennant. So all right. Better get started and beat the crowd home. That stuff in the ninth inning? That didn't mean anything.

A single by Al Dark. A single by Don Mueller. Irvin's pop-up. Lockerman's one-run double. Now the corniest possible sort of Hollywood schmaltz— stretcher bearers plodding away with an injured Mueller between them, symbolic of the Giants themselves.

There went Newcombe and here came Ralph Branca. Who's at bat? Thomson again? He beat Branca with a home run the other day. Would Charlie Dressen order him walked, putting the winning run on base, to pitch to the dead-end kids at the bottom of the batting order? No, Branca's first pitch was called a strike.

The second pitch—well, when Thomson reached first base he turned and looked toward the left-field stands. Then he started jumping straight up in the air, again and again. Then he trotted around the bases, taking his time.

Ralph Branca turned and started for the clubhouse. The number on his uniform looked huge. Thirteen.

Fisk's HR in 12th Beats Reds

PETER GAMMONS—*Boston Globe*—10/22/1975

And all of a sudden the ball was there, like the Mystic River Bridge, suspended out in the black of the morning.

When it finally crashed off the mesh attached to the left-field foul pole, one step after another the reaction unfurled: from Carlton Fisk's convulsive leap to John Kiley's booming of the "Hallelujah Chorus" to the wearing off of numbness to the outcry that echoed across the cold New England morning.

At 12:34 a.m., in the 12th inning, Fisk's histrionic home run brought a 7–6 end to a game that will be the pride of historians in the year 2525, a game won and lost what seemed like a dozen times, and a game that brings back summertime one more day. For the seventh game of the World Series.

For this game to end so swiftly, so definitely, was the way it had to end. An inning before, a Dwight Evans catch that Sparky Anderson claimed was as great as he's ever seen had been one turn, but in the ninth a George Foster throw ruined a bases-loaded, none-out certain victory for the Red Sox. Which followed a dramatic three-run homer in the eighth by Bernie Carbo as the obituaries had been prepared, which followed the downfall of Luis Tiant after El Tiante had begun, with the help of Fred Lynn's three-run, first-inning homer, as a hero of unmatched majesty.

So Fisk had put the exclamation mark at the end of what he called "the most emotional game I've ever played in." The home run came off Pat Darcy and made a winner of Rick Wise, who had become the record 12th pitcher in this 241-minute war that seemed like four score and seven years.

But the place one must begin is the bottom of the eighth, Cincinnati leading, 6–3, and the end so clear. El Tiante had left in the top of the inning to what apparently was to be the last of his 1975 ovations; he who had become the conquering king had been found to be just a man, and it seemed so certain. Autumn had been postponed for the last time.

Only out came an Implausible Hero, to a two-out, two-on situation against Rawlins J. Eastwick III, and Carbo did what he had done in Cincinnati. Pinch hitting, he sent a line drive into the center-field bleachers, and the chill of lachrymose had become mad, sensuous Fenway again. Followed by the point and counterpoint.

In the ninth, a Denny Doyle walk and Carl Yastrzemski single had put runners at first and third, which sent Eastwick away and brought in lefthander Will McEnaney, who walked Fisk to load the bases and pitch to Lynn.

Lynn got the ball to the outfield, but only a high, twisting fly ball down the left-field line that George Foster grabbed at the line and maybe 80 feet in back of third base. Third-base coach Don Zimmer said he told Doyle not to go, but he went anyway, and Foster's throw got to Johnny Bench in time for the double play. As the Red Sox shook their heads, mumbling "bases loaded, nobody out in the ninth," the Reds had their hero in Foster, who had put them ahead in the seventh with a two-run double.

Then in the 11th, the Reds had it taken away from them by Dwight Evans. With Ken Griffey at first, one out, Joe Morgan crashed a line drive toward the seats in right. Evans made his racing, web-of-the-glove, staggering catch as he crossed the warning track ("It would have been two rows in"—Reds bullpen catcher Bill Plummer), then as Griffey in disbelief stopped halfway between second and third, Evans spun and fired in. Yastrzemski, who had moved to first for Carbo's entrance to left, retrieved it off to the right of the coach's box, looked up, and guess who was standing on first base, waiting for the ball? Rick Burleson, who had raced over from shortstop. So Dick Drago, who worked three scoreless innings, the Red Sox, and a seventh game all had been saved.

When it was over, it was almost incomprehensible that it had begun with Tiant trying to crank out one more miracle. But it had, and for four innings, the evening was all his. They had merchandized "El Tiante" tee shirts on the streets, they hung a banner that read "Loo-Eee For President" and everything the man did, from taking batting practice to walking to the bullpen to warm up to the rhumbas and tangos that screwed the Reds into the ground for four innings brought standing ovations and the carol, "Loo-Eee, Loo-Eee . . ."

El Tiante had a 3–0 lead from the first inning, when Lynn had followed Yastrzemski and Fisk singles by driving a Gary Nolan kumquat into the bleachers over the pitching mound of the Boston bullpen. Nolan did not last long, followed by a succession of seven, but the Billinghams, Carrolls, and Borbons had apparently done what they had to do.

And the abracadabra that had blinded the Reds before began to smudge. In the fifth, after Boston had lost two scoring opportunites, Luis walked Designated Bunter Ed Armbrister, and before he could hear his father incant Grande Olde Game No. 56 ("Walks…"), Pete Rose singled and Griffey became the first player in three games here to hit The Wall. Not only was it the first time anyone had scored off Tiant in Fenway in 40 innings, but as the ball caromed away to be retrieved by Evans, the park went silent. In his running, leaping try for the ball at the 379-foot mark, Lynn had crashed into the wall and slid down to the ground, his back hurt.

Lynn eventually was able to stay in the game, but by the time the inning was over Bench had become the second to tickle The Wall, with a single, and it was 3–3. Then when Foster sent his drive off the center-field fence in the seventh, it was 5–3, and when Tiant was left to start the eighth, Cesar Geronimo angled a leadoff home inside the right-field pole, El Tiante left to his chant and his ovations. And in the press box, *Sport Magazine* editor Dick Schaap began collecting the ballots that determined which Red got the World Series hero's automobile.

So, if the honey and lemon works on the throat and the Alka-Seltzer does the same for the heads, Fenway will not be alone tonight. She has one drama, and it is perhaps sport's classic drama.

Bill Lee and Don Gullett, the Cincinnati Reds and the Boston Red Sox, and a long night's journey into morning, a game suspended in time as Fisk's home run was suspended beyond the skyline, a game that perhaps required the four-day buildup it got.

Summertime has been called back for just one more day—for the seventh game of the World Series.

Reggie Jackson's Three Homers
RED SMITH—*New York Times*—10/19/1977

It had to happen this way. It had been predestined since November 29, 1976, when Reginald Martinez Jackson sat down on a gilded chair in New York's Americana Hotel and he wrote his name on a Yankee contract. That day became an instant millionaire, the big honcho on the best team money could buy, the richest, least inhabited, most glamorous exhibit in Billy Martin's pin-striped zoo. That day the plot was written for the last night—the bizarre scenario Reggie Jackson played out by hitting three home runs, clubbing the Los Angeles Dodgers into submission and carrying his supporting players with him to the baseball championship of North America. His was the most lurid performance in 74 World Series, for although Babe Ruth hit three home runs in a game in 1926 and again in 1928, not even the demigod smashed three in a row.

Reggie's first broke a tie and put the Yankees in front, 4-3. His second fattened the advantage to 7–3. His third completed arrangements for a final score of 8–4, wrapping up the championship in six games.

Yet that was merely the final act of an implausible one-man show. Jackson had made a home run last Saturday in Los Angeles and another on his last time at bat in that earthly paradise on Sunday. On his first appearance at the plate last night he walked, getting no official time at bat, so in his last four official turns he hit four home runs.

In his last nine times at bat, this Hamlet in double-knits scored seven runs, made six hits and five home runs and batted in six runs for a batting average of .667 compiled by day and by night on two seacoasts three thousand miles and three time zones apart. Shakespeare wouldn't attempt a curtain scene like that if he was plastered.

This was a drama that consumed seven months, for ever since the Yankees went to training camp last March, Jackson had lived in the eye of the hurricane. All summer long as the spike-shod capitalists bickered and quarreled, contending with their manager, defying their owner, Reggie was the most controversial, the most articulate, the most flamboyant.

Part philosopher, part preacher and part outfielder, he carried this rancorous company with his bat in the season's last fifty games, leading them to the East championship in the American League and into the World Series. He knocked in the winning run in the twelve-inning first game, drove in a run and scored two in the third, furnished the winning margin in the fourth and delivered the final run in the fifth.

Thus the stage was set when he went to the plate in last night's second inning with the Dodgers leading, 2–0. Sedately, he led off with a walk. Serenely, he circled the bases on a home run by Chris Chambliss. The score was tied.

Los Angeles had moved out front, 3–2, when the man reappeared in the fourth inning with Thurman Munson on base. He hit the first pitch on a line into the seats beyond right field. Circling the bases for the second time, he went into his home-run glide—head high, chest out. The Yankees led, 4–3. In the dugout, Yankees fell upon him. Billy Martin, the manager, who tried to slug him last June, patted his cheek lovingly. The dugout phone rang and Reggie accepted the call graciously.

His first home run knocked the Dodgers' starting pitcher, Burt Hooton, out of the game. His second disposed of Elias Sosa, Hooton's successor. Before Sosa's first pitch in the fifth inning, Reggie had strolled the length of the dugout to pluck a bat from the rack, even though three men would precede him to the plate. He was confident he would get his turn. When he did, there was a runner on base again, and again he hit the first pitch. Again it reached the seats in right.

When the last jubilant playmate had been peeled off his neck, Reggie took a seat near the first-base end of the bench. The crowd was still bawling for him and comrades urged him to take a curtain call but he replied with a gesture that said, "Aw, fellows, cut it out!" He did unbend enough to hold up two fingers for photographers in a V-for-victory sign.

Jackson was the leadoff batter in the eighth. By that time, Martin would have replaced him in an ordinary game, sending Paul Blair to right field to help protect the Yankees' lead. But did they ever bench Edwin Booth in the last act?

For the third time, Reggie hit the first pitch but this one didn't take the shortest distance between two points. Straight out from the plate the ball streaked, not toward the neighborly stands in the right but on a soaring arc toward the unoccupied bleachers in dead center, where the seats are blackened out to give batters a background. Up the white speck climbing, dwindling, diminishing, until it settled at last halfway up those empty stands, probably 450 feet away.

This time he could not disappoint his public. He stepped out of the dugout and faced the multitude, two fists and one cap uplifted. Not only the customers applauded.

"I must admit," said Steve Garvey, the Dodgers' first baseman, "when Reggie Jackson hit his third home run and I was sure nobody was listening, I applauded into my glove."

Mohammed Ali
JACK NEWFIELD—*Village Voice*—4/30/1979

Float like a butterfly. Sting like a bee. And exit like a hero.

Muhammad Ali, after many rehearsals, is reportedly ready to retire for good, nineteen years after winning an Olympic gold medal for America as Cassius Clay.

We have burdened Ali with many identities. Symbol of the sixties. Draft dodger. Muslim evangelist. Most famous human on earth. Exile. People's champ. Braggart. Huckster. Manchild. Poet. Rebel. Survivor. He can be as funny as Richard Pryor. He can be as eloquent as Jesse Jackson. He is as charismatic as the Ayatollah.

But basically he is a fighter, the greatest fighter of the age. He danced like Nureyev. He could stick like Manolete. And he could think like Einstein.

What follows are basically a fan's notes, a farewell tribute to a public man who gave me pleasure, who gave me memories that are treasured. A man who showed how a life might be lived, and what personal values are important.

Twelve years ago this week—on April 28, 1967—Ali refused to take the "one step forward" at his army induction center in Houston, Texas. At that moment in history, the Vietnam war was still a popular war. And the Black Muslims to which Ali belonged were perceived by white American as a menacing and alien conspiracy. That same day, the New York State Athletic Commission withdrew its official recognition of Ali as heavyweight champion of the planet and suspended his license. Ali was not yet arraigned, indicted, tried, or convicted. He was never given a hearing or time for an appeal. He was stripped of his crown by a press release.

For three and a half years he was not allowed to fight. Ali and his lawyers drifted around the country like vagabonds looking for a location that would let him work. Seventy-two cities refused to give him a license. Seattle and Detroit were close to letting him fight, but then politicians and vigilantes held press conferences, and the permission evaporated. No white politician in the land would go on record to defend Ali's right to fight. He went broke. And he was robbed of his prime. We will never see what Ali was like between the ages of twenty-five and twenty-eight, because he was not permitted to work during the three years that an athlete's body is at its peak.

Three memories.

The first time I saw Ali was in the March of 1963, at Madison Square Garden. He had already knocked out Archie Moore and was promised a chance at the champ, Sonny Liston, if he could beat Doug Jones that night in the old Fiftieth Street Garden. I had worked at the Garden a few years before and was able to acquire a free ticket to see the twenty-one-year-old kid still named Cassius Clay.

Jones was a solid professional. He had recently knocked out Bob Foster, and the contest with Jones was a hard, close fight. But one could glimpse Ali's unripe genius that night. He had the fastest hands I ever saw. He seemed to have a built-in radar system that helped him slip punches at the last second. He charmed the crowd with the antic Ali Shuffle. And he could dance all night. He was on his toes all ten rounds. That night, on display as a work-in-progress, was Ali's original and distinctive style.

The Ali style of Constant Movement—dancing, sticking the jab, throwing a fast, hurtful combination, dancing to the left, dancing to the right, sticking, moving—this method would revolutionize boxing the way that Charlie Parker's bop improvisations changed jazz, or Hemingway's spare cadences influenced a generation of writers. Watch Sugar Ray Leonard, the fighter of the future, and you will see the echo of Muhammad.

After he won the close decision, in his dressing room, Ali recited his latest poem: "Don't bet on Sonny, and save your money." A year later, Ali, an 8-to-1 underdog, knocked out Sonny Liston.

In the autumn of 1967, I saw Ali speak at a college in Chicago. A smart-ass questioner asked him: "Isn't it a contradiction for you to participate in a violent sport like boxing but object to the violence in Vietnam? What's the difference?"

Ali's reply, which seemed spontaneous to me, was: "Man, there ain't no referees in Vietnam, that's the difference."

In September of 1979, I wrote a *Voice* piece on Ali. I spent two days with him and was struck by his sense of himself as a historical figure, and his understanding of how much he is a symbol and vessel of the dreams of blacks all over the world. He had just seen Howard Sackler's play about Jack Johnson, *The Great White Hope*, and kept saying that he would "never go out a loser" the way Jack Johnson did, the way Joe Louis did, the way Sugar Ray Robinson did. Ali has a powerful sense of racial history and symbolism, and he has a perfect sense of this history as it applies to boxing. He has said that only white heavyweight champions Gene Tunney and Rocky Marciano retired with the title. He wants to be the first great black champion to do this. And that is why, despite the $10 million temptation of one last big fight, it appears that he soon will retire—with the crown in his custody.

Ali's secret asset has been his pride, his will to win, and his self-knowledge. God gave him the hand speed and the gift of dancing legs. But time inevitably eroded Ali's body; it was diminished during his three and a half years of exile; and then he had to use up everything he held in reserve to win the third epic war with Joe Frazier. But as age deteriorated Ali's natural gifts, he began to create new ways to win.

Ali is like Picasso. He has gone through three or four different periods, adding different philosophies and colors to his palette through the years. He beat Doug Jones with his youth. He beat Cleveland Williams with his punching power. He beat Joe Frazier with his heart. He beat George Foreman with his imagination. He beat Leon Spinks with his memory.

But to me, the most impressive quality that Ali has is the way he has survived defeat, handles defeat emotionally, and come back from it stronger than ever.

Losing is the hardest thing of all for an athlete. Losing a fight, which is one on one, where you can't blame a teammate, is the most crushing form of defeat to accept and come to terms with. One defeat destroyed George Foreman's whole career. He believed he was invincible. When he lost for the first time, his self-confidence could not be restored and he disintegrated as a boxer.

Three fighters over nineteen years managed to defeat Ali: Ken Norton, Joe Frazier, and Leon Spinks. And Ali beat each of them in return bouts. Ali's pride was able to recover from defeat, learn from it; he was driven to redeem himself from each loss. Ali believed in his own myth even more than his fans did. The myth said he was "The Greatest."

Ali loved fun too much to endure the pain and boring discipline of training. The three times he lost he did not train faithfully. But each rematch with a conqueror, he punished his body in training. At six in the morning, no one knows whether you have run two miles or six miles. Ali ran six miles. Out of pride. He went to the woodshed three times and rebuilt his ego.

In his book, *The Greatest*, Ali described his hospitalization after Ken Norton broke his jaw. In the hospital, he received a gloating note that said: "THE BUTTERFLY HAS LOST ITS WINGS, THE BEE HAS LOST ITS STING. You are through, you loudmouthed braggart. Your mouth has been shut for all times. It's a great day for America. You are finished."

Ali wrote: "Later I tape it up on the wall of the gym so that every day I train, I remember the butterfly has got to get back its wings and the bee has to get back its sting. Of all the messages that came to me while I was in Claremont Hospital, this is the one I like best. It's funny, but those who hate me the most sometimes inspire me the most."

When Ali's reflexes began to slow, when his magical radar screen broke down, he learned and perfected other skills. Like taking a punch. In 1974, he treated his hands sore with calcium deposits, with hot wax and cortisone. This added to his punching power as his legs lost their spring.

When he confronted Foreman in Zaïre, Ali was the betting underdog. He psyched the unstable Foreman by leading the black African multitude between rounds in the "Ali! Ali! Bomaye!" chant. He made the crowd his choir. He invented the rope-a-dope strategy in the second round and let Foreman punch himself into a panting exhaustion. This tactic was an improvisation of Ali's and he stuck with it despite handlers' pleadings that he abandon it.

The Ali who met Spinks last September was a chess player. His speed was almost all gone. He was nearly thirty-seven years old. Spinks, at twenty-five, had beaten him seven months earlier. But Ali possessed self-knowledge. He knew his body. He knew exactly how much stamina he had left, how many seconds of each round he could dance, how many punches he had to throw to win each round. He was a genius-miser with his hoarded energy; he spent just enough to win a round, just enough to deflate Spinks' confidence, just enough to dominate the fight mentally.

When he beat Spinks, Ali won the heavyweight championship of the world for the third time. Nobody in the history of the sport had ever accomplished that.

Brecht said we should pity the land that needs heroes. But I think heroes are valuable, and necessary. Ali is a saving remnant of heroism.

He was the best in the world at what he did. He has class. He has principles he suffered for. He proved that courage, self-knowledge, and determination can prevail against great odds. He said no to the Vietnam war at a time when wise men from Harvard were bombing women and children. He gave, through his exploits, a feeling of dignity to the dispossessed and the hopeless.

Float like a butterfly. Sting like a bee. And go out a winner.

A Slugger, Right from the First Tee

JIM MURRAY—*Los Angeles Times*—12/1/1985

Nobody ever played golf the way Arnold Palmer did.

Arnold Palmer played golf the way Dempsey fought, the way Ruth hit, or the way a tiger hunted.

There was something primal about Arnold Palmer on the spoor of a golf championship, something that stirred emotions the way cowboy heroes did in the Saturday afternoon serials. Splendor in the grass. The perils of Palmer were as exciting as any ever concocted for Pearl White. He made everybody else on the leader board a villain. His defeats were tragedies, his victories everybody's.

He was America's Team long before the Dallas Cowboys were.

He turned a golf round into Dempsey-Firpo. A war. He didn't play a course, he invaded it. He waded into it like a guy jumping through a skylight with a Luger. He wasn't Ben Hogan, he was Hulk Hogan.

No one had ever gone around a course like this before. Not Snead, Hogan, Jones, Hagen, Harry Vardon. Not even Jack Nicklaus would. Sam Snead had this sweet swing you could pour on waffles. Hogan treated the course with the cold contempt of an executioner. Jones relied on elegant shotmaking.

There was nothing elegant or sugary about Palmer's method. Arnold's approach was passionate. His shirt came out, his hair got mussed, his pants wrinkled. Arnold mugged a course, he didn't romance it. Arnold made a 2 or a 12. He wasn't interested in self-defense.

He looked and acted like an athlete. He was strong enough to hit a ball out of the Pacific Ocean, and did. He could go in the rough and smash a ball out off debris so thick that the ball, chunks of rock, cans, bottles, a few squirrels, tree trunks and parts of old Volkswagens would come flying out together. And most of them landed on a green.

He paced a course like a predatory animal. He was tireless. Whenever a tournament took five rounds or 36 holes, Palmer was a four-hole favorite.

He loved the game. Watching Palmer play golf was like watching Willie Mays play center field. It wasn't a game, it was a love affair. They were made for each other.

The Scots invented the game, but Palmer popularized it. He brought the truck drivers in. He took it out of Long Island and Palm Beach and put it on the Pennsylvania Turnpike. Palmer was lucky there was golf, but golf was lucky there was Palmer. Babe Ruth saved baseball, Red Grange made pro football and Bill Tilden may have lifted tennis into the spotlight, but it was Arnold Daniel Palmer who put golf in prime time.

In 1957, Arnold Palmer won four tournaments and only $27,803. Between 1957 and 1960, he won eighteen tournaments, including two Masters and a U.S. Open, and banked only $188,136.

In 1982, Curtis Strange won $263,378 and no tournaments. Between 1980 and 1984, Curtis Strange won $1,213,668 on only four tour victories.

That, in a nutshell, is what Arnold Palmer, with a little help from his friends, did for golf.

Arnold Palmer won 61 golf tournaments, not counting two British Opens, the Australian Open and 17 other events around the world. He won 8 majors (Masters, PGA, U.S. and British Opens), but his near-misses were as spectacular as victories. He won one U.S. Open but was in a playoff for three other ones. Billy Casper didn't win the 1966 Open—Arnold Palmer lost it. Arnold characteristically forgot the live opposition when he got a seven-shot lead, and he began to play the ghost of Ben Hogan (who had set the Open scoring record to that time of 276). Not only did the ghost of Ben Hogan win, so did Billy Casper in person.

Palmer never won a PGA, but he lost by one shot three different times, once because he tried to hit a shot he would have needed a saw for and other times because he went for 3 when failure meant 6. He won two British Opens and lost a third (to Kel Nagle) by a shot on 18. He won four Masters and lost a fifth (to Gary Player) by trying to chip in instead of settling for a tie. Arnold didn't play the cards he was dealt—he bluffed fate.

He never lagged a putt or laid up in his life. Would Babe Ruth bunt? Dempsey clinch? Nick the Greek fold to a raise?

Golf doesn't need higher purses, celebrity fields, an international flavor. It doesn't need any more college-boy clones. It needs a guy out of the steel country with hands like a blacksmith, wrists like ingots and a back like a New York taxicab. It needs a guy who will go after a course like a leopard out of a tree.

They're holding the "Skins Game," a fun departure from the humdrum of medal play, down here at Jack Nicklaus' brutish Bear Creek golf course this weekend. It's not to be mixed up with the Quad Cities or the Honda Classic; it's a star lineup of Nicklaus, Watson, Fuzzy Zoeller, but any lineup which has Palmer is already a galaxy.

Even so, a lot of people are surprised that this offbeat production garners more TV viewers than any golf show this side of the Masters.

That's like being surprised if Caruso sells out an opera or Heifetz a recital.

Golf has become a crowd shot at a Japanese football game. Or a crocodile farm. You see one, you've seen 'em all.

Arnold Palmer is 11 to 22 years older than anyone in the field at Bear Creek. But he's still star quality. He's still taking the 4-wood out even with trees and water and dry gulches between him and the hole. He still looks like Ruth going after a curveball when he goes at a tee shot. He still hasn't left a putt short or a ball he won't hit. His play is still a cross between reckless and catastrophic. He's still reaching for the course's throat.

And he's still leaving the competition ready to throw their clubs in the nearest creek. At the end of nine holes of the Skins Game Saturday, the 56-year-old was in an old familiar position, leader in the clubhouse, leading money winner on this tour with $45,000 to Tom Watson's $30,000 and Jack Nicklaus' $15,000. It's not 1960 anymore, but the field still has Arnold Palmer to catch. Come to think of it, so has all golf.

Webber College: Best Team You Never Saw
MITCH ALBOM—*Detroit Free Press*—3/28/1986

The gym is empty now. Just two baskets staring at each other across a hardwood floor. Flies circle overhead. The air is sticky. It's hot. It's still. It's dead. It's over.

Dies the season, dies the program. Almost nobody knows what went on here at Webber College and almost nobody ever will now. Most American eyes this weekend are on the NCAA Final Four in downtown Dallas. Millions will watch it. Millions will bet on it. It's a big story.

But this is a better story.

This is a story about a chance of a lifetime, a deal you'd be crazy to take and crazier to pass up. This is a story of a tiny college and its gunslinging president, named Buck, who gave a basketball coach, named Nick, a chance to bring a handful of kids from the streets of New York and Baltimore and Buffalo down to the middle of nothing in Florida, to an auditorium with two backboards nailed to the walls and red ants crawling on the floor, and to work a miracle.

And they almost won it all.

This is a story about the Webber College Warriors, who disappeared forever last week, and who might have been the best college basketball team you've never seen. They just ran out of time.

Imagine the conversation. You're a young basketball player who couldn't make Division I—maybe grades, maybe lack of recruiting—so you've been playing junior college ball, or maybe not playing at all, and you're just hanging around in August 1983 trying to decide what you should do next and the phone rings.

"This is Nick Creola," the voice began. "I'm the new coach at Webber College. I'm looking for a man of your caliber. I'll give you a full scholarship, you'll play right away, you'll get a chance to see sunny Florida. If you're interested, there'll be a plane ticket waiting for you next Thursday. Come down. Look around. If you like the place we'll sign you right there."

This was the sales pitch Creola used on his prospects—all of whom he'd collected in two weeks' time—and as he drove to the Orlando airport that Thursday he still had no idea how many of them would buy it. "I had no recruiting budget," he said. "What else could I do?"

He had taken the job himself only a few weeks before. Who takes a coaching job in August? At Webber College no less, a tiny business school on the curb of the Bible Belt, with 450 students and no gym. Heck, the whole basketball idea was just a publicity stunt by the school president.

It was a gimmick. An investment in advertising. It was crazy. Which means it was just the kind of thing G. W. (Buck) Cleven, a former bomber pilot turned college president, would do. Cleven, 67, is a big man, with white hair and ice-blue eyes. He rules Webber. He calls himself "a benevolent despot," keeps a .357 Magnum in the desk drawer, and once fired a shotgun at joyriders who were disturbing his campus. Get the picture?

Only now he wanted a basketball team. A nationally renowned basketball team. Get some ink for his college. So he hired Creola, who is short, tanned, muscular and a winner.

Creola was a successful junior college coach at Jamestown, N.Y.—his team was ranked No. 1 in the nation—and back then, in 1983, he was 40 and single and figured this Webber thing might help him move up in the coaching ranks. Of course, he had no idea whom he'd be coaching.

And then he got to the airport.

"I looked around the baggage area and there were five or six big black kids, and they were talking, some of them knew of one another, and I said to myself, 'Holy jeez. This town is in for the shock of their lives.'"

Why? Because this is not New York or Baltimore. This is the South, and changes come slowly, and Webber College is mostly white. It's hardly the setting for a super-sonic, inner-city-type basketball team. Drive out to Webber. If you can find it. Take route 27 to Fat Boy's Barbeque, turn right, and keep going. Don't look for any other landmarks, because there aren't any. Just some orange groves and baked grass as hard as bristle. And after a few miles, it's just sort of there. A handful of small yellow buildings. Webber College.

It was here that Creola brought players such as Rockin' Rodney Jones from Buffalo, and Big Joe Farmer from the Bronx, and Dennis Pope from Baltimore and Carl (Jete) Jeter and his brother Gary, and Joe Patterson, who can dribble the ball behind his back and between his legs and over his head while on one knee. Brought them into an auditorium with no air conditioning—it had to be at least 100 degrees—pointed to the makeshift baskets and said, "Let's go, let's get started."

The floor was carpeted—carpeted?—and the ball kept skipping away. Gnats stuck to the wet skin of the players. One player took off his socks and wrung the sweat out like a sponge. Creola, wearing shorts, leaned down on one knee to watch a drill and jumped up yelling, "What the hell?" and there were red ants all over his legs chewing on him.

A fight broke out that first practice, a fight between two players, and the others instinctively rushed in and broke it up. And then they looked at each other, sweat washing their faces, and there was a sudden realization that they either died through this separately or lived through it together.

"I owe you guys the chance to be national champions," Creola said that first day. "How can you get beat? How can you get beat with what you're going through here?"

They had nothing. But nothing plus desire is no longer nothing. It's a beginning.

There are only about 120 people on this earth who can tell you about that first game. It was played in a local high school gym and the few students who came brought their books, figuring on early boredom.

Creola's new team marched in: eight blacks, two whites, two Cubans and the coach. The first tap went up and Rodney Jones, a 6-foot-5 forward who can jump high enough from a standing position to bang his head on the rim, took the ball in for a reverse dunk. Heads turned. What was this? The Warriors laughed through that game, won it by something like 50 points, with alley-oops and slams and jams.

And they kept winning. They would later say their practices—in the hellhole of a gym—were harder than their games. It was movie material. These kids, mostly from northern cities, whirling and juking and sending a buzz through the state. Winning? Is that the word for 141–62? And 137–50? And 95–36? All real scores from Webber victories.

"The word spread on us like wildfire," Creola said. Once during a game against an NCAA Division II opponent—which is like Cyclops playing Harpo Marx—the big-school coach came over to Creola and promised to "take it easy" on his kids.

"Thanks," Creola said. The Warriors won by 22 points.

By the time that season ended, Webber was 34–5 and won the national championship of the National Little College Athletic Association. It wasn't magic. It was more like chemistry. The players were all similar; all good, flashy players who had somehow missed the boat for bigger schools. They had three common denominators: Creola, the dunk and poverty.

"The first time I had Joe Farmer at school," says Creola, "he opened up his suitcase and there was only a toothbrush inside. I said, 'Joe, where's your clothes?' And he said, 'Coach, I'm wearin' them.'" Creola raised money to buy Farmer and several others a decent wardrobe. He and assistant Steve Prevesk ran bingo games every Sunday night to help pay for the players' books.

Creola was tireless, selling ads for programs, coaching, phoning recruits, coaching, playing psychologist, coaching.

"We were like his family," says Jones. And they were all alone.

Let's face it. This was a team full of sleek, street-smart black players in a white Southern school in a white Southern community in a region where Ku Klux Klan activities were more than an occasional rumor.

There were incidents. A black player and a white student scuffled in a bar. Ugly feelings arose over the players' dating some of the white female students. This is a place where such emotions still bubble close to the surface. So when the school threw a party that first year to wish the team well in post-season play, most students boycotted.

But in the second year, things seemed to cool down. People got more used to the idea. A new gym was built. A real gym.

Things should have gotten easier. They didn't. Prevesk remembers returning from summer vacation and having this conversation with Cleven:

"Cleven said, 'Now listen to me, you son of a bleep. See this hand? This is my wedding ring. See this hand? This is my national championship ring. I don't need any more rings. Now we do things my way.'"

Those were the first notes of the death song. Cleven had bragged about how the team he dreamed up would win a title in its first year, and now that the Warriors had done it, he wasn't sure he wanted them around anymore. "We were stealing his thunder," Creola said.

Meanwhile, the Warriors had moved up a class, to the National Association of Intercollegiate Athletics, and were finding a different problem. No one would play them. Ten Division II schools were within a 90-mile radius, and not a single one wanted Webber on its schedule. The reason was obvious: They were afraid of losing.

Instead, Webber had to take games as far north as Georgia and as far south as Miami. The players traveled in a Dodge van, drove eight or nine hours, ate at McDonald's, listened to Walkmans, talked. Once they broke down in a town called Yeehaw Junction, and a few players got out to roam around. Then someone spotted a bull behind a fence and the players ran back into the van.

"Half these guys had never seen a bull in their lives," Prevesk said, laughing. "They didn't know what it was going to do."

They kept winning. It was a simple formula: Run fast. Lots of offense. A pressing defense that stole the ball often. And dunk, dunk, dunk.

"Every player on the team dunked," Creola said. "People used to come out just to see our warm-up drills. We had an alley-oop play from halfcourt that was our trademark. It was beautiful."

That season the Warriors went to Hawaii with money Creola had raised, and they beat everyone they played—including Chaminade, which had knocked off national powers Louisville and Southern Methodist. The team wound up 32-5 and made it to the district semifinals of the NAIA. There was talk of moving up yet again, to Division II. Things looked good.

And then the roof fell in.

The experiment was called off.

Buck Cleven—who had once been quoted as saying, "We're using basketball to let people know we're here. After that, the heck with it."—announced that Webber was dropping basketball after the 1985-86 season. A "one-year moratorium," he called it. "It will never come back," interpreted Creola.

The coach was crushed. So were his players. But at Webber, Buck Cleven makes all the rules. All the players could do was go out in a blaze. Go for the NAIA national title. And they went for it. Won 24 regular-season games and lost only one. Averaged more than 100 points a game. Led the nation in scoring.

And a funny thing happened.

Support.

People began to come out to the games. Signs started popping up. The racial tensions that had once existed had eased, if not to where we dream, at least to where we can coexist.

"A lot of times this school isn't fun," Prevesk said. "It's too small. But the team was something fun. Something to rally around."

Webber won its district championship and was headed to the nationals in Kansas City. In the last home game, the crowd actually stood up when the players were announced, and when the first basket was scored, a roll of toilet paper was thrown out on the court.

The Warriors' last home game. Their first roll of toilet paper.

In certain ways, it was as big as a victory can be.

There is no happy ending. Webber lost in the first round of the NAIA national tournament by four points. The program is over. The players are without a team. The coach is looking for a job. The gym is empty.

"It's taken a few years off my life, I'll tell you that," Creola said. "But what a few years! I wouldn't trade them."

It's tough to say how good the Webber Warriors were. Creola rated them a "low Division I team." Maybe. Who'll know now? No one good would play them. Their creator gave up on them.

Things are quiet around Webber now. Most players plan on transferring. So do other students. "I don't know 10 people coming back here," says Prevesk.

For a brief moment something special happened here. Something was taken from nothing, some colors of life were mixed together, black and white, and though there were problems at the beginning, toward the end they were learning how to get along. Basketball was teaching them. And one gets the feeling this is the way the game was before the NCAAs and TV cameras and recruiting violations.

Dies the season, dies the program. And it rests there, inside the quiet gym near the orange groves. The arc of what might have been, going stale with the heat.

Why Is Baseball So Much Better Than Football?
THOMAS BOSWELL—*Washington Post*—1/18/1987

1. Bands.
2. Half time with bands.
3. Cheerleaders at half time with bands.

4. Up With People singing "The Impossible Dream" during a Blue Angels flyover at half time with bands.

5. Baseball has fans in Wrigley Field singing "Take Me Out to the Ball Game" at the seventh-inning stretch.

6. Baseball has Blue Moon, Catfish, Spaceman and The Sugar Bear. Football has Lester the Molester, Too Mean and The Assassin.

7. All XX Super Bowls haven't produced as much drama as the last World Series.

8. All XX Super Bowls haven't produced as many classic games as either pennant playoff did this year.

9. Baseball has a bullpen coach blowing bubble gum with his cap turned around backward while leaning on a fungo bat; football has a defensive coordinator in a satin jacket with a headset and a clipboard.

10. The Redskins have 13 assistant coaches, five equipment managers, three trainers, two assistant GMs but, for 14 games, nobody who could kick an extra point.

11. Football players and coaches don't know how to bait a ref, much less jump up and down and scream in his face. Baseball players know how to argue with umps; baseball managers even kick dirt on them. Earl Weaver steals third base and won't give it back; Tom Landry folds his arms.

12. Vince Lombardi was never ashamed that he said, "Winning isn't everything. It's the only thing."

13. Football coaches talk about character, gut checks, intensity and reckless abandon. Tommy Lasorda said, "Managing is like holding a dove in your hand. Squeeze too hard and you kill it; not hard enough and it flies away."

14. Big league baseball players chew tobacco. Pro football linemen chew on each other.

15. Before a baseball game, there are two hours of batting practice. Before a football game, there's a two-hour traffic jam.

16. A crowd of 30,000 in a stadium built for 55,501 has a lot more fun than a crowd of 55,501 in the same stadium.

17. No one has ever actually reached the end of the restroom line at an NFL game.

18. Nine innings means 18 chances at the hot dog line. Two halves means B.Y.O. or go hungry.

19. Pro football players have breasts. Many NFLers are so freakishly overdeveloped, due to steroids, that they look like circus geeks. Baseball players seem like normal fit folks. Fans should be thankful they don't have to look at NFL teams in bathing suits.

20. Eighty degrees, a cold beer and a short-sleeve shirt is better than 30 degrees, a hip flask and six layers of clothes under a lap blanket. Take your pick: suntan or frostbite.

21. Having 162 games a year is 10.125 times as good as having 16.

22. If you miss your favorite NFL team's game, you have to wait a week. In baseball, you wait a day.

23. Everything George Carlin said in his famous monologue is right on. In football you blitz, bomb, spear, shiver, march and score. In baseball, you wait for a walk, take your stretch, toe the rubber, tap your spikes, play ball and run home.

24. Marianne Moore loved Christy Mathewson. No woman of quality has ever preferred football to baseball.

25. More good baseball books appear in a single year than have been written about football in the past 50 years. The best football writers, like Dan Jenkins, have the good sense to write about something else most of the time.

26. The best football announcer ever was Howard Cosell.

27. The worst baseball announcer ever was Howard Cosell.

28. All gridirons are identical; football coaches never have to meet to go over the ground rules. But the best baseball parks are unique.

29. Every outdoor park ever built primarily for baseball has been pretty. Every stadium built with pro football in mind has been ugly (except Arrowhead).

30. The coin flip at the beginning of football games is idiotic. Home teams should always kick off and pick a goal to defend. In baseball, the visitor bats first (courtesy), while the host bats last (for drama). The football visitor should get the first chance to score, while the home team should have the dramatic advantage of receiving the second-half kickoff.

31. Baseball is harder. In the last 25 years, only one player, Vince Coleman, has been cut from the NFL and then become a success in the majors. From Tom Brown in 1963 (Senators to Packers) to Jay Schroeder (Jays to Redskins), baseball flops have become NFL standouts.

32. Face masks. Right away we've got a clue something might be wrong. A guy can go 80 mph on a Harley without a helmet, much less a face mask.

33. Faces are better than helmets. Think of all the players in the NFL (excluding Redskins) whom you'd recognize on the street. Now eliminate the quarterbacks. Not many left, are there? Now think of all the baseball players whose faces you know, just from the last Series.

34. The NFL has—how can we say this?—a few borderline godfathers. Baseball has almost no mobsters or suspicious types among its owners. Pete Rozelle isn't as picky as Bowie Kuhn, who for 15 years considered "integrity of the game" to be one of his key functions and who gave the cold shoulder to the shady money guys.

35. Football has Tank and Mean Joe. Baseball has The Human Rain Delay and Charlie Hustle.

36. In football, it's team first, individual second—if at all. A Rich Milot and a Curtis Jordan can play 10 years—but when would we ever have time to study them alone for just one game? Could we mimic their gestures, their tics, their

habits? A baseball player is an individual first, then part of a team second. You can study him at length and at leisure in the batter's box or on the mound. On defense, when the batted ball seeks him, so do our eyes.

37. Baseball statistics open a world to us. Football statistics are virtually useless or, worse, misleading. For instance, the NFL quarterback-ranking system is a joke. Nobody understands it or can justify it. The old average-gain-per-attempt rankings were just as good.

38. What kind of dim-bulb sport would rank pass receivers by number of catches instead of by number of yards? Only in football would a runner with 1,100 yards on 300 carries be rated ahead of a back with 1,000 yards on 200 carries. Does baseball give its silver bat to the player with the most hits or with the highest average?

39. If you use NFL team statistics as a betting tool, you go broke. Only wins and losses, points and points against and turnovers are worth a damn.

40. Baseball has one designated hitter. In football, everybody is a designated something. No one plays the whole game anymore. Football worships the specialists. Baseball worships the generalists.

41. The tense closing seconds of crucial baseball games are decided by distinctive relief pitchers like Bruce Sutter, Rollie Fingers or Goose Gossage. Vital NFL games are decided by helmeted gentlemen who come on for 10 seconds, kick sideways, spend the rest of the game keeping their precious foot warm on the sidelines and aren't aware of the subtleties of the game. Half of them, in Alex Karras' words, run off the field chirping, "I kick a touchdown."

42. Football gave us The Fudge Hammer. Baseball gave us The Hammer.

43. How can you respect a game that uses only the point after touchdown and completely ignores the option of a two-point conversion, which would make the end of football games much more exciting.

44. Wild cards. If baseball can stick with four divisional champs out of 26 teams, why does the NFL need to invite 10 of its 28 to the prom? Could it be that football isn't terribly interesting unless your team can still "win it all"?

45. The entire NFL playoff system is a fraud. Go on, explain with a straight face why the Chiefs (10-6) were in the playoffs but the Seahawks (10-6) were not. There is no real reason. Seattle was simply left out for convenience. When baseball tried the comparably bogus split-season fiasco with half-season champions in 1981, fans almost rioted.

46. Parity scheduling. How can the NFL defend the fairness of deliberately giving easier schedules to weaker teams and harder schedules to better teams? Just to generate artificially improved competition? When a weak team with a patsy schedule goes 10-6, while a strong defending division champ misses the playoffs at 9-7, nobody says boo. Baseball would have open revolt at such a nauseatingly cynical system.

47. Baseball has no penalty for pass interference. (This in itself is almost enough to declare baseball the better game.) In football, offsides is five yards, holding is 10 yards, a personal foul is 15 yards. But interference: maybe 50 yards.

48. Nobody on earth really knows what pass interference is. Part judgment, part acting, mostly accident.

49. Baseball has no penalties at all. A home run is a home run. You cheer. In football, on a score, you look for flags. If there's one, who's it on? When can we cheer? Football acts can all be repealed. Baseball acts stand forever.

50. Instant replays. Just when we thought there couldn't be anything worse than penalties, we get instant replays of penalties. Talk about a bad joke. Now any play, even one with no flags, can be called back. Even a flag itself can, after five minutes of boring delay, be nullified. NFL time has entered the Twilight Zone. Nothing is real; everything is hypothetical.

51. Football has Hacksaw. Baseball has Steady Eddie and The Candy Man.

52. The NFL's style of play has been stagnant for decades, predictable. Turn on any NFL game and that's just what it could be—any NFL game. Teams seem interchangeable. Even the wishbone is too radical. Baseball teams' styles are often determined by their personnel and even their parks.

53. Football fans tailgate before the big game. No baseball fan would have a picnic in a parking lot.

54. At a football game, you almost never leave saying, "I never saw a play like that before." At a baseball game, there's almost always some new wrinkle.

55. Beneath the NFL's infinite sameness lies infinite variety. But we aren't privy to it. So what if football is totally explicable and fascinating to Dan Marino as he tries to decide whether to audible to a quick trap? From the stands, we don't know one-thousandth of what's required to grasp a pro football game. If an NFL coach has to say, "I won't know until I see the films," then how out-in-the-cold does that leave the fan?

56. While football is the most closed of games, baseball is the most open. A fan with a score card, a modest knowledge of the teams and a knack for paying attention has all he needs to watch a game with sophistication.

57. NFL refs are weekend warriors, pulled from other jobs to moonlight; as a group, they're barely competent. That's really why the NFL turned to instant replays. Now, old fogies upstairs can't even get the make-over calls right. Baseball umps work 10 years in the minors and know what they are doing. Replays show how good they are. If Don Denkinger screws up in a split second of Series tension, it's instant lore.

58. Too many of the best NFL teams represent unpalatable values. The Bears are head-thumping braggarts. The Raiders have long been scofflaw pirates. The Cowboys glorify the heartless corporate approach to football.

59. Football has the Refrigerator. Baseball has Puff the Magic Dragon, The Wizard of Oz, Tom Terrific, Big Doggy, Kitty Kaat and Oil Can.

60. Football is impossible to watch. Admit it: The human head is at least two eyes shy for watching the forward pass. Do you watch the five eligible receivers? Or the quarterback and the pass rush? If you keep your eye on the ball, you never know who got open or how. If you watch the receivers . . . well, nobody watches the receivers. On TV, you don't even know how many receivers have gone out for a pass.

61. The NFL keeps changing the most basic rules. Most blocking now would have been illegal use of the hands in Jim Parker's time. How do we compare eras when the sport never stays the same? Pretty soon, intentional grounding will be legalized to protect quarterbacks.

62. In the NFL, you can't tell the players without an Intensive Care Unit report. Players get broken apart so fast we have no time to build up allegiances to stars. Three-quarters of the NFL's starting quarterbacks are in their first four years in the league. Is it because the new breed is better? Or because the old breed is already lame? A top baseball player lasts 15 to 20 years. We know him like an old friend.

63. The baseball Hall of Fame is in Cooperstown, N.Y., beside James Fenimore Cooper's Lake Glimmerglass; the football Hall of Fame is in Canton, Ohio, beside the freeway.

64. Baseball means Spring's Here. Football means Winter's Coming.

65. Best book for a lifetime on a desert island: *The Baseball Encyclopedia*.

66. Baseball's record on race relations is poor. But football's is much worse. Is it possible that the NFL still has NEVER had a black head coach? And why is a black quarterback still as rare as a bilingual woodpecker?

67. Baseball has a drug problem comparable to society's. Pro football has a range of substance-abuse problems comparable only to itself. And, perhaps, The Hells Angels'.

68. Baseball enriches language and imagination at almost every point of contact. As John Lardner put it, "Babe Herman did not triple into a triple play, but he did double into a double play, which is the next best thing."

69. Who's on First?

70 Without baseball, there'd have been no Fenway Park. Without football, there'd have been no artificial turf.

71. A typical baseball game has nine runs, more than 250 pitches and about 80 completed plays—hits, walks, outs—in 2½ hours. A typical football game has about five touchdowns, a couple of field goals and fewer than 150 plays spread over three hours. Of those plays, perhaps 20 or 25 result in a gain or loss of more than 10 yards. Baseball has more scoring plays, more serious scoring threats and more meaningful action plays.

72. Baseball has no clock. Yes, you were waiting for that. The comeback, from three or more scores behind, is far more common in baseball than football.

73. The majority of players on a football field in any game are lost and unaccountable in the middle of pileups. Confusion hides a multitude of sins. Every

baseball player's performance and contribution are measured and recorded in every game.

74. Some San Francisco linemen now wear dark plexiglass visors inside their face masks—even at night. "And in the third round, out of Empire U., the 49ers would like to pick Darth Vader."

75. Someday, just once, could we have a punt without a penalty?

76. End-zone spikes. Sack dances. Or, in Dexter Manley's case, "holding flag" dances.

77. Unbelievably stupid rules. For example, if the two-minute warning passes, any play that begins even a split second thereafter is nullified. Even, as happened in this season's Washington–San Francisco game, when it's the decisive play of the entire game. And even when, as also happened in that game, not one of the 22 players on the field is aware that the two-minute mark has passed. The Skins stopped the 49ers on fourth down to save that game. They exulted; the 49ers started off the field. Then the refs said, "Play the down over." Absolutely unbelievable.

78. In baseball, fans catch foul balls. In football, they raise a net so you can't even catch an extra point.

79. Nothing in baseball is as boring as the four hours of ABC's *Monday Night Football*.

80. Blowhard coach Buddy Ryan, who gave himself a grade of A+ for his handling of the Eagles. "I didn't make any mistakes," he explained. His 5-10-1 team was 7-9 the year before he came.

81. Football players, somewhere back in their phylogenic development, learned how to talk like football coaches. ("Our goals this week were to contain Dickerson and control the line of scrimmage.") Baseball players say things like, "This pitcher's so bad that when he comes in, the grounds crew drags the warning track."

82. Football coaches walk across the field after the game and pretend to congratulate the opposing coach. Baseball managers head right for the beer.

83. The best ever in each sport—Babe Ruth and Jim Brown—each represents egocentric excess. But Ruth never threw a woman out a window.

84. Quarterbacks have to ask the crowd to quiet down. Pitchers never do.

85. Baseball nicknames go on forever—because we feel we know so many players intimately. Football monikers run out fast. We just don't know that many of them as people.

86. Baseball measures a gift for dailiness.

87. Football has two weeks of hype before the Super Bowl. Baseball takes about two days off before the World Series.

88. Football, because of its self-importance, minimizes a sense of humor. Baseball cultivates one. Knowing you'll lose at least 60 games every season makes self-deprecation a survival tool. As Casey Stengel said to his barber, "Don't cut my throat. I may want to do that myself later."

89. Football is played best full of adrenaline and anger. Moderation seldom finds a place. Almost every act of baseball is a blending of effort and control; too much of either is fatal.

90. Football's real problem is not that it glorifies violence, though it does, but that it offers no successful alternative to violence. In baseball, there is a choice of methods: the change-up or the knuckleball, the bunt or the hit-and-run.

91. Baseball is vastly better in person than on TV. Only when you're in the ballpark can the eye grasp and interconnect the game's great distances. Will the wind blow that long fly just over the fence? Will the relay throw nail the runner trying to score from second on a double in the alley? Who's warming up in the bullpen? Where is the defense shading this hitter? Did the base stealer get a good jump? The eye flicks back and forth and captures everything that is necessary. As for replays, most parks have them. Football is better on TV. At least, you don't need binoculars. And you've got your replays.

92. Turning the car radio dial on a summer night.

93. George Steinbrenner learned his baseball methods as a football coach.

94. You'll never see a woman in a fur coat at a baseball game.

95. You'll never see a man in a fur coat at a baseball game.

96. A six-month pennant race. Football has nothing like it.

97. In football, nobody says, "Let's play two!"

98. When a baseball player gets knocked out, he goes to the showers. When a football player gets knocked out, he goes to get X-rayed.

99. Most of all, baseball is better than football because spring training is less than a month away.

Who Has Won and Who Has Lost
BOB GREENE—*Chicago Tribune*—3/16/1994

SARASOTA, FLA.—Because the world tends to remember in shorthand, Michael Jordan's attempt to make it to the major leagues down here may be destined to be recalled for only a couple of things. One is that he wasn't good enough. The other thing that may be remembered is the national sports magazine that put him on its cover to make fun of him—the magazine that said Jordan and the White Sox were embarrassing baseball.

Had Jordan, in his grief in the aftermath of his father's murder, gone out and gotten publicly drunk every evening, had he been seen gambling every night in Las Vegas, it is doubtful that he would have been ridiculed any more mercilessly than he has been ridiculed down here. It is doubtful that a national sports magazine—a magazine that has for years attempted to recruit subscribers by offering videotapes of Jordan playing basketball—would have laughed at him on its cover.

But he committed the most serious crime of all, in the eyes of the sports world: He failed. He tried to do something and he did not succeed. When Jordan was asked by reporters to rebut the magazine story that called him an embarrassment, he would not display anger. What he did say is that everyone should be given a chance: "It should be a game that everyone has an opportunity to play—no matter who, Michael Jordan or Leroy Smith, it doesn't matter."

I did not see any stories in the press that explained the Leroy Smith line. Perhaps everyone thought it was just a name that Jordan was making up, a symbol for everyman. But there is a Leroy Smith.

When Jordan was 15, it was he and his friend Leroy Smith who walked together into a high school gym in North Carolina to see who would make the basketball team and who would be cut. Leroy Smith made it; Jordan did not. That was the day he was told that he was not good enough to play basketball. Had he believed the people who judged him then, we would never have heard his name. Even now, many times when Jordan is checking into a hotel on the road and does not want to be bothered by callers, he registers under the name Leroy Smith. It is a constant and self-imposed reminder to him: The world is always waiting to tell you you are no good.

He has tried his best down here—not just at baseball, but at all the things that go with it. One day at his house I saw him studying a booklet put out by the White Sox, containing pictures of all the players and staff members. He was looking at it for 20 minutes, and finally I figured out what he was doing. He was learning the names—matching the names with the faces. When he went into the clubhouse, he wanted to make sure that no one—ballplayer, locker attendant, equipment man—felt awkward about saying hello to him. He wanted to be able to say their names first.

The first player to arrive each sunrise, on days when things went badly he also insisted on staying late to take more hitting practice. He said there was a reason: "I never want to go home at the end of a day on a failing note. I want to go home feeling I've done something right." Some of the players who have publicly spoken well of him have been devastatingly unkind behind his back. He knows it. He has never responded.

Major league baseball is a sport in which many players are casually rude to fans, refusing to stop to sign autographs or even wave hello. Jordan, at the end of his hitless days, almost always worked his way down the stands, meeting the customers and signing whatever they handed to him. Jerry Reinsdorf, owner of the White Sox, stood in right field of Ed Smith Stadium after one game, observing Jordan with the fans, and said, "I hope the other players are watching him. They might finally learn something."

He has given as much effort as he was capable of, knowing day by day that it was not going to be sufficient, and he has not walked away. He has heard the mockery and the cruel remarks, and he has refused to be discourteous even to those who have belittled him the most. He has demonstrated that there is honor in trying to do something, and that there is no loss of dignity in coming up short.

A man of great accomplishment, he has decided to take the risk of appearing ordinary.

An embarrassment? What Jordan has done down here is an embarrassment? If the baseball experts say so. But if you have children, you ought to hope against hope every day of your life that they will some day grow up to embarrass you like this.

For Timeless Player, It Was Time
THOMAS BOSWELL—*Washington Post*—9/21/1998

Cal Ripken, and his inspiring streak of 2,632 consecutive games, ended tonight in the one way that few within baseball expected.

Perfectly.

Neither injury, nor old age, nor lost skill, nor clubhouse intrigue nor any bitter controversy snapped The Streak.

Instead, Ripken ended it himself. The legendary Baltimore Orioles third baseman did it with exquisite timing—not too soon and not too belatedly. Ripken managed this nationally awaited moment with no fanfare or self-celebration. At the last minute before a game against the New York Yankees, he told Manager Ray Miller: Not tonight.

Best of all, Ripken ended his streak—which he had more than enough clout and health to continue indefinitely—voluntarily. It was in the best interests of the team and its future. So he did it.

"It's time to change the subject. It's time to return the focus to the team. . . . I'm a realist. The timing was right," said Ripken, who even stunned his teammates with a decision he had thought about for weeks, but kept secret until 30 minutes before game time. "Every time I told somebody before the game, they got that stare in their eyes that a deer gives you when your headlights hit him."

Over the 16 years since he missed his previous game, in 1982, many of his teammates have asked, jokingly, what would Ripken do with himself if he couldn't play? Tonight, they got their answer. By the fourth inning, he was out in the bullpen—the only place where a player can interact with fans without breaking a rule or interrupting the game.

Ripken was signing autographs.

By the sixth inning, he was warming up the outfielders by playing catch between innings, like a bullpen catcher or old coach. In the seventh, with a warmup jacket on, despite a warm evening, so he could hide his famous No. 8 and not cause a commotion, Ripken was out in center field beyond the wall, shaking the hands of bleacher fans.

"I wanted to scream and yell and say, 'Thank you' to everyone. And tell them it was okay. Don't be sad. Be happy," Ripken said. "I wanted to celebrate it, not mourn it."

Sad? Who's sad? When you do everything right for your entire career, then end your milestone streak on your own terms and in your own low-key, classy style, that's just a different kind of beauty.

Of all the records set in baseball, perhaps Ripken's mark, more than any other, deserved a clean, untarnished and dignified ending. Yet, hard as it is to believe, that same incredible mark was one that baseball insiders worried would end with ugliness, embarrassment or recriminations.

One of Ripken's greatest strengths is his absolute stubbornness—a family trait. Would he ever see the wisdom of missing a game? Or would a manager, general manager or even owner Peter Angelos, who has shown a mean streak at times, order him benched? Several days ago, a prominent member of the Orioles' organization told me, "I hope Cal takes a day off this season before somebody makes him take one next spring."

That might have been in the cards. And Ripken might well have sensed it. No player understands every aspect and nuance of the game better than this son of a career coach and manager. No one knows better than Ripken how significantly his stats have slipped this season.

His .273 batting average is just three points below his career average. And, with only nine errors this season, he's one of the best fielders at his position in the game. He's played every game this season for a good reason: The Orioles have had nobody better. In that sense, his streak has not been tainted at all.

But Ripken's long-formidable power is almost gone—14 homers and 61 RBI. In an era of mammoth offense, he's one of the worst run producers among major league third basemen. In recent days, he's resorted to a desperation batting stance too grotesque to describe. At midseason, he was asked, "Is your old power gone for good?" He didn't blink or duck. It was a baseball question. "In the past, I've never known when it'll suddenly come back. Hitting is timing. We'll see."

Nonetheless, it hasn't returned. "Cal looks like he's cheating to get to some pitches. And when he does hit it, the ball doesn't jump off his bat anymore," said one scout at tonight's game. "There's no shame in that. He's 38. And he's still a solid player."

Ever since he broke Lou Gehrig's mark of 2,130 straight games on Sept. 6, 1995, in one of the most moving events in baseball in the last quarter century, Ripken has claimed he'd "know when it was time" to snap the skein. Many times he explained that the streak would end "within the context of the game."

In other words, there would come a moment when it would be obvious that, if there were no streak, it would be normal baseball procedure for him not to play. Most assumed the ultra-fit Ripken, who has never been trimmer or stronger, was referring to an injury.

Now, we know that injury and age never got the last word on Ripken. And neither did hubris, that other bane of normal men. Suddenly, tonight, everything came together to make it obvious to Ripken that this was a suitable end.

It was the Orioles' last home game of the season. The night's opponent was a mighty Yankees team, worthy of Lou Gehrig or Babe Ruth. The Orioles had been (realistically) eliminated from the wild-card race. At such times, it is considered good form for veterans to step aside and let the organization's top prospects and late-season call-ups show their stuff and get their cleats wet. The most prominent of all Orioles prospects is, ironically, a third baseman—Ryan Minor. Ripken scratched himself from the lineup. Minor played.

One final piece of timing made this evening perfect. Ripken may have lost some of his timing at the plate, but not in his heart, not in his sense of what's right for his game.

On the night of 2,131, baseball needed Ripken as its standard-bearer more than the sport had needed any player at any time since Ruth saved the game with his home runs and his smile in the wake of the Black Sox scandal of 1919. Ever since that moment, as Ripken hit home runs in Nos. 2,129, 2,130 and 2,131, he has signed more autographs—no one disputes this—than any other modern player. Maybe any five modern players.

In fact, long after midnight, Ripken returned to the Camden Yards field tonight to wave, shake hands and sign for the thousand fans who simply would not leave.

No interview, no charity appearance to promote adult literacy, no opportunity to help revive baseball has been too much for Ripken.

Now, it's Mark McGwire and Sammy Sosa's turn. Ripken showed them, and everybody else in the sport, how to act in the spotlight, how to grow larger when history demands it of you and how to enjoy the game and its adoring fans as they deserve to be appreciated.

Ripken's time on top—as the greatest power-hitting shortstop in American League history and as the Iron Man—has come to an end.

However, one distinction is still left to Ripken. Baseball has never had a more universally beloved player. Nor has it ever had one who was raised up as the embodiment of the game for better reasons.

That has not changed. That's a streak that will go on forever.

Her Blue Haven
BILL PLASCHKE—*Los Angeles Times*—8/19/2001

Bill Plaschke predicted doom for the Dodgers in 2001. . . . Plaschke criticized. . . . Plaschke forgot. . . . Plaschke compared unfairly. . . . The Dodgers need encouragement, not negativity. . . .

That was part of a 1,200-word screed e-mailed to me last December, a holiday package filled with colorful rips. It was not much different from other nasty letters I receive, with two exceptions.

This note contained more details than the usual "You're an idiot." It included on-base percentages and catchers' defensive statistics. It was written by someone who knew the Dodgers as well as I thought I did.

And this note was signed. The writer's name was Sarah Morris. She typed it at the bottom.

Most people hide behind tough words out of embarrassment or fear, but Sarah Morris was different. She had not only challenged me to a fight, but had done so with no strings or shadows.

I thought it was cute. I wrote her back. I told her I was impressed and ready for battle.

Little did I know that this would be the start of a most unusual relationship, which eight months later is being recounted from a most unusual place. I am writing this from the floor, Sarah Morris having knocked me flat with a punch I never saw coming.

May I ask you a question? For two years I have been running my own Web site about the Dodgers. I write game reports and editorials. How did you become a baseball editorialist? That is my deam.

This was Sarah's second e-mail, and it figured. Every time I smile at someone, they ask me for a job.

Her own Web site? That also figured. Everybody has a Web site. The Dodgers guess there are more than two dozen Web sites devoted to kissing the almighty blue.

So my expert wasn't really an expert, but rather a computer nerd looking for work. I didn't need any more pen pals with agendas.

But about that last line. I chewed my lower lip about it. The part about "my deam."

Maybe Sarah Morris was just a lousy typist. But maybe she was truly searching for something, yet was only one letter from finding it. Aren't all of us sometimes like that?

It was worth one more response. I wrote back, asking her to explain.

I am 30 years old. . . . Because I have a physical handicap, it took me five years to complete my AA degree at Pasadena City College. . . . During the season I average 55 hours a week writing five to seven game reports, one or two editorials, researching and listening and/or watching the games.

Physical handicap. I paused again. I was in no mood to discuss a physical handicap, whatever it was.

I have had these discussions before, discussions often becoming long, teary stories about overcoming obstacles.

Courageous people make me jealous. They make me cry. But at some point, they have also made me numb.

Then I read the part about her working 55 hours a week. Goodness. This woman didn't only follow the Dodgers, she covered them like a newspaper reporter.

But for whom? Sarah called her Web site "Dodger Place." I searched for it, and found nothing. I checked all the Dodger search links, and found nothing.

Then I reread her e-mail and discovered an address buried at the bottom: http://members.tripod.com/spunkydodgers.

I clicked there. It wasn't fancy, rather like a chalkboard, with block letters and big type.

There was a section of "News from a Fan." Another section of "Views by a Fan." But she covered the team with the seriousness of a writer.

The stories, while basic, were complete. Sarah's knowledge was evident.

But still, I wondered, how could anybody find it? Is anybody reading?

Nobody ever signs my guestbook.

Does anybody correspond?

I get one letter a month.

I read the Web site more closely and realized that she does indeed receive about one letter a month—always from the same person.

So here was a physically handicapped woman, covering the Dodgers as extensively as any reporter in the country, yet writing for an obscure Web site with an impossible address, with a readership of about two.

That "deam" was missing a lot more than an r, I thought.

The days passed, winter moved toward spring, and I had more questions.

Sarah Morris always had answers.

I started my own Web site in hopes of finding a job, but I have had no luck yet. I have gone to the Commission of Rehabilitation seeking help, but they say I'm too handicapped to be employed. I disagree.

So what if my maximum typing speed is eight words per minute because I use a head pointer to type? My brain works fine. I have dedication to my work. That is what makes people successful.

I don't know how to look for a job.

A head pointer? I remember seeing one of those on a late-night commercial for a hospital for paralyzed people.

It looked frightening. But her stories didn't look frightening. They looked, well, normal.

Now I find out she wrote them with her head?

I asked her how long it took her to compose one of her usual 1,200-word filings.

3–4 hours.

While pondering that the average person can bang out a 1,200- word e-mail in about 30 minutes, I did something I've never before done with an Internet stranger.

I asked Sarah Morris to call me.

I wanted to talk about the Dodgers. I wanted to talk about her stories.

But, well, yeah, I mostly wanted to talk about why someone would cover a team off television, typing with her head for an invisible readership.

I have a speech disability making it impossible to use the phone.

That proved it. My first impression obviously had been correct. This was an elaborate hoax.

She didn't want to talk to me because, of course, she didn't exist.

I thought to myself, "This is why I never answer all my mail. This is why I will never go near a chat room."

The Internet has become more about mythology than technology, people inventing outrageous lives to compensate for ordinary realities.

So, I was an unwitting actor in a strange little play. This woman writer was probably a 45-year-old male plumber.

I decided to end the correspondence.

Then I received another e-mail.

The first sentence read, "There are some facts you might want to know . . ."

In words with an inflection that leaped off the screen, Sarah Morris spoke.

My disability is cerebral palsy. . . . It affects motor control. . . . I have excessive movement, meaning when my brain tells my hands to hit a key, I would move my legs, hit the table, and six other keys in the process.

This was only the beginning.

When my mom explained my handicap, she told me I could accomplish anything that I wanted to if I worked three times as hard as other people.

She wrote that she became a Dodger fan while growing up in Pasadena. In her sophomore year at Blair High, a junior varsity baseball coach, Mike Sellers, asked her to be the team statistician. Her special ed teacher discouraged it, but she did it anyway, sitting next to the bleachers with an electric typewriter and a head pointer.

We had a game on a rainy day. The rain fell in the typewriter, making it unusable, so Mom wrote the stats when I told her. I earned two letters that I am proud of still.

She wrote that her involvement in baseball had kept her in school—despite poor grades and hours of neck-straining homework.

Baseball gave me something to work for. . . . I could do something that other kids couldn't. . . . Baseball saved me from becoming another statistic. That is when I decided I wanted to do something for the sport that has done so much for me.

And about that speech disability?

When I went to nursery school, teachers treated me dumb. This made me mad, but I got over it. I hate the meaning of "dumb" in the phrase "deaf and dumb." My speech disability is the most frustrating.

OK, so I believed her. Sort of. It still sounded odd.

Who could do something like this? I figured she must be privileged. Who, in her supposed condition, could cover a baseball team without the best equipment and help?

I figured she had an elaborate setup somewhere. I was curious about it. I figured she couldn't live too far from Pasadena. I would drive over one day and we would chat.

I live in Anderson, Texas. It's about 75 miles from Houston.

Texas? She didn't explain. I didn't ask. But that seemed like a long flight to see a little rich girl bang on an expensive keyboard.

By now, it was spring training, and she was ranting about Gary Sheffield, and I was hanging out in Vero Beach, and I would have forgotten the whole thing.

Except Sarah Morris began sending me her stories. Every day, another story. Game stories, feature stories, some with missing words, others with typographical errors, but all with obvious effort.

Then, fate. The Lakers were involved in a playoff series in San Antonio, I had one free day, and she lived about three hours away.

I wrote her, asking if I could drive over to see her. She agreed, but much too quickly for my suspicious tastes, writing me with detailed directions involving farm roads and streets with no name.

I read the directions and again thought, this was weird. This could be dangerous. I wanted to back out.

Turns out, I wasn't the only one.

I'm so nervous about tomorrow. I'm nothing special but a woman with disabilities. I don't know what makes a good journalism story. I don't know if I am it.

I pulled out of my San Antonio hotel on a warm May morning and drove east across the stark Texas landscape. I followed Sarah's directions off the interstate and onto a desolate two-lane highway.

The road stretched through miles of scraggly fields, interrupted only by occasional feed stores, small white churches and blinking red lights.

I rolled into the small intersection that is Anderson, then took a right turn, down a narrow crumbling road, high weeds thwacking against the car's window.

After several miles, I turned down another crumbling road, pulling up in front of a rusted gate, which I had been instructed to open.

Now, on a winding dirt road dotted with potholes the size of small animals, I bounced for nearly a mile past grazing cows. Through the dust, I spotted what looked like a old toolshed.

But it wasn't a shed. It was a house, a decaying shanty covered by a tin roof and surrounded by weeds and junk.

I slowed and stared. Could this be right?

Then I saw, amid a clump of weeds near the front door, a rusted wheelchair. P.S. We have dogs.

Do they ever. A couple of creatures with matted hair emerged from some bushes and surrounded the car, scratching and howling.

Finally, an older woman in an old T-shirt and skirt emerged from the front door and shooed the dogs away.

"I'm Sarah's mother," said Lois Morris, grabbing my smooth hand with a worn one. "She's waiting for you inside."

I walked out of the sunlight, opened a torn screen door, and moved into the shadows, where an 87-pound figure was curled up in a creaky wheelchair.

Her limbs twisted. Her head rolled. We could not hug. We could not even shake hands. She could only stare at me and smile.

But that smile! It cut through the gloom of the cracked wooden floor, the torn couch, the broken, cobwebbed windows.

A clutter of books and boxes filled the small rooms. There was a rabbit living in a cage next to an old refrigerator. From somewhere outside the house, you could hear the squeaking of rats.

Eventually I could bear to look at nothing else, so I stared at that smile, and it was so clear, so certain, it even cut through most of my doubts.

But still, even then, I wondered.

This is Sarah Morris?

She began shaking in her chair, emitting sounds. I thought she was coughing. She was, instead, speaking.

Her mother interpreted. Every sound was a different word or phrase.

"Huh (I) . . . huh-huh (want to show) . . . huh (you) . . . huh (something)."

Her mother rolled her through a path that cut through the piles of junk, up to an old desk on cinder blocks.

On the desk was a computer. Next to it was a TV. Nearby was a Dodger bobble-head doll of uncertain identity.

Her mother fastened a head pointer around her daughter's temples, its chin-strap stained dark brown from spilled Dr Pepper. Sarah then began carefully leaning over the computer and pecking.

On the monitor appeared the Dodger Place Web site. Sarah used her pointer to call up a story. Peck by peck, she began adding to that story. It was her trade-mark typeface, her trademark Dodger fan prose, something involving Paul Lo Duca, about whom she later wrote:

". . . Offensively, Lo Duca has been remarkable. Entering Friday's game, Lo Duca has batted .382 with five home runs and seventeen RBI. Last Tuesday Jim Tracy moved Lo Duca into the leadoff position. Since then, the Dodgers have won six and lost two. Lo Duca has an on-base percentage of .412. On Memorial Day Lo Duca had six hits, becoming the first Dodger to do so since Willie Davis on May 24, 1973. . . ."

She looked up and giggled. I looked down in wonder—and shame.

This was indeed Sarah Morris. The great Sarah Morris.

She began making more sounds, bouncing in her chair. Lois asked me to sit on a dusty chair. There were some things that needed explaining.

Times photographer Anacleto Rapping, who had been there earlier in the day, and I had been Sarah's first visitors since she moved here with her mother and younger sister from Pasadena nearly six years ago.

This shack was an inheritance from Sarah's grandmother. When Sarah's parents divorced, her mother, with no other prospects, settled here.

The adjustment from life in Southern California to the middle of scrubby field more than 30 miles from the nearest supermarket was painful. Sarah was up-rooted from a town of relative tolerance and accessibility to a place of many stares.

The place was so remote, when her mother had once dropped Sarah, helping her out of bed, and called 911, the emergency crew couldn't find the place.

"But the hardest thing for Sarah was leaving her Dodgers," Lois said.

So, she didn't. She used her disability money, and loans, to buy the computer, the television and the satellite dish that allows her to watch or listen to every game.

She doesn't have any nearby friends, and it's exhausting to spend the five hours required for shopping trips to the nearest Wal-Mart, so the Dodgers fill the void.

They challenge her on bad days, embrace her on good days, stay awake with her while she covers an extra-inning game at 2 a.m.

She covers so much baseball, she maintains the eerie schedule of a player, rarely awaking before 10 a.m., often eating dinner at midnight.

Through the cluttered house, the path for not only her wheelchair, but for the entire direction of her life, leads from her bedroom to the kitchen to the Dodgers.

The air-conditioning sometimes breaks, turning the house into a steam bath. Lois totaled their aging van last year when she hit a black cow on a starless night, then missed so much work that they barely had enough money for food.

Yet, Sarah spends nine hours, carefully constructing an analysis of Gary Sheffield, or two hours writing about a one-run victory in Colorado.

I asked what her Dodger Web page represented to her.

Freedom.

I asked how she feels when working.

Happy. Useful.

I had contacted Sarah Morris months earlier, looking for a fight. I realized now, watching her strain into the thick air of this dark room to type words that perhaps no other soul will read, that I had found that fight.

Only, it wasn't with Sarah. It was with myself. It is the same fight the sports world experiences daily in these times of cynicism and conspiracy theories.

The fight to believe. The fight to trust that athletics can still create heroes without rap sheets, virtue without chemicals, nobility with grace.

It is about the battle to return to the days when sports did not detract from life, but added to it, with its awesome power to enlighten and include.

In a place far from such doubt, with a mind filled with wonder, Sarah Morris brought me back.

I had not wanted to walk into those shadows. But two hours later, I did not want to leave.

Yet I did, because there was an airplane waiting, and an NBA playoff series to cover, big things, nonsense things.

Sarah asked her mother to wheel her outside. She was rolled to the edge of the weeds. I grasped one of her trembling hands. She grasped back with her smile.

I climbed into the car and rattled down the dirt road. Through the rear-view mirror, through the rising dust, I could see the back of Sarah Morris' bobbing head as she was wheeled back to that cinder- blocked desk.

For she, too, had a game to cover.

If you see Karros, please tell him to watch his knees in 1999. He used to bend them more than now.

Sarah sent me that e-mail recently. It was about the same time she'd sent me an e-mail saying she had finally saved enough money to begin attending a college about 45 minutes down the road in pursuit of her "deam."

I didn't get a chance to pass along her note to the slumping Karros, but it didn't matter.

A day later, he had a game-winning hit. The next game, a home run. The game after that, another homer.

If you watched him closely, you could see that he indeed was bending his knees again.

Eight months ago I wouldn't have believed it, but I could swear each leg formed the shape of an r.

IV: Humor

From Mark Twain to Will Rogers, from Art Buchwald to Russell Baker, from Hunter S. Thompson to Dave Barry—America's humor columnists are sublime, ridiculous, and sometimes, beneath it all, deadly serious.

The humor column was the most popular early newspaper column, offering a welcome break from the official opinions offered by editorials. "The so-called humorous column is the most personal thing in the newspaper," wrote Hallam Walker Davis in 1926's *The Column*. Initially, they tended to consist of light verse and doggerel.

Early American humor columnists often adopted an alterego. Samuel Clemens became Mark Twain, and other columnists went even further in adopting a character they would inhabit, usually a wise yokel: the country bumpkin newly arrived in the city who unleashes generally well-intentioned chaos and finds apartment dwellers an odd and stuffy tribe.

From Mark Twain's early journalism we've chosen a parable from his time at the *Buffalo Gazette*, "The Danger of Lying in Bed." Still appropriate to hypochondriacs and the fear-fueled, Twain crunches the numbers to prove that there is a greater probability of dying in bed than in a railway crash—thus thriftily advising against the extra expense of buying insurance with a train ticket.

The western writer Ambrose Bierce's wit was of a different sort, that of the unreconstructed cynic who refuses to suffer fools gladly. His *Devil's Dictionary* remains an unblinking American classic, defining, for example, a saint as "a dead sinner revised and edited."

Harry Golden's "Vertical Negro Plan" is segregation-era Swiftian satire. The iconoclastic editor and sole columnist of the *Carolina Israelite* newspaper, Golden achieved instant fame for proposing an inventive solution to the debate over whether black and white students should be able sit together in school or at lunch counters—remove the seats.

Art Buchwald and Russell Baker ruled humor columns for the *New York Herald Tribune* and the *New York Times*, respectively, in the 1960s and '70s. To read Buchwald is like listening to Woody Allen narrate a UN conference; he elevated absurdity to the point where it told the truth. Russell Bakers's dry wit employed precise wordplay. His "Francs and Beans"—named one of the 100 greatest pieces of journalism in American history by a panel at NYU—mocked an infamously expensive dinner restaurant critic Craig Claiborne enjoyed during the recession-era 1970s.

Hunter S. Thompson, author of *Fear and Loathing in Las Vegas*, briefly tried his hand at a column for the *San Francisco Examiner* in the 1980s. "The Hellfire Club" shows the good doctor in fine form, skewering the sexual hypocrisies of the Televangelist crowd. Carl Hiaasen is brilliant when it comes to biting humor rooted in the news, and Tony Kornheiser is one of the best humorists of the past several decades, despite the fact that he now concentrates on his work for ESPN.

Perhaps the best known modern humor columnist is Dave Barry. His popularity is sufficient that his classic columns still run in papers across the country despite his having retired from daily column-writing more than a decade ago. The three Barry pieces here include an early obscurity, "How to Argue Effectively," and "Pithy into the Wind," in which he "goes for the Pulitzer"—an award which he did ultimately win.

Great humor columns remind us that insight into the news doesn't need to taste like medicine—and sometimes satire is the best way to tell the truth.

The Danger of Lying in Bed

MARK TWAIN—*The Buffalo Express*—1/7/1871

The man in the ticket-office said:

"Have an accident insurance ticket, also?"

"No," I said, after studying the matter over a little. "No, I believe not; I am going to be traveling by rail all day today. However, tomorrow I don't travel. Give me one for tomorrow."

The man looked puzzled. He said:

"But it is for accident insurance, and if you are going to travel by rail—"

"If I am going to travel by rail I sha'n't need it. Lying at home in bed is the thing I am afraid of."

I had been looking into this matter. Last year I traveled twenty thousand miles, almost entirely by rail; the year before, I traveled over twenty-five thousand miles, half by sea and half by rail; and the year before that I traveled in the neighborhood of ten thousand miles, exclusively by rail. I suppose if I put in all the little odd journeys here and there, I may say I have traveled sixty thousand miles during the three years I have mentioned. AND NEVER AN ACCIDENT.

For a good while I said to myself every morning: "Now I have escaped thus far, and so the chances are just that much increased that I shall catch it this time. I will be shrewd, and buy an accident ticket." And to a dead moral certainty I drew a blank, and went to bed that night without a joint started or a bone splintered. I got tired of that sort of daily bother, and fell to buying accident tickets that were good for a month. I said to myself, "A man CAN'T buy thirty blanks in one bundle."

But I was mistaken. There was never a prize in the the lot. I could read of railway accidents every day—the newspaper atmosphere was foggy with them; but somehow they never came my way. I found I had spent a good deal of money in the accident business, and had nothing to show for it. My suspicions were aroused, and I began to hunt around for somebody that had won in this lottery. I found plenty of people who had invested, but not an individual that had ever had an accident or made a cent. I stopped buying accident tickets and went to ciphering. The result was astounding. THE PERIL LAY NOT IN TRAVELING, BUT IN STAYING AT HOME.

I hunted up statistics, and was amazed to find that after all the glaring newspaper headlines concerning railroad disasters, less than THREE HUNDRED people had really lost their lives by those disasters in the preceding twelve months. The Erie road was set down as the most murderous in the list. It had killed forty-six—or twenty-six, I do not exactly remember which, but I know the number was double that of any other road. But the fact straightway suggested itself that the Erie was an immensely long road, and did more business than any other line in the country; so the double number of killed ceased to be matter for surprise.

By further figuring, it appeared that between New York and Rochester the Erie ran eight passenger-trains each way every day—16 altogether; and carried a daily average of 6,000 persons. That is about a million in six months—the population of New York City. Well, the Erie kills from 13 to 23 persons of ITS million in six months; and in the same time 13,000 of New York's million die in their beds! My flesh crept, my hair stood on end. "This is appalling!" I said. "The danger isn't in traveling by rail, but in trusting to those deadly beds. I will never sleep in a bed again."

I had figured on considerably less than one-half the length of the Erie road. It was plain that the entire road must transport at least eleven or twelve thousand people every day. There are many short roads running out of Boston that do fully half as much; a great many such roads. There are many roads scattered about the Union that do a prodigious passenger business. Therefore it was fair to presume that an average of 2,500 passengers a day for each road in the country would be almost correct. There are 846 railway lines in our country, and 846 times 2,500 are 2,115,000. So the railways of America move more than two millions of people every day; six hundred and fifty millions of people a year, without counting the Sundays. They do that, too—there is no question about it; though where they get the raw material is clear beyond the jurisdiction of my arithmetic; for I have hunted the census through and through, and I find that there are not that many people in the United States, by a matter of six hundred and ten millions at the very least. They must use some of the same people over again, likely.

San Francisco is one-eighth as populous as New York; there are 60 deaths a week in the former and 500 a week in the latter—if they have luck. That is 3,120 deaths a year in San Francisco, and eight times as many in New York— say about 25,000 or 26,000. The health of the two places is the same. So we will let it stand as a fair presumption that this will hold good all over the country, and that consequently 25,000 out of every million of people we have must die every year. That amounts to one-fortieth of our total population. One million of us, then, die annually. Out of this million ten or twelve thousand are stabbed, shot, drowned, hanged, poisoned, or meet a similarly violent death in some other popular way, such as perishing by kerosene-lamp and hoop-skirt conflagrations, getting buried in coal-mines, falling off house-tops, breaking through church, or lecture-room floors, taking patent medicines, or committing suicide in other forms. The Erie railroad kills 23 to 46; the other 845 railroads kill an average of one-third of a man each; and the rest of that million, amounting in the aggregate to that appalling figure of 987,631 corpses, die naturally in their beds!

You will excuse me from taking any more chances on those beds. The railroads are good enough for me.

And my advice to all people is, Don't stay at home any more than you can help; but when you have GOT to stay at home a while, buy a package of those insurance tickets and sit up nights. You cannot be too cautious.

[One can see now why I answered that ticket-agent in the manner recorded at the top of this sketch.]

The moral of this composition is, that thoughtless people grumble more than is fair about railroad management in the United States. When we consider that every day and night of the year full fourteen thousand railway-trains of various kinds, freighted with life and armed with death, go thundering over the land, the marvel is, NOT that they kill three hundred human beings in a twelvemonth, but that they do not kill three hundred times three hundred!

First Entries in the Devil's Dictionary
AMBROSE BIERCE—*The Wasp*—3/5/1881

ALONE	in bad company.
AMBITION	an overmastering desire to be vilified by the living and made ridiculous by friends when dead.
BRIDE	a woman with a fine prospect of happiness behind her.
BRUTE	see husband.
CONSUL	in American politics, a person who having failed to secure an office from the people is given one by the Administration on condition that he leave the country.
EGOIST	a person of low taste, more interested in himself than in me.
FRIENDSHIP	a ship big enough to carry two in fair weather, but only one in foul.
GALLOWS	a stage for the performance of miracle plays.
HANDKERCHIEF	a small square of silk or linen used at funerals to conceal a lack of tears.
HUSBAND	one who, having dined, is charged with the care of the plate.
LITIGANT	a person ready to give up his skin in the hope of retaining his bones.
LOVE	a temporary insanity curable by marriage.
MARRIAGE	a master, a mistress and two slaves, making in all, two.
MERCY	an attribute beloved of offenders.
MISFORTUNE	the kind of fortune that never misses.
MOUTH	in man, the gateway to the soul; in woman, the outlet of the heart.
NEPOTISM	appointing your grandmother to office for the good of the party.

NOVEL	a short story padded.
OPPOSITION	in politics, the party that prevents the government from running amuck by hamstringing it.
OPTIMIST	a proponent of the doctrine that black is white.
PICTURE	a representation in two dimensions of something wearisome in three.
PLATITUDE	a moral without a fable.
PLATONIC	a fool's name for the affection between a disability and a frost.
POLITENESS	acceptable hypocrisy.
POSITIVE	mistaken at the top of one's voice.
PRAY	to ask that the laws of the universe be annulled in behalf of an unworthy petitioner.
PREJUDICE	a vagrant opinion without visible means of support.
QUILL	an implement of torture yielded by a goose and wielded by an ass.
RIOT	a popular entertainment given to the police by innocent bystanders.
SAINT	a dead sinner revised and edited.
SIREN	any lady of splendid promise and disappointing performance.
SUCCESS	the one unpardonable sin.
TRICHINOSIS	the pig's reply to pork chops.
VIRTUES	certain abstentions.
YEAR	a period of 365 disappointments.

Reform Administration
FINLEY PETER DUNNE—*Chicago Post*—October 1902

"Why is it," asked Mr. Hennessy, "that a rayform administration always goes to th' bad?"

"I'll tell ye," said Mr. Dooley. "I tell ye ivrything an' I'll tell ye this. In th' first place 'tis a gr-reat mistake to think that annywan ra-aly wants to rayform. Ye niver heerd iv a man rayformin' himsilf. He'll rayform other people gladly. He like to do it. But a healthy man'll niver rayform while he has th' strenth. A man doesn't rayform till his will has been impaired so he hasn't power to resist what th' pa-apers calls th' blandishments iv th' timpter. An' that's thruer in politics thin annywhere else.

"But a rayformer don't see it. A rayformer thinks he was ilicted because he was a rayformer, whin th' thruth iv th' matther is he was ilicted because no wan knew him. Ye can always ilict a man in this counthry on that platform. If I was runnin' f'r office, I'd change me name, an' have printed on me cards: 'Give him a chanst; he can't be worse.' He's ilicted because th' people don't know him an' do know th' other la-ad; because Mrs. Casey's oldest boy was clubbed be a polisman, because we cudden't get wather above th' third story wan day, because th' sthreet car didn't stop f'r us, because th' Flannigans bought a pianny, because we was near run over be a mail wagon, because th' saloons are open Sundah night, because they're not open all day an' because we're tired seein' th' same face at th' window whin we go down to pay th' wather taxes. Th' rayformer don't know this. He thinks you an' me, Hinnissy, has been watchin' his spotless career f'r twenty years, that we've read all he had to say on th' evils iv pop'lar sufferage before th' Society f'r the Bewildhermint iv th' Poor, an' that we're achin' in ivry joint to have him dhrag us be th' hair iv th' head fr'm th' flowin' bowl an' th' short card game, make good citizens iv us an' sind us to th' pinitinchry. So th' minyit he gets into th' job he begins a furyous attimpt to convart us into what we've been thryin' not to be iver since we come into th' wurruld.

"In th' coorse iv th' twenty years that he spint attimptin' to get office, he managed to poke a few warrum laws conthrollin' th' pleasures iv th' poor into th' stachoo book, because no wan cared about thim or because they made business betther f'r th' polis, an' whin he's in office, he calls up th' Cap'n iv the polis an' says he: 'If these laws ar-re bad laws th' way to end thim is to enforce thim.' Somebody told him that, Hinnissy. It isn't thrue, d'ye mind. I don't care who said it, not if 'twas Willum Shakespere. It isn't thrue. Laws ar-re made to throuble people an' th' more throuble they make th' longer they stay on th' stachoo book. But th' polis don't ast anny questions: Says they: 'They'll be less money in th' job but we need some recreation,' an' that night a big copper comes down th' sthreet, sees me settin' out on th' front stoop with me countenance dhraped with a tin pail, fans me with his club an' runs me in. Th' woman nex' dure is locked up f'r sthringin' a clothes line on th' roof, Hannigan's boy Tim gets tin days f'r keepin' a goat, th' polis resarves are called out to protict th' vested rights iv property against th' haynyous pushcart man, th' stations is crowded with felons charged with maintainin' a hose conthrary to th' stachoos made an' provided, an' th' tindherline is all over town. A rayformer don't think anything has been accomplished if they'se a vacant bedroom in th' pinitinchry. His motto is 'Arrest that man.'

"Whin a rayformer is ilicted he promises ye a business administhration. Some people want that but I don't. Th' American business man is too fly. He's all right, d'ye mind. I don't say anything again' him. He is what Hogan calls th' boolwarks iv pro-gress, an' we cudden't get on without him even if his scales are a little too quick on th' dhrop. But he ought to be left to dale with his akels. 'Tis a shame to give him a place where he can put th' comether on millions iv people that has had no business thrainin' beyond occasionally handin' a piece iv debased money to a car conductor on a cold day. A reg'lar pollytician can't give away an alley without blushin', but a business man who is in pollytics jus' to see that th' civil sarvice law gets thurly enforced, will give Lincoln Park an' th' public libr'y to th' beef thrust, charge an admission price to th' lake front an' make it a felony f'r annywan to buy stove polish outside iv his store, an' have it all put down to public improvemints with a pitcher iv him in th' corner stone.

"Fortchnitly, Hinnissy, a rayformer is seldom a business man. He thinks he is, but business men know diff'rent. They know what he his. He thinks business an' honesty is th' same thing. He does, indeed. He's got thim mixed because they dhress alike. His idee is that all he has to do to make a business administhration is to have honest men ar-round him. Wrong. I'm not sayin', mind ye, that a man can't do good work an' be honest at th' same time. But whin I'm hirin' a la-ad I find out first whether he is onto his job, an' afther a few years I begin to suspect that he is honest, too. Manny a dishonest man can lay brick sthraight an' many a man that wudden't steal ye'er spoons will break ye'er furniture. I don't want Father Kelly to hear me, but I'd rather have a competint man who wud steal if I give him a chanst, but I won't, do me plumbin' thin a person that wud scorn to help himself but didn't know how to wipe a joint. Ivry man ought to be honest to start with, but to give a man an office jus' because he's honest is like ilicitin' him to Congress because he's a pathrite, because he don't bate his wife or because he always wears a right boot on th' right foot. A man ought to be honest to start with an' afther that he ought to be crafty. A pollytician who's on'y honest is jus' th' same as bein' out in a winther storm without anny clothes on.

"Another thing about rayform administhrations is they always think th' on'y man that ought to hold a job is a lawyer. Th' raison is that in th' coorse iv his thrainin' a lawyer larns enough about ivrything to make a good front on anny subject to annybody who doesn't know about it. So whin th' rayform administhration comes in th' mayor says: 'Who'll we make chief iv polis in place iv th' misguided ruffyan who has held th' job f'r twinty years?' 'Th' man f'r th' place,' says th' mayor's advisers, 'is Arthur Lightout,' he says. 'He's an ixcillent lawyer, Yale, '95, an' is well up on polis matthers. Las' year he read a paper on "The fine polis foorce iv London" befure th' annyal meetin' iv th' S'ciety f'r Ladin' th' Mulligan Fam'ly to a Betther an' Harder Life. Besides,' he says, 'he's been in th' milishy an' th' foorce needs a man who'll be afraid not to shoot in case iv public disturbance.' So Arthur takes hold iv th' constabulary an' in a year th' polis can all read Emerson an' th' burglars begin puttin' up laddhers an' block an' tackles befure eight a.m. An' so it is on ivry side. A lawyer has charge iv the city horseshoein', another wan is clanin' th' sthreets, th' author iv 'Gasamagoo on torts' is thryin' to dispose iv th' ashes be throwin' thim in th' air on a windy day, an' th' bright boy that took th' silver ware f'r th' essay on *ne exeats* an' their relation to life is plannin' a uniform that will be sarviceable an' constitchoochinal f'r th' brave men that wurruks on th' city dumps. An' wan day th' main rayformer goes out expictin' to rayceive th' thanks iv th' community an' th' public that has jus' got out iv jail f'r lettin' th' wather run too long in th' bath tub rises up an' cries: 'Back to th' Univarsity Settlemint.' Th' man with th' di'mon' in his shirt front comes home an' pushes th' honest lawyers down th' steps, an' a dishonest horse shoer shoes th' city's horses well, an' a crooked plumber does th' city's plumbin' securely, an' a rascally polisman that may not be averse to pickin' up a bet but will always find out whin Pathrolman Scanlan slept on his beat, takes hold iv th' polis foorce, an' we raysume our nachral condition iv illegal merrimint. An' th' rayformer spinds th' rest iv his life tellin' us where we are wrong. He's good at that. On'y he don't undherstand that people wud rather be wrong an' comfortable thin right in jail."

"I don't like a rayformer," said Mr. Hennessy.

"Or anny other raypublican," said Mr. Dooley.

Congress Is Funniest When It's Serious
WILL ROGERS—*New York Times*—6/8/1924

I just got back from Washington, D.C. (Department of Comedy). I had heard that the Congressional Show was to close on June the 7th, I don't see why they are closing then. They could bring that same show with the original cast they have, to New York, and it would run for years.

I am to go into Ziegfeld's new Follies, and I have *no* act. So I thought I will run down to Washington and get some material. Most people and actors appearing on the stage have some writer to write their material, or they reproduce some book or old masterpiece, but I don't do that. Congress is good enough for me. They have been writing my material for years and I am not ashamed of the material I have had. I am going to stick to them. Why should I go and pay some famous author, or even myself, sit down all day trying to dope out something funny to say on the stage! No sir, I have found that there is nothing as funny as things that have happened, and that people know that have happened. So I just have them mail me every day the *Congressional Record*. It is to me what the *Police Gazette* used to be to the fellow who was waiting for a haircut. In other words, it is a life saver.

Besides, nothing is so funny as something done in all seriousness. The material on which the *Congressional Record* is founded is done there every day in all seriousness. Each state elects the most serious man it has in the District, and he is impressed with the fact that he is leaving home with the expressed idea that he is to rescue his District from certain destruction, and to see that it received its just amount of rivers and harbors, post offices, and pumpkin seeds. Naturally you have put a pretty big load on that man. I realize that it is no joking matter to be grabbed up bodily from the leading lawyer's office of Main Street and have the entire populace tell you what is depending on you when you get to Washington. The fellow may be alright personally and a good fellow, but that Big League Idea of Politics just kinder scares him.

Now, they wouldn't be so serious and particular if they only had to vote on what they thought was good for the majority of the people of the U.S. That would be a cinch. But what makes it hard for them is every time a bill comes up they have a million things to decide that have nothing to do with the merit of the bill. They first must consider is, or was, it introduced by a member of the opposite Political Party. If it is, why then something is wrong with it from the start, for everything the opposite side does has a catch in it. Then the principal thing is of course, "what will this do for me personally back home?" If it is something that he thinks the folks back home may never read, or hear, of why then he can vote any way he wants to, but politics, and self preservations must come first, never mind the majority of the people of the U.S. If lawmakers were elected for life I believe they would do better. A man's thoughts are naturally on his next term, more than on his country.

The first day I got there it was a dandy show. In the House of Representatives they were arguing on the bill as to whether we could raise the elevation of the guns on our battleships. Now, when you stop to think, that would be just like arguing on, "Can we use bullets in our guns or must we just carry them and throw them at the enemy?" because naturally if you are allowed to have a gun at all you certainly ought to be allowed to point it any way that will get you the most good out of it. But most of them thought as our guns had always pointed toward the water instead of up in the air, why naturally, they should be kept pointing that way. Butler of Pennsylvania, and Britten, of Illinois, both members of the Naval communities, like to come to blows on it; both being Republicans, the Democrats urged them on in hopes they would murder each other.

Well, any way, they killed that bill instead of letting the Navy point the guns or elevate them where they thought best. They are to put them where Congress thinks they will do the least damage in case we ever have to use them in battle. The ones opposed to it were afraid Japan would object and get sore at us. That's why we wanted them elevated, to keep them from getting sore at us. If we had enough guns, and they all were elevated to the right height, no one would ever get sore at us.

Well, a friend from Texas, a member of the House, saw me sitting up in the gallery just soaking in all this gun raising patriotism, and he called attention and introduced me to the House of Representatives. Well, I felt that quite a compliment, but there was nothing I could do. An ordinary comedian like me would have no chance there. I was the most unfunny man in the entire building.

Then I went downstairs outside the Congress Hall and met all my old friends, Representatives from Oklahoma, Los Angeles, Texas, Kansas, Arizona, and from all over, and I want to tell you they are as fine a bunch of men as any one ever met in his life, they were all full of humor and regular fellows. That is, as I say, when you catch them when they haven't got politics on their minds, but the minute they get in that immense Hall they begin to get serious, and it's then that they do such amusing things. If we could just send the same bunch of men to Washington for the good of the nation, and not for political reasons, we could have the most perfect government in the world.

Tips on Horses
RING LARDNER—*The New York World*—11/1/1925

To the Editor of *The World*:

Once in every so often the undersigned receives a circular from the Horse Breeders ass'n of America or something, along with a request to give same all possible publicity to the end that people's interest in horses will be revived and roused up and not allow the genius equine to become extinct in our land from lack of attention. And just as often as one of those literary broadsides hits my happy home just so often do I feel it incumbrance on myself to come out flat-footed and open and above the boards and state my attitude towards what is known in exclusive livery stable circles as his highness le Horse.

Children, dogs and horses is regarded in this country as sacred items and it is considered pretty close to a felony to even make a face when any of the 3 is mentioned. Well, I am fond of children, at least four of them and can tolerate a few dogs provided they keep their mouths shut and ain't over a ft. high. But irregardless of less majesty and the deuce with same, I can't help from admitting at this junction that the bear mention of a horse has the same effects on me like red flags to a bull or gingerale to an Elk.

A horse is the most overestimated animal in the world with the possible exception of a police dog. For every incidence where a horse has saved a human life I can dig you up a 100 incidences where they have killed people by falling off them or trampling them down or both. Personally, the only horse who I ever set on their back throwed me off on my bosom before I had road him 20 ft. and did the horse wait to see was I hurt, no.

Devotees of horse flesh is wont to point out that King Richard the 3rd once offered his kingdom for one of them but in the 1st place he was not the kind of a man who I would pin any faith on his judgment of values and in the 2nd place the kingdom had been acquired by a couple of mild little murders and it was a case of easy come, easy go.

A study of some of the expressions in usage at the present day will serve to throw light on the real personality of a horse. Take for example the phrase "eat like a horse." The picture you get from this phrase is the picture of somebody eating without regard to ethics or good manners, the picture of a person who you would as least have a horse at the table as they.

Or take "horse laugh." This indicates the coarsest, roughest kind of a laugh and a person of breeding and refinement would pretty near as soon have their friends give them a head cold as the horse laugh. Or "Horse play." How often you hear theater goers complain that such and such a comedy has got too much horse play or observe parents order their kiddies to cut out the horse play. The answer is that a horse can't play nice like kittens or oxen or even wolfs, but has got to be ribald and rough in their sports as in everything else.

Defenders of le horse will no doubt point to the term "good, common horse sense," or the simile "work like a horse" as being proof of the beast's virtues, but if a horse has got such good common sense why do they always half to have a jockey show them the way around a fenced in race track where you couldn't possibly go wrong unless you was dumb, and as for working like a horse, I never met a horse who worked because he thought it was fun. They work for the same reason the rest of us works.

I will pass over what different horses has done to me in places like Saratoga, Belmont, Havana and New Orleans. Suffice it to say that none of them ever lived up to what I had been led to believe. And one day just last month I had to walk across 34th Street in N. Y. City and dodged my way amongst taxicabs, trucks and street cars and was just congratulating myself on making the trip unscathed when a horse reached out and snapped at me, a stranger.

Horses ain't been good in battle since trench warfare came into its own and besides you never heard of a horse volunteering for an army. . . . And do you think Paul Revere would even looked at a horse if all the taxis hadn't been engaged with the theater crowds that night?

Last, but not lease, have you ever been hit by a horsefly, which never would of been thought of only for his highness le horse.

Apology
WESTBROOK PEGLER—Scripps Howard—February 1936

GARMISCH-PARTENKIRCHEN—It is going to be pretty hard to do this, but right is right, as President Harding said, and I feel that I have done the Nazis a serious injustice, so this is my apology.

Two days ago these dispatches reported that the quaint little Bavarian town of Garmisch-Partenkirchen has the appearance of an army headquarters a few miles behind the Western Front during an important troop movement. That was wrong, and I can only plead that I was honestly mistaken and the victim of my own ignorance.

Those weren't troops at all, but merely peace-loving German workmen in their native dress, and those weren't army lorries which went growling through the streets squirting the slush onto the sidewalks, but delivery wagons carrying beer and wieners and kraut to the humble homes of the mountaineers in the folds of the hills. It is a relief to know this and a pleasure to be able to report that, after all, the Germans did not conduct their Winter Olympics in an atmosphere of war, which would have been very injurious to the Olympic ideal of peace through sporting competition.

My information comes from a kindly Bavarian cobbler in a long black overcoat who was standing in a cordon of cobblers along the main street Sunday afternoon during Adolph Hitler's visit to town to pronounce over the closing ceremonies the benison of a great protector of the world's peace.

"Are you a soldier?" I inquired, for I had been told that in Germany strangers often mistake for soldiers people who haven't nothing to do with the military establishment.

"Who, me?" he asked. "No, I'm a cobbler. All of us in the black costume are cobblers."

"Then why do you dress in military uniform?" I persisted.

"That's where you are wrong," said my cobbler friend. "This isn't a military uniform. It's a shoemaker's uniform, and this big toad stabber in the scabbard at my side, which may look like a bayonet to you, is merely a little knife which we use when we cobble."

"But," I asked, "why do you march in military formation through the scenes of international friendship?" The answer was that they don't really march at all. They just walk in step in columns of fours, because they like to walk that way. And it is an old custom of theirs to form cordons of military appearance along the curbs and just stand there by the hour for pleasure.

"But what about those other troops in the brown uniforms?"

"Troops?" said my friend. "Those are not troops. Those are gardeners who have always worn brown suits, which seem to be military but aren't. Just peace loving gardeners is what they are, and those blades which you see hanging from their belts are not bayonets, either, but pruning knives. It is an old Bavarian tradition.

"They too like to go for long walks in columns of fours and make gestures with spades, as soldiers sometimes drill with rifles, but they are not soldiers, I assure you, my friend. They are just kind-hearted gardeners who wouldn't hurt a potato bug. It is interesting to see them stack spades when they come to the end of a stroll in columns of fours. To some people unacquainted with our local customs they may seem to be performing a military drill with their spades, but nothing could be further from the truth. Thus far two of my military corps had been explained away as harmless and altogether peaceful workmen, but I thought I had him when I mentioned the men in the gray uniforms, also with scabbards at their sides, who seemed to be regular infantry. He laughed uproariously at this.

"Oh, those!" he said. "Those aren't infantry. How could you make that mistake? Those are plasterers, and the tin hats which you undoubtedly mistook for shrapnel helmets are an ancient tradition of Bavarian plasterers. Sometimes the plaster falls down, and it would knock them for a lot of loops if they didn't wear something for protection. Wait till I tell the foreman of the plasterers—I suppose you have been calling him the general—that you mistook his boys for soldiers. He will laugh himself dizzy."

Still, there were other men all dressed alike in blue-gray, with wings embroidered on their clothing. Undoubtedly those would be soldiers of the aviation branch, wouldn't they? But my friend the peace-loving cobbler in the black suit, which looked very military but wasn't, enjoyed another pleasant hysteric over that one too. Those, he said, were Bavarian white wings in native dress.

It is not easy to be proven wrong in a serious matter. I had seen as many as five thousand, perhaps even ten thousand, men in apparel which seemed to be that of soldiers, and had recklessly accused the peace-loving Nazi regime of converting the Winter Olympics into a military demonstration, which would have been a grave breach of manners. My troops had been explained into gentle civilians, and the marching to which I had referred had turned out to be nothing but a habitual method of going for nice long walks.

The motor trucks still seemed questionable, however, for they were painted in camouflage like the lorries used in the war.

"Yes, I know," my friend the cobbler explained, "but we have painted our motor trucks in eccentric designs and colors for hundreds of years. It makes them look nicer."

A foreman of the cobblers came by at the moment, and my friend put his hand to his cap in a gesture which resembled a military salute. I asked him about this, but he said he was only shading his eyes.

The Nazi press bureau released a quotation from a dispatch to the *New York Times* intimating that anyone reporting the presence of troops at the Olympic Games was a liar. I guess that's me, but the mistake was natural, as you can see. When thousands of men seem to march but don't in clothing and tin hats which seem to be military uniforms but aren't, and carry harmless utensils which appear to be bayonets but ain't, any stranger is likely to make the same mistake.

Death Pays a Social Call
DAMON RUNYON—King Features—c.1945

Death came in and sat down beside me, a large and most distinguished-looking figure in beautifully-tailored soft, white flannels. His expensive face wore a big smile.

"Oh, hello," I said. "Hello, hello, hello. I was not expecting you. I have not looked at the red board lately and did not know my number was up. If you will just hand me my kady and my coat I will be with you in a jiffy."

"Tut-tut-tut," Death said. "Not so fast. I have not come for you. By no means."

"You haven't?" I said.

"No," Death said.

"Then what the hell are you doing here?" I demanded indignantly. "What do you mean by barging in here without even knocking and depositing your fat Francis in my easiest chair without so much as by-your-leave?"

"Excuse me," Death said, taken aback by my vehemence. "I was in your neighborhood and all tired out after my day's work and I thought I would just drop in and sit around with you awhile and cut up old scores. It is merely a social call, but I guess I owe you an apology at that for my entrance."

"I should say you do," I said.

"Well, you see I am so accustomed to entering doors without knocking that I never thought," Death said. "If you like, I will go outside and knock and not come in until you answer."

"Look," I said. "You can get out of here and stay out of here. Screw, bum!"

Death burst out crying.

Huge tears rolled down both pudgy cheeks and splashed on his white silk-faced lapels.

"There it is again," he sobbed. "That same inhospitable note wherever I go. No one wants to chat with me. I am so terribly lonesome. I thought surely you would like to punch the bag with me awhile."

I declined to soften up.

"Another thing," I said sternly, "what are you doing in that get-up? You are supposed to be in black. You are supposed to look sombre, not like a Miami Beach Winter tourist."

"Why," Death said, "I got tired of wearing my old working clothes all the time. Besides, I thought these garments would be more cheerful and informal for a social call."

"Well, beat it," I said. "Just Duffy out of here."

"You need not fear me," Death said.

"I do not fear you Deathie, old boy," I said, "but you are a knock to me among my neighbours. Your visit is sure to get noised about and cause gossip. You know you are not considered a desireable character by many persons, although, mind you, I am not saying anything against you."

"Oh, go ahead," Death said. "Everybody else puts the zing on me so you might as well, too. But I did not think your neighbours would recognize me in white, although, come to think of it, I noticed everybody running to their front door and grabbing in their 'Welcome' mats as I went past. Why are you shivering if you do not fear me?"

"I am shivering because of that clammy chill you brought in with you," I said. "You lug the atmosphere of a Frigidaire around with you."

"You don't tell me?" Death said. "I must correct that. I must pack an electric pad with me. Do you think that is why I seem so unpopular wherever I go? Do you think I will ever be a social success?"

"I am inclined to doubt it," I said. "Your personality repels many persons. I do not find it as bad as that of some others I know, but you have undoubtedly developed considerable sales resistance to yourself in various quarters."

"Do you think it would do any good if I hired a publicity man?" Death asked. "I mean, to conduct a campaign to make me popular?"

"It might," I said. "The publicity men have worked wonders with even worse cases than yours. But see here, D., I am not going to waste my time giving you advice and permitting you to linger on in my quarters to get me talked about. Kindly do a scrammola, will you?"

Death had halted his tears for a moment, but now he turned on all faucets, crying boo-hoo-hoo-hoo.

"I am so lonesome," he said between lachrymose heaves.

"Git!" I said.

"Everybody is against me," Death said.

He slowly exited and, as I heard his tears falling plop-plop-plop to the floor as he passed down the hallway, I thought of the remark of Agag, the King of the Amalekites, to Samuel just before Samuel mowed him down: "Surely the bitterness of death is past."

The Vertical Negro Plan
HARRY GOLDEN—*Carolina Israelite*—May 1956

Those who love North Carolina will jump at the chance to share in the great responsibility confronting our Governor and the State Legislature. A special session of the Legislature (July 25–28, 1956) passed a series of amendments to the State Constitution. These proposals submitted by the Governor and his Advisory Education Committee included the following:

(A) The elimination of the compulsory attendance law, "to prevent any child from being forced to attend a school with a child of another race."

(B) The establishment of "Education Expense Grants" for education in a private school, "in the case of a child assigned to a public school attended by a child of another race."

(C) A "uniform system of local option" whereby a majority of the folks in a school district may suspend or close a school if the situation becomes "intolerable."

But suppose a Negro child applies for this "Education Expense Grant" and says he wants to go to a private school too? There are fourteen Supreme Court decisions involving the use of public funds; there are only two "decisions" involving the elimination of racial discrimination in the public schools.

The Governor has said that critics of these proposals have not offered any constructive advice or alternatives. Permit me, therefore, to offer an idea for the consideration of the members of the regular sessions. A careful study of my plan, I believe, will show that it will save millions of dollars in tax funds and eliminate forever the danger to our public education system. Before I outline my plan, I would like to give you a little background.

One of the factors involved in our tremendous industrial growth and economic prosperity is the fact that the South, voluntarily, has all but eliminated VERTICAL SEGREGATION. The tremendous buying power of the twelve million Negroes in the South has been based wholly on the absence of racial segregation. The white and Negro stand at the same grocery and supermarket counters; deposit money at the same bank teller's window; pay phone and light bills to the same clerk; walk through the same dime and department stores, and stand at the same drugstore counters.

It is only when the Negro "sets" that the fur begins to fly.

Now, since we are not even thinking about restoring VERTICAL SEGREGATION, I think my plan would not only comply with the Supreme Court decisions, but would maintain "sitting-down" segregation. Now here is the GOLDEN VERTICAL NEGRO PLAN. Instead of all those complicated proposals, all the next session needs to do is pass one small amendment which would provide only desks in all the public schools of our state—no seats.

The desks should be those standing-up jobs, like the old-fashioned bookkeeping desk. Since no one in the South pays the slightest attention to a VERTICAL NEGRO, this will completely solve our problem. And it is not such a terrible inconvenience for young people to stand up during their classroom studies. In fact, this may be a blessing in disguise. They are not learning to read sitting down, anyway; maybe standing up will help. This will save more millions of dollars in the cost of our remedial English course when the kids enter college. In whatever direction you look with the GOLDEN VERTICAL NEGRO PLAN, you save millions of dollars, to say nothing of eliminating forever any danger to our public education system upon which rests the destiny, hopes, and happiness of this society.

My WHITE BABY PLAN offers another possible solution to the segregation problem—this time in a field other than education.

Here is an actual case history of the "White Baby Plan to End Racial Segregation":

Some months ago there was a revival of the Laurence Olivier movie, *Hamlet*, and several Negro schoolteachers were eager to see it. One Saturday afternoon they asked some white friends to lend them two of their little children, a three-year-old girl and a six-year-old boy, and, holding these white children by the hands, they obtained tickets from the movie-house cashier without a moment's hesitation. They were in like Flynn.

This would also solve the baby-sitting problem for thousands and thousands of white working mothers. There can be a mutual exchange of references, then the people can sort of pool their children at a central point in each neighborhood, and every time a Negro wants to go to the movies all she need to do is pick up a white child—and go.

Eventually the Negro community can set up a factory and manufacture white babies made of plastic, and when they want to go to the opera or to a concert, all they need do is carry that plastic doll in their arms. The dolls, of course, should all have blond curls and blue eyes, which would go even further; it would give the Negro woman and her husband priority over the whites for the very best seats in the house.

While I still have faith in the WHITE BABY PLAN, my final proposal may prove to be the most practical of all.

Only after a successful test was I ready to announce formally the GOLDEN "OUT-OF-ORDER" PLAN.

I tried my plan in a city of North Carolina, where the Negroes represent 39 per cent of the population.

I prevailed upon the manager of a department store to shut the water off in his "white" water fountain and put up a sign, "Out-of-Order." For the first day or two the whites were hesitant, but little by little they began to drink out of the water fountain belonging to the "coloreds"—and by the end of the third week everybody was drinking the "segregated" water; with not a single solitary complaint to date.

I believe the test is of such sociological significance that the Governor should appoint a special committee of two members of the House and two Senators to investigate the GOLDEN "OUT-OF-ORDER" PLAN. We kept daily reports on the use of the unsegregated water fountain which should be of great value to this committee. This may be the answer to the necessary uplifting of the white morale. It is possible that the whites may accept desegregation if they are assured that the facilities are still "separate," albeit "Out-of-Order."

As I see it now, the key to my Plan is to keep the "Out-of-Order" sign up for at least two years. We must do this thing gradually.

Political Poll in 1776
ART BUCHWALD—*New York Herald Tribune*—11/1/1962

The political pollster has become such an important part of the American scene that it's hard to imagine how this country was ever able to function without him.

What would have happened, for example, if there were political pollsters in the early days of this country?

This is how the results might have turned out.

When asked if they thought the British were doing a good job in administrating the Colonies, this is how a cross section of the people responded:

British doing good job / 63%

Not doing good job / 22%

Don't know / 15%

The next question, "Do you think the dumping of tea in the Boston Harbor by militants helped or hurt the taxation laws in the New World?"

Hurt the cause of taxation / 79%

Helped the cause / 12%

Didn't think it would make any difference / 9%

"What do you think our image is in England after the Minute Men attacked the British at Lexington?"

Minute men hurt our image in England / 83%

Gave British new respect for Colonies / 10%

Undecided / 7%

"Which of these two Georges can do more for the Colonies—George III or George Washington?"

George III / 76%

George Washington / 14%

Others / 10%

It is interesting to note that 80 percent of the people questioned had never heard of George Washington before.

The next question was, "Do you think the Declaration of Independence as it is written is a good document or a bad one?"

Bad document / 14%

Good document / 12%

No opinion / 84%

A group of those polled felt that the Declaration of Independence had been written by a bunch of radicals and the publishing of it at this time would only bring harsher measures from the British.

When asked whether the best way to bring about reforms was through terrorism or redress to the Crown an overwhelming proportion of Colonists felt appeals should be made to the King.

Reforms through petition / 24%

Reforms through act of terrorism / 8%

Don't know / 66%

The pollsters then asked what the public thought was the most crucial issue of the time.

Trade with foreign nations / 65%

War with Indians / 20%

The independence issue / 15%

The survey also went into the question of Patrick Henry.

"Do you think Patrick Henry did the right thing in demanding liberty or death?"

Did a foolhardy thing and was a trouble maker / 53%

Did a brave thing and made his point / 23%

Should have gone through the courts / 6%

Don't know / 8%

On the basis of the results of the poll the militant Colonials decided they did not have enough popular support to foment a revolution and gave up the idea of creating a United States of America.

Nixon Goes to the Mountain
ART BUCHWALD—*Washington Post*—4/23/1973

Last weekend President Richard Nixon went to Camp David alone, without family or aides. Press Secretary Ron Ziegler denies it, but it has been reliably reported that the President went up the top of the mountain to speak with God.

"God, God, why are you doing this to me?"

"Doing what, Richard?"

"The Watergate, the cover-up, the grand jury hearings, the Senate investigations. Why me, God?"

"Don't blame me, Richard. I gave you my blessing to win the election, but I didn't tell you to steal it."

"God, I've done everything you told me to do. I ended the war. I defeated poverty. I cleaned the air and the water. I defeated crime in the streets. Surely I deserve a break."

"Richard, I tried to warn you that you had sinful people working for you."

"When, God?"

"Just after the Committee to Reelect the President was formed. When I saw the people you had selected to head up the committee, I was shocked. We've got a long file on them up here."

"Why didn't You tell me, God?"

"I tried to, but Ehrlichman and Haldeman wouldn't let Me talk to you on the phone. They said they'd give you the message I called."

"They never told me, God."

"It figures. Then I sent you a telegram saying it was urgent that you contact Me."

"The only telegrams I read during that period were those in support of my bombing North Vietnam."

"Finally, Richard, I made one last effort. I showed up at a prayer meeting one Sunday at the White House and after the sermon I came up to you and said there were men among you who would betray you. Do you know what you did, Richard? You introduced me to Pat and then you gave Me a ballpoint pen."

"I didn't know it was you, God. So many people show up at these prayer meetings. Is that why you're punishing me—because I snubbed You?"

"I'm not punishing you, Richard. But even I can do just so much. If it were merely a simple case of bugging at the Watergate, I could probably fix it. But your Administration is involved in the obstruction of justice, the bribing of witnesses, the forging of papers, wiretapping, perjury, and using the mails to defraud."

"Good God, nobody's perfect!"

"I guess that's what the grand jury is saying."

"Look, I've got less than four years in which to go down as the greatest President in the history of the United States. Give me a break."

"You've got to clean house, Richard. Get rid of everyone who has any connection with the scandal. You must make it perfectly clear you were hoodwinked by everyone on your staff. You must show the American people that when it comes to the Presidency, no one is too big to be sacrificed on the altar of expediency."

"God, are you asking for a human sacrifice?"

"It would show your good faith, Richard."

"All right, I'll do it. Will you take Jeb Magruder, Richard Kleindienst and John Dean III?"

What kind of sacrifice is that?

"John Mitchell?"

"Keep going."

"Haldeman and Ehrlichman?"

"That's more like it."

"And then, God, if I sacrifice them, will you keep me out of it?"

"Richard, I can't work miracles."

How to Cure a Hangover
MIKE ROYKO—*Chicago Daily News*—12/27/1974

This is the time of year all sorts of advice is written about hangovers.

The articles usually touch on three key points: What a hangover is, how to avoid one, and how to cure it.

Defining a hangover is simple. It is nature's way of telling you that you got drunk.

I've never understood why nature goes to the bother, since millions of wives pass on the information.

Except for abstinence or moderation, there is no way to completely avoid a hangover.

But there are certain rules that, if followed, will ease the discomfort.

First, stick with the same drink you started with. By that I mean that if you started the evening drinking champagne, beer, and frozen daiquiris, stick with champagne, beer, and frozen daiquiris the rest of the evening.

Drink quickly. If you can do most of your drinking within the first hour of the party and quickly pass out, you will have regained consciousness and be well on your way to recovery while others are still gadding about. By the time the Rose Bowl game comes on, your eyeballs will have come out from behind your nose.

Be careful what you eat, especially well into the night. Especially avoid eating napkins, paper plates, and pizza boards.

If you follow these rules, you'll still have a hangover. So the question is, how to get through it with a minimum of agony.

It should be remembered that part of a hangover's discomfort is psychological.

When you awaken, you will be filled with a deep sense of shame, guilt, disgust, embarrassment, humiliation, and self-loathing.

This is perfectly normal, understandable, and deserved.

To ease these feelings, try to think only of the pleasant or amusing things that you did before blacking out. Let your mind dwell on how you walked into the party and said hello to everyone, handed your host your coat, shook hands, and admired the stereo system.

Blot from your mind all memories of what you later did to your host's rug, what you said to that lady with the prominent cleavage that made her scream, whether you or her husband threw the first punch. Don't dredge up those vague recollections of being asleep in your host's bathtub while everybody pleaded with you to unlock the bathroom door.

These thoughts will just depress you. Besides, your wife will explain it in detail as the day goes on. And the week, too.

If anything, you should laugh it off. It's easy. Using your thumb and forefinger, pry your tongue loose from the roof of your mouth, try to stop panting for a moment and say: Ha, ha. Again: Ha, ha. Now pull the blanket over your head and go back to sleep.

The other part of a hangover is physical. It is usually marked by throbbing pain in the head, behind the eyes, in the back of the neck, and in the stomach. You might also have pain in the arms, legs, elbows, chin and elsewhere, depending upon how much leaping, careening, flailing, and falling you did.

Moaning helps. It doesn't ease the pain, but it lets you know that someone cares, even if it is only you. Moaning also lets you know that you are still alive.

But don't let your wife hear you moan. You should at least have the satisfaction of not letting her have the satisfaction of knowing you are in agony.

If she should overhear you moaning, tell her you are just humming a love song the lady with the prominent cleavage sang in your ear while you danced.

Some people say that moaning gives greater benefits if you moan while sitting on the edge of your bathtub while letting your head hang down between your ankles. Others claim that it is best to go into the living room, slouch in a chair, and moan while holding one hand over your brow and the other over your stomach.

In any case, once you have moaned awhile, you can try medication.

Aspirin will help relieve your headache. But it might increase the pain in your stomach.

If so, Maalox will help relieve the pain in your stomach. But it will make your mouth dry.

Water will relieve the dryness in your mouth. But it will make you feel bloated.

So it is best to take the aspirin and the Maalox and just hold your tongue under the kitchen faucet. Or rest it in the freezer compartment of your refrigerator.

If you don't like to take pills, then the headache can be eased by going outside and plunging your head into a snowbank. Be sure it isn't a snow-covered hedge.

If you eat, make it something bland, such as a bowl of gruel. I don't know what gruel is, but it sounds very bland. If you don't know what gruel is either, then just make something that you think it might be.

Most experts recommend a minimum of physical activity, such as blinking your eyes during the bowl games and moving your lips just enough to say to your wife: "Later, we'll discuss it later."

On the other hand, you might consider leaping out of bed the moment you open your eyes, flinging the windows open to let the cold air in, and jogging rapidly in place while violently flapping your arms and breathing deeply and heavily.

This will make you forget your hangover because it will bring on a massive coronary.

Francs and Beans
RUSSELL BAKER—*New York Times*—11/18/1975

As chance would have it, the very evening Craig Claiborne ate his historic $4,000 dinner for two with 31 dishes and nine wines in Paris, a Lucullan repast for one was prepared and consumed in New York by this correspondent, no slouch himself when it comes to titillating the palate.

Mr. Claiborne won his meal in a television fund-raising auction and had it professionally prepared. Mine was created from spur-of-the-moment inspiration, necessitated when I discovered a note on the stove saying, "Am eating out with Dor and Imogene—make dinner for yourself." It was from the person who regularly does the cooking at my house and, though disconcerted at first, I quickly rose to the challenge.

The meal opened with a 1975 Diet Pepsi served in a disposable bottle. Although its bouquet was negligible, its distinct metallic aftertaste evoked memories of tin cans one had licked experimentally in the first flush of childhood's curiosity.

To create the balance of tastes so cherished by the epicurean palate, I followed with a pâté de fruites de nuts of Georgia, prepared according to my own recipe. A half-inch layer of creamy-style peanut butter is troweled onto a graham cracker, then half a banana is crudely diced and pressed firmly into the peanut butter and cemented in place as it were by a second graham cracker.

The accompanying drink was cold milk served in a wide-brimmed jelly glass. This is essential to proper consumption of the pâté, since the entire confection must be dipped into the milk to soften it for eating. In making the presentation to the mouth, one must beware lest the milk-soaked portion of the sandwich fall onto the necktie. Thus, seasoned gourmandisers follow the old maxim of the Breton chefs and "bring the mouth to the jelly glass."

At this point in the meal, the stomach was ready for serious eating, and I prepared beans with bacon grease, a dish I perfected in 1937 while developing my cuisine du depression.

The dish is started by placing a pan over a very high flame until it becomes dangerously hot. A can of Heinz's pork and beans is then emptied into the pan and allowed to char until it reaches the consistency of hardening concrete. Three strips of bacon are fried to crisps, and when the beans have formed huge dense clots firmly welded to the pan, the bacon grease is poured in and stirred vigorously with a large screw driver.

This not only adds flavor but also loosens some of the beans from the side of the pan. Leaving the flame high, I stirred in a three-day-old spaghetti sauce found in the refrigerator, added a sprinkle of chili powder, a large dollop of Major Grey's chutney and a tablespoon of bicarbonate of soda to make the whole dish rise.

Beans with bacon grease is always eaten from the pan with a tablespoon while standing over the kitchen sink. The pan must be thrown away immediately. The correct drink with this dish is a straight shot of room-temperature gin. I had a Gilbey's, 1975, which was superb.

For the meat course, I had fried bologna à la Nutley, Nouveau Jersey. Six slices of A&P bologna were placed in an ungreased frying pan over maximum heat and held down by a long fork until the entire house filled with smoke. The bologna was turned, fried the same length of time on the other side, then served on air-filled white bread with thick lashings of mayonnaise.

The correct drink for fried bologna à la Nutley, Nouveau Jersey is a 1927 Nehi Cola, but since my cellar, alas, had none, I had to make do with a second shot of Gilbey's 1975.

The cheese course was deliciously simple—a single slice of Kraft's individually wrapped yellow sandwich cheese, which was flavored by vigorous rubbing over the bottom of the frying pan to soak up the rich bologna juices. Wine being absolutely de rigueur with cheese, I chose a 1974 Muscatel, flavored with a maraschino cherry, and afterwards cleared my palate with three pickled martini onions.

It was time for the fruit. I chose a Del Monte tinned pear, which, regrettably, slipped from the spoon and fell on the floor, necessitating its being blotted with a paper towel to remove cat hairs. To compensate for the resulting loss of pear syrup, I dipped it lightly in hot-dog relish, which created a unique flavor.

With the pear I drank two shots of Gilbey's 1975 and one shot of Wolf-schmidt vodka (non-vintage), the Gilbey's having been exhausted.

At last it was time for the dish the entire meal had been building toward—dessert. With a paring knife, I ripped into a fresh package of Oreos, produced a bowl of My-T-Fine chocolate pudding which had been coagulating in the refrigerator for days and, using a potato masher, crushed a dozen Oreos into the pudding. It was immense.

Between mouthfuls, I sipped a tall, bubbling tumbler of cool Bromo-Seltzer, and finished with six ounces of Maalox. It couldn't have been better.

How to Argue Effectively
DAVE BARRY—*The Local Daily News*—1981

I argue very well. Ask any of my remaining friends. I can win an argument on any topic, against any opponent. People know this and steer clear of me at parties. Often, as a sign of their great respect, they don't even invite me. You too can win arguments. Simply follow these rules:

DRINK LIQUOR
Suppose you are at a party and some hotshot intellectual is expounding on the economy of Peru, a subject you know nothing about. If you're drinking some health-fanatic drink like grapefruit juice, you'll hang back, afraid to display your ignorance. But if you drink several large martinis, you'll discover you have strong views about the Peruvian economy. You'll be a wealth of information. You'll argue forcefully, offering searing insights and possibly upsetting furniture. People will be impressed. Some may leave the room.

MAKE THINGS UP
Suppose, in the Peruvian economy argument, you are trying to prove that Peruvians are underpaid, a position you base solely on the fact that you are underpaid, and you'll be damned if you're going to let a bunch of Peruvians be better off. Don't say: "I think Peruvians are underpaid." Say instead: "The average Peruvian's salary in 1981 dollars adjusted for the revised tax base is $1,452.81 per annum, which is $836.07 below the mean gross poverty level."

NOTE: Always make up exact figures. If an opponent asks you where you got your information, make that up too. Say: "This information comes from Dr. Hovel T. Moon's study for the Buford Commission published on May 9, 1982. Didn't you read it?" Say this in the same tone of voice you would use to say, "You left your soiled underwear in my bathroom."

USE MEANINGLESS BUT WEIGHTY-SOUNDING WORDS AND PHRASES
Memorize this list:
Let me put it this way
In terms of
Vis-à-vis
Per se
As it were
Qua
So to speak
You should also memorize some Latin abbreviations such as "Q.E.D.," "e.g.," and "i.e." These are all short for "I speak Latin, and you don't." Here's how to use these words and phrases. Suppose you want to say, "Peruvians would like to order appetizers more often, but they don't have enough money." You never win arguments talking like that. But you WILL win if you say, "Let me put it this way. In terms of appetizers vis-à-vis Peruvians qua Peruvians, they would like to order them more often, so to speak, but they do not have enough money per se, as it were. Q.E.D." Only a fool would challenge that statement.

USE SNAPPY AND IRRELEVANT COMEBACKS
You need an arsenal of all-purpose irrelevant phrases to fire back at your opponents when they make valid points. The best are:
You're begging the question.
You're being defensive.
Don't compare apples to oranges.
What are your parameters?
This last one is especially valuable. Nobody (other than engineers and policy wonks) has the vaguest idea what "parameters" means. Here's how to use your comebacks:
You say: "As Abraham Lincoln said in 1873 . . ." "Your opponent says: "Lincoln died in 1865." "You say: "You're begging the question."
You say: "Liberians, like most Asians . . ." Your opponent says: "Liberia is in Africa." You say: "You're being defensive."

COMPARE YOUR OPPONENT TO ADOLF HITLER
This is your heavy artillery, for when your opponent is obviously right and you are spectacularly wrong. Bring Hitler up subtly. Say, "That sounds suspiciously like something Adolf Hitler might say" or "You certainly do remind me of Adolf Hitler."

So that's it. You now know how to out-argue anybody. Do not try to pull any of this on people who generally carry weapons.

Spring Before Swine
RUSSELL BAKER—*New York Times*—2/6/1985

Because of all the morbid interest in the press these days, I am often asked what is the most disagreeable aspect of the journalist's trade. At one time my answer would have been "covering the Thanksgiving Day parade," a chore that can forever maim the spirit of any person not easily moved to superlatives by vast quantities of inflated rubber.

Later I amended this judgment after being sent to work in Washington. There the journalistic code required "objectivity," which forbade a reporter to write of, say, Senator Blattis: "Lying as usual, Senator Blattis declared today . . ."

This obligation to assist in dignifying inferior men was even more dispiriting than the obligation to gush with enthusiasm for rubber floats. It made you feel inhuman, as though you were nothing more than a megaphone for the convenience of frauds.

Last Saturday I again had occasion to revise my opinion of the horrors of the journalist's life. That day, bedridden and near death of a flu that left me too weak to resist, I was subjected by insensitive kin to a day of television that my fevered brain was powerless to block from its memory bank. It was Groundhog Day.

All day long it was Groundhog Day. Far into the night—Groundhog Day. No television news outlet had overlooked the great story. Time and again, I heard it repeated: Groundhog Day had been among us. Consequences would ensue.

Here I become foggy about details. Somewhere in someone's otherwise inoffensive town a groundhog had either cast a shadow or not—that is, the sun was either shining or not—and as a result there would or would not be six weeks of winter to be tolerated before spring arrived.

Even now, with my fever down to a comparatively sensible 105 degrees, I cannot remember how the groundhog's shadow influences meteorological developments. Does shadow-casting sunlight mean prolonged winter, or is it the other way around, and who cares anyhow, except the American press? (You can't blame television for this groundhog idiocy; our TV brethren are simply carrying on a story created by the print business.)

I was 6 years old when I first heard of Groundhog Day. An uncle who was ill at ease with children, but was trying hard to be a good fellow, told me about it. Even at the gullible age of 6, I could tell the whole business was nonsense. I could tell that my uncle thought it was nonsense, too.

Why was this sensible man—a man sensible enough to be ill at ease with children—telling me this nonsense? I wondered. I have since concluded that he was telling me because he had read about it in a newspaper and probably thought it was a piece of American folklore that uncles ought to pass down to future generations, even if it was nothing but rot.

I conclude as much because years later I myself was tempted to tell a nephew the same thing when he asked why they interrupted "Howdy Doody" for a bulletin about a groundhog's shadow. "This is American folklore, and I ought to lay it on the kid," I said to myself, but didn't since, being ill at ease with children, I didn't want him to think I was also an imbecile.

While suffering the Groundhog Day onslaught Saturday, I realized I had finally discovered the most disagreeable aspect of the journalist's trade: Groundhog Day. Every year, in blind obedience to some antique creed about what constitutes news, poor wretched journalists must trudge off to do the groundhog-shadow story and miserable defeated editors must display it on their pages and tubes in utter indifference to sensible suspicion that the world could not care less.

The groundhog story survives because the unthinking assumption that makes it a cute and amusing story is rarely challenged by an editor or reporter willing to say that the story is tiresome, foolish and trite.

Unfortunately, it is not only in tolerating the harmless foolishness of the groundhog story that the press shows mental fatigue. A more serious "groundhog" story is the annual Washington tale of the making of the Pentagon budget, which is invariably reported as a struggle among the Titans for the soul of the nation and the safety of all humanity. Just as invariably, the Pentagon obtains almost precisely the amount everyone had always known it would get long before the press gave its annual forecast of titanic struggle.

We are now sitting through the same old story again with plenty of cute feature stuff about unyielding Secretary Weinberger and bad blood between Republican Senate and White House. Get excited about that and you'll thrill to anything. In six weeks we'll have spring; in six months the Pentagon will have what it wants. So the world turns and we feed on warmed-over hash.

How to Keep the IRS from Finding Out You're Lying
DAVE BARRY—*Miami Herald*—2/27/1987

Each year at this time (11:30) we present helpful tips for preparing your federal income-tax return so you can obtain the maximum possible financial benefits combined with the minimum possible prison term. As usual, we wish to caution you that these helpful tips are not necessarily accurate or true or representative of human brainwave activity. These tips are here solely for the purpose of taking up space in the newspaper, similar to editorials, and before you attempt any of these maneuvers yourself, you should consult a trained accountant.

That's what we do. We consult with our accountant, Evan, every year at tax time, and he always tells us: "Dammit, you have to keep 'complete financial records.' These are 'not' complete financial records. These are expired service warranties from various fondue sets."

Evan is constantly nitpicking like this, but we keep him as our accountant, anyway, because he has attractive picture books in his office that you can look at while he attempts to imagine what your actual incomes and expenses might have been if you had thought to write them down. Also, he invited us to his wedding, and when the minister asked him if he would love and cherish his wife-to-be, Kathy, who works with him, he answered, right in front of the audience, and this a true quote: "Only until the end of tax season."

Paying our income taxes is especially important this year, because the government needs all the money it can get to combat that darned pesky federal budget deficit, which in 1987 will zzzzzzzzzzzzzzzz

Whoops! Sorry! It's just that the deficit has grown so large and boring that even we journalists can't write about it without our faces crashing down onto our word processors. The same thing happens when we try to write about the tragic situation over there in the war-torn Middle Easzzzzzzzzzzzzzzzzzzzzzzz

Back to tax tips. By now, you should have received your 1986 tax form in the mail from the Internal Revenue Service ("Your IRS: Working to Put You in Jail").

As in past years, my No. 1 tax-preparation tip is: "Never use round numbers for deductible expenses, because it will be obvious you're lying." To quote from Official IRS Information Pamphlet Number 2893-C, "How to Fill Out Your Tax Forms So You Don't Get Caught": "Taxpayers should try to make up numbers that look like they might be real, such as '$1,407.62,' or even '$3,219.83.'"

This is important, taxpayers. If you write a number like "$500," you might just as well add: "Go ahead and audit me, scuzzballs!" This is how they got mobster Al Capone, who put down, under Business Expenses, "Cement: $100,000." If he had put: "Cement: $100,000.79," they probably would never have nailed him (except that he also made the common taxpayer error of listing his occupation as "mobster").

Common taxpayer question: Well, what if you really "do" have a legitimate tax-deductible expense that by sheer random chance happens to be $500?

Answer: You should put a little explanatory note in the margin stating: "Really! I'm not lying! On this one!"

In the unlikely event that, despite following these tax tips, you "are" called in for an audit, do not become needlessly alarmed. Remember: The people who work for the IRS are just human beings like yourself, with normal families and homes and kitchens where they like to put live chipmunks into their Veg-O-Matics.

"Just kidding," IRS workers! You know how much you love to kid around! Please give me back my child!

Seriously, a tax audit is not the end of the world. All that happens is, you take your financial records to the IRS office, and they put you into a tank filled with giant stinging leeches. Many taxpayers are pleasantly surprised to find that they die within hours.

Still, it's probably better to avoid an audit altogether by obeying the tax law to the maximum extent you can, considering that neither you nor anybody else has ever actually seen it. And to help you get fired up, this year the IRS plans to produce a series of motivational TV commercials called "Taxpayers in Action," patterned after the highly successful armed-forces recruitment commercials that show young armed-forces personnel having fun helicopter adventures and learning valuable career skills, but never being shot at or getting mandatory comical haircuts or standing in the rain at 4:30 a.m. getting yelled at by angry men with no foreheads.

Similarly, the "Taxpayers in Action" commercials will stress the positive side of taxpaying, showing, for example, a group of happy taxpayers dancing around and triumphantly giving each other the "high-five" handshake after successfully getting through on the convenient IRS taxpayer assistance telephone hot line in less than 200 tries.

So the government has done its part, and now we taxpayers should do ours, by following the many helpful tips that have appeared in this column, thanks to all the research that I did, which caused me to drive 352,792.4 miles and eat innumerable business-related lunches.

Pithy into the Wind
DAVE BARRY—*Miami Herald*—3/29/1987

The burgeoning Iran-contra scandal is truly an issue about which we, as a nation, need to concern ourselves, because

(Secret Note To Readers: Not really! The hell with the Iran-contra affair! Let it burgeon! I'm just trying to win a journalism prize, here. Don't tell anybody! I'll explain later. Shhhh.)

when we look at the Iran-contra scandal, and for that matter the mounting national health-care crisis, we can see that these are, in total, two issues, each requiring a number of paragraphs in which we will comment, in hopes that

(. . . we can win a journalism prize. Ideally a Pulitzer. That's the object, in journalism. At certain times each year, we journalists do almost nothing except apply for the Pulitzers and several dozen other major prizes. During these times you could walk right into most newsrooms and commit a multiple ax murder naked, and it wouldn't get reported in the paper, because the reporters and editors would all be too busy filling out prize applications. "Hey!" they'd yell at you. "Watch it! You're getting blood on my application!")

we can possibly, through carefully analyzing these important issues—the Iran-contra scandal, the mounting national health-care crisis, and (while we are at it), the federal budget deficit—through analyzing these issues and mulling them over and fretting about them and chewing on them until we have reduced them to soft, spit-covered gobs of information that you, the readers, can

(. . . pretty much ignore. It's OK! Don't be ashamed! We here in journalism are fully aware that most of you skip right over stories that look like they might involve major issues, which you can identify because they always have incomprehensible headlines like "House Parley Panel Links Nato Tax Hike to Hondurans in Syrian Arms Deal." Sometimes we'll do a whole series with more total words than the *Brothers Karamazov* and headlines like: "The World Mulch Crisis: A Time to Act." You readers don't bother to wade through these stories, and you feel vaguely guilty about this. Which is stupid. You're not supposed to read them. We journalists don't read them. We use modern computers to generate them solely for the purpose of entering them for journalism prizes. We're thinking about putting the following helpful advisory over them: "Caution! Journalism Prize Entry! Do Not Read!")

gain, through a better understanding of these very important issues—the Iran-contra scandal; the health-care crisis (which as you may be aware is both national AND mounting); the federal budget deficit; and yes, let's come right out and say it, the Strategic Defense Initiative—you readers can gain a better understanding of them, and thus we might come to an enhanced awareness of what they may or may not mean in terms of

(. . . whether or not I can win a Pulitzer Prize. That's the one I'm gunning for. You get $1,000 cash, plus all the job offers the mailperson can carry. Unfortunately, the only category I'd be eligible for is called "Distinguished Social Commentary," which is a real problem, because of the kinds of issues I generally write about. "This isn't Distinguished Social Commentary!" the Pulitzer judges would say. "This is about goat boogers!" So today I'm trying to class up my act a little by writing about prize-winning issues. OK? Sorry.)

how we, as a nation, can, through a deeper realization of the significance of these four vital issues—health care in Iran, the strategic federal deficit, mounting the contras, and one other one which slips my mind at the moment, although I think it's the one that's burgeoning—how we can, as a nation, through Distinguished Social Commentary such as this, gain the kind of perspective and foresight required to understand

(. . . a guy like noted conservative columnist George Will. You see him, on all those TV shows where he is always commenting on world events in that snotty smartass way of his, with his lips pursed together like he just accidentally licked the plumbing in a bus-station restroom, and you quite naturally say to yourself, as millions have before you: "Why doesn't somebody just take this little dweeb and stick his bow tie up his nose? Huh?" And the answer is: Because a long time ago, for reasons nobody remembers anymore, George Will won a Pulitzer Prize. And now he gets to be famous and rich and respected for ever and ever. That's all I want! Is that so much to ask?!)

what we, and I am talking about we as a nation, need to have in order to deeply understand all the issues listed somewhere earlier in this column. And although I am only one person, one lone Distinguished Social Commentator crying in the wilderness, without so much as a bow tie, I am nevertheless committed to doing whatever I can to deepen and widen and broaden and lengthen the national understanding of these issues in any way that I can, and that includes sharing the $1,000 with the judges.

The Hellfire Club
HUNTER S. THOMPSON—*San Francisco Examiner*—2/22/1988

How long, O Lord, how long? Are these TV preachers *all* degenerates? Are they wallowing and whooping with harlots whenever they're not on camera? Are they *all* thieves and charlatans and whoremongers?

Another of the shameless buggers got whacked last week. Jimmy Swaggart, a 52-year-old howler from Baton Rouge known in some quarters as "the Mick Jagger of TV evangelism," got nailed in a nasty little sting operation down in New Orleans and was forced to resign his $145 million-a-year ministry for the same kind of sex crimes that his old rival Jim Bakker got busted for last year.

There were those, in fact, who said it was Swaggart himself who hatched the plot to disgrace Bakker and have him labeled for life as a brutal sodomite and a flagrant embezzler with a dope fiend for a wife and the IRS for a new partner, instead of Jesus.

Then Swaggart, crazed by hubris, tried to take out yet another of his rivals—Preacher Gorman from New Orleans—by calling him a sot, a pervert and a dangerous child molester who couldn't help himself.

So it was Gorman who turned up, last week, in possession of a set of malicious photographs of Big Jim slinking into one of those "third-rate romance, low-rent rendez-vous"-style motels with a known prostitute, or at least a woman of ill repute.

It reminded a lot of people of the naked lunacy that blew Gary Hart out of the '88 presidential race.

It was shame, they said. But you know how these people are. . . . The semen finally backs up into the brain; the eyes get too bright, and the synapses start fusing into each other. Instead of secret love-nests, they begin strutting into the Holiday Inn and going to orgies on the outskirts of town. . . .

Not much has changed with these powermongers since Caligula's time. Sex and power have a long history of feeding on each other. In 18th-century England, the king and half his ministers were involved in a whole network of strange and violent sex clubs, whipping parlors and half-secret cults that embraced everything from Satanism and human sacrifice to flagrant white slavery and public bestiality.

In the early years of the century, there were a large number of "Rakes' Clubs" in London, where the high point of most evenings was hitting the streets in a drunken, brainless frenzy and raping, beating and maiming every human being they could get their hands on.

Bargo Partridge in his classic *History of Orgies* said, "The Bucks and Gallants roamed the streets terrifying the elderly, beating up the watch [police], breaking windows, committing rape and sometimes even murder. Young girls were stood on their heads in the gutter, and elderly ladies popped into barrels and sent rolling down hills. . . . There were clubs called the Mohawks and the Man-Killers, which tried to out-do each other in the hideous game called 'tipping the Lion.' This consisted in crushing the nose, and simultaneously gouging out the eyes of the victims unfortunate enough to be waylaid by them. They also carried a piece of apparatus for distending mouths and slitting ears."

These were not *lower class* thugs, as in *Clockwork Orange*, but the sons of the aristocracy. There was no law for them. Only the rich and powerful were allowed to carry swords or ride horses—which put the poor at a certain disadvantage when gangs of rich drunkards swooped down on them in some dim-lit street after midnight. . . .

That was the Golden Age of what they used to call "gentlemen's clubs" in London. . . . But it couldn't last. There were too many losers wandering around with their noses crushed, their eyes gouged out and their mouths so stretched that they could take in a whole cantaloupe and still make idle conversation in a pub. Public opinion turned on the "wild boys," and their clubs were banished.

By the second half of the century, there was a whole new focus for the gentlemen's clubs—the worship of sex and extravagant public decadence. This was the time of the infamous Hellfire Club, which included among its inner circle the Prince of Wales, the Lord Mayor of London, Benjamin Franklin, the crazed Earl of Sandwich, the monstrous Earl of Bute, then prime minister of England.

These people didn't fool around. They raised the orgy to an art form unknown since Caligula or even the fiendish Mongol hordes of Genghis Khan, who begat a long line of rapists and treacherous sex maniacs who were said to lament the fact that the human body had so few orifices to penetrate that they were forced to create new ones with their own daggers in order that the whole clan could swarm on a victim at once.

Dilettantes like Hart, Bakker and Swaggart would have been turned away at the door of the Hellfire Club, rejected as humorless churls and cheap masturbators. . . . Their only "crimes," after all, have involved low rumors and innuendo and being seen in public with sluts and half-naked bimbos.

The Earl of Sandwich would have taken great pride in being accused of these things. He was so constantly involved in orgies that he had little time for his duties, which included running the British Navy and entertaining the Empire on five oceans. . . . And one of his main accomplishments during that time—in addition to inventing the sandwich—was to sell off the Hawaiian Islands, which cost England control of the whole Pacific Ocean for the next 200 years.

King George III, meanwhile, was so crazed with his own warped fantasies that he had little time to deal with a nasty little colonial insurrection that would come to be called the "American Revolution."

These were no *amateur* degenerates, like the ones we sneer at today. They put the whole British Empire on the road to ruin and thought nothing of it—nor cared, for that matter. . . . When the famous English navigator, Capt. Cook, sent word back to London that he had Hawaii and all of Polynesia in the palm of his hand—if only Sandwich would authorize a new mast for his crippled flagship—the earl ignored the request. A few weeks later, Capt. Cook was murdered by angry natives—but Sandwich never noticed.

So much for Empire. These boys liked their orgies, and *nothing* was going to interfere. These were giants. They had standards—not like these whimpering mashers who keep fouling our headlines today.

Maybe Alphonse Karr was wrong.

You're Never Too Young to Aim High
CARL HIAASEN—*Miami Herald*—8/5/1988

(A true news item: The National Rifle Association has offered to help Florida schools teach special courses in gun education, beginning as early as kindergarten.)

Sit down, boys and girls.

For today's NRA lesson, we're going to show you how to help Mommy and Daddy select the best handgun for your family. Yes, Billy?

"What about the snub-nosed Ruger, Mr. Rogers?"

Well, Billy, the Ruger Speed-Six Magnum is a nifty little weapon. I like it because it comes with a rubber combat stock instead of a walnut grip. Can any of you children tell me the disadvantages of a wooden stock on a small gun?

"It's a recoil control problem, Mr. Rogers."

You're exactly right, Maria. If Daddy and Mommy insist on buying one of these snubbie Magnums, make sure they trade the walnut grip for neoprene. They'll be amazed at the difference.

And, kids, while we're on the subject, who can tell me which Magnum bullet carries the most stopping power against a human target? Andrea?

"Um, I think it's the 110-grain factory load, Mr. Rogers."

No, Andrea, that's wrong. Remember last week's pop quiz on hollow points? Bobby, you've got your hand up.

"Yeah, Mr. Rogers. The 125-grain jacketed Magnum bullet has the most stop-ping power."

Good. But don't forget, boys and girls, there's one serious problem with the 125-grainers. Can you remember what it is? All together:

"MUZZLE FLASH, MR. ROGERS!"

That's right, kids. And why is muzzle flash so dangerous?

"BECAUSE MOST SHOOT-OUTS HAPPEN AT NIGHT!"

Correct. A white muzzle flash can blind you in the middle of a firefight, and we can't have that, can we?

"NO, MR. ROGERS."

Getting back to personal weapons, some of your mommies and daddies prob-ably prefer something more substantial to hide in the nightstand. Jimmy, take your thumb out of your mouth and tell me about the Beretta 92-F.

"Gee, Mr. Rogers, I kind of like the 92-F. I mean it's OK, for a 9mm."

Jimmy, I'm very disappointed. Obviously, you weren't paying attention yesterday when we talked about the repeated slide failures being experienced with the 92-F by U.S. armed forces personnel. Until more testing is done, Mommy and Daddy would be better off with the standard Model 84, a .380 auto. What is it now, Jimmy?

"The Model 84 only holds 13 bullets, Mr. Rogers. My daddy says he needs at least fifteen."

Fine, Mr. Smartypants, stick with the 92-F. Only I suggest you tell your fa-ther to avoid using high-pressure loads and replace the slide mechanism every 3,000 rounds. Otherwise, he'll be picking hot shells out of his nostrils.

"Mr. Rogers, can we play with our crayons now?"

Yes, after lunch we'll practice drawing more bank-robber silhouettes. Only this time, no big red noses. Andrea?

"Mr. Rogers, was it Mark David Chapman or John Hinckley who used a Charter Arms .38?"

Oh no, you don't—that one's going to be on Monday's quiz. Look it up your-self. Bobby, you've got a question?

"Yeah, my dad wanted to know if he could borrow your MAC-10 converter kit this weekend."

I don't see why not. Be sure to remind him that he wouldn't even need a converter kit if those liberal wimps in Congress hadn't banned the sale of fully automatic machine guns a few years ago. By the way, you kids are still taking those petitions door-to-door, I hope.

"YES, MR. ROGERS!"

Great. Now, boys and girls, we all know what time it is.

"Oh no, not the pledge again, Mr. Rogers."

That's right. Everybody stand and repeat: The only way . . .

"THE ONLY WAY . . ."

. . . you'll take my gun . . .

". . . YOU'LL TAKE MY GUN . . ."

. . . is to pry it from my cold dead fingers.

"Aw, come on, Mr. Rogers. Do we have to?"

Say it!

". . . IS TO PRY IT FROM MY COLD DEAD FINGERS."

Very good, children. Now let's all take a little nap before target practice.

I Ate Breakfast and Lived

LEWIS GRIZZARD—*Atlanta Journal-Constitution*—6/12/1991

There has been a lot of discussion, not to mention a *Time* cover, recently regarding the fact there's not much left we can eat without taking serious health risks.

Red meat causes cancer. Chicken and pork aren't safe. Seafood isn't inspected well enough. Everything that's good contains too much cholesterol.

Avoid caffeine, sugar, sodium, butter, anything that's fried, exotic sauces (I presume gravy comes under that) and never eat white bread.

Basically, that leaves broccoli as the only thing left to eat, and I'll be damned if I'm going to spend the rest of my life eating only what looks like the Jolly Green Giant's brain stem and has all the taste of a house plant.

I think a lot of this comes from some doctors and researchers who have a lot of free time on their hands. When I get free time, I go play golf. When some doctors and researchers have time to spare, they sit around and think of ways to make our lives less enjoyable.

Having always been something of a rebel (I never bought a leisure suit back in the '70s), I decided recently to test these new nutritional theories and go out and have a meal of everything that is bad for you and see if it, indeed, killed me.

I went to the Waffle House for breakfast. I love the Waffle House.

The food is consistent, they don't serve anything you can't pronounce, and the grease in the air cuts down on the amount of mousse I must put in my hair to keep my *GQ* look.

Here's what I ordered: Steak and eggs. One T-bone steak, cooked medium well, and two eggs, sunnyside up. I also had hash browns and white toast, heavily buttered. I had a cup of coffee—leaded—as I awaited my meal. I had a Coke —The Real Thing—with it.

The waitress, Margie, said to me, "I'll be glad to bring your order, but first you'll have to sign a release."

"A what?"

"A release saying if you eat all this and drop dead in the parking lot, we can't be held liable."

I signed the release.

The meal came.

It was swimming in grease and butter. There was enough cholesterol there to clog up the arteries of four grown elephants, if there are four grown elephants left.

I ate it anyway. Ate the whole thing.

That was ten days ago. I still feel fine.

I know what you're saying, "Well, just having one meal like that won't hurt you."

That's not the point. The point is, you've got to take a stand somewhere. If we don't say to health officials, "Enough is enough," they'll keep digging until they take all our pleasures away, Waffle Houses all over the country will be forced to close, and everybody will become vegetarians, and every vegetarian I ever met was pale, wimpish and without humor.

Not only that, but all those cows and pigs and chickens we used to eat will be running all over the place, becoming a nuisance to traffic and leaving a lot of stuff on the sidewalk we'll be stepping in.

To be perfectly honest about it, I'd rather give up a few extra years eating what I please than to live to be a miserable 106-year-old vegetarian who is always getting a lot of smelly stuff on his shoes.

All the Waffle House waitresses watched me as I walked into the parking lot after my meal, incidentally. When I didn't drop dead, they cheered.

Pardon My French
TONY KORNHEISER—*Washington Post*—2/26/1995

Je suis scandalise.

(I am outraged.)

The French are accusing us of spying on them.

Now let's get this straight. We marched in and liberated them from the clutches of Satan. In return, they gave us, like, eels on toast. And now they are accusing us of spying on them?

Hey, listen. We should be free to go over there and help ourselves to whatever we want. Not that there's much to take. Truffles? A fungus snuffled out of the ground by pigs?

Anyway, I don't want to get into gratuitous French-bashing. After all, the French have given the world many important people, including Marie Curie and, um, hang on a minute. There's Marie, definitely. She was one important chemistry babe. And . . . Charles de Gaulle! He is famous for signing the "letters of transit" in *Casablanca*. Isn't it funny how we keep coming back to the Nazis?

But I digress.

So anyway the ingrates, I mean the French, want to boot five Americans out of France on the grounds that we have been stealing their technological secrets. Like what, how to make a car that looks like a toaster? Have you driven a Citroen lately? They've actually put in a new option for a "crumb disposer."

Remember Renault's Le Car, which was constantly in Le Repair Shop?

How good can their technology be? It certainly hasn't helped them win any wars. French military technology, now there's an oxymoron. What's the first thing they teach in French war college, how to say "I surrender" in German?

But I digress.

I will say this for the French: They are not pikers. They just spent $20 million building a fabulous state-of-the-art yacht for the America's Cup. The keel fell off. You know what that is like, building a boat and the keel falls off? You know how pathetic that is? That is like building a bridge but accidentally making it out of pasta.

It is so typically French to purse their lips and assume that their stuff is so good that we'd want to steal it. We've already got everything good they make. (It was over for the French the day you could buy a Croissanwich at Burger King.)

Bread. Sauce. Wine. Perfume.

Am I leaving anything out?

Certainly not soap.

Please don't tell me about French culture.

The Singing Nun. I rest my case.

I know their movies were good at one time. But like Brigitte Bardot chaining herself to a flock of sheep, they have grown old and tiresome. Every year at Cannes they enter a film that reeks like Limburger and loses to something with Wesley Snipes. The French haven't made a decent movie in years, and of course they blame us for cheapening the art form, which is preposterous considering that they . . . no, I won't even mention Jerry Lewis.

French movies generally feature a young woman running around in her underpants. Sometimes she's in a forest; sometimes in a field of day lilies; sometimes she's a stewardess on the Concorde. All the adults in the movie are smoking Gauloises in that snotty way where they look as if they're pinching a derriere, and fretting about whether the Beaujolais nouveau tastes impish enough. It's quite existential. It's all mood and look. It's called film noir. The literal translation of film noir is: Get me out of this theater before I flambé myself until mort.

Their language is so prissy-sounding that you could be challenging someone to a street corner fight and it would sound like an Elizabeth Barrett Browning sonnet. What other language would have a wine named Pouilly Fuisse? Try bellying up to a bar in Detroit and ordering three fingers of that.

The French will eat anything that's cooked in butter. You could sautee a Chiclet in butter and slap some bearnaise sauce on it, and half of Paris would line up. And they're big on glands. They love glands. If it once was in a body and squirted out goo, they love it.

"Oooh, what ees thees?"

"It's the anal gland of a ferret."

"C'est magnifique."

Possibly I am sounding somewhat embittered. You would be embittered too if you stormed the beach at Normandy, armed only with an M-16 and a pack of unfiltered Luckies, and a belly full of churning guts . . .

Tony, you were no closer to Normandy than you are to Cyd Charisse's daughter, Myrna, who lives in Istanbul.

Well, true.

How can you condemn an entire noble nation of people so cavalierly?

I'll tell you how. When I was in high school, we had a French exchange student named Chris. (Which he pronounced Kweeeees.) He had a goatee that made him look like Maynard G. Krebs. He wore a beret. He couldn't play a single American sport. He threw like a girl. He never participated in guy talk, wherein we all sat around and lied about all the thousands of girls we were boinking. I always had total contempt for Chris. But when I went to my 10-year high school reunion, I got to chatting with the women and discovered that half of them had slept with Chris, including many of the ones who wouldn't sleep with me.

The Gaul of that guy!

Why Not the Worst?
GENE WEINGARTEN—*Washington Post*—12/2/2001

My little puddle jumper begins its descent into Elko, a charmless city of 20,000 in the northern Nevada desert. Eighteen seats, all filled. This is not because Elko is a hot tourist attraction; it is because almost everyone else onboard belongs to a mariachi band. These guys have identical shiny blue suits and shiny blue shirts and shiny blue ties and shiny blue-black hair, like Rex Morgan in the comics, and they seem embarrassed to have accepted a gig in a place as tacky as Elko.

Compared with my final destination, Elko is Florence during the Italian Renaissance.

When I tell the Elko rental car agent where I am headed, she laughs. Elkonians, who proudly sponsor a yearly civic event called the "Man-Mule Race," consider their neighbor 70 miles west to be an absolute clodhoppy riot.

"Don't sneeze," snorts the rental car woman, "or you'll miss it."

Yeah, I know. I went to Battle Mountain five weeks before, to see if it was dreadful enough to be anointed, officially, "The Armpit of America." I was exorbitantly convinced.

That first visit was in late August. This second one is in early October. In the interim, Everything Changed. With the nation united in mourning and at war, with the Stars and Stripes aflutter in places large and small, slick and hicky, the idea of poking fun at any one part of us became a great deal less funny. The zeitgeist had shifted. Snide was out.

I had to go back, to rethink things.

The road to Battle Mountain is flatter than any cliché—even pancakes have a certain doughy topology. On this route, there is nothing. No curves. No trees. It is desert, but it is lacking any desert-type beauty. No cacti. No tumbleweeds. None of those spooky cow skulls. The only flora consists of nondescript scrub that resembles acre upon acre of toilet brushes buried to the hilt.

You know you have arrived at Battle Mountain because the town has marked its identity on a nearby hill in enormous letters fashioned from whitewashed rock.

I have returned to this place to find in it not America's armpit, but America's heart. I am here to mine the good in it, to tell the world that Battle Mountain doesn't stink. That is my new challenge.

I hang a right off the highway at the base of the hill, which proudly proclaims, in giant letters:

BM

Man. This is not going to be easy.

Take a small town, remove any trace of history, character, or charm. Allow nothing with any redeeming qualities within city limits—this includes food, motel beds, service personnel. Then place this pathetic assemblage of ghastly buildings and nasty people on a freeway in the midst of a harsh, uninviting wilderness, far enough from the nearest city to be inconvenient, but not so far for it to develop a character of its own. You now have created Battle Mountain, Nevada.

The letter was signed by Seattle resident Peter Hartikka, one of 220 people who mailed in their nominations for the nation's foulest place. I had invited these letters in my humor column after discovering on the Web a dismayingly indiscriminate use of the term "Armpit of America." Hundreds of people were describing dozens of locations they happened to dislike. It seemed an unacceptable anarchy of scorn.

The nominations were, literally, all over the map. There were predictable urban cesspools (East St. Louis, Ill.; Elizabeth, N.J.). There were places of idiotic purpose (Branson, Mo.; Las Vegas, Nev.). There were places of legendary lack of class (Buffalo, N.Y.; Fargo, N.D.).

The winnowing proved easy. Several nominees bit the dust because they are proximate to someplace immeasurably better. Gary, Ind., and Camden, N.J., two of the nation's least appealing locales, won reprieves because of their nearness to Chicago and Philadelphia. The armpit must smother. It can permit no escape.

Likewise, many promising candidates succumbed to personal knowledge or basic research. Terre Haute, Ind., a bland and sullen city popular with the KKK, offers too many cultural opportunities to make the cut. Wilkes-Barre, Pa., may be awful, but next-door neighbor Scranton is awfuler, and Scranton has a certain likable pugnacity that comes from knowing you are famously crummy and not giving two hoots. The otherwise leprous Bridgeport, Conn., was spared because it produced my wife. (The winnowing was not entirely without bias.)

Butte, Mont., may have surrendered its soul and much of its natural beauty to rapacious mining interests, and its citizenry may be congenitally inhospitable, and the city may resemble a suppurating chancre sore and smell like the sulfurous Stygian River of Woe, but . . . actually, there is no but about Butte. Research confirmed its foulness and it might well have become The Armpit had it not been blown out by the competition.

There is a maxim in journalism that some stories are just too good to check out. What that means is that the juiciest of tips, when subjected to research, tend to desiccate and crumble. I feared this with Battle Mountain, but after two days of research, I was ablubber in juice.

The town began as a lie. Prospector George Tannihill christened it in 1866 as a mining district, saying he chose the name to commemorate the fierce battle he and 23 settlers led by a Capt. Pierson had heroically won against marauding Indians there in 1857. Nevada historians have since poked a few holes in this story: There appears never to have been a Capt. Pierson, or 23 settlers, or any attacking Indians, or a battle, or pioneer heroism, or, for that matter, a mountain. (There does appear to have been a year "1857.")

According to David Toll's *The Complete Nevada Traveler*, the Battle Mountain area has two famous alumni. The first was W. J. Forbes, the Mencken of the Southwest. His was a brilliant if quixotic journalistic march across California, Nevada and Utah, culminating in the creation of a Battle Mountain newspaper named *Measure for Measure* in 1873. Unfortunately, it was designed to appeal to people who liked to read and knew how to think. When it failed, Forbes spiraled into depression and drink. As summarized half a century later by Carson City journalist Sam Davis: "A friend found [Forbes] stiff and cold across his shabby bed. He had fought a fight against all odds all his life, was one of the brightest geniuses the coast had ever seen, but he . . . lived in communities where his mental brightness was more envied than appreciated."

Battle Mountain, where genius comes to die.

But no Battle Mountaineer past or present reached the level of fame attained by Civil War Gen. James H. Ledlie, who retired to the area after the war, and even has a railroad siding named after him. Ledlie's name actually found its way onto the lips of a president of the United States, and in a startling superlative. Ulysses S. Grant himself called Gen. Ledlie "the greatest coward of the Civil War."

A notorious gambler and drooling drunk, Ledlie had been in command of a division of Union soldiers in 1864 when a group of Pennsylvania coal miners boldly dug a tunnel underneath Confederate lines protecting Petersburg, Va., packed it with explosives and blew it up. Ledlie's troops were to have stormed the confused enemy, but the general was soused in his bunker and refused to come out. His men mounted the attack in leaderless disarray, and were slaughtered like rabbits.

Battle Mountain was built as a mining town, and still survives as one, but just barely. Gold prices have lately been low, and the local mines have been cutting back. The population has recently sunk to just under 4,000. Without money from mining, there isn't much to recommend it. Even God discourages visitors: In the summer, Battle Mountain temperatures hit 100 by day and plummet to 45 at night. Winters typically see a month or more at sub-zero.

It is valuable to research a town through published material; it is far more valuable to talk to people who know it well. I found that the surest way to get a spirited defense of a place was by phoning a reporter who works there. Journalists may be notorious for their negativity, but when *The Washington Post* calls to say it is thinking of identifying as the Armpit of America the city or town in which your career is unspooling, negativity often yields nicely to sputtering indignation. At least, that was the way it usually worked.

I telephoned Lorrie Baumann, editor of the *Battle Mountain Bugle*, and told her my idea.

"The Armpit of America?" she said.

"That's sort of the, um, concept."

Silence.

"Sounds about right," she said.

But it's a such a big country, I said, with so many crappy places. How could I be sure this was the 'pit?

Lorrie's response was as dry as a desert full of toilet brushes.

"I think a quick drive around downtown will answer any questions that might be lingering in your mind."

I ordered up a plane ticket.

Still, I had one more call. The tough one. I couldn't very well arrive unannounced.

Sharlene "Shar" Peterson is the executive director of the Battle Mountain Chamber of Commerce. She told me a little about the town, and then I told her what I was proposing to do.

She laughed, then didn't say much of anything for the longest time.

The Battle Mountain Chamber of Commerce was thinking.

Shar?

"Well, I mean, who wants to be called an armpit? But, you know . . ."

I sensed where she was going. I wanted to kiss her.

". . . This could be an asset. We're just a dying, ugly little mining town without a real identity. It could be an opportunity."

Is this a great country, or what?

"Listen," Shar said, a trace of concern creeping into her voice, "I have to tell you we now have a Super 8 Motel and a McDonald's. I hope that doesn't knock us out of the running."

And so I went. It was my first trip, the one where cynicism was still allowed.

Signs are designed to convey information, and the signage of Battle Mountain speaks with eloquence. I'm not just talking about the big, thundering messages, like the enormous BM. Humbler signs have their stories to tell, too.

Downtown Battle Mountain boasts three principal business establishments, each with its own marquee, each a triumph of misinformation. The most elaborate sign adorns the Owl Club; it is a huge neon triptych featuring a smiling hoot owl proudly serving up a tray of piping hot food, a cow dourly contemplating the words "Choice Steaks," and a big, blocky, authoritative "FAMILY DINING."

The Owl Club serves no food. It's a bar. Its restaurant is closed.

Two doors down is the Nevada Hotel, where several placards inside, yellowed with age and indifference, caution against "obscene" language. Outside, the Nevada Hotel's marquee is 20 feet high and transforms nightly into the defiantly gaptoothed "Nevada Ho el."

It is not a hotel. It's mostly a bar and restaurant. There are rooms but they have no TVs and no phones and they don't rent them out.

But my favorite sign is the one down the block, at Donna's Diner. If there exists in America a more eloquent testament to the Jughead shrug, a better paean to intellectual lassitude and inertia, I demand to see it. At some point in the past, evidently, Donna's Diner ordered itself up a fancy illuminated sign. And the sign came, and the letters came, and the time came to put the letters on the sign, and wuh-oh. Not enough room.

Now, there are several ways to deal with such a situation. You can order yourself up a bigger sign, or you can buy some smaller letters, or you can do what Donna's Diner did, which is this: "DONNA' DINER"

According to *The Complete Nevada Traveler*, Donna's Diner is "a local treasure." I headed there dubiously, because in my first half-hour in town I had not observed much in the way of riches. I'd seen age, but no quaintness. I'd seen buildings, but no architecture. There was a coin-operated community car wash, but no community park. There was a store that sells only fireworks, but none that sells only clothing. There was a brothel but no ice cream parlor. There were at least seven saloons, but no movie theater.

(There were entertainment opportunities. A flier advertised an event at the upcoming county fair, where a cow is led over a grid of numbered squares, and you bet on the numbers, and you win if the cow poops on your number.)

Sensing there must be more to Battle Mountain—a hidden sophistication behind its bucktoothed rustic front—I bellied up to an oilcloth-covered table at Donna's and signaled for service. I picked up a humor book that sits on every table and opened to a list of "Things That Will Not Impress City Women." One was, "Leaving the hanky from your nosebleed stuffed up there when you go dancing."

I told owner Jerry Williams I was trying to get a feel for the soul of the place, and I wondered if he could be a sort of ambassador for Battle Mountain, and tell me what there was to do.

"Do?"

"Right."

"In Battle Mountain?"

"Yes."

"Absolutely nothing."

Eventually, as I ate Donna's specialty sandwich—fried, breaded frozen shrimp on toast with green pepper and a slice of cheese the color of a traffic cone—Jerry opined that the two things people do are what people do in every city in Nevada, which is drink and gamble.

I am not a particularly knowledgeable gambler, but I have an image of what a casino is, thanks to James Bond. Casinos contain tuxedoed cads and rotters with slender mustaches, and ladies in sequined gowns that hug their behinds. There are dice tables, and blackjack tables, and roulette wheels, and games so complex and exotic they can only be played by persons from Zurich.

In Battle Mountain, casinos are basically drunks at slot machines. They play with the intensity and excitement of people sorting socks at a laundromat.

At the Nevada Hotel bar, there is a video poker machine at every bar stool. I was playing and losing, and drinking a beer. Beside me, mechanic Mel Langer was playing and losing, and drinking a beer. Mel is a mechanic. He said the people here are nice and friendly, but there isn't much to do.

Bartender Helen Lumpkin agreed. It's worst for the kids, she said, because they find excitement in the wrong places: "Fifteen-year-old girls with bellies out to here."

Mel looked around conspiratorially and lowered his voice.

"When I moved here seven years ago from California, the odd thing was, the thing I noticed, and I'm not being negative . . ."

He took a drink.

". . . I am just saying, without being faultfinding, don't get me wrong, what I noticed was the obesity of the women. Have you noticed that?"

Gallantly, I said I had not.

"Well, the men work in the mines day and night and there's nothing to do for the women except eat."

One thing to do is bird huntin'. There is nothing quite as delicious, or as beautiful, as ducks in the wild, with splendiferous iridescent greens and blues and broad chests of rich mahogany. Alas, there aren't that many ducks around Battle Mountain. Battle Mountain bird hunters tend to settle for something called a chukar, a bird with the peculiar habit of running up hills and flying down. Chukars don't make good eating, but locals are pretty proud of them just the same.

Helen has one in a glass showcase behind the bar. She showed it to me.

"So that's the famous chukar I've been hearing about," I said.

It's a scrawny little flapdoodly thing with mottled feathers and a hooked beak.

"Yep, that's the chukar."

It looks like a cross between a chicken and a pigeon, with the least fortunate features of each. It is the color of dirt.

"So there it is, then."

"There it is."

As you enter Battle Mountain, a large billboard promises two things: "Fine Dining" and "A Good Night's Rest." Having despaired of finding the first, I aspired to the second at the famous Owl Club, where rooms are only $29 because the place doesn't go in for fancy big-city amenities like a coffee maker in the room, or an iron, or a shoe-buffing cloth, or shampoo, or a clock, or a telephone, or spotless carpeting.

I sank into bed for my promised good night's sleep, which I admit, in all candor, was delivered exactly as advertised, the solemn covenant between Battle Mountain and its guests remaining intact right up until 4:21 a.m. when the Union Pacific rumbled and roared and clanged and whistled its way through downtown, about 200 feet away.

Breakfast was pretty good flapjacks at the counter at the Nevada Hotel, where I had come to discover for myself the niceness and hospitality that I'd been hearing tell of.

I soon found myself surrounded by guys who plainly did not like who I was or what I was doing there. Hubert Sharp, a short, square man with a short, square haircut, has been living in Battle Mountain for 20 years, and he informed me he would not live in Washington, D.C., "if you gave me title to the whole place." When I asked why, Hubert said something about the citizenry of Washington that was so offensive, it occurred to me he might have kin in Terre Haute.

Hubert and his pals Bill Elquist and Tom Beebe meet here some mornings, a sort of rump parliament of Battle Mountain. Tom used to be the sheriff. Bill, who owns a backhoe and does odd jobs, is one of three Lander County commissioners; the commissioners run the town, which has no mayor.

Pretty soon the door opened and a big guy named Max walked in and occupied a stool. Max is a pooh-bah. As the town's justice of the peace, he presides over all criminal and civil matters. I told him who I was and why I was there, and he grunted noncommittally, and picked up a fly swatter.

"Max, what's your last name?" I asked, pen in hand. A fly alighted on the counter.

"I'm not going to tell you."

"But you're the judge. You're a public official. You have to tell me."

Whap! The fly escaped.

"No, I don't," said Judge Max.

His name is Max Bunch. I learned that from Lorrie Baumann, the editor of the *Battle Mountain Bugle*. Lorrie knows everything. She does everything: Takes pictures, writes stories, edits stories. With her knowledge of the town, she has few illusions.

Nevada, she said, attracts people who have trouble fitting in anywhere else, and of those misfits, the ones who have trouble fitting in in Nevada go to small towns like Battle Mountain.

"For the folks who like it here," she said, "it's mostly a matter of not being able to imagine anything else."

When I'd asked Battle Mountaineers what they most wish they had, a startling number mentioned a Wal-Mart. The closest one is in Winnemucca, 52 miles away. No one mentioned what I would have mentioned, which is anything bespeaking age, history or architecture. The town once had a nice old train station. They tore it down.

In Battle Mountain, entropy reigns; architectural context is nonexistent. One of the prettier wooden houses, with two levels and a porch, is 40 feet from the 24-hour car wash, serve-yourself, $1. Corrugated aluminum and aluminum siding seem to be the building material of choice. There are a lot of trailers. One had a smaller trailer in the back yard.

"When I first came here a couple of years ago," Lorrie said, "Battle Mountain was in the middle of constructing a new jail. Well, when it opened, one of the county officials was speaking, and he said it's great we have a wonderful new jail but it's a pity that it is the nicest building in town."

I had one more question, and I was almost embarrassed to ask it: How could she bring herself to live here?

"I don't."

Lorrie Baumann lives in Winnemucca. That was the deal under which she took the job editing the *Battle Mountain Bugle*: that they didn't make her live in Battle Mountain.

Shar Peterson is a slim, attractive, intense woman with striking hair that appears to have been styled by a Van de Graaff generator. The executive director of the Battle Mountain Chamber of Commerce is always smiling, and she was smiling at this very moment, but I knew she wasn't glad to see me. After our first phone conversation, Shar had talked to some of the town mothers and fathers, who apparently had not shared her vision about the terrific publicity potential of this armpit thing. As Shar put it, "Some people are taking it as a negative."

Shar had apparently been strongly encouraged to dissuade me from my mission, to argue the case against the armpit. Once enthusiastic collaborators, we were, at the moment, potential antagonists.

I sat down. Laid my cards on the table.

"Shar," I said, "this is not a handsome town."

"We understand that," she said, her smile defiantly unbroken.

Shar was doing her level best to show me the highlights of Battle Mountain. It was not easy. It was, in fact, a grim little exercise in desperation salesmanship. Shar is an excellent guide and spin artist, but being executive director of the Battle Mountain Chamber of Commerce is a little like being regional sales manager for Firestone tires.

Heading out on Route 305, Shar pointed out several distant hills in the Shoshone mountain range.

"That looked better before the fires."

And:

"Usually, in different weather, that's a nice view of the valley."

And:

"The people aren't exactly xenophobic. You just have to earn their trust."

We saw several distant peaks with bald smears caused by mining. "They'll look normal afterwards. They'll just be a little less high."

Shar wanted to show me some of the nicer houses, but they were scattered around, so to get to them we had to pass homes that looked like the sort of place Snuffy Smith's wife, Loweezy, is forever brooming out.

Shar came here many years ago, when her husband got a good job in a local mine. He still has it, and so she is still here. She loves it, she said. She said it three times.

I said nothing. We passed one of the more expensive homes. It features a rather startling facade of faux boulders that sort of look like stone, the way cardboard sort of looks like oak.

"I have two choices," Shar said at last. "To make myself miserable or to learn to love where I am. Do you know what I mean?"

I did.

"Okay, maybe we're an armpit," Shar said. "If so, we're shaven, and clean, and sweet-smelling because out here in the desert, we're arid, extra dry. "

The woman is very good.

Doug Mills owns Battle Mountain's Mills Pharmacy, which was the only place in town I could find a "Battle Mountain" T-shirt for sale. It had a cartoon of a mining car filled with nuggets of something oddly brown that are either shining or stinking, depending on how you interpret the lines radiating from it. Doug is a major civic booster; he has a pet project he thinks can help turn the town's fortunes around.

Out at the airstrip are a few vintage airplanes. They just need a little restoration, Doug figures, and they could become the centerpiece of a Battle Mountain museum. His concept is something called "Planes, Trains and Automobiles," celebrating Battle Mountain's storied history involving all three transportation modes.

Trains, I understood. Battle Mountain was built by the railroads. What about planes?

Amelia Earhart, he said, once stopped here to refuel during a solo transcontinental autogiro flight.

Okaaaay. And automobiles?

Doug studied his shoes.

The town of Carlin, he said, which is real nearby, "was the home of the first Datsun dealership in Nevada."

I let this marinate in the silence.

"Well," Doug said, "you got to go with what you got."

Hang a left at Battle Mountain's only sort-of traffic light (it blinks red 24 hours a day), cross the railroad tracks, follow the big red arrows and you're at Donna's Battle Mountain Ranch (no relation to Donna' Diner). An enormous parking lot accommodates 18-wheelers, which tend to park outside for about 20 minutes at a time with the engines running. Donna's Battle Mountain Ranch, open 24 hours a day, Visa and MasterCard accepted, ATM on the premises, is probably the most successful retail business in town.

One hundred dollars an hour, three girls on call, take your pick: the one who is a little skinny, the one who is a little big, or the one who is a little old. They all seem nice and friendly and accommodating. It's all perfectly legal.

I was here only because I was ordered to come. When I asked Gene Sullivan, one of the three county commissioners, where I should go in town, he'd nodded solemnly in the direction of the railroad tracks. "Whorehouse," he said.

I figured he must have had his reasons. Probably he knew that the management would express its gratitude to the town that sustains it, and respect for the locals who are open enough to expose their vulnerability in the timeless transaction of the hungry heart.

The locals are louts and creeps, said Paula Navar, day manager, who tends bar beneath a painting of a voluptuous nude.

"They raise hell," she said. Most of the clients at Donna's Ranch are transients, drivers en route from one place to another. Paula said they're swell.

"They're gentlemen. It's the locals, when they come in, who cause the most trouble. They just don't know any better. With them it's 'whore' this and 'whore' that. Listen, I know whores. I've worked with whores. These ladies are not whores."

A middle-aged redhead with big glasses, Paula said she loves her job and loves and respects her bosses, if not the town.

Paula considers herself an outcast in Battle Mountain—an attractive single mother, perennially under suspicion by Battle Mountain wives as a potential home wrecker. She finds this funny.

"I don't want their husbands. I don't want to be married to Billy Bob."

Evening was approaching and it was almost time to leave, but I had one more place to visit. The literature about Battle Mountain said the sunsets are spectacular, if viewed from the prime sunset-viewing spot. So I went. I was alone, at the top of a hill, Battle Mountain behind me, squinting westward as the Earth wheeled and the sun began to sink behind the Shoshones.

The clouds were like shredded gauze, and slowly they glowed a resplendent, fiery orange against the baby-blue sky, outlined like the beard of a disapproving Celtic god. It all seemed beautiful and humbling, out there at the famous sunset-viewing site, above the NO DUMPING sign riddled with buckshot, beside the placard authorizing acceptance of "municipal solid waste," "construction and demolition debris," "tires," "dead animals," "medical waste" and "non-friable asbestos," out there alone with nothing but my thoughts and a disquieting fragrance carried on the west wind, out there at the dump.

Alas, the Earth kept wheeling. September 11 came and went and everything you have just read became impossible to publish. Which is why I have returned, with a new mission. A rescue mission.

Seattle photographer Brian Smale arrived the day before me, and began shooting on his own. He knew this was about the Armpit of America, but no one had told him about the new mission. So, when we finally meet up, Brian Smale is all smiles.

"This is easy!" he says. "This is like fishing with poison!"

Oh, man.

Karen Davis is the owner and chief hair stylist of Stewart's Styling Salon, a full-service beauty parlor that also sells china figurines, candles, clocks, leather jackets, celebrity posters and underpants.

"It's a small town," says Karen, "so you have to diversify or you'll never make it." She is 42, a Marilu Henner type, and she grew up in Battle Mountain and raised her children here. She is smart, sophisticated, the kind of woman who could succeed anywhere, but who has chosen to succeed here. I have decided she is to be my first triumphal interview in the Battle Mountain Reclamation Project.

So, it's a pretty okay place, then?

"There a lot of good people here," she says measuredly. "There's a lot to be said for living in the wide-open desert. People who can't see the beauty here are lacking something in themselves. "

So, it's a great place, then?

Karen says it can be a little difficult for people like her and her husband, who don't drink or gamble and who like culture and fine dining and nice clothes. But, she quickly adds, there's plenty to do when you're raising kids, because you are involved in their school activities.

Her kids are almost grown up, now?

"Yes."

And?

"And I want out of here so bad I could scream."

It is not coincidence that I have returned to this place during the week of October 1–6. This is to be Battle Mountain's finest hour. The town has been chosen to host an international event, the world championship human-powered vehicle race, in which competitors attempt to set a land-speed record on recumbent bicycles. The trials take place every night near dusk, out on Highway 305, just outside of town.

There are only a few dozen spectators, but it's a spectacular sight. The bikes are sleek. They look like bullets, encased in plastic aerodynamic shells, and they reach speeds of almost 80 mph, whizzing nearly soundlessly across the finish line, faster than you could ever imagine an engineless vehicle moving.

Afterward, I collar Matt Weaver, the bike racer surfer dude from California who started the event several years ago, and asked him what factor, or combination of factors, led him to choose, of all places on Earth, Battle Mountain.

Basically, Weaver explains, building up enormous speed on a bike requires a very long stretch of straight road, almost six miles. But it has to be more than straight. It has to be straight and flat, with virtually no gradient. So he got in his car, with sophisticated measuring instruments on the seat beside him, driving thousands of miles looking for a high enough level of flatness, on a flatness meter.

"So, I'm, like, wow, I'm never gonna find this, six miles of road flat enough," he says, "and then suddenly, I am on this stretch, and it says it's level one, and then level two, and then level three, and I'd never seen a level three, and then four, and five, and ding ding ding!"

So he chose Battle Mountain because it had a boring road?

"Very, very, very boring!" Matt corrects. But that's not all, he says.

Thank goodness.

It had to be a road that could be closed down easily for the races, he says, so it couldn't be in a place that's used a lot.

So it had to be a very, very, very boring road in a very, very, very boring place? "Exactly!"

The reclamation project is not going well at all. In a funk, I find myself shambling over to the most depressing place in town, the cemetery, where I notice something odd. The most recent headstone I can find is from 1988. Have Battle Mountaineers stopped dying? Is boredom some sort of elixir?

It makes no sense. I begin to explore, and finally, I literally stumble over the truth. It's a stone marker level with the ground. All the newer graves have no tombstones. They're easy to miss from a distance.

Here's one with two festive helium balloons tethered to it, dancing in the wind. It's the final resting place of Robert Nevarez, died 1999. There's a handwritten note tucked into his bucket of plastic flowers, and I consider reading it, but I haven't the heart.

The balloons say "Happy 18th Birthday!"

Which is when I realize I've been going about this all wrong. This isn't about architecture, roads, weather, cultural opportunities, or ugly little birds.

It's amazing what you can discover when you start to look in the right places.

From today's classifieds in the *Battle Mountain Bugle*:

"Several photos and negatives found in Turner Lane. They are miscellaneous shots of people fishing, and a school photo of an eighth-grader named Charlee. To pick them up, please . . ."

I think: Who on Earth would take that sort of time and effort for something so trivial? Not anybody where I come from. We're not boring enough.

On this day, Battle Mountain is transformed. It is homecoming weekend, when the undefeated Battle Mountain Longhorns are taking on the hated Mustangs from Lovelock High, in Pershing County. Nearly every store window is soaped up with pro-Longhorn or anti-Mustang slogans.

And suddenly, I remember something. Back when Shar was squiring me around town, she brought me to see Tom Reichert, the head of Lander County building and planning and economic development. Tom was one of those people who didn't really cotton to this whole armpit idea. He was polite, but prickly.

I dig through my notes.

"This is a very family-oriented place," he'd told me. "The number one adult entertainment in Battle Mountain is attending youth sports events. I guess it is embarrassing that we're so lacking in things to do, we have to concentrate on our kids."

Now, I'd talked to kids, asked them about growing up here, and mostly I got rolled eyes and vows to bomb out of there at the earliest possible moment.

Still, I have to say, a whole lot of kids seem to have spent a whole lot of time soaping the heck out of this town for homecoming.

Over at the Civic Center auditorium, high-schoolers are putting on a talent show. There are maybe 30 rows of seats, maybe 20 seats across. And in a town too small to support two fast food restaurants, every seat is filled, moms and dads and little brothers and sisters, crammed in the aisles and spilling out into the vestibule, craning to see and straining to hear, over an insufficient PA system, a high school girl lip-syncing Michael Jackson's "Billie Jean."

Afterward, everyone—kids, parents, teachers—repairs to the high school grounds, for the homecoming bonfire. There aren't many trees in these parts, so Battle Mountain High makes do with a giant mound of wooden forklift pallets donated by local businesses.

When ignited with gasoline, these frames make a better than passable bonfire, the flames licking 50 feet into the night sky, against the cheesy backdrop of high-rise signs for the McDonald's and Super 8 Motel, the pyre disbursing heat devils that dance on the grass like little tornadoes. Chipper, fresh-faced teenage girls in cheerleader costumes, girls no bigger than Labrador retrievers, are high-stepping and kicking and chanting in voices that squeak, "We are the mighty, mighty Longhorns," and even littler girls on the side are imitating their varsity big sisters, and the high school band is playing a spiritedly terrible "Born to Be Wild," and parents are whooping and cheering, passing cameras back and forth to remember this forever.

The bonfire throws a lot of heat. You really feel it. It stings your eyes, and reddens your face.

It's all about the football game, of course. The Longhorns have a shot at the state championship, but first they must destroy Lovelock. One cheerleader,

Natalie Ormond, 16, in full costume, has an arm in a sling. What's a broken arm? This is homecoming; you play hurt.

The game has started, but I am watching the grandstands, not quite believing my eyes, and doing some math, and not quite believing my numbers. I count 670 people here, plus the players, which amounts to approximately one-fifth the entire population of Battle Mountain. In the city of Washington, that would be like 115,000 people showing up for a game between the Ballou Knights and the Woodson Warriors.

The game is too close for comfort—Battle Mountain is leading 17–14 in the fourth quarter—when the Longhorns have to punt from their 40. A bad snap. Gasps from the crowd. Longhorn punter Nick Sandru is forced to tuck the ball and run. He cuts right, shakes a tackler, sheds another, and races 60 yards for the touchdown, and the game.

The crowd explodes. Out of the corner of my eye, I see a figure in jeans and a polo shirt racing down the sideline, jubilantly trailing the play, arms pumping the air. This is not a coach or a trainer. This is someone who got so beautifully caught up in the joy of this moment that all professional skepticism and cynicism have evaporated here in Battle Mountain, the place she doesn't want to live.

This is Lorrie Baumann, the hard-bitten newspaper editor.

The shirt that Rose Carricaburu is wearing has a photograph of the flag-raising at Iwo Jima, and beneath it, it says, "If you want to burn the flag, why don't you ask one of these guys for a match?" Rose owns this place, Rosa's Cantina, out across the railroad tracks, near the whorehouse.

A month after September 11, you can see plenty of American flags in town, though the pall that hangs over Washington and New York is not evident here. Osama bin Laden is unlikely to be targeting Battle Mountain. The can behind the bar is taking donations, but not for disaster relief. "We Love You, Sherry," it says. Sherry is the owner of a nearby bar, and she has a bum ticker, and they are raising money to maybe get her a new one.

Rose is collecting for a business rival?

"There are no rivals in Battle Mountain," she says.

A weathered-looking guy sidles over. He is James Hopper, who owns H&H Exploration. "There's a flag flying on my trackhoe," he says. "The terrorists, what they've done? They've screwed up! They vaporized those poor people in New York, and they brought the whole nation together. The way I see it, little town U.S.A. is just like Big Town U.S.A. We all have hearts, and we all bleed."

He extends a hand.

"The way I see it," Hopper says, "you're my friend. Right?"

Oh, man.

Brian the photographer and I are cruising the streets, one last tour through town, and I am explaining to him my dilemma. I don't want to officially declare

Battle Mountain the Armpit of America, and they don't want me to, and I don't have to, and, truth to tell, maybe it isn't. Sure, it's got some jerky people, but it has some wonderful people, too. Maybe it's not the armpit. Maybe there simply is no such body part, now.

On the other hand, Shar Peterson was right. Back there on the phone, before all this began, she was dead-on right. You don't have to be an economist, or a sociologist, or an architect, or a land-use planner, to understand that this place is in trouble. It's got almost nothing going for it.

In America in the 21st century, you need something. You need an identity. A personality. You need to be someplace someone's heard of. You need to be able to pass a word-association test. ("L.A." "Movies!" "Detroit." "Cars!")

There's no answer for "Battle Mountain." Yet.

That's my dilemma. Do I hurt them in order to help them?

Lord, give me a sign.

Brian sees it first. He stops the car, and looks up at the sky, and points. My jaw drops.

God may indeed work in mysterious ways. But one thing, surely, is no mystery: He uses available material. When He visits destruction upon the tropics, He doesn't send a blizzard, He summons the power of the warm seas and the tropical winds.

In Battle Mountain, He writes in flickering neon.

Above us looms the highest structure in town, the giant sign on stilts 40 feet above the gas station, an enormous red and yellow SHELL.

The S is burned out.

So here it is, for better or worse.

Having objectively examined the evidence, which is clear and convincing, and having reached its conclusion beyond a reasonable doubt, *The Washington Post Magazine* hereby confers upon the town of Battle Mountain, Nev., the title of Armpit of America, with all the privileges and responsibilities therein.

One hundred seventy years ago, a young Frenchman named Alexis de Tocqueville preceded me into America's heartland, determined to map out not so much the nation's appearance, but its soul. He came away impressed by the resourcefulness of the people, a resourcefulness born of the enormous freedoms conferred by democracy and an anarchic economy.

I find myself returning again and again to something Tom Reichert said to me. Tom is the economic development guy who didn't like the armpit idea one little bit. He argued and argued, and finally said, with some defiance:

"Well, if you're going to make us the armpit, fine. You do it. Maybe we can work up some sponsorships. Maybe Secret antiperspirant will buy new uniforms for the girls softball team."

That, Tom, is exactly the idea.

And it would be just the beginning.

I can't make this happen. I've just handed you a tool. The rest is up to the image-makers—people like you. And Shar, who better than anyone understands the possibilities. And Lorrie, who cares way more than she lets on. And Doug Mills, who might consider changing the wording on the Battle Mountain T-shirts he sells at his pharmacy, if you get my drift.

A renaissance for Battle Mountain? The way I see it, this is America, we're all in it together, and anything is possible. All it will take is a little sweat.

V: Crime

Big-city columnists working the crime beat are sharp-eyed, quick-witted, and seem perhaps a bit too much at home in the city's wild streets, back alleys, and shady precincts. They record the grisly body counts but do it with so much flair that at times they almost seem to be having fun.

A young Ernest Hemingway describes a stunning series of gangland murders connected with a vicious political campaign in Chicago, honing the tough, punchy style that would become legendary. Damon Runyon, covering the trial of a faithless wife who murdered her rich husband, scores a classic example of the kind of story Pete Hamill has dubbed "Murder at a Good Address."

True to their status as first cousins to the homicide cops, some columnists end up in the middle of the cases they write about. Walter Winchell tells how the gangster Lepke Buchalter, afraid of being killed by police, contacted Winchell, surrendered to him, and was then driven to FBI chief J. Edgar Hoover. When the demented Son of Sam serial killer wanted to talk to the world, he sent his twisted notes to Jimmy Breslin.

Chronicling crime can also inspire dark humor, as when Mike Barnicle recounts the slaying of four mafiosi in "Steak Tips to Die For" and the murderers' pathetic attempt at a clean getaway. The fact that Barnicle can pivot just two weeks later to describe the harrowing murder of a Cambodian immigrant family speaks to both his range and the possibilities of the crime column.

Writing about crime is not the same as writing about justice, which often eludes the case and the columnist. As Murray Kempton says of yet another gruesome killing: "After a while it seems useless to try to explain things that cannot possibly be excused."

Chicago Gang War

ERNEST HEMINGWAY—*The Toronto Star*—5/28/1921

Anthony d'Andrea, pale and spectacled, defeated candidate for alderman of the 19th ward, Chicago, stepped out of the closed car in front of his residence and, holding an automatic pistol in his hand, backed gingerly up the steps.

Reaching back with his left hand to press the door bell, he was blinded by two red jets of flame from the window of the next apartment, heard a terrific roar and felt himself clouted sickeningly in the body with the shock of the slugs from the sawed-off shot gun.

It was the end of the trail that had started with a white-faced boy studying for the priesthood in a little Sicilian town. It was the end of a trail that had wound from the sunlit hills of Sicily across the sea and into the homes of Chicago's nouveau riche. A trail that led through the penitentiary and out into the deadliest political fight Chicago has ever known.

But it was not quite the end. For the pale-faced D'Andrea, his body torn and huddled, his horn-rimmed spectacles broken, but hooked on, pulled himself to his knees and looking with his near-sighted eyes into the darkness jerked five shots out of his automatic pistol in the direction of the shot gun that had roared his death warrant.

For months D'Andrea had been entering his home, gun in hand, in the expectation of such a death. He knew he was doomed—but he wanted to protest the verdict. It is all part of the unfinished story of the gunman's political war that is raging in Chicago at present.

Anthony d'Andrea, who is dead in Jefferson Park Hospital today with 12 slugs in his body, was educated at the University of Palermo. He renounced a career in the church and went to the States.

In Chicago he became a foreign language teacher to some of the wealthiest families of the city, numbering among his pupils many of the newer members of society. D'Andrea became an American citizen in 1899, and in subsequent years embarked on various commercial enterprises. In a small way he was a real estate dealer, macaroni manufacturer and banker.

Secret service agents raided his home in 1902 on a tip that D'Andrea was the man who was flooding Chicago with spurious ten-cent pieces. Counterfeit coins were found by the government operatives at both D'Andrea's home and his macaroni factory. He was tried, pleaded guilty and sentenced to Joliet penitentiary. After serving thirteen months he was pardoned by President Roosevelt.

After coming out of the penitentiary he became an Italian labor leader and shortly announced his intention of entering politics. His first venture in politics was in 1914, when he was defeated as candidate for county commissioner.

In 1916 he first contested the seat of Alderman John Powers, who has been alderman from the 19th ward for twenty-five years. Although D'Andrea proved that he was not disfranchised due to his pardon by President Roosevelt, his past record defeated him.

His power over the Italians continued to grow, however, and the first of the murders that have marked the Powers-D'Andrea feud occurred when Frank Lombardi, a strong Powers adherent, was killed in his saloon.

This last election started off with the bombing of Alderman Powers' home. Then D'Andrea's headquarters was bombed while a meeting was in progress and many of his henchmen badly wounded.

Alderman Powers, who is known to the Italians as "Johnny de Pow," won the election of last November by about 400 votes. Immediately D'Andrea announced a contest—and a series of killings commenced.

Gaetano Esposito, a strong Powers worker, was tossed out of a speeding motor car, in the heart of the city, his body riddled with bullets.

Paul A. Labriola, municipal court bailiff, who many believed was being groomed by Powers to take his place, was shot by five men who cornered him on his way to court. After he had fallen, one of his assassins bent over him and fired five times into his back.

The same day Harry Raimondi, a fellow Sicilian of D'Andrea's and another strong Powers worker, was shot while in his own grocery store.

Police were informed that twenty-five Powers workers were on a proscription list. All were marked for death. No Powers man in the ward has felt sure of his life. Then came the first threat of reprisal and vengeance.

"D'Andrea is a dying man," Alderman Powers is reported to have said, "I can no longer keep my men in check."

Everything quieted down—and then D'Andrea was shot on May 11.

But the war in the 19th ward of Chicago is not yet over. There are hints, there are rumors, and there are whispers in the saloons and cafés and the question that is being whispered is, "Who will be the next man to die?"

There are many answers.

Murder in the Worst Degree
DAMON RUNYON—International News Service—5/9/1927

A chilly-looking blonde with frosty eyes and one of those marble, you-bet-you-will chins, and an inert, scare-drunk fellow that you couldn't miss among any hundred men as a dead setup for a blonde, or the shell game, or maybe a gold brick.

Mrs. Ruth Snyder and Henry Judd Gray are on trial in the huge weather-beaten old courthouse of Queens County in Long Island City, just across the river from the roar of New York, for what might be called for want of a better name, The Dumbbell Murder. It was so dumb.

They are charged with the slaughter four weeks ago of Albert Snyder, art editor of the magazine, *Motor Boating*, the blonde's husband and father of her nine-year-old daughter, under circumstances that for sheer stupidity and brutality have seldom been equaled in the history of crime.

It was stupid beyond imagination, and so brutal that the thought of it probably makes many a peaceful, home-loving Long Islander of the Albert Snyder type shiver in his pajamas as he prepared for bed.

They killed Snyder as he slumbered, so they both admitted in confessions— Mrs. Snyder has since repudiated hers—first whacking him on the head with a sash weight, then giving him a few whiffs of chloroform, and finally tightening a strand of picture wire around this throat so he wouldn't revive.

This matter disposed of, they went into an adjoining room and had a few drinks of whisky used by some Long Islanders, which is very bad, and talked things over. They thought they had committed "the perfect crime," whatever that may be. It was probably the most imperfect crime on record. It was cruel, atrocious, and unspeakably dumb.

They were red-hot lovers then, these two, but they are strangers now.

Mrs. Snyder, the woman who has been called a Jezebel, a lineal descendant of the Borgia outfit, and a lot of other names, came in for the morning session of court stepping along briskly in her patent-leather pumps, with little short steps.

She is not bad-looking. I have seen much worse. She is thirty-three and looks just about that, though you cannot tell much about blondes. She has a good figure, slim and trim, with narrow shoulders. She is of medium height, and I thought she carried her clothes off rather smartly. She wore a black dress and a black silk coat with a collar of black fur. Some of the girl reporters said it was dyed ermine; others pronounced it rabbit.

They made derogatory remarks about her hat. It was a tight-fitting thing called, I believe, a beret. Wisps of her straw-colored hair straggled out from under it. Mrs. Snyder wears her hair bobbed, the back of the bobbing rather ragged. She is of the Scandinavian type. Her parents are Norwegian and Swedish.

Her eyes are blue-green and as chilly-looking as an ice-cream cone. If all that Henry Judd Gray says of her actions the night of the murder is true, her veins carry ice water. Gray says he dropped the sash weight after slugging the sleeping Snyder with it once and that Mrs. Snyder picked it up and finished the job.

Gray, a spindly fellow in physical build, entered the courtroom with quick, jerky little steps behind an officer, and sat down between his attorneys, Samuel L. Miller and William L. Millard. His back was to Mrs. Snyder, who sat about ten feet distant. Her eyes were on a level with the back of his narrow head.

Gray was neatly dressed in a dark suit, with a white starched collar and subdued tie. He has always been a bit on the dressy side, it is said. He wears big, horn-rimmed spectacles, and his eyes have a startled expression. You couldn't find a meeker, milder-looking fellow in seven states, this man who is charged with one of the most horrible crimes in history.

He occasionally conferred with his attorneys as the examination of the talesmen was going forward, but not often. He sat in one position almost the entire day, half slumped down in his chair, a melancholy-looking figure for a fellow who once thought of "the perfect crime."

Mrs. Snyder and Gray have been "hollering copper" on each other lately, as the boys say. That is, they have been telling. Gray's defense goes back to old Mr. Adam, that the woman beguiled him, while Mrs. Snyder says he is a "jackal," and a lot of other things besides that, and claims that he is hiding behind her skirts.

Some say Mrs. Ruth Snyder "wept silently" in court yesterday. It may be so. I could detect no sparkle of tears against the white marble mask, but it is conceivable that even the very gods were weeping silently as a gruff voice slowly recited the blonde woman's own story of the murder of her husband by herself and Henry Judd Gray.

Let no one infer she is altogether without tenderness of heart, for when they were jotting down the confession that was read in the courtroom in Long Island City, Peter M. Daly, an assistant district attorney, asked her:

"Mrs. Snyder, why did you kill your husband?"

He wanted to know.

"Don't put it that way," she said, according to his testimony yesterday. "It sounds so cruel."

"Well, that is what you did, isn't it?" he asked in some surprise.

"Yes," he claims she answered, "but I don't like that term."

A not astonishing distaste, you must admit.

"Well, why did you kill him?" persisted the curious Daly.

"To get rid of him," she answered simply, according to Daly's testimony; and indeed that seems to have been her main idea throughout, if all the evidence the state has so far developed is true.

She afterward repudiated the confession that was presented yesterday, with her attorneys trying to bring out from the state's witnesses that she was sick and confused when she told her bloody yarn five weeks ago.

The woman, in her incongruous widow's weed, sat listening intently to the reading of her original confession to the jury, possibly the most horrible tale that ever fell from human lips, the tale of a crime unutterably brutal and coldblooded and unspeakably dumb.

Her mouth opened occasionally as if framing words, and once she said, not quite distinctly, an unconscious utterance, which may have been a denial of some utterance by the lawyer or perhaps an assurance to her soul that she was not alive and awake.

Right back to old Father Adam, the original, and perhaps the loudest "squawker" among mankind against women, went Henry Judd Gray in telling how and why he lent his hand to the butchery of Albert Snyder.

She—she—she—she—she—she—she—she. That was the burden of the bloodly song of the little corset salesman as read out in the packed courtroom in Long Island City yesterday.

She—she—she—she—she—she. 'Twas an echo from across the ages and an old familiar echo, at that. It was the same old "squawk" of Brother Man whenever and wherever he is in a jam, that was first framed in the words:

"She gave me of the tree, and I did eat."

It has been put in various forms since then, as Henry Judd Gray, for one notable instance close at hand, put it in the form of eleven long typewritten pages that were read yesterday, but in any form and in any language it remains a "squawk."

"She played me pretty hard." . . . "She said, 'You're going to do it, aren't you?'" . . . "She kissed me." . . . She did this. . . . She did that. . . . Always she—she—she—she—she ran the confession of Henry Judd.

And "she"—the woman accused—how did she take this most gruesome squawk?

Well, on the whole, better than you might expect.

You must remember it was the first time she had ever heard the confession of the man who once called her "Momsie." She probably had an inkling of it, but not its exact terms.

For a few minutes her greenish-blue eyes roared with such fury that I would not have been surprised to see her leap up, grab the window sash weight that lay among the exhibits on the district attorney's table, and perform the same offices on the shrinking Gray that he says she performed on her sleeping husband.

She "belabored him," Gray's confession reads, and I half expected her to belabor Gray.

Her thin lips curled to a distinct snarl at some passages in the statement. I thought of a wildcat and a female cat, at that, on a leash. Once or twice she smiled, but it was a smile of insensate rage, not amusement. She once emitted a push of breath in a loud "phew," as you have perhaps done yourself over some tall tale.

The marble mask was contorted by her emotions for a time, she often shook her head in silent denial of the astounding charges of Gray, then finally she settled back calmly, watchful, attentive, and with an expression of unutterable contempt as the story of she—she—she—she ran along.

Contempt for Henry Judd, no doubt. True, she herself squawked on Henry Judd, at about the same time Henry Judd was squawking on her, but it is a woman's inalienable right to squawk.

As for Henry Judd, I still doubt he will last it out. He reminds me of a slowly collapsing lump of tallow. He sat huddled up in his baggy clothes, his eyes on the floor, his chin in hand, while the confession was being read. He seems to be folding up inch by inch every day.

He acts as if he is only semiconscious. If he was a fighter and came back to his corner in his present condition, they would give him smelling salts.

The man is a wreck, a strange contrast to the alert blonde at the table behind him.

The room was packed with women yesterday, well-dressed, richly befurred women from Park Avenue, and Broadway, and others not so well dressed from Long Island City, and the small towns farther down the island. There were giggling young schoolgirls and staid-looking matrons, and my friends, what do you think? Their sympathy is for Henry Judd Gray!

I made a point of listening to their opinions as they packed the hallways and jammed the elevators of the old courthouse yesterday and canvassed some of them personally, and they are all sorry for Gray. Perhaps it is his forlorn-looking aspect as he sits inert, numb, never raising his head, a sad spectacle of a man who admits he took part in one of the most atrocious murders in history.

There is no sympathy for Mrs. Snyder among the women and very little among the men. They all say something drastic ought to be done to her.

If you are asking a medium-boiled reporter of murder trials, I couldn't condemn a woman to death no matter what she had done, and I say this with all due consideration of the future hazards to long-suffering man from sash weights that any lesser verdict than murder in the first degree in the Snyder-Gray case may produce.

It is all very well for the rest of us to say what *ought* to be done to the blonde throwback to the jungle cat that they call Mrs. Ruth Brown Snyder, but when you get in the jury room and start thinking about going home to tell the neighbors that you have voted to burn a woman—even a blonde woman—I imagine the situation has a different aspect. The most astonishing verdict that could be rendered in this case, of course, would be first degree for the woman and something else for the man. I doubt that result. I am inclined to think that the verdict, whatever it may be, will run against both alike—death or life imprisonment.

Henry Judd Gray said he expects to go to the chair, and adds that he is not afraid of death, an enviable frame of mind, indeed. He says that since he told his story to the world from the witness stand he has found tranquility, though his tale may have also condemned his blonde partner in blood. But perhaps that's the very reason Henry Judd finds tranquility.

He sat in his cell in the county jail over in Long Island yesterday, and read from one of the epistles of John.

"Marvel not, my brethren, if the world hate you. We know that we have passed from death unto life, because we love the brethren. He that loveth not his brother abideth in death. Whosoever hateth his brother is a murderer: and ye know that no murderer hath eternal life abiding in him."

A thought for the second Sunday after Pentecost.

In another cell, the blonde woman was very mad at everybody because she couldn't get a marcel for her bobbed locks, one hair of which was once stronger with Henry Judd Gray than the Atlantic cable.

Waiting for Lepke
WALTER WINCHELL—*New York Daily Mirror*—8/26/1939

The surrender of public enemy "Lepke" Buchalter to the government last night took place while scores of pedestrians ambled by, and two police radio cars waited for the lights to change, near Twenty-eight Street and Fifth Avenue.

The time was precisely 10:17 p.m., and the search for the most wanted fugitive in the nation was over. The surrender was negotiated by this reporter, whom G-man John Edgar Hoover authorized to guarantee "safe delivery."

After a series of telephone talks with persons unknown, and with the head of the FBI, Lepke appeared to drop out of the sky, without even a parachute. The time was 10:15. The scene was Madison Square between Twenty-third and Twenty-fourth Streets, where we had halted our car as per instructions.

The following two minutes were consumed traveling slowly north on Fourth Avenue and west on Twenty-seventh Street to Fifth Avenue, where the traffic lights were red—and to the next corner at Twenty-eight Street, where Mr. Hoover waited alone, unarmed and without handcuffs, in a government limousine. Hoover was disguised in dark sunglasses to keep him from being recognized by passers-by.

The presence of two New York police cruisers, attached to the Fourteenth Precinct, so near the surrender scene startled Hoover as well as Lepke. The G-man later admitted he feared "a leak."

Lepke, who was calmer than this chauffeur, was on the verge of rushing out of our machine into Hoover's arms. The police cruisers, ironically, were the first observed by this reporter in two hours of motoring to complete the surrender.

Not until the final seconds was there a sign of uniformed law. But it was too late. The long arm of the government had reached out and claimed another enemy. The Federal Bureau of Investigation and the city of New York had saved $50,000—the reward offered.

While pausing alongside one police car at the Twenty-seventh Street intersection for the lights, Lepke, who was wearing spectacles as part of his disguise, threw them to the corner pavement. They crashed noisily. Two passers-by, middle-aged men with graying temples, stopped and looked up at a building.

Apparently they thought a window had broken above. They never realized that the man for whom every cop in the land was searching was within touching distance.

After parking our car behind a machine which was parked behind Hoover's we shut off the ignition and escorted Lepke into Hoover's car.

"Mr. Hoover," we said, "this is Lepke."

"How do you do?" said Mr. Hoover affably.

"Glad to meet you," replied Lepke. "Let's go."

"To the Federal Building at Foley Square," commanded Hoover. His colored pilot turned swiftly south.

Lepke was a little excited. He seemed anxious to talk—to talk to anybody new—after being in the shadow for over two years with so many hunted men.

"You did the smart thing by coming in, Lepke," comforted Hoover.

"I'm beginning to wonder if I did," Lepke answered. "I would like to see my wife and kids, please?"

Mr. Hoover arranged for them to visit him shortly after Lepke was booked, fingerprinted, and Kodaked. He had $1700 on him. He gave $1100 to the boy and $600 to the jailer—for "expenses."

When the government car reached Fourteenth Street, we got out and went to the first phone to notify our editor, who groaned:

"A fine thing! With a World War starting!"

The negotiations which led to Lepke's surrender began in this manner. On Sunday night, August 5 last, a voice on the phone said:

"Don't ask me who I am. I have something important to tell you. Lepke wants to come in. But he's heard so many different stories about what will happen to him. He can't trust anybody, he says. If he could find someone he can trust, he will give himself up to that person. The talk around town is that Lepke would be shot while supposedly escaping."

"Does he trust me?" we inquired.

"Do you really mean that?" said the voice anxiously.

"Sure," we assured. "I'll tell John Edgar Hoover about it and I'm sure he will see to it that Lepke receives his constitutional rights and nobody will cross him."

"O.K., put it on the air tomorrow night if you can get that promise," and then he disconnected.

We wrote a brief radio paragraph which was addressed to Lepke, "if you are listening now," which said we would try to get him assurance of a safe delivery. The next afternoon, Sunday, we phoned Mr. Hoover and read him the paragraph.

"You are authorized to state," said Hoover, "that the FBI will guarantee it!"

Hoover and his assistant director, Clyde Tolson, came to the studio and witnessed our microphoning. They remained for the repeat broadcast to the coast an hour later—in case another phone call came in.

For two nights, voices contacted us by phone and said:

"You're doing very well. You'll hear more later. If he agrees to come in, he will do it through you. But he may change his mind. Good-by."

And then all the dickering abruptly stopped—until last Tuesday night. Then a person we had never seen before, or since, approached us at Fifty-third Street and Fifth Avenue and said: "Where can you be reached on a pay-station phone in an hour?"

We went to the nearest phone booth, where the stranger marked down the number and instructed: "This is about Lepke. This time it's important. Please be here in an hour."

He hastened away, hailed a passing cab, and taxied north.

When we so reported to Mr. Hoover, after what seemed to him like too much stalling, he was exasperated. For the first time in our seven years of knowing him, he barked at us:

"This is a lot of bunk, Walter. You are being made a fool of and so are we. If you contact those people again, tell them the time limit is up! I will instruct my agents to shoot Lepke on sight."

Promptly an hour later, right on the button, that pay-station phone tinkled. We didn't give the voice a chance to talk. "I just spoke to Hoover," we said breathlessly. "He's fed up. If Lepke doesn't surrender by four p.m. tomorrow, Hoover says no consideration of any kind will ever be given him. For every day he stays away it may mean an extra two years added to his sentence"

The voice interrupted: "He's coming in, but you simply have to wait until he can arrange things. He's willing to come in, but it can't be tomorrow. Maybe the next night. Where can you be reached tomorrow night at six?"

We gave him another phone number. He said he'd call—and the call came. But it didn't seem to be the same voice. This time the instructions included: "Drive up to Proctor's Theater in Yonkers."

How sure could we be that the "meet" was for the surrender of Lepke? We weren't sure at all. But we hoped to convince the G-men that we weren't being made any "goat-between"! And so we motored up to Yonkers, and before we reached Proctor's Theater a car loaded with strangers—faces we don't recall ever seeing before—slowly drew alongside. We heard a voice say, "That's him."

One of the men got out, holding his handkerchief to his face as though he intended to blow into it. He got into our car, sat alongside, and kept the kerchief to his face throughout the brief conversation.

"Go to the drugstore on the corner of Nineteenth Street and Eighth Avenue," he instructed. "There are some phone booths there. Get in one and appear busy. About nine p.m. somebody will come up to you and tell you where to notify the G-men to meet you."

At 8:55 p.m. we were in that drugstore. We ordered a Coke. The boy behind the counter looked at us as though we seemed familiar. Perhaps we imagined it. At any rate, we didn't get a chance to appear busy in the phone booth. A face met ours as we turned to look through the open door. The stranger jerked his head as though to telegraph "Come here." We joined him outside and walked to our car slowly.

"Go back in there and tell Hoover to be at Twenty-eighth Street on Fifth Avenue between 10:10 and 10:20," he instructed.

We did so. When we returned to the car, the man was at the wheel. He drove slowly, to kill time, for more than an hour. Up and down Eighth Avenue, Ninth, Tenth, in and out of side streets, down to Fourteenth, back to Twenty-third, and east to Madison Square, where he stopped the car and said:

"Just wait here—and good luck."

And so saying he left hurriedly. We took the wheel, turned our eyes left, and noticed many people across the street lounging around. It was very humid. Our clothes were dripping. The butterflies started to romp inside of us.

Suddenly a figure approached our car in haste. Out of the nowhere, it seems. He opened the door, got in, and said: "Hello. Thanks very much."

We released the brake and stepped on the gas. "We'll be with Mr. Hoover in a minute or two," we said. "He's waiting in his car at Twenty-eighth Street."

"Yes, I know," said Lepke. "I just passed him."

Marvin the Torch
JIMMY BRESLIN—*New York Herald Tribune*—c.1964

Marvin the Torch never could keep his hands off somebody else's business, particularly if the business was losing money. Now this is accepted behavior in Marvin's profession, which is arson. But he has a bad habit of getting into places where he shouldn't be and promising too many favors. This is where all his trouble starts.

There was this one time a few winters ago when he listened to a hard-luck story from a guy who had a custard stand, located on the wrong side of a big amusement park, that was a bad loser and the owner had no way to get rid of it. Marvin the Torch should have kept his mouth shut, but he had a couple of drinks with the fellow, and sure enough, he wound up promising to do something about it. So a week later, gas cans at his feet, he stood in front of the guy's custard stand. The custard stand was just an old boarded-up place and it was an insult to bring Marvin the Torch anywhere near it. Marvin the Torch is a man who has burned in the best industries.

But here he was, stuck with another favor, so he picked up the gas cans and went to work. As long as he was at it, Marvin decided to put a little spectacle into the job. Marvin the Torch wanted to try to make the roof blow straight up into the air without bending the nails in it.

Pioneering columnist Richard Harding Davis poses with future president (and subsequent *Kansas City Star* columnist) Theodore Roosevelt on the eve of the Rough Riders' charge up San Juan Hill in Cuba during the Spanish-American War.

H. L. Mencken, the *Baltimore Sun*'s iconic iconoclast, believed that newspaper men of his time lived "the life of kings."

Will Rogers—the humorist, movie star, and cowboy philosopher—was among the most beloved Americans of his day.

Heywood Broun, founder of the Newspaper
Guild, beams from across his desk.

The poet, novelist, and playwright
Langston Hughes wrote a column for the
Chicago Defender for two decades.

Dorothy Thompson testifies before a
congressional committee in high style.

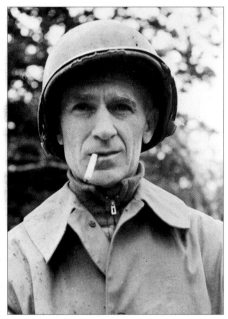

Ernie Pyle, the GI Journalist, was killed
in combat a year after winning the
Pulitzer Prize.

Walter Lippmann, arguably the most influential Washington columnist of the American Century.

Westbrook Pegler tries to focus his mind on the next target to be "Peglerized."

William F. Buckley Jr., godfather of the conservative movement, searches for the right word.

Damon Runyon surveys the racetrack.

Murray Kempton's perspective graced
newspapers for nearly fifty years.

Mike Royko, the soul of Chicago, reclines amid the debris of his office, circa 1980.

Jimmy Breslin, bold and boisterous, was the reigning champ among New York's newspaper columnists for decades.

Jack Newfield's muckraking column chronicled heroes and villains, always battling on the side of the underdog.

Legendary sports columnist Red Smith takes in another day at the office.

Texas humorist and fearless liberal, Molly Ivins—with hand on heart.

Pete Hamill—columnist, editor, and novelist—the consummate chronicler of life in New York.

Mary McGrory of the *Washington Star* puts her feet up at the Watergate hearings.

Boston's Mike Barnicle is a bridge between classic and contemporary newspaper columnists.

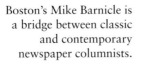

Peggy Noonan brings her patriotic grace to the pages of *The Wall Street Journal*.

"You just cover a lot of territory and you do it aggressively and you do it fairly and don't play favorites and you don't take prisoners," says *Miami Herald* columnist Carl Hiaasen.

The *Miami Herald*'s Leonard Pitts expressed America's outrage on 9/11.

Thomas L. Friedman translates his globe-trotting for the *New York Times* into best-selling books.

The Washington Post's Kathleen Parker surveys American life with a South Carolina perspective.

Steve Lopez, now of the *Los Angeles Times*, keeps the tradition of the reported column alive.

This would have been all right, except Marvin the Torch's fire caught a good south wind and the wind carried the fire straight over the amusement park and before the day was over, Marvin the Torch's favor job on the custard stand had also belted out most of a million-and-a-half-dollar amusement park.

He got into the restaurant business in Florida on one of these favors, and it nearly ruined him. Marvin was down there visiting restaurants which were not doing too well to see if he could drum up a few contracts. In one of the places he was eating at a table near the kitchen entrance when he noticed the chef hanging in the doorway with a disgusted look on his face during most of the meal.

"Business bad?" Marvin asked him.

"See for yourself," the chef said.

"Why don't you get yourself a cup of coffee and sit down with me," Marvin said.

Over coffee, Marvin carefully sold the chef on deal to "build an empty lot," as Marvin refers to his trade, on the site of the chef's restaurant. The chef liked the idea. Then, during a succeeding conference, a hitch developed. The chef said that after collecting the insurance and then coming up with Marvin's fee, he wouldn't have enough left to buy the new place he had his eye on.

Right here Marvin went ahead and opened his mouth. Some of his friends say he gets such a kick out of burning places down that he'll do anything for a deal. Whatever it is, Marvin wound up agreeing to waive his fee and take a partnership in the new restaurant the chef was going to get when Marvin burned his old one down.

Two weeks later, on a dark night, and with the chef visiting relatives two states away for alibi purposes, Marvin the Torch arrived at the restaurant with his team, which consisted of Benjamin, the blanket man, and a fellow named Lou, who drove. Now, arson is a three-man job. Two men pour, then one of the pourers comes out and becomes the blanket man. He holds an old car blanket and throws it over anyone coming out whose clothes are on fire. The driver counts the gas cans to make sure none is missing. In short, people don't pay you if they find gas cans in the ruins of your accidental fire. The Torch, of course, does the actual igniting.

Following the usual delay, the chef received his insurance money and bought his new restaurant. Marvin returned and the venture was off to a bright start. After a week, however, Marvin found that the chef couldn't cook. After two weeks, the customers started finding out. After a month, Marvin the Torch found the place was costing him money and he was telling the chef good-by.

"I'll be back around next season and stop around to see you," Marvin said. "If you're doing any good by then, we'll square up."

Marvin the Torch came back, all right. He came back a year later at four one morning and he belted out the restaurant with so much juice that the kitchen pots melted. But this still didn't satisfy him. In the end, he had had to do two jobs for the price of one.

"Favors," Marvin the Torch says in disgust. "Favors are for pyromaniacs, not professionals."

Breslin to .44 Killer: Give Up Now!
JIMMY BRESLIN—*New York Daily News*—6/5/1977

We put the letter on the table and read it again. In his opening paragraph he writes:

"Hello from the gutters of N.Y.C. which are filled with dog manure, vomit, stale wine, urine, and blood. Hello from the sewer of N.Y.C. which swallow up these delicacies when they are washed away by the sweeper trucks. Hello from the cracks in the sidewalks of N.Y.C. and from the ants that dwell in these cracks and feed on the dried blood of the dead that has settled into the cracks."

"He's a pretty good writer," somebody at the table said.

"Yes, he is," I said.

The letter was from the person who calls himself "Son of Sam." He prowls the night streets of New York neighborhoods and shoots at young girls and sometimes their boyfriends too, and he has killed five and wounded four. He sneaks up on victims with a .44 caliber pistol. Most of the young women had shoulder-length brown hair.

One of the victims was Donna Lauria, who was 18 last year when the killer shot her as she sat in a car with her girlfriend outside the Laurias' apartment house on Buhre Ave. in the Bronx. Donna Lauria was the only victim mentioned by the killer in this letter, which was sent to me at my newspaper in New York, *The Daily News*. So yesterday, I took the letter up to the fourth-floor apartment of Donna Lauria's parents and I sat over coffee and read the letter again and talked to the Laurias about it.

The killer had sent one communication before this one. He left a note to police after murdering a girl and boy as they sat in a parked car at a place only five blocks from where Donna Lauria had been killed. Both notes were handprinted.

Yesterday, in the sadness and tension of the Laurias' dining room, I read the letter again. Following the first paragraph, it read:

"J.B., I'm just dropping you a line to let you know that I appreciate your interest in those recent and horrendous .44 killings. I also want to tell you that I read your column daily and find it quite informative.

"Tell me Jim, what will you have July Twenty-Ninth? You can forget about me if you like because I don't care for publicity. However, you must not forget Donna Lauria and you cannot let the people forget her, either. She was a very sweet girl but Sam's a thirsty lad and he won't let me stop killing until he gets his fill of blood.

"Mr. Breslin, sir, don't think that you haven't heard from (me) for a while that I went to sleep. No, rather, I am still here. Like a spirit roaming the night. Thirsty, hungry, seldom stopping to rest; anxious to please Sam. I love my work. Now, the void has been filled.

"Perhaps we shall meet face to face someday or perhaps I will be blown away by cops with smoking .38s. Whatever, if I shall be fortunate enough to meet you I will tell you all about Sam if you like and I will introduce you to him. His name is 'Sam the Terrible.'

"Not knowing what the future holds I shall say farewell and I will see you at the next job. Or should I say you will see my handiwork at the next job? Remember Ms. Lauria. Thank you.

"In their blood

and

"From the Gutter.

"Sam's Creation" .44

"P.S.: J.B., please inform all the detectives working on the slayings to remain.

"P.S.: J.B., please inform all the detectives working on the case that I wish them the best of luck. 'Keep 'Em digging, drive on, think positive, get off your butts, knock on coffins, etc.'

"Upon my capture, I promise to buy all the guys working on the case a new pair of shoes if I can get up the money.

"Son of Sam"

Directly under the signature was a symbol the killer drew. It appears to be an X-shaped mark with the biological symbols for male and female and also a cross and the letter S.

When I finished reading the letter, Mike Lauria, the father, said to me, "What do you think?"

"Want to see for yourself?" the father was asked.

He pushed the letter away from him. "I don't want to see it."

"Let me," his wife, Rose, said.

"You don't want to see it," the husband said.

"Yes, I do. Because I have a lot of cards she used to get. Maybe the printing is the same."

Then the husband shrugged, "Go ahead, then."

We took out the page that mentioned her daughter and gave Rose Lauria the rest. Her large expressive brown eyes become cold as she looks at the printing. On the wall behind her was a picture of her daughter, a lovely brown-haired girl with the mother's features.

The mother put the pages down and looked up. "He's probably a very brilliant man, boy, whatever he is," she said. "His brain functions the opposite way."

She looked up at the picture of her daughter. "She was a dancer and a half. Everyplace you went, people used to praise her. Is it possible he saw her someplace and she didn't speak to him or something?"

"Who knows?" the husband said. "How can you say anything about a guy you don't even know?"

Nobody knows. The .44 killer appears to be saying that he is controlled by Sam, who lives inside him and sends him onto the streets to find young people to shoot. He does this at close range: One young woman, walking home from college, held a textbook up to her face and he put the gun up to the book and killed her.

The detectives, whose shoes he would buy, walk the streets at night and hope for a match with the man with the .44. "He's mine," one of them, a friend of mine, was saying Friday night. "The man is Jack the Ripper and I'm making a personal appointment with him."

The hope is that the killer realizes that he is controlled by Sam, who not only forces him into acts of horror but will ultimately walk him to his death. The only way for the killer to leave this special torment is to give himself up to me, if he trusts me, or to the police, and receive both help and safety.

If he wants any further contact, all he has to do is call or write me at *The Daily News*. It's simple to get me. The only people I don't answer are bill collectors.

The time to do it, however, is now. We are too close to the July 29 that the killer mentions in his letter. It is the first anniversary of the death of Donna Lauria.

"She was sitting in the car with her friend Jody Valente," Rose Lauria was saying. Jody Valente was wounded and has recovered. "Mike and I came walking up. We'd been to a wake. I went up to the car and I said, 'Tell me, Jody, what happened tonight.' She always used to tell me about her boyfriends. She said, 'It's a long story tonight. Donna'll tell you when she gets upstairs.' Now my husband says to Donna, 'What are you doing here at 1 a.m., you got to go to work tomorrow.' I said to him, 'What is she doing that's wrong?'

So we went upstairs. My husband says, 'I'm going to walk the dog.' He goes with the dog to the elevator and I hear Jody's horn blowing downstairs. I called out in the hall to my husband. He says to me, 'Well, go look out the window and see.' I look out and here's Jody screaming that Donna's been shot."

Rose Lauria, nervous now, got up from the table. "You know the last month when he killed the two more around here? My husband and I were at a wedding. We were supposed to meet some people after it. We left the wedding and I said to my husband, 'I don't want to go anywhere. Something's the matter. I want to go home.' And we just got inside at the same time the two got killed."

"She was pacing around here like a cat," Mike Lauria said.

He walked me downstairs to the street. He stood in an undershirt, with the sun glaring on his wide shoulders and he pointed to the spot where his daughter had been shot.

"She was starting to get out of the car when she saw this guy on the curb. Right where we are. Donna said to Jody, 'Who's this guy now?' Then the guy did what he did. Jody, she can't get herself to come near my wife. Forget about it. I saw her a couple of weeks ago. She spoke to me from the car. Told me she got engaged. She couldn't even look at me. I told her, 'All right, Jody, go ahead. I'll see you.' I let her go home."

He turned and walked back into his building. I took my letter from his daughter's killer and went down the street and out of his wounded life.

Head in a Box
PETE DEXTER—*Philadelphia Daily News*—8/13/1982

The boss's name is Tony Scarduzio, and Tuesday afternoon he goes out on the job with Jose Colon. Just to keep his hand in. "To make sure that things are being done to my specifications," he says.

Jose Colon is a parking-meter repairman. Somebody gets drunk in Camden and runs over a parking meter because he put a dime in and didn't get any bubble gum, Jose fixes that too.

It doesn't matter to Jose, he likes his job. "You don't have to go to school or nothing, and it's very enjoyable," he said.

So Jose and Tony are out on the truck, going up Broadway, when they come to a broken parking meter. It's broken in a way that they can only fix back at the shop, so Jose gets out a wrench to replace the head. While he is doing that, though, he happens to notice a white paper sack leaning against the stem.

"It's a nice paper sack," he said later, "got a label on it form some store on Germantown Avenue in Philly. It looks almost new, you know, a real nice paper sack, and somebody stapled it up. So I pick up the sack and it looks to me like there's a co-co-nut in there. I say, 'Hey, Tony, we better look inside. I think we found a co-co-nut.'"

Tony shrugs, and Jose opens it carefully, not wanting to damage a real nice paper sack, and looks inside. Tony waits, Jose just stares inside the sack. "Hey, Tony," he says after a minute, "there's a head inside this paper sack."

"A what?"

"It's not a coconut, Tony. It's a head." And Jose sees that his boss doesn't believe him, so he reaches in the sack and pulls the head out. A human skull. The jaw bone is missing and so are the teeth, but outside of that it is perfect. "It's not a coconut," Jose says again.

Tony says, "Oh my God!" and as soon as they fix the parking meter, they take the head over to Juvenile Division, where Tony has a friend who is a detective.

Tony and Jose go into the detective's office and put the sack in his hands. "I think I found Jimmy Hoffa," Tony says. The detective smiles and looks inside.

Then he stops smiling.

"I can't do anything about this," he says. "You better take it over to the administration building." And he hands the almost-new white paper sack with the head inside back to Tony, who gives it to Jose, and tells him to carry it over there.

On the way over, Jose stops to see his friend Kevin McKeel, who is also a supervisor for the city, and tells him to look inside the sack. Kevin does. "Surprised, huh?" Jose says.

And then he walks it the rest of the way to the police administration building, and has a short talk with the detectives' receptionist. "I bring in the bag and say, 'I found a head in the street,'" Jose says. "She says, 'This is serious. Do you really want me to go get a detective and tell him you got a head?'

"I tell her I'm not joking. I say, 'You want to look inside?' She don't want to, but another woman comes out of the office and she wants to look inside. I don't know who she was, she didn't say nothing after she looked. She just went back where she come from."

The receptionist, meanwhile, has located Sgt. Albert Handy, who comes out and takes the sack from Jose and checks inside, and then thanks him for bringing it over.

Sgt. Handy puts a tag on the skull and gives it to a detective to take over to the coroner's office in Cherry Hill. "We can't do anything about it here," he would say later.

So the detective drives the skull over to Jerry Healy, who is an investigator, and Jerry Healy puts another tag on it and sends it to Newark. "There was nothing we could do about it here," his wife would say later. Jerry was out collecting a body and couldn't be reached for comment.

And so, as the day ended, Jose was back at work in the street. Tony had gone back to work in his office. The skull was on a bus for Newark, and Sgt. Handy was working on new cases. "A man brings in a skull in a paper sack," Handy said. "It's nothing to stop work for." Sgt. Handy has been with the department fourteen years.

"Hey," he said, "this is Camden."

A Woman Burned While Police Had Their Danish
MURRAY KEMPTON—*Newsday*—11/9/1984

It is six years since the morning Nathan Giles Sr. accosted the car that Bonnie Anne Bush was driving to her Mount Sinai Hospital nursing post, forced her out with a gun, dragged her screaming into an abandoned West Side building, shot her and set her body afire.

Bonnie Bush's death did just about as much damage to the good name of the New York City Police Department as Kitty Genovese's did to Queen's reputation for conscientious citizenship. Kitty Genovese also screamed in the street through a protracted struggle with her murderer, and nobody who heard her called 911.

Kitty Genovese had been dead more than 20 years, and her ghost is still evoked whenever some moralist feels moved to arraign the callousness of this city's residents.

In Bonnie Bush's case, several citizens did their duty and the police botched theirs. The difference may be why Kitty Genovese's name has lasted so much longer than hers as a symbol of reproach to New Yorkers. Government is distinctly more efficient than the average citizen when it comes to erasing occasions for shame from the public memory.

Nathan Giles had a long struggle with Bonnie Bush before he got her to the killing floor. The first 911 call came at 8:03; there were four others, the last at 8:11. Antonio Reyes later swore that he ran up to a patrol car not many yards from the building into which the murderer had just dragged his victim. The two officers heard his story and went on eating their breakfast.

Meanwhile, back at 911, the headquarters operator had taken a succession of calls from witnesses to Bonnie Bush's peril and made such a hash of the information that the police details were scouring Manhattan Avenue for a criminal who had been identified as working his will at 15 West 102nd.

Bonnie Bush had been dead an hour when the Fire Department came to put out the blaze Giles had set, and reported a possible homicide to the police. It would be only speculation to suggest that she would still be alive if police had done their job, but then, after all, Kitty Genovese might still be just as dead if any of her neighbors in Queens had dialed 911. The point is that each of these women deserved even a small chance of rescue and survival, and Kitty Genovese was cheated of her chance by private citizens and Bonnie Bush by official servants.

The two policemen who had tarried over breakfast were put to a departmental trial and found guilty of having failed to "take fundamental police action." The punishment in each case was suspension for 30 days of vacation time, with the option to make up the loss with extra work. Thus does the department define its sensitivity to the standards of police conduct: Two patrolmen who refuse to bother with a call of mortal distress lose their vacations and Cybella Borges loses her job because she posed in the buff before she was even a patrolman.

Bonnie Bush's parents sued the city for the neglect they claimed had caused her wrongful death. Kenneth Besterman, plaintiff's counsel with Richard Winer, said yesterday that he had entered the case with minimal hope, because "the law is 103 percent against us." And the law is indeed clear-cut—a citizen cannot expect the police to protect him from felonious assault unless he gives them advance notice of its threat. If the police do not learn of the crime until after it starts, no subsequent negligence on their part adds up to a legal tort.

Yesterday it was announced that the City of New York had agreed to settle the claim by paying $150,000 to Bonnie Bush's estate. Assistant Corporation Counsel John Ryan credited this unheard-of generosity to "the prejudicial nature of the facts," even though they were "irrelevant." He spoke in cold tones of a government whose gelid habits make understandable its alarm that, whatever the law says, a jury might hear such a story and run wild in its outrage.

Etiquette at a Crime Scene
CARL HIAASEN—*Miami Herald*—6/20/1986

Shoppers at a West Kendall plaza got a special treat this week when a pair of bullet-riddled corpses were found in the trunk of a Lincoln parked in the lot.

Hundreds of spectators gathered in a festive atmosphere around the scene, many waiting up to six hours for the bodies to be extricated. Some onlookers drank lemonade while others took pictures and watched the death sedan through binoculars. A few even belly-crawled under parked cars to gain a closer vantage.

As the crowd grew, traffic actually backed up on Kendall Drive. "It was a nice day, they didn't have anything else to do, I guess," says Dr. Jay Barnhart, the medical examiner sent to the scene.

Look on the bright side. The fact that a routine trunk murder still draws an audience in Dade County proves we're not so desensitized to crime after all. If folks are so hungry for entertainment, maybe pro basketball really does have a chance down here.

Of course it's one thing to gather out of idle curiosity at a gruesome homicide, and quite another to make it a block party. As at all social occasions, there must be rules of etiquette.

Unfortunately the new maven of decorum, Miss Manners, has written virtually nothing about what is proper behavior at a crime scene. Such a guide is overdue in South Florida, where each day seems to offer a new Grisly Discovery.

Q. What should I wear?

A. Always pick out something that won't clash with the yellow police cordons; pastel greens and blues are nice. A sunbonnet can be fashionable, too. And choose sensible footwear—shoes with reinforced toes, so you can stretch and gawk.

Q. Where should I stand?

A. Upwind, always. Be considerate to fellow spectators. If somebody yells, "Down in front!" then sit down. Bring a lawn chair, or one of those portable stools you rent at golf tournaments. And stay off the fenders of the squad cars.

Q. Is it OK to bring the kids?

A. At burglaries, auto thefts, shopliftings—what the heck, unpack those strollers and give the little tykes a thrill! However, parental discretion is advised for most first-degree felony scenes.

Q. What about some helpful photo tips?

A. You'll want to use slide film, of course, so you can put together a carousel show for the neighbors. Bring a basic 35mm with a long lens, in case the police make you stand far away (they can be so fussy). And no need to hurry the focusing—one things about dead bodies, they tend to hold very still.

Q. What about souvenirs?

A. Usually it's unwise to try to collect souvenirs from a crime scene. Bullet fragments, shell casings, hair samples, ski masks, money satchels, bloody clothing—sure, the stuff would look swell in the rec room next to your bowling trophies. But, please, the crime lab gets first dibs.

Q. Do we have to bring our own food?

A. Meals and munchies are rarely served at major crime scenes, except for the occasional Sno-Cone vendor. If you're packing a picnic basket, finger food is best—chicken wings, ribs, tacos. Stuff you can heat up on the hibachi.

Q. Can we order some drinks?

A. Conveniently, many exciting homicides are committed in bars, and these establishments gladly serve bystanders. However, if the scene of the crime is a street or shopping mall, plan to bring a small Thermos—soft drinks and wine coolers are acceptable, though champagne is considered poor taste. The sound of the cork sets the cops on edge.

Q. What about wagering?

A. It's simply bad manners to make bets on how many days a body has been inside a car, the number of bullet holes, the length of the victim's rap sheet, or the amount of cash and cocaine in his pockets.

Q. How do we know when to applaud?

A. Some say you should clap when the body bags come out, others say hold the ovation until the coroner leaves. In any case, shouting out "Yo, Quincy!" is considered rude, as is coaxing the crowd into doing The Wave.

And please—no boat horns or cowbells. Have some respect.

Lucy's Blue Light
STEVE LOPEZ—*Philadelphia Inquirer*—3/12/1989

Not long ago, Lucy Perez's 14-year-old son gave her a three-speed bicycle. He told her that he had worked hard, selling flowers and shining shoes, and he wanted his mother to exercise and lose some weight.

The bike was put to good use. After Victor Corcino ran away from home the last time, Lucy would pedal around North Philadelphia, looking for her son. She would pedal east of Broad Street and west of Broad Street, through neighborhoods that used to be owned by people but are now owned drugs.

She prayed as she pedaled, hoping it was not too late.

A month ago her brother had a premonition and told Lucy to prepare for bad news about Victor. A week ago, she had her own vision. She says she saw a flash of light, and for her it symbolized death.

Last Tuesday, an awful feeling came over her. She went to Victor's room and touched his books, his clothes, his paintings. Things that were black, like his shoes, seemed to be alive. She saw some flowers and imagined a funeral.

About 2:15 p.m. Wednesday, Victor was shot near Ninth and Clearfield. The bullet entered his chest and came out his back.

Lucy, racing the ghosts, rushed to St. Christopher's Hospital. An hour later, the blue light was gone, and Victor with it. He had said he wanted to own a stove since he grew up.

She is in the car now, riding to the Medical Examiner's on a gorgeous day that is melting the late snow. She is wearing black, and in a few moments she will have to identify the body of her second of four sons.

Police don't know for sure that it was drugs, but that is where they're looking. Victor was arrested recently for selling marijuana, and it was the lure of money that put him on the corner where he was shot.

Lucy's brother had helped her look for Victor. Night after night.

"He told me he didn't want to be poor. He wanted to buy things," the brother says. "Jewelry. Clothes."

The search led Lucy's brother to Ninth and Clearfield, where the dealers are brokers of little boys' lives.

"I told them I'm Victor's uncle and I want to take him home. They said he's a runaway. He's ours now."

Another relative was chased away by men with bats and knives. The law of the streets said Victor was theirs. There is no court of appeals, here. There is no childhood.

"Ever since his father abandoned him, I think it hurt him in his heart," Lucy is saying in the car. "He ran away, the first time, right after his father left. He was like 9 years old."

And she was left to raise four kids in a neighborhood that waits to pluck them away. Lucy's back yard abuts the yard of the Mazzccua family. In December, the 17-year-old Keith Mazzccua was gunned down in a shootout on the street and his 11-year-old sister took a bullet in the leg. It was drug-related.

"I have students who can't read or write," says Sylvia Rider, principal of Kenderton School, which Mazzccua and Corcino children attend. "But talk about drugs, they're all fluent, they all have personal stories."

Victor graduated from Kenderton at 13. The Corcino kids are known for bright personalities and artistic talent—soldiers in the army of kids with Main Line potential and North Philly limitations.

The day after Victor was killed, the school nurse led students in a discussion about losing loved ones to tragedy. It's one subject that requires no remedial work.

On the way to the morgue, Lucy is looking at passing cars and people on the streets. Victor is everywhere. He is walking to school, he is selling flowers, he is opening the door of his store. The absurdity of routine movement of life is pulling soft tears out of her as the car pulses through traffic.

"I did the best I could do as a mother, God knows. I still serve the Lord, because I know that if I do, I'll get a second chance to be with Victor. That's what I live for now."

Lucy walks strong, with her brother, into the room where Victor lies. She comes out wearing his death, crying for all mothers and fathers of lost children, and for all the babies growing up in neighborhoods their parents used to own.

He was only a boy, and he died violently in a place where the murder of children is becoming small news, to the dishonor of us all.

The day Lucy went to the morgue, Ninth and Clearfield was crawling with dealers. A half-dozen worked the corner where Victor was shot, another half-dozen nearby.

They wore the stain of Victor's blood, as do all pushers and users, and they stood under the glare of Lucy's blue light.

Steak Tips to Die For
MIKE BARNICLE—*Boston Globe*—11/7/1995

Those who think red meat might be bad for you have a pretty good argument this morning in the form of five dead guys killed yesterday at the 99 Restaurant in Charlestown. It appears that the two late Luisis, Bobby, the father, and Roman, his son, along with their three pals, sure did love it because there was so much beef spread out in front of the five victims that their table-top resembled a cattle drive.

"All that was missing was the marinara," a detective was saying yesterday. "If they had linguini and marinara it would have been like that scene in *The Godfather* where Michael Corleone shoots the Mafia guy and the cop. But it was steak tips."

Prior to stopping for a quick bite, Roman Luisi was on kind of a roll. According to police, he recently beat a double-murder charge in California. Where else?

But that was then and this is now. And Sunday night, he got in a fight in the North End. Supposedly, one of those he fought with was Damian Clemente, 20 years old and built like a steamer trunk. Clemente, quite capable of holding a grudge, is reliably reported to have sat on Luisi.

Plus, it is now alleged that at lunch yesterday, young Clemente, along with Vincent Perez, 27, walked into the crowded restaurant and began firing at five guys in between salads and entree. The 99 is a popular establishment located at the edge of Charlestown, a section of the city often pointed to as a place where nearly everyone acts like Marcel Marceau after murders take place in plain view of hundreds.

Therefore, most locals were quick to point out that all allegedly involved in the shooting—the five slumped on the floor as well as the two morons quickly captured outside—were from across the bridge. Both the alleged shooters and the five victims hung out in the North End.

However, yesterday, it appears, everyone was playing an away game. For those who still think "The Mob" is an example of a talented organization capable of skillfully executing its game plan, there can be only deep disappointment in the aftermath of such horrendous, noisy and public violence.

It took, oh, about 45 seconds for authorities to track down Clemente and Perez. Clemente is of such proportions that his foot speed is minimal. And it is thought that his partner Perez's thinking capacity is even slower than Clemente's feet.

Two Everett policemen out of uniform—Bob Hall and Paul Durant—were having lunch a few feet away from where both Luisis and the others were having the last supper. The two cops have less than five years' experience combined but both came up huge.

"They didn't try anything crazy inside. They didn't panic," another detective pointed out last night. "They followed the two shooters out the door, put them down and held them there. They were unbelieveably level-headed, even when two Boston cops arrived and had their guns drawn on the Everett cops because they didn't know who they were, both guys stayed cool and identified themselves. And they are going to make two truly outstanding witnesses."

The two Boston policemen who arrived in the parking lot where Clemente and Perez were prone on the asphalt were Tom Hennessey and Stephen Green. They were working a paid detail nearby which, all things being equal, immediately led one official to cast the event in its proper, parochial perspective: "This ought to put an end to the argument to do away with paid details," he said. "Hey, ask yourself this question: You think a flagman could have arrested these guys?"

The entire event—perhaps four minutes in duration, involving at least 13 shots, five victims and two suspects caught—is a bitter example of how downsizing has affected even organized crime. For several years, the federal government has enforced mandatory retirement rules—called jail—on several top local mob executives.

What's left are clowns who arrive for a great matinee murder in a beat-up blue Cadillac and a white Chrysler that look like they are used for Bumper-Car. The shooters then proceed to leave a restaurant filled with the smell of cordite and about 37 people capable of picking them out of a lineup.

"Part of it was kind of like in the movies, but part of it wasn't," an eyewitness said last night. "The shooting part was like you see in a movie but the fat guy almost slipped and fell when he was getting away. That part you don't see in a movie. But what a mess that table was."

"We have a lot of evidence, witnesses and even a couple weapons," a detective pointed out last evening. "But the way things are going in this country it would not surprise me if the defense argues that these guys were killed by cholesterol."

New Land, Sad Story
MIKE BARNICLE—*Boston Globe*—11/23/1995

Three Cadillac hearses were parked on Hastings Street outside Calvary Baptist Church in Lowell Tuesday morning as an old town wrestled with new grief. Inside, the caskets had been placed together by the altar while the mother of the dead boys, a Cambodian woman named Chhong Yim, wept so much it seemed she cried for a whole city.

The funeral occurred two days before the best of American holidays and revolved around a people, many of whom have felt on occasion that God is symbolized by stars, stripes and the freedom to walk without fear. But a bitter truth was being buried here as well because now every Cambodian man, woman and child knows that despite fleeing the Khmer Rouge and soldiers who killed on whim, nobody can run forever from a plague that is as much a bitter part of this young country as white meat and cranberry sauce.

The dead children were Visal Men, 15, along with his two brothers Virak, 14, and Sovanna, 9, born in the U.S.A. They were shot and stabbed last week when the mother's friend, Vuthy Seng, allegedly became enraged at being spurned by Chhong Yim, who chose her children over Seng.

There sure are enough sad stories to go around on any given day. However, there aren't many to equal the slow demise of a proud, gentle culture—Cambodian—as it is bastardized by the clutter and chaos we not only allow to occur but willingly accept as a cost of democracy.

The three boys died slowly; first one, then the other in a hospital and, finally, the third a few days after Seng supposedly had charged into the apartment with a gun and a machete. He shot and hacked all three children along with their sister, Sathy Men, who is 13 and stood bewildered beside her howling mother, the two of them survivors of a horror so deep their lives are forever maligned.

At 10:45, as the funeral was set to begin, two cops on motorcycles came up Hastings ahead of a bus filled with children from Butler Middle School. The boys and girls walked in silence into the chapel to pray for the dead who have left a firm imprint on their adopted hometown.

The crowd of mourners was thrilling in its diversity. There were policemen, firefighters, teachers and shopkeepers. The young knelt shoulder-to-shoulder with the old. There were Catholic nuns and Buddhist priests. There were friends of the family as well as total strangers summoned only by tragedy.

A little after 11 a.m., Hak Seng, who drove from Rhode Island, parked his car by the post office and headed toward Calvary Baptist Church.

"I am late. I got lost," Hak Sen said.

"Are you a friend of the family?" he was asked.

"No," he replied. "I do not know them. I come out of respect and sadness. We all make a terrible journey to come here to America and this is very, very bad."

Hak Sen said he and his family were from Battambang Province, along the Thai-Cambodian border. He said that he served in the army before Pol Pot took over his country and that he and his family were forced to flee but not all made it to the refugee camps.

"I am lucky man," Hak Sen pointed out. "I survive. My wife, she survive and two of our children, they survive."

"Did you lose any children?" he was asked.

"Yes," he said. "I lose three boys, just like this woman. Three boys and our daughter. They all dead. The malaria kill them in the jungle. There was not enough food and no water and they were young and could not fight the disease and they died. They all dead. My mother and father too."

The innocent children inside the church as well as all the big-hearted citizens of Lowell along with the majority of people who will buy a paper or carve a turkey today simply have no idea of the epic, tragic struggle of the Cambodians. They left a country where they were killed for owning a ballpoint pen or wearing a pair of eyeglasses to arrive in this country where, each day, we become more and more narcoticized by the scale of violence around us.

At the conclusion of the service, Lowell detectives Mike Durkin, John Boutselis and Phil Conroy helped carry the caskets to the hearses. The procession wound slowly through city streets, pausing for a few seconds outside the Butler School, where pupils lined both sides of the road like grieving sentries as the entourage entered Westlawn Cemetery.

"This is as sad as it gets," said Roger LaPointe, a cemetery worker. "We cut the first two graves the end of last week but the funeral director told us we better hold on. When the third boy died, we had to cut it some more. It's an awful thing. That hole just kept getting bigger."

A Bullet's Impact
MITCH ALBOM—*Detroit Free Press*—12/29/2000

One night. One town. One bullet. One kid.

The kid was Justin Mello, barely 16 years old, a popular soccer player at Anchor Bay High School with a melting smile, a tall, athletic frame, a freshly minted driver's license, and a dream of buying his father's GMC truck with the money earned working at a pizza shop.

The bullet came from a 9-millimeter handgun. It was fired just inches from Mello's head as he knelt, execution style, in a cooler filled with dough and cheese. The bullet ripped through Mello's skull and exited his forehead. When they found his body, he was still on his knees.

The town was New Baltimore, population 7,000, a quiet, waterfront community in Macomb County, where there hadn't been a murder since before Justin was born.

The night was Saturday, Oct. 21.

"Before this," sighs a lawyer in the case, "the biggest problem in New Baltimore was the fish flies."

Not anymore.

One night. One town. One kid. One bullet. Follow its flight, and you witness a devastation that far exceeds its caliber, a swath that cuts a community in two. You see children weeping and parents numb with grief. You see a soccer team wearing armbands and a makeshift tombstone on a high school lawn. You see accused murderers, in chains, being cheered outside a courthouse. You see witnesses changing their stories. You see a Christmas tree in a suburban home, devoid of presents for the oldest boy. You see a father, in a hospital, as a yellow body bag is unzipped. He looks at the face that used to be so bright, used to be his son, and now is forever shattered by the hole of . . .

One bullet. Follow its flight. It begins with the simple pull of a trigger, late one autumn night. . . .

This much, they all agree on:

At 9:30 p.m. on Oct. 21, Justin Mello, his friend and soccer teammate Dan Buchman, and a store manager, Jeffrey Arwada, were working the night shift at Mancino's Pizza and Grinders on 23 Mile Road near Jefferson. There were no customers. They played the radio and sang along with it. Dan and Justin, to pass the time, threw sausage pieces at each other and laughed.

The phone rang. Justin answered, then handed the call to Jeff. Someone wanted a take-out order—but with a delayed delivery.

Don't bring it until 10:45, the caller said.

"We're not allowed to do that," Jeff replied.

The caller said he knew the owner. He insisted it was OK. Bring it at 10:45. Jeff relented.

At 10 p.m., Dan's shift was over. He told Justin, "I'll see you tomorrow at soccer practice." He punched him lightly in the arm, and Justin smiled and said, "See ya."

At 10:25 p.m., Jeff left Mancino's with the pizza. He had difficulty with the address, which was in a mobile home park. When he finally found the number, he knocked on the door. A woman answered and looked puzzled.

"I didn't order any pizza," she said. . . .

The call had been a setup.

This is what happened next:

Back at Mancino's, someone entered through the front door, locked it, took money from the cash register, forced Justin into the cooler, shot him in the back of the head, left him there, bleeding to death, and ran out the back. Whoever it was also turned the lights off, all except for the "open" sign in the window.

Shortly after 11 p.m., Jeff returned.

He immediately sensed something was wrong. He saw the place was dark, but why was the "open" sign still on? He saw cheese unpacked on the counter. He saw crumbs that hadn't been cleaned. He went into the cooler. There he found Justin's body, still on its knees, bleeding in the corner. He frantically called 911.

"He's unconscious," Jeff said. "He's bleeding real bad from his head. . . ."

Meanwhile, a few blocks away, Henry Mello sat in his living room and looked at his watch. He was worried. Justin was usually home by 11:30. It was now 12:15 a.m. With his wife, Denise, asleep, Henry jumped in the family van and drove to the shop. He saw police cars. He saw yellow tape.

"What do you want?" an officer barked. "Why are you here?"

"I'm looking for my son, Justin Mello."

The officer's expression changed. "Um . . . you're going to have to go to the police station, sir."

Henry's heart began to race. At the station he was met by the police chief, who took him inside and said, "Mr. Mello, there's been a robbery. There's been a shooting. There was one person in the store and he was taken to Mount Clemens General Hospital. . . ."

He paused.

"And he's deceased."

One bullet was all it took to kill Justin Mello. This, according to those who knew him, was the kind of kid we lost.

The kind who sat down next to you if you looked upset, and made a face, or cracked a joke.

The kind who, after every soccer game, went to the referees and shook their hands.

The kind who slid his palm on the chair as you were about to sit down, or who grabbed you from behind and laughed, or who raced to the most comfortable stool in science lab, said, "Ha! I got it!" then gave it to you anyhow.

The kind who banged pots and pans on New Year's Eve, the kind who worked at the student-run candy shop and slipped his friends free taffy, the kind who, even at age 16, could be seen playing with the neighborhood children, rolling in the grass, giving them horsey rides.

Girls called him "Babe." Or "Muffin Butt." Guys called him "Mello Yellow."

He was working to save money for his father's 1994 Sonoma truck, and had put away $4,000.

He was nominated for the National Honor Society.

He was a defender on the soccer team.

He was 6-feet-1.

He was dead.

"At the hospital, they took me into an emergency room," Henry Mello, 48, says now, his expression a dull gaze. "There were four or five steel tables. I didn't really see anything. Then the doctor walked up and there was this yellow bag laying there, and he started to unzip it. I walked over, and it was Justin. . . ."

He stops. He inhales. He is sitting at a dining room table, near a small plate of fruit and cookies put out for a visitor. Next to him sits his wife, Denise, 44, who looks devastated even when she smiles, and their 18-year-old daughter, Leah, a college student who was sleeping in her apartment when she got the call saying her kid brother was dead.

In the adjacent den is the Mellos' youngest child, 12-year-old Trevor, who is playing a video game near a large Christmas tree. As is often the case when a child is lost, the air in the house seems heavy, the weight of a ghost.

"He was shot in the back of his head," Henry continues. "And the bullet came out just above his eye. It was bad. They closed up the bag. Then Denise came in. . . ."

"He told me I shouldn't see the body," Denise says.

"I didn't think she'd want to go."

"But I felt like I had to. . . ."

"To have them unzip this bag. . . ."

"When I saw him, I was in shock. . . ."

"It's such a cold thing."

"I couldn't cry."

"And I couldn't stop."

Police in New Baltimore wanted this case solved. Theirs was not a town for murders. It was a place where people fished, where they bowled, where visitors took boats out on Anchor Bay and Lake St. Clair. Bloody murders, senseless violence, a dead body in a pizza cooler—this was all so alien.

Working with outside help from county, state and federal authorities, a task force was assembled to find the killer. Initially, police were optimistic about physical evidence—blood, fingerprints, something—but one by one, the cards came up blank.

They combed rooftops and dredged a nearby pond. No gun was found.

They sent divers into Lake St. Clair. Still no gun.

Fingerprints proved inconclusive. Search warrants yielded nothing.

The pizza shop had a surveillance system, but there was no tape in the video recorder.

And their first suspect, a 28-year-old Macomb County man found hiding under a bed in Detroit, was cleared after passing a lie-detector test.

Crime scenes dry up quickly. Several days after the shooting, there was still no one in custody.

Meanwhile, the community ached for justice, even as it mourned the loss of a favorite son. Mancino's, which remained closed, became a virtual shrine, ringed by flowers, candles, poems and stuffed animals. So did the large white anchor by the front lawn of Anchor Bay High School. It was painted with messages—God Bless, See You When We Get There—and became a gathering spot for confused and angry teens trying to make sense of what was, for many, their first exposure to death.

The soccer team, for which Justin had been a rugged, steady defender known for seeing the field, protecting his area, and occasionally, though legally, laying into an opposing player, had a district playoff game scheduled Monday night. The coach, Bob Grammens, called a team meeting and asked the players whether they wanted to cancel.

They said no.

Instead they would dedicate the game to Justin and would win it in his memory.

Although soccer matches at Anchor Bay High usually draw about 100 people, more than 2,000 came out for this one. The players wore armbands with Justin's No. 20. There was a moment of silence at the start, and a special memorial performance by the dance team at halftime.

"There was every kind of kid in the crowd," recalls Don Dziuk, an assistant coach. "I mean, kids who would never come to sports events were there. So were their parents, their grandparents. We won the game and people were running onto the field. The whole night, looking back, was surreal."

And then came the cold daylight.

Justin's body was on view Tuesday and Wednesday. The crowds at the funeral home were so enormous, people had to wait in line to get in. Many of the mourners didn't even know Justin. But this is the kind of town he lived in, the kind where murder is foreign and unfathomable, and grieving is a communal emotion.

At one point, with the hallways packed, Leah, Justin's older sister, entered a sitting room stuffed with crying teenagers. She edged to the front and said, "I want you to tell me about my brother."

And one by one, each kid stood up and said something. Some told stories. Some read poems. One teenager after another, talking about a dead boy's practical jokes, about his comforting ways, about his eyes and his smile. It was as if they had lost a healer, and were now trying to heal themselves.

The funeral itself was almost too much to bear. Henry stood and read a "letter" from Justin in heaven.

"Dear Dad,

"How ya doin? Do you see it? I know you do. . . . Our whole community is in such pain right now. . . .

"Please apologize to everyone at the soccer game for me. . . . I started to cry. I had no idea that would cause the rain to come. I know the guys on the team didn't mind, but I'm sorry I got the fans all wet. . . .

"Please take this strength and use it to heal our family . . . use it to heal our community. . . . Seek out those people that are hurting. Tell them to cry, to kick things. . . . Then, when they are done, tell them to remember me for all of the kind and good things they are saying about me. . . .

"I love you, Dad. Keep the faith.

"Justin."

One bullet. One kid. One town. One grave.

Not everyone in New Baltimore is on the soccer team or in the National Honor Society. Follow that bullet now, as it rivets through a fraternity of underachievers, kids for whom pot, beer, an odd job and the occasional party are enough.

Three young men, Jonathan Kaled, 18, Frank Kuecken, 19, and Matthew Daniels, 16, seem to fit the profile. Kaled, who recently dropped out of Anchor Bay High, had a rap sheet of minor offenses, including drug possession and breaking into a Jeep. Daniels also had dropped out of Anchor Bay High, and had several minor scrapes with the law. Kuecken, who dropped out of Hazel Park High in 1999, had been working as a pressman at a tool company.

All three youths, who had known each other and worked together as stock boys in a market—until Kaled was caught stealing beer in a trash can—had been at a bonfire party in nearby New Haven the night of the murder. The party was reportedly rife with marijuana and alcohol.

Still, all three, Kaled, Kuecken and Daniels, began the morning of Oct. 26 —Justin's funeral day—as free men.

Before the next sunrise, they were being held for murder.

According to State Police Lt. Charles Schumacher, who works with COMET, a multi-jurisdictional task force, police were following tips from former Mancino's employees. One of them, Schumacher says, claimed he overheard Kaled talking about what an easy robbery Mancino's would make. After more questioning and more witnesses, the trio was taken in for questioning.

All three were read their Miranda rights. Each was interrogated separately. Only Daniels had a parent with him, his mother. The questioning began between 8 and 9 at night.

By the wee hours Friday morning, police had two signed confessions.

Kaled confessed to shooting Justin Mello, claiming that it was an accident, that he went into Mancino's alone, that he intended only to rob the place, that the gun went off as he was backing up.

Kuecken confessed to driving the getaway truck and offered two versions in two separate interviews, both implicating Kaled in the shooting.

Daniels confessed nothing, although Kaled and Kuecken said he supplied the gun and later got rid of it.

When news leaked that the police had three young men in custody, a wave of relief went through New Baltimore, followed by ripples of anger that the guilty parties could be homegrown.

Kids wrote messages to Justin, saying, "They got the guys who did it." Others wrote letters to the Mello family, wishing speedy justice. The newspapers reported that the suspected killers had confessed.

For a brief moment, the bullet seemed to have come to rest.

Then the families of the charged teens hired lawyers.

And a few days later, everything changed.

Jonathan Kaled has a pudgy build and wears his hair short. A few nights after confessing to murder, he sat in a cell at the Macomb County Jail and told James Howarth a different story.

Howarth, a veteran attorney, had been through this before. He had no desire to take on a small town, a police force or Schumacher, a man he says he knows and respects. "I told the family before I went to see Jonathan that this was not a case I wanted unless I was completely convinced he didn't do it."

By the time he left the jail, Howarth was convinced.

Kaled—whom Howarth describes as "a highly susceptible 18-year-old who does not hold up well to pressure"—said his confession was coerced. He said he only signed it to stop the incessant questioning.

The truth, Kaled said, is that he was nowhere near Mancino's.

The truth, Kaled said, is that he was at the bonfire party all night.

The truth, Kaled said, is that he was innocent.

Howarth listened, and his mind was made up.

Kaled—like Kuecken—would plead not guilty.

"If there was something to back up the piece of paper my client signed—one scrap of evidence, a gun, a fingerprint, a fiber, anything!—then I would be highly concerned that I was representing a guilty person rather than an innocent one," Howarth says. "But the fact is, he's an 18-year-old who probably has attention deficit disorder. They question him from 8:30 at night to 1:30 in the morning. He's questioned by highly skilled officers, then gets 'softened up' by local guys—the classic good cop, bad cop thing.

"The local guys say, 'We know you. We know your family. We think this is terrible, but those guys are coming back for more questions. Maybe it's not as bad as they say. Maybe you went into that pizza place just to rob it and you accidentally shot the kid.' . . .

"And all of a sudden, that's what my client says."

The accusations are vehemently denied by Schumacher and Robert Merrelli, a Macomb County assistant prosecutor. Both say the interrogations were legitimate.

"I was there, overseeing it," Schumacher says. "And everything was done by the book."

Adds Merrelli: "Both of these suspects gave details only the people who committed the crime could have known."

Still, Howarth and Paul Stablein, the lawyer who represents Kuecken, not only plan to, in effect, put the police on trial, they also will try to raise reasonable doubt with several other factors, including:

- A group of party-goers from the bonfire that night, who plan to testify that all three men were there at the time of the killing.
- The disturbing fact that in late November, two former employees of the New Baltimore Mancino's, Dennis Bryan, 20, and David Baumann, 19, were arrested in Kentucky after holding up a Super 8 motel as part of a multi-state crime spree. Police found a collection of guns in their possession. (None matched the Mello killing.) More disturbingly, in their crime spree, the two allegedly murdered a Subway sandwich shop employee in St. Augustine, Fla. He was killed in almost identical fashion as Mello: shot in a cooler, execution style. And police found a map in the suspects' possession that had several red marks on it, including one on Detroit.

FBI agents already have questioned the two men about the Mello murder. Both denied involvement, even though Bryan admitted guilt in the other crimes.

Says Schumacher: "We were looking for those two even before we found (Kaled and Kuecken). The fact is, there is nothing to suggest they were in Michigan at the time of the murder. We had an FBI guy talk to Bryan in Kentucky, and Bryan told him, 'Look, I admitted to all the other stuff. If I did the one in Michigan, why wouldn't I tell you?'"

For Howarth—whose client, like Kuecken, is facing murder charges and up to life in prison when the trial starts next month—that is not good enough.

"You have to wonder about the gusto with which they went after those men in Kentucky," Howarth says, "especially when they think they've got their killer in jail already."

A 9mm bullet is smaller than a pinky fingernail, about the size of a pencil eraser. Yet the tiny bullet from Oct. 21, whose shell ripped through Justin's head, hit the cooler floor and came to rest in a wad of pizza cheese, continues to rip through New Baltimore as if freshly fired.

For the first preliminary hearing at 42nd District Court, Kaled, Kuecken and Daniels were led out in chains and bulletproof vests. They were greeted by cheers of "We love you!" and "We're with you!" from supporters gathered outside the courthouse.

Some of the chanting came from the trio's teenaged friends—what Judge

Cassidy referred to as the "subculture of miscreants"—and caused many in the community to shudder, including Justin's parents, Henry and Denise, who witnessed the display on their way into the courthouse.

"It made me mad," Henry says, back in the family dining room. "First of all, why are these kids not in school? Did their parents sign off notes that say, 'OK, you can go cheer for your friend?'"

Adds Denise: "I'm just appalled that anyone can do this to a family. They have no idea how many lives it affects. And it's forever. It's forever. . . .

"I believe when they went in with a gun, they knew they were going to kill somebody. . . . The moral decline of all this . . . I don't know, it seems like anything goes. It doesn't matter what you do, because your parents are always there to pull you out. You get parents who don't use court-appointed lawyers; they hire lawyers to get their kids a lesser sentence.

"A lesser sentence? I mean, you've got a confession.

"A confession!"

She shakes her head and looks down. And in that gush of emotion, she has crystallized the rumblings in her community.

On the one hand, there is no gun, no fingerprints, no hairs, no bloody clothes or previous convictions of violent crime. All the police have is two confessions by two high school dropouts currently sitting in Macomb County Jail. The charges against Daniels were dismissed—although Judge Cassidy firmly said he thought Daniels was guilty—because Daniels never confessed, and, under law, Kaled and Kuecken cannot be forced to incriminate him.

On the other hand, these are signed confessions. And, what's more, Schumacher says Kaled told police that he took Justin's wallet before shooting him. He described the contents of that wallet—$40, a driver's license, two photos— even though the wallet had never even found. When police called the Mello family, they verified the wallet's contents. How would Kaled know that if he wasn't there?

Schumacher also has a witness who identified Kuecken's Ford truck as being in front of Mancino's at the time of the murder.

As to the witnesses who will claim Kaled and Kuecken were at the party all night? Well. There seems to be dispute over how many actually will testify. Schumacher says many of them have changed their stories more than once.

Then again, so have some of the witnesses who originally told police that Kaled, Kuecken and Daniels might be guilty. One such witness, Joe Gosselin, first told police he overheard a robbery plot, then recanted the story when asked to write it down. He now says he was harassed.

"I can't believe that," Schumacher says. "I shook his hand and told him he was an honest man. Next thing you know, he's taking it all back. . . ."

And on it goes, a bullet that won't stop hitting the walls.

Had Justin Mello not been at Mancino's that night, he would have played in that district soccer playoff game. He would have worn his No. 20 uniform. He would have come home afterward and relived the game with his parents. And he would have bugged his father about that GMC truck.

"He used to check the Blue Book prices," Henry says, "and he'd say, 'Dad, it's coming down. . . .'"

"Sometimes, when I'm driving my truck now, I think, 'Justin should be doing this.' If it needs a new battery, 'Justin should be buying it.' If it needs gas, 'Justin should be filling it up.' This truck is supposed to be his. . . ."

He shakes his head.

"It's supposed to be his. . . ."

What is supposed to be. That is the true victim in New Baltimore. Small towns are supposed to be safe. Parents are supposed to be able to leave 16-year-olds on their own, without worrying about them dying. Schools are supposed to be for learning, not memorial services. Children are supposed to outlive their parents.

What is supposed to be . . .

Dan Buchman, the other Mancino's worker, was the last good friend to see Justin alive. He thinks a lot about that night, what might have been if he stayed, why Justin, not him. He thinks about when he told his buddy, "See you at soccer practice tomorrow," and he rabbit-punched his arm and Justin smiled and said, "See ya."

"That's the thing I miss the most," Buchman says now, his voice a scratchy mix of adolescent tones, "his big smile, you know? The way you'd go to school in the morning and you'd feel a hit on your shoulder and you'd turn around and there he was."

And now, nothing. They turn around and all they see is an empty locker, an empty chair, an empty soccer jersey, an empty bed. In the end, this is not about Kaled and Kuecken, or the two guys in Kentucky, or the way police interrogate, or "a subculture of miscreants."

It's about the loss of an innocent, and the innocence lost.

One night. One kid. One town shattered. The heartache, the horror, that one little bullet can do.

VI: CIVIL RIGHTS & CIVIL LIBERTIES

The early ancestor of the newspaper columnist was the pamphleteer and polemicist—writing often on the thorny issues of race, rights, and liberties that have preoccupied our nation since her founding.

Side by side with the struggle for equality has been the permanent battle for constitutional free speech: the right to speak one's mind, the right to be heard. Every journalist depends on those First Amendment rights, but not everyone is willing to stand up and fight for them with ferocity.

Facing popular support for a San Jose lynch mob—whose apologists included newspapers and then-California Governor James Rolphe—Heywood Broun replies to an editorial that stated "nobody that we've talked to appears to disagree with the mob" by saying simply, "All right; talk to me."

Writing in the 1930s, Dorothy Thompson grapples with the question of whether a pro-Nazi group in Connecticut has the right to spread its views: "We are asked to admit that the belief in democracy includes hospitality for our would-be murderers, who do not even bother any longer to deny that their strategy is planned for them abroad. Well, does it?"

Good question.

I. F. Stone forthrightly calls the willingness to shut off the free speech rights of Nazi sympathizers "the panic of faltering spirits," and hails a controversial Supreme Court decision.

Facing the brutal illogic of segregation, Langston Hughes uses satire to illustrate the injustice. Likewise, in the fight for civil rights, Murray Kempton and Jack Newfield travel down South and chronicle the struggle for racial justice with courage and compassion.

Eugene Patterson confronts the Birmingham Church bombing and finds plenty of blame to pass around the South in "A Flower for the Graves," written from his perch at the *Atlanta Constitution* and read aloud on the CBS Evening News at the request of Walter Cronkite. Max Lerner coins an inspirational aphorism writing about the courage of students attempting to integrate Little Rock in the face of hate: "The turning point in the process of growing up is when you discover the core of strength within you that survives all hurt." Meanwhile, William F. Buckley Jr. strikes a conservative contrarian tone in the wake of race riots, pointing out that "a man who breaks into a store to hijack himself a case of whiskey can hardly be said to be engaged in the advancement of colored people."

Columnists eventually picked up the question of gay rights: Pete Dexter finds a case of pure-and-simple job discrimination and renounces his own, mistaken idea that gays don't need anti-bias protection. Anna Quindlen warns even the outwardly politically correct against presenting "a veneer of tolerance atop a deep pool of hatred, distrust, and estrangement."

Cynthia Tucker salutes her niece for embodying the hope of immigration while William Raspberry analyzes the meaning of America electing her first black president—raising, once again, the questions of color and the Constitution that have been fought out in the news pages since America's founding.

The Destiny of Colored Americans
FREDRICK DOUGLASS—*North Star*—11/16/1849

It is impossible to settle, by the light of the present, and by the experience of the past, any thing, definitely and absolutely, as to the future condition of the colored people of this country; but, so far as present indications determine, it is clear that this land must continue to be the home of the colored man so long as it remains the abode of civilization and religion. For more than two hundred years we have been identified with its soil, its products, and its institutions; under the sternest and bitterest circumstances of slavery and oppression— under the lash of Slavery at the South—under the sting of prejudice and malice at the North—and under hardships the most unfavorable to existence and population, we have lived, and continue to live and increase. The persecuted red man of the forest, the original owner of the soil, has, step by step, retreated from the Atlantic lakes and rivers; escaping, as it were, before the footsteps of the white man, and gradually disappearing from the face of the country. He looks upon the steamboats, the railroads, and canals, cutting and crossing his former hunting grounds; and upon the ploughshare, throwing up the bones of his venerable ancestors, and beholds his glory departing—and this heart sickens at the desolation. He spurns the civilization—he hates the race which has despoiled him, and unable to measure arms with his superior foe, he dies.

Not so with the black man. More unlike the European in form, feature and color—called to endure greater hardships, injuries and insults than those to which the Indians have been subjected, he yet lives and prospers under every disadvantage. Long have his enemies sought to expatriate him, and to teach his children that this is not their home, but in spite of all their cunning schemes, and subtle contrivances, his footprints yet mark the soil of his birth, and he gives every indication that America will, for ever, remain the home of his posterity. We deem it a settled point that the destiny of the colored man is bound up with that of the white people of this country; be the destiny of the latter what it may.

It is idle—worse than idle, ever to think of our expatriation, or removal. The history of colonization society must extinguish all such speculations. We are rapidly filling up the number of four millions; and all the gold of California combined would be insufficient to defray the expenses attending our colonization. We are, as laborers, too essential to the interests of our white fellow-countrymen, to make a very grand effort to drive us from this country among probable events. While labor is needed, the laborer cannot fail to be valued; and although passion and prejudice may sometimes vociferate against us, and demand our expulsion, such efforts will only be spasmodic, and can never prevail against the sober second thought of self-interest. *We are here*, and here we are likely to be. To imagine that we shall ever be eradicated is absurd and ridiculous. We can be remodified, changed, and assimilated, but never extinguished. We repeat, therefore, that *we are here;* and that this is *our* country; and the question for the philosophers and statesmen of the land ought to be, What principles should dictate the policy of the action towards us? We shall neither die out, nor be driven out; but shall go with this people, either as a testimony against them, or as an evidence in their favor throughout their generations. We are clearly on their hands, and must remain there for ever. All this we say for the benefit of those who hate the Negro more than they love their country. In an article, under the caption of "Government and its Subjects," (published in our last week's paper,) we called attention to the unwise, as well as the unjust policy usually adopted, by our Government, towards its colored citizens. We would continue to direct attention to that policy, and in our humble way, we would remonstrate against it, as fraught with evil to the white man, as well as to his victim.

The white man's happiness cannot be purchased by the black man's misery. Virtue cannot prevail among the white people, by its destruction among the black people, who form a part of the whole community. It is evident that white and black "must fall or flourish together." In the light of this great truth, laws ought to be enacted, and institutions established—all distinctions, founded on complexion, ought to be repealed, repudiated, and for ever abolished—and every right, privilege, and immunity, now enjoyed by the white man, ought to be as freely granted to the man of color.

Where "knowledge is power," that nation is the most powerful which has the largest population of intelligent men; for a nation to cramp, and circumscribe the mental faculties of a class of its inhabitants, is as unwise as it is cruel, since it, in the same proportion, sacrifices its power and happiness. The American people, in the light of this reasoning, are, at this moment, in obedience to their pride and folly, (we say nothing of the wickedness of the act,) wasting one sixth part of their energies of the entire nation by transforming three millions of its men into beasts of burden.—What a loss to industry, skill, invention, (to say nothing of its foul and corrupting influence,) is *Slavery!* How it ties the hand, cramps the mind, darkens the understanding, and paralyses the whole man! Nothing is more evident to a man who reasons at all, than that America is acting an irrational part in continuing the slave system at the South, and in oppressing its free colored citizens at the North. Regarding the nation as an individual, the act of enslaving and oppressing thus, is as wild and senseless as it would be for Nicholas to order the amputation of the right arm of every Russian solider before engaging in a war with France. We again repeat that Slavery is the peculiar weakness of America, as well as its peculiar crime and the day may yet come when this visionary and oft repeated declaration will be found to contain a great truth.

To an Anxious Friend
WILLIAM ALLEN WHITE—*Emporia Gazette*—7/27/1922

You tell me that law is above freedom of utterance. And I reply that you can have no wise laws nor free entertainment of wise laws unless there is free expression of the wisdom of the people—and, alas, their folly with it. But if there is freedom, folly will die of its own poison, and the wisdom will survive. That is the history of the race. It is proof of man's kinship with God. You say that freedom of utterance is not for time of stress, and I reply with the sad truth that only in time of stress is freedom of utterance in danger. No one questions it in calm days, because it is not needed. And the reverse is true also; only when free utterance is suppressed is it needed, and when it is needed, it is most vital to justice.

Peace is good. But if you are interested in peace through force and without free discussion—that is to say, free utterance decently and in order—your interest in justice is slight. And peace without justice is tyranny, no matter how you may sugarcoat it with expedience. This state today is in more danger from suppression than from violence, because, in the end, suppression leads to violence. Violence, indeed, is the child of suppression. Whoever pleads for justice helps to keep the peace; and whoever tramples on the plea for justice temperately made in the name of peace only outrages peace and kills something fine in the heart of man which God put there when we got our manhood. When that is killed, brute meets brute on each side of the line.

So, dear friend, put fear out of your heart. This nation will survive, this state will prosper, the orderly business of life will go forward if only men can speak in whatever way given them to utter what their hearts hold—by voice, by posted card, by letter, or by press. Reason has never failed men. Only force and repression have made the wrecks in the world.

A Fine Lesson for the Whole Nation
HEYWOOD BROUN—*New York World-Telegram*—11/28/1933

Comment on the San Jose lynching constitutes an obligatory column.

In the beginning it seemed to me as if this thing were so monstrously and obviously evil that it would be enough to say calmly and simply, "Here is one more sadistic orgy carried on by a psychopathic mob under the patronage of the moronic governor of a backward state."

To my amazement I found not only condonation but actual praise for the lynchers in no less than three New York newspapers. I read of "the vigilantes" and "the pioneer spirit" and so on.

Let us examine the evidence to see if there is any reason at all to ascribe the deed to the full-flowered resentment of an aroused public spirit.

Here is the story of the lynching as told by an eighteen-year-old ranch boy who asserted that he was leader of the movement:

"I was the first one of the gang to break into the jail. I came to town in the afternoon and saw the crowd around the jail. I decided to organize a 'necktie' party. Mostly I went to the speakeasies and rounded up the gang there. That is why so many of the mob were drunk. The word got spread around that it was going to be a Santa Clara University student lynching. But I'm not a Santa Clara student. I didn't go to college. I knew Brooke Hart by sight, but never had spoken to him. I thought that his terrible murder should be avenged. I found that several hundred others thought the same thing."

In other words, a farm boy who came into town for a spree managed to hit upon a drunken crowd which was willing to defend the American home and its institutions for the fun of it.

Governor Rolph has called it "a fine lesson to the whole nation." And a New York newspaper says in its leading editorial, "Nobody that we've heard of or talked to appears to disagree with the mob or disapprove of what Governor Rolph said."

All right; talk to me. Or better still read these selections from a United Press dispatch:

"Thurmond was unconscious, and probably dead, when the noose was placed around his neck. He had been beaten and kicked senseless. A boy, not more than sixteen, climbed to the top of a shed and shouted in a shrill voice, 'Come on, fellows!' He was the leader the mob had been waiting for. A new cry went up, 'Let's burn 'em!' Thurmond's body was cut down. It was drenched with gasoline. A match was touched to it, but only his torn clothing burned."

Governor James Rolph, Jr., has been quoted as saying that he would like to turn over all jail inmates serving sentences for kidnapping into the custody of "those fine, patriotic San Jose citizens, who know how to handle such a situation."

"Thousands of men, women and children looking on in carnival spirit cheered with a lustiness which could be heard for blocks."

"Both were dragged across the park, their bruised and torn bodies leaving trails of blood."

And so the fine old pioneer spirit of California, under the leadership of that fine old nature lover, Jim Rolph, has ended kidnapping in the great commonwealth of California. And what has it left in its wake? It has left an obscene, depraved and vile memory in the minds of thousands who stood about and cheered lustily.

"Some of the children were babies in their mothers' arms."

If it were possible to carry on a case history of every person in the mob who beat and kicked and hanged and burned two human beings I will make the prophecy that out of this heritage will come crimes and cruelties which are unnumbered. The price is too high.

Every mother and father of a son wants to have him protected against the danger of kidnapping. But how would you like it if it were your sixteen-year-old boy who climbed to the top of a shed and shouted in a shrill voice, "Come on, fellows!"?

Governor James Rolph, Jr., has said with audacious arrogance, "If anyone is arrested for the good job I'll pardon them all."

It does not lie within the power of the governor of California to pardon the men and boys and women and children who cried out, "Let's burn 'em!" For them there is no pardon this side of the Judgment Seat. To your knees, Governor, and pray that you and your commonwealth may be washed clean of this bath of bestiality into which a whole community has plunged.

You, James Rolph, Jr., stand naked in the eyes of the world. "I'll pardon them all," you say. Is this to be the measure of justice in California? Men with blood and burnt flesh on their hands are to be set free. Mooney must remain in jail. Freedom for the guilty. Punishment for the innocent.

Governor, very frankly, I don't believe you can get away with it. There must be somewhere some power which just won't stand for it.

Rebellion in Connecticut
DOROTHY THOMPSON—*New York Herald Tribune*—12/13/1937

The dilemma of Southbury, Connecticut, raises a question which is tremendously important to the position of democracy, here and everywhere else. It involves the whole issue of civil liberties, and the question of how democracy, in the modern world, can defend itself.

Without revealing the purpose for which he wished it, Wolfgang Jung, of Stamford, Connecticut, purchased, some time ago, 178 acres of land in the village of Southbury. The German-American Bund, it now develops, was the real purchaser, and the purpose is to erect on this land a German-American Bund camp. I wish to be scrupulously correct, so I do not call this a 'Nazi' camp. Nevertheless, the fact that the present German government has publicly, through the foreign minister and elsewhere, announced that it intends to retain the allegiance of German citizens everywhere in the world, and that it has the right to expect that all men and women of German blood, wherever they may live, and whatever their citizenship may be, will collaborate to further the interests of the German Reich.

These German camps fly the swastika flag, train their adherents in the Nazi ideology and announce that their objective is to fight the Jews and Communism.

Now, this little village of Southbury, inhabited, I have no doubt, by no Communists at all, but by self-respecting, law-abiding American citizens, doesn't want this German-American Bund camouflaged Nazi camp in its midst. These camps attract over week-ends—it has been demonstrated, in Long Island and New Jersey—hundreds and perhaps thousands of trippers. From that point of view, such a camp can be an economic asset to any near-by community. Communities, by and large, have been anxious—to take a somewhat parallel example—to get C.C.C. camps established near-by. They mean that local merchants have an extended market. But the village of South-bury is queasy about this particular outfit. It held a town meeting on November 23, and voted 122 to 41 to try to keep them out. But they cannot be kept out in any direct way. So the village is driven to passing a zoning law, which will prohibit any activity on the camp site except private housing or farming, and therewith make the camp impossible.

Thus the village of Southbury is forced to take a roundabout way to prevent there being set up in its midst a training school for agitators of an alien ideology, and actual representatives of a foreign power. For make no mistake about it: the Nazi theology is strictly authoritarian, and the pope of this new religion lives in Berlin, and not in Washington.

And it isn't only the Nazis. There's another religion which is recruiting zealots in this country, and it has a pope, too. His name is Stalin and his residence is Moscow, and he has no interest whatsoever in the peace and prosperity of the United States of America.

The German-American Bund, of course, flies the American flag alongside the swastika, which stands for precisely everything that the Constitution of the United States abhors; and the Communist camps and Communist meetings fly the Red flag alongside these same Stars and Stripes, and also deplore every-thing that America has ever stood for.

The Communist Party in the United States has not a vestige of democratic organization. The orders do not come from the workers who join it; the policy is not made in the United States; it is established by the party line, and that party line is laid down in Moscow. I once went to the trouble of mapping out in considerable detail just what that party line has been, over a period of years, and who the personnel charged to carry it out have been. Most of the original personnel have been eliminated by prison or death, and the policy has been strictly geared to the exigencies of the foreign situation of Soviet Russia, from year to year. At the moment, the party line is the defense of democracy against Fascism, and yesterday an election was held in Moscow to "prove" Russia's democracy under the new constitution.

Elections of the same kind were held by carpetbaggers in the South in 1870. They are simon-pure hokum. The Communist Party believes now, as always, that so-called western democracy is merely a cloak for capitalism, which they are out to destroy, along with the democratic state, and they were a thousand times more sincere from 1918 to 1932 when they made that perfectly plain, and admitted that they were a conspirational organization out to overthrow the capitalist-democratic order by violence.

They are now out to overthrow it by seepage. They get their members into every labor organization under false pretenses. They camouflage themselves under relief groups for Spain, and organizations against war and Fascism. They don't deny their own Communism, because the Lie doesn't mean any more to a Communist than it does to a Nazi. It is perfectly justifiable if it serves the Cause. And if they don't wreck the labor unions of this country, and especially the C.I.O., it will be a wonder.

The problem of democracy is how to defend itself against this kind of thing, without thereby becoming just like the thing it is fighting. If this country were like Germany or Russia, the problem would be simple. After Baron von Neurath's recent speech, we should have deported every unnaturalized German from the United States, and we should long ago have deported every unnaturalized Russian. And we shuld suppress these organizations by force and out their officers into prison. If you don't believe it, just try starting on German or Russian or Italian soil a League for the Defense of American Democracy.

But the very basis of American democracy is the Bill of Rights and freedom of speech, assemblage and propaganda, in times of peace.

It is a fundamental American tenet that the people have the right to change the form of government under which they live, and that individuals and organizations have the right to agitate for such a change if they believe that the form they have is no longer compatible with their happiness and welfare. One doesn't have to quote radicals in support of this. It was made brilliantly clear by none other than Alexander Hamilton.

But that right does not, it seems to me, include gracious hospitality for agitators who take their orders from foreign powers, and attempt under these foreign orders, to influence our domestic and foreign policy. Or does it? The chief aim of Communist agitation in this country at present is not to improve the status of American workers, but to see to it that in case of a world war this country is lined up on the side of Russia. The chief aim of Nazi agitation, carried on through its own nationals or blood-brothers, is to see that we remain rigidly isolationist—or join a possible coming war on the side of Germany.

The democratic world has absolutely no technique for handling this kind of thing. We are asked to admit that the belief in democracy includes hospitality for our would-be murderers, who do not even bother any longer to deny that their strategy is planned for them abroad. Well, does it?

I confess that I do not know the answer to this question—and it is one of the greatest questions that one can ask. Any American citizen certainly has the right to believe in socialism. And he has the right to believe in any mystic blood-and-soil theory he chooses. But the issue has, really, nothing to do, any longer, with socialism or racism. It has become a conspiracy of foreign powers, fought out on American soil. So what?

There Ought to Be a Law
LANGSTON HUGHES—*Chicago Defender*—4/24/1948

"I have been up North a long time, but it looks like I just cannot learn to like white folks."

"I don't care to hear you say that," I said, "because there are a lot of good white people in this world."

"Not enough of them," said Simple, waving his evening paper. "If there was, they would make this American country good. But just look at what this paper is full of."

"You cannot dislike *all* white people for what the bad ones do," I said. "And I'm certain you don't dislike them all because once you told me yourself that you wouldn't wish any harm to befall Mrs. Roosevelt."

"Mrs. Roosevelt is different," said Simple.

"There now! You see, you are talking just as some white people talk about the Negroes they *happen* to like. They are always 'different.' That is a provincial way to think. You need to get around more."

"You mean among white folks?" asked Simple. "How can I make friends with white folks when they got Jim Crow all over the place?"

"Then you need to open your mind."

"I have near about *lost* my mind worrying with them," said Simple. "In fact, they have hurt my soul."

"You certainly feel bad tonight," I said. "Maybe you need a drink."

"Nothing in a bottle will help my soul," said Simple, "but I will take a drink."

"Maybe it will help your mind," I said. "Beer?"

"Yes."

"Glass or bottle?"

"A bottle because it contains two glasses," said Simple, spreading his paper out on the bar. "Look here at these headlines, man, where Congress is busy passing laws. While they're making all these laws, it looks like to me they ought to make one setting up a few Game Preserves for Negroes."

"What ever gave you that fantastic idea?" I asked.

"A movie short I saw the other night," said Simple, "about how the government is protecting wild life, preserving fish and game, and setting aside big tracts of land where nobody can fish, shoot, hunt, nor harm a single living creature with furs, fins, or feather. But it did not show a thing about Negroes."

"I thought you said the picture was about 'wild life.' Negroes are not wild."

"No," said Simple, "but we need protection. This film showed how they put aside a thousand acres out West where the buffaloes roam and nobody can shoot a single one of them. If they do, they get in jail. It also showed some big National Park with government airplanes dropping food down to the deers when they got snowed under and had nothing to eat. The government protects and takes care of buffaloes and deers—which is more than the government does for me or my kinfolks down South. Last month they lynched a man in Georgia and just today I see where the Klan has whipped a Negro within an inch of his life in Alabama. And right up North here in New York a actor is suing a apartment house that won't even let a Negro go up on the elevator to see his producer. That is what I mean by Game Preserves for Negroes—Congress ought to set aside some place where we can go and nobody can jump on us and beat us, neither lynch us nor Jim Crow us every day. Colored folks rate as much protection as a buffalo, or a deer."

"You have a point there," I said.

"This here movie showed great big beautiful lakes with signs up all around:
NO FISHING—STATE GAME PRESERVE
But it did not show a single with a sign up:
NO LYNCHING
It also showed flocks of wild ducks settling down in a nice green meadow behind a government sign that said:
NO HUNTING
It were nice and peaceful for them fish and ducks. There ought to be some place where it is nice and peaceful for me, too, even if I am not a fish or a duck.

"They showed one scene with two great big old longhorn elks locking horns on a Game Preserve somewhere out in Wyoming, fighting like mad. Nobody bothered with them elks or tried to stop them from fighting. But just let me get in a little old fist fight here in this bar, they will lock me up and the Desk Sergeant will say, "What are you colored boys doing, disturbing the peace?" Then they will give me thirty days and fine me twice as much as they would a white man for doing the same thing. There ought to be some place where I can fight in peace and not get fined them high fines."

"You disgust me," I said, "I thought you were talking about a place where you could be quiet and compose your mind. Instead, you are talking about fighting."

"I would like a place there I could do both," said Simple. "If the government can set aside some spot for a elk *to be a elk* without being bothered, or a fish *to be a fish* without getting hooked, or a buffalo *to be a buffalo* without being shot down, there ought to be some place in this American country where a Negro can be a Negro without being Jim Crowed. There ought to be a law. The next time I see my congressman, I am going to tell him to introduce a bill for Game Preserves for Negroes."

"The Southerners would filibuster it to death," I said.

"If we are such a problem to them Southerners," said Simple, "I should think they would want some place to preserve us out of their sight. But then, of course, you have to take into consideration that if the Negroes was taken out of the South, who would they lynch? What would they do for sport? A Game Preserve is for to keep people from bothering anything that is living.

"When that movie finished, it were sunset in Virginia and it showed a little deer and its mama laying down to sleep. Didn't nobody say, 'Get up, deer, you can't sleep here,' like they would to me if I was to go to the White Sulphur Springs Hotel."

"'The foxes have holes, and the birds of the air have nests; but the Son of man hath not where to lay his head.'"

"That is why I want a Game Preserve for Negroes," said Simple.

Free Speech Is Worth the Risk
I. F. STONE—*I. F. Stone's Journal*—5/18/1949

In principle, the majority and the minority of the United States Supreme Court were separated by a mere hair's breadth in deciding the successful appeal of the Jew-baiting suspended priest, Terminiello, against a $100 fine for breach of the peace.

The majority left untouched an earlier decision which permits local authorities to punish when hatemongers use so-called "fighting words"—derisive racial or religious epithets likely to precipitate a rumpus. The minority agreed that free speech protects advocacy of "fascism or communism" and allows speakers to "go far" in expressing sentiments hostile to Jews, Negroes, Catholics, or other minority groups.

It was in deciding where the line shall be drawn between the permitted and the prohibited in this area that the Court nicely illustrated Mr. Justice Holmes' astringent dictum, "General propositions do not decide concrete cases."

The majority, through Justice Douglas, reversed Terminiello's conviction on the ground that the Illinois trial judge went too far in ruling that "breach of the peace" was broad enough to allow the prosecution of any speech which "stirs the public to anger . . . dispute . . . unrest."

The decision is given unusual interest because Justice Jackson, with his experience at the Nuremberg trials fresh in mind, protested bitterly for the minority that "if the court does not temper its doctrinaire logic with a little practical wisdom, it will convert the Constitutional Bill of Rights into a suicide pact."

In the Terminiello case, as in most questions of law, the Court had to choose between two dangers. Justice Jackson and the minority are impressed with the danger that fascist or revolutionary movements may utilize the basic freedoms of the Constitution to destroy it. Chief Justice Vinson, though dissenting, did not take a position on the merits. But Justices Jackson, Burton, and Frankfurter obviously prefer the risk of some infringement on basic liberties to the risk of permitting antidemocratic movements to get out of hand. The majority, Justices Douglas, Black, Murphy, Rutledge, and Reed, are more fearful of the risk that officials will abuse this power and limit the open discussion which is the foundation of a free society.

Justice Jackson's distillations from German experience do not impress me; they embody commonly current misconceptions. The German people did not succumb to Hitlerism because there was too much freedom in their laws but because there was too little freedom in their hearts. The Weimar Republic could be energetic enough in dealing with the Left. There as elsewhere it was demonstrated that it is the Left rather than the Right which ultimately bears the impact of these shoddy rationalizations about turning the Bill of Rights into a suicide pact. This is the panic of faltering spirits.

The choice the Court had to make was difficult because the dangers either way are real enough. But you cannot have freedom without the risk of its abuse. The men who wrote the Bill of Rights were willing to take their chances on freedom. This willingness to take risk, whether in theology, science, or monetary investment, is the prime characteristic of the whole period of human history which encompasses the Reformation, capitalism, and rationalism in one great burst of human energy. The world has seen any number of closed systems, from the ancient Roman Catholic to the modern Communist, which sought to eliminate risk by relying on revelation of one kind or another, and on this basis justified inquisition and purge. But everything we know from the past teaches us that suppression in the long run provides an illusory security, and this is why, though a socialist, I am also a libertarian.

Almost every generation in American history has had to face what appeared to be a menace of so frightening an order as to justify the limitation of basic liberties—the Francophiles in the days of the Alien and Sedition Laws, the abolitionists, the anarchists, the Socialists in the days of Debs; fascists, anti-Semites, and Communists in our own time. Each for various people seemed to provide compelling arguments for suppression, but we managed to get through before and will, I hope, again without abandoning basic freedoms. To do so would be to create for ourselves the very conditions we fear.

I am, I suppose, exactly what Terminiello in his harangues meant by an "atheistic, communistic, zionistic Jew." I would not demean myself or my people by denying him the right to say it. I do not hold the liberties I enjoy as an American in so little esteem that I am prepared to run from them like a rabbit because someone else uses them to say what I suppose ought to disturb me deeply. It does not disturb me.

I do not think the danger from fascist ideas on the Right can be met by imprisonment any more than can the danger from revolutionary ideas on the Left. All history testifies to the contrary. The judges of the minority who would have permitted some measure of suppression in my protection are not men whose championship I care to have. In too many recent cases I have seen how current anti-Red hysteria has kept them from doing the humane, the just and rightful thing.

I learned in Israel what men here once learned at Lexington—not to scare easily. If there is a growth of unemployment and mass misery, it will be exploited by the Right as well as the Left, and anti-Semitism will grow like any other fungus on the muck of despair. This gutter paranoia can only be prevented by fighting the conditions in which it can breed, and for that fight we need more and not less freedom of discussion, even though it be at the price of a few Terminiellos.

The Wrong Man
MURRAY KEMPTON—*New York Post*—8/15/1957

TRAVELERS REST, SOUTH CAROLINA—Claud Cruell and Sherwood Turner did not know each other very well, even as a Negro knows a white man. Claud Cruell was old enough, for one thing, to be Sherwood Turner's father. He had, in fact, known Sherwood Turner's father; they had grown up together in these hills near the North Carolina border.

No one prospers to excess in that country. Claud Cruell was thirty-three years old twenty-five years ago when he got the $500 it cost him to buy the fifty-two acres which form the basis of his one-hundred-acre farm tract.

"They gave it to me," he says, "because no one else wanted it." He and his brothers farmed it and worked it over mostly for corn; they were Negroes surrounded by white neighbors. The size of his acreage is no measure of wealth; he and his wife, Fanny, made most of their cash income taking in laundry from ten white families in their neighborhood, carrying it down the hill to a stream below their house and beating it clean on rocks with sticks.

Six years ago Claud Cruell began building his house. It took him five years; when he had finished he and his wife moved from their old cabin into this brick house with its wide porch and its square columns which is almost too much room for a couple in their late fifties without children. Still life had been kinder and more peaceful for Claud Cruell an old Negro, than for Sherwood Turner, a young white man. Sherwood Turner had stomach trouble; he worked on the rarest of occasions; he was on what passes for public relief in Greenville County. The children kept coming; about a year ago there were seven when the landlord told Sherwood Turner he would have to move out. That afternoon he met Claud Cruell and asked if he could rent the old cabin.

"I told him," says Claud Cruell, "that it wasn't worth living in. But he said he had to have something, so I let him have it for $5 a month, which wasn't too little for what it was worth."

"I think," says Sherwood Turner still, "that he's as good a colored man as I've ever seen in my life. I hate to say this, but he's holped [sic] me when none of my brothers would holp me.

"I remember once I came out of the hospital and we didn't have food in the house, and Claud put me and Goldie and the children in his car and took us down to the store and bought us $15 worth of groceries."

It may have been putting them in the car and carrying them down to buy them groceries which started the rumors about Claud Cruell. That, and the Turner children playing on the Cruells' large and empty porch. "Claud thought the world of the kids, and they think the world of him," says Sherwood Turner now.

The Klan is far away from the hills, at least thirteen miles away to the south in Greenville. There are perhaps twenty active Klansmen, truck drivers most of them, with Elvis Presley haircuts. On Saturday night, July 20, they met and elected young Marshall Rochester, a sash-and-door factory hand, as their president. Rochester said that something had to be done. Someone present had a dim recollection that there was something about a Negro man and a white woman having an affair in the town of Travelers Rest.

Two Klansmen with their wives and their children went berry-picking to look at the terrain over the following afternoon. Sherwood Turner passed them as he was driving Goldie down the hill to the Greenville Hospital for a kidney operation. He left the children alone in their cabin, in the care of Marie, the oldest of them, who is eleven. As the sun went down, Marie grew lonely, and went to the Cruells' house to ask if they could sleep there. They were asleep when there was a rattling at the door and Claud Cruell looked up to see the avenging army of the Klan around him.

They put a chain around his arm and beat him. He kept saying that he was the wrong man, and they went on beating him. At last they left him and took his wife and put her in the car and rode her around, cursing her and telling her to stop mixing with white people, and dumped her out. While they were hitting Claud Cruell, little Marie got up with the gun her father had left her, and they took it away, and wanted to know why she had so few clothes on around these niggers. In her statement to the police, Marie Turner referred over and over to Daddy Claud.

Fanny Cruell walked home to find her husband sitting outside in the car, bowed over. He had sent the children home. He said he didn't see much sense in calling the police. But Sherwood Turner called the sheriff Bob Martin and the deputies came out and took the depositions. Sheriff Martin talked to the neighbors and satisfied himself that the Klan had picked the wrong man.

A visitor drove by Marshall Rochester's dirty red house on a rutty dirt road; it was dark at 9:30. He and the Klan seemed somehow irrelevant; what was relevant and unanswerable was the question of the dark passion that moves a man to use up his weekend avenging a rumor in a strange county thirteen miles away.

The Cruells have suspended their laundry business until they get their morale back. The Turners, upon the sheriff's advice, moved away last week. Claud Cruell sat on his porch in the dark glasses his eye doctor prescribed. "Yes, sir," he said, "I miss the children. A fellow can't help but miss children for a while."

Goldie Turner, returned from the hospital, was away from her new home. "She went out to see if she could pick a few beans and get us some money," said her husband. "I didn't want to move out of there, but if a bunch would get up there and start shooting these kids, it would be terrible." He said again that Claud Cruell had been kind when nobody else was. There was about the children the awful stale smell of unwiped, unwashed vomit. Little Marie, her shoulder pulled up against the weight, was carrying a huge pail of water into the house.

It cannot be counted among the least of the South's sorrows that she and her brothers and sisters have been parted from the best and kindest friends not of their blood that they have ever had.

Faubus and Little Rock: Scars are for the Young
MAX LERNER—*New York Post*—9/23/1957

I have been reading the debates on the power of a governor in the face of the Federal power—about how to interpret what Justice Holmes said once in the case of *Moyer v. Peabody* as against what Justice Hughes said later in the case of *Sterling v. Constantin*, and while there is usually enough of the old fire horse in me to respond to these alarms I am not really agitated. The final source of constitutional law is what takes place in the mind of a youngster growing up in America. The true test of our governments, state and Federal, is what their acts do to our young people, white and black alike.

How absurd the nullifiers are today is best shown when you look at the picture—republished in every European newspaper and weekly—of Dorothy Counts walking in a Charlotte street with a little rabble of jeering, screaming, spitting children around her. The apparatus of government, civil and military alike, is reduced to a monstrous evil when it is used to strike terror into Dorothy Counts and leave a scar on her heart. Government exists, as society exists, to protect children, not to wound them.

I hope we won't pass judgment too easily on Dorothy Count's parents for giving up the fight and pulling her out of school. She walked straight in that picture, and her pride seemed to sit on her firmly poised head with a quiet grace. But what the picture didn't show was the ravaged heart within, which was too young to build a wall of immunity against the jeers and insults.

It takes a deal of courage, for parents and child alike, to be in the front ranks of the struggle for equal rights in Southern schools. The weeding-out process is a tough one, and only the sturdy can hope to survive. There are white children to throw sticks at you, to spit at you, to chant insulting choruses. There are grownups from the White Citizens Councils to spur the tormenters to further ardors if their zeal and hate lag. It is hard for a child, at fifteen, not to feel her heart tighten at this.

There is cruelty of a sort, of course, in every school. The thoughts of youth are not always tender thoughts, nor are its songs always the songs of innocence. But whatever petty persecutions your child may suffer—and inflict—in the relatively secure harbor of his school, try to imagine what it would be like to send him off every morning to be battered by the waves of certain and organized hatred. In the South today the constitutional arguments and the political maneuvering are being carried on by men who are old with the corruption of the ages, but the scars are for the young.

Yet scars can hasten the process of growing up. It is a fearful price for the young to pay, but the fact is that the hate-ridden school of yesterday—fighting off every effort toward the beginnings of equality—becomes the integrated school of today. "Say not the struggle naught availeth."

With all our emphasis on concord we make a mistake sometimes in thinking that conflict is wholly destructive. It isn't. For those whom it doesn't destroy it can be a creative experience. The night before Elizabeth Eckford went to school, at Little Rock, she read the lines in the Psalms, "The Lord is my light and my salvation; whom shall I fear? The Lord is the strength of my life; of whom shall I fear?" Despite her lonely long walk back from the line of the Faubus militia who kept her out of the "white" school, Elizabeth says quietly that she is not going back to the Jim Crow school.

Elizabeth plans to study law. Another of the Little Rock girls will be a schoolteacher, still another a social worker. If the Faubus militia putsch has no other results, it is likely to strengthen these girls in their resolve to go through with their careers.

Something does come out of this struggle then, as something has always come out of every struggle for freedom. There are people who will tell you that the South has gone beyond the point of no return, that is can never accept the mandate of justice and rejoin a Union where children have an equal fighting chance at what life offers. Such people can learn from the quiet confidence of Elizabeth Eckford, who will never waver in her purpose, no matter what hurts she must suffer.

This is an education in itself—perhaps a better education than the schoolbooks will ever be able to give. The turning point in the process of growing up is when you discover the core of strength within you that survives all hurt. Am I wrong in thinking that a whole young generation of American Negroes is coming up which is being hardened in this baptism of fire, and which will furnish a new and great leadership in the days ahead?

They might perhaps, at another time, have grown up to be just mediocre people. But history has placed them *there*, at the right spot and the right time to give their lives a meaning beyond anything they might otherwise have had. Even a Faubus has his uses.

I do not mean to pass over the young white children in the South. They too pay a high price for the struggle—the price of hate. But there are a few who sit down by the young Negro newcomers in the classroom, and eat with them in the lunchroom, and walk home with them. It takes courage for them, but it is a courage that redeems the soul of the South.

He Went All the Way
MURRAY KEMPTON—*New York Post*—9/22/1958

Mose Wright, making a formation no white man in his county really believed he would dare to make, stood on his tiptoes to the full limit of his sixty-four years and his five feet three inches yesterday, pointed his black, workworn finger straight at the huge and stormy head of J. W. Milam and swore that this was the man who dragged fourteen-year-old Emmett Louis Till out of his cottonfield cabin the night the boy was murdered.

"There he is," said Mose Wright. He was a black pigmy standing up to a white ox. J. W. Milam leaned forward, crooking a cigaret in a hand that seemed as large as Mose Wright's whole chest, and his eyes were coals of hatred.

Mose Wright took all their blast straight in his face, and then, for good measure, turned and pointed that still unshaking finger at Roy Bryant, the man he says joined Milam on the night-ride to seize young Till for the crime of whistling suggestively at Bryant's wife in a store three miles away and three nights before.

"And there's Mr. Bryant," said Mose Wright and sat down hard against the chair-back with a lurch which told better than anything else the cost in strength to him of the thing he had done. He was a field Negro who had dared try to send two white men to the gas chamber for murdering a Negro.

He sat in a court where District Attorney Gerald Chatham, who is on his side, steadily addressed him as Uncle Mose and conversed with him in a kind of pidgin cotton-picker's dialect, saying "axed" for "asked" as Mose Wright did and talking about the "undertaker man."

Once Chatham called him "Old Man Mose," but this was the kindly, contemptuous tolerance of the genteel; after twenty-one minutes of this, Mose Wright was turned over to Defense Counsel Sidney Canton and now the manner was that of an overseer with a field hand.

Sidney Carlton roared at Mose Wright as though he were the defendant, and every time Carlton raised his voice like the lash of a whip, J. W. Milam would permit himself a cold smile.

And then Mose Wright did the bravest thing a Delta Negro can do; he stopped saying "sir." Every time Carlton came back to the attack, Mose Wright pushed himself back against his chair and said "That's right" and the absence of the "sir" was almost like a spit in the eye.

When he had come to the end of the hardest half hour in the hardest life possible for a human being in these United States, Mose Wright's story was shaken; yet he still clutched its foundations. Against Carlton's voice and Milam's eyes and the incredulity of an all-white jury, he sat alone and refused to bow.

If it had not been for him, we would not have had this trial. It will be a miracle if he wins his case; yet it is a kind of miracle that, all on account of Mose Wright, the State of Mississippi is earnestly striving here in this courtroom to convict two white men for murdering a Negro boy so obscure that they do not appear to have even known his name.

He testified yesterday that, as Milam left his house with Emmett Till on the night of August 28, he asked Mose Wright whether he knew anyone in the raiding party. "No, sir, I said I don't know nobody."

Then Milam asked him how old he was, and Mose Wright said sixty-four and Milam said, "If you knew any of us, you won't live to be sixty-five."

And, after the darkened car drove off, with his great-nephew, Mose Wright drove his hysterical wife over to Sumner and put her on the train to Chicago, from which she has written him every day since to cut and run and get out of town. The next day, all by himself, Mose Wright drove into nearby Greenwood and told his story in the sheriff's office.

It was a pathetic errand; it seems a sort of marvel that anything was done at all. Sheriff George Smith drove out to Money around 2 p.m. that afternoon and found Roy Bryant sleeping behind his store. They were good friends and they talked as friends about this little boy whose name Smith himself had not bothered to find out.

Smith reported that Roy had said that he had gone down the road and taken the little boy out of "Preacher's" cabin, and brought him back to the store and, when his wife said it wasn't the right boy, told him to go home.

Sheriff Smith didn't even take Bryant's statement down. When he testified to it yesterday, the defense interposed the straight-faced objection that this was after all the conversation of two friends and that the state shouldn't embarrass the sheriff by making him repeat it in court. Yet, just the same, Sheriff Smith arrested Roy Bryant for kidnaping that night.

When the body supposed to be Emmett Till's was found in the river, a deputy sheriff drove Mose Wright up to identify it. There was no inquest. Night before last, the prosecution fished up a picture of the body which had been in the Greenwood police files since the night it was brought in, but there was no sign the sheriff knew anything about it, and its discovery was announced as a coup for the state. But, with that apathy and incompetence, Mose Wright almost alone has brought the kidnapers of his nephew to trial.

The country in which he toiled and which he is now resigned to leaving will never be the same for what he has done. Today the state will put on the stand three other field Negroes to tell how they saw Milam and Bryant near the murder scene. They came in scared; one disappeared while the sheriff's deputies were looking for him. They, like Mose Wright, are reluctant heroes; unlike him, they have to be dragged to the test.

They will be belted and flayed as he was yesterday, but they will walk out with the memory of having been human beings for just a little while. Whatever the result, there is a kind of majesty in the spectacle of the State of Mississippi honestly trying to convict two white men on the word of four Negroes.

And we owe that sight to Mose Wright, who was condemned to bow all his life, and had enough left to raise his head and look the enemy in those terrible eyes when he was sixty-four.

A Flower for the Graves
EUGENE PATTERSON—*Atlanta Constitution*—9/16/1963

A Negro mother wept in the street Sunday morning in front of a Baptist Church in Birmingham. In her hand she held a shoe, one shoe, from the foot of her dead child. We hold that shoe with her.

Every one of us in the white South holds that small shoe in his hand.

It is too late to blame the sick criminals who handled the dynamite. The FBI and the police can deal with that kind. The charge against them is simple. They killed four children.

Only we can trace the truth, Southerner—you and I. We broke those children's bodies.

We watched the stage set without staying it. We listened to the prologue unbestirred. We saw the curtain opening with disinterest. We have heard the play.

We—who go on electing politicians who heat the kettles of hate.

We—who raise no hand to silence the mean and little men who have their nigger jokes.

We—who stand aside in imagined rectitude and let the mad dogs that run in every society slide their leashes from our hand, and spring.

We—the heirs of a proud South, who protest its worth and demand it recognition—we are the ones who have ducked the difficult, skirted the uncomfortable, caviled at the challenge, resented the necessary, rationalized the unacceptable, and created the day surely when these children would die.

This is not time to load our anguish onto the murderous scapegoat who set the cap in dynamite of our own manufacture.

He didn't know any better.

Somewhere in the dim and fevered recess of an evil mind he feels right now that he had been a hero. He is only guilty of murder. He thinks he has pleased us.

We of the white South who know better are the ones who must take a harsher judgment.

We, who know better, created a climate for child-killing by those who don't.

We hold that shoe in our hand, Southerner. Let us see it straight, and look at the blood on it. Let us compare it with the unworthy speeches of Southern public men who have traduced the Negro; match it with the spectacle of shrilling children whose parents and teachers turned them free to spit epithets at small huddles of Negro school children for a week before this Sunday in Birmingham; hold up the shoe and look beyond it to the state house in Montgomery where the official attitudes of Alabama have been spoken in heat and anger.

Let us not lay the blame on some brutal fool who didn't know any better.

We know better. We created the day. We bear the judgment. May God have mercy on the poor South that has so been led. May what has happened hasten the day when the good South, which does live and has great being, will rise to this challenge of racial understanding and common humanity, and in the full power of its unasserted courage, assert itself.

The Sunday school play at Birmingham is ended. With a weeping Negro mother, we stand in the bitter smoke and hold a shoe. If our South is ever to be what we wish it to be, we will plant a flower of nobler resolve for the South now upon these four small graves that we dug.

Marching to Montgomery
JACK NEWFIELD—*Village Voice*—4/1/1965

It was the Ecumenical Council, a hootenanny, a happening, and a revolution all rolled into one. And it happened in Montgomery, "Cradle of the Confederacy."

A broken-down hipster, the *Realist* sticking out of his dungarees, marched alongside an Episcopal bishop clutching the Holy Bible. There were the kamikazes of the Student Nonviolent Coordinating Committee—SNCC—in their blue denim overalls, mud-caked boots, and crash helmets, next to middle-class housewives who won't ride the subways after dark. There were nuns in flowing black habits arm in arm with jowly labor leaders who discriminate in their unions.

There were rabbis, junkies, schoolboys, actors, sharecroppers, intellectuals, maids, novelists, folk-singers, and politicians—10,000 motives and 40,000 people marching to Montgomery behind James Forman who hates the oppressor and Martin Luther King who loves the oppressed.

There were hundreds of high school and college youngsters—that new breed of revolutionary that has somehow grown up inside the bowels of prosperous America. There were kids who rioted against HUAC, vigiled against the Bomb, invaded Mississippi last summer, and turned Berkeley upside down. They are a new generation of insurgents, nourished not by Marx or Trotsky, but by Camus, Lenny Bruce, Bob Dylan, and SNCC. Their revolution is not against capitalism, but against what they deem to be the values of an enlightened America—Brotherhood Weeks, factories called colleges, desperation called success, and sex twice a week.

And there were thousands of clergymen symbolizing the revolution within a revolution—the nun with suntan cream on her face who marched all the way from Selma, priests, ministers, rabbis with yarmulkas. There was a huge sign: "Lutherans are Here Because Christ Cared." Another read: "Kansas Mennonites Support Civil Rights." And another: "SMU Marches for Freedom."

On the streets of the Confederacy's cradle, that "coalition of conscience" Bayard Rustin and Michael Harrington have tried to will into existence, materialized spontaneously. A line of marchers, strung out as far as the eye could see, sang "America the Beautiful" and made it sound like a revolutionary anthem.

The day that was to end in triumph and tragedy began in sleepy whimsy at 4 a.m. last Thursday for the 104 participants in the Village Independent Democrats' "Fly-In" as they pulled out of the West Side Airlines Terminal singing ironic songs about their pilgrimage.

They sang in spirited atonality that quickly disintegrated into anarchy songs like "Stars Fell on Alabama" and "I'm Alabamy Bound" and "Swanee" and "Dixie."

"Alabama, here I come," roared Bill Tatum, "VIDers, don't be late, open up that capitol gate. Alabama, here I come, right back where I started from . . ."

The "Welcome to Montgomery" sign at Dannelly Airport reinforced the ironic mood of the pilgrims, especially for those who noticed that billboard just outside the airport that read: "Get the U.S. out of the U.N. or get the U.N. out of the U.S."

Within twenty minutes the small airport lounge became congested as flights from Boston and St. Louis also landed, disgorging eager, smiling, scrubbed and middle-class faces, some on top of clerical collars.

A white minister from Martin Luther King's Southern Christian Leadership Conference (SCLC) greeted new arrivals, urged them to leave the city "as soon as the rally is over because it will be dangerous," and directed them to shuttle buses to the City of St. Jude, a Roman Catholic complex where the marchers had camped the night before. On the SCLC minister's lapel was a button that said "GROW." He explained it stood for "Get Rid of Wallace."

At St. Jude the predominant mood was gaiety, as thousands upon thousands of visitors swelled the great serpentine line of march that coiled around the vast, muddy athletic field.

Small clusters sang freedom songs during the two hours it took for the whole line to unwind onto the streets toward the capitol, four miles away. The visitors sang off-key versions of better-known freedom songs, while local Negroes, led by either SNCC or SCLC staff members, sang raucous, sassy, taunting songs that came out of the Movement in Alabama's Black Belt. A group of about 5,000 from St. Louis stood in a large circle, one small, Negro woman calling out chorus after chorus of "We Shall Overcome."

Other demonstrators milled around the staging area like conventioneers, wearing name tags and introducing themselves to strangers, pronouncing their home towns with accents of pride—Montreal, Berkeley, Boston, Detroit—and their association with equal pride—ADA, the United Auto Workers, NAACP, the University of Virginia, the American Legion (Gramercy Park chapter).

At noon, under one of the day's brief showers, the procession began to move out, with the bloody-shoed 300 who had marched all the way in the vanguard. With them were barefoot Joan Baez; James Baldwin, nervously smiling, just back from Scandinavia; the angelic-looking Montgomery seamstress Rosa Parks, who ignited the mythic bus boycott a decade ago; and SNCC's John Lewis, who walked the whole way from Selma and who had suffered head injuries on "Bloody Sunday" at the Alabama River Bridge. And there was Martin Luther King, to whom Negroes of the Black Belt now sing "Glory, Glory Hallelujah" and then kiss his hand.

The streets in the Negro slums of Montgomery were of mud and clay. There were row upon row of run-down shacks, with the very old, the very young, the unemployed sitting on porches.

At first the nonmarchers were timid and shy. It was as if shame made them look down rather than at the masses that surged past them. But slowly, they looked up, to wave, and when the marchers began to shout, "Join us, come on," many accepted the invitation and probably protested their plight for the first time in their lives. Marching through the slums was like taking LSD for the soul.

One bent old woman ran off her porch and kissed a white marcher. Children, dirty and scrawny, ran alongside, singing the songs and chanting the slogans of freedom. A very old man, his cane resting between his legs, sat on his porch steps and wept.

About a mile from the capitol we reached the downtown section of Montgomery, with its banks, hotels, movies, stores, office buildings, and clean asphalt streets. The sidewalks were almost deserted except for a sprinkling of hecklers and the federal troops at each intersection, standing at attention, their rifles at their sides.

But against the windows of the office buildings were pressed the white faces of the South. Some shook their heads "no" or gave the thumbs-down sign when the marchers waved at them. A beautiful woman of about twenty-five stood on the balcony of the Jefferson Davis Hotel, and when the demonstrators waved at her, this flower of Southern womanhood made the traditional obscene gesture of one finger up.

On the lawn of an elegant home a hunched, elderly maid stood in the midst of her sullen employers. She was smiling and waving a white handkerchief at the procession. One wonders what was happening in the minds of her employers at that moment.

Remarked Edward Koch, the Village Democratic leader: "Walking through the Negro section made me feel like I was walking through Paris again with the liberation army. The white section was what it must have been like marching through Germany."

From the window of the Alabama Bible Society Building hung a blow-up of the picture Senator Eastland introduced into the *Congressional Record* prior to the March on Washington to prove Martin Luther King was "part of the Communist conspiracy." The photograph shows King at a rally in 1957 at Highlander Folk School.

Dexter Avenue is the eight-lane street that leads into the white stone capitol building. As the procession turned the corner of that final leg of the journey, the marchers suddenly broke into "America the Beautiful" and sang it with a passion normally associated in the Movement with "We Shall Overcome."

"America, America, God shed his grace on thee. And crown thy good with brotherhood, from sea to shining sea," they sang. Hundreds of schoolchildren waving little American flag. Ahead loomed the dome of the capitol with its Alabama and Confederate flags blowing in the breeze.

By 2 p.m. all 40,000 marchers, including about 10,000 whites, arrived at the foot of the capitol and stretched out several blocks down Dexter Avenue. The symbolism of the scene was inescapable. At the spot where Jefferson Davis was inaugurated, where George Wallace shouted in his inaugural in 1961, "Segregation now, segregation tomorrow, segregation forever," the largest civil-rights demonstration in the history of the South sang "We Shall Overcome"—black and white, together—"We are not afraid today."

In the shadow of the red-brick Dexter Avenue Baptist Church, from whose pulpit Martin Luther King led the bus boycott ten years earlier, the huge rally was turning into a kind of coronation of Dr. King.

"Who is your leader?" the Reverend Ralph Abernathy asked the throng. The answer swelled up. "Martin Luther King!" The only exceptions were veterans of SNCC, who yelled, "De Lawd of Slick." But even that invidious distortion of SCLC was probably shouted as much in respect as in cynicism.

(The bitterness lurking in the background was based on the fact that SNCC, which had been alone in Dallas County since late 1962, had great difficulty working in harness with King after SCLC took over the Selma campaign in January. There had been serious disputes over strategy and tactics, since King's basic goal is integration and SNCC's is a revolution.)

After two hours of speeches by every major leader of the civil-rights movement, King was finally introduced to the crowd. Like the multitude in Washington in 1963, they had become fatigued and restless; many had been awake as long as twenty hours. Overhead, a helicopter and a Piper Cub circled noisily. Behind the platform two dozen green-helmeted Alabama conservation police guarded the steps of the capitol building. Behind them stood a number of members of the Alabama legislature.

Then King began, his resonant voice and preacher's alliterative rhythm slowly rousing the audience from boredom. From behind him on the platform came counterpoints of "Amen" and "Tell it, Brother" from other ministers.

In Washington he invoked the phrase, "I have a dream," the way a blues singer repeats a key phrase. In Montgomery, facing the capitol, it was, "We are on the move now," that became the launching pad for a series of crescendo-like thrusts.

"We are on the move now," he said. "The burning of our churches will not deter us. We are on the move now. The bombing of our homes will not dissuade us. We are on the move now." Now the throng responded with shouts of "Yes, Lord," and "Amen."

"The beating of our clergymen will not divert us. We are on the move now. Yes, we are on the move now, and no wave of racism can stop us."

King climaxed his speech by repeating four times with rising fervor, "Glory Glory Hallelujah." And then the cooks, maids, and janitors were crying and cheering at the same time.

There were supposed to be twenty-six shuttle buses waiting after the rally to ferry demonstrators from the capitol to the airport five miles away. But twenty-one of the drivers called in sick, and for two hours thousands milled around in a muddy lot a block behind the capitol while fives buses tried to do all the work. There was pushing, shoving, and maneuvering each time a bus pulled in. Finally an SNCC worker with a walkie-talkie told the crowd, "Come on, you're acting like kids. This ain't the New York subway."

By dusk, the troops had disappeared and the last handful waited unprotected in the lot, feeling fear for the first time during the day.

Chaos reigned at the airport. Hundreds sprawled on the lawn, picnicking, sleeping, and singing. Huge lines pointed to the lavatories and phones; there were no snack counters. All outgoing flights were late.

After an hour's delay the VID flight was ready to be boarded, except that there was no ladder available. So for another hour, the 104 weary passengers stood in a cramped line, twenty yards away from the plane, while a ladder was searched—or, as some suspected, hidden.

Meanwhile, a few yards away, the dean of all civil rights leaders, seventy-seven-year old Asa Philip Randolph, had collapsed from exhaustion, and Bayard Rustin and Michael Harrington tended him while dispatching friends to find a doctor. The Montgomery police seemed uninterested.

"It's my fault," Rustin mumbled. "I never should have gotten him up at 2 a.m. and he never should have walked those four miles."

At 10:45 New York time, the VID flight left the Cradle of the Confederacy amid complaints to the Civil Aeronautics Board about the delay and caustic reflections on "Southern hospitality." There was no singing on the flight back. Most of the passengers slept. A few talked about the future of the civil-rights movement, agreeing at the outset that Montgomery was just a skirmish in a long war whose end still lies beyond the rim of history.

Steve Berger, an aide to reform Congressman Jonathan Bingham, said the new voting rights bill was "pretty bad and very poorly drawn." Others, activists of the Movement, thought no legislation could possibly deal with the specter of firing, beating, and murder that faces any Negro who tries to register in the Black Belt. Other militants spoke eagerly of the next battle—the continuing attempt to unseat the five Congressmen from Mississippi by the Freedom Democratic Party.

Elizabeth Sutherland, who works for SNCC in New York, sat reading a private legal memorandum on the proposed voting bill, pointing out all its flaws and loopholes. "I just hope the registrars don't get their hands on this memo," she said.

And there was speculation about what would happen in the Black Belt now that the "civil-rights tourists," Dr. King, the federal troops, and the outside journalists were leaving and the Negroes were left alone to confront the Jim Clarks, the racist registrars, and those terrible faces that looked down from those windows.

When the plane landed at Kennedy Airport, its passengers were told it had already happened—murder. Nobody said anything memorable or poetic. They just cursed.

Are the Rioters Racists?
WILLIAM F. BUCKLEY JR.—Universal Press Syndicate—7/29/1967

Add to the judgment of Governor Richard J. Hughes of New Jersey that the riots are unrelated to civil rights the judgment of Mayor Jerome P. Cavanaugh of Detroit, also a Democrat, that of Governor George Romney of Michigan, a Republican, and that of Governor Ronald Reagan of California, ditto. It is easy enough to see what these gentlemen mean. A man who breaks into a store to hijack himself a case of whiskey can hardly be said to be engaged in the advancement of colored people. And it is certainly true that most of those who are roaming the streets like drunken janissaries pillaging and razing our cities are not engaged in the forwarding of any certified ideals.

Even so the riots are, in a critical sense, related to civil rights broadly understood—i.e., they are politically motivated. The point is that those who have succeeded in transforming local disturbances into wholesale insurrections seem to have been motivated by racial animosities which rise, or are said to rise, from a concern for the distribution of power.

Most obviously, there is H. Rap Brown, successor, as chairman of the Student Nonviolent Coordinating Committee, to Stokely Carmichael (who is nowadays in Havana giving the Communists a postgraduate course in the art of revolution). Mr. Brown lectured on Tuesday in Cambridge, Maryland, and urged his listeners to "burn this town down. . . . Don't tear down your own stuff," he cautioned. "When you tear down the white man, brother, you are hitting him in the money. Don't love him to death. Shoot him to death. . . . You better get yourselves some guns. . . . This town is ready to explode." And explode it promptly did—though ironically it was the Negro section of town that was demolished, not the white section.

The volunteer firemen declined to move their fire engines into streets manned by snipers acting on Mr. Brown's injunction to shoot whitey to death, the position of the firemen being that they had volunteered for fire duty, not combat duty. Here, in other words, was a pretty clear case of civil-rights involvement, if one is still prepared to think of Mr. Brown and SNCC as related to civil rights.

The snipers played a critical role elsewhere as well, for instance in Newark. *Life* magazine reported an extraordinary interview held with several of the snipers during mid-fighting. These were no more routine looters than Danton and Robespierre were routine executioners. They calmly explained that their purpose in sniping was not to kill the police (you may have noticed that in fact very few policemen were killed) but rather to exacerbate the situation so as to hone the revolutionary spirit and, while at it, to permit an effective redistribution of goods. How else, one sniper asked, can you get color TV into the hands of those who do not have it? (An interesting note for the International Revolutionary Bulletin Board: Man is born free, but everywhere he is without color TV.)

Once again, these gentlemen are related to the civil-rights movement, even as Malcolm X and the Black Muslims are related to the civil-rights movement, however much it can be said that they perverted that movement. In other words, a hard taxonomic look at the riots places them other than in the category of wanton crime. They are racist and political in character, even if most of the participants can be said to have been moved only by a concern for free liquor and color TV. How many of those who stormed the Bastille or the Winter Palace were true idealists? Yet no one doubts that those assaults were revolutionary in their final meaning, even if panty raiding was the spirit of the mob.

In short, if one subtracts from the situation those who were motivated by malevolent racism, you have pretty well defused the riots, which without the snipers document nothing very much more than the tiresome commonplaces that there are reserves of anarchy in all of us and that demagogy, especially if armed by a righteous rhetoric, can bring those reserves to violent life.

Well, the FBI has now issued a bulletin on riot control for use by local police forces, and we can assume that the FBI will penetrate the racist organizations and abort some of the riots planned for the future. But there is work for the moralizers to do, and in order to speak effectively, they will have to speak the truth. The truth is that some of the civil-rights rhetoric of recent years has provided the phony justifications for violence which the Carmichaels and the Browns and, yes, some of our principal journalists have leaned on in explaining the disasters they are partly responsible for creating.

The Power of One
ANNA QUINDLEN—*New York Times*—4/28/1993

Now we have the numbers game. How many gay people are there in the nation? Ten percent? One percent? Four percent? It depends on whom you ask, what survey you read, how statisticians and sex experts crunch the numbers, which respondents tell the truth and which don't. How many marched in Washington on Sunday for the civil rights of gay men and lesbians? Three hundred thousand? Half a million? A million or more? It depends on whether you ask the park police or the march organizers.

But at some level none of it matters at all.

I know that gay men and lesbians have ample reason to believe their political clout in America, the most quantifying of countries, will be measured by their numbers. I know, too, that those who want to prove that homosexuality is a "deviant lifestyle" are anxious to show that the demands are disproportionate to the number of demanders, as though the right to be treated fairly depended on a head count.

But it's the power of one that really brings change. No one's head is truly turned around by a faceless sea of folks seen from a distance marching on the capital, or by numbers on sexual behavior from a research center.

It's the power of one that does it.

It's the power of one man like Sergeant Jose Zuniga, who was the Sixth Army's 1992 soldier of the year and a medic in the Golf War. Before the march he stood before the television cameras and so before the world and said, with a chestful of medals, that he was proud to be a soldier, and he was proud to be gay.

Right that minute, maybe, some fellow vets and fellow Americans wrote him off. But there have to be people who have worked with him, trained with him, fought with him, who are now forced to reexamine their attitudes toward gay men, to compare their prejudices with what they know of this one individual.

Maybe in the beginning those people will decide that Sergeant Zuniga is the exception, and that the rule is that gay men are predatory, effeminate, unfit for service. They may embrace the old "Okay, but . . ." analysis, which we have seen with blacks, with Latinos, with women and now with gay people. It goes like this: "Jose is okay, but the rest of them . . ."

Stereotypes fall in the face of humanity. You toodle along, thinking that all gay men wear leather after dark and should never, ever be permitted around a Little League field. And then one day your best friend from college, the one your kids adore, comes out to you. Or that wonderful woman who teaches third grade is spotted leaving a lesbian bar in the next town.

And the ice of your closed mind begins to crack.

Day by day, this is how the world will change for gay men and lesbians, with the power of one—one person who doesn't fit into the straight world's fact pattern and so alters it a tiny bit, irrevocably. A revered actor who was typecast in tough-guy roles. A beloved female friend who cannot be transformed into a hate object. Coming out is a powerful thing.

It is why the march, one of the biggest civil rights demonstrations in the history of this country, was most powerful when it reflected not quantity, but quality. A sunburned man in chinos. Two silver-haired women hand in hand, smiling. A woman pushing a stroller. Sure, there were men in lipstick and women in buzz cuts. And women in lipstick and men in buzz cuts. Like straight people, gay people are a diverse group. To paraphrase Gloria Steinem on turning fifty, this is what gay looks like.

In recent years gay men and lesbians have moved purposefully ahead in the civic arena, putting money behind candidates, crafting antidiscrimination legislation, demanding that their relationships be formally recognized. No matter what their numbers, they've become a formidable political force.

But a veneer of tolerance atop a deep pool of hatred, distrust, and estrangement is no more than a shiny surface, as civil rights leaders can testify from decades of experience. The numbers in Washington were not as important as the faces, the sheer humanity of one person after another stepping forward, saying: Look at me. I am a cop, a mother, a Catholic, a Republican, a soldier, an American. So the ice melts. The hate abates. The numbers, finally, all come down to one.

Out of the Closet and Open to Legal Attack
PETE DEXTER—*Sacramento Bee*—6/13/1994

It has been my belief ever since the issue first came up that there was no need for special laws to protect the rights of homosexuals. That they are protected by the same laws that protect the rest of us.

It has also been my belief that homosexuals—particularly men, who, taken as a group, do significantly better financially than the rest of society—are not suffering the kind of economic discrimination that certain vocal members of the homosexual community insist is the case.

Which left me biased, I suppose, when I came across the story in *The New Yorker* magazine last week of Daniel Miller of Harrisburg, Pennsylvania, who was fired after five exemplary years from the firm of Donald L. DeMuth Management Consultants when Mr. DeMuth found out he was gay.

He was given no severance pay and ordered out of his office by the end of the day.

Miller, a certified public accountant with an M.B.A. from Penn State, thought DeMuth had called him into the office to offer him a partnership. (I can't tell you how many times that's happened to me.)

Anyway, a month and a half after he was fired, Miller opened his own management firm in Harrisburg—across the river from DeMuth's firm, which is in Camp Hill—and in no time at all had taken about one-third of DeMuth's business away.

This in spite of a letter DeMuth sent to his clients saying, in part, "Right now Dan is on his own. If he ever wants to grow, I question who he will be able to attract as an associate. While there may be other homosexual practice management consultants and CPAs, to the best of my knowledge I've never met one. . . . It's well known that homosexuals are significantly at risk for AIDS. While I have no knowledge of Dan's medical condition, consider getting the results of a blood test from him if you are considering using his services on a long-term basis."

Still, a number of DeMuth's clients—mostly doctors and dentists—were happy enough with Miller's work to change firms. He understood computers, for one thing, and DeMuth did not.

So time passed, and DeMuth discovered Miller's business was costing him about $100,000 a year in billings. DeMuth went to his lawyer and invoked a clause in Miller's employment agreement that, in the event he quit or was fired "for cause," called for penalties if he started a competing practice.

Specifically, 125 percent of whatever money he made from DeMuth's old clients.

Now, at this point it is worth remembering that Miller had signed the agreement when he went to work for DeMuth. He signed, he said later, thinking he had no choice.

Among the reasons DeMuth included as "just cause" for termination were moral turpitude, being charged with a felony, use of illicit drugs, intoxication while working, insulting DeMuth's family or clients, engaging in sexual activities in the office, and homosexuality.

It is also worth pointing out that at the time he signed the agreement, Miller says he had never had sexual activity with another man, and was in fact dating and thinking of marrying a woman. Only later did he admit to himself that he was gay.

All right, so Miller signed the agreement, put in five good years at the office and then came out of the closet.

DeMuth fired him and then sued when he opened his own office. Miller countersued, but his suit was thrown out of court because the state of Pennsylvania has no law on the books prohibiting discrimination against homosexuals.

The case went to court in June of last year, and there was no real argument from either side about what had happened.

In his instructions to the jury, Judge Kevin Hess of the Cumberland County Court of Common Pleas said that the jury was not to consider the fairness of the contract Miller had been made to sign.

"Mr. Miller cannot avoid the consequences of a contract between himself and Mr. DeMuth simply by claiming that he did not intend to be bound by it," the judge said. "An agreement need not be reduced to writing to be enforceable. Oral or verbal agreements between the parties are valid. And the law will enforce them."

Given those instructions, the jury deliberated a day and a half and came back—all members but one (a unanimous finding is not necessary in a civil trial)—with a finding that Miller, who, in spite of the fact he was only trying to save himself professionally and financially after having been fired for his sexual orientation, owed DeMuth $126,648.

As mentioned earlier, I have argued that there is no need for special legislation protecting the civil rights of homosexuals. I have argued they didn't need it.

And as the case of *Donald DeMuth vs. Daniel Miller* illustrates, a lot of the time I don't know what the hell I'm talking about.

Strangling the NAACP
CARL T. ROWAN—*Baltimore Sun*—8/5/1994

It is sickening to watch the death of the National Association for the Advancement of Colored People, a once-proud organization now being strangled by two incredibly arrogant leaders.

This oldest and once most-feared, most-respected of all the nation's civil rights groups will soon sink into pitiable irrelevance, bankruptcy and shame unless a majority of its board of directors can rescue it from its chairman, William F. Gibson, a South Carolina dentist, and its executive director, Benjamin F. Chavis Jr.

Unfortunately, that may be impossible because Gibson has stacked the board in ways that seem to shield him and Chavis from dismissal, even in the face of egregiously bad judgment and conduct.

On Sunday, NAACP members and financial supporters across the nation saw on TV an admission by Chavis and Gibson that they committed more than $300,000 in "hush" money to a fired woman who threatened a lawsuit charging employment discrimination and sexual harassment.

Chavis admitted to paying Mary E. Stansel $82,400–$64,000 directly out of NAACP funds and $18,400 from secret donors. Chavis pledged to pay her $250,000 more if he could not find Stansel a job paying at least $80,000 a year. Stansel has sued for the $250,000.

Chavis said he paid Stansel "to protect the NAACP from exposure to false and slanderous allegations." Gibson said he approved the payments to protect the integrity of the NAACP.

Almost nothing could do more to destroy the organization's integrity and reputation than these payoffs. Who is going to give more money to the NAACP when the chairman and executive director use its coffers as a private piggy bank when one of them wants to avoid personal embarrassment?

Where do Gibson and Chavis find authority to commit $332,000 in "hush" money without informing or gaining the approval of the NAACP's budget committee, the personnel committee or the full board?

The NAACP faithful, such as Marc Stepp in Detroit, who have been working doggedly to raise funds to erase the organization's $3 million deficit, surely feel betrayed. They know that the futile effort to pay Stansel for silence was not made to protect the NAACP; they have read where NAACP attorney Abbey G. Hairston was quoted as saying that the money was paid to protect Chavis, who was "literally scared to death."

The courts can decide the merits of Stansel's charges (from the lawsuit she filed, despite the keep-quiet payments) and the later Chavis suit (the NAACP court action charging her with violating the deal). But we do not need a judicial decree to tell us that Gibson and Chavis have shown such terrible judgment and atrocious arrogance that they ought to resign their posts immediately or be ousted.

I have written before that the NAACP was doomed to impotence when Gibson became chairman and decided that he, not the executive director, would have the last word on everything. He provoked a deep schism within the board of directors but kept power by loading it with aged, conservative black Southern cronies who would rubber stamp even his most outrageous decisions.

At the time Chavis was chosen to succeed Benjamin Hooks as executive director, I noted publicly that Gibson hovered over Chavis at every moment by way of saying that the real power still rested with the chairman.

So, as in the dictatorships of the old Soviet Union and China, a cult of personality began to suck the lifeblood out of the NAACP. And Gibson's cult followers may foolishly excuse him and Chavis for an action that was stupid and comes perilously close to unlawful use of funds contributed by a trusting, hoping public.

Can a majority of this 64-member board be such Gibson sycophants that they will tolerate meekly this autocratic, unconscionable use of NAACP funds?

If they fail to oust Gibson and Chavis, the NAACP will never again be a meaningful force in the councils of power in America.

Coming Out Against Cultural Pollution
STANLEY CROUCH—*New York Daily News*—1/28/2005

We might be on the verge of a real revolution.

It appears that black entertainers will no longer be allowed to denigrate their audiences while hiding behind so-called authenticity.

The recent decision on the part of Samuel L. Jackson to turn down a role offered him opposite the rapper 50 Cent is just one indication of something important that is going on in our culture at this moment. More and more people are deciding to take public what they say behind closed doors and come out against the cultural pollution that holds such a prominent position in the rap idiom.

This is more than a bit startling, because ours is a time in which anything black that makes money gets an automatic pass, especially if it is not illegal. No high moral tone is being projected by the civil-rights establishment, black politicians or any of the others we would expect to be leaders or, at least, to be concerned when such a scurrilous product projects images of young black men as thugs and young black women as sluts who are hot to trot and drop their drawers at the slightest provocation.

Anyone who has studied American popular culture knows that this sort of thing must be considered the new minstrelsy, if only for its consistent ignorance, gold teeth and buffoon attire. The greatest irony is that black "authenticity" has been defined downward to such an extent that these contemporary buffoons, vulgarians and misogynists are defined as the purest black young men, the ones who are "keeping it real."

Comedian Chris Rock had the best reply to that when he said: "Keeping it real. Yeah, real dumb." Rock was problematic at the same time because even though he never missed an opportunity on any of his HBO comedy shows to hold rap and rappers up to ridicule, he submitted to their powerful positions by presenting rappers at the end of almost every show.

Last fall, the black women at Spelman College in Atlanta raised a stink when the rapper Nelly was supposed to appear on campus. They considered his material indefensible and would not have it. He stayed away.

But everything went raw when *Essence*, the most popular black women's magazine, called for a movement to "take back the music" in this month's issue. *Essence* questioned the images of hos, bitches and freaks that rap constantly offers up of black women in lyrics and videos.

Such images were unquestionably hateful, and there was no easing around that fact or forgiving the hatred because it worked as part of a product that was hustled to the tune of millions of dollars in a number of cases.

In a poll taken on the *Essence* Web site, 2,667 people voted, and 72.5 percent took the position that what they hear on urban radio "makes me cringe."

This all adds up to one of the most important moments in the rejection of vile images in popular entertainment. No longer can only the generation that listens to or buys a product be allowed to claim "ownership" of it. It is no longer a closed discussion. Pollution is anybody's business who is within its range. The fact that teenage girls, young women, their mothers and their grandmothers are joining up with their brothers, fathers and grandfathers means something special.

Nobody white would be allowed to get away with selling such a product. It's about time we started seeing some equality.

Living Proof of Immigration's Marvelousness
CYNTHIA TUCKER—*Atlanta Journal-Constitution*—5/14/2006

"Life is beautiful, the world is marvelous, and I love everyone!!!!!!"

My 7-year-old niece—seven-and-a-half, she insists—e-mailed me that message a few weeks back, a reflection of the boundless enthusiasm only a small child can muster.

At the time, I hardly shared her cheeriness. Listening as the rhetoric surrounding immigration grew coarser—with unmistakable signals of an unwholesome nativism, if not outright racism, seeping in from the fringes—I worried that her future wouldn't be as bright as I had hoped. You see, my niece, Maria Irene Vazquez, is a multiethnic child, a "black-xican," as I call her. My sister is married to a man who was born in Mexico.

My e-mail box had been crammed with messages describing illegal workers from south of the border as "criminals" who bring down property values in respectable neighborhoods, grifters who exploit social services that rightfully belong to taxpaying citizens and gatecrashers who refuse to learn our language or customs. One of my e-mail correspondents includes the word "wetback" every time he writes me on immigration. Others sprinkle enough uses of they and them and those people in their missives to remind me of the rhetoric used by white Southerners who resisted desegregation in the 1960s. I wondered if Irene's multiethnic heritage would only expose her to multiple demeaning stereotypes.

There are clearly legitimate worries about the burdens of illegal immigration. Communities with a huge influx of newcomers have struggled to accommodate schoolchildren who speak little English, to provide health care to uninsured pregnant women and to enforce housing codes in areas where undocumented workers crowd together in tight quarters.

But those legitimate concerns can be drowned out by the bigoted messages of xenophobes such as D. A. King, a Cobb County man who has emerged as one of the loudest local critics of illegal immigrants. Though he insists he supports legal immigration, he rails against cultural change.

A frequent contributor to a right-wing, invective-filled Web site called VDARE.com, King once wrote in a column, after attending a rally supporting illegal immigrants as a "counterprotester": "I got the sense that I had left the country of my birth and been transported to some Mexican village, completely taken over by an angry, barely-restrained mob. . . . My first act on a safe return home was to take a shower."

King could easily be speaking that dismissively of Irene's family; her paternal heritage includes a history of illegal labor and immigration rules flexed and bent, if not shattered. Her grandfather entered this country on a tourist visa in 1983 but stayed on after the visa expired and worked in construction.

Though his English is less-than-fluent, he is now an American citizen. He works hard; he loves baseball; he frequents Home Depot. What could be more American?

Repeating the pattern of earlier immigrants—Irish, Italian, Polish, Chinese and others—his children and grandchildren have taken to this country and adopted its values. One grown son is a high-school-educated construction worker. A grown daughter—a mother with three children, one in college—is a teacher's assistant who hopes eventually to complete her own college degree. Another son, my brother-in-law, José, graduated summa cum laude in engineering from the University of Houston, later earning a doctorate. He is the newly minted CEO of a small naval architecture consulting firm in New Orleans.

Little Irene, meanwhile, is much like any other indulged child of the American middle class. She attends a trendy private school; she competes in chess tournaments and takes gymnastics classes; she has Crocs, a portable DVD player and a passport. Call me biased, but I don't get the impression she and her paternal kin are ruining the country.

As it turns out, neither do most other Americans. A newly released *New York Times*/CBS poll shows that most of my fellow citizens reject the exclusionary rhetoric of the D. A. Kings, along with the harsh sanctions proposed by hardline Republicans in the U.S. House, who would make illegal border crossings a felony. Sixty-one percent of poll respondents said illegal immigrants who have been in the United States at least two years should be given the chance to apply for legal status; 66 percent oppose building a fence along the southern border.

I was heartened by those views. Irene may yet grow up in a world that embraces her mixed heritage, that encourages her bilingualism, that endorses her unique contributions to America—a world as marvelous as she believes it to be.

A Path Beyond Grievance
WILLIAM RASPBERRY—*Washington Post*—11/8/2008

It's been said that the ascendancy of Barack Obama signals the beginning of a "post-racial" America.

I wish. What we have witnessed, I think, is something less profound but still hugely significant. Obama's election means that in America, including at the highest levels of our politics, race is no longer an automatic deal-breaker. That's a major step forward in the thinking of white America.

For black America, Obama may be the harbinger of a different transformation: the movement away from what might be called the civil rights paradigm. Since the astounding success of the civil rights movement nearly half a century ago, America's black leadership has been a civil rights leadership, focused almost exclusively on grievance—America owes us the right to vote, to enjoy places of public accommodation, to attend nonsegregated schools, to be free of the laws that underlie American-style apartheid.

America listened, and changed.

What more recent black leaders have not acknowledged is that there are some problems that the grievance model cannot address. The schools black children attend don't work as well as they should—but most often for reasons that have less to do with white attitudes than with our own. Many black children—and too many of their parents—don't value education. If they do, they see it as a debt owed rather than a prize to be earned. Their resulting under-education renders them specially vulnerable to the vicissitudes of the job market. Black communities are beset by crime and violence but, again, less because of racism than because of lack of discipline in those communities. One key reason for this failure of discipline is the dissolution of black families—not because of discrimination but because black Americans lead the nation in fatherlessness, having allowed marriage to fall to an all-time-low priority.

Obama tried to talk about some of this during his campaign, frequently pointing out that government can do little to improve education unless parents take control of the television, read to their children and check their homework.

The point is not to deny that America's black communities still suffer horribly from poor education, dim employment prospects and other crippling (and heritable) ills but to observe that these problems no longer lend themselves to civil rights—or grievance-based—solutions.

How has Obama come to see so clearly the need for black America's active and confident participation in solving its problems?

First, he is supremely confident in his own ability to succeed at whatever he sets out to do, and his experience may lead him to see the power of self-confidence in general. Second, he grew up without the encumbrance of a personal link to American slavery. It is easy even for the descendants of slavery to forget how powerfully that not-so-distant experience guides our sense of destiny. We tend to see slavery as a palpable, almost genetic, experience; that is one reason so many black Americans initially had trouble accepting Obama, with his Kenyan father and white American mother, as authentic.

But while our handed-down "remembrance" of slavery makes us super-conscious of (and, we imagine, steels us against) white America's racist possibilities, it does two other things as well. It leads us too easily to a racial explanation of all that goes wrong in our community, and it encumbers us with the burden of doubt as to what this country will let us do—and be.

Obama certainly did not escape American racism; his skin saw to that. But he did escape the encumbrance of "genetic" slavery; the people who raised him saw to that.

You begin to understand what a different script he follows when he tells you about his upbringing. His mother resolved early on to get him back to the States from her overseas work. Why? "My son's an American, and he needs to know what that means," he quotes her as saying. He recalls his (white) grandfather taking him to watch the recovery of a U.S. astronaut team, waving a miniature flag and remarking that "Americans can do anything they put their minds to."

How many African American parents proffer their children another script: They won't let you succeed (except as entertainers and athletes). If you expect to do well elsewhere, you have to be twice as good.

We imagine that we are preparing our children for the real world. But is not Obama's world also real?

His ascendancy to the most powerful political position in the world does not mean an end to black problems—including the problem of racial discrimination. But it may allow our children to begin to see life as a series of problems and possibilities and not just a list of grievances.

VII: LOCAL VOICES

Anybody who's been telling stories on deadline for a while must eventually hunt for big game: the fine art of explaining some important truth about a place to the world—including, most importantly, its own citizens.

These local voices ring true today. Margaret Fuller's 1846 observation about New York City—"Life rushes wild and free, but too fast"—could have been penned last week. Likewise, Fanny Fern's 1867 tale of meeting one of the "unrecognized heroes" of the Civil War speaks to the reintegration to daily life that soldiers' still face among their unassuming neighbors.

The short-story writer O. Henry—the pen-name of William Sydney Porter — practiced his craft by writing local dispatches for the Houston Post which presaged his most famous work.

A local column can be an unembarrassed love letter, like Herb Caen's ode to San Francisco: "a long white sail fluttering home at dusk past the amber lights of the bridge that only a dreamer could have built."

Occasionally it might include a cut-the-crap slap in the city's face, like Mike Royko's 1967 take on a newly unveiled Picasso in Chicago, comparing it to "some giant insect that is about to eat a smaller, weaker insect . . . Everybody said it had the spirit of Chicago. And from thousands of miles away, accidentally or on purpose, Picasso captured it." Molly Ivins cheerfully tweaks her home state while explaining why so many county music stars from a certain part of Texas sing about sin and redemption: "Lubbock will by-God let you know what sin is. So you can go out and do it, and enjoy it."

Most of all, the reader gets the sense of a place through depictions of unforgettable local characters, such as the lifelong loan shark gently eulogized by John Smith in the *Las Vegas Review-Journal*: "A gentlemen in a violent racket filled with predators . . . He was not a saint and made no such pretenses." Kathleen Parker shares the life-changing power of a South Carolina high school teacher.

These are remarkable characters and remarkable places brought to life by writers eager to share the same amazed, exuberant shout Steve Lopez gave his adopted hometown, Philadelphia: "Is this a great city or what?"

She Bids Farewell to New York

MARGARET FULLER—*New York Daily Tribune*—8/1/1846

Farewell to New York City, where twenty months have presented me with a richer and more varied exercise for thought and life, than twenty years could in any other part of these United States.

It is a common remark about New York, that it has at least nothing petty or provincial in its methods and habits. The place is large enough: there is room enough, and occupation enough, for men to have no need for small cavils or scrutinies. A person who is independent, and knows what he wants, may lead his proper life here, unimpeded by others.

Vice and crime, if flagrant and frequent, are less thickly coated by hypocrisy than elsewhere. The air comes sometimes to the most infected subjects.

New York is the focus, the point where American and European interests converge. There is no topic of general interest to men, that will not betimes be brought before the thinker by the quick turning of the wheel.

Too quick that revolution,—some object. Life rushes wild and free, but *too fast.* Yet it is in the power of every one to avert himself from the evil that accompanies the good; he must build for his study, as did the German poet, a house beneath the bridge; and then all that passes above and by him will be heard and seen, but he will not be carried away with it.

Earlier views have been confirmed, and many new ones opened. On two great leadings, the superlative importance of promoting national education by heightening and deepening the cultivation of individual minds, and the part which is assigned to woman in the next stage of human progress in this country, where most important achievements are to be effected, I have received much encouragement, much instruction, and the fairest hopes of more.

On various subjects of minor importance, no less than these, I hope for good results, from observation, with my own eyes, of life in the old world, and to bring home some packages of seed for life in the new.

These words I address to my friends, for I feel that I have some. The degree of sympathetic response to the thoughts and suggestions I have offered, through the columns of the *Tribune*, has indeed surprised me, conscious as I am of a natural and acquired aloofness from many, if not the most popular tendencies of my time and place. It has greatly encouraged me, for none can sympathize with thoughts like mine, who are permanently ensnared in the meshes of sect or party; none who prefer the formation and advancement of mere opinions to the free pursuit of truth. I see, surely, the topmost bubble or sparkle of the cup is no voucher for the nature of its contents throughout, and shall, in future, feel that in our age, nobler in that respect than most preceding ages, each sincere and fervent act or word is secure, not only of a final, but a speedy response.

I go to behold the wonders of art, and the temples of old religion. But I shall see no forms of beauty and majesty beyond what my country is capable of producing in myriad variety, if she has the soul to will it; no temple to compare with what she might erect in the ages, if the catchword of the time, a sense of *divine order*, should be no more than a mere word of form, but a deeply-rooted and pregnant idea in her life. Beneath the light of a hope that this may be, I say to my friends once more a kind farewell!

The History of Our Late War
FANNY FERN—*New York Ledger*—1/26/1867

Many able works have already appeared on this subject, and many more will doubtless follow. But *my* History of the War is yet to be written; not indeed *by* me, but *for* me.

A history which shall record, not the deeds of our Commanders and Generals, noble and great as they were, because these will greatly fail of historical record and prominence; but *my* history shall preserve for the descendants of those who fought for our flag, the noble deeds of our *privates*, who shared the danger but missed the glory. Scatted far and wide in remote villages—hidden away in our mountains—struggling for daily bread amid our swarming cities, are these unrecognized heroes. Traveling through our land, one meets them everywhere; but only as accident, or chance, leads to conversation with them, does the plain man by your side become transfigured in your eyes, till you feel like uncovering your head in his presence, as when one stands upon holy ground. Not only because they were brave upon the battle-field, but for their sublime self-abnegation under circumstances when the best of us might be forgiven our selfishness; in the tortures of the ambulance and hospital—quivering through the laggard hours, that might or might not bring peace and rest and health. Oh! what a book might be written upon the noble unselfishness *there* displayed; not only towards those who fought *for* our flag, but *against* it. The coveted drop of water, handed by one dying man to another, whose sufferings seemed the greater. The simple request to the physician to pass *his* wounds by, till those of another, whose existence was unknown to him until a moment before, should have been alleviated. Who shall embalm us these?

Last summer, when I was away in the country, I was accustomed to row every night at sunset on a lovely lake near by. The boatman who went with me was a sunburnt, pleasant-faced young man, whose stroke at the oar it was poetry to see. He made no conversation unless addressed, save occasionally to little Bright-Eyes, who sometimes accompanied me. One evening, as the sun set gloriously and the moon rose, and the aurora borealis was sending up flashes of rose and silver, I said, "Oh, this is too beautiful to leave. I *must* cross the lake again." I made some remark about the brilliance of the North Star, when he remarked simply, "That star was a good friend to me in the war." "Were you in the war?" asked I; "and all these evenings you have rowed a loyal woman like me about this lake, and I knew nothing of it!"

Then, at my request, came the story of Andersonville, and its horrors, told simply, and without a revengeful word; then the thrilling attempt at escape, through a country absolutely unknown, and swarming with danger, during which the North Star, of which I had just spoken, was his only guide. Then came a dark night, when the friendly star, alas! disappeared. But a watch, which he had saved his money to obtain, had a compass on the back of it. Still of what use was that without a light? Our boatman was a Yankee. He caught a glowworm and pinched it. It flashed light sufficient for him to see that he was heading for one of our camps, where, after many hours of travel, he at last found safety, sinking down insensible from fatigue and hunger, as soon as he reached it. So ravenously did he eat, when food was brought, that a raging fever followed; and when he was carried, a mere skeleton, to his home on the borders of the lovely lake where we were rowing, whose peaceful flow had mocked him in dreams in that seething, noisome prison pen, he did not even recognize it. For months his mother' watched his sick-bed, till reason and partial health returned—till by degrees he became what he then was.

When he had finished, I said, "Give me your hand—*both of 'em*—and God bless you!"—and—then I *mentioned* his jailers! Not a word of bitterness passed his lips—only this: "I used to gasp in the foul air at Andersonville, and think of this quiet, smooth lake, and our little house with the trees near it, and long so to see them again, and row my little boat here. But," he added, quietly, "*they* thought they were as right as we, and they *did* fight well!"

I swallowed a big lump in my throat—as our boat neared the shore, and he handed me out—and said, penitently, "Well, if *you* can forgive them, I am sure I ought to; but it will be the hardest work I ever did."—"Well, it is strange," said he: "I have often noticed it, since my return, that you who stayed at home feel more bitter about it, than we who came so near dying there of foul air and starvation."

Postscripts
O. HENRY—*Houston Post*—1895–1896

WHAT IT WAS
There was something the matter with the electric lights Tuesday night, and Houston was as dark as Egypt when Moses blew the gas out. They were on Rusk Avenue, out on the lawn, taking advantage of the situation, and holding as close a section as possible.

Presently, she said:

"George, I know you love me, and I am sure that nothing in the world can change my affection for you, yet I feel that something has come between us, and although I have hesitated long to tell you, it is paining me very much."

"What is it, my darling?" asked George, in the agony of suspense. "Speak, my own, and tell me what it is that has come between you and me?"

"I think, George," she softly sighed, "it is your watch."

And George loosened his hold for a moment and shifted his Waterbury.

A GOOD STORY SPOILED

A few nights ago in a rather tough saloon in a little town on the Central Railroad, a big, strapping desparado, who had an unenviable reputation as a bad man generally, walked up to the bar and in a loud voice ordered everybody in the saloon to walk up and take a drink. The crowd moved quickly to the bar at his invitation, as the man was half drunk and undoubtedly dangerous when in that condition.

One man failed to accept the invitation. He was a rather small man, neatly dressed, who sat calmly in his chair, gazing idly at the crowd. A student of physiognomy would have been attracted to the expression on his face, which was with a cool determination and force of will. His jaw was square and firm, and his eye gray and steady, with that particular gray glint in the iris that presses more danger than any other kind of optic.

The bully looked around and saw someone had declined his invitation.

He repeated it in a louder voice.

The small man rose to his feet and walked cooly toward the desparado.

"Excuse me," he said in a low but determined tone, "I'm a little deaf and didn't hear you the first time. Gimme whiskey straight."

And another story was spoiled for the papers.

A STARTLING DEMONSTRATION

What a terrible state of affairs it would be if we could read each other's minds! It is safe to say that if such were the case, most of us would be afraid to think above a whisper.

As an illustration, a case might be cited that occurred in Houston. Some months ago a very charming young lady came to this city giving exhibitions in mind reading, and proved herself to be marvelously gifted in that respect. She easily read the thoughts of the audience, finding many articles hidden by simply holding the hand of the person secreting them, and read sentences written on little slips of paper at some considerable distance from her.

A young man in Houston fell in love with her, and married her after a short courtship. They went to housekeeping, and were for a time as happy as mortals can be.

One evening they were on the porch of their residence holding each other's hands, and wrapt in the close communication of mutual love, when she suddenly rose and knocked him down the steps with a large flower-pot. He arose astonished, with a big bump on his head, and asked her, if it were not too much trouble, to explain.

"You can't fool me," she said with flashing eyes. "You were thinking of a red-headed girl named Maud with a gold plug in her front tooth and a light pink waist and a black silk skirt on Rusk Avenue, standing under a cedar bush chewing gum at twenty minutes to eight with your arm around her waist and calling her 'sweetness,' while she fooled with her watch chain and said: 'Oh, George, give me a chance to breathe,' and her mother was calling her to supper. Don't you dare to deny it. Now, when you can't get your mind on something better than that, you can come in the house and not before."

The door slammed and George and the flower-pot were alone.

Don Quixote and His Last Windmill
BEN HECHT—*Chicago Daily News*—1921

Sherwood Anderson, the writer, and I were eating lunch in the back room of a saloon. Against the opposite wall sat a red-faced little man with an elaborate mustache and a bald head and a happy grin. He sat alone at a tilted round table and played with a plate of soup.

"Say, that old boy over there is trying to wigwag me," said Anderson. "He keeps winking and making signs. Do you know him?"

I looked and said no. The waiter appeared with a box of cigars.

"Mr. Sklarz presents his compliments," said the waiter, smiling.

"Who's Sklarz?" Anderson asked, helping himself to a cigar. The waiter indicated the red-faced little man. "Him," he whispered.

We continued our meal. Both of us watched Mr. Sklarz casually. He seemed to have lost interest in his soup. He sat beaming happily at the walls, a contagious elation about him. We smiled and nodded our thanks for the cigars. Whereupon after a short lapse, the waiter appeared again.

"What'll you have to drink, gentlemen?" the waiter inquired.

"Nothing," said Anderson, knowing I was broke. The waiter raised his continental eyebrows understandingly.

"Mr. Sklarz invites you, gentlemen, to drink his health—at his expense."

"Two glasses," Anderson ordered. They were brought. We raised them in silent toast to the little red-faced man. He arose and bowed as we drank.

"We'll probably have him on our hands now for an hour," Anderson frowned. I feared the same. But Mr. Sklarz reseated himself and, with many head bowings in our direction, returned to his soup.

"What do you make of our magnanimous friend?" I asked. Anderson shrugged his shoulders.

"He's probably celebrating something," he said. "A queer old boy, isn't he?"

* * *

"What'll it be, gentlemen?" he inquired, smiling. "Mr. Sklarz is buying for the house."

For the house. There were some fifteen men eating in the place. Then our friend, despite his unassuming appearance, was evidently a creature of wealth! Well, this was growing interesting. We ordered wine again.

"Ask Mr. Sklarz if he will favor us by joining us at our table for this drink," I told the waiter. The message was delivered. Mr. Sklarz arose and bowed but sat down again. Anderson and I beckoned in pantomime. Mr. Sklarz arose once more, bowed and hesitated. Then he came over.

As he approached a veritable carnival spirit seemed to deepen around us. The face of this little man with the elaborate black mustache was violent with suppressed good will and mirth. He beamed, bowed, shook hands and sat down. We drank one another's health and, as politely as we could, pressed him to tell us the cause for his celebration and good spirits. He began to talk.

He was a Russian Jew. His name was Sklarz. He had been in the Russian army years ago. In Persia. From a mountain in Persia you could see three great countries. In Turkey he had fought with baggy-trousered soldiers and at night joined them when they played their flutes outside the coffee-houses and sang songs about women and war. Then he came to America and opened a box factory. He was very prosperous and the factory in which he made boxes grew too small.

So what did he do but take a walk one day to look for a larger factory. And he found a beautiful building just as he wanted. But the building was too beautiful to use for a factory. It should be used for something much nicer. So what did he do then but decide to open a dance-hall, a magnificent dance-hall, where young men and women of refined, fun-loving temperaments could come to dance and have fun.

* * *

"When does the dance-hall open?" Andersen asked. Ah, in a little while. There were fittings to buy and put up first. But he would send us special invitations to the opening. In the meantime would we drink to health again? Mr. Sklarz chuckled. The amazing thing was that he wasn't drunk. He was sober.

"So you're celebrating," I said. Yes, he was celebrating. He laughed and leaned over the table toward us. His eyes danced and his elaborate mustache made a grotesque halo for his smile. He didn't want to intrude on us with his story, but in Persia and Turkey and the Urals he found life very nice. And here in Chicago he also found life very nice. Life was very nice wherever you went. And Anderson quoted, rather imperfectly, I thought:

Oh, but life went gayly, gayly
In the house of Idah Dally;
There were always throats to sing
Down in the river bank with spring.

Mr. Sklarz beamed.

"Yes, yes," he said, "down the river benk mit spring." And he stood up and bowed and summoned the waiter. "See vat all the gentlemen vant," he ordered, "and give them vat they vant mit my compliments." He laughed, or, rather, chuckled. "I must be going. Excuse me," he exclaimed with a quick little bow. "I have other places to call on. Good-by. Remember me—Sam Sklarz. Be good—and don't forget Sam Sklarz when there are throats to sing down the river benk mit spring."

He watched him walk out. His shoulders seemed to dance, his short legs moved with a springly lift.

"A queer old boy," said Anderson. We talked about him for a half hour and then left the place.

* * *

Anderson called me up the next morning to ask if I had read about it in the paper. I told him I had. A clipping on the desk in front of me ran:

"Sam Sklarz, 46 years old and owner of a box factory on the West Side, committed suicide early this morning by jumping into the drainage canal. Financial reverses are believed to have caused the end of his life. According to friends he was at the verge of bankruptcy. His liabilities were $8,000. Yesterday morning Sklarz cashed a check for $700, which represented the remains of his bank account, and disappeared. It is believed that he used the money to pay for personal debts and then wandered around in a daze until the end. He left no word of explanation behind."

About New York
MEYER BERGER—*New York Times*—1/23/1959

Last Friday a welfare worker led a slender, pale old man into the old Straus mansion at 9 East Seventy-first Street. Franciscan nuns run the Eye, Ear, Nose and Throat Division of St. Clare's Hospital there.

The old man was blind. His clothes were shabby. His sunken cheeks were stubble-covered. He tried to sit on the elevator floor as it lifted to the second floor. In dimly lighted Room 203, to which he was assigned, he tried to sit on the floor again.

The welfare woman said: "He has lived a long time in Bowery flophouses. When there are no seats in flophouses, the men sit on the floor."

The old man was shaved, bathed, and put into pajamas. He gave his history as though through a veil. His memory failed now and then. He said he was Laurence Stroetz, born in Fifth Street between Avenues A and B on Aug. 10, 1877, when the Lower East Side was mostly German.

His father was Frank Stroetz, who played cornet for Squadron A of the Old National Guard in the Seventies. The family had a grocer's shop at 165 Second Street. He could remember some of his brothers and sisters—Frank, Hannah, Barbara, Madeline, Annie, Mary.

"All gone, now?" he was asked, and he nodded. The listeners were conscious of mental gropping behind the sightless, cataract-covered eyes that might once have been blue. He said, "My wife was Maud Baker." He repeated, "Maud Baker."

"She gone?" He nodded.

"No children?" He said, "No children."

Violin Lessons Long Ago

By last Monday the old man had mellowed under the kindly treatment of dark-clad Franciscan sisters and the white-clad nuns who are nurses. He told of life on the East Side in his boyhood, of how he had taken violin lessons there and of playing in his twenties with professional orchestras.

He said he had been two years with Victor Herbert in the Pittsburg Symphony Orchestra; with the orchestra in the old Academy of Music in Fourteenth Street next to Tony Pastor's. He told of playing in the Savoy and in the Lyceum when Billie Burke was in "Mrs. Dot," long, long ago. He snatched each memory from the past with difficulty.

He kept talking about Charlie, who had been his guide and companion in one Bowery flophouse or another the last thirty years. He said: "When my eyes began to go, Charlie was my boss in a restaurant in Radio City. I had a broom and a pan. I picked up cigarette butts and napkins. Charlie had his own office."

It took a long time before the old man could better identify Charlie: "He slept in the Majestic, same as me, and in the Alabama." Those are Bowery lodging houses. "He brought my coffee. Charlie was good to me." Then he remembered Charlie's last name:

"Charlie was a Frenchman. He pawned my old violin for me. I used to play in the Hotel Oriental in Coney Island. I played in Beethoven Hall and in the Liederkranz. Charlie Messier—he was a good pianist. He led the boys' choir in the old Mariners' Temple when Dr. Hubbell was there. I played in the Church of The Land and Sea. Mrs. Morris was organist."

The mental scraps had to be fetched before they fled. At 82 they don't stay put, the old man said. A few times he fell asleep. His head fell to his chest and his white lion's mane—he looks like Franz Liszt—caught feeble light that came through the hospital window.

Nun's Violin Recalled

Nurse Josephine Wynne spoke with Sister Pauline Marie. They remembered that Sister Francis Marie had in her room the old Biotte violin that had belonged to her sister, the nun Sister Anthony Marie. Sister Anthony Marie died in St. Clare's three years ago. Cardinal Spellman had found the instrument for her in Rome more than thirty years ago.

The staff talked with Sister Mary Fintan, who has charge of the hospital. With her consent they brought the old violin to Room 203. It had not been played for years, but Laurence Stroetz groped for it. His long white fingers stroked it. He tuned it, with some effort, and tightened the old bow. He lifted it to his chin and the lion's mane came down.

It was 8 'o clock. Dinner was over. Room 203 was all but dark. Only diffused light filtered in through the silent corridor through the partly open door. The old man had told the nuns he had not played since Charlie pawned his violin, but the pale fingers rippled up and down the strings as he sought touch.

He played "Sidewalks of New York," true, but quavery. The fingering was stronger in Handel's "Largo," in "Humoresque," and "The Blue Danube." Before each number, the old man muttered the composer's name and hummed opening bars to recapture lost melody. The nuns, the patients and the nurses were silent.

LISTENERS ATTRACTED

An audience assembled in the tilted corridor as the strains quivered and hung in the quiet, as they fled in thin echo. Laurence Stroetz murmured another tune, barely heard by the nuns and the nurses. Then he played it, clear and steady. It was Gounod's "Ave Maria."

Black-clad and white-clad nuns moved lips in silent prayer. They choked up. The long years on the Bowery had not stolen Laurence Stroetz's touch. Blindness made his fingers stumble down to the violin bridge, but they recovered. The music died and the audience pattered applause. The old violinist bowed and his sunken cheeks ceased in a smile.

Next week eye surgeons at St. Clare's will try to remove the cataracts. If they do, the Welfare Department will try to place the old violinist in a nursing home to get him off the Bowery. If someone could offer a violin that he could call his own again, he would know ecstasy.

"It would make me feel good," he told the sisters. "It would be wonderful."

Ah, San Francisco
HERB CAEN—*San Francisco Examiner*—5/5/1953

Twin Peaks blooming in green freshness at the end of drab Market Street, the sun reflecting fiercely on the windshields of a thousand cars filing across the Bay Bridge, the East Hills softly golden at the end of a perfect spring day, Alcatraz looking suddenly like an enchanted isle as it sits and stares dreamily at its own perfect reflection in the still waters . . . Ah, San Francisco.

Harold Zellerbach riding democratically in the front seat with his chauffeur as his black limousine drones through the Broadway Tunnel, the Oriental sharpies with patent-leather shoes and hair to match enjoying the warm sun on the fringe of Portsmouth Square, the plain-clothes coppers cruising around in the overly plain sedans that shout, "Police!" louder than any sign, the good jazz of Cal Tjader filtering out of the Blackhawk and getting lost under the stars that shine down on Turk Street too . . . Oh, San Francisco!

The red-and-blue stacks of an American President Liner shimmering in the sun as the great liner floats like a mirage past the Marina, the silhouette of the clipper ship *Balclutha* adding a touch of square-rigged glamour to the water-front, an ancient trolley rattling past Lotta's Fountain exactly as it has done for forty long years, the red beacons atop the Clay-Jones and Bellaire apartments blinking back and forth from Nob Hill to Russian, like pulse beats in the night sky . . . Ah, Baghdad-by-the-Bay.

The big signs that invite you to the little joints along Broadway, the newsboy who was once a stockbroker hollering his headlines off in the ticker-taped heart of Montgomery Street, the motorists who drive the wrong way in one-way streets and answer your warning honk with a pickle-faced look, the dozens of mailboxes clustered at the entrances to the smelly tenements in Chinatown, jammed together like the people who live upstairs . . . Oh, cool gray city of love, hate, filth, beauty and incense and garlic in the air.

The people who take a Sunday drive through Golden Gate Park and gnash their ulcers in irritation because they can't drive through its beauties fast enough, the bobby-soxers and the grandmothers eyeing each other curiously as they wait at the Curran stage entrance for an autograph from Jack Benny, the withered little man who peddles his sacks of lavender on Grant Avenue near the entrance to flower-bowered Podesta Baldocchi, unemployed B-girls wandering along Mason Street in search of a guy who'll buy them a real drink for a change . . . Ah, Queen City of the West, with white, pennant-topped towers that reach to the sky and gutters that need cleaning and mansions with marble halls and streets that need sweeping.

A Powell Street cable waddling slowly across the Broadway Tunnel's concrete bridge as though it's not quite safe for cables to cross bridges, longshoremen playing catch like kids in the shadows of the great piers that have known so much strife, the thin-faced artists of Little Bohemia showing their wares on the sidewalks and trying not to look disappointed when passers-by keep passing by, the polo players and the soccer players in the Park and the yachtsmen in their self-conscious blues in Yacht Harbor and the near-nudes baking to a turn and turning to bake on the Marina Green. . . . Oh, Pearl of the Pacific, treasure of the trade winds, mecca of the mariner, sanctuary of the screaming sea gull, port of call for half the world and beloved landmark for the other half.

The Post Street clerks who pause to stare appraisingly at the $10,000 trifles in the windows of Shreve's and then move on with a silent shrug to indicate that they weren't quite satisfied with the quality, girls shrieking on the rides at the beach and sounding exactly like every girl who has ever shrieked on the ride anywhere, the old men who sit alone in the side-street hotel lobbies and then walk alone to eat in cafeterias where they can be alone together and share their misery in unspoken understanding . . . Ah, city of sophistication and culture and hammer murders and shakedowns, and people who are overcrowded together and never speak to each other.

The Negro children of Sutter Street staring out of their cracked windows at the tennis players in their white-white shorts chasing a white-white-white ball across the courts of the California Tennis Club, a jet plane leaving a vapor trail smudged across the blue sky like a sky writer who started a message and then forgot it, springtime's young lovers parked at Land's End to enjoy the view of each other, the grown-up kids who hang around Earle Swenson's ice cream parlor at Union and Hyde and say, "Gee, thanks" (just like their children) when Earle rewards them with a free sample, the unemployed guys in their dirty non-working clothes clustered on Howard Street to discuss their last meal and wonder where the next one is coming from . . . Oh, big-little town of wide views from dark alleys.

An extravagant sunset fading so fast you can't fully all the work that must have gone into it, a long white sail fluttering home at dusk past the amber lights of the bridge that only a dreamer could have built, the ceaseless nighttime hum of life and tires and lights and horns in this worldly town that never quite finds time to go to sleep, and then—the moon rising fast out of the far-off east of bean whitely down on the hills and valleys and restless waters of the tiny city that has no boundaries . . . San Francisco. Ah, San Francisco.

Picasso and the Cultural Rebirth of Chicago
MIKE ROYKO—*Chicago Sun-Times*—8/16/1967

Mayor Daley walked to the white piece of ribbon and put his hand on it. He was about to give it a pull when the photographers yelled for him to wait. He stood there for a minute and gave them that familiar blend of scowl and smile.

It was good that he waited. This was a moment to think about, to savor what was about to happen. In just a moment, with a snap of the mayor's wrist, Chicago history would be changed. That's no small occurrence—the cultural rebirth of a big city.

Out there in the neighborhoods and the suburbs, things probably seemed just the same. People worried about the old things—would they move in and would we move out? Or would we move in and would they move out?

But downtown, the leaders of culture and influence were gathered for a historical event and it was reaching a climax with Mayor Daley standing there ready to pull a ribbon.

Thousands waited in and around the Civic Center plaza. They had listened to the speeches about the Picasso thing. They had heard how it was going to change Chicago's image.

They had heard three clergymen—a priest, a rabbi, and a Protestant minister—offer eloquent prayers. That's probably a record for a work by Picasso, a dedicated atheist.

And now the mayor was standing there, ready to pull the ribbon.

You could tell it was a big event by the seating. In the first row on the speakers platform was a lady poet. In the second row was Alderman Tom Keane. And in the third row was P. J. Cullerton, the assessor. When Keane and Cullerton sit behind a lady poet, things are changing.

The only alderman in the front row was Tom Rosenberg. And he was there only because it was a cultural event and he is chairman of the City Council's Culture Committee, which is in charge of preventing aldermen from spitting, swearing, and snoring during meetings.

The whole thing had been somber and serious. The Chicago Symphony Orchestra had played classical music. It hadn't played even one chorus of "For He's a Jolly Good Fellow."

Chief Judge John Boyle had said the Picasso would become more famous than the Art Institute's lions. Boyle has vision.

Someone from the National Council of Arts said it was paying tribute to Mayor Daley. This brought an interested gleam in the eyes of a few ward committeemen.

William Hartmann, the man who thought of the whole thing, told of Picasso's respect for Mayor Daley. Whenever Hartmann went to see Picasso, the artist asked:

"Is Mayor Daley still mayor of Chicago?"

When Hartmann said this, Mayor Daley bounced up and down in his chair, he laughed so hard. So did a few Republicans in the cheap seats, but they didn't laugh the same way.

After the ceremony, it came to that final moment the mayor standing there holding the white ribbon.

Then he pulled.

There was a gasp as the light blue covering fell away in several pieces. But it was caused by the basic American fascination for any mechanical feat that goes off as planned.

In an instant the Picasso stood there unveiled for all to see.

A few people applauded. But at best, it was a smattering of applause. Most of the throng was silent.

They had hoped, you see, that it would be what they had heard it would be.

A woman, maybe. A beautiful soaring woman. That is what many art experts and enthusiasts had promised. They had said that we should wait—that we should not believe what we saw in the pictures.

If it was a woman, then art experts should put away their books and spend more time in girlie joints.

The silence grew. Then people turned and looked at each other. Some shrugged. Some smiled. Some just stood there, frowning or blank-faced.

Most just turned and walked away. The weakest pinch-hitter on the Cubs receives more cheers.

They had wanted to be moved by it. They wouldn't have stood there if they didn't want to believe what they had been told—that it would be a fine thing.

But anyone who didn't have a closed mind—which means thinking that anything with the name Picasso connected must be wonderful—could see that it was nothing but a big, homely metal thing.

That is all there is to it. Some soaring lines, yes. Interesting design, I'm sure. But the fact is, it has a long stupid face and looks like some giant insect that is about to eat a smaller, weaker insect. It has eyes that are pitiless, cold, mean.

But why not? Everybody said it had the spirit of Chicago. And from thousands of miles away, accidentally or on purpose, Picasso captured it.

Up there in that ugly face is the spirit of Al Capone, the Summerdale scandal cops, the settlers who took the Indians but good.

Its eyes are like the eyes of every slum owner who made a buck off the small and weak. And of every building inspector who took a wad from a slum owner to make it all possible.

It has the look of the dope pusher and of the syndicate technician as he looks for just the right wire to splice the bomb to.

Any bigtime real estate operator will be able to look into the face of the Picasso and see the spirit that makes the city's rebuilding possible and profitable.

It has the look of the big corporate executive who comes face to face with the reality of how much water pollution his company is responsible for and then thinks of the profit and loss and of his salary.

It is all there in that Picasso thing—the I Will spirit. The "I will get you before you will get me" spirit.

Picasso has never been here, they say. You'd think he's been riding the L all his life.

A not-so-classic Christmas story about a not-so-silent day in Pershing Square
JACK SMITH—*Los Angeles Times*—12/25/1983

No matter how much I try to resist it, at least until Christmas Eve, the Yuletide spirit usually gets to me when I'm not expecting it, at some unguarded moment, from some improbable quarter.

I was ambushed by it the other day in downtown Los Angeles. I was not unaware of the seasonal seductions of that neighborhood. The elevators were playing carols. The store windows were festive. The Santa Belles were out on their corners, dancing to keep their legs warm and ringing their little bells. But I had steeled myself against these familiar sirens and thought I was safe when I took the shortcut through Pershing Square.

There was not much chance of catching the Christmas spirit from the shabby fringe of derelicts around the ornamental pool. They dozed in the sun, nipped from bottles in brown paper sacks, scanned remnants of discarded newspapers, quarreled with the pigeons and peered back into the hazy past, looking for some long-lost fork in the road.

Two men stood side by side in front of the war memorial singing "Silent Night." One was about five feet tall and wore a shapeless coat that would have looked big on Boris Karloff. The other wore a limp fedora that hid his face except for the mouth and a threadbare overcoat so large he didn't seem to be wearing it so much as living in it.

Their appearance alone might have attracted no attention in the park, being a kind of protective coloration; but their singing was hard to ignore, and now and then one of their captive audience would turn his head in their direction and stare in silent wonder.

The smaller man was the leader. He sang in a tenor voice that evidently had known much abuse and given vent to much anguish and passion. He worked it to the very edge of its capacity, rubbing its raw edges painfully against the underside of the high notes, falling heroically short of the Savior in "Christ the Savior is born" and sinking mercifully into "heavenly peace." He sang with his eyes shut, his face swollen and purple from the effort.

His partner wrestled the harmony with a mixture of foolhardiness and caution, like an over-the-hill matador fighting a mean young bull. His voice might have been deep and resonant once. It would come on strong for a phrase and then fade out. As he sang he rocked perilously back and forth, his open mouth vanishing under the brim of his hat when he bent forward and appearing in full flower for a moment on the backswing before rolling out of sight.

It wasn't simply the quality of their performance or the incongruity of their appearance that kept me there, but the growing realization that they didn't stop when they finished the song. They were no sooner through the final "heavenly place" than the smaller man would throw his shoulders back, fill his lungs, turn himself purple, and start all over again:

"Si . . . uh . . . lent night!

Ho . . . uh . . . ly night!"

His partner would turn to face him at each of these reprises as if stupefied by this new demand on his overextended powers. He would stand dumb until he made sure the song was launched again beyond recall, then once more he would lean backward, his gray mouth opening valiantly, and attack the harmony, not far off the pitch and almost on the beat.

"All is calm,
All is bright!"

They had sung it through three times and started again when I walked on to Fifth and Hill and beyond their reach, wondering at the indestructibility of the Christmas spirit. Evidently it was the only carol they knew, but it was a miracle, I thought, that even "Silent Night" had survived, fairly intact, the disenchantments they must have suffered.

I won't say that I myself was infused with the Christmas spirit by that threadbare "Silent Night," but I couldn't very well say "humbug" either. Nobody was going to take those old men riding through the snow on a one-horse open sleigh or stuff them full of plum pudding and fill their stockings with the things they wanted; yet they seemed to be bursting with good will anyway and were moved to spread it among their fellows.

What resistance I still had was caved in the next night when we drove up to Descano Gardens for the preview opening of the annual Nine Days of Christmas at Hospitality House.

It was cold but exhilarating—something like riding in an open sleigh, I thought—as the tram took us from the gate to the house through tunnels of overhanding oaks. White camellias swam toward us through the dark, and here and there our headlights shone on clusters of red berries tackled to the trees.

We emerged from the oaks to see the lighted house, like a house in a fairy take, and suddenly the night was filled with angelic singing. It came from a chorus of schoolchildren who stood outdoors, huddled together in their coats and mittens. An utterly disarming sound—sweet, vibrant, innocent and supple. No orchestra could simulate its poignancy, and only the most vigilant ear could catch its undercurrent of throttled mischief.

The house was warm and bright and crammed with handmade gifts and decorations and the sounds and scents of Christmas past. A child who wakened to Christmas Day in a house like this, I thought, would never forget it, and fifty years later, long after he had taken some wrong fork in the road, he might stand in Pershing Square, wrapped in rags, and pour out the memory of it to the pigeons and the sky:

Silent night
Holy night.

I was hooked.

"Lubbock": Her Teeth Are Stained But Her Heart Is Pure
MOLLY IVINS—*Dallas Times-Herald*—2/13/1987

When in the course of human events one is called upon to explain Lubbock art, the oxymoron, to San Francisco, the city of sophisticates, one might well take a dive.

Duty called. Some outfit in San Francisco is putting on a program in April entitled "The Texans' Project," which consists of a bunch of Lubbock artists and musicians doing art and music. In my semi-official capacity as a person supposedly capable of explaining Texas to normal people, this theater asked me to explain to San Franciscans why so many great musicians come from Lubbock. How fortunate that I know:

Because there is nothing else to do in Lubbock.

Except perhaps for Wednesday Fellowship Night.

This is not a cheap shot at Lubbock. This is fact.

Another reason there is so much music in Lubbock is because people there know what sin is. Lubbock is a godly place, so it follows as night the day that there should be a lot of country music and down-home rock, with their consequent and probably inevitable accompaniment of drinking and dancing and other forms of enjoyable sin. The sheer beauty of having something as clear-cut as Lubbock to rebel against is almost enough to make me move there.

What is a teenager in San Francisco to rebel against, for pity's sake? Their parents are all so busy trying to be non-judgmental, it's no wonder they take to dyeing their hair green. But Lubbock will by-God let you know what sin *is*. So you can go out and do it, and enjoy it.

Lubbock is full of They-Sayers and They Say that if you sin long enough, you will become An Example to Us All. However, if you should become sufficiently rich and famous in the process, they will also put you in the Lubbock Music Hall of Fame—along with Buddy Holly, Bob Wills, Waylon Jennings, Mac Davis, Joe Ely and the like.

Also, we should give a little credit to the musical history of Lubbock, which for many years harbored the late lamented Cotton Club, the finest honky-tonk in all of West Texas. Kent Hance, the former congressman from Lubbock who fell into Republicanism and came to electoral grief, reports, "When I was in college we went to the Cotton Club to dance, to pick up girls and to drink beer out of Coca-Cola cups in case a minister came in, and it would embarrass him and you both. Outside they had soap and water so you could wash that stamp off your hand when you left at the end of the night, so it wouldn't show Sunday morning at church.

"The dancin' started at 9, and everbody'd dance until 11:30 and then everbody'd go out to the parkin' lot and fistfight or somethin' else and then go back in to dance until 2. Which is how a whole lot of great cheatin' songs and tragedy love songs came to be written."

Good Lord, Lubbock, Texas. Well, about 88.3 percent of the world there is sky, and if you are used to that, it feels like freedom and everywhere else feels like jail. I have no idea what that has to do with Lubbock art, but maybe someone can think of a connection. I should probably explain more to the people in San Francisco about Lubbock weather, but I reckon hearing Joe Ely is close to a Lubbock tornado, and he'll be out there.

It is extremely difficult to develop either pretensions or affectations in Lubbock. Without getting laughed out of town. Which probably does account for a lot about the music. Lubbock is sometimes called "the Hub City of the Plains"—actually the Lubbock Chamber of Commerce is the only thing that ever calls it that—and I think it was Jimmie Gilmore who once observed, "Plain is the opposite of fancy."

Hance says the failures of Lubbock music deserve some attention, too. "Not everybody from Lubbock has been able to sing well. I knew a guy from Matador named Robin Dorsey who wanted to be a country-western writer. He wrote a song about his girlfriend, who was from Muleshoe, called 'Her Teeth Are Stained But Her Heart Is Pure.' And she quit him. And he had her name, Patty, tattooed on his arm which ever after cut down on his social life because we always had to fix him up with girls named Patty. So he wrote a tragedy love song about it, 'I Don't Know Whether to Kill Myself or Go Bowling.'"

One of my favorite Lubbock songs that never made it big is "I Wish I Was in Dixie Tonight, But She's Out of Town." The others are all too dirty to print.

So, come April, San Francisco will meet Lubbock. Lord have mercy. I just don't think those people out there are *ready*.

True Confessions
STEVE LOPEZ—*Philadelphia Inquirer*—12/24/1989

Call it intuition. Call it instinct. When the city has embarrassed two weeks ago in the famous Snow Bowl at Veterans Stadium, something told me a local politician had to have a hand in it.

Think about it, folks. A nationally televised debacle. A complete and total lack of class.

Use your head.

And so, before 65,000 fans file into nonalcoholic Veterans Stadium today to watch the Eagles play the Cardinals, I'd like to tell you one more story about the famous Eagles-Cowboys Snow Bowl.

Have you guessed the politician?

Using telepathy, I count 478,000 votes for Councilman Fran Rafferty.

Wrong.

Hey, I was disappointed too.

All right, I'm going to turn the story over to Eric Brosz, a paving contractor and a season ticket holder from Worchester, Montgomery County. He was sitting in Row 2600 level north side, 50-yard line.

"At the start of the game, well, there's four guys in front of us, they came in drunk, they each had cans of Budweiser, and during the moment of silence for Doug Scovil [the Eagles coach who died], they started spelling out EAGLES."

The hooligans mocked the national anthem, They insulted everyone who walked by. One of them puked before halftime. And in the fourth quarter they started throwing snowballs.

No. They weren't politicians.

The politician was on their left, wearing a powder blue ski cap that said Finland on it. Brosz heard the hooligans refer to him once or twice as Ed. He looked closer.

Ed Rendell.

You know him. Former district attorney, perennial candidate. Ran for governor. Ran for mayor.

Brosz says the snowball throwing got nastier. One of the four rowdies hit No. 15 for the Cowboys.

"Right between the shoulder blades," says Brosz, who started looking around for security guards.

He couldn't find anybody. But he thought Rendell, the city's former chief law enforcement official, might take action.

He did.

"Rendell says to this one guy, 'I'll bet you $20 you can't reach the field.' I couldn't believe it."

So the guy loads a good one. He winds up, lets it rip. A howitzer.

"It lands at the feet of the back judge—the same referee who got hit in the head earlier," Brosz says.

"Rendell pulls out his wallet, rips out a 20, and pays the guy."

I called Rendell

"Were you at the game? Yes. First row, 600 level? Yes. Wearing a powder blue Finland cap? Yes.

Did you bet the guy $20 he couldn't reach the field with a snowball?

"No."

No such thing?

"No. I was trying to talk guys out of throwing snowballs."

Rendell said I could ask the guy he was with. Attorney Cliff Haines.

I left a message for Haines, but I pretty much gave up on the story. Somebody was lying, but how could I know who?

An hour later, the phone rang.

"Steve, Ed Rendell again."

He just called to say he'd lied.

I swallowed some teeth but maintained my composure.

He said he got to thinking. He felt like a hypocrite. He had to call.

"I'm sorry I didn't tell you the truth originally."

Hey, no harm done. I mean it. Rendell said he thought if the guy got $20, he might stop throwing snowballs.

Maybe it's good he isn't mayor or governor. Can you imagine him in contract negotiations?

"What I did was stupid. To say 'I bet you can't reach the field,' maybe in some small way, encouraged them."

Former D.A. Ran for governor.

Rendell asked whether I'd talked to Haines. No, I said.

"If he calls you back, I'm sure he'll lie for me. He's the finest lawyer in Philadelphia. No way you'll get him to tell you the truth."

I'm not making this up. We said goodbye. The phone rang. Cliff Haines.

This is easier than opening Christmas presents.

Were you at the game, Cliff? Yes. The 600 level with Ed Rendell? Yes. Did Ed bet some guy $20 he couldn't reach the field with a snowball?

"No."

OK, pop quiz. Was former D.A. Ed Rendell's worst mistake to (A) bet a drunken hooligan he couldn't reach the field, (B) lie about it, (C) confess, or (D) take his friend down with him?

My vote is C. Too honest. Why do you think he can't win an election?

I said it before. I'll say it again.

Is this a great city or what?

Moneylender Jasper Speciale Last of a Different Breed
JOHN L. SMITH—*Las Vegas Review-Journal*—1/2/1992

The diner was nearly empty when the imperially slim fellow pushed open the door.

Jasper Speciale looked tired and gaunt, but he managed a smile, handshake and few terse words. His sport shirt buttoned up tight, his mind of a steak sandwich and the business of the day, he was always a gentleman.

Despite chronic lung problems, he managed to make the rounds and often turned up at the city's best delis and restaurants. Despite the word that he had retired from illegal bookmaking and moneylending trades, it was obvious he had no intention of spending his remaining years at a Palm Springs spa or a Florida beach. Perhaps the sporting zeal is what kept the twinkle in his brown eyes long after his lungs had soured.

Speciale's tired lungs finally gave out Saturday. The convicted loan shark, illegal bookmaker and unique Las Vegas character died in a local hospital. He was 68 and left a fascinating street legend.

You have heard of Valley Bank. Speciale was the president of Sidewalk Savings and Loan.

Although loan sharks with hearts of gold do not exist. Speciale was a gentlemen in a violent racket filled with predators. He loaned $500 to countless cabbies and poker players. At high interest, of course; that's the Shylock's rub.

It didn't make him the worst guy in Las Vegas, and his personality assured his place in the annals of local lore.

Fellows possessing Speciale's old-school panache were plentiful a generation ago. Unfortunately, they have been largely replaced by glorified dope dealers and punks with pistols.

Born Gaspare Anedetto Speciale July 13, 1923, in New York City, he was not a saint and made no such pretenses. Many of the occupations in the world of his youth were by their nature illegitimate. His pursuit of sports betting was a natural. The fact that it was illegal and influenced by New York's La Cosa Nostra families constituted the cost of doing business.

At a time other kids were memorizing multiplication tables, young Jasper was booking football games in New York schoolyards. He was 8.

By the time Speciale was a teen-ager, his bookmaking expertise was attracting attention from the cops and the wise guys.

He was arrested 19 times in New York. Bookmaking is not the street's most egregious sin. But in mob-muscled New York, those who play in the street pay the boys to prevent being hit by a bus.

Tuberculosis slowed him in youth, and chronic lung ailments shadowed him throughout his life.

So did the law.

From 1944 to 1959, he was nicked eight times for illegal bookmaking. His candy store was known for its tasty treats and sweet odds.

After migrating to Las Vegas in the early 1960s, he operated the Tower of Pizza and later Jasper's Manhattan Florist. The food was good and the posies smelled nice, but mostly Speciale was booking bets and lending C-notes.

He eventually was charged with felonies, and in 1976 was sentenced to four years for loan sharking and obstructing justice.

His health steadily diminished in recent months, but you can bet your mortgage he was still working. It was in his blood.

"He only booked sports, that's all he done," a friend from Speciale's New York days said with respect. "He was honorable. He never had nothing to do with them guys."

Them, being people connected to New York's mob families. Authorities vehemently disagree, and say Speciale had long business relationships with the Genovese and Gambino families.

None of that matters now.

Presuming he was still taking bets, someone will acquire his customers. Assuming he was still a one-man teller machine, someone will collect the debts.

The beat will go on, but the street won't be the same.

His critics won't remember the Speciale whose golf tournament raised thousands for charity. They don't know about the dozen poor children he sponsored in the Dominican Republic. They won't believe his biggest collections in recent years came on Sunday morning as he escorted the baskets through the congregation at our Lady of Las Vegas.

It didn't make Speciale's work legal, but it made him a human being with good qualities to place in the left-hand column next to his faults.

I'll let others tally the old-school sportsman's final record.

A Sprig of Verbana and the Gifts of a Great Teacher
KATHLEEN PARKER—*Washington Post*—4/14/2010

One of President Obama's consistent education themes has been the wish that every child cross paths with that one teacher who hits the light switch and changes one's life.

Each time he expresses some iteration of that thought, I suspect thousands or millions think briefly of the person who held that distinction in their life. The light master. Or, in my case, the one who extended an imaginary sprig of verbena and, holding it to his nose, inhaled deeply in a gesture of solidarity with William Faulkner.

That scene took place in my 11th-grade English class, oh, a few years ago. The teacher was mine for only three months, but he changed my life in a flicker of light. I thought of him Monday when—if you'll grant me this small indulgence—I was awarded the Pulitzer Prize for Commentary.

On such occasions, one is expected to recognize those who have helped along the way. But also on such occasions, one is likely to be a bit distracted and unable to remember one's own name, much less those that deserve mention. I would like to correct the record with one who stands out and who, as it happens, is celebrating his 50th year of teaching.

I materialized in James Gasque's class in March of the school year for reasons that will have to wait for another day. Suffice to say, I knew no one and had come from a small high school in central Florida where, for some reason, no one had bothered to teach the diagramming of sentences.

Thus, my fellow students at Dreher High School in Columbia, S.C., were way ahead of me when Mr. Gasque finally called on me to identify some part of a sentence he had written on the blackboard. His back to the class with chalk in hand, he stood poised to write my instructions.

Every living soul knows the feeling of helplessness when a crowd of peers awaits the answer you do not know. Whatever I said was utterly ridiculous, I suppose, because all my classmates erupted in peals of laughter.

I have not forgotten that moment, or the next, during all these years. As I was trying to figure out how to hurl myself under my desk, Mr. Gasque tossed me a sugarcoated, tangerine-colored lifesaver from the good ship lollipop.

He whirled. No perfectly executed pirouette can top the spin executed by

Mr. Gasque that day. Suddenly facing the class, he flushed crimson and his voice trembled with rage.

"Don't. You. Ever. Laugh. At her. Again," he said. "She can out-write every one of you any day of the week."

It is not possible to describe my gratitude. Time suspended and I dangled languorously from a fluff of cloud while my colleagues drowned in stunned silence. I dangle even now, like those silly participles I eventually got to know. Likely no one but me remembers Mr. Gasque's act of paternal chivalry, but I basked in those words and in the thought that what he said might be true. I started that day to try to write as well as he said I could. I am still trying.

Mr. Gasque's even greater gifts belong to all who ever sat in his class. That sprig of verbena, a recurring symbol in *The Unvanquished*, stays in my mind because it also symbolizes the great passion Mr. Gasque brought to teaching and to the literature he loved.

During my 12 weeks or so in his class, we devoured *The Unvanquished* and John Steinbeck's *Of Mice and Men*. I remember every word and sensation.

"I've always wanted to lean down from my back stoop and pluck a sprig of verbena," he said, inhaling deeply. Exhaling and tilting his head back, he closed his eyes and seemed to drift off into some lemony-scented world where verbena is the smell of courage. I closed my eyes and followed him.

A couple of decades later, having moved back to South Carolina, I went looking for Mr. Gasque, toting a pot of verbena. He didn't remember me, but upon hearing my tale, asked that I speak to his class. Afterward, his cheeks streaked with tears, he presented me with two lined pieces of notebook paper—my essay on *The Unvanquished*.

Obama is right about the power of teachers. Thank you, Mr. Gasque.

VIII: Hard Times

There comes a time when everyone needs an extra dose of courage—a reminder that others have been through similar situations before and that the sun still rises. Hard times can bring out the best in a newspaper columnist. Detailing tragedies and disasters is part of the job description—it comes with the drama built in.

Westbrook Pegler's "The Death of Frankie Jerome" captures a man struggling with a murder he committed in the ring, attending the funeral alongside the victim's friends and family. Struggling through the Great Depression stung Woody Guthrie, but not as much as hearing his fellow migrant workers derided for taking public relief. As Nazis swept through Europe, Walter Lippmann warned that "liberty without discipline cannot survive." Jimmy Breslin's columns following the assassination of John F. Kennedy are masterpieces of American journalism, especially "A Death in Emergency Room One" and "It's an Honor." Of course, not all hard times are historic events. The grief of dealing with the loss of a loved one is felt in John Leonard's disarming "On Losing a Friend."

In our own day, the aftermath of the attacks of September 11th brought out inspired columns by Peggy Noonan that captured the spirit of New York City, in its pain and perseverance. She called on the patriotic grace we needed to assimilate the facts of loss into our lives and begin to rise again. Likewise, Chris Rose's "Letter to America," written in the wake of Hurricane Katrina, speaks of the spirit of New Orleans and of a people determined to keep their character intact even as death crowded in.

The Death of Frankie Jerome
WESTBROOK PEGLER—United News Syndicate—1/18/1924

A yellow-haired kid with a mashed nose and scalloped lips dipped his fingers in the holy water fount of St. Jerome's Church, crossed himself with the fist that killed Frankie Jerome and went to his knees on the cold marble to pray, when all that was left of the little fellow was wheeled up the aisle to the altar yesterday for the funeral mass that preceded the journey to the grave.

Bud Taylor of Terra Haute, Ind., had been very happy for a moment last Friday night when he realized that he had been the first one to knock out the "Bronx Spider." As he bent his tousled head in a shadowy corner of the big church he wished to God he hadn't been the one to do it.

The church was full of people, most of them prizefighters, managers, bottle-holders and ring-siders, and a lot of them had not been to church in so long a time that all they recollected of the procedure was that a fellow is supposed to take off his bowler hat and kneel down.

John Doherty and Mrs. Doherty, the father and mother of Frankie, were in a front pew with the little widow and her baby girl. Outside the church, the police reserves were handling a crowd of Frankie's friends.

On the night that Frankie dropped Jack Kid Wolfe seven times in one round at the Velodrome, equaling a record that Jack Dempsey achieved at the expense of Jess Willard, these friends had raised a roar that drowned the rattle of the L and the croupy whooping of the tug whistles in the Harlem River near by. Now they were as silent as they had been noisy and the stillness was a tribute to the "Spider," just as the racket had been on that long-ago summer night.

Nine big open automobiles wheeled into file, burgeoning with flowers as the bearers came down the steps with Frankie on their shoulders. It took a long time to get the procession under way because there were sixty-five carriages in the line. It seemed that all the Bronx was going to the end of the journey with the "Spider," the boy who fought in the Great War before he was 21 and fought till his body was worn out in the ring.

Father Ryan got out of his vestments and into his clerical black in time to get aboard the last hack in the procession and lurch over the humpy roads of the Bronx to the cemetery, where he dribbled a handful of loam over the brink of the unfathomable abyss. He thumped on the box that contained the spindling kid.

Father Ryan didn't blame himself at all. He was the one who had first taught Frankie Doherty to turn his thumbs out and his knuckles up and to hit straight with all the drive of his body and character behind every blow. Frankie had been "one of the kids who fooled around the basement of St. Jerome's" about eight years ago, and Father Ryan had tied the first laces about the bony wrists of the bellicose acolyte for a slam-bang bout in the cellar of the church where the altar boys still maul one another for the joy of fighting.

Being a bit of a handy man in a fight himself, Father Ryan taught Frankie how to roll with a punch, how to upset a right swing with a left stab to the shoulder, and how to swing in with a right cross to the nubbin of the chin while his man was off keel. He taught Frankie the rudiments of the business of Billy Gibson when he took hold of the boy as a professional, had Benny Leonard to teach him the rest.

"The boy is dead," Father Ryan said, when the carriages had rumbled back over the bridge. "He led a good life. He married a good wife and he was as good as his marriage vows. I wish all men were as good as Frankie Jerome was. There'd be no need of preachers, then. Green be his memory. A square shooter was Frankie Doherty."

Migration Workers Take Lots of Abuse
WOODY GUTHRIE—*People's Daily World*—5/3/1939

The *Times* carried quite a story about the flood, drout an' dust—bowlers a comin' to Calif in their rickety, rundown jallopies, their little handful of belongings, an' their children . . . only, says the *Times*, to dig into some of the Relief Gold.

The tale, written by Kenneth Somebody, an' paid for by Mr. Somebody Else, was wrote up for the whole purpose of givin' the Refugees another black eye.

The Migration Workers was compared to Hollywood, Reno, and Wilshire Gold-Diggers . . . only the "Gold" that the Workers dug, was sposed to come from the Taxpayers' & Property Owners' stach.

The story was spun around the conditions of the Refugees a livin' in the various Trailor Cities thet are strung around over the country, the conditions in which the children must live in destitution, want, filth and despair.

Scene on Life in a Trailer Camp City was painted to call your attention to the untold, inhumane suffering that these people are willing to go thru—just for some of that "Easy Relief Money."

How the Sheriff's Force "cleared out the Jungles" and drove the Shack-dwellers out of River Bottom, set fire to their Cardboard Houses, and destroyed their patch-work shelters—was told about—not to make you feel your heart in a genuine sorrow for your brothers and sisters of our American Race that's got to live in such places, but to try to make you believe that there Underprivilidged people are designing in their hearts to "Dig some Easy Gold"—off you taxpayers.

The Author was trying to make you believe that these weather beaten, brow-beaten, homeless people are really robbers at heart and he gave some typical conversations of some Oklahoma people who were living like wild hogs in a boggy river bottom in order to get some of that easy Relief Gold.

No, Kenneth . . . it ain't the "Easy Relief Money Us Folks is After"—it's jest a chance to work an' earn our livin'—sorta like you earn yore livin'.

You've got your Gift of writin'—an' that's the way you work an' earn your meal ticket here in this old world. An' each one of us has got our little Job that we hope to do in order to pay our keep.

We can gather in the crops, an' we can drive Tracters, an' Draglines, an' Shovels, an' Cranes, an' Cement Mixers, an' Picks, an' Hammers, an' lots of things like that.

'Course we aint as educated as you are—'cause you're a mighty smart feller. But we'd like fer our children to grow up an' be big, smart, educated fellers like you. ("Course if any of 'em ever got so educated thet they took to a robbin' or a runnin' the rest of the folks—well, we just naturally wouldn't claim him no more.)

Personal, I've been in Calif. 2 years—'cause the dust and the cold, run me out of Texas . . . an' I ain't never applied for relief of any kind yet. An' for the past year I've averaged makin' less than $1 a day.

But before I'd make my livin' by a writin' articles that make fun of Hungery Folks, an' the Workin' Folks, I'd go on Relief.

Yrs Trly Woody

To First and Last Things
WALTER LIPPMANN—*New York Herald Tribune*—5/25/1940

Behind all questions of politics and armaments, of personalities and parties, there is the question whether a self-governing people will impose upon itself a self-discipline strong enough to insure its own defense. The question is put to a final and desperate test in Western Europe today, and in the Americas it is the question on which depends the future of this hemisphere as a hemisphere of freedom. Liberty without discipline cannot survive. Without order and authority in the spirit of man the free way of life leads through weakness, disorganization, self-indulgence, and moral indifference to the destruction of freedom itself.

The tragic ordeal through which the Western world is passing was prepared in the long period of easy liberty during which men forgot the elementary truths of human existence. They forgot that their freedom was achieved by heroic sacrifice; they became so accustomed to freedom that they thought it was as normal as the air they breathe, and they came to believe that the heroic virtues were antiquated and that sacrifice was a bore and bother. They forgot that their rights were founded on their duties, and they thought that to get while the getting was good, whether by private smartness or by collective pressure, was the normal and natural thing to do. They forgot that unless they bear themselves so that the eternal values of truth, justice, and righteousness are perpetually revealed to them, they will not know how to resist the corrosion of their virtue or how to face the trials that life will bring to them upon this earth. They had become too comfortable and too safe and too sophisticated to believe the first things and the last things which men have been inspired to understand through generations of suffering, and they thought it clever to be cynical, and enlightened to be unbelieving, and sensible to be soft.

And so, through suffering, they must rediscover these first and last things again, and be purified once more by repentance.

The free people of the Western world have lived upon a great inheritance which they have squandered recklessly. When they were put to the test, they had come to the point where they took the blessings of this inheritance so totally for granted that they no longer knew, and their schools had almost ceased to teach them, and their leaders were afraid to remind them, how the laws and the institutions and the great controlling customs of our civilization were made. They thought that the God whom they believed in dimly or not at all had conferred these blessings upon them gratuitously, that somehow they, as distinguished from their own ancestors and from millions of their fellow beings in less fortunate lands, were exempt from the labors and the sacrifices and the trials of man. They did not know that the products of civilization which they so greedily consumed are not the enduring inheritance of man.

These pleasant things are no more than an estate accumulated by the labor of the father and easily ruined by the dissipation of his son.

They did not believe any longer that the true inheritance of man is the capacity to produce these products, to preserve the estate by remaking it. Only that. All that has been conferred upon man is the capacity to know what is good and the freedom of will to strive for it.

What is left of our civilization will not be maintained, what has been wrecked will not be restored, by imagining that some new political gadget can be invented, some new political formula improvised which will save it. Our civilization can be maintained and restored only by remembering and rediscovering the truths, and by re-establishing the virtuous habits on which it was founded. There is no use looking into the blank future for some new and fancy revelation of what man needs in order to live.

The revelation has been made. By it man conquered the jungle about him and the barbarian within him. The elementary principles of work and sacrifice and duty—and the transcendant criteria of truth, justice, and righteousness—and the grace of love and charity—are the things which have made men free. Men can keep their freedom and reconquer it only by these means. These are the terms stipulated in the nature of things for the salvation of men on this earth, and only in this profound, this stern, and this tested wisdom shall we find once more the light and the courage we need.

A Death in Emergency Room One

JIMMY BRESLIN—*New York Herald Tribune*—11/24/1963

DALLAS—The call bothered Malcolm Perry. "Dr. Tom Shires, STAT," the girl's voice said over the page in the doctor's cafeteria at Parkland Memorial Hospital. The "STAT" meant emergency. Nobody ever called Tom Shires, the hospital's chief resident in surgery, for an emergency. And Shires, Perry's superior, was out of town for the day. Malcolm Perry looked at the salmon croquettes on the plate in front of him. Then he put down his fork and went over to a telephone.

"This is Dr. Perry taking Dr. Shires' page," he said.

"President Kennedy has been shot. STAT," the operator said. "They are bringing him into the emergency room now."

Perry hung up and walked quickly out of the cafeteria and down a flight of stairs and pushed through a brown door and a nurse pointed to Emergency Room One, and Dr. Perry walked into it. The room is narrow and has gray tiled walls and a cream-colored ceiling. In the middle of it, on an aluminum hospital cart, the President of the United States had been placed on his back and he was dying while a huge lamp glared in his face.

John Kennedy had already been stripped of his jacket, shirt, and T-shirt, and a staff doctor was starting to place a tube called an endotracht down the throat. Oxygen would be forced down the endotracht. Breathing was the first thing to attack. The President was not breathing.

Malcolm Perry unbuttoned his dark blue glen-plaid jacket and threw it onto the floor. He held out his hands while the nurse helped him put on gloves.

The President, Perry thought. He's bigger than I thought he was.

He noticed the tall, dark-haired girl in the plum dress that had her husband's blood all over the front of the skirt. She was standing out of the way, over against the gray tile wall. Her face was tearless and it was set, and it was to stay that way because Jacqueline Kennedy, with a terrible discipline, was not going to take her eyes from her husband's face.

Then Malcolm Perry stepped up to the aluminum hospital cart and took charge of the hopeless job of trying to keep the thirty-fifth President of the United States from death. And now, the enormousness came over him.

Here is the most important man in the world, Perry thought.

The chest was not moving. And there was no apparent heartbeat inside it. The wound in the throat was small and neat. Blood was running out of it. It was running out too fast. The occipitoparietal, which is a part of the back of the head, had a huge flap. The damage a .25-caliber bullet does as it comes out of a person's body is unbelievable. Bleeding from the head wound covered the floor.

There was a mediastinal wound in connection with the bullet hole in the throat. This means air and blood were being packed together in the chest. Perry called for a scalpel. He was going to start a tracheotomy, which is opening the throat and inserting a tube into the windpipe. The incision had to be made below the bullet wound.

"Get me Doctors Clark, McCelland, and Baxter right away," Malcolm Perry said.

Then he started the tracheotomy. There was no anesthesia. John Kennedy could feel nothing now. The wound in the back of the head told Dr. Perry that the President never knew a thing about it when he was shot, either.

While Perry worked on the throat, he said quietly, "Will somebody put a right chest tube in, please."

The tube was to be inserted so it could suction out the blood and air packed in the chest and prevent the lung from collapsing.

These things he was doing took only small minutes, and other doctors and nurses were in the room and talking and moving, but Perry does not remember them. He saw only the throat and chest, shining under the huge lamp, and when he would look up or move his eyes between motions, he would see this plum dress and the terribly disciplined face standing over against the gray tile wall.

Just as he finished the tracheotomy, Malcolm Perry looked up and Dr. Kemp Clark, chief neurosurgeon in residency at Parkland, came in through the door. Clark was looking at the President of the United States. Then he looked at Malcolm Perry and the look told Malcolm Perry something he already knew. There was no way to save the patient.

"Would you like to leave, ma'am?" Kemp Clark said to Jacqueline Kennedy. "We can make you more comfortable outside."

Just the lips moved. "No," Jacqueline Kennedy said.

Now, Malcolm Perry's long fingers ran over the chest under him and he tried to get a heartbeat, and even the suggestion of breathing, and there was nothing. There was only the still body, pale white in the light, and it kept bleeding, and now Malcolm Perry started to call for things and move his hands quickly because it was all running out.

He began to massage the chest. He had to do something to stimulate the heart. There was not time to open the chest and take the heart in his hands, so he had to massage on the surface. The aluminum cart was high. It was too high. Perry was up on his toes so he could have leverage.

"Will somebody please get me a stool," he said.

One was placed under him. He sat on it, and for ten minutes he massaged the chest. Over in the corner of the room, Dr. Kemp Clark kept watching the electrocardiogram for some sign that the massaging was creating action in the President's heart. There was none. Dr. Clark turned his head from the electrocardiogram.

"It's too late, Mac," he said to Malcolm Perry.

The long fingers stopped massaging and they were lifted from the white chest. Perry got off the stool and stepped back.

Dr. M.T. Jenkins, who had been working the oxygen flow, reached down from the head of the aluminum cart. He took the edges of a white sheet in his hands. He pulled the sheet up over the face of John Fitzgerald Kennedy. The IBM clock on the wall said it was 1 p.m. The date was November 22, 1963.

Three policemen were moving down the hall outside Emergency Room One now, and they were calling to everybody to get out of the way. But this was not needed, because everybody stepped out of the way automatically when they saw the priest who was behind the police. His name was the Reverend Oscar Huber, a small seventy-year-old man who was walking quickly.

Malcolm Perry turned to leave the room as Father Huber came in. Perry remembers seeing the priest go by him. And he remembers his eyes seeing that plum dress and that terribly disciplined face for the last time as he walked out of Emergency Room One and slumped into a chair in the hall.

Everything that was inside that room now belonged to Jacqueline Kennedy and Father Oscar Huber and the things in which they believe.

"I'm sorry. You have my deepest sympathies," Father Huber said.

"Thank you," Jacqueline Kennedy said.

Father Huber pulled the white sheet down so he could anoint the forehead of John Fitzgerald Kennedy. Jacqueline Kennedy was standing beside the priest, her head bowed, he hands clasped across the front of her plum dress that was stained with blood which came from her husband's head. Now this old priest held up his right hand and he began the chant that Roman Catholic priests have said over their dead for centuries.

"*Si vivis, ego te absolvo a peccatis tuis. In nomine Patris et Filii et Spiritus Sancti, amen.*"

The prayer said, "If you are living, I absolve you from your sins. In the name of the Father and of the Son and of the Holy Ghost, amen."

The priest reached into his pocket and took out a small vial of holy oil. He put the oil on his right thumb and made a cross on President Kennedy's forehead. Then he blessed the body again and started to pray quietly.

"Eternal rest grant unto him, O Lord," Father Huber said.

"And let perpetual light shine upon him," Jacqueline Kennedy answered. She did not cry.

Father Huber prayed like this for fifteen minutes. And for fifteen minutes Jacqueline Kennedy kept praying aloud with him. Her voice did not waver. She did not cry. From the moment a bullet hit her husband in the head and he went down onto his face in the back of the car on the street in Dallas, there was something about this woman that everybody who saw her keeps talking about. She was in shock. But somewhere, down under that shock some place, she seemed to know that there is a way to act when the President of the United States has been assassinated. She was going to act that way, and the fact that the President was her husband only made it more important that she stand and look at him and not cry.

When he was finished praying, Father Huber turned and took her hand. "I am shocked," he said.

"Thank you for taking care of the President," Jacqueline Kennedy said.

"I am convinced that his soul had not left his body," Father Huber said. "This was a valid last sacrament."

"Thank you," she said.

Then he left. He had been eating lunch at his rectory at Holy Trinity Church when he heard the news. He had an assistant drive him to the hospital immediately. After that, everything happened quickly and he did not feel anything until later. He sat behind his desk in the rectory, and the magnitude of what had happened came over him.

"I've been a priest for thirty-two years," Father Huber said. "The first time I was present at a death? A long time ago. Back in my home in Perryville, Missouri, I attended a lady who was dying of pneumonia. She was in her own bed. But I remember that. But this. This is different. Oh, it isn't the blood. You see, I've anointed so many. Accident victims. I anointed once a boy who was only in pieces. No, it wasn't the blood. It was the enormity of it. I'm just starting to realize it now."

Then Father Huber showed you to the door. He was going to say prayers.

It came the same way to Malcolm Perry. When the day was through, he drove to his home in the Walnut Hills section. When he walked into the house, his daughter, Jolene, six and a half, ran up to him. She had papers from school in her hand.

"Look what I did today in school, Daddy," she said.

She made her father sit down in a chair and look at her schoolwork. The papers were covered with block letters and numbers. Perry looked at them. He thought they were good. He said so, and his daughter chattered happily. Malcolm, his three-year-old son, ran into the room after him, and Perry started to reach for him.

Then it hit him. He dropped the papers with the block numbers and letters and he did not notice his son.

"I'm tired," he said to his wife, Jennine. "I've never been tired like this in my life."

Tired is the only way one felt in Dallas yesterday. Tired and confused and wondering why it was that everything looked so different. This was a bright Texas day with a snap to the air, and there were cars on the streets and people on the sidewalks. But everything seemed unreal.

At 10 a.m. we dodged cars and went out and stood in the middle lane of

Elm Street, just before the second street light; right where the road goes down and, twenty yards further, starts to turn to go under the overpass. It was right at this spot, right where this long crack ran through the gray Texas asphalt, that the bullets reached President Kennedy's car.

Right up the little hill, and towering over you, was the building. Once it was dull red brick. But that was a long time ago when it housed the J. W. Deere Plow Company. It has been sandblasted since and now the bricks are a light rust color. The windows on the first three floors are covered by closed venetian blinds, but the windows on the other floors are bare. Bare and dust-streaked and high. Factory-window high. The ugly kind of factory window. Particularly at the corner window on the sixth floor, the one where this Oswald and his scrambled egg of a mind stood with the rifle so he could kill the President.

You stood and memorized the spot. It is just another roadway in a city, but now it joins Ford's Theatre in the history of this nation.

"R.L. Thornton Freeway. Keep Right," the sign said. "Stemmons Freeway. Keep Right," another sign said. You went back between the cars and stood on a grassy hill which overlooks the road. A red convertible turned onto Elm Street and went down the hill. It went past the spot with the crack in the asphalt and then, with every foot it went, you could see that it was getting out of range of the sixth-floor window of this rust-brick building behind you. A couple of yards. That's all John Kennedy needed on this road Friday.

But he did not get them. So when a little bit after 1 o'clock Friday afternoon the phone rang in the Oneal Funeral Home, 3206 Oak Lawn, Vernon B. Oneal answered.

The voice on the other end spoke quickly. "This is the Secret Service calling from Parkland Hospital," it said. "Please select the best casket in your house and put it in a general coach and arrange for a police escort and bring it here to the hospital as quickly as you humanly can. It is for the President of the United States. Thank you."

The voice went off the phone. Oneal called for Ray Gleason, his bookkeeper, and a workman to help him take a solid bronze casket out of the place and load it onto a hearse. It was for John Fitzgerald Kennedy.

Yesterday, Oneal left his shop early. He said he was too tired to work.

Malcolm Perry was at the hospital. He had on a blue suit and a dark blue striped tie and he sat in a big conference room and looked out the window. He is a tall, reddish-haired thirty-four-year-old, who understands that everything he saw or heard on Friday is a part of history, and he is trying to get down, for the record, everything he knows about the death of the thirty-fifth President of the United States.

"I never saw a President before," he said.

It's an Honor

JIMMY BRESLIN—*New York Herald Tribune*—11/26/1963

WASHINGTON—Clifton Pollard was pretty sure he was going to be working on Sunday, so when he woke up at 9 a.m., in his three-room apartment on Corcoran Street, he put on khaki overalls before going into the kitchen for breakfast. His wife, Nettie, made bacon and eggs for him. Pollard was in the middle of eating them when he received the phone call he had been expecting.

It was from Mazo Kawalchik, who is the foreman of the gravediggers at Arlington National Cemetery, which is where Pollard works for a living. "Polly, could you please be here by eleven o'clock this morning?" Kawalchik asked. "I guess you know what it's for."

Pollard did. He hung up the phone, finished breakfast, and left his apartment so he could spend Sunday digging a grave for John Fitzgerald Kennedy.

When Pollard got to the row of yellow wooden garages where the cemetery equipment is stored, Kawalchik and John Metzler, the cemetery superintendent, were waiting for him.

"Sorry to pull you out like this on a Sunday," Metzler said.

"Oh, don't say that," Pollard said. "Why, it's an honor for me to be here."

Pollard got behind the wheel of a machine called a reverse hoe. Gravedigging is not done with men and shovels at Arlington. The reverse hoe is a green machine with a yellow bucket which scoops the earth toward the operator, not away from it as a crane does. At the bottom of the hill in front of the Tomb of the Unknown Soldier, Pollard started the digging [Editor Note: At the bottom of the hill in front of the Custis-Lee Mansion.]

Leaves covered the grass. When the yellow teeth of the reverse hoe first bit into the ground, the leaves made a threshing sound which could be heard above the motor of the machine. When the bucket came up with its first scoop of dirt, Metzler, the cemetery superintendent, walked over and looked at it.

"That's nice soil," Metzler said.

"I'd like to save a little of it," Pollard said. "The machine made some tracks in the grass over here and I'd like to sort of fill them in and get some good grass growing there, I'd like to have everything, you know, nice."

James Winners, another gravedigger, nodded. He said he would fill a couple of carts with this extra-good soil and take it back to the garage and grow good turf on it.

"He was a good man," Pollard said.

"Yes, he was," Metzler said.

"Now they're going to come and put him right here in this grave I'm making up," Pollard said. "You know, it's an honor just for me to do this."

Pollard is forty-two. He is a slim man with a mustache who was born in Pittsburgh and served as a private in the 352nd Engineers battalion in Burma in World War II. He is an equipment operator, grade 10, which means he gets $3.01 an hour. One of the last to serve John Fitzgerald Kennedy, who was the thirty-fifth President of this country, was a working man who earns $3.01 an hour and said it was an honor to dig the grave.

Yesterday morning, at 11:15, Jacqueline Kennedy started walking toward the grave. She came out from under the north portico of the White House and slowly followed the body of her husband, which was in a flag-covered coffin that was strapped with two black leather belts to a black caisson that had polished brass axles. She walked straight and her head was high. She walked down the bluestone and blacktop driveway and through shadows thrown by the branches of seven leafless oak trees. She walked slowly past the sailors who held up flags of the states of this country. She walked past silent people who strained to see her and then, seeing her, dropped their heads and put their hands over their eyes. She walked out the northwest gate and into the middle of Pennsylvania Avenue. She walked with tight steps and her head was high and she followed the body of her murdered husband through the streets of Washington.

Everybody watched her while she walked. She is the mother of two fatherless children and she was walking into the history of this country because she was showing everybody who felt old and helpless and without hope that she had this terrible strength that everybody needed so badly. Even though they had killed her husband and his blood ran onto her lap while he died, she could walk through the streets and to his grave and help us all while she walked.

There was mass, and then the procession to Arlington. When she came up to the grave at the cemetery, the casket already was in place. It was set between brass railings and it was ready to be lowered into the ground. This must be the worst time of all, when a woman sees the coffin with her husband inside and it is in place to be buried under the earth. Now she knows that it is forever. Now there is nothing. There is no casket to kiss or hold with your hands. Nothing material to cling to. But she walked up to the burial area and stood in front of a row of six green-covered chairs and she started to sit down, but then she got up quickly and stood straight because she was not going to sit down until the man directing the funeral told her what seat he wanted her to take.

The ceremonies began, with jet planes roaring overhead and leaves falling from the sky. On this hill behind the coffin, people prayed aloud. They were cameramen and writers and soldiers and Secret Service men and they were saying prayers out loud and choking. In front of the grave, Lyndon Johnson kept his head turned to his right. He is President and he had to remain composed. It was better that he did not look at the casket and grave of John Fitzgerald Kennedy too often.

Then it was over and black limousines rushed under the cemetery trees and out onto the boulevard toward the White House.

"What time is it?" a man standing on the hill was asked. He looked at his watch. "Twenty minutes past three," he said.

Clifton Pollard wasn't at the funeral. He was over behind the hill, digging graves for $3.01 an hour in another section of the cemetery. He didn't know who the graves were for. He was just digging them and then covering them with boards.

"They'll be used," he said. "We just don't know when."

"I tried to go over to see the grave," he said. "But it was so crowded a soldier told me I couldn't get through. So I just stayed here and worked, sir. But I'll get over there later a little bit. Just sort of look around and see how it is, you know. Like I told you, it's an honor."

Two Minutes to Midnight: The Very Last Hurrah
PETE HAMILL—*Village Voice*—6/13/1968

It was, of course, two minutes to midnight and the Embassy Room of the Ambassador Hotel was rowdy with triumph. Red and blue balloons drifted up through three golden chandeliers to bump against a gilded ceiling. Young girls with plastic Kennedy boaters chanted like some lost reedy chorus from an old Ray Charles record. The crowd was squashed against the bandstand, a smear of black faces and Mexican-American faces and bearded faces and Beverly Hills faces crowned with purple hair. Eleven TV cameras were turning, their bright-blue arc lights changing the crowd into a sweaty stew. Up on the bandstand, with his wife standing just behind him, was Robert Kennedy.

"I'd like to express my high regard for Don Drysdale," Kennedy said. Drysdale had just won his sixth straight shutout. "I hope we have his support in this campaign." There was a loud cheer. He thanks Rafer Johnson and Rosey Grier (cheers) and Jesse Unruh (timid cheer) and Cesar Chavez (very loud cheer), and he thanked the staff and the volunteers and the voters, and the crowd hollered after every sentence. It was the sort of scene that Kennedys have gone through a hundred times and more: on this night, at least, it did not appear that there would be a last hurrah. Kennedy had not scored a knockout over Eugene McCarthy; but a points decision at least would keep his campaign going.

"I thank all of you," Kennedy was saying. "Mayor Yorty has just sent a message that we have been here too long already" (laughter). "So my thanks to all of you, and now it's on to Chicago . . ."

I was at the rear of the stand, next to George Plimpton. Kennedy put his thumb up to the audience, brushed his hair, made a small V with his right hand, and turned to leave. The crowd started shouting: "We want Bobby! We want Bobby!" Plimpton and I went down three steps, and turned left through a gauntlet of Kennedy volunteers and private cops in brown uniforms.

We found ourselves in a long grubby area called the pantry. It was the sort of place where Puerto Ricans, blacks and Mexican-Americans usually work to fill white stomachs. There were high bluish fluorescent lights strung across the ceiling, a floor of raw sandy-colored concrete, pale dirty walls. On the right were a rusty ice machine and shelves filled with dirty glasses. On the left, an archway led into the main kitchen and under the arch a crowd of Mexican-American cooks and busboys waited to see Kennedy. Against the left wall, three table-sized serving carts stood end to end, and at the far end were two doors leading to the press room, where Kennedy was going to talk to reporters.

Kennedy moved slowly into the area, shaking hands, smiling, heading a platoon of reporters, photographers, staffers, the curious, TV men. I was in front of him, walking backward. I saw him turn to his left and shake the hand of a small Mexican cook. We could still hear the chants of "We want Bobby" from the Embassy Room. The cook was smiling and pleased.

Then a pimply messenger arrived from the secret filthy heart of America. He was curly-haired, wearing a pale-blue sweatshirt and blue jeans, and he was planted with his right foot forward and his right arm straight out and he was firing a gun.

The scene assumed a kind of insane fury, all jump cuts, screams, noise, hurtling bodies, blood. The shots went pap-pap-pap-pap-pap, small sharp noises like a distant firefight or the sound of firecrackers in a backyard. Rosey Grier of the Los Angeles Rams came from nowhere and slammed his great bulk into the gunman, crunching him against a serving table. George Plimpton grabbed the guy's arm, and Rafer Johnson moved to him, right behind Bill Barry, Kennedy's friend and security chief, and they were all making deep animal sounds and still the bullets came.

"Get the gun, get the gun."

"Rafer, get the gun!"

"Get the fucking gun!"

"No," someone said. And you could hear the stunned horror in the voice, the replay of odd scenes, the muffle of drums. "No. No. Noooooooooooo!"

We knew then that America had struck again. In this slimy little indoor alley in the back of a gaudy ballroom, in this shabby reality behind the glittering façade, Americans were doing what they do best: killing and dying, and cursing because hope doesn't last very long among us.

I saw Kennedy lurch against the ice machine, and then sag, and then fall forward slowly, to be grabbed by someone, and I knew then that he was dead. He might linger a few hours, or a few days; but his face reminded me somehow of Benny Paret the night Emile Griffith hammered him into unconsciousness. Kennedy's face had a kind of sweet acceptance to it, the eyes understanding that it had come to him, the way it had come to so many others before him. The price of the attempt at excellence was death. You saw a flicker of that understanding on his face, as his life seeped out of a hole in the back of his skull, to spread like spilled wine across the scummy concrete floor.

It was as if all of us there went simultaneously insane: A cook was screaming, "Kill him, kill him now, kill him, kill him!" I tried to get past Grier, Johnson, Plimpton, and Barry to get at the gunman. The Jack Ruby in me was rising up, white, bright, with a high singing sound in the ears, and I wanted to damage that insane little bastard they were holding. I wanted to break his face, to rip away flesh, to hear bone break as I pumped punches into that pimpled skin. Budd Schulberg was next to me; I suppose he was trying to do the same. Just one punch. Just one for Dallas. Just one for Medgar Evers, just one for Martin Luther King. Just one punch. Just one. One.

Kennedy was lying on the floor, with black rosary beads in his hand, and blood on his fingers. His eyes were still open, and as his wife, Ethel, reached him, to kneel in an orange-and-white dress, his lips were moving. We heard nothing. Ethel smoothed his face, running ice cubes along his cheeks. There was a lot of shouting, and a strange chorus of high screaming. My notes showed that Kennedy was shot at 12:10, and was taken out of that grubby hole at 12:32. It seemed terribly longer.

I don't remember how it fits into the sequence, but I do have one picture of Rosey Grier holding the gunman by his neck, choking life out of him.

"Rosey, Rosey, don't kill him. We want him alive. Don't kill him, Rosey, don't kill him."

"Kill the bastard, kill that sum of a bitch bastard," a Mexican busboy yelled.

"Don't kill him, Rosey."

"Where's the doctor? Where in Christ's name is the doctor?"

Grier decided not to kill the gunman. They had him up on a serving table at the far end of the pantry, as far as they could get him from Kennedy. Jimmy Breslin and I were standing up on the table, peering into the gunman's face. His eyes were rolling around, and then stopping, and then rolling around again. The eyes contained pain, flight, entrapment, and a strange kind of bitter endurance. I didn't want to hit him anymore.

"Where the fuck is the doctor? Can't they get a fucking doctor?"

"Move back."

"Here comes a doctor, here's a doctor."

"Move Back!"

Kennedy was very still now. There was a thin film of blood on his brow. They had his shoes off and his shirt open. The stretcher finally arrived, and he trembled as they lifted him, his lips moved, and the flashbulbs blinked off one final salvo and he was gone.

The rest was rote: I ran out out into the lobby and picked up my brother Brian and we rushed to the front entrance. A huge black man, sick with grief and anger and bitterness, was throwing chairs around. Most landed in the pool. The young Kennedy girls were crying and wailing, knowing, I suppose, what the guys my age discovered in Dallas: Youth was over. "Sick," one girl kept saying. "Sick. Sick. What kind of country is this? Sick. Sick." Outside, there were cops everywhere and sirens. The cops were trying to get one of the wounded into a taxi. The cabbie didn't want to take him, afraid, I suppose, that blood would sully his nice plastic upholstery.

When we got through the police barricades, we drove without talk to the Hospital of the Good Samaritan, listening to the news on the radio. The unspoken thought was loudest: The country's gone. Medgar Evers was dead, Malcolm X was dead, Martin Luther King was dead, Jack Kennedy was dead, and now Robert Kennedy was dying. The hell with it. The hatred was now general. I hated that pimpled kid in that squalid cellar enough to want to kill him. He hated Kennedy the same way. That kid and the bitter Kennedy haters were the same. All those people in New York who hated Kennedy's guts, who said "eccch" when his name was mentioned, the ones who creamed over Murray Kempton's vicious diatribes these past few months—they were the same. When Evers died, when King died, when Jack Kennedy died, all the bland pundits said that some good would come of it in some way, that the nation would go through a catharsis, that somehow the bitterness, the hatred, the bigotry, the evil of racism, the glib violence would be erased. That was bullshit. We will have our four-day televised orgy of remorse about Robert Kennedy and then it will be business as usual.

You could feel that as we drove through the empty L.A. streets, listening to the sirens screaming in the night. Nothing would change. Kennedy's death would mean nothing. It was just another digit in the great historical pageant that includes the slaughter of Indians, the plundering of Mexico, the enslavement of black people, the humiliation of Puerto Ricans. Just another digit. Nothing would come of it. While Kennedy's life was ebbing out of him, Americans were dropping bombs and flaming jelly on Orientals. While the cops fingerprinted the gunmen, Senator Eastland's Negro subjects were starving. While the cops made chalk marks on the floor of the pantry, the brave members of the National Rifle Association were already explaining that people commit crimes, guns don't (as if Willie Mays could hit a homerun without a bat). These cowardly bums claim constitutional rights to kill fierce deer in the forests, and besides, suppose the niggers come to the house and we don't have anything to shoot them with? Suppose we have to fight a nigger man to man?

America the Beautiful: with crumby little mini–John Waynes carrying guns to the woods like surrogate penises. Yes, the kid I saw shoot Kennedy was from Jordan, was diseased with some fierce hatred for Jews. Sam Yorty, who hated Kennedy, now calls Kennedy a great American and blames the Communists. Hey Sam: You killed him too. The gun that kid carried was American. The city where he shot down a good man was run by Sam Yorty. How about keeping your fat pigstink mouth shut.

At the approach to the Good Samaritan Hospital the cops had strung red flares across the gutter, and were stopping everyone. A crowd of about seventy-five people were on the corner when we arrived, about a third of them black. I went in, past those black people who must have felt that there was no white man at all with whom they could talk. A mob of reporters was assembling at the hospital entrance. The cops were polite, almost gentle, as if they sensed that something really bad had happened and that many of these reporters were friends of the dying man.

Most of the hospital windows were dark, and somewhere up there Robert Kennedy was lying on a table while strangers stuck things into his brain looking for a killer's bullet. We were friends, and I didn't want him to die; but if he were to be a vegetable, I didn't want him to live either.

We drove home, through the wastelands around L.A. and the canyons through the mountains to the south. When I got home, my wife was asleep, the TV still playing out its record of the death watch. Frank Reynolds of ABC, a fine reporter and a compassionate man, was so upset he could barely control his anger. I called some friends and poured a drink. Later I talked to my old man, who came to this country from Ireland in flight from the Protestant bigots of Belfast forty years ago. I suppose he loved John Kennedy even more than I did, and he has never really been the same since Dallas. Now it had happened again.

"If you see Teddy," he said, "tell him to get out of politics. The Kennedys are too good for this country."

I remembered the night in 1964, in that bitter winter after John Kennedy's murder, when Robert Kennedy appeared at a St. Patrick's Day dinner in Scranton, Pennsylvania. He talked about the Irish, and the long journey that started on the quays of Wexford and ended in Parkland Hospital. He reminded them of the days when there were signs that said "No Irish Need Apply" (and it was always to his greatest dismay that so many sons of Irishmen he came across in New York were bigots and haters). Bob told them about Owen O'Neill, an Irish patriot whose ideals had survived his martyrdom. Men were crying as he read the old Irish ballad:

> Oh, why did you leave us, Owen?
> Why did you die?. . .
> We're sheep without a shepherd,
> When the snow shuts out the sky.
> Oh, why did you leave us, Owen?
> Why did you lie?

I didn't know. There was some sort of answer for John Kennedy, and another for Robert Kennedy. But I had learned that I knew nothing finally, that when my two young daughters present the bill to me in another ten years, I won't have much to say. I sat there drinking rum until I was drunk enough to forget that pimpled face cracking off the rounds into the body of a man who was a friend of mine. Finally, easily, with the sun up, I fell asleep on the couch. I didn't have any tears left for America, but I suppose not many other Americans did either.

On Losing a Friend

JOHN LEONARD—*New York Times*—3/2/1977

My father sang tenor, drank rye and died young. I was 23 years old at the time, and a continent away, and hadn't seen much of him since age 8. Relatives advised me of his death by wiring for some money to help bury him. My grandmother used to say he could have been another Dennis Day, on the radio. But he wasn't very good at life. I inherited his small bones, and whenever I am not being very good at life, when I am stuck in a procrastination that is actually a form of panic, I look at my hands and wonder if, like a recessive gene, his surrender is inside of me.

I remember standing in the control room of a radio station in Berkeley, Calif., with the telegram, trying to decide what expression to put on my face, what behavior to select. According to Freud, this was a significant moment in my life. We are so practiced in our self-consciousness that we've got it down to a disease. I was shopping for an appropriate emotion. What I bought was stupidity. To be stupid in front of the fact of death was, I thought, a kind of cleverness.

Some people weep, some drink, some keen, some platitudinize, some go to bed and don't get up for awhile, some take charge and make telephone calls and arrangements. I get stupid. I haven't had to do so often. A few of us are tourists. Decade after decade goes by, and the worst we have to face are sprained ankles and disappointments. We go to hospitals because that's where children are born. Or we take our children to hospitals when they have concussions or pneumonia. (My son, for instance, is the one to whom concussions and pneumonia happen, as if he is being punished for his excellence. Maybe bad luck skips a generation.) Cats die. My friends went to graduate school instead of Vietnam.

There was one friend, six years ago, who was punished for his excellence. He was so good at life that we couldn't even bring ourselves to envy him. He edited a magazine, and wrote books, and ate and drank and smoked too much, and was the wittiest person I knew. But no one ever accused God of a sense of humor. He died on an operating table. I was called in the middle of the night, because it was known we were to publish an unfavorable notice of his new book in a magazine that had already gone to press. People wanted me to stop the print-run, as though a book review could possibly pertain to the larger unfairness. It was their way of being stupid in front of the fact of death.

For this friend, there was an elaborate memorial service. Diplomats and journalists attended, famous names said graceful things, and a party followed. I suppose we were too scared not to have a party. By midnight, the friends of my friend were telling their favorite stories about him, repeating his best jokes, attempting impersonations. They had formed a circle, not a wailing wall, and passed around champagne, which they drank directly from upended bottles, as if they were characters in a novel of brave, doomed youth. I appreciate the theory of a wake, or an exorcism. Nevertheless, I put on my stupidity and went home.

This is not much of a dossier on death, is it? Thin. Hearsay. The telephone that rings in the middle of the night—nobody is calling to announce that you have won a lottery. You have always lost this lottery. My eyes are weak. When in the morning, not yet having put on my glasses, I go to the door to pick up my copy of *The New York Times* and see a banner headline, a black smear, I want to close the door and go back to bed and be stupid. Banner headlines in the morning *Times* are usually the same as telephone calls in the middle of the night. Another Kennedy is dead.

I used to think that the Kennedys were dying—or going mad—for me, in my stead. They were using up all the available bad luck, the senselessness. It wasn't necessary to be stupid about the Kennedys: the networks would cope, and someone would sing "The Battle Hymn of the Republic," and everybody would write books, and you could go into the other room and count your children and they would still add up, and then it was all right to cry or be angry, to make fists with your brain, to throw up. You were safe, and didn't have to choose a behavior. The behavior would choose you.

Now of course, another friend has died, on the tennis court, of a heart attack, at age 49. It was not the birthday present I wanted. By definition, our friends are those people the world can least afford to lose. We are getting to be of an age when it is difficult to grow new friends; we haven't the energy, the time to cultivate; each one gone is a permanent impoverishment. We are also getting to be of an age when our friends are doing a lot of the dying; each one gone is a surprise, but the surprises now are more likely to arrive once a year than every six years or two decades. To deflect this bad news requires the sort of permanent stupidity even I am not clever enough to sustain.

He was, though, a particular friend, and particularly suspicious of the impulse to generalize. The best of editors, he demanded evidence. No train of thought was allowed without freight cars of facts. Fiercely honest—his friends were not spared—he would have been the first to admit that his poker-playing left much to be desired, he didn't know how to tell a joke, and he couldn't carry a tune. He hated television. He loved food, tennis, truth and—because of a highly developed sense of the preposterous—frogs. He owned just one tie, which stayed in a drawer in the desk in his office, waiting for the publisher of this newspaper to convoke a solemn lunch. He would be wherever you were, when there was trouble. He wanted to be young again. Too briefly, he was.

His admirable sons, who have perhaps inherited his sense of the preposterous as I inherited father's small bones, decided to bury him without a tie, in the tennis clothes he was wearing when the universe made a criminal mistake. There was, in the memorial rites last Thursday, a want of ceremony. Informality honored him. It occurs to me, however, that—in the clumsy way men in this country mismanage their emotions—I never got around to telling Al Marlens that I loved him. And so I thought that this time around I would be stupid in public.

If You're Expecting One-Liners
Jim Murray—*Los Angeles Times*—7/1/1979

OK, bang the drum slowly, professor. Muffle the cymbals. Kill the laugh track. You might say that Old Blue Eye is back. But that's as funny as this is going to get.

I feel I owe my friends an explanation as to where I've been all these weeks. Believe me, I would rather have been in a press box.

I lost an old friend the other day. He was blue-eyed, impish, he cried a lot with me, laughed a lot with me, saw a great many things with me. I don't know why he left me. Boredom, perhaps.

We read a lot of books together, we did a lot of crossword puzzles together, we saw films together. He had a pretty exciting life. He saw Babe Ruth hit a home run when we were both 12 years old. He saw Willie Mays steal second base, he saw Maury Wills steal his 104th base. He saw Rocky Marciano get up. I thought he led a pretty good life.

One night a long time ago he saw this pretty girl who laughed a lot, played the piano and he couldn't look away from her. Later he looked on as I married this pretty lady. He saw her through 34 years. He loved to see her laugh, he loved to see her happy.

You see, the friend I lost was my eye. My good eye. The other eye, the right one, we've been carrying for years. We just let him tag along like Don Quixote's nag. It's been a long time since he could read the number on a halfback or tell whether a ball was fair or foul or even which fighter was down.

So, one blue eye missing and the other misses it a lot.

So my best friend left me, at least temporarily, in a twilight world where it's always 8 o'clock on a summer night.

He stole away like a thief in the night and he took a lot with him. But not everything. He left a lot of memories. He couldn't take those with him. He just took the future with him and the present. He couldn't take the past.

I don't know why he had to go. I thought we were pals. I thought the things we did together we enjoyed doing together. Sure, we cried together. There were things to cry about.

But it was a long, good relationship, a happy one. It went all the way back to the days when we arranged all the marbles in a circle in the dirt in the lots in Connecticut. We played one o'cat baseball. We saw curveballs together, trying to hit them or catch them. We looked through a catcher's mask together. We were partners in every sense of the word.

He recorded the happy moments, the miracle of children, the beauty of a Pacific sunset, snowcapped mountains, faces on Christmas morning. He allowed me to hit fly balls to young sons in uniforms two sizes too large, to see a pretty daughter march in halftime parades. He allowed me to see most of the major sports events of our time. I suppose I should be grateful that he didn't drift away when I was 12 or 15 or 29 but stuck around over 50 years until we had a vault of memories. Still, I'm only human. I'd like to see again, if possible, Rocky Marciano with his nose bleeding, behind on points and the other guy coming.

I guess I would like to see Reggie Jackson with the count 3 and 2 and the Series on the line, guessing fastball. I guess I'd like to see Rod Carew with men on first and second and no place to put him, and the pitcher wishing he were standing in the rain someplace, reluctant to let go of the ball.

I'd like to see Stan Musial crouched around a curveball one more time. I'd like to see Don Drysdale trying to not laugh as a young hitter came up there with both feet in the bucket.

I'd like to see Sandy Koufax just once more facing Willie Mays with a no-hitter on the line. I'd like to see Maury Wills with a big lead against a pitcher with a good move. I'd like to see Roberto Clemente with the ball and a guy trying to go from first to third. I'd like to see Pete Rose sliding into home headfirst.

I'd like once more to see Henry Aaron standing there with that quiet bat, a study in deadliness. I'd like to see Bob Gibson scowling at a hitter as if he had some nerve just to pick up a bat. I'd like to see Elroy Hirsch going out for a long one from Bob Waterfield, Johnny Unitas in high-cuts picking apart a zone defense. I'd like to see Casey Stengel walking to the mound on his gnarled old legs to take a pitcher out, beckoning his gnarled old finger behind his back.

I'd like to see Sugar Ray Robinson or Muhammad Ali giving a recital, a ballet, not a fight. Also, to be sure, I'd like to see a sky full of stars, moonlight on the water, and yes, the tips of a royal flush peeking out as I fan out a poker hand, and yes, a straight two-foot putt.

Come to think of it, I'm lucky. I saw all of those things. I see them yet.

"Are You John Lennon?"
JIMMY BRESLIN—*New York Daily News*—12/9/1980

That summer in Breezy Point, when he was eighteen and out of Madison High in Brooklyn, there was the Beatles on the radio at the beach through the hot days and on the jukebox through the nights in the Sugar Bowl and

Kennedys. He was young and he let his hair grow and there were girls and it was the important part of life.

Last year, Tony Palma even went to see *Beatlemania*.

And now, last night, a thirty-four-year-old man, he sat in a patrol car at Eighty-second Street and Columbus Avenue and the call came over the radio: "Man shot, One West Seventy-second Street."

Palma and his partner, Herb Frauenberger, rushed through the Manhattan streets to an address they knew as one of the most famous living places in the country, the Dakota apartments.

Another patrol car was there ahead of them, and as Palma got out he saw the officers had a man up against the building and were handcuffing him.

"Where's the guy shot?" Palma said.

"In the back," one of the cops said.

Palma went through the gates into the Dakota courtyard and up into the office, where a guy in a red shirt and jeans was on his face on the floor. Palma rolled the guy over. Blood was coming out of the mouth and covering the face. The chest was wet with blood.

Palma took the arms and Frauenberger took the legs. They carried the guy out to the street. Somebody told them to put the body in another patrol car.

Jim Moran's patrol car was waiting. Moran is from the South Bronx, from Williams Avenue, and he was brought up on Tony Bennett records in the juke-boxes. When he became a cop in 1964, he was put on patrol guarding the Beatles at their hotel. Girls screamed and pushed and Moran laughed. Once, it was all fun.

Now responding to the call, "Man shot, One West Seventy-second," Jim Moran, a forty-five-year-old policeman, pulled up in front of the Dakota and Tony Palma and Herb Frauenberger put this guy with blood all over him in the backseat.

As Moran started driving away, he heard people in the street shouting, "That's John Lennon!"

Moran was driving with Bill Gamble. As they went through the streets to Roosevelt Hospital, Moran looked in the backseat and said, "Are you John Lennon?" The guy in the back nodded and groaned.

Back on Seventy-second Street, somebody told Palma, "Take the woman." And a shaking woman, another victim's wife, crumpled into the backseat as Palma started for Roosevelt Hospital. She said nothing to the two cops and they said nothing to her. Homicide is not a talking matter.

Jim Moran, with John Lennon in the backseat, was on the radio as he drove to the hospital. "Have paramedics meet us at the emergency entrance," he called. When he pulled up to the hospital, they were waiting for him with a cart. As Lennon was being wheeled through the doors into the emergency room, the doctors were on him.

"John Lennon," somebody said.

"Yes, it is," Moran said.

Now Tony Palma pulled up to the emergency entrance. He let the woman out and she ran to the doors. Somebody called to Palma, "That's Yoko Ono."

"Yeah?" Palma said.

"They just took John Lennon in," the guy said.

Palma walked into the emergency room. Moran was there already. The doctors had John Lennon on a table in a trauma room, working on the chest, inserting tubes.

Tony Palma said to himself, I don't think so. Moran shook his head. He thought about his two kids, who know every one of the Beatles' big tunes. And Jim Moran and Tony Palma, older now, cops in a world with no fun, stood in the emergency room as John Lennon, whose music they knew, whose music was known everywhere on earth, became another person who died after being shot with a gun on the streets of New York.

A Short Story About the Vietnam War Memorial
MOLLY IVINS—*Dallas-Times Herald*—11/30/1982

She had known, ever since she first read about the Vietnam War Memorial, that she would go there someday. Sometime she would be in Washington and would go and see his name and leave again.

So silly, all that fuss about the memorial. Whatever else Vietnam was, it was not the kind of war that calls for some "Raising the Flag at Iwo Jima" kind of statue. She was not prepared, though, for the impact of the memorial. To walk down into it in the pale winter sunshine was like the war itself, like going into a dark valley and damned if there was ever any light at the end of the tunnel. Just death. When you get closer to the two walls, the number of names start to stun you. It is terrible, there in the peace and the pale sunshine.

The names are listed by date of death. There has never been a time, day or night, drunk or sober, for thirteen years she could not have told you the date. He was killed on August 13, 1969. It is near the middle of the left wall. She went toward it as though she had known beforehand where it would be. His name is near the bottom. She had to kneel to find it. Stupid clichés. His name leaped out at her. It was like being hit.

She stared at it and then reached out and gently ran her fingers over the letters in the cold black marble. The memory of him came back so strong, almost as if he were there on the other side of the stone, she could see his hand reaching out to touch her fingers. It had not hurt for years and suddenly, just for a moment, it hurt again so horribly that it twisted her face and made her gasp and left her with tears running down her face. Then it stopped hurting but she could not stop the tears. Could not stop them running and running down her face.

There had been a time, although she had been an otherwise sensible young woman, when she had believed she would never recover from the pain. She did, of course. But she is still determined never to sentimentalize him. He would have hated that. She had thought it was like an amputation, the severing of his life from hers, that you could live on afterward but it would be like having only one leg and one arm. But it was only a wound. It healed. If there is a scar it is only faintly visible now at odd intervals.

He was a biologist, a t.a. at the university getting his Ph.D. They lived together for two years. He left the university to finish his thesis and before he could line up a public school job—teachers were safe in those years—the draft board got him. They had friends who had left the country, they had friends who had gone to prison, they had friends who had gone to Nam. There were no good choices in those years. She thinks now he unconsciously wanted to go even though he often said, said in one of his last letters, that it was a stupid f—in' war. He felt some form of guilt about a friend of theirs who was killed during the Tet offensive. Hubert Humphrey called Tet a great victory. His compromise was to refuse officer's training school and go as an enlisted man. She had thought then it was a dumb gesture and they had a half-hearted quarrel about it.

He had been in Nam less than two months when he was killed, without heroics, during a firefight at night by a single bullet in the brain. No one saw it happen. There are some amazing statistics about money and tonnage from that war. Did you know that there were more tons of bombs dropped on Hanoi during the Christmas bombing of 1972 than in all of World War II? Did you know that the war in Vietnam cost the United States $123.3 billion? She has always wanted to know how much that one bullet cost. Sixty-three cents? $1.20? Someone must know.

The other bad part was the brain. Even at this late date, it seems to her that was quite a remarkable mind. Long before she read C. P. Snow, the ferociously honest young man who wanted to be a great biologist taught her a great deal about the difference between the way scientists think and the way humanists think. Only once has she been glad he was not with her. It was at one of those bizarre hearings about teaching "creation science." He would have gotten furious and been horribly rude. He had no patience with people who did not understand and respect the process of science.

She used to attribute his fierce honesty to the fact that he was a Yankee. She is still prone to tell "white" lies to make people feel better, to smooth things over, to prevent hard feelings. Surely there have been dumber things for lovers to quarrel over than the social utility of hypocrisy. But not many.

She stood up again, still staring at his name, stood for a long time. She said, "There it is," and turned to go. A man to her left was staring at her. She glared at him. The man had done nothing but make the mistake of seeing her weeping. She said, as though daring him to disagree, "It was a stupid, f—in' war," and stalked past him.

She turned again at the top of the slope to make sure where his name is, so whenever she sees a picture of the memorial she can put her finger where his name is. He never said goodbye, literally. Whenever he left he would say, "Take care, love." He could say it many different ways. He said it when he left for Vietnam. She stood at the top of the slope and found her hand half-raised in some silly gesture of farewell. She brought it down again. She considered thinking to him, "Hey, take care, love," but it seemed remarkably inappropriate. She walked away and was quite entertaining for the rest of the day, because it was expected of her.

She thinks he would have liked the memorial. He would have hated the editorials. He did not sacrifice his life for his country or for a just or noble cause. There just were no good choices in those years and he got killed.

A Fool's Errand

BOB HERBERT—*New York Times*—5/4/2000

Paul Conover and I met Michael Farmer during basic training at Fort Dix, N.J., in the mid-1960's. Conover and I were friends from Montclair. Farmer was a kid from Atlantic City, a 17-year-old who mumbled so badly you could never be sure what he was saying. He was big and good-looking, but the first impression was that he wasn't too swift.

One night Farmer came over to our barracks—uninvited—while Conover and I, who were a couple of years older and light-years cooler, were sitting on the floor, spit-shining our combat boots. Very tentatively and very politely, Farmer asked if he could join us.

I told him to get lost. Farmer must not have understood because he promptly sat down, took off his boots and, over the next few minutes, proved to my satisfaction that he was as dumb as he sounded.

First he told us he had joined the Army. Conover grinned and rolled his eyes. Then Farmer said he was in love with a girl in Atlantic City and planned to marry her. I shook my head. This was not a person worth spending time with. As a draftee, all I wanted was for my hair to grow back and to be reunited with that gleaming symbol of freedom and the good life, my Thunderbird.

But Conover liked Farmer and told him to come back the next night.

"He mumbles," I said.

But Conover said, "Ah, he's all right."

So Farmer came back, night after night, to smoke cigarettes, listen to Motown music, mumble about his girlfriend and polish boots. To my chagrin, I started to like him, though I still needed a translator to understand him. For the longest time I thought his girlfriend's name was Merlin. It was Marilyn.

Farmer and Conover became very close. Eventually both of them were sent to Vietnam. I got lucky and was sent to Korea, which was no walk in the park. But it wasn't Vietnam.

The impact of the war on Conover and Farmer was strange. When Farmer came back, he seemed more sure of himself, more open and fun-loving, less insecure. He and Marilyn were married.

Conover, the most happy-go-lucky guy I had ever known, was a wreck. He was nervous. Jumpy. Some nights he would drink like a fiend. The cheerful optimism that had once defined his personality was gone.

He wouldn't really talk about Vietnam. All I ever heard him say was, "Didn't know I could get so scared."

Then the unthinkable happened. Farmer, who had enlisted for four years and was still in the service, got orders to go back to Vietnam. We told him not to go. Call your congressman, we said. Fight this thing. But Farmer didn't know how.

It's not hard to guess what happened. Farmer's second tour lasted only a few months. I was in the back of my father's upholstery shop one afternoon when Conover walked in.

"Farmer didn't make it," he said. And then he started crying.

A year passed. I got a job with a newspaper. Conover got married. Other buddies got killed in the war, which began to look like it might go on forever. My sister's boyfriend got shot.

I didn't realize it, but Conover's struggle was winding down. He wouldn't make it, either. I never got the story straight. All I know is that he got his hands on a gun, and one night he waited in a car outside his house for his wife to come home. When she showed up he shot her dead. Then he killed himself.

Sunday was the 25th anniversary of the end of the war, which I cannot think about without thinking of Farmer and Conover. Neither had a clue about the politics or the history or the egos that sucked them up like dust from a carpet and consigned them to their pointless fate. Vietnam was a fool's errand, and the young and the ignorant went to their doom by the tens of thousands.

When David Brinkley, appalled by the carnage, asked Lyndon Johnson why he didn't just pull out of Vietnam, thus saving many lives, Johnson replied, "I'm not going to be the first American president to lose a war."

A couple of years ago I visited the Vietnam Memorial in Washington. I found Farmer's name, and then, not thinking, looked for Conover's. Of course, it wasn't there. But his short life and that of his wife, whose name I don't know, were wasted by Vietnam just a surely as the lives of those 58,000 other Americans listed on that bitter wall.

His Delicious, Mansard-Roofed World
PEGGY NOONAN—*Wall Street Journal*—10/26/2001

I found the words on a yellow Post-it I'd stuck on the side of the bookcase in my office about a year ago. It had gotten covered up by phone numbers and pictures and doctor's appointment cards, and yesterday, looking for a number, I found it—a piece of yellow paper with the words "His delicious mansard-roofed world." It took me aback. And I remembered what it was.

That night I had been out with friends—it was last fall—and it was fun, and I got home thinking, simply, of something we all should think of more and I don't think of enough: how wonderful it is to be alive, the joy of it, the beauty. And as I thought it—this is the part I remember most sharply—a scene came into my mind of a little French town with cobblestone streets and sharply slanting roofs on 18th-century buildings. Which made me think, in turn, in a blink, of New York, and its older architecture uptown and off the park, the old mansions off Fifth Avenue with sloping mansard roofs, and how this is the world we live in.

And I thought at that moment, with those pictures in my head: "His delicious, mansard-roofed world." He being God. I wrote down the words on a Post-it and put it on the bookcase, thinking some day I'd use them in writing about . . . something. Maybe joy. Maybe: us. Or maybe I'd just see them and think: That was a nice moment.

Anyway, the words captured for me a moment of thought.

And last night I found them and thought: *Oh—they speak of a moment in time.*

Yesterday afternoon, I was with a teenage friend, taking a cab down Park Avenue. It was a brilliant day, clear and sparkling, and as the cab turned left at 86th Street the sun hit the windows in one of those flashes of bright gold-yellow that can, on certain days or at certain times, pierce your heart. We had been quiet, not talking, on the way to see a friend, when I said, "Do you . . . find yourself thinking at all of the ways in which you might be feeling differently about the future if September 11th had never happened?"

"Oh yes," she said, softly. "Every day."

And she meant it. And neither of us said any more and neither of us had to.

There are a lot of quiet moments going on. Have you noticed? A lot of quiet transformations, a lot of quiet action and quiet conversations. People are re-aligning themselves. I know people who are undergoing religious conversions, and changes of faith. And people who are holding on in a new way, with a harder grip, to what they already have and believe in.

Some people have quietly come to terms with the most soul-chilling thoughts. A young man I know said to me last week, as we chatted in passing on the street, "I have been thinking about the end of the American empire." And I thought: *Oh my boy, do you know the import, the weight, of the words you are saying?* And then I thought *Yes, he does. He's been thinking, quietly.*

Some people are quietly defining and redefining things. I am one of them. We are trying to define or paint or explain what the old world was, and what the new world is, and how the break between them—the exact spot where the stick broke, cracked, splintered—could possibly have been an hour in early September.

One thing that passes through our minds is what to call the Old World—"The Lost World," or "The Golden Age," or "Then." We don't have to know yet what to call the New World, and cannot anyway because it hasn't fully revealed itself, and so cannot be named.

But if we can name the Old World, we'll at least know exactly what it is we think we've lost. And this is a funny little problem, because if you go out onto your street right now, if you live anyplace but downtown Manhattan or Arlington, Va., the world outside looks exactly—exactly—like the one that existed a year ago. The pumpkins in the stores, the merry kids, the guy who owns the butcher shop outside smoking in his apron. Everything looks the same. Same people, same stores, same houses.

And yet we all feel everything has changed. And we're right.

People say things like, "We have lost a sense of certainty," and I nod, for it is true. But on the other hand, I didn't feel so certain about the future last year. Did you?

People say we have lost the assumption that what we had would continue. Or, this being America, get better.

Certainly people who were carefree have lost their carefreeness. And with no irony I think: *That's a shame. Carefreeness is good.*

Lately when I think of the Old World I think of an insult that I mean as a tribute. It is the phrase *the narcissism of small differences*. In the world that has just passed, careless people—not carefree, careless—spent their time deconstructing the reality of the text, as opposed to reading the book. You could do that then. The world seemed so peaceful that you could actively look for new things to argue about just to keep things lively. You could be on a faculty and argue over where Jane Austen meant to put the comma, or how her landholding father's contextually objective assumptions regarding colonialism impacted her work. You could have real arguments about stupid things. Those were the days! It's great when life is so nice you have to invent arguments.

But the big thing I remember as we approached the end of the Old World, the thing I had been thinking for years and marveled over and also felt mildly anxious about, was this: You could go out and order and eat anything in a restaurant. And I had a sense that this wouldn't last forever, and some day we'd look back on these days fondly.

I would actually think that. It actually seemed to me marvelous that we could order anything we wanted. Raspberries in February! Bookstores, shoe stores, computer stores, food stores. We could order anything. Www-dot-gimme-dot-com.

I think the general feeling was a lovely optimism, which was captured in a great '80s phrase: "The future's so bright, I gotta wear shades."

This was the thing: abundance. Not only of food but of potential, of hope, of the kid from the project's dream of being the next J. Lo, or West Point cadet, or millionaire. Every middle-class kid in the suburbs thought it absolutely within his grasp to be the next Steven Spielberg or Russell Crowe, or to play Martin Sheen's assistant on *The West Wing*, or run the record industry or direct commercials.

Abundant dreams. There was peace—crime down for the first time in a generation, the world relatively quiet, and in the suburbs they were starting to sleep with the windows open again! And material goods, things from the factory and the farm. As Kevin Spacey says in the commercial for his new movie, "Your produce alone has been worth the trip!"

God, it was the age of abundance.

Or maybe just: The Abundance.

I know people who are feeling a sense of betrayal at the big change, as if they thought history were a waiter in a crisp white jacket, and though they ordered two more of the same, instead—instead!—he brought them, on a pretty silver platter, something quite dreadful.

They feel betrayed because they thought what we have been living through the past four decades or so was "life." But it wasn't, it was "Superlife."

In the long ribbon of history life has been one long stained and tangled mess, full of famine, horror, war and disease. We must have thought we had it better because man had improved. But man doesn't really "improve," does he? Man is man. Human nature is human nature; the impulse to destroy coexists with the desire to build and create and make better. They've both been with us since the beginning. Man hasn't improved, the weapons have improved.

In the early 20th century the future was so bright they had to invent shades. They had everything—peace, prosperity, medical and scientific breakthroughs, political progress, fashion, glamour, harmless tasty scandals. The Gilded Age. And then all of a sudden they were hit by the most terrible war in all of European history, the most terrible plague in all of modern history (the Spanish flu) and on top of it all the most terrible political revolution in the history of man. And that was just the first 18 years.

People always think good news will continue. I guess it's in our nature to think that whatever is around us while we're here is what will continue until we're not.

And then things change, and you're surprised. I guess surprise is in our nature too. And then after the surprise we burrow down into ourselves and pull out what we need to survive, and go on, and endure.

But there's something else, and I am thinking of it.

I knew for many years a handsome and intelligent woman of middle years who had everything anyone could dream of—home, children, good marriage, career, wealth. She was secure. And she and her husband had actually gotten these good things steadily, over 25 years of effort, and in that time they had suffered no serious reverses or illnesses, no tragedies or bankruptcies or dark stars. Each year was better than the previous.

It was wonderful to see. But as I came to know her I realized that she didn't think she had what she had because she was lucky, or blessed. She thought she had them because she was better. She had lived a responsible, effortful life; of course it had come together. She had what she had because she was good, and prudent.

She deserved it. She was better than the messy people down the block.

She forgot she was lucky and blessed!

You forget you're lucky when your luck is so consistent that it confounds the very idea of luck. You begin to think your good fortune couldn't be luck, it must have been . . . talent. Or effort. Or superiority.

The consistency of America's luck may have fooled many of us into forgetting we were all lucky to be born here, lucky to be living now, lucky to have hospitals and operas and a film industry and a good electrical system. We were born into it. We were lucky. We were blessed.

We thought we were the heirs of John Adams, Ulysses S. Grant, Thomas Edison, Jonas Salk, Mr. Levitt of Levittown. And we are. But still, every generation ya gotta earn it. It doesn't mean you're better; it means you're lucky, and ya gotta earn it.

How did our luck turn bad, our blessings thin out?

Great books will be written about that. But maybe from this point on we should acknowledge what we quietly know inside: It was a catastrophic systems failure, a catastrophic top-to-bottom failure of the systems on which we rely for safety and peace.

Another way to say it: The people of the West were, the past 10 years or so, on an extended pleasure cruise, sailing blithely on smooth waters—but through an iceberg field. We thought those in charge of the ship, commanding it and steering it and seeing to its supplies, would—could—handle any problems. We paid our fare (that is, our taxes) and assumed the crew would keep us safe.

We thought our luck would hold, too.

The people—us, you and me, the sensuous man on the deck—spent a lot of time strolling along wondering, *What shall I pursue today, gold or romance? Romance or gold? I shall ponder this over a good merlot.* We were not serious. We were not morally serious. We were not dark. We banished darkness.

The American people knew, or at least those paying attention knew, that something terrible might happen. But they knew the government had probably done what governments do to protect us. The people did not demand this; the government did not do it. Bad men were allowed in; bad men flourished here, fit right in, planned their deeds. They brought more bad men in after them. They are here among us now; they send anthrax through the mail and watch our reaction, predicating their next move perhaps upon our response.

Our intelligence system failed—but then for a quarter century we had been denying it resources, destroying its authority, dismantling its mystique. Our immigration system failed—but then in many ways it had been encouraged to fail. Our legal system failed.

One of our greatest institutions, American journalism, failed. When the editors and publishers of our great magazines and networks want you to worry about something—child safety seats, the impact of air bags, drunken driving, insecticides on apples—they know how to make you worry. They know exactly how to capture your attention. Mathew Shepard and hate crimes, Rodney King and racism: The networks and great newspapers know how to hit Drive and go from zero to the American Consciousness in 60 seconds. And the networks can do it on free airwaves, a gift from our government.

Did the networks and great newspapers make us worry about what we know we should have worried about? No. Did they bang the drums? No. Did they hit this story like they know how to hit a story? No.

In January 2001 the Homeland Security report, which declared flatly that international terrorism would inevitably draw blood on American soil, was unveiled. They called a news conference in a huge Senate office building. Congressmen came, and a senator, Pat Roberts of Kansas. Only a half dozen reporters showed up, and one, from the greatest newspaper in the nation, walked out halfway through. It was boring.

Every magazine and newspaper had, over the past 10 years, a front-page story and a cover on the madmen in the world and the weapons they could seize and get and fashion. But they never beat the drum, never insisted that this become a cause.

Why? In part I think for the same reason our political figures didn't do anything. It would have been bad for ratings. *The people don't want serious things at 10 o'clock on a Tuesday night, they want Sela Ward falling in love.* I will never, ever forget the important Democrat who told me over lunch why Bill Clinton (president of the United States, January 1993 through January 2001) had never moved and would never move in a serious way to deal with the potential of nuclear and biological terrorism. Because it doesn't show up in the polls, he said. Because it doesn't show up in the focus groups.

It was a catastrophic systems failure, top to bottom. And we all share in it, some more than others.

Except.

Except those who did the remarkable things that day, Sept. 11, 2001—the firemen who charged like the Light Brigade, the businessmen who said, "Let's roll." Which is, in part, why we keep talking about them. To remind ourselves who we are in the midst of the systems failure. They did the right thing just by being what they were, which gave us inspiration just when we needed it most.

And now we have to turn it all around.

Great books, as I said, will be written about these days, and the war on which we are embarked, on how it began and why America slept, and what America did when it awoke. Much awaits to be learned and told.

And what we must do now, in our anger and defensiveness, is support, assist and constructively criticize the systems that so catastrophically failed. For those systems still reign and we still need them. And they are trying to function now, and trying to protect us, with the same sense of loss we all share and the added burden of a mind-bending sense of remorse, frustration, anger and pain.

Where are we right now? We have reached the point in the story where the original trauma is wearing off (except in our dreams, where it's newly inflicted), where expressions of solidarity and patriotism are true but tired, and questions about exactly how well our institutions are handling this—not in the past but right now—are rising.

It all began 45 days ago. We know who did the bombings because they were on the planes, and they left receipts.

But we do not know who their confederates here were, do not know who is spreading the anthrax that has hit Florida, New York and Washington, do not know the dimensions of the threat at home.

Authority figures are doubted. The letter carriers don't trust their superiors to take care of them, and how they feel is legitimate and understandable. The workers in the newsrooms, reassured by the boss that if they were going to get anthrax they would have had it by now, do not trust what they're being told, or the tellers. And that is legitimate and understandable.

We are reading anxious reports. Yesterday I read that the Nuclear Regulatory Commission had admitted it kept nuclear plant vulnerability studies out and about and available for any citizen to see in their libraries. (Q: What were they thinking? A: They weren't thinking; they were feeling, and what they were feeling was lucky.)

More and more one senses we're going to have to be taking as much responsibility for ourselves—and on ourselves—as we can. Doing our own research, taking our own actions, making our own decisions, and acting on our own guts.

A week after Sept. 11, I was on a TV show where I said I'd been thinking about *Mrs. Miniver*, the 1942 movie with Greer Garson as the doughty British matron who saw her family—and thus her country—through the Blitz. I said that we were all going to have to be Mrs. Minivers now; we're going to have to keep the home front going.

I keep waiting for some talk show or news show to do the Mrs. Miniver segment, telling us what to do in case of real and terrible trouble.

And no one is doing it.

So we must all be doing it ourselves. I am researching and talking to experts. Next week I will talk about "How to Be Mr. and Mrs. Miniver"—from how much water to buy to where to put it and how to get everyone in your ambit together. I will share everything I'm told and hear. And let me tell you why I think, in all this mess, we must gather together and talk about how to get through it together, as citizens. *Because our systems are not fully working yet.*

It's a murky time. We're all feeling a little bit lonely, and all of us at one moment or another have the existential willies. Those who have 13 kids and 34 grandchildren are feeling as alone as those who are actually all alone.

We'd all best handle as much as we can ourselves, in and with our own little units.

It may become a terrifically tough time. But we are not alone, as you well know. God loves faith and effort, and he loves love. He will help us get through this, and to enjoy Paris and New York again, and to breathe deep of his delicious, mansard-roofed world.

Amen.

Open Letter to America
CHRIS ROSE—*New Orleans Times Picayune*—9/6/2005

Dear America,

I suppose we should introduce ourselves: We're South Louisiana.

We have arrived on your doorstep on short notice and we apologize for that, but we never were much for waiting around for invitations. We're not much on formalities like that.

And we might be staying around your town for a while, enrolling in your schools and looking for jobs, so we wanted to tell you a few things about us. We know you didn't ask for this and neither did we, so we're just going to have to make the best of it.

First of all, we thank you. For your money, your water, your food, your prayers, your boats and buses and the men and women of your National Guards, fire departments, hospitals and everyone else who has come to our rescue.

We're a fiercely proud and independent people, and we don't cotton much to outside interference, but we're not ashamed to accept help when we need it. And right now, we need it.

Just don't get carried away. For instance, once we get around to fishing again, don't try to tell us what kind of lures work best in your waters.

We're not going to listen. We're stubborn that way.

You probably already know that we talk funny and listen to strange music and eat things you'd probably hire an exterminator to get out of your yard.

We dance even if there's no radio. We drink at funerals. We talk too much and laugh too loud and live too large and, frankly, we're suspicious of others who don't.

But we'll try not to judge you while we're in your town.

Everybody loves their home, we know that. But we love South Louisiana with a ferocity that borders on the pathological. Sometimes we bury our dead in LSU sweatshirts.

Often we don't make sense. You may wonder why, for instance—if we could only carry one small bag of belongings with us on our journey to your state—why in God's name did we bring a pair of shrimp boots?

We can't really explain that. It is what it is.

You've probably heard that many of us stayed behind. As bad as it is, many of us cannot fathom a life outside of our border, out in that place we call Elsewhere.

The only way you can understand that is if you have been there, and so many of you have. So you realize that when you strip away all the craziness and bars and parades and music and architecture and all that hooey, really, the best thing about where we come from is us.

We are what made this place a national treasure. We're good people. And don't be afraid to ask us how to pronounce our names. It happens all the time.

When you meet us now and you look into our eyes, you will see the saddest story ever told. Our hearts are broken into a thousand pieces.

But don't pity us. We're gonna make it. We're resilient. After all, we've been rooting for the Saints for 35 years. That's got to count for something.

OK, maybe something else you should know is that we make jokes at inappropriate times.

But what the hell.

And one more thing: In our part of the country, we're used to having visitors. It's our way of life.

So when all this is over and we move back home, we will repay to you the hospitality and generosity of spirit you offer to us in this season of our despair.

That is our promise. That is our faith.

IX: Farewells

The columns collected here are not obituaries; they are appreciations and celebrations. Columnists have the opportunity to present an individual's life in a larger context. These are, in some ways, public eulogies. Biographies writ small, they help sum up the lessons of a life and its enduring spirit.

Sometimes it's a personal tribute to a loved one, like William Allen White's salute to his daughter Mary or Jimmy Breslin's eulogy for his wife. More often such columns are about public figures who helped define their era, like Damon Runyon's rumination on the sudden death of FDR or Walter Lippmann's transcendent tribute to the pioneering spirit of Amelia Earhart. Sometimes it's a bit of both, such as Grantland Rice on his friend Babe Ruth in "Game Called" or Jimmy Cannon's de-mythologizing in "The Earnest Hemingway I Knew."

Not all farewells are said with sadness—Westbrook Pegler's unsentimental take on the death of Huey Long did not try to honor the man; instead, Peg warned that Huey could have been an "American Mussolini."

The pairings make all the difference, like Chicago icon Mike Royko on the death of the city's powerful mayor, Richard Daley: "He wasn't graceful, suave, witty, or smooth. But, then, this is not Paris or San Francisco. He was raucous, sentimental, hot-tempered, practical, simple, devious, big, and powerful. This is, after all, Chicago."

And few hit a more perfect pitch than George Will on the passing of Ronald Reagan: "If you seek Ronald Reagan's monument, look around and consider what you do *not* see. The Iron Curtain that scarred a continent is gone, as is the Evil Empire responsible for it." It is exceeded only by his tribute to "A Mother's Love, Clarified."

In all cases, these columns are a tribute to the impact one person's life can make, whether for family, friends, or fellow countrymen.

Mary White
WILLIAM ALLEN WHITE—*Emporia Gazette*—5/17/1921

The Associated Press reports carrying the news of Mary White's death declared that it came as the result of a fall from a horse. How she would have hooted at that! She never fell from a horse in her life. Horses have fallen on her and with her—"I'm always trying to hold 'em in my lap," she used to say. But she was proud of few things, and one of them was that she could ride anything that had four legs and hair. Her death resulted not from a fall, but from a blow on the head which fractured her skull, and the blow came from the limb of an overhanging tree on the parking.

The last hour of her life was typical of its happiness. She came home from a day's work at school, topped off by a hard grind with the copy on the High School Annual, and felt that a ride would refresh her. She climbed into her khakis, chattering to her mother about the work she was doing, and hurried to get her horse and be out on the dirt roads for the country air and the radiant green fields of spring. As she rode through the town on an easy gallop, she kept waving at passers-by. She knew everyone in town. For a decade the little figure in the long pigtail and the red hair ribbon has been familiar on the streets of Emporia, and she got in the way of speaking to those who nodded at her. She passed the Kerrs, walking the horse in front of the Normal Library, and waved at them; passed another friend a few hundred feet farther on, and waved at her.

The horse was walking and, as she turned into North Merchant Street she took off her cowboy hat, and the horse swung into a lope. She passed the Tripletts and waved her cowboy hat at them, still moving gaily north on Merchant Street. A *Gazette* carrier passed—a high school boyfriend—and she waved at him, but with her bridle hand; the horse veered quickly, plunged into the parking where the low-hanging limb faced her and, while she still looked back waving, the blow came. But she did not fall from the horse; she slipped off, dazed a bit, staggered, and fell in a faint. She never quite recovered consciousness.

But she did not fall from the horse, neither was she riding fast. A year or so ago she used to go like the wind. But that habit was broken, and she used the horse to get into the open to get fresh, hard exercise and to work off a certain surplus energy that welled up in her and needed a physical outlet. The need has been in her heart for years. It was back of the impulse that kept the dauntless little brown-clad figure on the streets and country roads of the community and built into a strong, muscular body what had been a frail and sickly frame during the first years of her life. But the riding gave her more than a body. It released a gay and hardy soul. She was the happiest thing in the world. And she was happy because she was enlarging her horizon. She came to know all sorts and conditions of men; Charley O'Brien, the traffic cop, was one of her best friends. W. L. Holtz, the Latin teacher, was another. Tom O'Connor, farmer-politician, and the Rev. J. H. J. Rice, preacher and police judge, and Frank Beach, music master, were her special friends, and all the girls, black and white, above the track and below the track, in Pepville and Stringtown, were among her acquaintances. And she brought home riotous stories of her adventures. She loved to rollick; persiflage was her natural expression at home. Her humor was a continual bubble of joy. She seemed to think in hyperbole and metaphor. She was mischievous without malice, as full of faults as an old shoe. No angel was Mary White, but an easy girl to live with for she never nursed a grouch five minutes in her life.

With all her eagerness for the out-of-doors, she loved books. On her table when she left her room were a book by Conrad, one by Galsworthy, *Creative Chemistry* by E. E. Slosson, and a Kipling book. She read Mark Twain, Dickens, and Kipling before she was ten—all of their writings. Wells and Arnold Bennett particularly amused and diverted her. She was entered as a student in Wellesley for 1922; was assistant editor of the High School Annual this year, and in line for election to the editorship of the Annual next year. She was a member of the executive committee of the High School Y.W.C.A.

Within the last two years she had begun to be moved by an ambition to draw. She began as most children do by scribbling in her schoolbooks, funny pictures. She bought cartoon magazines and took a course—rather casually, naturally, for she was, after all, a child with no strong purposes—and this year she tasted the first fruits of success by having her pictures accepted by the High School Annual. But the thrill of delight she got when Mr. Ecord, of the Normal Annual, asked her to do the cartooning for that book this spring, was too beautiful for words. She fell to her work with all her enthusiastic heart. Her drawings were accepted, and her pride—always repressed by a lively sense of the ridiculousness of the figure she was cutting—was a really gorgeous thing to see. No successful artist ever drank a deeper draft of satisfaction than she took from the little fame her work was getting among her school-fellows. In her glory, she almost forgot her horse—but never her car.

For she used the car as a jitney bus. It was her social life. She never had a "party" in all her nearly seventeen years—wouldn't have one; but she never drove a block in her life that she didn't begin to fill the car with pickups! Everybody rode with Mary White—white and black, old and young, rich and poor, men and women. She like nothing better than to fill the car with long-legged High School boys and an occasional girl, and parade the town. She never had a "date,"nor went to a dance, except once with her brother, Bill, and the "boy proposition" didn't interest her—yet. But young people—great spring-breaking, varnish-cracking, fender-bending, door-sagging carloads of "kids"—gave her great pleasure. Her zests were keen. But the most fun she ever had in her life was acting as chairman of the committee that got up the big turkey dinner for the poor folks at the county home; scores of pies, gallons of slaw; jam, cakes, preserves, oranges, and a wilderness of turkey were loaded into the car and taken to the county home. And, being of a practical turn of mind, she risked her own Christmas dinner by staying to see that the poor folks actually got it all. Not that she was a cynic; she just disliked to tempt folks. While there, she found a blind colored uncle, very old, who could do nothing but make rag rugs, and she rustled up from her school friends rags enough to keep him busy for a season. The last engagement she tried to make was to take the guests at the county home out for a car ride. And the last endeavor of her life was to try to get a rest room for colored girls in the High School. She found one girl reading in the toilet, because there was no better place for a colored girl to loaf, and it inflamed her sense of injustice and she became a nagging harpy to those who, she thought, could remedy the evil. The poor she always had with her, and was glad of it. She hungered and thirsted for righteousness; and was the most impious creature in the world. She joined the Congregational Church without consulting her parents; not particularly for her soul's good. She never had a thrill of piety in her life; and would have hooted at a "testimony." But even as a little child she felt the church was an agency for helping people to more of life's abundance, and she wanted to help. She never wanted help for herself. Clothes meant little to her. It was a fight to get a new rig on her; but eventually a harder fight to get it off. She never wore a jewel and had no ring but her High School class ring, and never asked for anything but a wrist watch. She refused to have her hair up; though she was nearly seventeen. "Mother," she protested, "you don't know how much I get by with, in my braided pigtails, that I could not with my hair up." Above every other passion of her life was her passion not to grow up, to be a child. The tomboy in her, which was big, seemed to loathe to be put away forever in skirts. She was a Peter Pan, who refused to grow up.

Her funeral yesterday at the Congregational Church was as she would have wished it; no singing, no flowers except the big bunch of red roses from her brother Bill's Harvard classmen—heavens, how proud that would have made her! And the red roses from the *Gazette* forces, in vases, at her head and feet. A short prayer; Paul's beautiful essay on "Love" from the Thirteenth Chapter of First Corinthians; some remarks about her democratic spirit by her friend, John H. J. Rice, pastor and police judge, which she would have deprecated if she could; a prayer sent down for her by her friend Carl Nau; and, opening the service the slow, poignant movement from Beethoven's Moonlight Sonata, which she loved, and closing the service a cutting from the joyously melancholy first movement of Tchaikovsky's Pathetic Symphony, which she liked to hear in certain moods, on the phonograph; then the Lord's Prayer by her friends in High School.

That was all.

For her pallbearers only her friends were chosen: her Latin teacher, W. L. Holtz; her High School principal, Rice Brown; her doctor, Frank Foncannon; her friend, W. W. Finney; her pal at the *Gazette* office, Walter Hughes; and her brother Bill. It would have made her smile to know that her friend, Charley O'Brien, the traffic cop, had been transferred from Sixth and Commercial to the corner near the church to direct her friends who came to bid her good-by.

A rift in the clouds in a gray day threw a shaft of sunlight upon her coffin as her nervous, energetic little body sank to its last sleep. But the soul of her, the glowing, gorgeous, fervent soul of her, surely was flaming in eager joy upon some other dawn.

American Mussolini
WESTBROOK PEGLER—Scripps Howard—3/24/1936

Within a few months I have seen three dictatorships in operation, and the experience confirms my belief that the death of Huey Long removed a terrible menace to the liberty of the United States. This may sound high-powered, but I have been seeing some grim demonstrations of the condition which we narrowly escaped. It is alarming to realize that a majority of the people of Louisiana regarded Huey as their friend, and were not only willing but eager to sign over their citizenship to him.

This was not so shocking when it happened in Italy, Germany and Austria, because those people had always lived under the authority of kings and armies. But the citizenship of the American was supposed to be a possession worth fighting for. Huey himself denied that he had dictatorial ambitions, insisting, on the contrary, that he was the protector of the common man, and I do not deny that he liked poor people better than businessmen and the rich, although he hated poor people who opposed him.

But Mussolini and Hitler both say the same thing, and, like Huey, they proceed on the theory that the common man is too dumb to know what is best for him.

By trick and stratagem Huey Long had abolished the Legislature in Louisiana, and the two houses which were jumping through hoops for him at the time of his death were just as farcical as the so-called legislative bodies which answer the commands of the dictators in Rome and Berlin.

Elections in Louisiana also had been reduced to absurdity by the application of various laws which Huey had enacted, particularly the law permitting him to engage unlimited numbers of poll inspectors at $5 each to protect the purity of the ballot.

Huey himself snickered as he pronounced the worlds "purity of the ballot" in explaining the purpose of this bill to the committee in Baton Rouge. For his legislature knew that it really granted him the power to buy votes at $5 each, sufficient to control the result in any doubtful precinct and charge the cost to the public treasury.

Like Mussolini and Hitler, Huey was organizing a terrorist organization under the authority of the State Department of Criminal Investigation, with no limit on the number of operatives or the amount to be spent meeting the payroll. He already had the courts and the lawyers under control, and the Department of Criminal Investigation, if it had reached its full development, would have been a terrible force.

In Germany the Brown Shirts have now been superseded by the army and have lost most of their old power, but they were a bad lot when they were running wild. They could drag a man out of his bed at night and put him away in a concentration camp without the merest pretense of a trial. And often when a Brown Shirt happened to owe money to the prisoner, the accused was executed for treason or shot in the back while attempting to escape.

It was the same in Italy in the early years of Fascism, and it would have been the same in our country under Huey Long if he had lived and enjoyed a few more of the political breaks which were bringing him along so alarmingly up to the day of his death.

Another characteristic that Huey shared with Il Duce and Der Fuehrer was his cruelty toward people who wouldn't quit to him. He enjoyed seeing unarmed men beaten by his armed guards. He enjoyed feeling that a machine gun was mounted at his hotel in Baton Rouge, ready to pour it into anyone who opposed him. And if he had lived to develop his dictatorship he would not have hesitated to fire on the common man.

For Huey had the heart and soul of a demagogue and dictator, and his closest associates in the development of his power were men of the same brutal type as Goebbels, Streicher, Roehm and the rest of Hitler's handy men.

Huey used to boast of the mileage of paved roads and the bridges which he had built and of the grandeur of his state capitol and the buildings of the state university. But Mussolini and Hitler also boast of their roads and bridges, railroad stations and model tenements. But the state capitol of Louisiana had ceased to be a Legislature and the university, like Heidelberg and Munich, was no longer free.

Huey lynched freedom in the university when he kicked out of school half a dozen students of journalism for criticizing him in print, and his university president was a promising candidate for the office of director of education under the national dictatorship. He also had a clergyman lined up for the job of national bishop, and his system of persecuting his opponents by raising their taxes was a method of confiscation adjusted to the early stage of an elastic plan. He refused to permit any inspection of the public treasury accounts, and his appeal to enthusiasm in public appearance was as magnetic as Mussolini's or Hitler's, with the additional menace of good-natured hilarity.

He could make the suckers laugh. There is no denying that he was a good fighter; all dictators are. But Huey was stealing the freedom of the very people he claimed to love, and he might have had them completely at his mercy in four years more.

Probably his method was impulsive rather than studied, but he was following exactly the system that had made slaves of the Italians and Germans. It is no laughing matter that such a man with such a plan was hell bent for national power when mere chance cut him down.

Amelia Earhart
WALTER LIPPMANN—*New York Herald Tribune*—7/8/1937

I cannot quite remember whether Miss Earhart undertook her flight with some practical purpose in mind, say, to demonstrate something or other about aviation which will make it a little easier for commercial passengers to move more quickly around the world. There are those who seem to think that an enterprise like hers must have some such justification, that without it there was no good reason for taking such grave risks.

But in truth Miss Earhart needs no such justification. The world is a better place to live in because it contains human beings who will give up ease and security and stake their own lives in order to do what they themselves think worth doing. They help to offset the much larger number who are ready to sacrifice the ease and the security and the very lives of others in order to do what they want done. No end of synthetic heroes strut the stage, great bold men in bulletproof vests surrounded by squads of armed guards, demonstrating their courage by terrorizing the weak and the defenseless. It is somehow reassuring to think that there are also men and women who take the risks themselves, who pit themselves not against their fellow beings but against the immensity and the violence of the natural world, who are brave without cruelty to others and impassioned with an idea that dignifies all who contemplate it.

The best things of mankind are as useless as Amelia Earhart's adventure. They are the things that are undertaken not for some definite, measurable result, but because someone, not counting the costs or calculating the consequences, is moved by curiosity, the love of excellence, a point of honor, the compulsion to invent or to make or to understand. In such persons mankind overcomes the inertia which would keep it earthbound forever in its habitual ways. They have in them the free and useless energy with which alone men surpass themselves.

Such energy cannot be planned and managed and made purposeful, or weighed by the standards of utility or judged by its social consequences. It is wild and it is free. But all the heroes, the saints and the seers, the explorers and the creators partake of it. They do not know what they discover. They do not know where their impulse is taking them. They can give no account in advance of where they are going or explain completely where they have been. They have been possessed for a time with an extraordinary passion which is unintelligible in ordinary terms.

No preconceived theory fits them. No material purpose actuates them. They do the useless, brave, noble, the divinely foolish and the very wisest things that are done by man. And what they prove to themselves and to others is that man is no mere creature of his habits, no mere automaton in his routine, no mere cog in the collective machine, but that in the dust of which he is made there is also fire, lighted now and then by great winds from the sky.

FDR: A Great Man Passes By
DAMON RUNYON—*New York American*—4/14/1945

The funeral cortege of the late President Roosevelt, a comparatively small, war-begrimed cavalcade, passed through the streets of Washington this morning from the railroad station to the White House, where simple religious services were held this afternoon before the body was taken to his old home in Hyde Park for burial tomorrow.

The procession was the only touch of military pomp to the funeral of the dead chieftain of the mightiest armed force on the face of the earth.

Hundreds of thousands of the people of Washington packed the sidewalks along Constitution and Pennsylvania Avenues, and watched the passing of the mournful troop.

At the corner of 12th Street and Constitution Avenue stood a well-dressed, confident-appearing man, a prosperous businessman, perhaps, with a boy in his mid-teens but tall for his years. He could look over the heads of most of those wedged in 10-deep ahead of him.

"I remember his smile, father," the boy was saying. "I mean I remember it from the pictures of him in the newsreels. It was such a wonderful smile. It crinkled his face up all around his eyes."

"Yes, he smiled a lot," the man said. "I used to say he smiled to think of the way he had fellows like me over a barrel. I hated him.

I hated him most of the 12 years he lived in this town. I mean I hated him politically. Now I wonder why. He only did the best he could. No man could do more."

Against a sky of crystal, flocks of silvery planes roared overhead at intervals, gleaming in the sunlight. But when the noise of their motors had died away the whole city seemed strangely quiet.

The shrill whistles of the traffic policemen, the clip-clop of feet hurrying over the pavements and the low hum of human voices were the only sounds and they carried far in the eerie silence.

It was as if by signal everyone had said, "Let us all be very quiet," and the whole community fell into restrained mood as it awaited the passing of the funeral party this morning.

Yet one knew that at this very moment, across two oceans, the American guns this man who lies dead had mobilized were bombing what was at once the thunder of his triumph and the vast volleys for those who died in the service of their country, as he had undoubtedly died.

"He wore funny hats, father," the boy said. "I remember the one he had on when he was in North Africa to see the soldiers, and he was riding in a jeep. He turned his hat up in the front and back. He wore funny hats when he went fishing, too."

"Yes, and I used to think his head was too big for them—for any hat," the man said. "I know now that was a foolish idea. Why should he have been swell headed—a great man like him? What crazy things I said about him!"

It was hot. Sweat ran down the faces of the steel-helmeted soldiers standing along the street in heavy flannel shirts. There were no parade troops. They wore crumbled-looking uniforms, they looked field stained.

A man, coatless and bareheaded, carrying a sleepy-looking child in his arms, held the youngster up so it could see over the heads of the crowd and softly said, "Look, look."

Some day that child may be telling its grandchildren that she saw the funeral of President Roosevelt as grandparents used to tell of seeing the funeral of President Lincoln.

Mothers leading children by the hands instructed them to wiggle in between the close-packed spectators to the front lines. No one complained about the children.

Everyone talked in a low voice. There was an impatient turning of heads as some people setting up empty boxes on which to stand chatted loudly for a moment, their voices disturbing the funeral hush.

Small boys perched in the trees along the avenue now green in the early spring.

Footloose soldiers and sailors including officers wandered through the crowd. Canadian service girls in their spic and span uniforms and long black stockings stepped smartly along the street.

Heads showed in clusters at every window in the low temporary war buildings and on the steps and in every jutting place on the solemn looking government buildings that would afford a foothold.

Tradesmen wearing aprons and artisans wearing overalls pressed against the police lines.

Now the trump of drums, at first faint and far-off, but quickly getting stronger, broke the silence and then came the wail of a funeral march played by a band, and an auto loaded with officers passed, then a squad of motorcycle policemen on their machines. The street signals on the avenue kept changing to "stop" and "go" all through the procession.

The people stood with their arms folded, those in back of the front row teetering on their tiptoes trying to get at least a fleeting glimpse of the procession.

The Marine band, the musicians in white caps and blue uniforms, their great silver horns flashing, footed it along to the slow strains of funeral music.

"They say he always had to wear a terrible steel brace like poor little Jackie Clark and like Cousin Nellie, too," the boy said. "They say he suffered greatly just as they do. Is that true, father? He must have been very brave."

"Yes," the man said, "he suffered greatly. I read once he fought all the better because he fought in chains. He was a game man. That I always said. A very game man. No man could be gamer."

Now came a battalion from Annapolis, the cadet officers with drawn swords, the cadets in blue uniforms with white caps and white leggings and guns slanted across their shoulders.

Then a battalion of field artillery, the soldiers sitting stiffly upright on their gun carriers which moved four abreast, the engines throttled down so that they made scarcely any noise.

Used-looking field pieces painted a dingy red were towed behind trucks loaded with their crews, and the faces of all these soldiers seemed absolutely expressionless under their helmets.

"I remember so many little things about him, father," said the boy. "I remember his nose-glasses. I often wondered how he kept them on his nose, even when he was out in a storm. He never seemed to mind what kind of weather it was."

"Yes," the man said, "I guess all the people will remember little things about him in the years to come. I once said that when it came to weather he didn't mind hell or high water if he had to put one of his ideas across. But it was a snide remark. I made too many snide remarks about him in his lifetime."

Another band, some colored artillerymen marching on foot, then a band of sailor musicians, their dolorous march music throbbing on the still air.

A battalion of bluejackets and then a battalion of women's armed force units, the Wacs and Waves and women Marines marching rather loosely in the absence of quickstep music.

Movie cameramen on trucks weaved along the line of march. The crowd watched in silence.

And now at last came the flag-swathed casket on an artillery caisson drawn by six strapping the big gray horses in a brightly polished harness, four of them mounted by soldiers.

The President's flags were borne just behind the caisson and then came the automobiles loaded with the great men of the nation. But with the passion of the casket, the crowd began breaking up, still strangely silent. They had seen the funeral cortege of a fellow citizen, who in other nations and other times would have had the death panoply of a Caesar but who, as it was, probably had more than he would have wished.

"I remember when he got his little dog Fala," the boy said. "I think they must have loved each other a good deal, father, as much as my Mugs and I love each other. You could tell it in the newsreels when they were together. I think he must have been a very kind man to be so nice to a little dog. I hope they take good care of Fala."

"Yes," the man said, "he was a kind man. He was kind to many people. I used to say I hated him when he was alive but now it is difficult for me to pick out one reason why. How could I hate a kind man?"

Babe Ruth: Game Called
GRANTLAND RICE—North American Newspaper Alliance—8/17/1948

Game called by darkness—let the curtain fall,
No more remembered thunder sweeps the field.
No more ancient echoes hear the call
To one who wore so well both the sword and shield.
The Big Guy's left us with the night to face,
And there is no one who can take his place.
Game called—and silence settles on the plain.
What is the crash of ash against the sphere?
Where is the mighty music, the refrain
That once brought joy to every waiting ear?
The Big Guy's left us, lonely in the dark,
Forever waiting for the flaming spark.
Game called—what more is there for one to say?
How dull and drab the field looks to the eye.
For one who rules it in a golden day
Has waved his cap to bid us all good-bye.
The Big Guy's gone—by land or sky or foam
May the Great Umpire call him "safe at home."

The greatest figure the world of sport has ever known has passed from the field. Game called on account of darkness. Babe Ruth is dead.

There have been mighty champions in their day and time from John L. Sullivan to Jack Dempsey—such stars as Bobby Jones, Ty Cobb, Walter Johnson, on and on, who walked along the pathway of fame.

But there has been only one Babe Ruth—one Bambino, who caught and held the love and admiration of countless millions around the world.

From the time he appeared on the big league scene with the Boston Red Sox in 1914, to the day his playing career ended more than 20 years later, Ruth was the greatest all-around ballplayer in the history of the game. He was a brilliant left-handed pitcher—the top power hitter of all time—a star defensive outfielder who could be rated with the best.

He was the one ballplayer who was a master of offense and defense—the nonpareil in both.

But Ruth was something more than a great ballplayer. He was an emblem, a symbol. No other athlete ever approached his color, not even the colorful Jack Dempsey, who had more than his share.

Babe Ruth's appeal to the kids of this nation was something beyond belief. He loved them and the kids knew it. There was nothing phony about his act. The kids knew the Babe was the greatest home run hitter of all time—that he was one of the greatest pitchers of all time—that he was an able place-hitter—that he could do more with a bat and a baseball than any player that ever lived. And the Babe could. But they also knew he was their pal.

I was present when he drove 60 miles one night before a world series game in Chicago to see a sick boy. "And if you write anything about it," he said, "I'll kick your brains out." He meant it that way.

Oddly enough, the Babe and Walter Johnson, the two stars on offense and defense, the mighty hitter and the whirlwind pitcher, died from the same cause—a tumor attached to the brain.

And once again, oddly enough, it was Babe Ruth who was Johnson's nemesis in the box and at the bat. He told me once that he had beaten Johnson six times by the scores of 1 to 0. And even the great Johnson was none too keen about facing him from the firing hill.

I've been a close friend of Babe Ruth since 1919, nearly 30 years ago when the Red Sox and Giants traveled north from spring training together.

The true story of Babe's life will never be written—the story of wrecked cars he left along the highway—the story of the night he came near dropping Miller Huggins off a train—the story of the $100,000 or more he lost in Cuba one racing winter. (The Babe told me it was $200,000.)

The story of the ribald, carefree Babe who ignored all traffic signals. I was riding home with Ruth one night after a game of golf. The Babe was late. He ignored red lights and everything else in a big car. I begged Babe to let me get out and take a taxi. The Babe only laughed.

"These cops are my pals," he said. "A funny thing happened yesterday. Maybe I'd had a shot or so too much. Anyways, my car stalled. A big cop came up and asked me what the matter was.

"'It won't run,' I said.

"'You're drunk,' the cop said.

"I hit him in the nose.

"'Now I know you're drunk, you so-and-so,' the cop said.

"He showed me out of the way and drove me home."

One day the Babe was going the wrong way on a road to some golf club.

"Hey, this is a one-way street," some traffic cop hollered.

"I'm only driving one way, you dumb—," the Babe said.

The cop, enraged, came rushing up, "Oh, hello Babe," he said. "I didn't know it was you. Drive any way you want to."

I sat one day with Babe at St. Albans, his golf club. The Babe took out a .22

rifle, and he and a pal began shooting away the door knob at $1 a shot. The Babe missed some guy who had just opened the door by two inches. "He should have knocked," the Babe said.

Just one day with Babe was a big adventure. There was the time he planted a small explosive bomb in some pal's car and almost blew up the place, including the Babe and myself. "I didn't know it was that strong," was all he said.

He was rough, rowdy, swaggering figure, more profane than anyone I ever hope to meet again, with a strong sense of decency and justice and fair play. He was a sportsman, if I ever saw one. He wanted no advantage at any start.

There was the day Miller Huggins was going to fine Ruth $5,000. He had been absent two days. The fine was to be plastered after the game. All baseball writers were notified. The Babe appeared before the game, red-eyed and dazed-looking. He was in terrible shape. He hit two home runs and a triple. Huggins forgot the fine.

These are among the true stories of Babe Ruth, who had no regard for the conventions of the common or normal man, whether this included actions or words. But, beyond all this, he was open-hearted, friendly, always cheerful, a great guy to be with.

I can still hear the roar of voices wherever he was. There was nothing quiet and sedate about the Babe.

He could recall few names. "I caught back of him for 10 years," Mickey Cochrane once told me. "But he never knew my name. It was 'Hello, kid.'"

Driving around, Babe always responded to those who called out, "Hey, Babe." His reply was "Hello, Mom," or "Hello, Pop."

"They can't forget my funny-looking pan," he said once. They won't forget his funny-looking pan soon. His records were terrific, but they meant little when compared to the man who was so far above all the records he ever set. I've never seen him turn a mean trick.

No game will ever see his like, his equal again. He was one in many, many lifetimes. One all alone.

The Earnest Hemingway I Knew
JIMMY CANNON—*New York Post*—7/3/1961

Death assumed many shapes in the novels of Ernest Hemingway. It was the foul breath of a hyena, or a heavy emptiness squatting on the chest, or a puff of wind blowing across a summer's day, or a leopard lying frozen in the snows of a high mountain. But death, as I think of my friend and the foe that obsessed him, becomes a sniper in the tree.

It always kept him within range. The sniper made all the trips he took and accompanied him on every voyage. The tree was there where no trees grew.

Concealed and still, the assassin waited with a hunter's patience which Hemingway respected. Death was the enemy and he hated it, but he admired it for its hunter's skill.

It never intimidated him, nor did he honor it by glancing over his shoulder at it, as the rest of us do. He knew the unseen rifleman would find him no matter where he hid, and he followed no strange roads to avoid it. It didn't matter how often it missed. There would always be a final bullet in the chamber. The trick was to make it waste ammo.

The sniper used Hemingway's own gun yesterday. That wouldn't surprise Ernest, because he understood death better than any writer of this time. It was sneaky, but it was always there. One way or another, death gets the job done.

Dying with grace was important to Hemingway. He humiliated death, and the sharpshooter often had him in the sights, but the aim wasn't good. It was a bad match and Hemingway, more than most, understood he had to lose. But he made it tough with a glorious obstinacy, and he taunted death as a matador might tell his contempt to a bull with a calculated recklessness.

The losers become majestic in Hemingway's work, because they accept their violent deaths with pride and dignity. He was haunted by the sniper, but he never ran from it but seemed to enjoy being as close to it as he could get.

I remember a night in Paris 1945 when a message was given to me by the telephone operator in the office of the *Stars and Stripes*. The scrawl advised me to contact Hemingway at the Ritz. I called him, and he said he wanted to see me.

"Come alone," Ernest said, brusquely.

There was no electricity and no heat in the Ritz. In bed, with newspapers spread around the candlelit room, Hemingway lay bulkily under the blankets in his correspondent's uniform. He was bleary and his voice was a sort of groaning when he talked. His breath rasped, and his forehead glinted with the jewelry of sweat.

"Got — — cold," he said in that curious shorthand he often used, which was spoken cablese.

"You ought to be in a hospital," I said.

"I'm all right," he replied. "But they took my kid."

His son, "Bumbly," a second lieutenant of the OSS, had been captured as he guided a German spy back to the enemy lines.

"He was hit," he said. "They threw grenades. That's all I know."

I sat with him that night as the wind bent the flame of the candle. He seemed to be strangling on phlegm and spat frequently on the carpet that the newspapers made.

Not once again did he mention his boy, but he was sick with more than the pneumonia he had. Grief was a private matter, and he never allowed me to console him. He changed the subject when I tried.

The sniper was there with us in the darkness of that room, quiet in the unseen tree. Toward morning Ernest, who had been drinking from a bottle of cognac on the floor near the bed, spoke of it.

"I'm going to be killed," he said.

"You will," I said, "if you don't go to a hospital."

"In combat," he said. "I know it."

Coming across France, because he knew the country, Hemingway had an outfit of his own. They were irregular soldiers of the Maquis, and he had used them for purposes of reconnaissance. This caused other correspondents to complain, and the army was investigating if Hemingway had violated the rules of the Geneva Convention, which prohibit journalists from bearing arms.

"They are trying to ruin me," he said. "But I want you to promise that you'll tell how it was. I want someone I trust to do it. I won't live to defend myself."

I left him when he drifted off into sleep. I called him the next day before I went back to cover the Third Army, and he mumbled sleepily that the cold was breaking up.

Couple of afternoons later I was at the command post of Buck Lanham, who would be the colonel in *Across the River*, when Hemingway pulled up in a jeep. He had a bottle of cognac in each pocket of his field jacket, and he shuddered with the fire of his fever and the sudden chills.

"My doctors cured me," he said.

The brandy got him though, and he made assaults with the regiment and stayed with it until the Battle of the Bulge was over.

The sniper must have been disappointed, because Hemingway wasn't young anymore then and the only physician he used to fight off pneumonia was brandy. But he wore the patch of the Fourth Infantry Division on his field jacket and considered himself a soldier of the division.

The troops had an affection for him that didn't depend on his fame. He went with them on the attacks and never asked for privileges that his age or his position were entitled to. He was, I believe, the greatest American writer.

There Was Only One Casey

WELLS TWOMBLY—*San Francisco Examiner*—9/30/1975

On casual inspection, the old man looked like a woodcarver's first attempt at a gargoyle. The face was crude and drooping, even when it was new. The eyes were watery and mournful, like a human basset hound. The ears were large and foolish. The hands were hopelessly gnarled. The legs looked like two Christmas stockings stuffed with oranges.

Luckily, greatness doesn't necessarily come in attractive wrappings. Up close, the old man was genuinely beautiful, not exactly in the category of Robert Redford, but beautiful just the same. It was the beauty of a rare antique, tenderly rendered and gracefully aged. It was the beauty of a three-hundred-year-old handcrafted pipe, rubbed by a thousand hands and redolent of a thousand aromatic tobaccos. This was a precious original and, of millions of words that will be written about Charles Dillon Stengel in the next few days, none of them will quite do him justice.

He was one of a handful of baseball characters whose reputations did not exceed their true personalities. The fact is that Yogi Berra was never anything but a quiet, humorless, somewhat grumpy New Jersey businessman, whose humor was largely created by Joe Garagiola anyway. Bo Belinsky was just another charming scoundrel who like girls, which made him about as kooky as five-sixths of America's male population. Dizzy Dean was a big depression-era red-neck who loved beer. As a young man he was bumptious. As a senior citizen, he was a bore.

But the Casey Stengel of real life was better than the Casey Stengel of the printed page. The problem was a mechanical one, which was never solved. He could not be properly transmitted. However, the best literary men of his time worked on it. Oh, how they worked. Still, it never came out quite right, especially the rambling, shattered syntax of his speech, which was a flagrant put-on. Only a very few people understood what Stengel was doing. He led them through a merry maze built entirely of semantic disgraces. He did it on purpose.

Early one morning when he was between jobs, he sat in the tower at Wrigley Field in Los Angeles trying to make Gene Autry a pauper by sucking up so much booze that the singing cowboy would have to get his guitar and make a come-back. The more he tucked away, the more lucid he became. A twenty-five-year-old baseball writer who covered the Los Angeles Angels and delivered a column nobody read out in the San Fernando Valley was utterly amazed. "That jargon of yours is just a joke," he gasped.

"Son," said Casey in that gravel-driveway voice of his. "This is gonna be our little secret, isn't it?"

The man was a clever and articulate comic who spoke two languages. When he was unguarded he would talk in this straightforward, highly lucid English, which nobody paid any attention to. When there were reporters and other assorted individuals present he spoke in tongues. It was a tangled rat's nest of verbiage that bore only a scant resemblance to the Mother Tongue so heartily endorsed by the queen of England. Even the mightiest of journalists cowed when he turned on the juice.

When he was managing the wretched New York Mets of the early 1960s he attempted to describe what the fans were like. It was a fine, feathered piece of literature. "These fans are very rabid like they were very collegiate or something because it takes four hours for us to leave our dressing room after a game, which is good because the concession people sell a lot of hot dogs, which is good for our business and I like that. I expect that very soon they will carry one of my players out on their shoulders like he just caught a touchdown for Yale. They are very patient and that's good. These fellows of ours are going to keep right on improving because they are better than most folks think and not as bad as they used to be, because it would be hard to be as bad as that."

There were people who thought Charles Dillon Stengel was a bad manager, just because he had wretched teams in Boston, Brooklyn, and New York. They said that Harpo Marx could have won ten pennants in 12 years with the Yankee clubs that Casey had. That was a mistake. Oh, occasionally he would fall asleep on the bench during night games when he was fronting for the Mets, but that was strictly an epilogue to his years with the Yankees. Even that most cynical of athletes-turned-author, Jim Bouton, said that Stengel knew exactly what he was doing when he had Mickey Mantle and Whitey Ford working for him.

There was this pitcher named Hal Stowe who thought that all he had to do to make the major-league roster was to act like he belonged. He did none of the things other rookies were asked to do. He drank and went to dinner with Mantle and Ford. He did not run in the outfield and he made no overt attempt to impress Stengel. There was one place open on the roster, but Stowe failed to qualify.

"It's true that Hal Stowe pitched pretty good this spring," said Stengel in straight language. "But I noticed that he never ran in the outfield, that he never did all the things he was supposed to do. He never really hustled and he never really worked at it. That's why he didn't make the squad cut, he could bull-bleep everybody but the manager."

Just two years later, Stowe used the same act and managed to a put a move on Ralph Houk, the hand-clapping, cigar-chewing militarist who replaced Stengel. The pitcher went north and opened the season with the Yankees because Houk thought he looked and acted like a big leaguer and that was very, very important. Stengel was no so easily confused. When he worked for the Mets the club came up with a nineteen-year-old first baseman named Greg Goossen, whom everybody gurgled about.

"In ten years, Greg Goossen has a great chance of being twenty-nine years old," he said. It wasn't cruel. It was accurate. Sure enough, just ten years later, Goossen did turn twenty-nine, but not with any major-league baseball club.

One afternoon before a World Series game, Stengel took a young Mickey Mantle out to right field at the old ball park in Brooklyn and started to explain how to play caroms off the concave wall. Mantle wanted to know how his manager knew so much about it.

"I used to play right field for the Dodgers!" growled Stengel. "Do you think I was born old?"

So there will be a World Series this year and Casey Stengel will not be present. He was always good for a story. One afternoon it was raining in Baltimore and there he stood with a foot on the rail. "Pardon me, Casey," said a columnist, "it's lousy outside and I need help." He went on for an hour.

Standing nearby was a slim, quivering journalist from a small-town paper. When he was through rescuing the veteran, he turned to the rookie, gave him about 15 minutes and ended up with: "Listen, I got a secret, exclusive story I don't want to give to nobody else. I got to bed late and get up early. You gotta meet me at 6 a.m., but bring some Scotch and we'll break things together."

The man was beautiful. If he's dead, it's only a rumor. Don't bother to print it.

Daley Embodied Chicago
Mike Royko—*Chicago Sun-Times*—12/21/1976

If a man ever reflected a city, it was Richard J. Daley of Chicago.

In some ways, he was this town at its best—strong, hard-driving, working feverishly, pushing, building, driven by ambitions so big they seemed Texas-boastful.

In other ways, he was this city at its worst—arrogant, crude, conniving, ruthless, suspicious, intolerant.

He wasn't graceful, suave, witty, or smooth. But, then, this is not Paris or San Francisco.

He was raucous, sentimental, hot-tempered, practical, simple, devious, big, and powerful. This is, after all, Chicago.

Sometimes the very same Daley performance would be seen as both outrageous and heroic. It depended on whom you asked for an opinion.

For example, when he stood on the Democratic National Convention floor in 1968 and mouthed furious crudities at smooth Abe Ribicoff, tens of millions of TV viewers were shocked.

But it didn't offend most Chicagoans. That's part of the Chicago style—belly to belly, scowl to scowl, and may the toughest or loudest man win.

Daley was not an articulate man, most English teachers would agree. People from other parts of the country sometimes marveled that a politician who fractured the language so thoroughly could be taken so seriously.

Well, Chicago is not an articulate town, Saul Bellow notwithstanding. Maybe it's because so many of us aren't that far removed from parents and grandparents who knew only bits and pieces of the language.

So when Daley slid sideways into a sentence, or didn't exit from the same paragraph he entered, it amused us. But it didn't sound that different from the way most of us talk.

Besides, he got his point across, one way or another, and usually in Chicago style. When he thought critics should mind their own business about the way he handed out insurance business to his sons, he tried to think of a way to say that they should kiss his bottom. He found a way. He said it. We understood it. What more can one ask of the language?

Daley was a product of the neighborhoods and he reflected it in many good ways—loyalty to the family, neighbors, old buddies, the corner grocer. You do something for someone, they do something for you. If somebody is sick, you offer the family help. If someone dies, you go to the wake and try to lend comfort. The young don't lip off to the old, and everybody cuts his grass, and takes care of his property. And don't play your TV too loud.

That's the way he liked to live, and that's what he thought most people wanted, and he was right.

But there are other sides to Chicago neighborhoods—suspicion of outsiders, intolerance toward the unconventional, bigotry and bullying.

That was Daley, too. As he proved over and over again, he didn't trust outsiders, whether they were long-hairs against war, black preachers against segregation, reformers against the Machine, or community groups against his policies. This was his neighborhood-ward-city-county, and nobody could come in and make noise. He'd call the cops. Which he did.

There are those who believed Daley could have risen beyond politics to statesmanship had he embraced the idealistic causes of the 1960s rather than obstructing them. Had he used his unique power to lead us toward brotherhood and understanding, they say, he could have achieved greatness.

Sure he would have. But to have expected that response from Daley was as realistic as asking Cragin, Bridgeport, Marquette Park, or any other white Chicago neighborhood to celebrate Brotherhood Week by having black gang leader Jeff Fort to dinner. If Daley was reactionary and stubborn, he was in perfect harmony with his town.

Daley was a pious man—faithful to his church, a believer in the Fourth of July, apple pie, motherhood, baseball, the Boy Scouts, the flag, and sitting down to dinner with the family, and deeply offended by public displays of immorality.

And, for all the swinging new lifestyles, that is still basically Chicago. Maybe New York will let porn and massage houses spread like fast-food franchises, and maybe San Francisco will welcome gay cops. But Chicago is still a square town. So City Hall made sure our carnal vices were kept to a public minimum. If old laws didn't work, they got new laws that did.

On the other hand, there were financial vices.

And if somebody in City Hall saw a chance to make a fast bundle or two, Daley wasn't given to preaching. His advice amounted to: Don't get caught.

But that's Chicago, too. The question has never been how you made it, but if you made it. The town was built by great men who demanded the drunkards and harlots be arrested, while charging them rent until the cops arrived.

If Daley sometimes abused his power, it didn't offend most Chicagoans. The people who came here in Daley's lifetime were accustomed to someone wielding power like a club, be it a czar, emperor, king, or rural sheriff. The niceties of the democratic process weren't part of the immigrant experience. So if the Machine muscle offended some, it seemed like old times to many more.

Eventually Daley made the remarkable transition from political boss to father figure.

Maybe he couldn't have been a father figure in Berkeley, California; Princeton, New Jersey; or even Skokie, Illinois. But in Chicago there was nothing unusual about a father who worked long hours, meant shut up when he said shut up, and backed it up with a jolt to the head. Daley was as believable a father figure as anyone's old man.

Now he's gone and people are writing that the era of Richard J. Daley is over. Just like that.

But it's not. Daley has left a legacy that is pure Chicago.

I'm not talking about his obvious legacy of expressways, high-rises, and other public works projects that size-conscious Chicagoans enjoy.

Daley, like this town, relished a political brawl. When arms were waving and tempers boiling and voices cracking, he'd sit in the middle of it all and look as happy as a kid at a birthday party.

Well, he's left behind the ingredients for the best political donnybrook we've had in fifty years.

They'll be kicking and gouging, grabbing and tripping, elbowing and kneeing to grab all, or a thin sliver of the power he left behind.

It will be a classic Chicago debate.

He knew it would turn out that way, and the thought probably delighted him.

I hope that wherever he is, he'll have a good seat for the entire show. And when they are tangled in political half-nelsons, toeholds, and headlocks, I wouldn't be surprised if we hear a faint but familiar giggle drifting down from somewhere.

John Wayne's True Grit
MIKE ROYKO—*Chicago Sun-Times*—6/13/1979

During the late 1960s, I had a serious falling out with a liberal friend. He was against the Vietnam War, and so was I. He didn't like Richard Nixon or George Wallace or J. Edgar Hoover, and I didn't either.

But I was a John Wayne fan and he couldn't understand that. John Wayne, he argued, stood for everything that was wrong. He glorified war, violence, justice by the gun, male chauvinism, simple-minded solutions, and even racism in the casual way he shot down Indians. So how could I like a man who represented all of that?

My answer drove him up the wall and almost ended our friendship. "You're right," I told him. "But I still like John Wayne. His movies make me feel good."

That was about it. I can't remember *not* being a John Wayne fan. Other movie cowboys were more popular than Wayne when I was a kid. But there was something unreal about them. Roy Rogers, for example, never shot anyone, except in the wrist, and seemed to be in love with his horse, Trigger. Gene Autry never shot anyone, except in the wrist, and he played guitar and sang in an adenoidal voice.

Then John Wayne came along, and he shot people in the heart, and drank whisky, and treated his horse like a horse. In fact, he treated women like he treated his horse. He seemed real because he reminded me of the men in my neighborhood.

I never went to a John Wayne movie to find a philosophy to live by or to absorb a profound message. I went for the simple pleasure of spending a couple of hours seeing the bad guys lose.

And I still refuse to go to movies that have unhappy endings, or movies in which the villain wins, or movies in which the hero whines, or movies in which the hero isn't a hero, but a helpless wimp. If I want to become depressed, why should I spent three dollars at the movies. I can go to work, instead.

That's why the Duke's fans went to his movies. We knew he would not become bogged down in red tape, or fret about losing his pension rights, or cringe when his boss looked at him, or break into a cold sweat and hide in his room, or moan about his impotence, or figure the odds and take the safe way out.

He would do exactly what he did in *True Grit,* my choice as his greatest movie, when he rode out to bring in Dirty Ned Pepper, whom he had once shot in the lip.

As all John Wayne freaks recall, he was alone, as a hero should be, and he was sitting on his horse confronting Ned Pepper across a long, lovely valley. Ned Pepper was accompanied by several villainous friends.

Wayne informed Dirty Ned he was bringing him in—dead if need be.

And Dirty Ned sneered and said something like: "That's mighty bold talk for a one-eyed old fat man."

Who can ever forget the look of thunderous rage that enveloped John Wayne's face. True, he was fat. True, he was old. True, he had only one eye. But did Dirty Ned have to be so rude as to mention it?

Ah, it was a wonderful moment. And it got better when Wayne, in a voice choking with anger, snarled: "Fill yer hand, you sonofabitch!"

And it got even better when he snuck the reins between his teeth, drew a pistol with one hand, a repeating rifle with the other, and galloped full speed into the valley, steering his horse with his teeth and blazing away with both weapons.

At the time, a movie critic—a man in his thirties—wrote that he was so overwhelmed by the scene that he abandoned his critical poise and stood on his seat in the theater, waving his arms and screaming: "Go, John, go!"

I didn't get quite that carried away, being of a more mature age. I simply stomped my feet and put my fingers between my teeth and whistled as loud as I could.

Foolishness? Maybe. But I hope we never become so cool, so laid back, so programmed, that nobody has that kind of foolish, odds-defying, damn-the-risk spirit.

After all, what makes some firemen drop the hose and run into a burning building to carry somebody down an icy ladder? It's not the pension, or the thirty days of vacation, or the civil service guarantees. What makes one man drop his briefcase, kick off his shoes, and dive off the Michigan Avenue bridge into the Chicago River to try to rescue a prospective suicide, while everyone else just watches? What makes an occasional politician enrage his constituents and risk defeat by damning the consequences and taking a position that is right, but unpopular? What make some lawyers take on lost causes for no fee, and pound away for frustrating years until they get an ounce of justice?

I don't know the answer, but I'll bet that down deep, they're all John Wayne fans, and would have put the reins between their teeth, too.

Now that he's gone, I don't know what we'll do. I just can't see somebody like Johnny Travolta confronting Ned Pepper.

He'd probably ask him to dance.

She Said Goodby with Charm
JIMMY BRESLIN—*New York Daily News*—6/11/1981

Jimmy Breslin's wife, the former Rosemary Dattolico, was buried yesterday. She died Tuesday morning after a long illness. Breslin wrote the following eulogy and read it at the funeral services at Our Lady of Mercy Catholic Church in Forest Hills, Queens. We wanted to share it with our readers.

About a year ago, when she was unwell to the point where even she became unsure, she offered during prayer to her God a suggestion that she thought was quite good.

Her youngest had experienced difficulty through the start of his schooling. Then suddenly, he had expressed great interest in attending one school.

His mother developed great faith in the situation.

And so, she proposed, give me this year while my son goes to this school. Let me try to help him as best I can. Then that should do it. He will be on his way.

And I will be perfectly happy to be on my way.

Providing the school works out.

The year went by and the youngest attended school and she lived despite the gloomy signs given by her body. For a period, she simply willed herself to improve. The mind over a blood count.

And her youngest suddenly grew. A plant nourished.

Whatever she asked for, she appeared to be receiving.

And now, the other day, from the depths of a hospital bed, with her body in revolt, she looked up and said, "The report card was pretty good. But now I don't feel like keeping my part of the deal."

Which was her notion of fairness. For all her life, she believed that true even-handedness meant that those in need always were allowed more.

And now, at the end, she desired to follow her own counsel.

So as she left us, she did so with that most elusive of qualities, a little bit of charm.

We of her family who remain have a special burden. We have lived with nobility.

She was a person who regarded life as one long attempt to provide a happy moment or so for another person.

Always, she was outraged by those who rushed about, shouldering past others, their sides lathered with effort, horses in some cheap race, as they pawed for material success.

She knew that life belonged to those who seek out the weary, sit with the defeated, understand the clumsy.

And do this not as some duty. But do it with the cheerful realization that we are a part of it all.

She thought the word "duty" meant that each day there should be a word or gesture that would cause someone else to smile over the life about them. Her contempt was reserved for those who would not attempt this. Who are you, she would rail, to go through a day, knowing that another day is to follow, and another after that, and knowing that it is all ceaseless, and still you refuse to join with us and help soften the path of those about you?

She was a woman utterly unspoiled. I thank God for the high privilege of having known her so well.

She ran my life and those of her children almost totally. She leaves us with a tradition of decency that we must attempt to carry on. Her strength was such that even if those of us here today stumble now and then, I think the Rosemary Dattolico line of decency will reveal itself time after time in whatever generations there are to come.

As was said of another aristocrat such as this one:

Earth, receive an honored guest.

King of Cool
MICHAEL KELLY—*Washington Post*—5/20/1998

Do not blame it on the bossa nova. Nor on rock-and-roll nor soul nor jazz nor rhythm and blues. It wasn't Elvis or the Beatles or the Rolling Stones. It wasn't Washington or Hollywood or the Upper West Side. It wasn't Ted Kennedy and it wasn't Richard Nixon. It wasn't the Years of Rage or the Me Decade or the Decade of Greed. It wasn't the Commies or the Beats, or the hippies or the yippies, or the Panthers or the druggies, or the yuppies or the buppies, or the NIMBYs or the DINKs, or even the ACLU.

No, if you want to finger any one person, place or thing for what went wrong with America, you need look no further than that accidental one man validation of the great-man theory of history, Francis Albert Sinatra, 1915–1998. Yes— The Voice, the Chairman of the Board, Old Blue Eyes, the leader of the (rat) pack, the swinger in chief—he's the culprit. It's all Frankie's fault.

American popular culture—which is more and more the only culture America has, which is more and more the only culture everyone else in the world has (we live, as the gormless Al Gore keeps chirpily and horrifyingly reminding us, in a global village)—may be divided into two absolutely distinct ages: Before Frank and After Frank.

Sinatra, as every obit observed, was the first true modern pop idol, inspiring in the 1940s the sort of mass adulation that was to become a familiar phenomenon in the '50s and '60s. One man, strolling onto the set at precisely the right moment in the youth of the Entertainment Age, made himself the prototype of the age's essential figure: the iconic celebrity. The iconic celebrity is the result of the central confusion of the age, which is that people possessed of creative or artistic gifts are somehow teachers—role models—in matters of personal conduct. The iconic celebrity is idolized—and obsessively studied and massively imitated—not merely for the creation of art but for the creation of public self, for the confection of affect and biography that the artist projects onto the national screen.

And what Frank Sinatra projected was: cool. And here is where the damage was done. Frank invented cool, and everyone followed Frank, and everything has been going to hell ever since.

In America, B.F., there was no cool. There was smart (as in the smart set), and urbane, and sophisticated, and fast and hip; but these things were not the same as cool. The pre-Frank hip guy, the model of aesthetic and moral superiority to which men aspired, is the American male of the 1930s and 1940s. He is Humphrey Bogart in *The Big Sleep* or *Casablanca* or Archie Goodwin in Rex Stout's Nero Wolfe novels. He possesses an outward cynicism, but this is understood to be merely clothing; at his core, he is a square. He fights a lot, generally on the side of the underdog. He is willing to die for his beliefs, and his beliefs are, although he takes pains to hide it, old-fashioned. He believes in truth, justice, the American way, and love. He is on the side of the law, except when the law is crooked. He is not taken in by jingoism but he is himself a patriot; when there is a war, he goes to it. He is, after his fashion, a gentleman and, in a quite modern manner, a sexual egalitarian. He is forthright, contemptuous of dishonesty in all its forms, from posing to lying. He confronts his enemies openly and fairly, even if he might lose. He is honorable and virtuous, although he is properly suspicious of men who talk about honor and virtue. He may be world-weary, but he is not ironic.

The new cool man that Sinatra defined was a very different creature. Cool said the old values were for suckers. Cool was looking out for number one always. Cool didn't get mad; it got even. Cool didn't go to war: Saps went to war and, anyway, cool had no beliefs it was willing to die for. Cool never, ever, got in a fight it might lose; cool had friends who could take care of that sort of thing. Cool was a cad and boastful about it; in cool's philosophy, the lady was always a tramp, and to be treated accordingly. Cool was not on the side of the law; cool made its own laws. Cool was not knowing but still essentially idealistic; cool was nihilistic. Cool was not virtuous; it reveled in vice. Before cool, being good was still hip; after cool, only being bad was.

Quite a legacy. On the other hand, he sure could sing.

Reagan: An Optimist's Legacy
GEORGE F. WILL—*Washington Post*—6/6/2004

One measure of a leader's greatness is this: By the time he dies the dangers that summoned him to greatness have been so thoroughly defeated, in no small measure by what he did, it is difficult to recall the magnitude of those dangers or of his achievements. So if you seek Ronald Reagan's monument, look around and consider what you do *not* see.

The Iron Curtain that scarred a continent is gone, as is the Evil Empire responsible for it. The feeling of foreboding—the sense of shrunken possibilities—that afflicted Americans 20 years ago has been banished by a new birth of the American belief in perpetually expanding horizons.

In the uninterrupted flatness of the Midwest, where Reagan matured, the horizon beckons to those who would be travelers. He traveled far, had a grand time all the way, and his cheerfulness was contagious. It was said of Dwight Eisenhower—another much-loved son of the prairie—that his smile was his philosophy. That was true of Reagan, in this sense: He understood that when Americans have a happy stance toward life, confidence flows and good things happen. They raise families, crops, living standards and cultural values; they settle the land, make deserts bloom, destroy tyrannies.

Reagan was the last president for whom the Depression—the years when America stopped working—was a formative experience. Remarkably, the 1930s formed in him a talent for happiness. It was urgently needed in the 1980s, when the pessimism of the intelligentsia was infecting people with the idea that America had passed its apogee and was ungovernable.

It also was said then that the presidency destroyed its occupants. But Reagan arrived at the office, looked around and said, "This is fun. Let's saddle up and go for a ride." Which he did, sometimes in the middle of the afternoon. Scolds, who thought presidents were only serious when miserable, were scandalized.

In an amazingly fecund 27-month period, Margaret Thatcher, Pope John Paul II and Reagan came to office. The pope and the president had been actors. Reagan said he wondered how presidents who have *not* been actors could function. Certainly the last century's greatest democratic leaders—Churchill, FDR—mastered the theatrical dimension of politics.

Good actors, including political actors, do not deal in unrealities. Rather, they create realities that matter—perceptions, aspirations, allegiances. Reagan in his presidential role made vivid the values, particularly hopefulness and friendliness, that give cohesion and dynamism to this continental nation.

A democratic leader's voice should linger in his nation's memory, an echo of his exhortations. Reagan's mellifluous rhetoric lingers like a melody that evokes fond memories. Because of demagogues, rhetoric has a tainted reputation in our time. However, Reagan understood that rhetoric is central to democratic governance. It can fuse passion and persuasion, moving free people to freely choose what is noble.

He understood the axiom that people, especially Americans, with their Founders' creed and vast reservoirs of decency, more often need to be reminded than informed. And he understood the economy of leadership—the need to husband the perishable claim a leader has on the attention of this big, boisterous country.

To some, Reagan seemed the least complicated of men—an open book that the country had completely read. However, he had the cunning to know the advantage of being underestimated. He was more inward than he seemed. And much tougher. The stricken fields of American and world politics are littered with those who did not anticipate the steel behind his smile.

The oldest person ever elected president had a sure sense of modernity, as when he told students at Moscow University that mankind is emerging from the economy of muscle and entering the economy of mind. "The key," he said, "is freedom," but freedom grounded in institutions such as courts and political parties. Otherwise, "freedom will always be looking over its shoulder. A bird on a tether, no matter how long the rope, can always be pulled back."

Reagan was a friendly man with one close friend. He married her. He had one other great love, for the American people, a love intense, public and reciprocated.

Presidents usually enter the White House as shiny and freshly minted dimes and leave tarnished. Reagan left on the crest of a wave of affection that intensified in response to the gallantry with which he met illness in his final years.

Today, Americans gratefully recall that at a turbulent moment in their national epic, Reagan became the great reassurer, the steadying captain of our clipper ship. He calmed the passengers—and the sea.

A Mother's Love, Clarified
GEORGE F. WILL—*Washington Post*—7/13/2006

NEWPORT BEACH, CALIF.—The long dying of Louise Will ended here recently. It was time. At 98, her body was exhausted by disease and strokes. Dementia, that stealthy thief of identity, had bleached her vibrant self almost to indistinctness, like a photograph long exposed to sunlight.

It is said that God gave us memory so we could have roses in winter. Dementia is an ever-deepening advance of wintery whiteness, a protracted paring away of personality. It inflicts on victims the terror of attenuated personhood, challenging philosophic and theological attempts to make death a clean, intelligible and bearable demarcation.

Is death the soul taking flight after the body has failed? That sequence—the physical extinguished, the spiritual not—serves our notion of human dignity. However, mental disintegration mocks that comforting schemata by taking the spirit first.

In the very elderly the mind can come and go, a wanderer in time, and a disintegrating personality can acquire angers and jagged edges that are, perhaps, protests against a growing lightness of being. No one has come back from deep in that foreign country to report on life there. However, it must be unbearably frightening to feel one's self become light as a feather, with inner gales rising.

Dementia slowly loosens the sufferer's grip on those unique tokens of humanity, words. An early sign is a forgetfulness that results in repetitiveness, and fixation on the distant past.

For a while, one of Louise's insistently recurring memories was of spring 1918, a war year, and eastbound troop trains passing through Greenville, Pa. When the trains stopped, residents offered candy and magazines to the soldiers—but not to black units. That infuriated Louise's father, whose fury was a fine memory for Louise to have among those of a father who died at age 44.

To the end, even when virtually without speech, Louise could recognize her children, could enjoy music and being read from love letters written 75 years ago by Fred, her future husband. She could even laugh, in spite of the tormenting chasm between her remaining cognition and the prison of her vanished ability to articulate.

In 1951, in Champaign, Ill., for her 10-year-old son, she made a mother's sacrifice: She became a White Sox fan so she could converse with the argumentative Cubs fan who each evening dried the dishes as she washed. Even after much of her stock of memories had been depleted, she dimly knew that the name Nellie Fox (a second baseman) once meant something playful.

The aging that conquered Louise was, like war, a mighty scourge, and, like war, elicited nobility from those near its vortex. The nearest was Fred Will, who died eight years ago, at the end of his ninth decade.

A few years before his death, Fred, a reticent romantic, whose reticence may have been an effect of his tinge of melancholy, shared with his children some poetry he had written for Louise, including this from 1933:

> The warm sun
> beams through the clear air
> Upon glistening leaves.
>
> And the birds
> sweep in long arcs
> Over the green grass.
>
> They seem to say,
> "This might last forever!"
> But it doesn't.

But it lasted more than six decades, which is forever, as foreverness is allotted to us.

A retired professor of philosophy, Fred probably knew what Montaigne, quoting Cicero, meant when he said that to study philosophy is to prepare to die. Fred was, strictly speaking, philosophic about his wife's affliction. A common connotation of "philosophic" is placid acceptance of what can be comprehended but not altered. However, Fred's philosophic response to the theft of his wife by aging was much richer than mere stoicism grounded in fatalism. It was a heroic act of will, arising from clearsightedness about the long trajectory of Louise's life.

He understood this stern paradox: Families seared by a loved one's dementia face the challenge of forgetting. They must choose to achieve what dementia inflicts on its victims—short-term memory loss. They must restore to the foreground of remembrance the older memories of vivacity and wit.

"All that we can know about those we have loved and lost," Thornton Wilder wrote, "is that they would wish us to remember them with a more intensified realization of their reality. What is essential does not die but clarifies. The highest tribute to the dead is not grief but gratitude." Louise, released from the toils of old age and modern medicine, is restored to clarity.

X: The Pursuit
of Happiness

The column is the only place in the newspaper set aside for a nondenominational bit of wisdom, a moment of reflection to help make sense of the world. That's where "the pursuit of happiness" comes in.

America is unique in that our founders thought to add an idea so human to our Declaration of Independence. It is an open-ended invitation for people to live their lives to the best of their ability. Columns can be the secular sermons that help us remember what really matters in life, so these columns function as a coda—the pursuit of happiness is rarely a beat unto itself.

They begin with the aphorisms of "Poor Richard," penned by Benjamin Franklin before our nation's founding. Plucked out of the eighteenth-century English, many phrases are instantly recognizable, such as "Early to bed, early to rise, makes a man healthy, wealthy and wise." Such sayings form the basis of American folk wisdom, but they also aimed for a more practical outcome, aiding individuals in the accumulation of wealth through a productive and virtuous life. The classic "Yes, Virginia—There is a Santa Claus" is a defense of innocence against cynicism that is still reprinted in newspapers across the nation each Christmas.

Not all columnist advice is high-minded—Damon Runyon frankly tells young people to "get the money," while Murray Kempton seeks out Louis Armstrong's philosophy: "there's kicks everywhere." The imperfect joys of parenting are captured by Anna Quindlen in "The Days of Gilded Rigatoni" and Majorie Williams's last column, "The Halloween of My Dreams," will make you hug your kids a little closer.

Some of these columns are so beloved that they spawned cottage industries. Mary Schmich's graduation-exercise aphorisms went viral online, were misattributed to Kurt Vonnegut, and even turned into a song. Steve Lopez's series of columns about a homeless violinist he befriended in Los Angeles, "A Man in Three Suites," was turned into a movie, *The Soloist*. These columns remind us that the pursuit of happiness is an opportunity, not an entitlement. Everyone has to find their own path, guided by the hard-won wisdom of others.

Advice from *Poor Richard's Almanack*
BENJAMIN FRANKLIN—1757

A good example is the best sermon.

A house without woman and firelight, is like a body without soul or sprite.

A long life may not be good enough, but a good life is long enough.

A mob's a monster; heads enough, but no brains.

Anger is never without a reason, but seldom with a good one.

An old young man will be a young old man.

A quiet conscience sleeps in thunder.

A spoonful of honey will catch more flies than a gallon of vinegar.

Be always ashamed to catch thyself idle.

Beware of little expenses, a small leak will sink a great ship.

Beware of the young doctor and the old barber.

Blame-all and praise-all are two block-heads.

Blessed is he that expects nothing, for he shall never be disappointed.

Ceremony is not civility; nor civility ceremony.

Cheese and salt meat should be sparingly eat.

Content makes poor men rich; discontent makes rich men poor.

Dally not with other folks' women or money.

Death takes no bribes.

Diligence overcomes difficulties, sloth makes them.

Don't go to the doctor with every distemper, nor to the lawyer with every quarrel, nor to the pot for every thirst.

Drive thy business, or it will drive thee.

Drunkenness, that worst of evils, makes some men fools, some beasts, some devils.

Early to bed and early to rise, makes a man healthy, wealthy, and wise.

Employ thy time well, if thou meanest to gain leisure.

Experience keeps a dear school, yet fools will learn in no other.

Fear God, and your enemies will fear you.

Fear not death; for the sooner we die, the longer shall we be immortal.

Fish and visitors stink in three days.

Fools multiply folly.

Glass, china, and reputation are easily crack'd, and never well mended.

God helps them that help themselves.

Great good-nature, without prudence, is a great misfortune.

Great spenders are bad lenders.

Half the truth is often a great lie.

Half-wits talk much but say little.

Haste makes waste.

Have you somewhat to do tomorrow; do it today.

He is a governor that governs his passions, and he a servant that serves them.

He's a fool that cannot conceal his wisdom.

He's the best physician that knows the worthlessness of the most medicines.

He that cannot obey, cannot command.

He that goes far to marry, will either deceive or be deceived.

He that has a trade, has an office of profit and honor.

He that is of opinion money will do everything may well be suspected of doing everything for money.

He that lies down with dogs, shall rise up with fleas.

He that won't be counsell'd, can't be help'd.

If passion drives, let reason hold the reins.

If thou hast wit and learning, add to it wisdom and modesty.

If thou would'st live long, live well; for folly and wickedness shorten life.

If you'd have a servant that you like, serve yourself.

If you know how to spend less than you get, you have the philisopher's stone.

If you would be loved, love and be lovable.

If you would have guests merry with cheer, be so yourself, or so at least appear.

If you would not be forgotten as soon as you are dead and rotten, either write things worth reading, or do things worth writing.

If you would reap praise you must sow the seeds, gentle words and useful deeds.

In success be moderate.

I saw few die of hunger, of eating 100,000.

Keep your eyes wide open before marriage, half shut afterwards.

Late children, early orphans.

Laws too gentle are seldom obeyed; too severe, seldom executed.

Lend money to an enemy, and thou'lt gain him, to a friend and thou'lt lose him.

Let every New Year find you a better man.

Little strokes fell great oaks.

Lost time is never found again.

Mad kings and mad bulls, are not to be held by treaties and pack-thread.

Many have quarrel'd about religion, that never practiced it.

Meanness is the parent of insolence.

Men take more pains to mask than mend.

Money and good manners make the gentleman.

Most people return small favors, acknowledge middling ones, and repay great ones with ingratitude.

Neglect mending a small fault, and 'twill soon be a great one.

Nine men in ten are suicides.

No gains without pains.

No man e'er was glorious who was not laborious.

Nothing drys sooner than a tear.

Of learned fools I have seen ten times ten; of unlearned wise men I have seen a hundred.

Old boys have their playthings as well as young ones; the difference is only in the price.

One today is worth two tomorrows.

Pardoning the bad, is injuring the good.

Plough deep, while sluggards sleep.

Reading makes a full man, meditation a profound man, discourse a clear man.

Search others for their virtues, thyself for thy vices.

Sell not virtue to purchase wealth, nor liberty to purchase power.

Silence is not always a sign of wisdom, but babbling is ever a mark of folly.

Take counsel in wine, but resolve afterwards in water.

Take this remark from Richard, poor and lame, whatever is begun in anger, ends in shame.

The absent are never without fault, nor the present without excuse.

The bird that sits, is easily shot.

The devil sweetens poison with honey.

The doors of wisdom are never shut.

The eye of a master, will do more work than his hand.

The golden age never was the present age.

The honest man takes pains, and then enjoys pleasures; the knave takes pleasures, and then suffers pains.

The muses love the morning.

The noblest question in the world is, what good may I do in it?

There are no ugly loves, nor handsome prisons.

There is neither honor nor gain got in dealing with a villain.

The things which hurt, instruct.

The wise man draws more advantage from his enemies, than the fool from his friends.

The worst wheel of the cart makes the most noise.

Think of three things, whence you came, where you are going, and to whom you must account.

Tho' modesty is a virtue, bashfulness is a vice.

Those who are fear'd, are hated.

Three good meals a day is bad living.

Three may keep a secret, if two of them are dead.

'Tis easier to prevent bad habits than to break them.

To be intimate with a foolish friend, is like going to bed with a razor.

To lengthen thy life, lessen thy meals.

Up, sluggard, and waste not life; in the grave will be sleeping enough.

Virtue and happiness are mother and daughter.

Well done is better than well said.

When the well's dry, we know the worth of water.

Where there's marriage without love, there will be love without marriage.

Wink at small faults; remember thou hast great ones.

Wish not so much to live long as to live well.

Yes, Virginia—There Is a Santa Claus
FRANCIS PHARCELLUS CHURCH—*New York Sun*—9/21/1897

"DEAR EDITOR: I am 8 years old.

"Some of my little friends say there is no Santa Claus.

"Papa says, 'If you see it in THE SUN it's so.'

"Please tell me the truth; is there a Santa Claus?

"VIRGINIA O'HANLON.

"115 WEST NINETY-FIFTH STREET."

Virginia, your little friends are wrong. They have been affected by the skepticism of a skeptical age. They do not believe except [what] they see. They think that nothing can be which is not comprehensible by their little minds.

All minds, Virginia, whether they be men's or children's, are little. In this great universe of ours man is a mere insect, an ant, in his intellect, as compared with the boundless world about him, as measured by the intelligence capable of grasping the whole of truth and knowledge.

Yes, Virginia, there is a Santa Claus. He exists as certainly as love and generosity and devotion exist, and you know that they abound and give to your life its highest beauty and joy. Alas! how dreary would be the world if there were no Santa Claus. It would be as dreary as if there were no Virginias. There would be no childlike faith then, no poetry, no romance to make tolerable this existence. We should have no enjoyment, except in sense and sight. The eternal light with which childhood fills the world would be extinguished. Not believe in Santa Claus! You might as well not believe in fairies!

You might get your papa to hire men to watch in all the chimneys on Christmas Eve to catch Santa Claus, but even if they did not see Santa Claus coming down, what would that prove? Nobody sees Santa Claus, but that is no sign that there is no Santa Claus. The most real things in the world are those that neither children nor men can see. Did you ever see fairies dancing on the lawn? Of course not, but that's no proof that they are not there. Nobody can conceive or imagine all the wonders there are unseen and unseeable in the world.

You may tear apart the baby's rattle and see what makes the noise inside, but there is a veil covering the unseen world which not the strongest man, nor even the united strength of all the strongest men that ever lived, could tear apart. Only faith, fancy, poetry, love, romance, can push aside that curtain and view and picture the supernal beauty and glory beyond. Is it all real? Ah, Virginia, in all this world there is nothing else real and abiding.

No Santa Claus! Thank God! he lives, and he lives forever. A thousand years from now, Virginia, nay, ten times ten thousand years from now, he will continue to make glad the heart of childhood.

It's What the Home Folks Think of You That Really Counts
WILL ROGERS—*Tulsa Daily World*—5/24/1925

A few days ago I was asked by one of the big Ministers of New York City to come to a Luncheon and speak to over 300 Ministers and prominent Laymen. He sat in my dressing room for over an hour. I tried to explain to him that I was only a teller of jokes and that I would be all out of tune with the audience he would have. He is the Methodist Minister here who is building that wonderful big Church which will be the tallest building in New York. A Club, a home, a meeting place, a recreation place for everybody that is interested in trying to live a nice clean wholesome life, and wants to be thrown with people interested in the same thing.

Well, I had worked at affairs for every denomination in the World here in New York, because one is just as worthy as the other. Old New York, the so-called heartless city, houses some great people in every denomination in the world, and I can't see any difference in them. I haven't been able to see where one has the monopoly on the right course to Heaven.

I told him I didn't know what to talk about. Saying the erection of this wonderful Church, and Worth While Center, was of course understood as everyone knew that it was a wonderful undertaking. But, anyway, I went and never in my life did I face an audience with as little preparation. Well, I foundered around from one subject to another. The Minister in introducing me had said that I had been raised a Methodist and I had. So when I got off on that I just couldn't help but speak of a thing which I didn't want to speak of. I knew what would happen if I did.

Out of a large family of which I am the youngest, I have two sisters living. And I couldn't speak of any Church without bringing in the work that those two Sisters have done, in the little town in which they both live. It's Chelsea, Oklahoma, which means nothing in your life, but it has meant a lot to people who have lived in association with them.

They started in this little Western Town some 35 years ago. They helped build the Methodist Church, the first church there. They have helped every Church, they have helped every movement that they knew was for the best upbuilding of their community. They have each raised a large family of Boys and Girls who are today a credit to their community. They have carried on the same as thousands of Women have carried on in every small and Big Town in the World. They don't think they are doing anything out of the ordinary. They don't want credit. They do good simply because they don't know any other thing to do.

The reason I spoke of this personal thing is because I couldn't help it. My Wife was waiting at the train right then for me to see her off to the sickbed of one of these sisters. I didn't tell this to the Ministers because they are my sisters but because none of them who has given his entire life and time to God could have given any more than they have. They have given their all.

Now when I had finished my little talk to rush to the train to see my wife off, I had something happen that had never happened before and I have spoke at a great many affairs. The entire 300 stood up and offered a silent Prayer for my poor afflicted Sister. That was days ago.

Today, as I write this, I am not in the Follies, the carefree comedian who jokes about everything. I am out in Oklahoma, among my People, my Cherokee people, who don't expect a laugh for everything I say.

That Silent Prayer that those 300 Ministers uttered didn't save my sister. She has passed away. But she had lived such a life that it was a privilege to pass away. Death didn't scare her. It was only an episode in her life. If you live right, death is a Joke to you as far as fear is concerned.

And on the day that I am supposed to write a so called Humorous Article I am Back Home. Back home at the funeral of my Sister. I can't be funny. I don't want to be funny. Even Ziegfeld don't want me to be funny. I told him I wanted to go. He said: "I would hate you if you didn't." I told W. C. Fields, the principal comedian of the show. He said: "Go on, I will do something to fill in." Brandon Tynan, my friend of years, said: "Go home where you want to be and where you ought to be."

After all, there is nothing in the world like home. You can roam all over the World, but after all, it's what the people at home think of you that really counts. I have just today witnessed a Funeral that for real sorrow and real affection I don't think will ever be surpassed anywhere. They came in every mode of conveyance, on foot, in Buggies, Horseback, Wagons, Cars, and Trains, and there wasn't a Soul that come that she hadn't helped or favored at one time or another.

Now, we are in the South, of the South, and according to Northern standards we don't rate the Negro any too high. Well, I wish you could have seen the Negroes at her home on the day of the Funeral. Before her death, she said: "They are my folks, they have helped me for years, they are all my friends. When I am gone I don't want you Children at my Funeral to show any preference." That's the real South's real feelings for its real friends. Death knows no Denomination. Death draws no color line. Some uninformed Newspapers printed: "Mrs. C. L. Lane sister of the famous Comedian, Will Rogers." They were greatly misinformed. It's the other way around. I am the brother of Mrs. C. L. Lane, "the friend of Humanity." And I want to tell you that as I saw all these people who were there to pay tribute to her memory, it was the proudest moment of my life that I was her brother. And all the honors that I could ever in my wildest dreams hope to reach, would never equal the honor paid on a little western Prairie hilltop, among her people, to Maud Lane. If they will love me like that at the finish, my life will not have been in vain.

Magnificent Mammon
DAMON RUNYON—*New York American*—c.1935

This punk, maybe he was fourteen, fifteen years old, said he wanted to get my best advice to the youth of the land. I said, are you kidding, son? I said you would not take my best or even my worst advice if I gave it to you—you or any other kid.

I said I would not take it myself if I was your age.

He said, well give it to me, anyway. The teacher said you have been around since Noah built the ark and you ought to have something interesting to say, only make it short because I want to go to the football game.

I said all right, my boy, I will give you my best advice in three words:

Get the money.

I said that is my advice. Get the money.

Get it honestly, son, I said. The hazards and inconveniences of dishonest dough are too numerous to make it worth while. You not only run the risk of going to the can, but there is the matter of conscience that produces sleepless nights and waking hours of fear and brooding like an income tax return full of lies.

I said, then, there is the economic phase of dishonest jack, what with the fences and the mouthpieces and the other protection and assistance getting the most of the swag. Son, I said, if you had been a reader of my column in the old days you would often have read that I think honesty the best policy. Not so much from a moral standpoint but as an economic proposition.

Get the money by hard work and application, if necessary, though I am not opposed to getting it in a soft berth that requires little effort if you can find such a spot. I mean I am no booster for the old rags-to-riches routine if you can locate an easier path.

But get the money.

Son, I said, I am not even opposed to marrying for it. I said I do not approve of youth marrying rich old valises just for their money, though much of the money of this nation is in the hands of the V.P.'s left them by their late ever-loving husbands, and we ought to devise some means of jarring them loose from it.

But, I said, since arranged marriages with a dowry going with the dame have been in vogue in many countries and among many peoples for hundreds of years, I propose nothing sinful nor extraordinary in advising you, my boy, to fall in love with an heiress, if you must fall in love, and vice versa to the girls.

In any event, get the money.

You will hear that money is not everything, and that is true enough. It is only 99 percent of everything, and if you do not believe that there are millions of elderly persons in this nation that you can ask.

Get the money. Get rich if possible, my boy. It is my observation that the rich have all the best of it in this nation, and my studies of American History fail to disclose any time when this same situation did not prevail.

Calamities seldom befall the rich, or at least not in the same proportion that they do the poor or the worse-than-the-poor, the in-betweens, Mr. and Mrs. Mugg. The rich do not stand in line. They do not serve in the ranks. Son, I said, if you cannot get rich get as close to being rich as you can.

Get the money, I said.

Yes, I know the good book states that "Love of money is the root of all evil," but it also says "Money is a defense," and that is what I am talking about, money as a defense—a defense in youth against that irksome love in an attic or a housing project in middle age against the petty laws and regulations that annoy Mr. and Mrs. Mugg, and in old age against fear and disrespect.

Son, I said, get the money.

I must hurry to the football game, the punk announced.

Myriad-Minded Us
Westbrook Pegler—Scripps Howard—c.1938

Of all the fantastic fog-shapes that have risen off the swamp of confusion since the First World War, the most futile and, at the same time, the most pretentious, is the deep-thinking, hair-trigger columnist or commentator who knows all the answers just offhand and can settle great affairs with absolute finality three days or even six days a week.

Being one of these myself, I have been trying to figure out how we came to be. Some, I know, have been pontificating for twenty years and have come to regard themselves as intellectual landmarks and American institutions as permanent as Baseball.

But I am one of the green crop, come after the panic, and my confidence in the vast public importance of my opinions, to say nothing of their sanity, has not become a fixed habit.

It takes gall to sit down to a typewriter at a certain hour every afternoon to confront a long mile of white paper and presume to tell the people what it is all about to the extent of from 500 to 1000 words.

Tell them what what is all about, says you? Oh, just anything and everything.

What is it that you would like to be told all about by your favorite myriad-minded commentators? Economies, pig prevention, the Constitution, the law, politics, war, history, labor, the C.I.O. and the A.F. of L., housing, international relations, birth control, the infield fly rule, Fascism, Nazism and Communism, inflation, agriculture or phrenology? Name me something we can't tell you all about with absolute, irrefutable authority and no two, perhaps, in agreement on any single point.

We include experts on the budget who can't balance an expense account; economic experts who can't find the 5:15 on a suburban timetable much less read a balance sheet, labor experts who never did a lick of work in their lives, pundits on the mechanical age who can't put a fresh ribbon on their own type-writers and resounding authorities on the problem of the farmer who never even grew a geranium in a pot.

We are, in short, the berries of the Fourth Estate, so passionate and self-important these last few years that some of our number, not content with telling the world what and why so on paper, must even rear back at public meetings and snort and sweat in the faces of our fellow citizens in outbursts of courthouse forensics intended to make them think, or anyway think they do.

Not only that, but these oral remarks are sometimes deemed to be of such priceless originality and wisdom as to justify reprinting in full next day, lest some immortal truth be gone with the wind when the cleaners air out the joint.

What causes us? Well, as nearly as I can figure it out, this trade began as a sort of journalistic vaudeville intended to entertain the customers and exert a little circulation pull of a slightly higher tone than that of the comics. Actually, even now at our grimmest, we aren't one, two, six with a real good comic strip in which some evil man is plotting to put out a little girl's eyes or throw a little boy into a blast furnace, a reassuring fact, if you are considering the good sense of the nation, as the syndicate managers, in their nasty way, are always reminding us.

In the days of the wham-sock strips our trade was just olives, requiring a cultivated taste, and as the comics veered off into tragedy and we drifted into isms and causes, the salesmen on the road found, as they continue to find today, that it was much easier to peddle serious funnies than funny seriousness. The comic artists still ride in the big cars and spend their winters shooting in the eighties down South, while we drive the light models and interview ourselves day after solemn day on the state of the nation and the wrongs of a woeful world.

You might think that once in a great while we would run out of intelligence, and I often marvel at my own inexhaustible fund of knowledge, but it just keeps on bubbling up. Nowadays, numbers of our set even get into rather acrimonious clothesline spats figuring, like the old-time fight promoters, that a grudge fight is good for the gate. And the one sure way to drive a small competitor nuts, as Mr. Lippmann has demonstrated in several instances where efforts were made to smoke him out, is to ignore him as though he didn't exist.

Maybe I should be writing like this, revealing secrets of the trade and all, but I just to got to thinking it over and, honest to God, it is getting plumb ridiculous.

Even to Judas
HEYWOOD BROUN—*New York World-Telegram*—12/24/1938

EDITORS' NOTE: President Franklin Delano Roosevelt read this column to the nation in his 1938 Christmas radio address.

We were sitting in a high room above the chapel and although it was Christmas Eve my good friend the dominie seemed curiously troubled. And that was strange, for he was a man extremely sensitive to the festivities of his faith.

The joys and sorrows of Jesus were not to him events of a remote past but more current and living happenings than the headlines in the newspapers. At Christmas he seems actually to hear the voice of the herald angels.

My friend is an old man, and I have known him for many years, but this was the first time the Nativity failed to rouse him to an ecstasy. He admitted to me something was wrong. "Tomorrow," he said, "I must go down into that chapel and preach a Christmas sermon. And I must speak of peace and good-will toward men. I know you think of me as a man too cloistered to be of any use to my community. And I know that our world is one of war and hate and enmity. And you, my young friend, and others keep insisting that before there can be brotherhood there must be the bashing of heads. You are all for good-will to men, but you want to note very many exceptions. And I am still hoping and praying that in the great love of God the final seal of interdiction must not be put on even one. You may laugh at me, but right now I am wondering about how Christmas came to Judas Iscariot."

It is the habit of my friend, when he is troubled by doubts, to reach for the Book, and he did so now. He smiled and said, "Will you assist me in a little experiment? I will close my eyes and you hold out the Bible to me. I will open it at random and run my fingers down a page. You read me the text which I blindly select."

I did as he told me and he happened on the twenty-sixth chapter of St. Matthew and the twenty-fourth verse. I felt sorry for him, for this was no part of the story of the birth of Christ but instead an account of the great betrayal.

"Read what it says," commanded the dominie. And I read: "Then Judas, which betrayed Him, answered and said, 'Master, is it I?' He said unto him, 'Thou has said.'"

My friend frowned, but then he looked at me in triumph. "My hand is not as steady as it used to be. You should have taken the lower part of my finger and not the top. Read the twenty-seventh verse. It is not an eighth of an inch away. Read what it says." And I read, "And He took the cup and gave thanks and gave it to them, saying, 'Drink ye all of it.'"

"Mark that," cried the old man exultantly. "Not even to Judas, the betrayer, was the wine of life denied. I can preach my Christmas sermon now, and my text will be 'Drink ye all of it.' Good-will toward men means good-will to every last son of God. Peace on earth means peace to Pilate, peace to the thieves on the cross, and peace to poor Iscariot."

I was glad, for he had found Christmas and I saw by his face that once more he heard the voice of the herald angels.

The Kicks
MURRAY KEMPTON—*New York Post*—8/20/1954

Louis Armstrong blesses New York these nights at a place in the Fifties called Basin Street.

Armstrong carries his unique imperial scepter with him wherever he goes, and his court chamber, here as everywhere else, is a narrow dressing room unprotected against any man who wants to walk in and ask him for the gift and the secret of laughter.

He sits there at midnight between sets in his shorts and with a handkerchief on his head rubbing his scarred and ravaged lips with a special salve he discovered in Germany during some royal tour in the Twenties.

No man is denied the balm of his touch, for he is alone and walks by himself only in those moments when he looks at the ceiling and plays his slow, sweet song of memory and loss and desire.

A man walked in and said he hadn't known "Pops" was in town until he had seen the marquee and he had come in because he had told his kid that he would listen to Armstrong whenever he could.

When was Louis coming out to teach his kid the trumpet? And Armstrong said he was afraid he couldn't make it this trip, but he'd send a book of his old choruses like "You're Next" and "Cornet Chop Suey."

Someone had written the notes down from listening to the old records and made a book out of them, he said.

It was as though it were the most normal thing in the world to have stood in a barn in Chicago thirty years ago and blown a notion into a low fidelity recording machine and then had some musicologist come along now and listen to the old records and set them down in a book.

It is a rare thing to have written the book when all you thought you were doing was making $50 at a recording date. Louis Armstrong knows that he is history, but he is arrogant only with the gravediggers who come around and ask him to conform to his stature with the ages.

"They ask me my favorite band," he says, "and I tell them Guy Lombardo. They say you don't really mean that. And I say you asked me, didn't you."

The legend of jazz is death and defeat; its saints died beaten and broke; the legend says that it should be that way. They should drink like Bix Beiderbecke or be cheated and broken and lose their teeth like Joe Oliver, because the legend says they should be destroyed seeking notes that aren't in the registers of their horns.

But Louis Armstrong defies that invented destiny of destruction; he endures and to mix in his own person all men, the pure and the cheap, clown and creator, god and buffoon.

"You got to take care of yourself. You got to flush yourself out and you got to watch those germs. You got to keep before the public. Don't let them tell you you got to take top billing or nothing. Your instrument's your billing.

"I done everything in my time, and there were kicks all the time. I got kicks on that coal cart when I was fifteen. In fifty-four years you get lots of kicks. I've played with everyone.

"There's kicks anywhere. When I first came to New York, I stood up with the Vincent Lopez band and some old man stood up in front and played the same thing an octave higher. I went home that week and that's when I made 'When You're Smiling.'"

The name Vincent Lopez does not appear in the legend, but it is part of Louis Armstrong's life, and no part of his life is devoid of kicks because it does not fit the legend.

His vocalist, Velma Middleton, came in and said, "Pops, I never can get to you for the chicks," and he laughed and some boys came in and he said, "Ah, the cats," and everyone laughed. "My disciples," he said.

His soiree was over and he put on his pants to have his picture taken, as a favor to a press agent, picked up his handkerchiefs and went back on the stand. His band was loose and careless, for that's how Armstrong feels these nights.

They clowned awhile and then, of a sudden, he put up his horn and played "When You're Smiling," as he had heard that nameless forgotten old man do it thirty years ago, on the melody, the notes high, a little slow and longing, and he was walking on that plain alone.

The press agent at Basin Street was saying that he came down every night, which was more, after all, than anyone owes a client, because he could not stop listening to Louis.

He was saying I suppose that after all these years, Louis Armstrong has become the River Mississippi, pure like its source, flecked and choked with jetsam like its middle, broad and triumphant like its end. It is never the same river, but its ends are like its beginnings, and there aren't many rivers left like it.

When God Created Fathers
ERMA BOMBECK—*Dayton Journal Herald*—6/17/1973

When the good Lord was creating fathers, he started with a tall frame.

A female angel nearby said: "What kind of father is that? If you're going to make children so close to the ground, why have you put fathers up so high? He won't be able to shoot marbles without kneeling, tuck a child in bed without bending, or even kiss a child without a lot of stooping."

And . . . God smiled and said, "Yes, but if I make him child-size, who would children have to look up to?"

And when God made a father's hands, they were large and sinewy.

The angel shook her head sadly and said: "Do you know what you're doing? Large hands are clumsy. They can't manage diaper pins, small buttons, rubber bands on pony tails, or even remove splinters caused by baseball bats."

And God smiled and said: "I know, but they're large enough to hold everything a small boy empties from his pockets at the end of a day, yet small enough to cup a child's face."

And then God molded long, slim legs and broad shoulders.

The angel nearly had a heart attack. "Boy, this is the end of the week, all right," she clucked. "Do you realize you just made a father without a lap? How is he going to pull a child close to him without the kid falling between his legs?"

And God smiled and said: "A mother needs a lap. A father needs strong shoulders to pull a sled, balance a boy on a bicycle, or hold a sleepy head on the way home from the circus."

God was in the middle of creating two of the largest feet anyone had ever seen when the angel could contain herself no longer. "That's not fair. Do you honestly think those large boats are going to dig out of bed early in the morning when the baby cries? Or walk through a small birthday party without crushing at least three of the guests?"

And God smiled and said: "They'll work. You'll see. They'll support a small child who wants to 'ride a horse to Banbury Cross,' or scare off mice at the summer cabin, or display shoes that will be a challenge to fill."

God worked throughout the night, giving the father few words, but a firm, authoritative voice; and eyes that saw everything, but remained calm and tolerant.

Finally, almost as an afterthought, he added tears. Then he turned to the angel and said, "Now, are you satisfied that he can love as much as a mother?"

The angel shutteth up.

When God Created Mothers

ERMA BOMBECK—*Dayton Journal Herald*—5/12/1974

When the good Lord was creating mothers, he was into his sixth day of overtime when the angel appeared and said, "You're doing a lot of fiddling around on this one."

The Lord said, "Have you read the specs on this order?

"She has to be completely washable, but not plastic;

"Have 180 movable parts . . . all replaceable;

"Run on black coffee and leftovers;

"Have a lap that disappears when she stands up;

"A kiss that can cure anything from a broken leg to a disappointed love affair;

"And six pairs of hands."

The angel shook her head slowly and said, "Six pairs of hands? No way."

"It's not the hands that are causing me problems," said the Lord. "It's the three pairs of eyes that mothers have to have."

"That's on the standard model?" asked the angel.

The Lord nodded. "One pair that sees through closed doors when she asks, 'What are you kids doing in there?' when she already knows. Another here in the back of her head that sees what she shouldn't but what she has to know, and of course the ones here in front that can look at a child when he goofs up and say, 'I understand and I love you' without so much as uttering a word." "Lord," said the angel, touching his sleeve gently, "come to bed. Tomorrow . . . "

"I can't," said the Lord. "I'm so close to creating something so close to myself. Already I have one who heals herself when she is sick . . . can feed a family of six on one pound of hamburger . . . and can get a 9-year-old to stand under a shower."

The angel circled the model of a mother very slowly and sighed. "It's too soft."

"But tough!" said the Lord excitedly. "You cannot imagine what this mother can do or endure."

"Can it think?"

"Not only think, but it can reason and compromise," said the Creator.

Finally the angel bent over and ran her finger across the cheek. "There's a leak," she pronounced. "I told you that you were trying to put too much into this model."

"It's not a leak," said the Lord, "it's a tear."

"What's it for?"

"It's for joy, sadness, disappointment, pain, loneliness and pride."

"You are a genius," said the angel.

The Lord looked somber. "I didn't put it there."

Memories of Leaner Times Fed by Image of Hungry Bum
PETE DEXTER—*Sacramento Bee*—2/22/1987

The kid was big, but he was a kid.

He was standing beside the drive-in window at Church's Fried Chicken on North Broad, asking the people who came by for money. "Do you have some change so I could get somethin' to eat, sir?" He said it like it was memorized.

It was early last week, the weather was catching up with the season. He had taken his arms out of his shirtsleeves and put them underneath, trying to stay warm, so when he tapped on the window I figured he had at least a machete under there.

"Get the f-ck out of here," I said. I did that without thinking about it, the same way you check for cars before you cross the street.

He looked at me, I looked at him. He took his hand off the car and put it back underneath his shirt. He began to shake, then he moved away. I turned on the radio to put the kid out of mind. If there is anything you have to know in a city, it's how to put things out of mind. If you can't do it, you better not be here.

I have been in Philadelphia more than six years. It took a while, but I can do that now.

The kid moved back to the corner of the building, stared at the car. I could see him in the side mirror. He looked like he was seventeen or eighteen, but you couldn't tell. He looked cold in every way there is to be cold. I put him out of mind again, but every time I looked in the mirror, he was standing there, black and cold and angry, and he wouldn't move away.

I don't know exactly when it happened, but somewhere along the line I got tired of victims in groups—women, blacks, Puerto Ricans, gay, and all the self-promotional bull that went with it—then I got tired of victims in person. I didn't want to see the mother and father nodded out on heroin at the Fox Theater Sunday afternoon while their four-year-old kid tried to wake them up anymore.

I didn't want to see old people who had been mugged, or fourteen-year-old alcoholics or abused children.

So, as much as you can in the city, I quit looking. At least I tried to only look once. There is too much of it to carry around with you.

And to do that, you have to forget that you have been hungry too.

The kid moved again, slowly across the parking lot to the garbage bin. He began going through it a piece at a time.

I was a couple of years older than this kid, but I went about a week once without anything to eat. In Minneapolis, in the coldest winter, I was hungry enough to go through garbage, but in the morning it had passed and what replaced it was just an empty, weak feeling, and later on a dizziness when I stood up. And much later, something inside that kept saying I was getting myself in serious trouble.

I wondered if the kid had heard that too. If he knew what it meant. I turned around and watched him a minute. He held the garbage close to his face, then put it back in the bin. A piece of paper stuck to his hand, and suddenly he was throwing things. Picking up cans and bags out of the bin and throwing them back, over and over. A beat-up gray cat with milk in her nipples jumped out of the other end of the bin.

He stopped and sat down, exhausted. He put his face in his hands, I said it out loud, so I could hear how it sounded. "Get the f-ck out of here."

I ordered two chicken dinners and drove back around the lot to where the kid was sitting. I don't think he recognized me because he got up, tapped on the window and asked for a quarter to buy something to eat. There was garbage stuck to his chin.

I gave him one of the chicken dinners and said I was sorry. "I didn't see you were hungry," I said. The kid was looking at a two-dollar box of chicken with something close to love.

"Thank you," he said. "Thank you very much, thank you . . ."

"I've been in the city too long."

He studied me a minute. "Me too," he said. Then he took the chicken and walked over to his spot near the garbage and sat down to eat it.

The cat came out of the weeds toward him, a step at a time. The kid looked up and saw her. He tore a piece of meat off the breast and stroked her coat while she ate.

The Days of Gilded Rigatoni
ANNA QUINDLEN—*New York Times*—5/12/1991

Breakfast will be perfect. I know this from experience. Poached eggs expertly done, the toast in triangles, the juice fresh squeezed. A pot of coffee, a rose in a bud vase. A silver tray. I will eat every bit.

Breakfast will be perfect, except that it will be all wrong. The eggs should be a mess, in some no man's land between fried and scrambled, the toast under-done, the orange juice slopped over into the place where the jelly should be, if there were jelly, which there is not. Coffee lukewarm, tray steel-gray and sus-piciously like a cookie sheet. I get to eat the yuckie parts. I know this from ex-perience.

Today is Mother's Day, and the room-service waiter at the hotel is bringing my breakfast. No hand print in a plaster-of-Paris circle with a ribbon through a hole in the top. Nothing made out of construction paper or macaroni spray-painted gold and glued to cardboard. This is a disaster. Any of the other 364 days of the year would be a wonderful time for a woman with small children to have a morning of peace and quiet. But solitary splendor on this day is like being a book with no reader. It raises that age-old question: If a mother screams in the forest and there are no children to hear it, is there any sound?

It has become commonplace to complain that Mother's Day is a manufactured holiday, cooked up by greeting-card moguls and covens of florists. But these complaints usually come from those who have forgotten to buy cards or order flowers. Or they come from grown-ups who find themselves on a one-way street, who are stymied each year by the question of what to give a mature woman who says she has everything her heart desires except grandchildren.

It has become commonplace to flog ourselves if we are mothers, with our limitations if we stay home with the kids, with our obligations if we take jobs. It's why sometimes mothers who are not working outside their homes seem to suggest that the kids of those who are live on Chips Ahoy and walk barefoot through the snow to school. It's why sometimes mothers with outside jobs feel moved to ask about those other women, allegedly without malice, "What do they do all day?"

And amid that incomplete revolution in the job description, the commercial Mother's Day seems designed to salute a mother who is an endangered species, if not an outright fraud. A mother who is pink instead of fuchsia. A mother who bakes cookies and never cheats with the microwave. A mother who does not swear or scream, who wears an apron and a patient smile.

Not a mother who is away from home on a business trip on Mother's Day. Not a mother who said "You can fax it to me, honey" when her son said he had written something in school and is now doomed to remember that sentence the rest of her miserable life.

Not an imperfect mother.

The Mother's Day that means something, the Mother's Day that is not a duty but a real holiday, is about the perfect mother. It is about the mother before she becomes the human being, when she is still the center of our universe, when we are very young.

They are not long, the days of construction paper and gilded rigatoni. That's why we save those things so relentlessly, why the sisterhood of motherhood, those of us who can instantly make friends with a stranger by discussing colic and orthodonture, have as our coat of arms a set of small handprints executed in finger paint.

Each day we move a little closer to the sidelines of their lives, which is where we belong, if we do our job right. Until the day comes when they have to find a florist fast at noon because they had totally forgotten it was anything more than the second Sunday in May. Hassle city.

The little ones do not forget. They cut and paste and sweat over palsied capital letters and things built of Popsicle sticks about which you must never ever say, "What is this?"

Just for a little while, they believe in the perfect mom—that is, you, whoever and wherever you happen to be. "Everything I am," they might say, "I owe to my mother." And they believe they wrote the sentence themselves, even if they have to give you the card a couple of days late. Over the phone you can say, "They don't make breakfast here the way you make it." And they will believe it. And it will be true.

Jon Will's Aptitudes
GEORGE F. WILL—*Washington Post*—5/3/1993

Jon Will, the eldest of my four children, turns 21 this week and on this birthday, as on every other workday, he will commute by subway to his job delivering mail and being useful in other ways at the National Institutes of Health. Jon is a taxpayer, which serves him right: He voted for Bill Clinton (although he was partial to Pat Buchanan in the primaries).

The fact that Jon is striding into a productive adulthood with a spring in his step and Baltimore's Orioles on his mind is a consummation that could not have been confidently predicted when he was born. Then a doctor told his parents that their first decision must be whether or not to take Jon home. Surely 21 years later fewer doctors suggest to parents of handicapped newborns that the parental instinct of instant love should be tentative or attenuated, or that their commitment to nurturing is merely a matter of choice, even a question of convenience.

Jon has Down syndrome, a chromosomal defect involving varying degrees of mental retardation and physical abnormalities. Jon lost, at the instant he was conceived, one of life's lotteries, but he also was lucky: His physical abnormalities do not impede his vitality and his retardation is not so severe that it interferes with life's essential joys—receiving love, returning it, and reading baseball box scores.

One must mind one's language when speaking of people like Jon. He does not "suffer from" Down syndrome. It is an affliction, but he is happy—as happy as the Orioles' stumbling start this season will permit. You may well say that being happy is easy now that ESPN exists. Jon would agree. But happiness is a species of talent, for which some people have superior aptitudes.

Jon's many aptitudes far exceed those few that were dogmatically ascribed to people like him not long ago. He was born when scientific and social understanding relevant to him was expanding dramatically. We know much more about genetically based problems than we did when, in the early 1950s, James Watson and Francis Crick published their discoveries concerning the structure of DNA, the hereditary molecule, thereby beginning the cracking of the genetic code. Jon was born the year before *Roe v. Wade* and just as prenatal genetic tests were becoming routine. Because of advancing science and declining morals, there are fewer people like Jon than there should be. And just in Jon's generation much has been learned about unlocking the hitherto unimagined potential of the retarded. This begins with early intervention in the form of infant stimulation. Jon began going off to school when he was three months old.

Because Down syndrome is determined at conception and leaves its imprint in every cell of the person's body, it raises what philosophers call ontological questions. It seems mistaken to say that Jon is less than he would be without Down syndrome. When a child suffers a mentally limiting injury after birth we wonder sadly about what might have been. But a Down person's life never had any other trajectory. Jon was Jon from conception on. He has seen a brother two years younger surpass him in size, get a driver's license and leave for college, and although Jon would be forgiven for shaking his fist at the universe, he has been equable. I believe his serenity is grounded in his sense that he is a complete Jon and that is that.

Some of life's pleasures, such as the delights of literature, are not accessible to Jon, but his most poignant problem is that he is just like everyone else, only a bit more so. A shadow of loneliness, an irreducible apartness from others, is inseparable from the fact of individual existence. This entails a sense of incompleteness—we *are* social creatures—that can be assuaged by marriage and other friendships, in the intimacy of which people speak their hearts and minds. Listen to the wisdom whispered by common locutions: We speak of "unburdening ourselves" when we talk with those to whom we talk most freely.

Now, try to imagine being prevented, by mental retardation and by physical impediments to clear articulation, from putting down, through conversations, many burdens attendant on personhood. The shadow of loneliness must often be somewhat darker, the sense of apartness more acute, the sense of incompleteness more aching for people like Jon. Their ability to articulate is, even more than for everyone else, often not commensurate with their abilities to think and feel, to be curious and amused, to yearn.

Because of Jon's problems of articulation, I marvel at his casual everyday courage in coping with a world that often is uncomprehending. He is intensely interested in major league baseball umpires, and is a friend of a few of them. I think he is fascinated by their ability to make themselves understood, by vigorous gestures, all the way to the back row of the bleachers. From his season-ticket seat behind the Orioles dugout, Jon relishes rhubarbs, but I have never seen him really angry. The closest he comes is exasperation leavened by resignation. It is an interesting commentary on the human condition that one aspect of Jon's abnormality—a facet of his disability—is the fact that he is gentleness straight through. But must we ascribe a sweet soul to a defective chromosome? Let us just say that Jon is an adornment to a world increasingly stained by anger acted out.

Like many handicapped people, Jon frequently depends on the kindness of strangers. He almost invariably receives it, partly because Americans are, by and large, nice, and because Jon is, too. He was born on his father's birthday, a gift that keeps on giving.

Advice, Like Youth, Probably Wasted on the Young
MARY SCHMICH—*Chicago Tribune*—6/1/1997

Inside every adult lurks a graduation speaker dying to get out, some world-weary pundit eager to pontificate on life to young people who'd rather be Rollerblading. Most of us, alas, will never be invited to sow our words of wisdom among an audience of caps and gowns, but there's no reason we can't entertain ourselves by composing a Guide to Life for Graduates.

I encourage anyone over 26 to try this and thank you for indulging my attempt.

Ladies and gentlemen of the class of '97:

Wear sunscreen.

If I could offer you only one tip for the future, sunscreen would be it. The long-term benefits of sunscreen have been proved by scientists, whereas the rest of my advice has no basis more reliable than my own meandering experience. I will dispense this advice now.

Enjoy the power and beauty of your youth. Oh, never mind. You will not understand the power and beauty of your youth until they've faded. But trust me, in 20 years, you'll look back at photos of yourself and recall in a way you can't grasp now how much possibility lay before you and how fabulous you really looked. You are not as fat as you imagine.

Don't worry about the future. Or worry, but know that worrying is as effective as trying to solve an algebra equation by chewing bubble gum. The real troubles in your life are apt to be things that never crossed your worried mind, the kind that blindside you at 4 p.m. on some idle Tuesday.

Do one thing every day that scares you.

Sing.

Don't be reckless with other people's hearts. Don't put up with people who are reckless with yours.

Floss.

Don't waste your time on jealousy. Sometimes you're ahead, sometimes you're behind. The race is long and, in the end, it's only with yourself.

Remember compliments you receive. Forget the insults. If you succeed in doing this, tell me how.

Keep your old love letters. Throw away your old bank statements.

Stretch.

Don't feel guilty if you don't know what you want to do with your life. The most interesting people I know didn't know at 22 what they wanted to do with their lives. Some of the most interesting 40-year-olds I know still don't.

Get plenty of calcium. Be kind to your knees. You'll miss them when they're gone.

Maybe you'll marry, maybe you won't. Maybe you'll have children, maybe you won't. Maybe you'll divorce at 40, maybe you'll dance the funky chicken on your 75th wedding anniversary. Whatever you do, don't congratulate yourself too much, or berate yourself either. Your choices are half chance. So are everybody else's.

Enjoy your body. Use it every way you can. Don't be afraid of it or of what other people think of it. It's the greatest instrument you'll ever own.

Dance, even if you have nowhere to do it but your living room.

Read the directions, even if you don't follow them.

Do not read beauty magazines. They will only make you feel ugly.

Get to know your parents. You never know when they'll be gone for good. Be nice to your siblings. They're your best link to your past and the people most likely to stick with you in the future.

Understand that friends come and go, but with a precious few you should hold on. Work hard to bridge the gaps in geography and lifestyle, because the older you get, the more you need the people who knew you when you were young.

Live in New York City once, but leave before it makes you hard. Live in Northern California once, but leave before it makes you soft. Travel.

Accept certain inalienable truths: Prices will rise. Politicians will philander. You, too, will get old. And when you do, you'll fantasize that when you were young, prices were reasonable, politicians were noble, and children respected their elders.

Respect your elders.

Don't expect anyone else to support you. Maybe you have a trust fund. Maybe you'll have a wealthy spouse. But you never know when either one might run out.

Don't mess too much with your hair or by the time you're 40 it will look 85.

Be careful whose advice you buy, but be patient with those who supply it. Advice is a form of nostalgia. Dispensing it is a way of fishing the past from the disposal, wiping it off, painting over the ugly parts and recycling it for more than it's worth.

But trust me on the sunscreen.

The Halloween of My Dreams
Marjorie Williams—*Washington Post*—11/3/2004

I was the one who insisted on the body glitter. Normally, you understand, I am a mother who pulls her daughter's shirt down and tucks it into her waistband every morning to keep her from showing her navel to the whole third grade. I make her scrub the supposedly water-soluble unicorn tattoos off her cheeks before she goes to school. I court her wrath by refusing to buy the kids' fashions that seem designed to clothe tiny hookers.

But after all, this was Halloween, the holiday that celebrates license. (A fifth KitKat bar after 9 p.m.? Why not?) Alice was determined to be a rock star, and I was happy to help her. Simple enough.

Yet my joy in conspiring with her felt so *big*. Usually I'm not much of a Halloween enthusiast, not since I was 13 or so. For a while, having children of my own brought me a new version of the old childhood thrill. One year Will came home from preschool and told me he'd learned about a new Halloween creature, one that lurches through the night swathed in flapping bandages.

"Oh," I said casually. "What's it called?"

"The MOMMIES!" he announced, with much more excitement than dismay.

But my delight lasted for only a few years before I returned to thinking of Halloween as just a silly, gaudy night that strains at symbolism—the floozy among the family of big holidays. I thought, for a while, that I had simply buckled under the demands of Costume Hell. ("I want to be a computer, but also my feet will be, like, a robot, and you can make me a head with glowing red eyes and a voice like Darth Vader.") But that explanation has become less and less convincing: At 11 and almost-9, after all, the kids have more and more fun making their own costumes, with minimal help. Really, I think that I'm just not one of those people who easily climbs into fantasy and achieves flight.

Recently, after my dear cousin Sally spent a night guarding my sleep in the hospital, we talked about the one part of the experience I remembered as clearly as she. When I'd finally taken aboard enough pain medicine to dull the effects of the procedure I'd just been through, I'd said clearly, out of my cloud of Dilaudid, "I love all these random thoughts. All my life I've worked so hard to get words and sentences into line. They had to have a *point*. I love floating along on all these random thoughts."

It made me hugely sad to see that my escapes from the taskmistress of literalism are still so rare and hard-won. And in the days before this Halloween, it was especially hard for me to avoid interpreting its elements too bluntly. If you have cancer, if you've had it for a while, at some point you start really *seeing* all those skulls and skeletons and Styrofoam headstones, all those children in hooded capes, bearing scythes on their little shoulders.

So how could I explain the euphoria of the 45 minutes Alice and I spent in her bedroom, colluding over her hair, giggling at her faux-leather, deeply fringed bell-bottoms? The pleasure of watching her strap on those awful silver platform shoes, like something I wore in 1973?

Because Alice was getting picked up to join friends for trick-or-treating, I kept my eye on the clock, and shooed her into the bathroom just in time to add make-up: grown-up lipstick, a layer of shimmery lip gloss over that, and an overall, emphatic scribble, on her neck and face, with the body-glitter crayon. Every other day of the year, any mother knows that glitter is the work of Satan, but last

Sunday it lit her skin with a dew of every color.

We could hear her friends pull up to the curb. As her momentum carried her to the top of the stairs, Alice looked back and tossed me a radiant smile. She had become my glimmering girl: She looked like a rock star. She looked like a teenager. She looked absolutely stunning. She thundered down the stairs in those shoes, and as the front door slammed behind her, it came to me—what fantasy I had finally, easily entered this Halloween.

I'd just seen Alice leave for her prom, or her first real date. I'd cheated time, flipping the calendar five or six years into the future. The character I'd played was the 52-year-old mother I will probably never be.

It was effortless.

Man of the Streets, in Three Suites
STEVE LOPEZ—*Los Angeles Times*—12/4/2005

FIRST SUITE: THE APARTMENT

He's a lucky man, Nathaniel Anthony Ayers. At least in some ways. Despite the imagined voices and daily flutter of scattered thoughts, he has a burning passion.

For him, the city is an orchestra, a labyrinth of musical references and inspiration. He sees a swaying palm and hears a violin. A bus roars by and gives him a bass line. He hears footsteps and imagines Bach and Brahms.

"I can't survive," Nathaniel once told me, "if I can't hear Los Angeles the way I like to hear it."

That's why he doesn't want to give up sleeping on the streets. I've told him that if he'd be willing to move into an apartment, he would have the freedom to devote even more time to music. As it is, he lugs his belongings around in a shopping cart, tugging an anchor through the city. If he locked up his things, he could travel lighter, with just his fiddle or cello.

But Nathaniel can't see the advantages. After years on the streets, his schizophrenia untreated, he's at home outdoors in a world of his own making.

He needed a nudge.

The staffers at Lamp, the skid row agency that has been working with Nathaniel most of the year, helped me devise a plan in late October. A downtown apartment, complete with all the supportive services Nathaniel needs, had become available. At the same time, a member of the Los Angeles Philharmonic had graciously offered to give Nathaniel cello lessons. Now if we could just get Nathaniel to see that the apartment would be the perfect location.

Thanks, Nathaniel said, but he'd rather have the lessons in the 2nd Street tunnel.

With all due respect, I told him, a member of a world-class orchestra might balk at the idea, even if Nathaniel had studied at Juilliard. In the end, he gave in.

As a warmup, I went to the apartment with Nathaniel, trying to get him comfortable there. The building is on a quiet street that seems miles from skid row, with a courtyard where bougainvillea flows over an arbor.

Nathaniel sat on a bench in the garden, took bow in hand and played Beethoven, followed by Bach. Several residents stopped to listen on their way through the courtyard, stunned, as people often are, at the bedraggled source of such refinement.

Let's go check out the room, I said when he broke. Maybe the acoustics are good.

The apartment was small, plain, perfect. Nathaniel liked the light that fell through the window, filtered by an oleander that scratched lightly at the screen.

He took a seat on the bed and played Schubert, and in the embrace of the music, eyes closed, he was home.

SECOND SUITE: THE LESSON

Nathaniel was nervous about the encounter, worried he wasn't good enough to burn the time of a professional. So too was Peter Snyder. The cellist, a 33-year member of the Los Angeles Philharmonic, couldn't know what he was in for.

"It so moved me that I simply have to do something," he had written to me after meeting Nathaniel at Disney Hall. The orchestra had invited Nathaniel to a rehearsal, and Snyder had felt a connection with him during a brief chat.

One Monday last month, I picked up Snyder at Disney and we drove down off the hill, through downtown and across to skid row, a six-minute trip across the universe. Nathaniel was waiting in the courtyard with his shopping cart, two violins and a cello. We moved into the apartment and I asked Nathaniel when he last had a lesson.

Early 1970s, he said. Right before a concert in Aspen.

"Did you play in Aspen?" Snyder asked.

"Yes, but I got in trouble with the psychiatrists there," Nathaniel said without explanation. "Straitjacket."

He mentioned the names of several teachers and mentors; Snyder knew them all.

"I brought you something," Snyder said, showing Nathaniel the sheet music to Pablo Casals' "Song of the Birds." "It's something appropriate, because you're kind of a wandering bird."

Nathaniel responded by telling Snyder there was a battle in the tunnels between Don Quixote and Colonel Sanders.

"That's a nice story," Snyder said kindly.

Without an invitation, Nathaniel began playing, and Snyder was instantly impressed.

"You know," he said when Nathaniel paused, "you're a very natural player."

For several minutes they talked music, a conversation that was way over my head. Snyder would later write to me: "The way in which he compared the philosophies of different composers and their visions is extraordinary."

Snyder took his own cello and began to play.

"Do you know this?" he asked.

"Bouree," Nathaniel said, from the Bach suite in C major for unaccompanied cello.

As Snyder continued, Nathaniel was riveted. He leaned forward and stared at the fingering. Then a smile suddenly took shape.

Next it was Nathaniel's turn to impress. Snyder asked if he could play Bach, and Nathaniel showed his chops.

"I'm amazed," Snyder said. "I know many talented people who don't have as pretty a sound."

As Nathaniel continued, Snyder leaned in to me.

"He might be a musical genius," he said. "It's not unusual to find someone with his aptitude. What is unbelievable is to see someone without recent training play so well."

Snyder told Nathaniel he ought to seriously consider keeping the apartment as a sanctuary—a safe place to connect spiritually with his music.

Thanks, Nathaniel responded quickly, but he preferred playing on the streets and in the tunnel.

"How about making this deal," Snyder said. "You come here as often as you can, so maybe we can have another lesson."

Nathaniel fidgeted like a teenager, then repeated his preference for the tunnel.

"Think of this as a clean, quiet tunnel," Snyder suggested.

Nathaniel was sitting by the window and his own shadow fell before him. The idea seemed to grow on him.

"I wouldn't have thought of it," he said. "Yeah. This is a brand new tunnel."

THIRD SUITE: THE CONVERSATION

Nathaniel stayed away from the apartment for days after the lesson, then surprised everyone by asking to leave his cart there for several hours while he copied sheet music at the public library. But that was it. He didn't go back, and he said he had no interest in the apartment for anything but lessons from Peter Snyder.

"Will you give me violin lessons?" I asked Nathaniel the day after Thanksgiving.

Sure, he said.

"Great," I said. "I'd like to do it at the apartment."

He's a smart man—cagey, even—and good at sniffing out a ruse. I think Nathaniel was on to me, but he agreed.

I didn't envy the poor man. I took guitar lessons for several years, but didn't even know how to hold a violin. We sat in the courtyard last Wednesday and Nathaniel was patient and gentle, making me think teaching could one day give him new meaning and pay his bills. He had selected a simple piece of music for me to try but quickly gave up on it and asked me to just try and get something—anything—out of the violin.

What I got sounded like the torture of several small animals.

"There," Nathaniel said. "You get a sound and work with it. It's frustrating, but if you admire the violin, you'll weather the frustrations. Desire, discipline, diversity."

Nathaniel had a white shirt tied over his head. In one pocket of his blue cardigan was a tennis ball, in the other a dinner roll. He took out a copy of Beethoven's Ninth and began playing effortlessly.

By the time he switched to cello, he had drawn a crowd. One resident approached with a battery-operated drill and gunned it in rhythm with the music. Two other residents stopped and said they were musicians.

I suggested they start a band.

Nathaniel liked the idea, and he also liked it when another resident, wowed by his moves on cello, handed him a dollar.

"Dynamic," the resident said.

When everyone was gone but the two of us, I steered the conversation to Nathaniel's mother, who died several years ago.

You know, I said, she'd probably like to know you have a safe place to lay your head at night.

"I lost a god and I gained a god," he told me. His mother died in Cleveland, but he came to Los Angeles and found a statue of Beethoven in Pershing Square.

"It's rough out there," he said, "but as long as I can look at Beethoven, I'll be all right."

As I struggled with the violin, a man named James walked up, stood next to the "Smoking Prohibited" sign and lit a cigarette.

"Excuse me, sir," said Nathaniel, who hates smoke. "You can't smoke here."

"Who are you?" asked James. "You don't live here."

"I do too live here," Nathaniel snapped. "I have a place."

It was music to my ears. On some level, maybe Nathaniel had already begun thinking of the apartment as home, even if he hadn't spent a night in it.

"Where's your place?" James asked.

Nathaniel told him the room number.

"You're in violation of the city ordinance against smoking in that spot," Nathaniel persisted.

"Well, so what? I don't have a house on wheels."

"You see?" Nathaniel said, standing next to his cart. "I knew it was personal."

"You need soap and water," James said.

"You're killing yourself and everyone else," Nathaniel retorted.

"Get a doctor," James said. "Get some help."

If Nathaniel was hurt by that, it didn't show. I wondered how many times in 30-plus years he's been insulted that way.

"You know what?" James asked. "It's a shame you allowed yourself to give up."

"I didn't give up," Nathaniel said.

"You're a young man, strong, you could get a job. You're a musician and you should encourage someone else. You can't encourage no one looking like that. . . . Look at all that talent gone to waste."

Nathaniel shrugged as he got his cart ready to leave.

"You gave up," James went on, reciting what sounded like a speech he'd heard a few times. "You push a cart and say, 'I quit. I quit on life.' . . . I can't stand to see you like that. I don't even know you, but I love you as a human being."

Nathaniel was ready to go. He told James he hadn't quit anything. Then he thanked him for trying to help, and pointed once more to the room he hasn't yet slept in.

"That is my place," he said.

Maybe one day it will be.

---

45 Life Lessons—and Five to Grow On
REGINA BRETT—*Cleveland Plain Dealer*—5/28/2006

To celebrate growing older, I once wrote the 45 lessons life taught me.

It is the most-requested column I've ever written. My odometer rolls over to 50 this week, so here's an update:

1. Life isn't fair, but it's still good.
2. When in doubt, just take the next small step.
3. Life is too short to waste time hating anyone.
4. Don't take yourself so seriously. No one else does.
5. Pay off your credit cards every month.
6. You don't have to win every argument. Agree to disagree.
7. Cry with someone. It's more healing than crying alone.
8. It's OK to get angry with God. He can take it.
9. Save for retirement starting with your first paycheck.
10. When it comes to chocolate, resistance is futile.
11. Make peace with your past so it won't screw up the present.
12. It's OK to let your children see you cry.
13. Don't compare your life to others'. You have no idea what their journey is all about.
14. If a relationship has to be a secret, you shouldn't be in it.
15. Everything can change in the blink of an eye. But don't worry; God never blinks.

16. Life is too short for long pity parties. Get busy living, or get busy dying.
17. You can get through anything if you stay put in today.
18. A writer writes. If you want to be a writer, write.
19. It's never too late to have a happy childhood. But the second one is up to you and no one else.
20. When it comes to going after what you love in life, don't take no for an answer.
21. Burn the candles, use the nice sheets, wear the fancy lingerie. Don't save it for a special occasion. Today is special.
22. Overprepare, then go with the flow.
23. Be eccentric now. Don't wait for old age to wear purple.
24. The most important sex organ is the brain.
25. No one is in charge of your happiness except you.
26. Frame every so-called disaster with these words: "In five years, will this matter?"
27. Always choose life.
28. Forgive everyone everything.
29. What other people think of you is none of your business.
30. Time heals almost everything. Give time time.
31. However good or bad a situation is, it will change.
32. Your job won't take care of you when you are sick. Your friends will. Stay in touch.
33. Believe in miracles.
34. God loves you because of who God is, not because of anything you did or didn't do.
35. Whatever doesn't kill you really does make you stronger.
36. Growing old beats the alternative—dying young.
37. Your children get only one childhood. Make it memorable.
38. Read the Psalms. They cover every human emotion.
39. Get outside every day. Miracles are waiting everywhere.
40. If we all threw our problems in a pile and saw everyone else's, we'd grab ours back.
41. Don't audit life. Show up and make the most of it now.
42. Get rid of anything that isn't useful, beautiful or joyful.
43. All that truly matters in the end is that you loved.
44. Envy is a waste of time. You already have all you need.
45. The best is yet to come.
46. No matter how you feel, get up, dress up and show up.
47. Take a deep breath. It calms the mind.
48. If you don't ask, you don't get.
49. Yield.
50. Life isn't tied with a bow, but it's still a gift.

To Old Times
PEGGY NOONAN—*Wall Street Journal*—8/25/2007

Once I went hot-air ballooning in Normandy. It was the summer of 1991. It was exciting to float over the beautiful French hills and the farms with crisp crops in the fields. It was dusk, and we amused ourselves calling out "Bonsoir!" to cows and people in little cars. We had been up for an hour or so when we had a problem and had to land. We looked for an open field, aimed toward it, and came down a little hard. The gondola dragged, tipped and spilled us out. A half dozen of us emerged scrambling and laughing with relief.

Suddenly before us stood an old man with a cracked and weathered face. He was about 80, in rough work clothes. He was like a *Life* magazine photo from 1938: "French farmer hoes his field." He'd seen us coming from his farmhouse and stood before us with a look of astonishment as the huge bright balloon deflated and tumbled about.

One of us spoke French and explained our situation. The farmer said, or asked, "You are American." We nodded, and he made a gesture—I'll be back!—and ran to the house. He came back with an ancient bottle of Calvados, the local brandy. It was literally covered in dust and dry dirt, as if someone had saved it a long time.

He told us—this will seem unlikely, and it amazed us—that he had not seen an American in many, many years, and we asked when. "The invasion," he said. The Normandy invasion.

Then he poured the Calvados and made a toast. I wish I had notes on what he said. Our French speaker translated it into something like, "To old times." And we raised our glasses knowing we were having a moment of unearned tenderness. Lucky Yanks, that a wind had blown us to it.

That was 16 years ago, and I haven't seen some of the people with me since that day, but I know every one of us remembers it and keeps it in his good-memory hoard.

He didn't welcome us because he knew us. He didn't treat us like royalty because we had done anything for him. He honored us because we were related to, were the sons and daughters of, the men of the Normandy Invasion. The men who had fought their way through France hedgerow by hedgerow, who'd jumped from planes in the dark and climbed the cliffs and given France back to the French. He thought we were of their sort. And he knew they were good. He'd seen them, when he was young.

I've been thinking of the old man because of Iraq and the coming debate on our future there. Whatever we do or should do, there is one fact that is going to be left on the ground there when we're gone. That is the impression made by, and the future memories left by, American troops in their dealings with the Iraqi people.

I don't mean the impression left by the power and strength of our military. I mean the impression left by the character of our troops—by their nature and generosity, by their kindness. By their tradition of these things.

The American troops in Iraq, our men and women, are inspiring, and we all know it. But whenever you say it, you sound like a greasy pol: "I support our valiant troops, though I oppose the war," or "If you oppose the war, you are ignoring the safety and imperiling the sacrifice of our gallant troops."

I suspect that in their sophistication—and they are sophisticated—our troops are grimly amused by this. Soldiers are used to being used. They just do their job.

We know of the broad humanitarian aspects of the occupation—the hospitals being built, the schools restored, the services administered, the kids treated by armed forces doctors. But then there are all the stories that don't quite make it to the top of the heap, and that in a way tell you more. The lieutenant in the First Cavalry who was concerned about Iraqi kids in the countryside who didn't have shoes, so he wrote home, started a drive, and got 3,000 pairs sent over. The lieutenant colonel from California who spent his off-hours emailing hospitals back home to get a wheelchair for a girl with cerebral palsy.

The Internet is littered with these stories. So is Iraq. I always notice the pictures from the wire services, pictures that have nothing to do with government propaganda. The Marine on patrol laughing with the local street kids; the nurse treating the sick mother.

A funny thing. We're so used to thinking of American troops as good guys that we forget: They're good guys! They have American class.

And it is not possible that the good people of Iraq are not noticing, and that in some way down the road the sum of these acts will not come to have some special meaning, some special weight of its own. The actor Gary Sinise helps run Operation Iraqi Children, which delivers school supplies with the help of U.S. forces. When he visits Baghdad grade schools, the kids yell, "Lieutenant Dan!"—his role in *Forrest Gump*, the story of another good man.

Some say we're the Roman Empire, but I don't think the soldiers of Rome were known for their kindness, nor the people of Rome for their decency. Some speak of Abu Ghraib, but the humiliation of prisoners there was news because it was American troops acting in a way that was out of the order of things, and apart from tradition. It was weird. And they were busted by other American troops.

You could say soldiers of every country do some good in war beyond fighting, and that is true enough. But this makes me think of the statue I saw once in Vienna, a heroic casting of a Red Army soldier. Quite stirring. The man who showed it to me pleasantly said it had a local nickname, "The Unknown Rapist." There are similar memorials in Estonia and Berlin; they all have the same nickname. My point is not to insult Russian soldiers, who had been born into a world of communism, atheism, and Stalin's institutionalization of brutish ways of being. I only mean to note the stellar reputation of American troops in the same war at the same time. They were good guys.

They're still good.

We should ponder, some day when this is over, what it is we do to grow such men, and women, what exactly goes into the making of them.

Whatever is decided in Washington I hope our soldiers know what we really think of them, and what millions in Iraq must, also. I hope some day they get some earned tenderness, and wind up over the hills of Iraq, and land, and an old guy comes out and says, "Are you an American?" And they say yes and he says, "A toast, to old times."

ABOUT THE COLUMNISTS

The columnists whose work is collected in *Deadline Artists* are fascinating characters in their own right. Understanding the outlines of their personal journeys can help readers further appreciate their work and perspective. The following brief biographical sketches focus on their careers as columnists and contain quotes that capture their spirit or approach to writing.

"There is only one inviolable rule in newspaper columning," wrote Hallam Walker Davis in his 1926 book *The Column* "and that is, 'Be Yourself.'" A glance at these biographies will show that these vivid personalities would not have done it any other way.

MITCH ALBOM (1958–) Mitch Albom is an author, radio host, television commentator, screenwriter, playwright, musician, and philanthropist. What's more, he splits his twice-weekly column for the *Detroit Free Press* between sports and civic issues. His books include the best-selling *Tuesdays with Morrie*, a work of inspirational nonfiction. Albom has been named best sports columnist thirteen times and best feature writer seven times by the Associated Press. He has used his financial success to start four separate charities, most impacting his adopted hometown of Detroit. His advice to fellow newspaper journalists confronting competition with cable TV, the Internet, and talk radio: "We have to arrest the readers' attention. . . . When we do what we do best, which is stylize, write, detail, flow, extrapolate, then we win, because they can never do that."

JOSEPH AND STEWART ALSOP (1910–1989 and 1914–1974, respectively) The influential brothers Alsop started the syndicated column "Matter of Fact" in 1946. Anti-communist abroad and anti-anti-Communist at home, they help define the contours of cold war–era policy, coining terms such as "Hawks" and "Doves." "As columnists," they wrote, "we always regard ourselves as reporters. We tried . . . never to print a column lacking at least one previously unpublished and significant item of factual information."

JACK ANDERSON (1922–2005) An investigative "muckraking" columnist, Jack Anderson was an influential Washington outsider who specialized in exposing political corruption. He began as an assistant to Drew Pearson, whose political-gossip column "Washington Merry-Go-Round," was published in nearly a thousand newspapers at the time. In 1969, Anderson took over the column entirely and improved the quality of investigative reporting. The father of nine children, Anderson won the Pulitzer Prize for National Reporting in 1972 by exposing Nixon administration outreach to Pakistan during a war with India. He was subsequently placed on Nixon's Enemies List and was targeted for LSD poisoning by the CIA, the odd subject of the 2010 book *Poisoning the Press: Richard Nixon, Jack Anderson, and the Rise of Washington's Scandal Culture* by Mark Feldstein.

RUSSELL BAKER (1925–) A Pulitzer Prize–winning humor columnist for the *New York Times*, Russell Baker brought satire and irreverence to the nation's editorial pages for the better part of four decades. The Virginia native is the author of two memoirs, editor of several anthologies, and he served as the host of PBS's *Masterpiece Theater*. His column "Francs and Beans" was listed as one of the hundred best pieces of American journalism of the twentieth century by a panel convened by New York University. The author Neil Postman described Baker as ". . . like some fourth-century citizen of Rome who is amused and intrigued by the Empire's collapse but who still cares enough to mock the stupidities that are hastening its end."

MIKE BARNICLE (1943–) Barnicle is to Boston what Royko was to Chicago and Breslin is to New York—an authentic voice who comes to symbolize a great city. Almost a generation younger than Breslin & Co., Barnicle also serves as the keeper of the flame of the reported column. A speechwriter after college, Barnicle's column with the *Boston Globe* ran from 1973 to 1998. He has subsequently written for the *New York Daily News* and the *Boston Herald*, logging an estimated four thousand columns in the process. He is also a frequent guest on MSNBC's *Morning Joe* and *Hardball* as well as a featured interview in Ken Burns's *Baseball: The Tenth Inning* documentary.

DAVE BARRY (1947–) The Pulitzer Prize–winning humorist for the *Miami Herald* proved so popular that he gave up his column in 2005 to concentrate on writing books and spending time with his family. He has said that he worked seven days a week to make his column sound like he "dashed it off while carpet-chewing drunk." Barry won the Pulitzer Prize in 1988 "for his consistently effective use of humor as a device for presenting fresh insights into serious concerns"—a year after he mocked the prize in his classic column "Pithy into the Wind." Barry has defined a sense of humor as "a measurement of the extent to which we realize that we are trapped in a world almost totally devoid of reason. Laughter is how we express the anxiety we feel at this knowledge."

MEYER BERGER (1898–1959) Still renowned as "a reporter's reporter," Meyer Berger started the *New York Times*'s long-running "About New York" column in 1939. A master of local color and street-level storytelling, Berger won the Pulitzer Prize in 1950 for his feature detailing a murder spree in Camden perpetrated by a war vet named Howard Unruh. Berger gave the prize money to Unruh's mother. He was selected to write the official history of the *New York Times* to mark the paper's centennial and he holds the distinction of being the only Jewish American newspaper columnist to have been blessed by the pope. Some of his best work was posthumously anthologized in *Meyer Berger's New York*.

AMBROSE BIERCE (1842–1914?) Proud to be known as "the wickedest man in San Francisco," Ambrose Bierce brought vicious cynicism and sarcasm to the columns he wrote for the *San Francisco Examiner* and other papers. He stumbled onto column writing while working as a watchman at the Treasury office in San Francisco after serving as a Union soldier in the Civil War. Bierce's fiction, notably the short story "Occurrence at Owl Creek Bridge" helped add to his fame. His evolving work, "The Devil's Dictionary," excerpted in *Deadline Artists*, appeared in various papers and periodicals, including *The Wasp*. Bierce is believed to have been killed in battle after traveling to Mexico to ride with Pancho Villa's army at the age of seventy-two.

ERMA BOMBECK (1927–1996) "Socrates of the Ironing Board" as *Life Magazine* once described her, Erma Bombeck was one of the most successful and widely syndicated humor columnists of her time. Her story took on Horatio Alger proportions—a Dayton Housewife begins to write a column about her daily travails called "At Wit's End." It gets picked up by a national syndicate and is soon read in nine hundred papers around the country. Prosperity ensues. Bombeck also wrote a dozen books, boasting titles like *The Grass is Always Greener Over the Septic Tank* and *Motherhood: The Second Oldest Profession*.

THOMAS M. BOSWELL (1947–) The *Washington Post* columnist began covering sports for the paper in 1969, shortly after graduating from Amherst College. He also serves as a sports commentator on NPR and was a featured interview in Ken Burns's *Baseball* documentary. His books include *Why Time Begins on Opening Day* and several anthologies. Among his best-known quotes: "A major golf tournament is 40,000 sadists watching 140 masochists" and "There is no substitute for excellence—not even success."

JIMMY BRESLIN (1930–) The archetypal New York newspaper columnist, he is regarded by contempories as one of the all-time greats. The Queens Irish native inspired a generation of writers with his front-page columns and recurring characters. Breslin's best work found uncommon angles to breaking news—interviewing the attending emergency room surgeon after JFK's assassination and the cop who piled John Lennon's dying body into the back of his patrol car. Breslin grew to embody many stereotypes—the hard-drinking, chain-smoking newsman, brilliant but bullshit intolerant, rumpled but hyper-literate and able to write on deadline like an unsentimental angel. Says Breslin: "Rage is the only quality which has kept me, or anybody I have ever studied, writing columns for newspapers."

REGINA BRETT (1956–) a *Cleveland Plain Dealer* columnist, Brett's candid account of overcoming a breast cancer diagnosis in 1998 made her column an inspiration to readers. Initially, her columns ran in the *Akron Beacon Journal*, where she won a National Headliner Award. Brett has written over two thousand columns in her career and hosts a radio show. Her column "45 Life Lessons" went viral online and is often misattributed to a ninety-year-old woman. She was a Pulitzer Prize finalist for commentary in 2008 and 2009. Her first book, *God Never Blinks: 50 Lessons for Life's Little Detours*, was published in April 2010.

DAVID S. BRODER (1929–2011) Known as the "Dean of the D.C. Press Corps," Broder earned a reputation as a fair-minded, hardworking reporter writing an influential column. He was generous with his younger colleagues and resisted being pigeonholed by either partisanship or ideology. He won the Pulitzer Prize for Commentary in 1973 for his coverage of the Nixon White House. A survey by *The Washingtonian* by editorial page editors and members of Congress found Broder to be "Washington's most highly regarded columnist" because of "overall integrity, factual accuracy and insight." Not content to simply cover politics through the prism of official Washington, he often traveled the country, believing that columnists should spend "a lot of time with voters . . . walking precincts, knocking on doors, talking to people in their living rooms. If we really got clearly in our heads what it is voters are concerned about, it might be possible to let their agenda drive our agenda."

DAVID BROOKS (1961–) A twice-weekly touchstone for the center-right, David Brooks' columns in the *New York Times* mine deep territory looking to brain science and theology as well as American history to understand the impulses of our body politic. Since serving on the staff of the *National Review* and *The Weekly Standard*, Brooks has declared his political independence, arguing that the GOP needs to reconnect with the legacy of Hamilton and Lincoln and writing an early column encouraging then-senator Barack Obama to run for president. A regular on-air commentator on the *PBS NewsHour*, Brooks's books include *Bobos in Paradise* and 2011's *The Social Animal*.

HEYWOOD BROUN (1888–1939) Perhaps the preeminent liberal columnist of his day, Broun was a Harvard dropout and the founding president of the American Newspaper Guild. His talents allowed him to tackle subjects ranging from art to sports to war to politics—and he was an outspoken advocate of the idea that journalism could help solve society's ills. During the Great Depression, he used his column as an occasional employment agency, helping to find work for roughly one thousand individuals. In 1930, he ran for Congress unsuccessfully as a Socialist. Rumpled and resistant to authority, Broun found himself frequently fired, but his skill and temperament allowed him to find work easily. An easygoing man of appetites, he was a member of the storied Algonquin Round Table and a friend of the Marx Brothers. He wrote more than a dozen books and was a frequent voice on the radio. President Franklin Delano Roosevelt read Broun's column "Even to Judas" aloud to the nation on a 1938 Christmas radio address. Broun died suddenly a week after his fifty-first birthday. More than three thousand mourners crowded St. Patrick's Cathedral.

ART BUCHWALD (1925–2007) A syndicated satirist for more than fifty years, Art Buchwald published more than thirty books and won the Pulitzer Prize for Commentary in 1982. The son of Austrian-Hungarian immigrants, Buchwald ran away from home to join the Marines during World War II. After attending the University of Southern California on the GI Bill, Buchwald decamped for France, where he began writing a humor column. In 1962, he transferred his column to the United States under the title "Capitol Punishment." His writing riffed off newspaper headlines, extending narratives to absurd extremes and adding new characters—for example, God speaking to Richard Nixon as Watergate unfolds. When once asked why he chose to write humor, Buchwald replied, "Getting even. I am constantly trying to avenge hurts from the past." After his death in 2007, a video obituary was posted online, beginning with the columnist beaming into the camera, saying: "Hi. I'm Art Buchwald, and I just died."

WILLIAM F. BUCKLEY JR. (1925–2008) Godfather of the modern conservative movement, Buckley was a prolific author, bon vivant, ideological entrepreneur, television host, one-time mayoral candidate, and founder of the *National Review*. Through his Universal

Press Syndicate column, Buckley wrote three pieces a week that reached 350 papers. His vivid personality disarmed (some) critics while galvanizing a movement; his intellectual achievement was to reshape the landscape of American political debate without sacrificing the breadth of his interests or enthusiasms. "If there is a common thread in Buckley's writings," George Will wrote in the preface of the posthumous column anthology *Athwart History*, "it is the compatibility of seriousness, even occasional indignation, with an unfailing sense of merriment about the pleasures of intellectual combat."

HERB CAEN (1916–1997) Writing a column at the *San Francisco Chronicle* for nearly sixty years, Herb Caen was a beloved local legend in the city he called "Baghdad by the Bay." His column, "It's News to Me," was a collection of short items, pieced together by ellipses—a style that he called "three dot journalism." He is credited for coining both "beatnik" and "hippie"—contributions to the language that alone would justify a career. Shortly before his death, Caen won a special Pulitzer Prize in 1996 "for his extraordinary and continuing contribution as a voice and conscience of his city." In his will, Caen funded a public fireworks festival for the people of San Francisco, which culminated with the image of a typewriter hovering above the bay. His public memorial service was among the largest attended in the city's history, and a street was renamed "Herb Caen Way."

JIMMY CANNON (1909–1973) Greenwich Village–born Jimmy Cannon gained his fame writing sports columns for New York dailies and for a time was the highest paid sportswriter in the nation, making $1,000 a week. His range and access was aided by friendships with the hard-drinking rich and famous, including Frank Sinatra and Ernest Hemingway. Fellow New York columnist Pete Hamill paid Cannon tribute by writing: "It was Cannon who made me want to be a newspaper man. He wrote a sports column, but it was always more than that. In some ways the hero of the column was its style, an undisciplined personal mixture of New York street talk, soaring elegance, Hemingway and Algren, deep Celtic feeling, city loneliness, prohibition violence, and a personal belief in honor."

ROBERT J. CASEY (1890–1962) This South Dakota native served in the First World War as an artilleryman at Verdun and Argonne, earning three citations for bravery. After being discharged as a captain after the war, Casey joined the *Chicago Daily News*, where he stayed for the next twenty-seven years. He worked as a columnist and foreign correspondent, covering the Prohibition-era Chicago Gang Wars and then the Second World War, from the Battle of Britain to the immediate aftermath of Pearl Harbor. He traveled extensively throughout Southeast Asia, publishing accounts of his adventures under the titles "Vest Pocket Anthology" and "Such Interesting People." He was named Press Veteran of the Year in 1955 by the Chicago Press Veterans Association. His papers are archived at the Newberry Library in Chicago.

FRANCIS PHARCELLUS CHURCH (1839–1906) The author of the most reprinted newspaper piece in American history is also among the least known. Francis Pharcellus Church was trained to be a lawyer but instead pursued the newspaper life. His father was the editor of the *New York Chronicle*. He and his brother William founded *The Galaxy*, a literary magazine that published articles by Walt Whitman and Mark Twain, ultimately merging with *The Atlantic Monthly*. In 1897, Church was writing editorials for Charles Dana's *New York Sun*. The paper received a letter from eight-year-old Virginia O'Hanlon, asking if there was a Santa Claus. Church wrote the immortal response quickly and anonymously. Church was married to Elizabeth Wickham but died childless. His contribution to American literature is reprinted in newspapers across the country and around the world each Christmas.

BOB CONSIDINE (1906–1975) He began writing a column about local high school tennis for the *Washington Post* and ended up covering World War II, the cold war and corresponding with presidents. In the interim, Bob Considine's daily sports column was syndicated in more than one hundred papers. After the attack on Pearl Harbor, Considine shifted gears to serve as a war correspondent, covering the South Pacific and cowriting the classic *Thirty Seconds over Tokyo*. He ultimately wrote or edited twenty-five books and was awarded numerous journalism prizes for his interviews and profiles. His immortal lede for "Louis Knocks Out Schmeling" earned the column's inclusion in *The Best American Sports-writing of the 20th Century.* In 1973, he wrote what is considered the shortest column ever published: "I have nothing to say today." In his last column, he wrote, "I'll croak in the newspaper business. Is there any better way to go?"

STANLEY CROUCH (1945–) The *New York Daily News* columnist is also an accomplished jazz critic and novelist. He writes the liner notes to jazz trumpeter Wynton Marsalis's albums and often combines music criticism with his political column, notably denouncing gangsta rap for its promotion of violence, sexism, homophobia, and glorification of crime. His books include *Notes of a Hanging Judge: Essays and Reviews, 1979–1989* and the novel *Don't the Moon Look Lonesome*. In 1993, he was awarded the MacArthur Foundation's "Genius" Award.

RICHARD HARDING DAVIS (1864–1916) The pioneering war correspondent and columnist helped create the image of the swashbuckling international reporter, writing of bullets that sound like "humming-birds on a warm summer's day." He first made his name covering the devastation of the Johnstown Flood and then focused his attention overseas, often becoming a part of the action he chronicled. Davis participated in his friend Teddy Roosevelt's charge up San Juan Hill in the Spanish-American War, being named an honorary "Rough Rider" in its aftermath. David helped established Roosevelt's fame and had become a celebrity in his own right. He covered the Russian-Japanese war from the Japanese perspective and traveled extensively to hot-spots around the world. His account of the German army marching into Belgium at the outset of the First World War, "Like a River of Steel, It Flowed Gray and Ghostlike," is considered a classic of war reporting. Davis authored many thinly veiled fictional accounts of his adventures, including *Captain Macklin* and *Soldiers of Fortune*. He died suddenly at his home in Mount Kisco, New York, shortly before his fifty-second birthday.

PETE DEXTER (1943–) A National Book Award–winning novelist for *Paris, Trout* in 1988, Pete Dexter first made his name as a columnist for the *Philadelphia Daily News* and the *Sacramento Bee* in the 1970s and '80s. His wry, self-effacing style fronted a razor-sharp mind that enjoyed confrontation. His reported columns show remarkable range—alternately compassionate, cold-eyed, and funny. The best of his newspaper work was collected in the highly recommended 2007 book *Paper Trails*.

FREDERICK DOUGLASS (1818–1895) A runaway slave turned self-made man and American moral leader, Frederick Douglass founded the abolitionist newspaper the *North Star* in Rochester, New York, in 1847. Its motto was: "Right is of no Sex—Truth is of no Color—God is the Father of us all, and we are all Brethren." Remembered as an orator and pioneering civil rights leader, Douglass was also an accomplished editor, essayist, and author. He wrote for numerous newspapers throughout his life and wrote books including *The Life and Times of Frederick Douglass* and *My Bondage and My Freedom*. He served as a U.S. marshal and U.S. minister to Haiti under Republican administrations in the post–Civil War nineteenth century.

MAUREEN DOWD (1952–) The Pulitzer Prize–winning *New York Times* columnist is known for her jaunty, personality-driven political columns. A native of Washington, D.C., where her father was a police inspector, Dowd attended Catholic University and began work at the *Washington Star* as an editorial assistant, becoming a feature writer and sports columnist. The *New York Times's* White House correspondent in the first Bush administration, she was given a column upon the retirement of Anna Quindlen. Dowd quickly established a distinctive style, drawing out the character of administration officials, complete with nicknames. She won the 1999 Pulitzer for her commentary in the wake of the Monica Lewinsky affair. In 2000, Dowd won the Damon Runyon Award for outstanding contributions to journalism.

FINLEY PETER DUNNE (1867–1936) Creator of the turn-of-the-century American mainstay, Mr. Dooley, Finley Peter Dunne was a Chicago journalist who gained national prominence through his humorous columns. Mr. Dooley was a fictitious Irish saloonkeeper who dispensed wisdom in a dialect brogue to a fictitious steel mill worker named Mr. Hennessey. Many of Dooley's sayings became American aphorisms, such as "A fanatic is a man that does what he thinks th' Lord wud do if He knew th' facts iv th' case." Dunne sold several successful volumes of Mr. Dooley columns and counted prominent figures like President Theodore Roosevelt as both fans and friends.

FANNY FERN (1811–1872) Fanny Fern was the adopted name of Sara Willis Parton, the first professional female newspaper columnist in American history and the highest-paid columnist of her time. Publishing her work for the *New York Ledger* uninterrupted between 1856 and 1872, Fern commanded $100 a week for her popular column. The first anthology of her work, *Fern Leaves*, sold an astounding seventy thousand copies. Her semi-autobiographical first novel, *Ruth Hall,* was likewise a success. The thrice-married Fern was an early suffragist, once used her column to defend Walt Whitman from criticism after the publication of *Leaves of Grass*, and lived on Eighteenth Street in the Gramercy Park area of Manhattan. Parton requested that her headstone read simply "Fanny Fern."

BENJAMIN FRANKLIN (1706–1790) This founding father always referred to himself as a "publisher" first—at a time when the trade meant being an owner, editor, and journalist. Apprenticing at his brother James's *New England Courant*, young Benjamin filed a series of letters from a fictitious character named Silence DoGood. When he achieved his own press in Philadelphia more than a decade later, he created *Poor Richard's Almanack*, offering practical advice on how to live a prosperous and virtuous life and selling some ten thousand copies a year. Franklin remained involved in all aspects of early American civic life, establishing the Library Society and the Franklin Inn Club, a Philadelphia club for journalists and writers.

THOMAS L. FRIEDMAN (1953–) Thomas Friedman is a Minnesota native turned prophet of globalization and three-time Pulitzer Prize winner. His *New York Times* column is read around the world. He became Beirut bureau chief six weeks before the Israeli invasion of Lebanon in 1982, and his frontline reporting gave him enduring insights into the Middle East conflicts, bringing his first Pulitzer and forming the basis of his award-winning book *From Beirut to Jerusalem,* ultimately translated into twenty-five languages. He then served as the *Times*'s a chief diplomatic correspondent during the end the cold war and revived the paper's foreign affairs column in 1995. "I tried to do two things with the column when I took it over," he explained. "First was to broaden the definition of foreign affairs and explore the impacts on international relations of finance, globalization, environmentalism, biodiversity, and technology, as well as covering conventional issues like conflict, traditional diplomacy, and arms control. Second, I tried to write in a way that would be accessible to the general reader and bring a broader audience into the foreign policy conversation—beyond the usual State Department policy wonks." Friedman's other best-selling books include *The Lexus and the Olive Tree* and *The World Is Flat*.

MARGARET FULLER (1810–1850) Legendary editor Horace Greeley hired Fuller to be a literary and social critic for the *New York Tribune*, making her the first female member of the staff. Fuller was already well-known as coeditor of *The Dial*, a transcendentalist publication. In 1846, she bade farewell to New York, having convinced Greeley to send her to Europe as a foreign correspondent (another first) to cover the Roman Revolution. While in Italy she met her husband and had a son. They were all lost in a shipwreck off the coast of Fire Island, only miles away from New York.

PETER GAMMONS (1945–) A Boston-based baseball-columnist, Gammons joined the *Boston Globe* in 1969 and ESPN in 1988. His in-print and on-air commentary have made him one of the best known sports-writers of his era. He was named National Sportswriter of the Year in 1989, 1990 and 1993. In 2006, Gammons released an album titled *Never Slow Down, Never Grow Old*. The City of Boston proclaimed January 9, 2009, "Peter Gammons Day."

HARRY GOLDEN (1902–1981) Founder, editor, publisher, and writer of the *Carolina Israelite*, Harry Golden was born in the Ukraine and raised on New York's Lower East Side. After losing his job in the stock-market crash of 1929 and serving three years for mail fraud in a federal penitentiary, Golden moved to Charlotte, North Carolina. His irregularly published newspaper combined humor, Jewish folklore, and contemporary politics, including Golden's support for civil rights in the still segregated South, the subject of his most famous column, "The Vertical Negro Plan." His collection *Only in America* became a national bestseller as Golden's unabashed patriotism and humorous approach to social criticism made him a beloved figure in his lifetime. The *New York Post* proclaimed: "His is the voice of sanity amid the braying of jackals. He combines the cool lucidity of a Montaigne with the gusto of a pushcart peddler."

BOB GREENE (1947–) Robert Bernard "Bob" Greene was a twenty-four-year veteran of the *Chicago Tribune*, where he won numerous awards for his columns before resigning in 2002. Greene's friendship with basketball great Michael Jordan provided material for many columns as well as one of two of his twenty-four books. Often writing from the baby boomer perspective, Greene has written about his experiences as a roadie for rocker Alice Cooper as well as touring with '60s surf-rock duo Jan and Dean. A column he wrote on a library destroyed by fire resulted in the donation of twenty thousand books and $25,000. An Ohio native and father of two children, Greene has written a column for *Esquire* and done on-air commentary for ABC's *Nightline*. He resigned from the *Chicago Tribune* under pressure after an inappropriate encounter from a decade earlier became public. He currently writes a weekly column for CNN.com.

LEWIS GRIZZARD (1946–1994) This Southern humorist was once called "a Mark Twain for our Time" by the *New York Times*. The Georgia-born Grizzard wrote for the *Atlanta Journal-Constitution* his entire career, taking a "good ole boy" anti-PC attitude mixed with a sweetness for Southern life. He was the author of eighteen books—one sample title is *Elvis Is Dead and I Don't Feel Too Good Myself*—and his column was syndicated in 450 newspapers across the country at the height of his popularity. "Writing a daily column is like being married to a nymphomaniac," Grizzard once said. "The first two weeks is fun."

WOODY GUTHRIE (1912–1967) This archetypal American folksinger—an inspiration to Bob Dylan and many others—also wrote a newspaper column called "Woody Sez" for the *People's Daily World* in the 1930s. The composer of "This Land Is Your Land" and author of the memoir *Bound for Glory* was later the subject of a biography by *Time* magazine political columnist Joe Klein.

PETE HAMILL (1935–) Pete Hamill began delivering newspapers in Brooklyn and became one of the most respected journalists of his generation. He started as a columnist for the *New York Post* in 1965 and ultimately went on to serve as editor of that newspaper as well as its rival, the *New York Daily News*. His subjects range from war to politics to sports, music, and the attacks of 9/11. He has written a celebrated memoir, *A Drinking Life*, numerous New York City–based novels (*Snow in August, Forever*), and two anthologies of his journalism, *Irrational Ravings* and *Piecework*. He even won a Grammy for writing the liner notes to Bob Dylan's classic *Blood on the Tracks*. Hamill is the recipient of numerous awards, including the Ernie Pyle Lifetime Achievement Award from the National Society of Newspaper Columnists and the A. J. Liebling Lifetime Achievement Award from the Boxing Writers of America

BEN HECHT (1894–1964) The *Chicago Daily News* columnist became a pioneering Hollywood screenwriter, using his journalist experience to write *The Front Page* and other award-winning films. The son of Russian Jewish immigrants, Hecht served as a war correspondent in Berlin in 1918 and 1919. Upon returning to the *Daily News,* Hecht proposed a column to be called "One Thousand and One Afternoons," composing a short story each day, rooted in reportage. As his editor, Henry Justin Smith, explained, "The idea [was] that just under the edge of the news as commonly understood, the news often flatly unimaginatively told, lay life; that in this urban life there dwelt the stuff of literature, not hidden in remote places, either, but walking the downtown streets, peering from the windows of skyscrapers, sunning itself in parks and boulevards." The column was influential and successful for a time. His real-world experience made him attractive to Hollywood, where he stayed for the remainder of his life, writing or assisting with the scripts of *Scarface, Gone with the Wind* (uncredited), *Gunga Din, His Girl Friday, Wuthering Heights,* and *Underworld.* He wrote and directed the film *Angels Over Broadway* and was active in Zionist causes that aided the creation of the State of Israel.

W. C. HEINZ (1915–2008) William Charles Heinz joined the staff of the *New York Sun* after graduating from Middlebury College. Intending to cover sports, he instead soon found himself covering the Second World War from the front lines. After the war's end he got his wish and returned to New York to begin writing a column for the *Sun* called "The Sports Scene." His column "Death of a Racehorse," written on a manual typewriter on scene at the racetrack is regarded as one of the best sports articles ever written and been called the "Gettysburg Address" of sportswriting. Following the shuttering of the *New York Sun,* Heinz wrote primarily for magazines. He cowrote Vincent Lombardi's *Run to Daylight* and the novel *M*A*S*H,* which was turned into a celebrated film and television series. His sportswriting was collected in two anthologies, *American Mirror* and *What a Time It Was.*

ERNEST HEMINGWAY (1899–1961) The archetypal American novelist began as a newspaper reporter for the *Kansas City Star* and the *Toronto Star,* filing dispatches from Chicago, Paris, Barcelona, and Germany. Much of Hemingway's journalism is captured in the anthology *By-line: Ernest Hemingway.* In later years, with his reputation established, Hemingway occasionally filed features and columns from war-zones for the *New York Times.* He credited the *Kansas City Star*'s style guide for providing the foundation of his writing: "Use short sentences. Use short first paragraphs. Use vigorous English. Be positive, not negative."

DANIEL HENNINGER (1946–) The Deputy Editor of the *Wall Street Journal* editorial page, Henninger writes the weekly "Wonderland" column. He shared the *Wall Street Journal*'s Pulitzer Prize for coverage of the September 11th attacks and was a Pulitzer finalist for editorial writing in 1987 and 1996. He has won numerous journalistic awards.

O. HENRY (1862–1910) O. Henry is the pen name for William Sydney Porter, the famed short-story writer of "The Gift of the Magi" and other American fables, Porter worked as a columnist for the *Houston Daily Post* in 1895 and 1896. Previously, Porter had tried to establish a satirical magazine called *The Rolling Stone* in Austin, Texas, achieving critical but not commercial success. At the invitation of the *Houston Post*'s editor, Porter began a column called "Postscripts and Pencillings" at the salary of $25 a week. It foreshadowed the style and tone that would later become famous under the name O. Henry. "Postscripts" proved popular, but Porter abruptly stopped filing copy after he was indicted for embezzling from a prior employer and fled to Central America before serving time in a federal prison in Ohio. Thereafter, he decamped for New York City and found his fortune as a popular short-story writer. O. Henry's *Houston Post* columns have been collected in a single volume called *Postscripts*.

BOB HERBERT (1945–) Born in Brooklyn and raised in New Jersey, Bob Herbert's journalism career began at the *Newark Star-Ledger* after a stint in the U.S. Army. He moved over to the *New York Daily News* and then became an on-air national correspondent reporting for NBC News. In 1993, he reached the peak as an Op-Ed page columnist at the *New York Times*, writing columns on politics, urban affairs, and social trends. In 2005, he published *Promises Betrayed: Waking Up from the American Dream*. In 2011, he resigned his column. Herbert has been awarded the Meyer Berger Award and the American Society of Newspaper Editors Award.

CARL HIAASEN (1953–) A columnist, novelist, and humorist, Carl Hiaasen captures the absurdity of his native Florida's excesses. A *Miami Herald* columnist since 1985, Hiaasen is among the most versatile contemporary columnists, touching on politics, corruption, crime, corporate greed, and environmental devastation. Two collections of his columns have been published to date: *Kick Ass* and *Paradise Screwed*. On the job of writing a column, Hiaasen believes: "You just cover a lot of territory and you do it aggressively and you do it fairly and you don't play favorites and you don't take any prisoners. It's the old school of slash-and-burn metropolitan column writing. You just kick ass. That's what you do. And that's what they pay you to do."

ART HOPPE (1925–2000) A mainstay of the *San Francisco Chronicle* for more than forty years, Hoppe's humor columns could be laced with a serious message. That was certainly the case with "To Root Against Your Country," written at the height of opposition to the Vietnam War. *The Chronicle* ran Hoppe's column five days a week and it was syndicated to more than one hundred papers. He was as much identified with San Francisco as his competitor Herb Caen, but Hoppe's columns presented stories developed in a style similar to that of his friend Art Buchwald. In 1996, he was awarded the Ernie Pyle lifetime achievement award from the National Society of Newspaper Columnists.

LANGSTON HUGHES (1902–1967) Famous as a poet and playwright, Langston Hughes also wrote a weekly column for the *Chicago Defender* from the 1940s to the 1960s, a leading African-American paper billed as "The World's Greatest Weekly." Beginning in 1943, Hughes created a character named Jesse B. Simple to use as a foil for addressing issues of the day, from the Second World War to racial discrimination. The column and character proved so popular that Hughes eventually filled five books with his musings, beginning with *Simple Speaks His Mind* in 1950.

MOLLY IVINS (1944–2007) A Texas humorist and fighting liberal, Molly Ivins always gave her readers a good time. A columnist for the *Dallas Times-Herald*, the *Fort Worth*

Star-Telegram, and Creators Syndicate, Ivins pulled no punches, as when she remarked that Pat Buchanan's "Culture War" speech at the 1992 Republican convention "probably sounded better in the original German." But she could also express powerful, understated sentiment, as with her classic column "A Short Story about the Vietnam War Memorial." In books such as *Molly Ivins Can't Say That, Can She?,* she expressed her love of her Lone Star State even as she mocked its excesses, saying, "God gave me Texas politics to write about. How can I not be funny?" This defiant left-libertarian died of breast cancer while still in her prime, but she left a rollicking legacy. "So keep fightin' for freedom and justice, beloveds, but don't you forget to have fun doin' it," she once advised. "Lord, let your laughter ring forth. Be outrageous, ridicule the fraidy-cats, rejoice in all the oddities that freedom can produce. And when you get through kickin' ass and celebratin' the sheer joy of a good fight, be sure to tell those who come after how much fun it was."

PETER R. KANN (1942–) While covering the Vietnam War for the *Wall Street Journal,* Kann received a telegram from his editors telling him to stay out of harm's way. Kann cabled back: "Message Unreceived." He won a Pulitzer Prize in 1972 for reporting on the India–Pakistan War. Kann was appointed publisher of the *Wall Street Journal* in 1988 and served as CEO of the Dow Jones Company from 1993 to 2006. "We believe facts are facts and that they are ascertainable through honest, open-minded, and diligent reporting," he once wrote. "We thus believe that truth is attainable by laying fact upon fact, much like the construction of a cathedral. News, in short, is not merely a matter of views. And truth is not merely in the eye of the beholder."

MICHAEL KELLY (1957–2003) Armed with piercing insight and perfect pitch, Michael Kelly was one of the best political and culture writers of his generation. A frequent contributor to the pages of the *Washington Post,* Kelly was the editor of *The New Republic* and *The Atlantic Monthly.* He was the author of *Martyr's Day* and the posthumous collection *Things Worth Fighting For.* He died covering the 2003 invasion of Iraq. Even a quick survey of his writing will instill an appreciation of a rare talent. As Robert Vare wrote, "Mike's voice was a musical instrument that he played in many different keys."

MURRAY KEMPTON (1917–1997) He began as a copyboy for H. L. Mencken and became a newspaper legend in his own right. Four days a week for almost forty years, Murray Kempton graced New York City newspaper pages, first at the *New York Post* and then finishing his career at *Newsday.* He was known for a courtly personal style, riding a bicycle around New York in a three-piece suit, listening to Bach on headphones. His writing could be wise, kind, and incisive. It was collected in *America Comes of Middle Age* and *Rebellions, Perversities, and Main Events.* As David Remnick wrote in 1994: "Murray Kempton is the greatest of all living newspapermen and his beat stretches from the Vatican to the social clubs of the Mob. He is a moralist who does not preach; an artist who reports."

MICHAEL KINSLEY (1951–) The columnist and editor of publications ranging from *The New Republic* to *Slate* to the *Los Angeles Times,* and founding cohost of CNN's *Crossfire,* Kinsley has staunchly—but not dogmatically—defended the Democratic

Party on air as well as in print for decades. The author of three collections of his columns, including *Please Don't Remain Calm: Provocations and Commentaries*, Kinsley announced in 2001 that he had been diagnosed with Parkinson's disease. He is currently a columnist at Politico.com. Among his contributions to political discourse is his definition of a gaffe in Washington: when a politician tells the truth.

TONY KORNHEISER (1948–) The former *Washington Post* sports and humor columnist, Kornheiser is now best known for his ESPN show *Pardon the Interruption* and his radio show. In 1997, he was a runner-up for the Pulitzer Prize for Commentary. Collections of his humor columns include: *Pumping Irony, Bald as I Wanna Be,* and *I'm Back for More Cash: A Tony Kornheiser Collection (Because You Can't Take Two Hundred Newspapers into the Bathroom).*

CHARLES KRAUTHAMMER (1950–) One of the most influential conservative columnists writing today began his career in politics as a speechwriter for liberal Democratic vice president Walter Mondale. He is also unique among the ranks of columnists in that he is an MD—a licensed psychiatrist—and partially paralyzed due to a car accident in medical school. Krauthammer was awarded the Pulitzer Prize for Commentary in 1987, two years after he began writing his weekly column for the *Washington Post*. He had previously worked at *Time* and *The New Republic*. Krauthammer is credited for developing the term "Reagan Doctrine" and he coined "Bush Derangement Syndrome" in a 2003 column: "the acute onset of paranoia in otherwise normal people in reaction to the policies, the presidency—nay—the very existence of George W. Bush."

NICHOLAS D. KRISTOF (1959–) The two-time Pulitzer Prize–winning *New York Times* columnist's official bio states that he "has lived on four continents, reported on six, and traveled to more than one hundred forty countries, plus all fifty states, every Chinese province and every main Japanese island. He's also one of the very few Americans to be at least a two-time visitor to every member of the Axis of Evil." In 1990, he and his wife Sheryl WuDunn won a Pulitzer Prize for reporting on the Tiananmen Square massacre. Together, they are the authors of three books, including *Half the Sky: From Oppression to Opportunity for Women Worldwide.* In 2006, Kristof won the Pulitzer Prize for Commentary, earning accolades "for his graphic, deeply reported columns that, at personal risk, focused attention on genocide in Darfur and that gave voice to the voiceless in other parts of the world." Kristof was the subject of a 2009 documentary, *Reporter,* and established himself as an early adaptor of digital journalism, becoming the first *Times* columnist to blog and use Twitter. "I'm not surprised to see him emerge as the moral conscience of our generation of journalists," said his one-time college classmate Jeffrey Toobin. "I am surprised to see him as the Indiana Jones of our generation of journalists."

RING LARDNER (1885–1933) He began as a sportswriter in South Bend, Indiana, but Ring Lardner achieved fame with his wide-ranging column, "In the Wake of the News" and through his satirical short stories collected in bestsellers like *You Know Me Al.* He also was dispatched to cover the First World War. Lardner was one of the few correspondents to recognize that the fix was in while covering the 1919 "Black Sox"–thrown World

Series. The young Ernest Hemingway was an admirer of Lardner's style, sometimes signing his high school newspaper pieces "Ring Lardner, Jr." The great sports columnist Grantland Rice was a close friend and neighbor in East Hampton, New York.

JOHN LEONARD (1939–2008) The celebrated literary critic wrote the weekly "Private Lives" column for the *New York Times* from 1977 to 1980. Known for his passionate liberal views, he nonetheless worked at *The National Review* before becoming the *New York Times* Book Review's editor at age thirty-one. In later years, he wrote columns for *Newsday* and *The Nation*, as well as criticism for *New York* magazine and serving as the on-air television critic for CBS's *Sunday Morning*. His books include *Private Lives in the Imperial City* and *The Last Innocent White Man in America*. "The library is where I've always gone," Leonard wrote, "for transcendence, of course, a zap to the synaptic cleft, the radioactive glow of genius in the dark; but also to get more complicated; for advice on how to be decent and brave; for narrative instead of scenarios, discrepancies instead of euphemism. In the library, that secretariat of dissidents, they don't lie to me." "When I start to read John Leonard," his friend Kurt Vonnegut said, "it is as though I, while simply looking for the men's room, blundered into a lecture by the smartest man who ever lived."

MAX LERNER (1902–1992) A Russian immigrant, Lerner wrote a controversial column for the *New York Post* beginning in 1949. Embracing the role of a public intellectual, Lerner's liberal views won him the admiration of Elizabeth Taylor and a place on the Nixon Enemies List. In later life, he wrote movingly of his struggle with illness and found grudging respect for President Ronald Reagan. Two hundred of his columns were anthologized in *The Unfinished Country*.

WALTER LIPPMANN (1889–1974) Walter Lippmann was the premiere pundit at the heart of the American Century, and his column ran from 1931 to 1971. He was a counselor to presidents whose work was carefully read by all who worked in the corridors of power. As a student at Harvard, he studied under George Santayana and William James and served as an assistant to Lincoln Steffens. He later helped draft Woodrow Wilson's Fourteen Points and served on the staff of General Pershing in Army Intelligence. He was an editor at *The New Republic* and the *New York World*, before starting his syndicated column "Today and Tomorrow." He wrote over forty books, including the 1922's classic (and controversial) *Public Opinion*. "We have missed the meaning of history, then, if today we are 'Jeffersonians' opposed to 'Hamiltonians' or vice versa," Lippmann wrote in a 1943 column titled "The Living Past." "To be partisan today as between Jefferson and Hamilton is like arguing whether men or women are more necessary to the procreation of the race."

STEVE LOPEZ (1953–) An award-winning columnist at the *Los Angeles Times* and *Philadelphia Inquirer*, Steve Lopez is the son of Spanish and Italian immigrants. His work has been anthologized in *Land of Giants* and he has written three novels to date. His series of columns about his friendship with the homeless and schizophrenic bassist Nathaniel Anthony Ayers inspired *The Soloist*, a 2009 film starring Robert Downey Jr. and Jamie Foxx. "I've always tried to keep readers wondering what might be next, whether it's a postcard from a corner of a forgotten neighborhood, someone's struggle against the system, or a good chop to the teeth of a public official," Lopez says. "I used to listen to Thelonious Monk when I wrote, just to remind myself there's no point in doing it if you can't find a way to write like no one else and make a story your own."

CHARLES McDOWELL (1926–2010) The Washington columnist for the *Richmond Times-Dispatch*, McDowell was nationally syndicated from 1954 until his retirement in 1998. He wrote three books—a history of the 1964 presidential campaign titled *Campaign Fever* and two collections of humor columns. His unassuming Southern style and distinctive voice made him a favorite for television commentary and documentaries, including Ken Burns's *Congress* and *The Civil War*. "Through his voice," Burns remembered, "he brought himself, Charley McDowell, with all his humor and sensitivity and a kind of confidence that things are going to be OK in the end. It was that confidence that informed his writing and thinking. He was a great reporter, a great writer, but most of all a great person."

MARY McGRORY (1918–2004) The Boston native worked her way up from being a secretary at the *Boston Herald-Traveler* to becoming one of the most influential and admired Washington columnists of her era. From the Army-McCarthy hearings to the Kennedy administration to Watergate, McGrory's presence was a Washington staple and her column captured the tone of the times. She worked for the *Washington Star* until it folded and then moved to the *Washington Post*, writing her column until shortly before her death. She won the Pulitzer Prize in 1975 for her columns on Watergate. "No great men call me," she once said proudly. "You know who calls me? Losers. I am their mark. . . . If you want to abolish land mines. If you want to reform campaign spending . . . if you want to save children from abuse, or stupid laws, or thickheaded judges, you have my telephone number. . . . All the places of little hope, that's my constituency."

H. L. MENCKEN (1880–1956) The "Sage of Baltimore" is among the most revered American columnists—a transcendent skeptic, an equal opportunity offender. Writing for the *Baltimore Sun* and cofounding *The American Mercury*, Henry Louis Mencken courted controversy as a critic and satirist. He was particularly impatient with the ignorance that paraded as populism and the politicians who catered to it. His coverage of the Scopes Monkey trial brought him national renown, and he was the thinly-veiled inspiration for the character E. K. Hornbeck played by Gene Kelly in the film *Inherit the Wind*. He wrote over forty books, many of which are still in print. "A newspaper reporter, in those remote days" he wrote in his memoir *Newspaper Days*, "had a grand and gaudy time of it, with no call to envy any man."

JIM MURRAY (1919–1998) The longtime *Los Angeles Times* sports columnist was so beloved that Ronald Reagan showed up at a tribute dinner to offer ten minutes of unscripted remarks. The nationally syndicated Murray could be funny, sarcastic, and often disarmingly personal with his column—the only cardinal sin, as he saw it, was to bore readers. A 1990 winner of the Pulitzer Prize for Commentary, Murray filed his last column on the day he died. Looking back gratefully at a life in sportswriting he said, "Somebody had to sit on the curb and watch the parade go by."

JACK NEWFIELD (1938–2004) This modern muckraker wrote for the *Village Voice* for twenty-four years before bringing his column to the *New York Daily News*, the *New York Post*, and the *New York Sun*. He was the author of ten books, received the George Polk Award for Investigative Journalism in 1980 and was awarded an Emmy for his documentary on Don King in 1991. A friend and confidant of Bobby Kennedy and Muhammad Ali, he was unafraid to take on the rich, powerful, and corrupt. When eccentric millionaire Abe Hirschfeld bought the *New York Post* in 1993, Newfield's column about his new boss asked "Who Is This Nut?" "I do have an underlying set of principles," Newfield wrote when he was ill with cancer. "Tell the truth no matter what. . . . Also, I tend to defend underdogs and the powerless. I often find the official version of events is not the true story. I have never wanted to be a stenographer for those in power."

PEGGY NOONAN (1950–) The *Wall Street Journal* columnist began her career as a writer and producer for CBS News. She was a Special Assistant and Speechwriter for President Ronald Reagan. Her memoir of the Reagan Era, *What I Saw at the Revolution,* has become a classic. Her *Wall Street Journal* columns after the attacks of September 11, 2001, helped heal a city and a nation struggling to assimilate the facts of loss into their lives, and were published in the collection *A Heart, a Cross and a Flag.* Noonan's eight books to date include a biography of Ronald Reagan, *When Character Was King,* and *Patriotic Grace: What It Is and Why We Need It Now.*

KATHLEEN PARKER (1952–) A voice of sanity from South Carolina, Kathleen Parker captures the common sense of Main Street America in her columns for the *Washington Post*. Witty, sly, and self-effacing, Parker's center-right sensibility keeps her political opponents from successfully stereotyping her. She won the H. L. Mencken Award for commentary in 1993 writing for the *Orlando Sentinel*, and the Pulitzer Prize in 2010.

EUGENE PATTERSON (1923–) The Georgia-born editor of the *Atlanta Constitution* in the turbulent 1960s also published a column seven days a week. During World War II, he served as a tank platoon leader in General Patton's Third Army. After his time in Atlanta, Patterson served as Managing Editor of the *Washington Post* and the *St. Petersburg Times* as well as head of the Poynter Institute. A collection of his work— *The Changing South of Gene Patterson: Journalism and Civil Rights, 1960–1968*—was published in 2002. "I was regarded as a Southern turncoat by many of my critics," Patterson said. "But I didn't think I was. I thought I was leading us in the direction the South had to go, which was toward justice."

WESTBROOK PEGLER (1894–1969) One of the most talented and widely read columnists of his time, Pegler's fighting spirit shone through in prose of uncommon wit and clarity. In his prime, he was an equal opportunity offender, criticizing Democrats and Republicans as well as Communists and Fascists with equal enthusiasm. Targets of his attacks were said to have been "Peglerized." In 1938, *Time* magazine wrote, "Pegler's place as the great dissenter for the common man is unchallenged." In 1941, Pegler became the first columnist to win a Pulitzer Prize for Reporting, uncovering criminal racketeering in labor unions. Pegler lost a libel suit in 1954 and was fired by the Hearst syndicate in 1962. He once commented to his friend Murray Kempton that his increasing unhinged-ness did not start with his hatred of Eleanor Roosevelt: "It began when I quit sports and went cosmic. It finished when I began writing on Monday to be printed on Friday." As alcoholism consumed him, he moved further and further to the right, ending his distinguished career writing for a journal published by the John Birch Society. The subject of at least two biographies, Pegler's work was also anthologized in should-be classics like *T'ain't Right* and *The Dissenting Opinions of Mr. Westbrook Pegler.*

LEONARD PITTS JR. (1957–) Winner of the 2004 Pulitzer Prize for Commentary, the *Miami Herald's* Leonard Pitts writes about race, politics, and culture. His column written on September 11, 2001, "We'll Go Forward from This Moment," became a national expression of rage, grief, and resolve. His celebrated column series "What Works?" looks at programs with proven success in helping African-American children. The onetime music critic is the author of a novel, *Before I Forget,* and a collection of columns, *Forward from This Moment.*

BILL PLASCHKE (1958–) Born in Louisville, Kentucky, Plaschke has written for the *Los Angeles Times* since 1987 and been a columnist since 1996. A four-time winner of "Sports Columnist of the Year" by the Associated Press, Plascke is a regular panelist on ESPN's *Around the Horn.* His column "Her Blue Haven" was selected for the annual "Best American Sports Writing" anthology. One collection of his columns has been published to date: *Plaschke: Good Sports, Spoil Sports, Foul Balls and Odd Balls.*

SHIRLEY POVICH (1905–1998) For seventy-five years, Shirley Povich wrote for the *Washington Post*—as enduring a relationship as American journalism is ever likely to see. He became the nation's youngest sports columnist at age twenty and continued his column for the next seventy-one years, ceasing only for military service during World War II. His ledes are the stuff of legend—for example, here is Povich after witnessing Don Larsen's perfect game in the 1956 World Series. "The million-to-one shot came in. Hell froze over. A month of Sundays hit the calendar. Don Larsen today pitched a no-hit, no-run, no-man-reaches-first game in a World Series." He and his wife, Ethy, were the parents of television journalist Maury Povich and two other children, David and Lynn. Many of his best columns were collected in his acclaimed memoir *All Those Mornings . . . at The Post.*

ERNIE PYLE (1900–1945) Ernie Pyle is the quintessential GI journalist and the patron saint of war correspondents. His syndicated Scripps Howard column brought the facts and feel of the Second World War to the home front. He lived on the front lines with the troops—"the God-Damned Infantry," as he christened them. His columns had the informal style of a letter back home but they did not shy away from the cold facts. His column "The Death of Captain Waskow" is among the best writing to come out of the war. Previously, Pyle studied at Indiana University and worked as the nation's first aviation columnist before buying a home in Albuquerque. He wrote a column encouraging Congress to pay active duty soldiers an additional $10 a month as "combat pay," leading to the passage of the proposal, known as the "Ernie Pyle bill." On April 18, 1945, Pyle was killed by Japanese machine-gun fire on the island of le Shima, off the coast of Okinawa. His last words to a soldier standing next to him were, "Are you all right?" Soldiers erected a gravesite monument that read, "At this spot the 77th Infantry Division lost a buddy, Ernie Pyle." Pyle was portrayed by Burgess Meredith in the movie *The Story of G.I. Joe*. His wartime journalism was collected in four books: *Ernie Pyle in England, Here Is Your War, Brave Men,* and *Last Chapter*.

ANNA QUINDLEN (1953–) Winner of the 1992 Pulitzer Prize for Commentary, Anna Quindlen began her career at the *New York Post* and then moved to the *New York Times*, where she wrote the storied "About New York" column from 1981 to 1983 and then created her "Life in the 30s" column. In 1990, she became the third woman to have a regular column on the *Times's* Op-Ed page. In 1995, she left newspapers to become a novelist. Her columns have been collected in *Loud and Clear, Thinking Out Loud,* and *Living Out Loud*.

WILLIAM RASPBERRY (1935–) The 1994 Pulitzer Prize winner for commentary, William Raspberry was a pioneering and popular African-American columnist for the *Washington Post*, beginning in 1966 and continuing for four decades. He retired to run a parent-training program called "Baby Steps" in his native Mississippi. Raspberry often wrote about education as well as urban affairs. He sometimes challenged liberal orthodoxies, arguing that affirmative action should be tied to economic need rather than race. He still writes occasional columns, such as the included "A Path Beyond Grievance," written after the election of Barack Obama.

JAMES RESTON (1909–1995) The Scottish-born Reston twice won the Pulitzer Prize for his work at the *New York Times* and received the Presidential Medal of Freedom. He served as a longtime columnist as well as executive editor of the *Times*. He was sometimes accused of being too close to those in power, but he was also included in President Richard Nixon's Enemies List. In his "retirement," Reston bought and ran the weekly *Vineyard Gazette*. He wrote several books, including a collection of columns called *Sketches in the Sand* and a memoir, *Deadline*. "[Reston] felt that journalism and government were integral parts of the fabric of the country," wrote Reston's biographer John F. Stacks in 2002's *Scotty*, "working in different ways toward the same goal: helping the country deal with threats to its health and survival from abroad and at home."

GRANTLAND RICE (1880–1954) He was known as "the Dean of American sportswriters" and helped the American sports column evolve, adopting a literary style and becoming a star in his own right. The Tennessee native's syndicated column, "The Sportlight," shone on the athletic heroes of his day—Babe Ruth, Jack Dempsey, Seabiscuit and, especially, the Notre Dame backfield he christened "The Four Horsemen." At the end of his career, Rice estimated that he'd written an average of three thousand words a day and traveled fifteen thousand miles a year in pursuit of good stories. He was the play-by-play announcer of the 1922 World Series, the first broadcast in its entirety. He also wrote verse, at least one line of which lodged itself in the American consciousness:

"When the One Great Scorer comes to mark against your name, He writes—not that you won or lost—but how you played the game."

EUGENE ROBINSON (1955–) The 2009 Pulitzer Prize winner for commentary, Robinson joined the *Washington Post* in 1980 and worked his way up from covering City Hall to a foreign correspondent to becoming a columnist in 2005. A native of Orangeburg, South Carolina, and a University of Michigan graduate, Robison is a frequent cable news commentator and the author of three books, including *Disintegration: The Splintering of Black America.* "The great thing about a column," he once said, "is that you have a license to feel."

WILL ROGERS (1879–1935) This cowboy philosopher, humorist, and movie star was among the most beloved celebrities of his day. His column, "Will Rogers Says," was syndicated by the *New York Times.* Will was beloved for his "cool mind and warm heart," offering wisdom that harkened back to his Oklahoma roots. Among his enduring aphorisms: "I never met a man I didn't like" and "everybody is ignorant, only on different subjects." An early aviation enthusiast (often typing his columns out en route), Rogers was killed in an Alaskan crash with aviator Wiley Post. He was mourned in cities and small towns, from the East Coast to the West.

ELEANOR ROOSEVELT (1884–1962) The First Lady of the United States wrote a newspaper column, "My Day," for United Feature Syndicate from 1935 to 1962. It began as a daily diary type item written from the White House but she continued the column after her husband's death and the subjects turned more serious and policy driven. Roosevelt's column remained a popular vehicle for her influence in American political debates until her death.

THEODORE ROOSEVELT (1858–1919) After leaving the White House at age fifty, President Theodore Roosevelt became the editor of *The Outlook* magazine, which served as a base of operations for his adventures. He had always been an author, writing eighteen books and numerous articles over his lifetime. In September 1917, he became a columnist for the *Kansas City Star*, due to his friendship with the paper's founder, William Rockhill Nelson, and TR's growing concern about the lack of U.S. preparation for intervention in World War I. "The Star would be guilty of false modesty if it did not frankly confess its happiness in the acquisition of Colonel Roosevelt to its organization in the capacity of a regular contributor," the paper announced. Roosevelt called himself a "cub reporter." He dictated his columns and sent them into the newsroom via telegraph, continuing the practice until his death in 1919.

CHRIS ROSE (1960–) He has been called "the Crescent City's Bard"—a humorist and longtime columnist for the *New Orleans Times-Picayune* who became perhaps the foremost chronicler of the aftermath of Hurricane Katrina. He was a finalist for the 2006 Pulitzer Prize for Commentary and is the author of *1 Dead in Attic*, a bestselling collection of stories about New Orleans in the four months after Katrina. Rose grew up in the suburbs of Washington D.C. and received a degree in Journalism from the University of Wisconsin-Madison in 1982. Like his adopted hometown, Rose's work is infused with irreverence, flashes of humor illuminating the dark.

CARL T. ROWAN (1925–2000) He was raised in a tiny Tennessee town but left with a burning drive to see the world—an ambition that first took him to the U.S. Navy during WWII, then on to the *Minneapolis Tribune* as a reporter sent to cover the Montgomery bus boycott at the dawn of the civil rights movement. Rowan went on to report from India, Pakistan, and Southeast Asia, where his columns caught the eye of policymakers and led to government stints as ambassador to Finland and director of the U.S. Information Agency—a pioneering appointment for an African-American at the time. He returned to journalism in 1966, commencing a thirty-two-year run as a Washington-based columnist for the *Chicago Sun-Times* and a well-regarded Beltway pundit. At the peak of his influence, Rowan's syndicated column reached half of all homes in the U.S. that received newspapers.

MIKE ROYKO (1932–1997) For more than forty years, Mike Royko was the voice of Chicago. He grew up over his family's tavern and began writing a five-day-a-week column in 1956, switching newspapers three times but never leaving the Windy City. He challenged City Hall and celebrated the little guy, especially those who gathered at his favorite watering hole, the Billy Goat Tavern. Syndicated in over six hundred papers, Royko created characters to tell his stories, including Slats Grobnik, and was the first to call California's Jerry Brown "Governor Moonbeam." Jimmy Breslin called him "the best journalist of his time" and Royko won the Pulitzer Prize for Commentary in 1972. Royko's only book was an unflattering look at Chicago's longtime mayor, John Daley, titled *Boss*, but columns were collected in two posthumous anthologies. Royko's memorial service was held on a sunny day in Wrigley Field.

DAMON RUNYON (1884–1946) Best known today as the author of *Guys and Dolls*, this chronicler of Broadway's characters was born in Pueblo, Colorado, in the waning days of the Wild West. He established his column at the *New York American*, establishing himself as one of the most versatile and distinctive columnists in U.S. history, developing a dialogue style known to devotees as "Runysonese." Runyon covered crime, politics, war, humor, and sports with equal mastery. On one notable adventure, he rode into Mexico with General Pershing on the hunt for Pancho Villa. His short stories were developed into nearly a dozen feature films and more than fifty radio plays, making Runyon one of the wealthiest writers of the time. Runyon was an inveterate gambler and night owl who nonetheless gave up drinking at age thirty in exchange for the hand of the first of his two wives. After his death due to throat cancer, the result of a heavy smoking habit, his ashes were scattered over Manhattan and a still enduring cancer research fund was established in his name.

WILLIAM SAFIRE (1929–2009) A onetime Nixon speechwriter turned *New York Times* columnist, Safire developed a reputation as one of the most thoughtful chroniclers of contemporary politics. A self-described "pundit" and "libertarian-conservative," Safire also authored the weekly "On Language" column in the *New York Times Magazine*. He was the author of *Safire's Political Dictionary* and won the Pulitzer Prize in 1978 for investigating President Carter's budget director's financial dealings. Among Safire's rules for writers: "Remember to never split an infinitive. Take the bull by the hand and avoid mixing metaphors. Proofread carefully to see if you words out. Avoid clichés like the plague. And don't overuse exclamation marks!!"

MARY SCHMICH (1953–) The *Chicago Tribune*'s Mary Schmich is perhaps the only columnist who has a number one hit record. Her June 1, 1997, column "Advice, Like Youth, Probably Wasted on the Young"—written as the commencement address she would have given that year if asked—went viral in the early years of the Internet, often misattributed to Kurt Vonnegut. Its wise advice and irreverent perspective resonated across generations. In 1998, Schmich wrote a book building off the column called *Wear Sunscreen* and in 1999 director Baz Lurhmann wrote a song that turned its words into lyrics over a trance beat, which went to the top of the charts in several countries. Sadly, Schmich's skills as a barrelhouse piano player were not employed. Mary Schmich currently splits her time between her column and writing the comic strip *Brenda Starr*.

JACK SMITH (1916–1996) For forty-two years, Jack Smith was the chronicler of Los Angeles life, as associated with his city as Herb Caen was with San Francisco and Mike Royko was with Chicago. As a columnist, he wrote five days a week, compiling an estimated six thousand columns. He was a witness to Los Angeles's growth, the creation of a southern Californian suburban identity. After his death, a museum exhibit was devoted to his career and civic contributions. "Critics have despised us in Los Angeles as worshippers of money, health, sex, surf, and sun," Smith once said. "Not quite true. We don't worship those things; we just rather get used to them, since they happen to be so available."

JOHN L. SMITH (1960–) The chronicler of Casino-land, Smith has written four columns a week for the *Las Vegas Review-Journal* since 1988. His character studies involve "aging boxers, two-bit mobsters, bookmakers, loan-sharks and waitresses at Denny's—preferably a combination of two or more." He has written five books to date, including an anthology of his columns titled *On the Boulevard*.

RED SMITH (1905–1982) Walter "Red" Smith's 1976 Pulitzer Prize for Commentary cited "the erudition, the literary quality, the vitality and freshness of viewpoint" he brought to the most widely syndicated sports column of his time. Writing about sports for five decades and covering forty-five World Series, Smith didn't become a columnist until age forty and reached the *New York Times* at an age at which many men retire. But his excellence was appreciated by readers and competitors alike, especially given his five-day-a-week output. His *New York Times* colleague Dave Anderson paid tribute to Smith the day after his death, writing: "Red Smith was, quite simply, the best sportswriter. Put the emphasis on 'writer.' Of those who have written sports for a living, no one else ever had the command of the language, the turn of the phrase, the subtlety of the skewer as he did."

I. F. STONE (1907–1989) An iconoclastic and controversial journalist, Isidor Feinstein "Izzy" Stone was the sole proprietor of *I. F. Stone's Weekly* between 1953 and 1973. He was previously a reporter for the *New York Post*, Washington editor of *The Nation*, and foreign correspondent for *PM*. Stone's leftist views led to his being blacklisted in the early 1950s and striking out on his own. (While Stone was an early Soviet sympathizer who eventually became a critic of the USSR, posthumous allegations that he was, for a time, a Soviet spy have been strenuously denied). To his contemporary critics, he replied, "I may be just a goddamn Jew Red to you, but I'm keeping Jefferson alive!" Stone's journalistic style was to pour over voluminous public government documents that other reporters ignored. Late in life, he went back to college to receive a degree in classical languages and wrote a surprise bestseller, *The Trial of Socrates*. Whatever your politics, Stone's mission statement is worth contemplating: "To write the truth as I see it; to defend the weak against the strong; to fight for justice; and to seek, as best I can, to bring healing perspectives to bear on the terrible hates and fears of mankind, in the hope of someday bringing about one world, in which men will enjoy the differences of the human garden instead of killing each other over them."

ERNEST LAWRENCE THAYER (1863–1940) On June 3, 1888, a poem called "Casey" appeared on the pages of the *San Francisco Examiner* under the byline "Phinn." It was written by a twenty-five-year-old former editor of the *Harvard Lampoon* named Ernest Lawrence Thayer. He had been a classmate of the *Examiner*'s young owner, William Randolph Hearst, and was hired to serve as a humor columnist for the fledgling paper. It was Thayer's final offering as columnist—he went back east to work in his family's textile mills in Worcester, Massachusetts. The first public performance of the poem by the actor De Wolf Hopper occurred two months later—Hopper would go on to recite the play more than one thousand times on the vaudeville circuit.

DOROTHY THOMPSON (1893–1961) Sometimes called "The First Lady of American Journalism," Dorothy Thompson was the most influential female columnist of the 1930s and '40s. A pioneer in her field, she was the Berlin bureau chief for the *New York Post* in the late 1920s and became an early and outspoken opponent of the Nazis' rise. She was the first foreign journalist to be expelled from Germany, in 1934. Her syndicated column "On the Record" began in 1936, and she simultaneously served as an NBC radio correspondent, reaching 8 million readers and 5 million listeners. When Hitler invaded Poland in 1939, she spoke on the radio for fifteen consecutive nights denouncing the action and the world war she had warned was coming. Married for a time to the novelist Sinclair Lewis, Thompson was a charismatic and colorful figure. Among her aphorisms: "Only when we are no longer afraid do we begin to live."

HUNTER S. THOMPSON (1937–2005) The great gonzo journalist tried his hand at a weekly column for the *San Francisco Examiner* in the late 1980s. The results were decidedly mixed, though they formed the basis for his collection *Generation of Swine*. But you couldn't blame the editors or the good doctor for trying—Thompson's best political reporting, captured in *Fear and Loathing on the Campaign Trail '72*, mainlines the mixture of ambition, chaos, patriotism, and insanity beneath presidential campaigns. The edgiest humorist who emerged in the wake of the sixties, Hunter warned that "absolute truth is a very rare and dangerous commodity in the context of professional journalism."

CYNTHIA TUCKER (1955–) An *Atlanta Journal-Constitution* columnist and 2007 Pulitzer Prize–winner for Commentary, Cynthia Tucker has become a leading voice in contemporary political debates in print and on-air. She grew up in the end of seg-regation and did not attend an integrated school until she was seventeen. Tucker served as the editorial page editor of the *Journal-Constitution* and now lives in Wash-ington, D.C. Her column is syndicated in twenty-fve papers. Her Pulitzer award cited "her courageous, clear-headed columns that evince a strong sense of morality and per-suasive knowledge of the community."

MARK TWAIN (1835–1910) Mark Twain is the pen name of Samuel Clemens, the Mis-sissippi river boat pilot who ran west to seek his fortune and found himself writing for newspapers. Clemens wrote for the *San Francisco Daily Morning Call*, the *Virginia City Territorial Enterprise*, and the *Sacramento Union*. Those experiences, plus the travelogues he composed after a Pacific voyage, helped develop the humorous persona of Mark Twain, who would help define American literature. The column "The Danger of Lying in Bed" uses statistics about the risks of rail crashes to tell a comic tale with a serious underlying point. It was published simultaneously in the *Buffalo Express* newspaper and as Twain's column in *The Galaxy* in 1871.

WELLS TWOMBLY (1935–1977) Wells Twombly was named one of the six best sports-writers in the nation by *Esquire* magazine in 1974, His inventive columns graced the *San Francisco Examiner* six days a week until his untimely death at age forty-two. His work was anthologized in *Best Sports Stories* for sixteen of the twenty years of his professional career. "There Was Only One Casey" was included in the anthology *Best American Sports-writing of the Century*. "I try to be as literate as I can be. Anybody who writes down to a reader in this age of higher education is living in the past," Twombly once commented. "I don't want anybody skimming through anything I write. I've been battling the Who-What-Where-Why-When and KISS (Keep it Simple Stupid) crowd ever since I started. Lord, we're in a war with television. I try to recreate scenes for readers, take them places where even the damned camera can't go."

GENE WEINGARTEN (1951–) "Below the Beltway" is the name of Gene Weingartern's weekly humor column for the *Washington Post*. Weingarten has won two Pulitzer Prizes for Feature Writing in 2008 and 2010. He coauthors the comic strip *Barney & Clyde* with his son Dan. Among his books are *Old Dogs Are the Best Dogs* and *The Hypochondriac's Guide to Life. And Death.*

ORSON WELLES (1915–1985) The legendarily ambitious actor and director wasn't sat-isfied with *Citizen Kane* and *The Mercury Theatre*. In 1945, he embarked on a column titled "Orson Welles Today." Syndicated by the *New York Post*, it balanced Welles's views on foreign policy and domestic politics in the closing days of World War II. At the time, Welles was considering a future career in politics. This little-remembered period in his life is well captured in the "Actor Turns Columnist" chapter in volume two of Simon Callow's biography of Welles, *Hello Americans*. Welles summed up the challenges of a regular column, telling his editor: "It takes a huge daily toll, it calls for enthusiasm and love and energy . . . getting that piece off is the toughest, most thankless day's work I've ever been faced with."

WILLIAM ALLEN WHITE (1868–1944) He was born, lived, and died in the town Emporia, Kansas, but his voice reached across the nation. William Allen White was an editor, author, and leading Progressive Republican—the voice of Midwest common sense. He bought the *Emporia Gazette* for $3,000 in 1895 and used the papers' editorials as his own column, combining the personal with the political. He asked, "What's the Matter with Kansas?" attacking the unintended consequences of populist reformers and labor unions that had left Kansas at a competitive disadvantage with other states. He took on the Ku Klux Klan and won a Pulitzer Prize in 1923 for a three-paragraph editorial backing free speech, counseling "If there is freedom, folly will die of its own poison." His editorial on the death of his daughter Mary was also widely reprinted. He posthumously won a 1947 Pulitzer Prize for his autobiography and the University of Kansas Journalism School is named in his honor.

MARJORIE WILLIAMS (1958–2005) The *Washington Post* columnist was diagnosed with fourth-stage liver cancer the day she was told that her column would be nationally syndicated. She was a writer of uncommon grace and precision, the daughter of a successful publishing executive who left that business to become a writer in her own right, penning profiles for *Vanity Fair* and then the *Post*. She achieved an Op-Ed page column in 2000 and was diagnosed with cancer a year later, outlasting the months-to-live diagnosis by four years. "The Halloween of My Dreams" was her final column and is included in a masterful collection of her work, *The Woman at the Washington Zoo: Writings on Politics, Family, and Fate,* which was edited by her husband, *Slate* columnist Timothy Noah, and won the PEN American Center's Martha Albrand Award for First Nonfiction.

GEORGE F. WILL (1941–) The conservative columnist and author is among the most widely syndicated writers working today. The son of an Illinois philosophy professor and a graduate of Oxford University, the bow-tied Will worked at *The National Review* before graduating to the *Washington Post* editorial page. He is a baseball devotee and a religious agnostic, an independent-minded Burkean conservative who is willing to criticize Republican presidents as well as Democrats on matters of principle. Readers of *Deadline Artists* might be surprised to find that of his four columns included here, two—at his suggestion—were not about politics but about his family: on the enthusiasms of his son Jon Will, who has Down syndrome, and the passing of George Will's mother after a long battle with Alzheimer's.

WALTER WINCHELL (1897–1972) Considered the innovator of the modern gossip column, Winchell's influence extended into the realm of domestic and foreign politics for a time. At its peak, his *New York Mirror* column was syndicated to eight hundred papers and a spin-off radio and then television program expanded his audience considerably. Holding court at the Stork Club, writing dispatches consisting of short paragraphs separated by ellipsis, Winchell was feared, hated, and respected. Columnist Ben Hecht memorably said Winchell wrote "like a man honking in a traffic jam." He boosted political allies in power, and attacked his opponents mercilessly. He was an early and vocal critic of Nazism but also a defender of McCarthyism, which ultimately contributed to his decline in popularity. When Winchell died, his funeral was sparsely attended.

ACKNOWLEDGMENTS

Compiling *Deadline Artists* has been an enjoyable education. We have tried to include the best of the past in one volume, and we relied on many people's advice and insight to help refine our judgment.

Among these are: Roy Peter Clark of the Poynter Institute; Janie Eisenberg; David Dunbar; Don Fry; Brooke Kroeger, Director of the Arthur L. Carter Journalism Institute at New York University; Seth Lipsky of Columbia School of Journalism; Rick Mastroianni of the Newseum; The National Society of Newspaper Columnists; Matt Pottinger; Sam Riley of Virginia Tech; Steve Shepard of the CUNY Journalism School; Glenn Stout; and Richard J. Tofel, General Manager of ProPublica.

Many working columnists generously gave their time to help us with this project, including: Mike Barnicle, Jimmy Breslin, David Brooks, Stanley Crouch, Thomas Friedman, Pete Hamill, Carl Hiaasen, Peggy Noonan, and Kathleen Parker. A special thanks to our friend and one-time colleague, Jack Newfield, who was an inspiration and a sounding board as this project was first conceived.

We would like to thank our agent, Ed Victor, and our publisher, Peter Mayer at Overlook Press and the whole Overlook team, especially our editor Rob Crawford, cover designer David Shoemaker, book designer Bernard Schleifer, and publicity team, Jack Lamplough and Katherine Gales.

We literally could not have completed this book without the help of many dedicated researchers, including (in chronological order): Jemma Futterman, Mirva Lempiainen, Rachel Stern, Herpreet Grewal, Sophia Tewa and Stephanie Lowe. Photo Editor and researcher Sarah Hughes was instrumental in securing the photos of classic columnists.

Among the many books we surveyed were *The Column* by Hallam Walker Davis (1926); *The Columnists: A Surgical Survey* by Charles Fisher (1944); *A Treasury of Great Reporting* by Louis L. Snyder & Richard B. Morris (1949); *A Treasury of American Political Humor* by Leonard C. Lewin; *Pundits, Poets and Wits* by Karl E. Meyer (1990); *The American Newspaper Column* by Sam G. Riley (1998); *Biographical Dictionary of American Newspaper Columnists* by Sam G. Riley; *Crusaders, Scoundrels, Journalists: The Newseum's Most Intriguing Newspeople*, edited by Eric Newton (1999).

We'd like to thank our co-workers at *The Daily, The New York Post*, NY1, *The Daily Beast, Newsweek* and CNN. And of course, our families and friends.

John: I would like to thank my bride Margaret for her love and support. My parents for their lifetime of love and encouragement—and my brother, cousin, aunts, uncles, godparents and especially my grandmother, for giving me the blessing of a great family. Tina Brown, Harry Evans, Edward Felsenthal, Randall Lane, Andrew Kirk and everyone at Newsbeast for creating an exciting place to work that is always evolving. I'm also proud to be part of the CNN team and thank Ken Jautz, Janelle Rodriguez, Sam Feist, Lucy Spiegel and Rich Galant, in particular. For all my friends—and you know who you are— Thank You.

Jesse: I would like to thank Rupert Murdoch, Col Allan and all of my colleagues at *The Daily, The Post, The Telegraph* and *The Sun* for the fantastically fun and exciting career as a newspaperman I have had so far. I would also like to thank my family—Mom, Dad, Jack, Kate, Francois and Hilary—and Rebecca for their understanding and forgiveness for all the missed holidays, long nights, late dinners and cancelled plans that come with this career.

Errol: I would like to thank my parents, Edward and Tomi Louis; my wife, Juanita Scarlett and our son Noah Louis; and my sisters, Pamela Louis, Lisa Burton and Ellen Louis. I also thank my good friends Eric Daniels, Al Jackson, Fred Moten and the Rev. Eugene Rivers, who inspired and shaped hundreds of my columns. And many thanks to my ex-editors: Arthur Browne, Seth Lipsky, and the late Andrew Cooper—three old-school newspapermen for whom writing was not a job but a privilege.

PERMISSIONS

ABOUT THE EDITORS

JOHN AVLON is senior columnist for *Newsweek* and *The Daily Beast* as well as a CNN contributor. He is the author of *Independent Nation: How Centrists Can Change American Politics* and *Wingnuts: How the Lunatic Fringe Is Hijacking America*. Previously, Avlon was the chief speechwriter and deputy communications director for New York City Mayor Rudy Giuliani as well as a columnist and associate editor for the *New York Sun*. After the attacks of September 11, 2001, he and his team were responsible for writing the eulogies for the firefighters and police officers killed in the destruction of the World Trade Center. Avlon's essay on the attacks, "The Resilient City," concluded the anthology *Empire City: New York Through the Centuries* and won acclaim as "the single best essay written in the wake of 9/11."

JESSE ANGELO is Editor-in-Chief of *The Daily*, which launched in February 2011 as the first national news brand built from scratch for the iPad and other emerging platforms. He is also Executive Editor of the *New York Post*. He arrived at the Post in 1999 and after stints reporting news, gossip and business, he was appointed Metropolitan Editor in June 2001 at age 27. Angelo directed the paper's news coverage for almost a decade—through the 9/11 terror attacks, the two wars that followed, the 2003 Northeast blackout, and countless classic *Post* stories. He also oversaw the *Post's* website and the creation of its popular iPad app. A native New Yorker, Angelo worked as a reporter for *The Sun* in London and the *Daily Telegraph* in Sydney before joining the *Post*. He graduated magna cum laude from Harvard College.

ERROL LOUIS is the Political Anchor of NY1 News, where he hosts "Inside City Hall," a nightly prime-time show about New York City politics. Prior to joining NY1, Louis was a *New York Daily News* columnist from 2004 to 2010, writing on a range of political and social affairs and serving on the paper's editorial board. He also hosted a weekday talk show on AM1600 WWRL and was named the city's Best Columnist & Radio Show Host by the *Village Voice* in 2010. Prior to joining the *Daily News*, Louis was Associate Editor of the *New York Sun*, where he published columns from 2002 to 2004. He is a CNN Contributor.